MILWAUKEE TELEVISION HISTORY
THE ANALOG YEARS

WTMJ-TV photo

MILWAUKEE TELEVISION HISTORY
THE ANALOG YEARS

DICK GOLEMBIEWSKI

MARQUETTE UNIVERSITY PRESS
MILWAUKEE, WISCONSIN

MARQUETTE UNIVERSITY PRESS
MILWAUKEE, WISCONSIN 53201-3141
FOUNDED 1916

LIBRARY OF CONGRESS CATALOGING-IN-PUBLICATION DATA

Golembiewski, Dick, 1957-
  Milwaukee television history : the analog years / Dick Golembiewski.
    p. cm.
  Includes bibliographical references and index.
  ISBN-13: 978-0-87462-055-9 (hardcover : alk. paper)
  ISBN-10: 0-87462-055-4 (hardcover : alk. paper)
  1. Television broadcasting—Wisconsin—Milwaukee—History. I. Title.
  PN1992.3.U5G653 2008
  791.4509775'95—dc22
                                                                    2008044452

∞ The paper used in this publication meets the minimum requirements of the
American National Standard for Information Sciences—
Permanence of Paper for Printed Library Materials, ANSI Z39.48-1992.

© 2008 Richard G. Golembiewski
All rights reserved.

DUST JACKET PHOTO CREDITS

Front cover: Jim Wulliman adjusting the TV. MPTV photo.
Back flap: Upper: Murl Deusing. UWM Libraries, Archives Dept.
   Lower: Some of the WITI-TV on-air team in 1964: Standing L-R: Carl Zimmermann, Earl
   Gillespie, Jim Major, Larry Ebert and Tom Hooper. WITI photo.
Back cover: Top: Howard & Rosemary Gernette in August of 1968. WISN-TV photo.
   Bottom left: Jack DuBlon manipulating Albert the Alley Cat (upper) and Albert the Alley Cat
   (lower). WITI photos.
   Bottom center: Bill Carlsen on an early WTMJ-TV weather set. UWM Libraries, Archives Dept.
   Bottom right: The CBS 58 Ten at 10:00 News team in 2008. Weigel Broadcasting Co. photo.

www.marquette.edu/mupress/

MARQUETTE UNIVERSITY PRESS
MILWAUKEE

The Association of Jesuit University Presses

Editor's note: All illustrations not otherwise attributed are by the author
or from his personal collection.

CONTENTS

Foreword	7
Preface	9
Funding Acknowledgment	13
Acknowledgments	15
1. Fundamentals and Early Experiments	17
2. WTMJ-TV (Channels 3 & 4)	37
3. The "Freeze" and UHF	125
4. WCAN-TV (Channel 25)	141
5. WOKY-TV/WXIX/WUHF/WVTV (Channels 19 & 18)	159
6. WTVW/WISN-TV (Channel 12)	213
7. WITI-TV (Channel 6)	271
8. WMVS/WMVT (Channels 10 & 36)	331
9. WCGV-TV (Channel 24)	409
10. WVCY-TV (Channel 30)	431
11. WKRW-TV/WHKE/WPXE (Channel 55)	451
12. WDJT-TV (Channel 58)	455
13. WJJA/WBME (Channel 49)	469
14. WWRS-TV (Channel 52)	473
15. Low-Power, Class-A and Translator Stations	479
Afterword	489
Index	493

DEDICATION

This work is dedicated to my parents, who put up with my brother and me when we watched test patterns early in the morning and later with me when I watched "Nightmare Theatre" at 1:00 a.m.

It's also dedicated to the on-air talent, engineers, managers, and owners who conceived, constructed, and put the stations on the air. Thanks for the memories!

FOREWORD

When Dick Golembiewski called to invite me to breakfast, I had no inkling that he was going to ask me to write the "Foreword" to this wonderful book. If I had glimpsed his ulterior motive, I would have dropped breakfasts from my schedule on the spot.

"But I'm not a writer!" I whined over coffee. Dick had a response to every objection I raised. Now, since reading and editing my efforts, I'm sure that he has a deeper appreciation of my lack of literary ability!

What finally convinced me to tackle the "Foreword" was a conversation I had with a student at Marquette University. When I asked the young man what he wanted to do in broadcasting, he said, "I want to do what you do." As I thought for a moment on how to respond, I realized that I couldn't be supportive. I told him that he was facing a much steeper hill than I had had to climb. The reason had to do with the many changes in radio and television programming which had taken place in the forty years since I began my career.

In 1967 virtually every station in most markets produced at least one, and sometimes two, local, non-news programs daily. It was hosting these shows that allowed me and many others to hone our – in my case meager – talents. Locally, that meant people like Bob Sherwood, Bob Barry, Bob Beringer (How did I make it without the name of "Bob?"), along with such lights as Howard and Rosemary Gernette, Bob Trent, Hank Stoddard and Gordon Hinkley. What we shared was the opportunity to push our limits and try new things: in-studio interviews, man-on-the-street segments, etc. We got to try controversial topics, celebrity interviews, political and social commentary and, generally, whatever we could talk our program directors into supporting. The key point is that each station had a "place" for us to grow our wings.

When I left Milwaukee in 1973, it was to host a daily TV talk show in Washington, D.C. Again, my program was one of many produced locally there. After heading to L.A. in 1976 to host a series of game shows I was still able to keep my interviewing skills alive by guest-hosting on one of the six or seven locally-produced talk shows.

Those opportunities, largely, no longer exist. The "syndication button" made a program director's life immeasurably easier. He/she could push that button and up popped "Regis and Kelly." By the way, Regis made a handsome living hosting local shows for a number of years before he was syndicated. Rather than oversee the production, budget, talent hiring and nurturing and keeping a sharp eye on the ratings

Jim Peck began his TV career as a member of the announcing staff at WISN-TV. He later worked for WVTV and WTMJ-TV before moving on to Washington, D.C. and Los Angeles. He now hosts "I Remember" on Milwaukee Public Television, as well as the Saturday morning shows on WTMJ radio. (MPTV photo)

books, now a program director simply bought a syndicated show (Phil Donahue, Dinah Shore, Regis, Dr. Laura) and got a good night's sleep. The PD's bottom line looked better and there was far less work – and fewer headaches. We "wannabees" sometimes got a bit too close to the edge, and could alienate sponsors. Then it fell to the program director to bail us out, and keep us from being fired. It is a different world now.

Of course, radio and television are vastly different from their early years. You may be surprised to learn that WTMJ-TV was originally Channel 3, not the Channel 4 we have lived with for so long. You may not be aware of the battle over frequencies and how public television came to be. Does anyone remember needing to have a separate antenna for UHF stations? The same goes for sitting spellbound in front of a thirteen inch television screen staring at a "Test Pattern." Do you even know what that was? It shocks my grandchildren to realize that I remember a time BEFORE television! I also remember my father almost convincing us that no one needed to add color to TV programs. I guess that all of this merely points out the remarkable changes we have seen over the past decades.

Personally, I am indebted to Dick Golembiewski for conceiving this book and then spending all those years researching and writing it. *Milwaukee Television History: The Analog Years* is an invaluable reference tool for anyone interested in the history of television in Milwaukee. But it is much more than that. It is a reminder of the hopes many had for the new medium. It is a memory trip through a revolutionary period. It is a record of change – not always for the better, but of a constant change nevertheless.

So I say to my friend, Dick: "Thank you for giving us this book. I can't imagine how difficult it must have been to comb records and interview countless people who were there at the beginning. Through you we can meet those people, and learn the story of television in Milwaukee."

Jim Peck
September, 2008

PREFACE

"How on earth did you ever get interested in Milwaukee TV history?" That's a question I'm asked a lot nowadays. My entire life I've been involved in a number of interests: motorsports and race engineering, films, folk music, and others. Some folks know me as a mechanical engineer – and for many years a professor at the Milwaukee School of Engineering (MSOE). Others knew me as "Dick Nitelinger," the DJ who produced and hosted "Folk City" on WMSE from 1984-1992, while still others figured out that the Dick Golembiewski doing "Milwaukee Talking" immediately after that show for a couple of years was the same person! Some know me as an occasional race engineer, or as a faculty advisor, official, judge and past chairman of the Society of Automotive Engineers (SAE) student design competitions' committee.

I've always been fascinated by local broadcasting. Growing up on the south side of Milwaukee, I never got to see the "tower farm" along the Milwaukee River, but when making the occasional visit downtown, or looking across the Menomonee Valley from Mitchell Park, the tower atop the Sheraton-Schroeder Hotel called attention to the fact that a TV station was broadcasting from that building! I dreamt of what might be taking place inside.

In late 1995, I stumbled across *Scary Monsters* magazine, and noticed that the publisher dedicated some articles to the TV horror hosts from around the country. I inquired of publisher Dennis Druktenis if he was interested in a story about Milwaukee's "Dr. Cadaverino" – a host I watched as a teenager. I sent an inquiry with some questions to WITI, and got a one-page letter in return from Anne Clausen (then the head of research and programming) along with copies of some newspaper clippings. I was hooked! My research led me to the periodicals section of the Milwaukee Public Library, where I began poring through the microfilm of local newspapers to verify dates, etc.

My article on the good doctor appeared in September of 1996. I was going through a devastating, unilateral divorce, which led me to pursue a career change. I found that immersing myself in some project helped me to maintain my sanity. I began documenting the history of Milwaukee's other TV horror hosts and shows, and interviewed both Rick Felski ("Tolouse NoNeck") and Bob Hersh ("The Advisor") for articles. My friend Bob Schwarz suggested that I might want to write something about Milwaukee's old UHF stations, and mentioned WCAN-TV and WOKY-TV. I'd never heard of them, and was intrigued. Back to the library I went. There I began to dig out the story of our local stations.

I moved to the Charlotte, NC area in July of 1999 to become head of R&D for what turned out to be a stillborn Indy car chassis manufacturer. While there, I struck up a correspondence with the late Tom Snyder – who had helped Bob Hersh write scripts for "The Advisor's Mystery Theater" on WXIX. Tom told me about WCAN-TV and Lou Poller. He later told me about the Du Mont Vitascan color system that he'd seen at WITI in Milwaukee. He and Bob Schwarz inspired me to dig further into our city's TV history.

I accumulated a lot of information, and in September of 2000, I began working on a website dedicated to Milwaukee's TV horror hosts and shows. Included was a side page on the city's TV history. It soon became the online source for information on the subject. The Milwaukee Public Library included a hard copy in their local history room, and added the side page to their card catalog.

As I dug further into my research, I discovered that Milwaukee – and not New York, Chicago or Los Angeles – was the scene of a number of firsts: The Journal Co. filed the very first application for a commercial TV license with the FCC in 1938. The first female program and news directors in a major market were both at Milwaukee stations. The first regular schedule of colorcasts by an educational TV station took place here, as did the first long-distance test of a digital over-the-air signal. The battle to put WMVS-TV on the air was fought at the national, state and local levels, and the city was deeply involved in the VHF vs. UHF battle that began in the 1950s.

With all of that history, I decided to share that information, and write this book. Little did I know that I would spend thousands of hours and several years doing the research, obtaining and cleaning up graphics, writing, editing, and obtaining the required permissions. It was worth it!

Television has changed a great deal since my youth. By the time I was born, there were five stations on the air in Milwaukee. Before I was two years-old, all three networks and the educational station were on VHF, while the sole independent station was on UHF.

In those days, local stations produced a lot of their own programming. As kids, we watched "Cartoon Alley" on WITI-TV, "Pops' Theater" on WISN-TV, "Kids' Klub" on WTMJ-TV and "Children's Fair" on WMVS-TV. I remember watching wrestling from the South Side Armory. "Bowling with the Champs" was a staple on Sunday mornings in our house, and we watched Bill Carlsen for the weather. Hollywood films had been released to television, and they made up a large part of our local stations' programming.

To those of us who grew up during those times, the memories of the locally-produced shows are very precious. We still talk about them many years later.

As time went on, the local shows became too expensive for the stations to produce compared to buying syndicated reruns. The children's shows died as the baby boomers got older and the Federal Trade Commission promulgated policies that prohibited product tie-ins. VCRs and later DVD players came on the market, and many viewers liked the convenience of watching a film whenever they wanted to. Although some stations continued to show a few, Hollywood films, a staple of local stations' programming since the mid-to-late 1950s, were for the most part relegated to cable channels.

After the area was wired for cable, the situation changed significantly. Deregulation of broadcasting and the relaxation of public service requirements also contributed. Local programming focused on news/weather/sports. Few local documentaries were produced, and those that were usually came from the city's public television stations. The news/weather/sports shows were filled with more and more fluff and entertainment rather than hard news.

With the transition to digital television (DTV) scheduled for February 17, 2009, it seemed appropriate to reminisce about the city's television history. For some of you, this will be a trip down memory lane. Younger readers will learn about a time when local stations produced many of their own shows – which they may have heard their parents and grandparents speak of.

One problem with this type of project is the fact that stations either never saved, or discarded, many of their historical materials. Most are focused on their current operations and the next rating book. History has little priority. Fortunately, many materials were saved, and I'm grateful for having been granted access to them. In some cases, individuals saved them from the dumpster!

Nowadays another problem has arisen: electronic media has made the exchange of information easy and almost instantaneous, but as a result, much of our history is not being properly preserved. In television's early days, preserving the programming was expensive. In Milwaukee, only WMVS-TV had a kinescope unit. Even after videotape came on the scene, few local programs were preserved, as the cost of the tape drove stations to erase and reuse them after programs aired.

While few local programs were preserved from the early days of local television, stations documented many of them with still photographs. Many of those have found their way into this tome. The television sections of the Sunday newspapers featured many photos and stories about local programming. Many of those same still photos were also used in promotional ads which ran in the newspapers or *TV Guide*. Tim Cuprisin still writes a column on radio and TV that appears in the *Milwaukee Journal Sentinel* each weekday, but the Sunday section has been reduced to pages of listings in a format similar to others around the country. The programs have become easy and inexpensive to save, but the stations no longer run print ads or document their history with still photos.

Hence one of my motivations for writing this book: The side page on Milwaukee TV history on my website has proven to be very popular. An advantage of electronic media is that it can be updated very quickly, and that page has grown considerably since its humble beginning in 2002. Nonetheless, historians and archivists are struggling with the fact that much of our history is no longer being properly preserved in a permanent form that doesn't require equipment to view. Accordingly, I thought it appropriate to compile what I've documented in a book, which future generations can use to study how television broadcasting started in Milwaukee.

One of my goals was to strike a balance between many competing areas of research. License battles, local programming, community impact, political battles and technical background are all contained herein. The Milwaukee TV history side page on my website is laid out chronologically. This book's chapters cover individual stations in the order of their founding. As such, there is some duplication of material to facilitate reading each chapter out-of-order if desired. Feel free to explore, skim, and return to the material that interests you for a detailed discussion. Another goal was to provide detailed documentation of sources for those who might do similar research in the future. I hope that I've succeeded!

Nowadays, some historical writers seem to want to follow the philosophy of their broadcasting counterparts and deal only in short bites. Others have chosen to emulate fiction writers, who use conflict as the basis for their storytelling; dates and other pertinent details are often eliminated if they don't contain the required conflict or contribute significantly to the storyline. Still others add their own analysis or commentary to historical events. There is nothing wrong with those additions, but I've chosen to restrict such comments (primarily to this preface and the afterword) and present a detailed look at what happened, which can then serve as a reference.

I've been fortunate to receive the cooperation of the Milwaukee television stations. All understood that this was a historical tome and not a public relations piece. While a few corrected facts after reading preliminary drafts, none tried to influence my philosophy or approach.

This has been a great project for me to complete. I've met many of the pioneers of local television, and their stories have been priceless! I hope that you'll enjoy reading them as much as I enjoyed compiling and bringing them to you!

Some folks have asked if I'll do a similar tome on Milwaukee radio. If this proves to be popular, I may!

Dick Golembiewski
September, 2008

SPECIAL ACKNOWLEDGMENT

Funding for this book's publication was provided by a grant from John and Kathleen Retzlaff, in memory of Kathleen's late husband, Wardwell Chase Rosenberg, better known to Milwaukeeans as "Ward Chase."

Ward was born in Chicago on April 30, 1926. He was drafted into the Army in WWII, but never saw action. He obtained a bachelor's degree in speech from Northwestern University in 1949. Later that year he began his broadcasting career at WBAY radio in Green Bay, Wisconsin. Four years later, he shifted over to the new medium of television when WBAY-TV went on the air. In 1956, Ward left Green Bay for the larger Milwaukee market. His first position was that of a newscaster at WOKY radio. In 1957, he returned to TV, joining the staff of WITI-TV. In 1959 he moved to the newly-independent WXIX.

Ward will perhaps best be remembered for his "Mac the Mailman" live television program, on which he was the principal character. (See chapters 5 & 7.)

Kathleen's favorite photo of her late husband as "Mac the Mailman" (Courtesy of John & Kathleen Retzlaff; all rights reserved)

As time passed, Ward transitioned into teaching at Spencerian College in Milwaukee. While at Spencerian, he obtained a master's degree in education, administration and supervision, from the University of Wisconsin – Milwaukee. Then he joined the staff of the Milwaukee Area Technical College (MATC), where he became a full-time instructor. Ward taught courses in English, speech, and broadcasting. While teaching became his vocation, broadcasting remained an avocation. Even while teaching, he remained in broadcasting in a limited way. He hosted a weekend

Ward Chase doing his big band show at WISN. (Courtesy of John & Kathleen Retzlaff; all rights reserved)

big band show on WISN, a classical music show on WFMR, and a jazz show on WYMS. He retired from MATC in 1991 after twenty years of service.

Ward Chase passed away on August 22, 1996, after a long illness.

The author and publisher wish to express their grateful appreciation to John and Kathleen Retzlaff for their support.

(The Retzlaffs are looking for kinescope, film, or audio recordings of Ward Chase's programs or appearances. If any reader is aware of such material and is willing to share, please contact the author.)

ACKNOWLEDGMENTS

A project like this requires the input of many, many individuals. My friend Bob Schwarz and the late Tom Snyder provided the initial inspiration, but many others contributed.

The stations themselves provided me with unprecedented access to their archives. I am eternally grateful.

Milwaukee is blessed with an incredible public library system. This book couldn't have been completed without the resources available in the central library. I have spent thousands of hours pouring through microfilm of old newspapers, *TV Guide* and other magazines. I now know the idiosyncrasies of each microfilm reader! The library has *Broadcasting* magazine going back to 1937, and that was a source of much information, as FCC data is compiled there. I spent many hours pouring through clippings in the Frank P. Zeidler Humanities and Local History Room – so much so that many of the librarians now know me by name! Thanks to Assistant Coordinator, Arts & Humanities Mary Milankovich, archival assistant Gayle Ecklund, photo librarian Rose Fortier, and all of the librarians and library aides who provided me with assistance.

Sarah Johnson in the *Milwaukee Journal Sentinel*'s photo archives helped me dig through their extensive collection. Ellen Engseth did the same for the *Milwaukee Journal* Stations Collection in the University of Wisconsin–Milwaukee archives. Matt Blessing and Susan Stawicki helped me with the late Art Olszyk's files, and those on radio station WHAD in Marquette University's archives. Likewise Gary Shimek helped me find some early WIAO/WSOE materials in the MSOE archives.

I'm proud to be a life-member of the Milwaukee Broadcasters' Club, which was founded by Don Metzger and the late Lee Rothman. Through the club, I've met many of the people who contributed to this tome. My thanks to Don for providing me with contact information when requested.

The list of those who provided information, photos, granted interviews or helped in some way is long. I hope that I haven't missed anyone!

Thanks to: Ward Allen, Carl Ames, Stu Armstrong, Tom Axtell, Bob Bach, Kun Chae Bae, Shawn Barland, Bob Barry, Jane Bartell, Joe Bauer, Barbara Becker, Glenn Bishop, Jill Bishop, Robert Block, Dennis Brechlin, Ellis Bromberg, Pat Buckett, Fay Campion, Frank Carmichael, Kurt Carmichael, Joan Christopherson-Schmidt, Walter Clare, Anne Clausen, Bryce Combs, Karen Copper, Marvin Cox, Steve Cox, Jack Crowley, Randall Davidson, Steve Dhuey, Andy Eliason, Vic Eliason, Ralph Evans III, Jim Feeley, Rick Felski, Marv Fishman, Dick Flanigan, David Ford, Jill Geisler, Rosemary Gernetzke, Larry Grzegorek, Darlyne Haertlein, Al Hajny, Jim Hall, Amy Hansmann, Nels Harvey, Wayne Hawk, Bob Hersh, Bob Higley, Ruane Hill, Gordon Hinkley, Ed Hinshaw, Bill Howe, Neil Jaehnert, Aye Jaye, Kevin Johnson, Paul Johnson, Paul Joseph, Dan Kallenberger, Tony Karr, Doug Kiel, Tom Koester, Jack Krause, Ron Kurer, Jack Lee, Michelle Lehman, Sister Gilmary Lemberg, George Liberatore, Julie Lindemann, Joe Loughlin, Michael Love, Jim Major, Budde Marino, Judy Marks, Dean Maytag, Steve McVoy, Adine Mikolajczak, Irv Miller, Bruce Nason, Tom Nielsen, Steve Olszyk, Dale Palecek, Cherie Lee Parcher, Bunny Raasch, B.J. Rafenstein, Budd Reth, John & Kathleen Retzlaff, Artie Rickun, Sue Riordan, Jerry Robinson, Jim Robertson, Stephan Roselin, Ed Rosenthal, Greg Sahs, Harvey Scales, Al Scheel, Bill Scherbarth, Thom Schlais, Jeff Schimetz, Jim Schneider, Gregg Schraufnagel, Gary Seymour, Tom Shanahan, Amy Shelander-Burkee, Bob Sherwood, John Shimon, Scott Shuster, Kelly Skindzelewski, Mike Sroka, Paul Staszak, Chuck Steinmetz, Hank Stoddard, Andrew Stone, John Stone, Jerry Sundt, John Sveum, Paul K. Taff, Jim Thomas, John Torres, Gordie Trantow, Tom Trethewey, Bob Truscott, Sprague Vonier, Jan Wade, Bill Watson, Richard Wenzel, Jim Windsor, Garrett Wollman, Lori Wucherer, Jim Wulliman, Bob Wundrock, Thay Yang, Ron Yokes, and Carl Zimmermann.

Jim Peck not only wrote the foreword, but recommended people to interview, and provided me with contact information.

Ralph Evans, III was an invaluable source re: the Bartell stations. He was also kind enough to review chapters 1 and 3 for their technical content.

Milwaukee historian John Gurda provided much-needed encouragement when I was first thinking about writing this book.

Pete Draves helped me scan some large format negatives from the MPTV archives. My long-time friend from my days at Harley-Davidson, Karl Nilson loaned me his scanner which was able to handle the beautiful 4"x5" negatives in the WTMJ-TV archives.

My friend Hal Erickson, who writes on movie and television history, provided information on early children's shows and syndicated cartoons. He also compiled the list of network shows cleared by WXIX/WUHF/WVTV over the years.

Special thanks to Mike Drew, John Gurda, and Dr. Ruane Hill for reviewing advance copies of the book.

John & Kathleen Retzlaff not only provided historical materials related to Kathleen's late husband Ward Chase Rosenberg, but also a much-needed grant in his memory that helped with the production costs.

Finally, thanks to Andrew Tallon and Maureen Kondrick of the Marquette University Press, who believed in this project and found the way to make it happen!

CHAPTER I
FUNDAMENTALS AND EARLY EXPERIMENTS

Television may seem like a modern invention, but the technology goes back almost two centuries. Alexandre Edmond Becquerel published the findings of his experiments in the electrochemical effects of light in 1839, and even demonstrated a primitive photocell, which produced an electrical current when exposed to light.[1] Interest intensified when the element selenium was found to have electrochemical properties.

At the same time, researchers began to model the human eye. Of particular interest was the discovery of "persistence of vision." Because of that phenomenon, the illusion of motion could be successfully made if still images were "flashed" by the viewer quickly. Motion pictures use the phenomenon by projecting entire images on a screen. It became apparent that if a successful television system was to transmit more than still photographs, it would have to scan and reproduce images fast enough to take advantage of the persistence of vision.

A series of still pictures that create the illusion of motion.

Initial experiments used mechanical scanning systems. In 1884, German researcher Paul Nipkow suggested that an image might be scanned by projecting it through a series of holes arranged in a spiral pattern around the periphery of a rotating disc. As the disc rotated, a different portion of the scene would pass through each hole. Each represented a different line of the overall picture.[2] This was the first "sequential scanning" system. The resolution, or picture quality, was determined by the number of lines, and therefore the number of holes in the rotating disc, each revolution of which produced a single "frame." The frame was refreshed each revolution when the scanning process started over. The speed with which the frame was refreshed is referred to as the "flicker" rate. Both the scanning and flicker rates were a direct function of how fast the disk spun.

Since the number and arrangement of the holes, as well as the rotation speed could be varied, there was a need for those factors to be standardized.

In Nipkow's proposed system, a brightly illuminated scene would be scanned by his rotating disc. As the light passed through one of the holes, it would strike a photocell, which then produced an electrical signal. That signal would

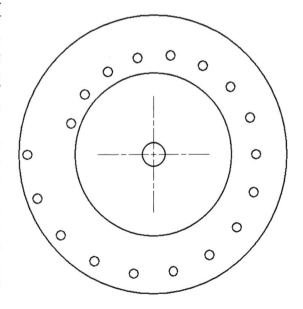

A disc of the style proposed by Nipkow.

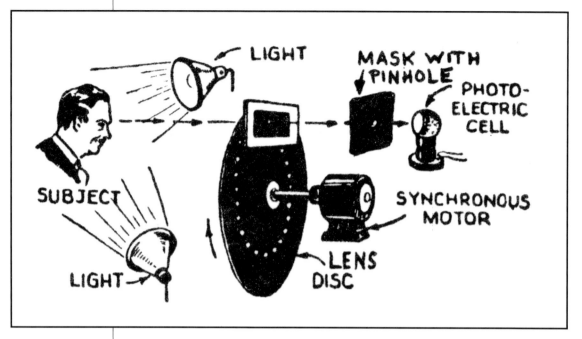

In the system proposed by Nipkow, the reflected light was scanned by the rotating disc, and picked up by the photocell. Later improvements included adding lenses to the scanning disc as shown here. While the scanning method has changed, modern TV systems do the same thing.

be sent to a receiver. That receiver would contain a high-intensity light source, the brightness of which was modulated by the electrical output of the transmitter's photocell. That light would be passed through another rotating disc, which was identical, and synchronized to the scanning disk. The output would be projected onto a screen.

Nipkow never constructed his proposed system, but it would serve as the basis for a number of early television experiments.

A second proposed system reversed the position of the light source and photocell. In the "flying-spot" method, the light passed through the holes in the rotating disc, producing a narrow beam, which scanned the scene. Photocells then picked up the reflected light. The system was first proposed in a French patent issued to Rignoux and Fournier in 1908.[3]

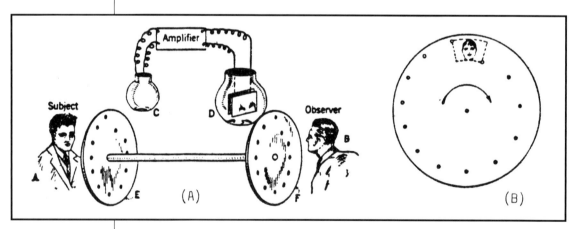

In this illustration of a simplified scanning disc system, the common shaft illustrates that both the camera and the receiving discs must be synchronized. The resulting image is composed of a series of curved lines.

While the two systems solved the problems of scanning and receiving, there remained two problems: First, selenium was rather slow to respond to changes in light intensity. Second, no suitable light source had been developed for the receiver.[4] Eventually, both problems were solved by the introduction of more sensitive photosensitive chemicals, as well as neon tube light sources.

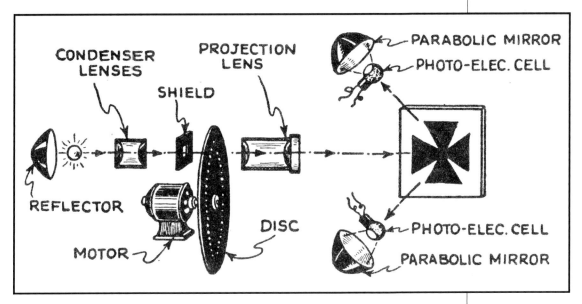

As mechanical systems were still being developed, so was the cathode-ray tube. In it, a beam of electrons (cathode-ray) was produced when an electrical potential is applied across a vacuum tube. When it hit the specially-treated glass surface, fluorescence was produced. The beam could be deflected by the use of electrically charged plates.

Meanwhile, Charles Francis Jenkins had become interested in motion pictures, and he introduced a system of prismatic rings designed to replace a projector's shutter. That interest led him to investigate television.

Jenkins used two sets of rings to scan an image. Light passing through one rotating prism scanned an image vertically, while a second did so horizontally. The output signal then had its amplitude modulated and transmitted using standard radio methods. Similar prisms in the receiver had to be synchronized with those in the scanner. Jenkins transmitted his first still photograph (facsimile) in May of 1922. A year later, he successfully transmitted both moving images and motion picture film. In 1925, he demonstrated his system. The images produced were crude, and had only 48 lines.

In England, John Baird had begun experimenting with television. Using a double-spiral of lenses and a radially-slotted Nipkow disc, he made his first demonstration in 1925.

In April of 1927, AT&T demonstrated a television system using a fifty-hole Nipkow disc, and the flying-spot method. One demonstration was made by a closed-circuit connection via a wire, while the second utilized a visual signal broadcast over 1575 kHz, an audio signal broadcast over 1450 kHz and a synchronizing pulse (to sync the Nipkow discs in the scanner and receiver) broadcast over 185 kHz.

All radio transmission in the U.S. was undergoing a period of chaos. Broadcasting by radio had been started by all kinds of groups. Attempts by Secretary of Commerce Herbert Hoover to regulate radio broadcasting and assign frequencies were ruled illegal by the courts, and stations used whatever frequency they desired, regardless of interference issues. The Radio Act of 1927 established the Federal Radio Commission (FRC) to regulate and oversee radio broadcasting. (See section entitled Federal Regulation of the Airwaves.)

In the "flying-spot" system, the light source passes through the scanning disc as it rotates, and reflects off of the object to be scanned as a narrow beam, which is then reflected by the parabolic mirrors and picked up by the photocells. The light path is just the opposite of that we normally think of. In fact, the subject to be scanned must be in complete darkness. (Television News, March-April, 1932)

FEDERAL REGULATION OF THE AIRWAVES

When experiments with radio first began in the early twentieth century, there was no government control over it. With the outbreak of WWI, the federal government chose to take over control of domestic frequencies in the interest of national defense. After the war, many governments, such as that of Great Britain, chose to retain both control and ownership of the radio spectrum, and formed government-controlled broadcasting systems. In the U.S., the federal government chose to allow private interests to run broadcasting stations. Regulation was via the Radio Act of 1912, which placed control in the hands of the Department of Commerce.

The Radio Act of 1912 was written when radio transmissions were primarily ship-to-shore. It was inadequate to regulate broadcasting. To solve the problems that had arisen from the growth of radio broadcasting, Commerce Secretary Herbert Hoover called four National Radio Conferences between 1922 and 1925. The second in March of 1923 addressed the problems associated with increasing the number of signals on the broadcast spectrum. The Conference recommendations included the equitable distribution of frequencies to local areas and discussed wavelengths, power, time of operation and apparatus. More importantly, the Conference suggested three concepts that have not changed with time and technology: The first recognized that broadcasting usually covers a limited area and encouraged local community involvement in the licensing process. The second acknowledged the limited amount of frequency space in the electromagnetic spectrum and supported the assignment of one consistent wavelength to a broadcaster. The third proposed that once a broadcaster was assigned a certain frequency, it should not have to move that placement due to new regulations.[5] A subsequent bill passed in the U.S. House of representatives, but stalled in the Senate Interstate Commerce Committee, primarily because of opposition from the radio industry, which did not want to give the secretary of commerce the ability to refuse licenses to those he thought were trying to monopolize radio.[6]

Hoover v. Intercity Radio (1923) held that the government could not refuse a license to an interested party, but could designate a frequency and police interferences.[7] In *United States v. Zenith Radio Corporation* (1926), a federal judge ruled the Commerce Department had no jurisdiction to regulate radio.[8] The result was what FRC Commissioner Orestes Caldwell called "anarchy in the ether" in a speech in Chicago on June 11, 1927.[9]

Some sort of regulation was necessary, so Congress passed the Radio Act of 1927. The Act established the Federal Radio Commission (FRC) to regulate and oversee radio broadcasting. As a result, the federal government officially retained ownership of the airwaves, but allowed private interests to operate broadcasting facilities under licenses it issued. Provision was made for the renewal of such licenses after three years, depending on the holder's ability to serve the "public interest, convenience, and necessity."[10]

Shortcomings in the original Act led to the enactment of The Communications Act of 1934. It established the Federal Communications Commission (FCC), which replaced the FRC.

The Act outlines a four-step process for granting frequencies. An entity that applies for a construction permit (the right to build a broadcast station) must seek a specific channel, antenna location, coverage area, proposed times of operation and power level of preference. If that applicant is selected for a grant, the FCC issues them a construction permit. When the station is built, the owners must prove their transmitter and antenna can perform to FCC standards, and they can then apply for a license to cover. Usually, applicants must also prove U.S. citizenship, good character free of criminal records, sufficient financial resources and proof of expert technical abilities.[11]

It is under that process that the FCC still grants the use of radio and television frequencies to broadcasters.

That same year, the FRC allowed experimental television broadcasting to begin in what had been the "standard" radio band (550-1500 kHz), using a 10 kHz bandwidth. It also allowed television experiments to take place in the 1500-2000 kHz band.[12] Such broadcasts were limited to one hour per day. None were allowed between 6:00 and 11:00 p.m., in order to prevent interference with commercial radio.[13] By 1929, experimental television broadcasting was limited to 1:00-6:00 a.m.[14]

Several television stations took to the airwaves in 1928, sparking a minor "boom." General Electric began broadcasting television programs over W2XB (popularly called WGY – now WRGB) in Schenectady, NY between 1:30 and 2:00 p.m. every Tuesday, Thursday and Friday on its AM radio frequency. The pictures of men "talking, laughing or smoking"[15] were primarily field tests meant for the firm's engineers.[16] WRNY in New York City, which was owned by *Radio News* publisher Hugo Gernsback, began television tests in August. WLEX in Lexington, Massachusetts began telecasting film programming, and WCFL in Chicago did so as well. In Washington, D.C., Jenkins, who had abandoned his rotating prism system for a 48-hole Nipkow disc, started experimental telecasts on W3XK. Other stations soon followed – although the 10 kHz bandwidth allowed meant that the definition was limited to 48 lines. In addition, all of the stations broadcast using different standards.

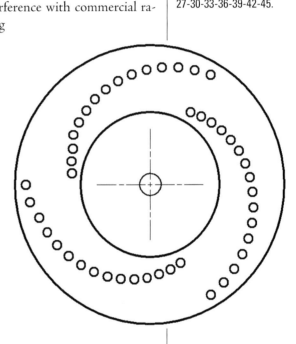

In Sanabria's 45-line, interlaced disc, each field consisted of 15 lines. Field 1 scanned lines: 1-4-7-10-13-16-19-22-25-28-31-34-37-40-43, field 2, lines: 2-5-8-11-14-17-20-23-26-29-32-35-38-41-44 and field 3, lines: 3-6-9-12-15-18-21-24-27-30-33-36-39-42-45.

In 1928, the Radio Manufacturers Association (RMA, now the Electronic Industries Association) established a committee to study television standards. Those recommended were based on mechanical systems, and did not take into account fully-electronic versions which were just starting to show promise. The proposed standards did not include guidance on all issues needed to establish commercial broadcasting. As a result, the FRC refused to accept the RMA standards, and instead chose to allow continued experimentation until such time as the technical development would result in a quality level sufficient to allow commercial broadcasting to begin.

An interlaced frame consists of two or more fields, which when put together form the entire image. An NTSC television picture contains two interlaced fields per frame.

Shown here is the inside of a Western Television Corp. Empire State receiver showing the triple spiral of interlaced scanning holes. This model includes lenses. Note the neon bulb that provided the image. Equipment similar to this was used by the Journal Co. for its television experiments in the early 1930s. (Courtesy of the Early Television Museum)

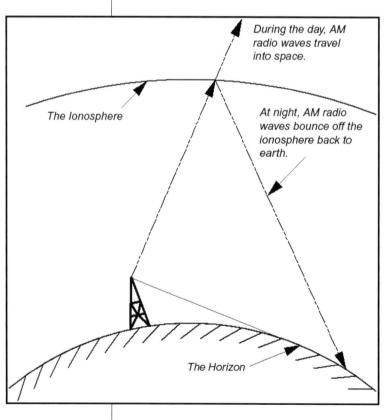

During the daytime, medium-wave transmissions (AM radio) follow the groundwave, and can be received for some distance beyond the horizon. At night, medium-waves bounce off of the ionosphere and can be received well beyond the horizon – often thousands of miles away. The phenomenon is known as "skywave propagation." Shortwaves (3-30 MHz) do the same during the day, which is why they can travel very long distances.

As a result of such experimentation, 100 kHz bandwidths were recommended in order to provide sufficient picture definition. In 1929, the FRC allocated four channels for experimentation: 2-2.1, 2.1-2.2, 2.75-2.85, and 2.85-2.95 MHz. It also allocated 2.2-2.3 MHz, but specified that it could only be used in the southern and southwestern portions of the country, so as to avoid interference with Canadian radio.[17] Since these were shortwave frequencies, stations hundreds of miles apart could interfere with each other. Experimental stations avoided the problem by agreeing to broadcast only at pre-scheduled times.[18]

One of the problems with mechanical systems was that the picture flickered unacceptably, as the frame rate was limited by the speed at which the discs spun. A young Chicago inventor, Ulises Sanabria, improved upon the Nipkow disc by using three separate spirals consisting of 15 holes each. Thus, each time the disc rotated, the image was scanned three times. The spacing between the holes in each spiral was such that every second line of the image was scanned by each spiral. The full image was still called a "frame," and each set of scanned lines was known as a "field." Thus three fields made up a frame. Because of the persistence of vision, it appeared as if the image was being scanned three times as fast, thus reducing the amount of flicker. Sanabria assigned his patent for "interlacing" to the Western Television Corp. of Chicago, which had been formed to sell equipment he developed. The early experiments by the Journal Co. in Milwaukee were made using one of those systems. (See chapter 2.)

In 1931, the FRC allocated television to what is now the very high frequency (VHF)[19] band. Experimental broadcasts were authorized in the 43-46 MHz, 48.5-50.3, and 60-80 MHz bands with no limits on the bandwidth used.[20] That was significant. The "standard" broadcast band is now known as "medium wave" and is used for AM radio. Those frequencies have unique properties which allow them to follow the earth's surface (groundwave propagation) and bounce off of the ionosphere at night (skywave propagation). That allows them to be transmitted great distances.

Skywave propagation does not normally occur with VHF frequencies[21], which follow a line of sight. As such, their range is shorter, and is dictated not only by the transmitter power, but also by the height of the sending and receiving antennas. Broadcasters worked on problems associated with VHF transmission throughout the 1930s.

"APEX" RADIO

Television, like FM broadcasting, uses higher frequencies than the standard broadcasting band (which is now known as AM radio). The problems associated with those frequencies were explored by experimental radio broadcasters beginning in 1934.

Called "Apex" radio, the experiments were initially designed to see if the increased bandwidth available at the higher frequencies would allow for greater fidelity than what was then attainable. It was also thought that static produced by thunderstorms might be diminished. Apex radio used amplitude modulation, but broadcast in what are now known as the VHF or shortwave bands. Because VHF waves do not follow the contour of the earth as well as the medium waves used in the standard broadcast band, and do not bounce off of the ionosphere at night (skywave propagation), the FCC thought that they might also prove to be a way to reduce interference between stations. Skywave propagation was particularly troublesome, and it was such interference from stations in Florida, Ohio and Maine, that led to the development of directional antenna arrays by Milwaukee station WTMJ in the late 1920s-early 1930s.

Manufacturers did not produce sets which could receive the VHF signals, so hobbyists built their own. Because the signals were for the most part line of sight, ending just over the horizon, it became necessary to mount the antennas for "Apex" stations as high as possible and early stations mounted them atop mountains, or tall buildings.

In Milwaukee, The Journal Co. received a construction permit for experimental Apex station W9XAZ on March 30, 1934. It broadcast on 31.6 MHz using the transmitter the company had used for experimental, mechanical-scanning television broadcasts. In November of 1936 the station's frequency was shifted to 26.4 MHz and its power increased to 500 watts. That meant that the station was broadcasting at the high end of the shortwave band, and as a result, its signal was picked up in Los Angeles, England and New Zealand.[22]

On Monday, November 30, it began a regular schedule by broadcasting WTMJ programming from noon until 11:00 p.m. daily.[23] On December 10, it originated its first program: the testimonial dinner for University of Wisconsin athletic director and head football coach Harry Stuhldreher. The dinner was sent to W9XAZ from Madison by wire, and then sent to listeners from the transmitter atop the Schroeder Hotel.[24] On December 13, the station announced that it would soon begin originating Marquette University home basketball games, boxing matches from the Eagles' Club, and other sporting and special events.[25] The first was the game against Iowa at the Marquette Gymnasium on Saturday, January 2, 1937. The play-by-play was called by WTMJ's announcer Russ Winnie.[26] W9XAZ became the first Apex station to originate its own programming.[27] The station also cleared network programming that previously could only be heard on Chicago stations WCFL, WENR and WMAQ. The *Milwaukee Journal* carried the station in its listings through Wednesday, July 7, 1937.

Because manufacturers did not produce radios capable of receiving Apex radio signals, W9XAZ held a contest in which listeners were encouraged to develop adapters. Prizes were awarded for the best two sets of plans.[28] The winners were two brothers: Robert and Lloyd Wilson, partners in the Home Radio Service store, each submitted his own design. Robert's two-tube design took first prize because of its superior performance, while Lloyd's single-tube version impressed the judges with its simplicity.[29]

As reported in *Broadcasting*, W9XAZ was one of the few stations in the country with proven high fidelity. Its distortion from microphone input to transmitter output was only 2 1/2 percent. Frequency response was flat from 20 Hz to 17,000 Hz within one decibel.[30]

On November 1, 1937, the FCC allocated seventy-five channels between 41.020 and 43.980 MHz to Apex radio. Each channel was 0.04 MHz wide.[31] Precedent was set on February 1, 1938, when the Commission reserved twenty-five of those channels (between 41 and 42 MHz) for educational use.

Problems worked out around the country included those associated with high towers, such as icing. Apex experiments also discovered that while the VHF signals did not bounce off of the ionosphere at night, under the right conditions lower in the atmosphere (thermal inversion), the signals would travel further than the horizon.[32]

In 1940, the Journal Co. began broadcasting on its experimental FM station W9XAO. (The call letters had earlier been used by a Chicago mechanical television station.) Journal Co. engineers asked the FCC to suggest tests it might run comparing FM to Apex radio.[33] W9XAZ went back on the air so that the tests could be conducted.

The FRC still did not consider television development sufficiently advanced for commercial broadcasting to begin, and it refused to issue technical standards. Despite pressures from the industry, that policy would continue until 1941. Instead it encouraged experimentation, with the hope that the technology would advance sufficiently so as to result in a television system of "permanent interest to the public." The FRC initiated a policy in which the industry would develop standards, which the Commission would accept or reject. During this time it did eventually accept a standard that called for left-to-right and top-to-bottom scanning.

As such, television licenses were experimental, and did not allow commercial broadcasting. A licensee was required to file periodic reports with the FRC indicating the station's hours of operation, the general results of broadcasting, and what technical studies were being undertaken.[34]

In the meantime, both CBS and RCA-NBC had begun mechanical television experiments in New York. In 1928, RCA-NBC broadcast a now famous 60-line picture of "Felix the Cat" using a flying-spot scanner. In July of 1931, RCA announced that its television laboratories would be moved to The Empire State Building. In late 1931 and early 1932, RCA-NBC conducted its last mechanical TV experiments, which featured a 120-line picture with 24 frames/second.

In Chicago, WCFL had begun telecasting in 1928. Western Television Corp. began operating W9XAO in 1930, and by 1931 it had begun broadcasting on a regular schedule. Radio station WMAQ, had begun telecasting on station W9XAP in

1930. It was originally owned by the *Chicago Daily News*, and was later purchased by NBC. It also used Western Television equipment, and the audio was broadcast over WMAQ. Programming was scheduled so as not to interfere with W9XAO.

The mechanical television era came to an end primarily because the definition available was insufficient to provide programming acceptable to the general public. Short-wave transmission allowed signals to be broadcast over long distances, but the bandwidth assigned was too low. Nonetheless, those early experiments resulted in interlaced pictures, as well as both horizontal and vertical synchronizing pulses, and standards for scanning. The scanning method, however, would change dramatically.

In 1917, Vladimir Zworykin began working on television research at the Russian Wireless Telephone and Telegraph Co. Zworykin had been a student of Boris Rosing at the St. Petersburg Technological Institute. Rosing had been doing television research, and on July 25, 1907, he applied for a patent for a television system using a cathode ray tube as a receiver.[35] On March 2, 1911, Rosing applied for a patent for a means of securing exact synchronization between the transmitter and the receiver.[36] Zworykin studied electrical engineering under Rosing in 1910-1912, and took part in his experiments.[37] The experience would influence Zworykin's future work.

In 1919, Zworykin moved to the United States, and was hired by Westinghouse the following year. There, he began television research. A year later, he went to work for the C&C Development Co. of Kansas City, Missouri. After two years there he returned to Westinghouse, and on December 29, 1923, he applied for a patent on an all-electronic television system.[38] Included in his invention was a camera tube he called the "iconoscope," which came from the Greek words *eikon* (image) and *skopein* (to view).[39] Unfortunately, Zworykin would not demonstrate his invention until 1928, a fact which would enter into later battles over his patent.

Meanwhile, a young high school student, Philo T. Farnsworth, had begun studying various science magazines. In February of 1922, he had won a prize from *Science and Invention* magazine for a "magnetized anti-theft automotive ignition system." Farnsworth and his family had recently moved to Utah, and he had enrolled at the high school in nearby Rigby, Idaho. There he pestered a chemistry teacher, Justin Toleman, for permission to take the senior chemistry course. At first, Toleman turned the enthusiastic youngster down, but later relented under Farnsworth's pestering, and allowed him to take the class – for no credit. Farnsworth soon outpaced the rest of the class, and Toleman found himself giving advanced lessons to the young scholar after school. Farnsworth was particularly interested in radio waves and light-sensitive chemicals.

Inspired by his science magazines, Farnsworth's thoughts turned to television. One day, he was mowing a field. As he turned back to look at the freshly mown hay, he noticed that it had fallen into neat rows, each alternating in direction from the one above it. It suddenly struck him that it might be possible to produce a sys-

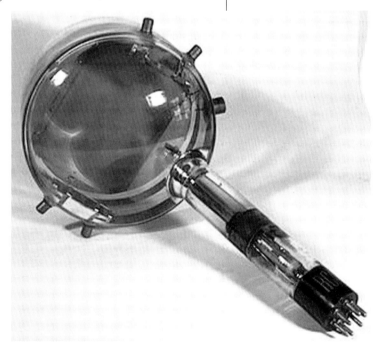

A model 1850 Iconoscope from 1939. (Courtesy of the Early Television Museum)

tem for scanning images electrically in a series of horizontal rows, and then putting them back together the same way.

Farnsworth kept the idea to himself. Then one afternoon in late February of 1922, Justin Toleman arrived for one of his afternoon tutoring sessions with Farnsworth. He found that his young student had covered his blackboard with schematic drawings and mathematical equations. When he asked what they represented, Toleman was told "television," and Farnsworth went on to disclose to him how he proposed to make an electrical system work. At one point, as Farnsworth clarified a particular point, he reached for the closest sheet of paper – a page from Toleman's notebook – and jotted down a crude sketch of his proposed camera device.[40]

Westinghouse showed little interest in Zworykin's television work, and consequently he traveled to New York to meet with RCA chairman David Sarnoff in late December of 1928 or early January of 1929. In that meeting, Sarnoff asked the scientist what it would take to develop a practical television. Zworykin reportedly answered "two years and one hundred thousand dollars"[41]. Sarnoff later hired him to conduct television research, but it would take much more time and money before a practical television system would be developed.

Meanwhile, Farnsworth had graduated from high school, secured some funding, and had begun research into what he called an "image dissector." In 1927, he filed a patent application for a "Television System." In September of that year, he demonstrated it in his San Francisco laboratory. It was the first demonstration of electronic television. In April of 1930, his laboratory was visited by Zworykin.

A Farnsworth "Image Dissector." (Courtesy of the Early Television Museum)

In 1930, Farnsworth was issued a patent for his "Television System," touching off an infringement battle with RCA and Zworykin over the latter's 1923 patent application. There was no doubt that Zworykin's application preceded Farnsworth's, but patent law at the time required that an invention be "reduced to practice," and that meant that a working prototype had to be produced.

Farnsworth had disclosed his idea to his patent attorneys in 1926. He had built a prototype and demonstrated a working system in 1927 – the year he applied for the patent. In order to prove "priority of invention," he would have to show that he conceived of the idea before Zworykin.

Farnsworth's attorneys found Justin Toleman, who still had the notebook Farnsworth had sketched the schematic in back in 1922. Toleman gave a deposition in the matter, but a patent examiner ruled that it did not corroborate Farnsworth's claim. However, Zworykin ran into a problem: he could not produce any evidence that the system described in his 1923 patent application could actually produce a scanned image in the manner described.

Attorneys for both sides filed final briefs on April 16, 1934, and a final hearing was held the following week. On July 22, 1935, the patent examiner ruled in Farnsworth's favor, and granted him priority. RCA appealed the decision, but on March

6, 1936, the Patent Office's Board of Appeals upheld the original findings of the examiner.

As early as 1933, the RMA reconstituted its television committee to re-examine standards given the trend toward electronic – as opposed to mechanical – systems. At the FCC's 1936 hearings on television standards, the RMA Allocations Committee recommended that seven channels between 42 and 90 MHz be allocated for television – each with a bandwidth of 6 MHz. The recommendation also included a provision for television experimentation above 125 MHz. The RMA Standards Committee recommended RCA's proposed standards, which called for 441 lines of definition at 30 frames per second, and amplitude modulation (AM) sound.

As a result of the hearings, in May of 1936, the FCC allocated three groups of television frequencies: 42-56 MHz, 60-86 MHz, and any two adjacent frequencies above 110 MHz (except for 400-401 MHz).[42]

In June of 1936, RCA and NBC began broadcasting a series of experimental, all-electronic television shows from the Empire State Building.

On October 13, 1937, the FCC allocated 19 VHF channels between 44 and 294 MHz for TV. Each channel was 6 MHz wide. The new allocations became effective on October 13, 1938. Twelve of the nineteen channels were above 150 MHz. Those frequencies were thought at the time to be useful only for television relay networks, but some manufacturers thought that the seven channels allocated between 44 and 108 MHz were sufficient for commercial television to begin. The FCC still refused to issue technical standards, and wanted experimentation to continue.

In April of 1938, the FCC promulgated Rule 103.8, which limited experimental television licenses to those stations engaged in R&D in the technical phases of broadcasting. On September 10 of that year, it appointed a committee made up of three commissioners, to study the status of television subsequent to recommending standards and allowing commercial broadcasting to begin.[43]

RCA wanted to profit from its research and development investment, and advocated that the FCC allow commercial broadcasting to begin as soon as possible. Despite the lack of standards, on October 20, 1938 RCA announced that it would make its television equipment available for purchase by broadcasters, and would authorize its licensees to manufacture receivers under its patents. It also announced that it would begin regular television programming on April 30, 1939 – the opening of the World's Fair in New York. It also announced that it would sell 1000 watt transmitters for both visual and aural signals.[44] RCA hoped that interest from stations would spark a conference on television standards.

Other manufacturers disagreed. The president of Zenith, E.F. McDonald, in a message to his stockholders, said that, "The offering for sale of television receivers at the time in view of the present status of the art is, in my opinion, unfair to the public, and premature, both for economic and technical reasons"[45]. He further stated that giving the go-ahead to commercial television at the time would burden the public with the cost of replacement receivers.[46]

In Milwaukee, The Journal Co., which lost its experimental license for W9XD when the FCC introduced Rule 103.8, decided to help push the matter of commercialization, when it announced on November 6 that it had filed an application for a commercial television construction permit the previous day.[47] The FCC formally accepted the application on November 14.[48] It was the first application ever filed for commercial television. The FCC referred the application to its committee which was studying the status of television.[49]

On March 13, 1939, the FCC announced new allocations for the higher frequencies. Television was allocated the same nineteen channels it received in 1937. The allocations were effective as of April 13.[50]

On April 30, 1939, RCA began broadcasting from the New York World's Fair over experimental station W2XBS, which transmitted on 45.25 MHz visual and 49.75 MHz aural. There, Franklin Roosevelt became the first U.S. president to appear on television.

On May 2, W2XBS broadcast its first variety show. On May 17, it telecast a Princeton-Columbia baseball game was telecast from Baker Field in New York.

On May 22, 1939, the FCC committee, which had been established to study television, issued its first report. It recommended that further experimentation be encouraged, and warned against the danger of freezing television's improvement by the premature adoption of standards.[51] Further, the industry had divided, with RCA, Farnsworth and GE supporting the proposed RMA standards, while Philco, Zenith, and Du Mont objected. The FCC would not set standards as long as the industry itself was divided, for fear that doing so would create a monopoly for one group of manufacturers.

On June 1, W2XBS televised the first heavyweight boxing match: Max Baer vs. Lou Nova, from Yankee Stadium, and on August 26, it telecast the first Major League Baseball game: a double-header between the Cincinnati Reds and the Brooklyn Dodgers at Ebbets Field. On September 30, it televised the first college football game: Fordham vs. Waynesburg, at Randall's Island, New York.

ELECTRONIC SCANNING AND "BLANKING PERIODS"

One of the standards that had to be worked out was how scanning of the image would be done by the camera tube. Like mechanical TV, the picture is scanned left-to-right, top-to-bottom.

However, unlike a Nipkow disk, a cathode ray would have to be turned off as it moved back to the right after scanning a line, or when returning to the top of a field

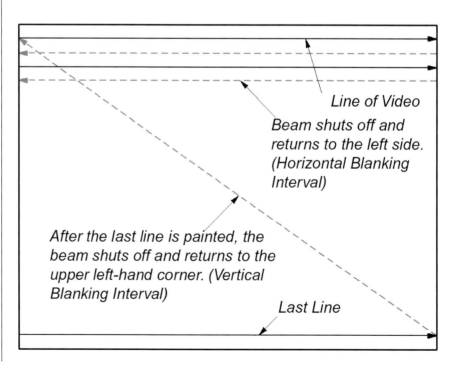

The horizontal and vertical blanking intervals.

after scanning was completed. Those segments were referred to as the horizontal and vertical "blanking periods."

The vertical blanking period is used to transmit other information, and was used by Du Mont to flash a strobe light for studio illumination in its Vitascan color system in the 1950s. (See chapter 7.) Of the 525 lines per frame in an NTSC television frame, only 483 are used for the picture.

Once it began regularly scheduled public telecasting, RCA had to come to an arrangement with Philo Farnsworth. The company had started as a radio patent pool, and had become very profitable by buying up the rights and then licensing them to others. It had never paid royalties. On October 2, 1939, RCA and Farnsworth signed a nonexclusive, cross-licensing agreement.[52] RCA would finally pay royalties. It was reported that the RCA attorney who signed the agreement, Otto Schairer, had tears in his eyes.[53]

That same month, RCA decided to test market television. It picked the small town of Newburgh, New York, some sixty miles north of Manhattan. There, it stocked local appliance stores, dropped prices by one-third, ran weekly advertisements in the local newspaper, and invited the town's 30,000 residents to demonstrations in local stores. In a few weeks, two hundred sets were sold. Another four hundred were sold in the next few months[54]

On October 22, the first NFL game was televised by W2XBS: the Brooklyn Dodgers vs. the Philadelphia Eagles from Ebbets Field in Brooklyn.

The FCC Television Committee issued its second report on November 15, 1939. Reversing its earlier stand, it recommended that experimental stations be allowed to operate on a limited commercial basis. Only seven of the nineteen channels allocated for television were deemed to be technically suitable at the time, and the committee recommended that metropolitan areas with populations in excess of 1,000,000 be assigned three channels, those between 500,000-1,000,000 two, and one to those with less than 500,000 persons. It also recommended that the commission adopt the proposed RMA standards.[55]

Draft rules for limited commercialization were published by the FCC on December 22, 1939. They called for two classes of stations. Class I stations would be limited to experimental broadcasts. Class II stations would be allowed to run advertisements and charge for production, but not for transmission costs.[56]

In January of 1940, the FCC held television hearings. Edwin Armstrong objected to the idea of allowing commercial television broadcasting to begin, until after the Commission had allocated spectrum space for commercial FM broadcasting.[57] He wanted the lower portion of the VHF band allocated to FM, and higher frequencies for television.[58] Du Mont and Zenith objected to the synchronization technique proposed by the RMA.[59]

Before making a decision, members of the Commission toured television laboratories on the east coast, in order to get a feel for the state-of-the-art. On February 28 the FCC announced that limited commercial television broadcasting would be allowed as of September 1. However, it declined to set standards, and warned the public against purchasing receivers which might become obsolete as the technical state-of-the-art progressed. It also refused to allocate spectrum space until after its FM hearings concluded.[60]

In reaction, Philco pulled out of the RMA, and all manufacturers save for RCA and Farnsworth voted to consider new standards.[61]

Despite the language in the FCC's order that nothing should be done to encourage a large public investment in television receivers, RCA, as it had in Newburgh, cut the price of receivers by one-third in NYC.[62] It began running newspaper advertisements there on March 20. RCA's competitors were aghast, as was the FCC, and three days later the Commission rescinded its limited authorization. It announced that new hearings would be held in April. In doing so, the Commission stated that:

> *Promotional activities directed to the sale of receivers...may react in the crystallizing of transmission standards at present levels. Moreover, the possibility of one manufacturer gaining an unfair advantage over competitors may cause them to abandon the future research and experimentation.*[63]

At the instigation of RCA[64], Minnesota Senator Ernest Lundeen called for hearings to see if the FCC had exceeded its authority. Fierce exchanges took place between representatives of the FCC and RCA, but no action was taken as a result of the hearings.

Meanwhile, the Commission began its own hearings on April 8. Opposition to fixed standards was still heard from Philco and Du Mont. On May 27 the FCC voted unanimously not to issue standards until the industry could reach an agreement.[65] In its report, the Commission also recommended a "multiple ownership" proviso, in which no entity could own more than three television stations.

On April 13, Du Mont received a construction permit for W2XWV in New York. At the same time, the FCC announced that commercial FM broadcasting could begin as of January 1, 1941. To make more room for FM, it reallocated the VHF band. The 42-44 MHz band, previously used by government and educational services, was combined with television channel 1 (44-50 MHz) and allocated for FM. What had been TV channel 2 was now called channel 1, and a new channel 2 was allocated to 60-66 MHz.[66]

In June of 1940, W2XBS and Philco's W3XE provided thirty-three hours of coverage of the Republican National Convention from Philadelphia. It was the first political convention covered by television.[67]

On June 18, the FCC announced tentative approval for twenty-three television applications. It also announced that it would consider nineteen other outstanding applications. One of those was the Journal Co.'s.[68] On October 29, The Journal Co. received a construction permit for experimental television station W9XMJ.

To solve the television standards problem, the RMA and the FCC formed the National Television System Committee (NTSC), which was charged with recommending technical standards.

The first meeting of the NTSC was held on July 31.[69] Panels began meeting in September. Initially, there were three points of contention that had to be resolved: the number of scanned lines per frame, the synchronization technique, and whether there should be fixed standards at all. Philco had demonstrated a system which used 625 lines of definition. Du Mont still advocated a flexible system, in which the number of lines and frame rate could be varied depending upon the programming.

On August 6, 1940, W9XBK in Chicago, owned by Balaban & Katz/Paramount, received a television construction permit.

On September 4, 1940, CBS demonstrated its field-sequential color system, in a broadcast from the Chrysler Building in New York over W2XAB. In it, a mechanical, spinning disk, with red, green and blue filters spun in front of the image to be scanned. A similar disk, synchronized with that at the camera end, reproduced the color at the receiver.[70] To get all of the necessary information within a 6 MHz channel, the CBS system used only 343 lines of definition. Most manufacturers, with investments in monochrome television, were not supportive, of the system.

On January 27, 1941, the NTSC recommended standards which included 441 lines of definition, at 30 frames per second – again, the same as the RMA had proposed. One change made was to recommend the use of frequency modulation (FM) for sound. In its decision, it rejected the CBS color system, as well as Du Mont's proposed flexibility in the number of lines and the frame rate.[71] The FCC scheduled hearings on television standards for March 20.

The NTSC continued its studies, prior to the hearings.[72] During them, it changed its standard from 441 to 525 lines[73] per frame on the recommendation of the Bell Telephone Laboratories.[74] It also recommended that field tests be made of competing synchronization techniques, and the best method picked. Du Mont objected to the 525-line standard, and continued to advocate a flexible one which would allow for 375-800 lines per frame at 15-30 frames per second, so as to allow for the reception of both high-definition black & white or lower definition color broadcasts, as proposed by CBS.[75]

On April 30, the FCC approved the NTSC standards, and authorized commercial broadcasting to begin as of July 1.[76] In doing so, it rejected the CBS color proposal. The new regulations called for 18 VHF channels between 50 and 294 MHz, as allocated the previous year. As originally drafted, the rules required commercial stations to broadcast thirty hours per week. Opposition was expressed during the March hearings, and the requirement was reduced to fifteen hours per week. Despite opposition from NBC and CBS, the FCC included in the new regulations a proviso which prevented any entity from owning more than three television stations.[77]

Because the general public invested in many receivers, the NTSC standards remained in effect – with subsequent modifications in 1953 for color – until digital television standards replaced them on February 17, 2009.

Despite the agreement on standards, the clouds of war had changed the public's attitude toward television, and receiver sales were sluggish. On May 27, President Roosevelt declared a state of unlimited national emergency.[78]

On July 1, 1941, W2XBS became WNBT, the first commercial television station in the United States. It aired its first commercial – for Bulova watches – at 2:30 p.m.[79] That same day, the CBS station, W2XAB, became commercial station WCBW and W3XE in Philadelphia became WPTZ.

The Japanese attack on Pearl Harbor put the country on a war footing, and on February 24, 1942 new television construction was frozen by the Defense Communication Board and the FCC.[80] Nonetheless, the General Electric station in Schenectady, New York became WRGB on March 1.

The decision to halt new television construction was reiterated by the newly formed War Production Board on April 24.[81] At a special television conference held by the FCC on April 4, broadcasters petitioned the FCC for a reduction in the requirement that they broadcast for a minimum of fifteen hours each week. As a consequence, on May 12th the Commission reduced the programming requirement for commercial stations to four hours per week.[82] The handful of stations operating broadcast civil defense programs. WPTZ in Philadelphia went dark during the war, but W9XBK in Chicago became WBKB on October 13, 1943, and Du Mont's W2XWV, became commercial station WABD on May 2, 1944.

As the war progressed, discussions were held with regard to post-war frequency allocations, and on April 27, 1944 CBS proposed a high-definition color system, using channels with 16 MHz bandwidths in the untested UHF band.[83] Other television broadcasters took issue with CBS' ideas.[84]

On May 16 of that year, the FCC announced that it was modifying its multiple ownership rules to allow an entity to own up to five, as opposed to three, television stations.[85]

The FCC held hearings on the future of the radio spectrum between September 28[86] and November 2, 1944.[87] The military uses of radio had put new pressure on the FCC to allocate more space in the spectrum to them, and the expected growth of AM, FM and television after the war compounded the problem. The Radio Technical Planning Board testified that an agreement had been reached in which FM radio would be allocated to the 41-56 MHz band, with higher frequencies to be allocated to television. CBS concurred with the decision to give FM more space, and testified that television should be moved to the UHF band above 300 MHz. At the hearings, much restricted military propagation data was presented, and former FCC engineer Kenneth Norton submitted flawed data[88] that showed that sunspot activity anticipated in 1947-48 would produce interference in the FM band around 44 MHz.[89]

On January 15, 1945, the Commission announced a proposed frequency allocation plan for frequencies above 25 MHz (VHF). Based upon Norton's testimony, FM was to be shifted upward, with television channel 1 allocated to 44-50 MHz, amateur radio to 50-54 MHz, television channels 2-6 to 54-84 MHz, educational FM to 84-88 MHz, commercial FM to 88-102 MHz, and non-governmental uses to 102-108 MHz. Experimental television was to be moved to the UHF band. Hearings on the matter began on February 14.[90]

The FCC announced the allocation plan for 25-44 MHz on May 21, but held off on making a decision on the rest of the VHF band until after FM propagation studies could be made.[91] Anxious to free up the spectrum, FM and television broadcasters urged the FCC to immediately allocate the VHF band, with educational FM to be allocated to 50-54 MHz, commercial FM to 54-68 MHz, and commercial television to 68-74 and 78-108 MHz.

U.S. VHF TELEVISION CHANNEL ALLOCATIONS

Channel	Frequency (MHz)		
	1938	1940	1946
1	44-50	50-56	44-50*
2	50-56	60-66	54-60
3	66-72	66-72	60-66
4	78-84	78-84	66-72
5	84-90	84-90	76-82
6	96-102	96-102	82-88
7	102-108	102-108	174-180
8	156-162	162-168	180-186
9	162-168	180-186	186-192
10	180-186	186-192	192-198
11	186-192	204-210	198-204
12	204-210	210-216	204-210
13	210-216	230-236	210-216
14	234-240	236-242	
15	240-246	258-264	
16	258-264	264-270	
17	264-270	282-288	
18	282-288	288-294	
19	288-294		

*Deleted from television and reallocated to land-mobile use in 1948.

Despite objections from Edwin Armstrong and other FM pioneers (including The Journal Co. in Milwaukee)[92], the FCC allocated educational FM to 88-92 MHz, and commercial FM to 92-108 MHz on June 27, 1945. At the same time, it allocated part of the former FM band, 44-50 MHz, to TV channel 1. TV channels 2-6 were allocated to 54-88 MHz; channels 7-13 to 174-216 MHz.[93]

In September, the FCC issued draft television rules and regulations, which included a channel assignment plan for 178 metropolitan districts. The plan allowed for three different types of licenses: metropolitan, community and rural. Metropolitan licenses covered a single, major city. Community stations covered smaller cities, were allowed less radiated power, and could not interfere with metropolitan stations. Rural stations were allowed the most power, but were prohibited from covering more than one metropolitan area. Channels 1, 12 and 13 were allocated to community stations – one of which (using channel 1) was assigned to Racine-Kenosha. Milwaukee received VHF channels 3, 5, 8 and 10, while Madison received channel 3.[94]

Before hearings began on October 4, the Commission issued a revised Table of Channel Assignments. To eliminate possible co-channel interference, Madison was assigned channel 6 instead of channel 3. Milwaukee lost a channel and was assigned channels 3, 8 and 10.[95]

After the hearings, the FCC released its final Rules Governing Television Broadcast Stations on November 21, 1945. Milwaukee gained a channel back, and received channels 3, 6, 8 and 10. Madison received channel 9. Channel 1 was reserved exclusively for Community stations. Channels 2-13 could also be used for them as needed. Those assignments became effective on February 25, 1946. The new frequency allocations became effective on March 1, 1946.[96] Once the new regulations were released, the FCC began processing television applications, and issuing construction permits for new stations.

All was not well, however. CBS continued to push for UHF television. After a meeting on February 21-22, 1946, its Affiliates Advisory Board adopted a resolution asking the FCC to authorize commercial broadcasting of high-definition, color television in the UHF band.[97] Broadcasters, unwilling to risk the investment in black and white VHF television, if the industry was to shift, balked. The FCC admitted that thirteen channels might be insufficient, and that television might eventually have to be moved to the UHF portion of the spectrum. On March 22, 1946, Hearst Radio, Inc., which owned WISN radio in Milwaukee, asked the FCC to return its application for channel 4. (Despite the freeze on new television construction, it had filed an application on June 13, 1945.)

The Journal Company had filed an application for a commercial TV construction permit on July 15, 1941, and had received a construction permit for WMJT on September 16 of that year. It withdrew its construction permit (without prejudice) on May 14, 1946. Nationwide, 80 of 158 applications were withdrawn by the end of 1946. Reasons cited by the permitees were that they were going to wait for color broadcasting to begin, or that they had underestimated the capital required for TV broadcasting.[98] On May 16, The Journal Co. applied for a construction permit for an experimental station in the UHF band, which was granted by the FCC on June 21.[99] It later received the call letters W9XKY.

On September 27, 1946, CBS petitioned the FCC to immediately adopt standards and authorize commercial operation of UHF, color television. In its petition, CBS quoted a statement from the Commission from May of 1945, which stated that: "A truly nationwide competitive television system...must find its lodging higher up in the spectrum where more space exists, and where color pictures and superior monochrome pictures can be developed through the use of wider channels."[100]

After studying the matter, The Journal Co. concluded that black and white television was not likely to be replaced by color in the near future.[101] As such, on December 6, it applied for another commercial television construction permit, and the FCC issued them one on January 24, 1947. The call letters WTMJ-TV were later assigned to it.

The FCC began hearings on the future of television in December of 1946.[102] In mid-March of 1947, it denied CBS's petition for color television, stating that it was too early to adopt standards. One of the reasons cited was the bandwidth requirements proposed by CBS. The 16 MHz required would allow for only 27 channels in the UHF band (480-920 MHz). The FCC had as its goal the development of "a truly nationwide, competitive television system"[103], for which it believed more channels were necessary.

The decision was seen as the "go" signal for black and white television. In Milwaukee, it would take the establishment of WTMJ-TV to trigger more applications.

NOTES

1 R. M. Garrat Gerald and Albert H. Mumford, "The History of Television," *Proc. IEE*, 1952, 99, Part IIIA, 25.
2 Paul Nipkow, *Electrisches Teleskop*. German Patent No. 30,105, January 6, 1884.
3 Joseph H. Udelson, *The Great Television Race: A History of the American Television Industry 1925-1941* (Tuscaloosa: University of Alabama Press, 1982), 18-19.
4 Ibid, p. 19.
5 Joan Stuller-Giglione, *Allocation*. The Museum of Broadcast Communications (website), http://www.museum.tv/archives/etv/A/htmlA/allocation/allocation.htm
6 James C. Foust, *Big Voices of the Air: The Battle Over Clear Channel Radio* (Ames: Iowa State University Press, 2000), 18.
7 Ibid., 25.
8 *United States v. Zenith*, 12 Fed. 614 (1926).
9 "*Annual Report of the Federal Radio Commission for the Fiscal Year Ending June 30, 1927*. July 1, 1927, 10.
10 Federal Radio Commission, *General Order No. 37*, August 22, 1928.
11 Ibid.
12 "Hold Band Open for 'Visual Radio,'" *Milwaukee Journal*, April 5, 1927.
13 Federal Radio Commission, *Second Annual Report*, 1928, 21-22.
14 Federal Radio Commission, *Third Annual Report*, 1929, 2.
15 "Far Off Speakers Seen As Well As Heard Here in a Test of Television," *The New York Times*, April 8, 1927, 1.
16 *Great Television Race*, 35.
17 FRC, *Third Annual Report*, 22.
18 *Great Television Race*, 41-42.
19 In the 1930s, what we now call the VHF band was known as the "ultra high" band, which can cause confusion if one doesn't check the frequencies referenced.
20 Federal Radio Commission, *Fifth Annual Report*, 1931, 53-54.
21 Skywave propagation does occur on channel 2 due to refraction in the ionosphere during the two periods of high activity during the 22-year sunspot cycle.
22 "Milwaukee Station Using Apex Band Tells of Results: W9XAZ, With Own Schedule, Is Checked by Spotters," *Broadcasting*, May 15, 1937, 72.
23 BCL, "Riding the Airwaves: Station W9XAZ Goes on a New Schedule at Once" *Milwaukee Journal*, November 30, 1936.
24 BCL, "W9XAZ to Broadcast Dinner for Stuhldreher," *Milwaukee Journal*, December 10, 1936.
25 BCL, "Station W9XAZ to Offer Sports Schedule: Fights, Cage Games Will Be on Short Wave," *Milwaukee Journal*, December 13, 1936.
26 BCL, "Riding the Airwaves: Station W9XAZ Opens Sports Schedule Tonight," *Milwaukee Journal*, January 2, 1937.

27 "Apex Station on Its Own: Complete and Separate Schedule Is Broadcast by 26.4 mc. Subsidiary of WTMJ," *Broadcasting*, January 1, 1937, 36.
28 "Contest Opens for Short Wave Adapters: Cash Awards for Two Best Sets of Plans," *Milwaukee Journal*, January 3, 1937.
29 "Winners Are Selected in Short Wave Contest," *Milwaukee Journal*, March 28, 1937.
30 "Milwaukee Station Using Apex Band Tells of Results."
31 The public is generally not aware that the FCC has assigned channel numbers to AM and FM frequencies. Unlike television, the broadcasters and the public have not referred to the stations by channel number, but rather by the frequency.
32 The troposphere is the lower part of the atmosphere where weather occurs. Under the right conditions, usually involving a warm, dry air mass on top of a cooler, humid one (temperature inversion), radio waves in the portion of the radio spectrum used by television can be bent, and follow the curvature of the earth, rather than ending at the horizon.
33 T.J. Slovic, letter to the Journal Co. re: high frequency broadcast stations W9XAO and W9XAZ. March 6, 1940. *Milwaukee Journal* Stations. 1922-1969. Milwaukee Manuscript Collection 203. Wisconsin Historical Society. Milwaukee Area Research Center. UWM Libraries. University of Wisconsin-Milwaukee, (Box 2, folder 7).
34 FRC, *Third Annual Report*, 28.
35 Albert Abramson, *The History of Television, 1880-1941* (Jefferson: McFarland & Co., 1987), 26.
36 Ibid., p. 35.   37 Ibid., p. 37.   38 Ibid., p. 63.
39 Christopher Sterling and John Kittross, *Stay Tuned: A Concise History of American Broadcasting* (East Windsor: Wadsworth Press, 1990), 146.
40 Donald Stashower, *The Boy Genius and the Mogul: The Untold Story of Television* (New York: Broadway Books, 2002), 25.
41 Paul Schatzkin, *The Boy Who Invented Television: A Story of Inspiration, Persistence, and Quiet Passion* (Silver Spring: TeamCom Books, 2002), 87.
42 "FCC New Rules Issued," *Broadcasting*, June 1, 1936, 7, 48.
43 *Stay Tuned*, 150.
44 "RCA Ready to Sell Visual Transmitters," *Broadcasting*, October 15, 1938, 11.
45 "Early Television Start is Opposed by McDonald," *Broadcasting*, November 15, 1938, 20.
46 Ibid.
47 "Journal Makes Application to Use Television: Is First to Ask Commission for Permit to Transmit Radio Pictures to Public on Scheduled Programs," *Milwaukee Journal*, November 6, 1938. Also see: "WTMJ Seeks Television," *Broadcasting*, November 15, 1938, 20.
48 "Actions of the FCC," *Broadcasting*, December 1, 1938, 80.
49 "Television Study is Begun by FCC," *Broadcasting*, January 15, 1939, 64.
50 "Ultra-High Bands Allocated By FCC," *Broadcasting*, March 15, 1939, 80.
51 Federal Communications Commission, *Fifth Annual Report*, 1939, 45-46.
52 "RCA-Farnsworth Pact," *Broadcasting*, October 15, 1939, 75.
53 George Everson, *The Story of Television: The Life of Philo T. Farnsworth* (New York: Arno Press, 1974), 38.
54 James Von Schilling, *The Magic Window: American Television, 1939-1953* (Binghampton: The Haworth Press, 2003), 11-12.
55 "Relax Video Rules, FCC Group Urges," *Broadcasting*, November 15, 1939, 17, 81.
56 "Hearing Ordered on Proposed New Television Rules," *Broadcasting*, January 1, 1940, 19, 58.
57 "Commercial Video Draws Objections," *Broadcasting*, January 15, 1940, 32.
58 "Future of Television in Lap of the FCC: Hearings Indicate Industry Wants to Go Ahead," *Broadcasting*, February 1, 1940, 24-27, 62-71.
59 *Stay Tuned*, 150.
60 "FCC Approves Commercial Television: Sept. 1 Date Set, No Allocations Are Made," *Broadcasting*, March 1, 1940, 17.
61 *Stay Tuned*, 151.
62 "Drive to Promote Video Set Sales Started by RCA," *Broadcasting*, March 15, 1940, 86.
63 "FCC Reopens Television Hearings April 8: RCA is Called to Task for Video Activity," *Broadcasting*, April 1, 1940, 22, 50.
64 *Stay Tuned*, 151.

65 "Television Back on Experimental Shelf: FCC Ruling Demands an Industry Agreement on Standards," *Broadcasting*, June 1, 1940, 17, 88-89.
66 "One Thousand New FM Stations Foreseen," *Broadcasting*, June 1, 1940, 18-19, 90.
67 *Broadcasting*, July 1, 1940, 16.
68 "Hint of Commercial Television Noted in License Grants," *Broadcasting*, July 1, 1940, 28, 68.
69 "Standards Group Plots Course for Television Set-Up: Fly, Jett Offer Cooperation of FCC in Industry Study," *Broadcasting*, August 15, 1940, 50.
70 "Color Television by 1941 is Forecast: CBS Method Described as Utilizing Lag of Eyes," *Broadcasting*, September 15, 1940, 38, 42.
71 "FCC Orders Hearing on Video Report: Industry Group Urges Standards Similar to Prior Basis," *Broadcasting*, February 3, 1941, 18, 36a.
72 "Video Committee to be Continued: Will Carry On More Studies Prior to March 20 Hearing," *Broadcasting*, February 17, 1941, 8.
73 "RCA Seeks Television Unity to Avoid More False Starts," *Broadcasting*, March 24, 1941, 16, 48-49.
74 *History of Television*, 268.
75 *Broadcasting*, March 24, 1941.
76 Lewie V. Gilpin, "Television Authorized by FCC on a Full Commercial Basis," *Broadcasting*, May 5, 1941, 12.
77 Ibid.
78 Sol Taishoff, "No Immediate Change Seen From Crisis," *Broadcasting*, June 2, 1941, 7, 46.
79 "Novel Commercials in Video Debut: Three Stations Present July 1 Programs in New York," *Broadcasting*, July 7, 1941, 10.
80 "Freeze Order Leaves Room for Flexibility: Individual Facts to Guide FCC in Grants," *Broadcasting*, March 2, 1942, 9-10.
81 *Stay Tuned*, 209.
82 "Television Operators Granted Respite Allowing Four Hours Minimum Weekly," *Broadcasting*, May 18, 1942, 66.
83 "Build for Better Television – CBS," *Broadcasting*, May 1, 1944, 9, 65.
84 "Television Broadcasters Take Issue with CBS on Quality," *Broadcasting*, May 1, 1944, 67.
85 "5 Video Outlets May be Owned by One Company, FCC Rules," *Broadcasting*, May 22, 1944, 10, 62.
86 Bill Bailey, "FCC to Hear Claims for Spectrum Space: Extensive Study to Get Underway Sept. 28," *Broadcasting*, September 25, 1944, 13, 60.
87 Bill Bailey, "FCC Tackles Conflicting Space Demands: Close of Hearing Leaves Many Problems," *Broadcasting*, November 6, 1944, 11, 60-66.
88 "Propagation Error Claimed in Basic Material," *Broadcasting Telecasting*, April 3, 1950, 47.
89 *Stay Tuned*, 231.
90 "Allocation Proposals Announced by FCC," *Broadcasting*, January 16, 1945, 13, 66-68.
91 Bill Bailey, "FM Decision Delayed as FCC Allocates: Tests to Be Made; Upstairs TV Assured," *Broadcasting*, May 21, 1945, 13, 17.
92 "Briefs Filed in FCC Allocation Hearing," *Broadcasting*, February 26, 1945, 60-62.
93 "FCC Allocates 88-106 mc Band to FM," *Broadcasting*, July 2, 1945, 13-14.
94 "TV Rules and Regulations," *Broadcasting*, September 24, 1945, 79-80.
95 "TV Channel Assignment List Is Revised With 90 Changes," *Broadcasting*, October 8, 1945, 73, 75.
96 "Rules Governing Television Broadcast Stations," *Broadcasting*, December 3, 1945, 76.
97 "CBS Affiliates to Ask Licenses for Commercial Color Video," *Broadcasting Telecasting*, March 4, 1946, 76.
98 Federal Communications Commission, *12th Annual Report (1946)*, February 8, 1947, 17.
99 Walter J. Damm, "Television Plan Realignment Announced by The Journal Co.," *Broadcasting Telecasting*, May 13, 1946, 25, 29.
100 "CBS Asks Commercial Color Video Now," *Broadcasting Telecasting*, September 30, 1946, 4.
101 "'Milwaukee Journal' Plans to Reapply for Black-and-White Video Station," *Broadcasting Telecasting*, December 16, 1946, 83.
102 "FCC to Hear CBS Color Case Dec. 9: Order Implies Complete Probe of UHF Video to be Held," *Broadcasting Telecasting*, October 14, 1946, 20, 82.
103 "CBS Petition for Color TV Denied: Performance Under Plan Cited As Not Adequate In Reasonable Time," *Broadcasting Telecasting*, March 24, 1947, 14, 74.

CHAPTER 2
WTMJ-TV
CHANNELS 3 & 4

(WTMJ-TV)

The *Milwaukee Journal* was founded as an afternoon newspaper in 1882 by Lucius Nieman, who had been the managing editor of the *Milwaukee Sentinel*. Nieman was succeeded by Harry J. Grant.

By early 1922, radio was beginning to become popular, and representatives of the newspaper visited with Professor Earle M. Terry at the University of Wisconsin in Madison. Terry ran WHA, the university's radio station out of the physics department. It was one of the first stations to broadcast regular voice programming in the U.S., and could be picked up around the country.

The visitors offered the university a proposal. As detailed in a letter from Terry to university president Edward A. Birge, the newspaper offered to contribute $5,000 in order that WHA might increase its power sufficiently so as to cover the entire state during daytime. It also offered to contribute additional funds to be used to cover maintenance and operator's salaries during the time it utilized the station. In return, WHA would "agree to broadcast three or more times per week, according to a definite schedule, material furnished by the *Milwaukee Journal*." The programming "would consist of musical concerts, lectures, and talks by well-known persons, the nature of the service being similar to that now furnished by the Westinghouse Company, the *Chicago Tribune* and others." The project was to be "advertised as a co-operation between the university and the *Milwaukee Journal*." The agreement was to be effective for two years, after which time the university would retain ownership of all equipment purchased by the Journal Co.[1]

Birge brought the matter up at an informal meeting with some of the university's regents. In a letter to Harry Grant, Terry responded to the proposal by stating that "since the university is a state institution and its facilities must, accordingly, be available to all citizens of the state without discrimination, it is hardly at liberty to accept funds from any group of individuals or to enter upon any agreement whereby a particular group may secure privileges not available to citizens of the state at large." He continued by saying that unless "...the university is still at liberty to broadcast material for other papers in the state, it cannot accept your offer." Terry held open the possibility that the Journal Co. might amend its offer to reflect the views of the regents, but acknowledged that "...exclusiveness is one of the features which makes the proposition of value to you." He thanked Grant for the offer on behalf of Birge, and stated that by rejecting it, "the university is in no way discriminating against the *Milwaukee Journal*. He went on to say that: "As a matter of fact, offers of a similar nature in other fields of activity are not infrequently received, but the university has not been able to take advantage of them, for the reasons stated above"[2]

In a letter to Terry, Grant stated that the paper understood the university's position, and would not pursue the matter further.[3]

On April 26 of that year, WAAK went on the air as Milwaukee's first radio station and a service of the Gimbel brothers' department store on a wavelength of 360 meters (833 kHz).[4] Gimbels started the station as a way to sell radio receivers.

Four days later, the newspaper announced that it would sponsor a concert to be broadcast over WAAK on May 1, featuring Lionel Barrymore, who was in town appearing at the Davidson Theater. Also appearing were the Sophie Brandt Opera Company, local musicians and vocalists. The Kesselman-O'Driscol Music Co. provided a grand concert radiophone – one of only a few in the country – which was setup in the Shubert Theater, so that those without receivers might hear the concert.[5] Other speakers were set up at the Journal building and Lake Park Lutheran Church.[6] Radio matters at the newspaper were handled by Walter J. Damm, then manager of its promotion department.

On June 16, Milwaukee's second radio station, WCAY went on the air. It was owned by the Kesselman-O'Driscol Music Co. Since December 1, 1921, radio stations had been assigned two wavelengths: 360 meters[7] (833 kHz) for "broadcasting news, concerts and such matter," and 485 meters (619 kHz) for "broadcasting crop reports and weather forecasts." As such, WAAK and WCAY entered into an agreement to share the wavelength.[8]

The Journal Co. sponsored one of the first contests in the country for home-built radio receivers at the inaugural Milwaukee Radio Show held at the Auditorium June 21-25.[9] The show exposed the city to the new technology.

In October of 1921, WHAD began as an experiment in Marquette University's physics department by Father John B. Kramer.[10] It received a license on June 30, 1922, and began broadcasting Wednesday nights on September 27.[11] It featured broadcasts by students in the College of Music and other departments, as well as daily weather and market reports at noon.[12]

Milwaukee's fourth radio station went on the air on October 23. It was owned by the School of Engineering of Milwaukee (now the Milwaukee School of Engineering), and used the call letters WIAO.[13] The initial license was issued jointly on July 22 to the school and the Journal Co.'s afternoon rival the *Wisconsin News*, which was owned by the Hearst Corp. That newspaper began promoting WIAO from its first day on the air. The *Wisconsin News* began programming some shows on WIAO beginning in January of 1924.[14] The rivalry would drive future moves in radio – and later television.

In the spring of 1924 two people who had been associated with WAAK, Ray Mitchell and Dan Gellerup[15], formed the Milwaukee Civic Broadcasting Association. WCAY had gone silent and the equipment was about to be sold to the Metropolitan Church Association of Waukesha. Mitchell, had made a deal with the Antlers Hotel on North Second Street and West Wisconsin Avenue for studio space in exchange for on-air mentions, and he had done the same with the owner of WCAY, Lou Kesselman.[16] The new WCAY went on the air on June 9, 1924.[17]

That summer, The Journal Co. bought time on WCAY for a series of contests in which products advertised in the newspaper were used as prizes.[18]

On August 18, WIAO became WSOE.[19] The *Wisconsin News* opened its own studio from which it could broadcast over the station that October.[20] At the end of 1924, the School of Engineering announced that it had purchased all of the equipment from WCBD in Zion, Illinois (one of the nation's first religious broadcasters, and the "flat earth" station). That gave the station one of the most powerful transmitters in the nation, as well as two transmitting towers. The *Wisconsin News* announced at that time that it "would 'cooperate' with operation of the station."[21]

To compete, the Journal Co. entered into an agreement with Marquette University on January 23, 1925 for the joint operation of WHAD. The university had used very little of its available time until then. As a part of the agreement, the station was to be listed as "the Marquette University – *Milwaukee Journal*" station. The newspaper paid all expenses, with the exception of one-half of the transmitter operator's salary, and half of any expenses related to license renewals and transmitter repairs. Marquette retained the right to broadcast a ninety-minute program Friday nights originating from a new studio constructed in the university's science building by the newspaper.[22]

The new, more powerful, WSOE was dedicated on July 8, 1925[23], and the *Wisconsin News* took over all programming responsibility.

WCAY went silent in May of that year.[24] Ray Mitchell had a disagreement with the new owners of the Antlers Hotel, and moved his transmitter out of it. Hi Wood, Lou Kesselman and an engineer, H. L. Ford formed the WKAF Broadcasting Corporation.[25] WKAF began broadcasting on October 20, 1925.[26] George W. Browne later used the old WCAY transmitter to put WGWB on the air on October 18, 1926.[27]

By late 1926, The Journal Co. had developed WHAD's programming along several fronts. On November 1, an organ was ordered from Wurlitzer for installation in the Journal Co. building next to the radio studio. November 26 saw the station clear its first program via wire from NBC, featuring Mary Garden and Will Rogers. In response, 14,000 listeners wrote or cabled asking that WHAD become a part of the network.[28] On December 27, arrangements were made for remote broadcasts of the Civic Symphony Orchestra from the Pabst Theater. On December 22, the Marquette University – University of Wisconsin basketball game was broadcast from the Milwaukee Auditorium.[29]

The Federal Radio Commission (FRC) came into being with the passage of the Radio Act of 1927. The Act was signed into law by President Coolidge on February 23, 1927. It empowered the FRC to issue licenses to all broadcasters. In order to give the new commission time to issue them, Section 40 of the Act, provided that no station that held a license issued by the secretary of commerce would be subject to a penalty for broadcasting without one for a period of sixty days after it became effective. Stations throughout the country were faced with uncertainty as to whether the new Commission would renew their licenses.[30] The Journal Co. felt that its growth in the medium was limited because WHAD's transmitter was located within the city. It wanted to move it outside the city limits, and increase its power. In addition, its contract with Marquette precluded running commercials, at a time when it became obvious that was the direction broadcasting was headed.[31] In late 1926, it had entered into discussions aimed at settling some of those differences[32], but the two parties could not come to an agreement.

On April 18, 1927 Walter Damm, representing the Journal Co., conferred with FRC commissioner Henry J. Bellows in an attempt to see if he could get a new wavelength for WHAD. Bellows stated that no new frequencies could be added to Wisconsin. Instead, he recommended that the Journal Co. sever its relationship with Marquette, and purchase another station. In that way, Marquette could go back to operating WHAD, broadcasting a few hours per week. Bellows further recommended that the newspaper scrap the transmitting equipment of the station it would purchase, replace it with a new 1 kW Western Electric unit, and locate it outside the city.[33]

As a consequence, on April 20, The Journal Co. purchased WKAF for $16,350. On April 24, the FRC assigned temporary permits to all stations currently broadcasting.[34] On May 2, the Journal Co. applied for a construction permit for a new 1 kW transmitter to be located in Brookfield.[35] On May 6, the FRC issued it a construction permit for broadcasting on a frequency of 1150 kHz with 500 W of power. On May 10, the station was assigned the call letters WTMJ (The *Milwaukee Journal*).[36]

On May 24, the FRC announced a new allocation plan in which most stations' frequencies were shifted. The FRC assigned WTMJ a frequency of 1020 kHz. It was also ordered to share time with WHAD, with the understanding that once the station went on the air, it could do so at 1,000 watts, and WHAD would be moved to another frequency. The Journal Co., objected to the order to share time with WHAD, applied for a new construction permit on June 10, and asked for that provision to be dropped. The new frequency assignments took effect on June 15, and every station was granted a temporary permit with which to broadcast that was good for sixty days.[37] On July 6, the company received a letter from FRC Commissioner Bellows stating that it could begin broadcasting at a power of 1,000 watts.[38]

On Monday, July 25, 1927, WHAD broadcast until 7:30 p.m. It then signed off and WTMJ began broadcasting its inaugural program on the same frequency.[39] Numerous local artists were featured, including George Devine's Wisconsin Roof Orchestra.[40] Its director, Bill Carlsen, would later become WTMJ-TV's long-time weatherman. (See special section.) The following day, WTMJ broadcast its first program from the NBC "Red" network.[41] It began offering a regular schedule of network shows on August 15.[42]

In September of 1927, the FRC issued Special Order 105, which moved WHAD to a frequency of 1110 kHz, where it would share one-seventh time with WSOE. That allowed WTMJ to broadcast full time.[43]

To compete with WTMJ, the *Wisconsin News* entered into a lease arrangement with the School of Engineering for WSOE on November 15, 1927.[44] To reflect the new arrangement, they changed the station's call letters to WISN on January 23, 1928. That year, WTMJ affiliated with NBC.

With the issuance of its General Order 40 on August 30, 1928, the FRC assigned WTMJ to 570 kHz, and ordered it to share time with WHA in Madison. The Journal Co. objected, and filed applications (in order of preference) for 920, 940, 620, 610, 950, 590, and 570 kHz.[45] As a consequence, on October 12, the FRC assigned WTMJ to 620 kHz at 1,000 watts full time. The Journal Co. then withdrew all applications for other frequencies.[46] WTMJ remains on 620 kHz frequency to this day.[47]

With General Order 40, the FRC assigned "clear channels" on which no other station could broadcast, and the Journal Co. wanted one of them. The country had been divided into five zones, with clear channels assigned to each. Wisconsin was the fourth populous state in zone 4 – which also included Illinois, Missouri, Indiana, Minnesota, Iowa, Kansas, Nebraska, North and South Dakota – but no clear channel was assigned to it.[48] The Journal Co. requested that the Commission com-

CHAPTER 2 ~ WTMJ-TV: CHANNELS 3 & 4   41

bine WBBM's half of 770 kHz and WENR (670 kHz) into a single clear channel for WTMJ, which would broadcast with 50,000 watts of power.[49] The FRC's chief examiner opposed the request[50], and the petition was later dismissed by the full Commission.

As a newspaper, the *Milwaukee Journal* was interested in new technologies that would allow the transmission of still photographs via radio. In April of 1929, it began experiments with a process called Rayfoto. It was the first station west of New York to broadcast any pictures. At the same time, a minor "boom" was beginning in television, and several stations went on the air in Chicago. The Western Television Corp. had been formed there to produce mechanical scanning television equipment invented by a young engineer, Ulises Sanabria. (See chapter 1 for more on Sanabria.)

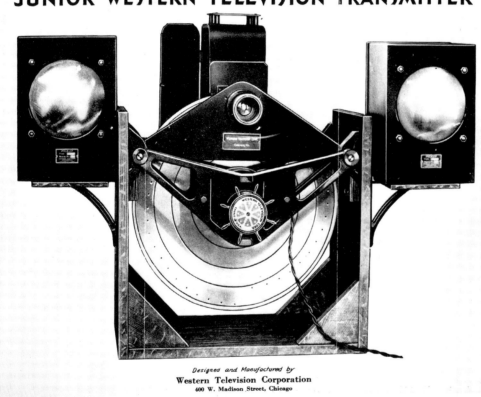

The Journal Co.'s early mechanical television experiments used Western Television equipment. (WTMJ-TV)

On May 5, 1930, the Journal Co. applied for an experimental television broadcasting license.[51] On December 19 of that year, it received a construction permit for an experimental television station, with facilities located in the Journal Co. building. There technicians installed a 500 watt transmitter and a 10 ft. antenna which was 35 feet above the ground. The transmitter was designed and built by John V. L. Hogan, one of the country's foremost radio engineers.[52] In the summer of 1931, the Journal Company's experimental facilities were moved to the 25th floor penthouse of the Schroeder (later the Sheraton-Schroeder, Marc Plaza, and now the Hilton) hotel.[53] A license was received for experimental television station W9XD on September 4, 1931, and Journal Co. engineers began television experiments using Western Television mechanical scanning equipment. Per FRC regulations then in effect, W9XD broadcast 1.5 hours before and after sunset.

During late 1932 and early 1933 the experimental work was moved back to the Journal Company building, and then back to the Schroeder Hotel in late 1933. Television experimentation ended that year, as mechanical television was being replaced by an all-electronic version. The Journal Company retained its license, however. The transmitter was later converted to an experimental high-fidelity, VHF, AM (Apex) radio unit in 1934. (See chapter 1.)

In April of 1938, the FCC's Rule 103.8 took effect. It limited experimental television licenses to those stations engaged in R&D in the technical phases of broadcasting. As a result, the Journal Co. allowed its license for W9XD to lapse on March 28. On September 10 of that year, the FCC appointed a committee made up of three commissioners, to study the status of television subsequent to recommending standards and allowing commercial broadcasting to begin.[54]

Manufacturers (primarily RCA), wanted to profit from their research and development investment, and advocated that the Commission allow commercial broadcasting to begin. Despite the lack of standards, RCA announced in October of 1938 that it would make its television equipment available for purchase by broadcasters, and would authorize its licensees to manufacture receivers under its patents.[55] As a direct result, on November 5, the Journal Company announced its intention to apply[56], and on November 14, it filed the first application for a commercial television construction permit in the U.S. On November 9, the company received a telegram from RCA chairman David Sarnoff praising them for their actions.[57] Since the FCC had not issued technical specifications, nor authorized commercial broadcasting to begin, it referred the Journal Company's application to its television committee on January 3, 1939.[58]

After its decision to allow commercial television broadcasting to begin, its subsequent rescinding of that decision, and the formation of the first NTSC (See chapter 1.), the FCC announced tentative approval for twenty-three television applications on June 18, 1940. It also announced that it would consider nineteen other outstanding applications. One of those was the Journal Co.'s.[59] On October 29, The Journal Co. received a construction permit for experimental television station W9XMJ.[60] The new station was to broadcast on channel 3 (then 66-72 MHz), at 1 kW of power for both its visual and aural signals.

In the 1930s, the Journal Co. had experimented with "Apex radio" – amplitude modulated broadcasting in the VHF band. (See chapter 1.) After FM became viable, the company applied for an experimental license on June 20, 1939. It received a construction permit for W9XAO On September 9. Experimental work had moved to the top of the Wisconsin Tower on the northwest corner of North 6th Street and West Wisconsin Avenues, from where the company would make its initial FM broadcasts.[61]

Testing began on January 15, 1940, and an experimental license was issued by the FCC on February 23. Hearings on commercial FM began later that month, and the "go" signal was given on March 20. W9XAO began broadcasting officially on April 22. On July 17, an application was filed for a commercial FM station to broadcast with 50 kW of power from a 200' tower located in Richfield. A construction permit for commercial FM station W55M[62] was issued on October 31.

To accommodate standard (AM), FM and television stations, the Journal Co. announced plans to build a new broadcasting facility on November 3, 1940.[63] It was named "Radio City," and would be built around a 389 seat auditorium, where broadcasts could be made before a live, studio audience. On February 23, 1941, it was announced that the new facility would be built on a tract of land west of the

CHAPTER 2 ~ WTMJ-TV: CHANNELS 3 & 4   43

"blue hole" area near North Humboldt Blvd. and East Capitol Drive, on the west bank of the Milwaukee River.[64]

On April 7, the FCC authorized W55M to begin broadcasting commercially on a temporary basis for sixty days. On June 25, ground was broken for "Radio City."[65]

On April 30, the FCC authorized commercial TV broadcasting to begin as of July 1.[66] In response, on July 15 the Journal Co. asked the Commission to modify its TV construction permit to allow for commercial broadcasting. On September 16, it received approval to broadcast commercially using the call letters WMJT (*Milwaukee Journal* Television).[67]

On September 27, the cornerstone was laid at Radio City in a formal ceremony. Attending were Wisconsin Governor Julius P. Heil, Milwaukee Mayor Carl Zeidler, Alderman Theodore R. Froemming of the twenty-first ward, FCC Chairman James Fly and Harry J. Grant, chairman of the board of The Journal Co.[68]

The Japanese attack on Pearl Harbor put the country on a war footing, and on February 24, 1942 new television construction was frozen by the Defense Communication Board and the FCC.[69] The decision to halt new television construction was reiterated by the newly formed War Production Board on April 24.[70]

All radio operations were transferred to Radio City on August 5[71], and the facility was formally opened on August 23.[72]

The Journal Co. put its television plans on hold. Phil Laeser, then the Journal Co.'s director of radio engineering, told Art Olszyk that the studio cameras and control room equipment had arrived and were stored in crates on the railroad siding immediately to the west of Radio City.[73] Some of the unused equipment was sold to the federal government, who used the vacuum tubes[74], while the rest was assigned to NBC for use in its already completed New York studios. The 300' self-supporting tower, slated for television, was used to receive short wave remote broadcasts for

Walter J. Damm (left), manager of radio and television for the Journal Co., helps to insert a time capsule in the cornerstone for Radio City. (UWM Libraries, Archives Department, Milw MSS 203)

Radio City in 1942. The original 300' television tower is still there. (Historic photo collection/ Milwaukee Public Library)

The Radio City auditorium would be used for live radio and TV broadcasts. (UWM Libraries, Archives Department, Milw MSS 203)

After WWII the Journal Co. began preparing for television with a series of training exercises. (WTMJ-TV photo)

WTMJ radio. Studio D, which measured 56' by 30' and was designed for television, was converted for radio rehearsals and broadcasts.[75]

As the war wound down, television plans continued, and staff training began on July 1, 1945.

In September of 1945, the FCC released its draft rules and regulations for postwar television. Included for the first time was a Table of Channel Assignments for cities. The VHF portion of the spectrum was re-allocated – including the portion used by television. (See chapter 1.) Channel 3 was now 60-66 MHz.[76] After hearings the Commission released its final Rules Governing Television Broadcast Stations on November 21, 1945. The city channel assignments became effective on

Although crude by today's standards, the post-WWII training helped radio people gain experience in the new medium of television. (WTMJ-TV photo)

Phil Laeser with some early television equipment. (WTMJ-TV photo)

February 25, 1946, while the new television frequency allocations became effective on March 1.[77]

All was not well however. CBS continued to push for color television in the untested UHF band. (See chapter 1.) The Journal Co. had some tough decisions to make. Lewis Herzog, assistant manager for radio and television, and Phil Laeser made a trip to the east coast in late January of 1946 in order to visit television equipment manufacturers, and assess the status of the medium. In a report to company management dated February 11, 1946, Herzog concluded that monochrome, VHF television was already obsolete. UHF color broadcasting was on the way, but still in the development stages. He recommended: "…that we delay as long as possible in making a decision on low-band television. Our hand may be forced in this respect by the FCC. Our Washington counsel advises us that the old construction permit which became dormant at the start of the war, is no longer considered by the Commission to be in existence, but that they are regarding it as a virtual application for a construction permit." He went on to say that: "In the meantime we should wait for further developments and particularly keep an eye on the following matters:

1. Most important of all, the activities of manufacturers in building transmitting and receiving equipment, particularly as regards to price.

2. FCC action on our so-called construction permit.

3. Any action on the part of Hearst Radio or any other firms or individuals who may file an application for a Milwaukee television of any type.

4. The Chicago television stations, especially NBC's activities in that city.

5. The progress made by AT&T in building the Chicago-Milwaukee relay link."[78]

The latter item was a proposed network connection.

Despite the fact that new television construction was frozen because of WWII, on June 13, 1945 Hearst Radio, Inc. had applied for VHF channel 4 (then 78-84

MHz).[79] Herzog reported that Hearst's president Major Stoerr: "...told me that while he plans to go ahead with low-band black and white television in Baltimore, he is making no immediate plans about Milwaukee for some time to come; the inference being that he, too, would delay action here unless his hand was forced by a competitive move."[80] Hearst asked the FCC to return its application on March 22.

Because of the uncertainty, on May 14, 1946 the Journal Co. asked the FCC to withdraw its construction permit (without prejudice) for WMJT. Nationwide, 80 of 158 applications were withdrawn by the end of that year. Reasons cited by the permitees were that they were going to wait for color broadcasting to begin, or that they had underestimated the capital required for TV broadcasting.[81] On May 16, The Journal Co. applied for a construction permit for an experimental station in the UHF band, which was granted by the FCC on June 21.[82] It later received the call letters W9XKY.

The FCC began hearings on the future of television in December of 1946.[83] The Journal Co. concluded that black and white television was not likely to be replaced by color in the near future.[84] As such, on December 6, it applied for another commercial television construction permit, and the FCC issued them one on January 24, 1947. Since the FCC changed its previous rules on call letters, and now allowed radio and television stations to use suffixes to distinguish between AM, FM and TV stations, the Journal Co. requested WTMJ-TV. Although the post-war regulations were based on 500 foot-tall towers, the company elected to use the 300' unit it had erected in 1941. (At the time it was built, it was the tallest structure the manufacturer would guarantee that would support the weight of a TV antenna.)

On February 7 & 10, 1947, members of the Journal Company staff were treated to demonstrations of the new television equipment.[85]

In mid-March, the FCC denied CBS' petition for color television, stating that it was too early to adopt standards.[86] March 15-22, Milwaukee residents got their first look at television when WTMJ-TV held demonstrations at the Milwaukee Home Show.[87] April 14-19, public demonstrations were held using the station's portable equipment at Schuster's department store on North 12th Street. Various household appliances were demonstrated. Private demonstrations for various clubs were held at Radio City the same month.[88] In early May, demonstrations were held at the downtown Boston Store. Later that month, the portable equipment was used to televise a speech by presidential candidate Harold Stassen to the overflow portion of the crowd at the Wisconsin Press Association banquet held at the Pfister Hotel. The same was done for a speech given to the Milwaukee Advertising Club by Eleanor Roosevelt at the Schroeder Hotel that month.[89]

In June, members of the WTMJ-TV staff visited the *Detroit News* (WWJ) and *St. Louis Post Dispatch* (KSD) television stations to get a feel for their operations. They were chosen as closely matching the type of operation the Journal Co. envisioned for Milwaukee, as opposed to larger stations in New York, Philadelphia and Chicago. That same month, an application was filed for a microwave relay station, so that remote broadcasts could be made without the use of AT&T co-axial lines.[90]

The transmitter arrived at Radio City on July 9. Later that month, the FCC granted the company a construction permit for microwave relay station W9XMK. "T-Day" was tentatively set for December 1, and TV set manufacturers guaranteed that stores would have an adequate supply. Because of the work on WTMJ-TV, little progress was made on the experimental UHF station, and the FCC granted a request to move the completion date to February 20, 1948.[91]

The transmitter was installed in August, and a formal announcement that "T-Day" would be on December 1 was made in The *Milwaukee Journal* on the 17th.[92]

Television demonstrations were held at the Milwaukee Home Show in March of 1947. (UWM Libraries, Archives Department, Milw MSS 203)

On September 6-7, 1,500 people viewed the TV antenna at Radio City before it was installed on the tower.[93] From the 25th to the 27th of that month, demonstrations were held in the radio department of Gimbel's downtown store.[94]

Prior to going on the air, WTMJ-TV had displays in the windows of area department stores. (UWM Libraries, Archives Department, Milw MSS 203)

CHAPTER 2 ~ WTMJ-TV: CHANNELS 3 & 4   49

In early October, WTMJ-TV began broadcasting test patterns. That same month, the station held another series of demonstrations in which government officials, educators, and others viewed test programs in the Radio City auditorium Wednesday nights.[95] Tests of the portable microwave pickup equipment were made from the South Side Armory (from where professional wrestling shows would be televised) and the Marquette University Gymnasium, from where an intra-squad game was televised.[96] The Journal Co. decided to initially broadcast five days-a-week – Wednesday through Sunday. Since December 1 was a Monday, "T-Day" was shifted to December 3.

Sprague Vonier was at WTMJ-TV from the beginning, and became program director, after the station's first, Jim Robertson, left to start WTTW in Chicago. He remembered that no one really knew what format television programming might take:

> There was an early conviction that television would be unlike radio, in that it would work in 20-minute (and even 5-minute) units, rather than half-hour units. The typical hour, so the theory went, would consist of three 20-minute shows, or fifteen minute shows and 5-minute nuggets. Jim even scheduled a couple of 5-minute acts in that way: a girl singer named Barbara and [a] brother & sister act in which they mugged phonograph records. The notion was short-lived; but we did wind up with a considerable number of 15-minute programs.[97]

Engineers Leroy Watson (left) and Henry Goeden aim WTMJ-TV's portable microwave dish from the roof of the South Side Armory during a test of the equipment in October of 1947. St. Stanislaus Catholic church is in the background, as is the author's high school alma mater. (Milwaukee Journal photo, ©2008 Journal Sentinel, Inc., reproduced with permission.)

On October 10, Schuster's department stores signed the first sponsorship contract with WTMJ-TV. It called for fifty-two quarter-hour variety programs (later named "Schuster's Open House") every Wednesday night.[98] Other sponsors signed included:
- Gettelman Brewing Co.: Wrestling From the South Side Armory
- Wadham's Division of Socony Vacuum: Marquette University home basketball games
- Taylor Electric Co.: High school basketball
- Perma-Stone Corp.: Boxing
- Gimbels: NBC Television Newsreel
- The Boston Store: How-To program
- Botany Mills: One minute film commercial[99]

A test program on November 11 was viewed by the general sales manager of the Philco Corp., who told a group of television dealers at the Pfister Hotel that WTMJ-TV's picture quality, was as good as that he'd seen in eleven other cities with TV stations he'd visited. The test consisted of a ping-pong game, newscast and films.[100]

(WTMJ-TV)

Finally, the big day arrived. At 8:00 p.m. on Wednesday, December 3, 1947, WTMJ-TV began formal broadcasting with a half-hour dedication ceremony. Live from Studio D, William E. Walker, assistant to Wisconsin Governor Oscar Rennebohm, and Milwaukee Common Council president Milton McGuire offered their congratulations.[101] NBC executive vice president Frank E. Mullen promised that the network would eventually provide connections between the east coast and Midwest – and eventually the west coast. The network's president, Niles Trammel, offered his congratulations on film.[102] According to Art Olszyk, Walter J. Damm used the occasion to take shots at the presidents of the American Federation of Musicians and the Screen Actors Guild, who forbade their members to take part in live television broadcasts. That meant that the WTMJ studio musicians, long a fixture on the company's radio broadcasts, could not participate.[103]

WTMJ-TV was the first television station in Wisconsin, and the fifteenth in the nation to broadcast commercially. It only broadcast for about twenty hours-per-week initially. Today, that may not seem like much, as stations regularly broadcast twenty-four hours a day. However, when WTMJ-TV went on the air, there was no network programming available. Videotape was some years away from availability, and stations had to broadcast live, or show what little film programming they could

CHAPTER 2 ~ WTMJ-TV: CHANNELS 3 & 4

Civic leaders gather to celebrate "T-Day," December 3, 1947. (WTMJ-TV photo)

obtain. Since the Hollywood studios considered television a competitor, it would be several years before feature films would be made available in any quantity. (See section entitled Movie Hosting.)

When it went on the air, WTMJ-TV only owned two RCA field television cameras and one film camera. As such, the cameras had to do double-duty. Jim Robertson joined the WTMJ radio staff as an announcer in 1943. In 1947 he was WTMJ-TV's first program director.[104] As he remembered:

> We only had two cameras. All of our engineers were radio guys, but they soon adapted. We would set up those two cameras in the lobby of Radio City and did an interview program called 'Meet Your Neighbor' at two o'clock in the afternoon, where we would interview people as they came in. Occasionally we had guests lined up ahead of time. Then the engineers would take the cameras out to the South Side Armory, or the Marquette Gymnasium, or on other remotes for high school sports.[105]

The lighting posed some problems in those early days, as Robertson recalled in his book *TeleVisionaries*:

> Our engineers rigged up what I think Bill Eddy at WBKB in Chicago had come up with. You know the kind of sealed lamp that you have now for outdoor yard lights, either floods or spots? They would rig up what was called a light

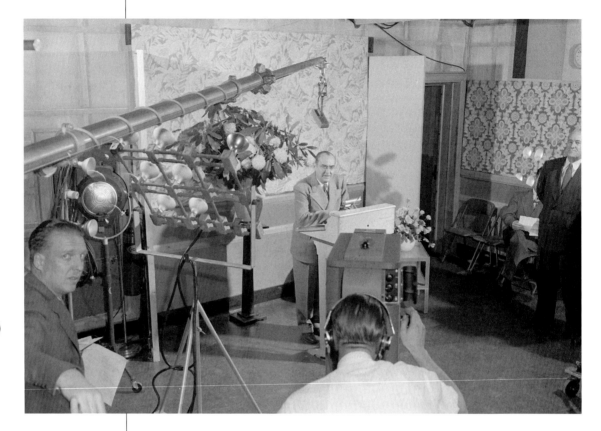

Walter Damm presides over WTMJ-TV's opening ceremony broadcast from Studio D in Radio City. (UWM Libraries, Archives Department, Milw MSS 203)

For its debut, WTMJ-TV set up receivers in both the Milwaukee Public Library/Museum and Radio City. (WTMJ-TV photo)

CHAPTER 2 ~ WTMJ-TV: CHANNELS 3 & 4

> **WTMJ-TV's First Day's Programming:**
> **December 3, 1947**
> * 8:00 p.m.   Television Dedication
> * 8:30 p.m.   Open House: A Look at Milwaukee's Future
> * 8:45 p.m.   Salute to Television
> * 9:00 p.m.   Television Newsreel
> * 9:15 p.m.   Sports Revue
> * 9:30 p.m.   Wisconsin Styles
> * 9:45 p.m.   Night Club: Variety Entertainment
> * 10:15 p.m. Golf Demonstration by Professional Francis Gallett.

tree – with either nine or sixteen of these – either three each way or four each way, into a kind of quadrangle of lights – a grid of lights. And they would have several of those, which could be moved around the studio. They generated quite a lot of heat.

When we got around to developing commercials for our brewery accounts in Milwaukee, one of the problems we had was that there was so much heat that the beer wouldn't pour properly! This was all live in those days, you know; you had to pour the beer right at the moment when the announcer was talking about it, and it took some doing to get that beer to get just the right head on it under the heat!"[106]

In the first week of January, 1948, the station received a shipment of new equipment, including two new RCA studio cameras.[107]

Around the country, sports promoters worried that telecasts might cause drops in attendance. In many cases, just the opposite occurred. The *Milwaukee Journal* reported that attendance at Golden Gloves boxing matches and a pro basketball double header at the Milwaukee Auditorium suffered no such drops. Attendance at wrestling matches at the South Side Armory actually went up, as new fans were made of viewers.[109] As such, The AAA Milwaukee Brewers announced in March of 1948, that they would not charge WTMJ-TV for the rights to broadcast games from Borchert Field at 8th and Chambers Streets, but they would pay the station for air time and production costs.[110]

Beginning on March 15, 1948, WTMJ-TV began its weekday programming an hour later – 3:00 p.m. – to make it easier for school children to watch its programming.[112] That same month, it reported that 1,666 TV sets had been installed in the area.[113] By April 1, the number had risen to 2,050 – of which 74% were in private homes.[114]

On May 17, Walter Damm announced that WTMJ-TV had signed an affiliation agreement with the NBC Midwest television network.[115] The network was for the time only in the Midwest, as there was no connection to either the east or west coasts. Most cities were connected via AT&T coaxial cable, but Milwaukee would be connected to Chicago via a three-station microwave relay network.[116] As such, WTMJ-TV could receive programming, but could not originate any. Damm committed the station to purchasing the connection. Jim Robertson:

> *AT&T had hearings to determine how they would allocate the hours on the network lines. Walter Damm said: 'You know what we're going to do? We're going to buy the lines from Chicago to Milwaukee and we're going to decide which of the network programs we're going to take.'*
>
> *I think that was a master stroke, because it meant that WTMJ-TV, when it carried network programming, carried NBC, CBS, ABC and Du Mont.*[117]

Professional Wrestling and TV were made for each other. Early TV stations needed programming, and turned to sports. Wrestling took place in a confined area and under lights – both of which were an advantage in the days of big cameras that needed a lot of illumination. The fact that the matches were choreographed by the wrestlers ensured that there was always plenty of action – that ended just in time for commercial breaks! WTMJ-TV closed its second broadcast day with live wrestling from the South Side Armory.

WTMJ-TV's original Studio D. Note the primitive lighting. (UWM Libraries, Archives Department, Milw MSS 203)

WTMJ-TV's original master control. (UWM Libraries, Archives Department, Milw MSS 203)

On February 9, 1948, WTMJ-TV took delivery of a $10,000 remote truck.[108] Here it is being used to cover the 1951 Labor Day parade. In the background is the Wisconsin Tower, from where the Journal Co. began FM broadcasts in 1940. (UWM Libraries, Archives Department, Milw MSS 203)

WTMJ-TV began broadcasting minor league Milwaukee Brewers' games from Borchert Field with a game against Toledo on April 27, 1948. Here, announcer Larry Clark calls the action shot by cameraman George Kasdorf. The broadcasts ended in 1950 after viewers objected to too much baseball — particularly Sunday doubleheaders.[111] (UWM Libraries, Archives Department, Milw MSS 203)

WTMJ-TV's early film room. (UWM Libraries, Archives Department, Milw MSS 203)

August 7-28, 1958, WTMJ-TV completed 37 remote broadcasts from the Wisconsin Centennial Exposition at State Fair Park. More than 100,000 visitors watched as Journal radio and television programs were broadcast from The Journal Communications Center and from Radio Hall.

ABC announced that it would begin Midwest network programming on September 20, originating from WENR-TV in Chicago.[118] All of the networks announced that they would provide kinescopes of their New York programs to their Midwest affiliates. FCC regulations prohibited networks from entering into exclusive contracts with affiliates.[119] As such, on September 11, WTMJ-TV announced that it would carry network programming from CBS and ABC in addition to NBC.[120]

At 5:00 p.m. on Monday night, September 20, 1948, network television was introduced to Milwaukee when WTMJ-TV broadcast a half-hour variety show originating from Chicago station WENR-TV by the ABC Midwest network. Although ABC broadcast two more network shows that evening, WTMJ-TV chose to switch to NBC at 6:00 p.m. when its Midwest network broadcast a show highlighting television "firsts" originating from KSD-TV in St. Louis. From 6:30-7:30 p.m., kinescopes of various NBC features were shown. That was followed by a local program highlighting WTMJ's long affiliation with NBC, which also featured a congratulatory message from Mayor Frank Zeidler. At 8:00 p.m., the station rejoined the NBC network. The first ten minutes of the ABC show were blurred, as was the first NBC program, but the problems were resolved by the time network programming resumed at 8:00 p.m.[121]

CHAPTER 2 ~ WTMJ-TV: CHANNELS 3 & 4   57

After network programming began, WTMJ-TV expanded its broadcasting to seven nights a week.[122]

On September 24, 1948 WTMJ-TV broadcast a Suburban Conference high school football game between Whitefish Bay and Shorewood. It was the first football game to be televised in the state.

Once WTMJ-TV began broadcasting, radio stations in the area began applying for TV construction permits. After the first round of hearings before the FCC, three applicants remained for the three available channels: WEMP (Ch. 6), WFOX (Ch. 8) and WISN (Ch. 10). All three were granted a joint petition on September 7 – the day before the second round of hearings were to begin – for an indefinite continuance. The three asked the Commission to immediately grant them construction permits.

Unfortunately, that same week, the FCC passed over six applications, and indicated that it would not make any further grants unless at least two hundred miles separated the proposed station from another on the same channel.[123]

The problem was that the Commission had contracted the distance stations needed to be separated by when it issued a proposed revision to the Table of Channel Assignments. Interference resulted – even though there weren't that many stations on the air yet. As a consequence, some thought that television might have to use the untested UHF band of frequencies.

A hearing on UHF began on September 20, and lasted for three days. At the end of that hearing, the Commission concluded that the matter was more complex than it had originally thought, and that more study was needed. There was a consensus that the UHF band would have to be used, but none as to how.[124] As a result, on September 30, it announced that all television applications would be put in pending files, that no hearings would be scheduled, and that no decisions would

As a city of immigrants, Milwaukee loved ethnic shows. In 1932 "Heinie and His Grenadiers" made its debut on WTMJ. "Heinie" was played by Jack Bundy. During WWII, the German connection was dropped – as was "Heinie." Bundy later went to WMAW, where he hosted "Heinie and His Band," and later became the station manager. The Grenadiers continued on WTMJ with Bob Heiss as the new host. On September 29, 1948, the show made its TV debut on WTMJ-TV. In 1954 it became the first locally-originated show to be broadcast in color. The Grenadiers' TV run ended on Friday, September 24, 1954. (WTMJ-TV photo)

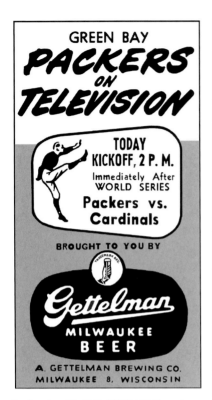

On October 10, 1948, WTMJ-TV broadcast its first Green Bay Packers' game – against the Chicago Cardinals from Wisconsin State Fair Park. On November 14, it broadcast the Packer-Bear game from Chicago – at the time the longest remote broadcast it had made.[127]

be made on cases already heard, until after the questions on channel allocations and assignments were settled.[125] At a news conference held to announce the freeze, FCC chairman Wayne Coy said that he expected the freeze to last "possibly six months."[126] It would not be lifted until 1952. (See chapter 3.)

One of the cases awaiting a decision was for Milwaukee. The three remaining applicants for the three available channels were confident that they would receive grants. The freeze changed all of that. That would lead to battles after the freeze was lifted.

Another affect of the freeze was to make WTMJ-TV the only television station in the city – and the state. It would enjoy a *de facto* monopoly for over five years, and as such, would consolidate its position. It would take many years for any other station to challenge its dominance.

The NBC Midwestern network included Milwaukee, Chicago, St. Louis, Cleveland, Detroit and Toledo. On October 30, NBC announced that AT&T would complete a coaxial cable link between Philadelphia and Cleveland in January.[128] That would join the Eastern and Midwestern networks.

The link-up of the Eastern and Midwestern networks was marked by a special two-hour telecast on Tuesday, January 11, 1949. All four networks, NBC, CBS, ABC, and Du Mont, cooperated with the program. After remarks by FCC Chairman Wayne Coy, and network officials, Milwaukee viewers were treated to CBS' Arthur Godfrey. Du Mont contributed a stage show featuring pianist Ted Steele and his orchestra, while ABC showed an episode of the *Stand by for Crime* drama. But the hit of the night was NBC's *Texaco Star Theater* starring Milton Berle.[129] "Uncle Miltie" was already that network's number one star, and Milwaukeeans were finally able to see him live.

In those early days, the station tried anything to fill time. Sprague Vonier:

The spring election in April of 1948 was the first to be televised by WTMJ-TV. The general election that November was the second. At the insistence of its parent, the Milwaukee Journal, the station broadcast from the newspaper's newsroom. Standing in the center is the station's assistant news editor Arthur Olszyk. (UWM Libraries, Archives Department, Milw MSS 203)

CHAPTER 2 ~ WTMJ-TV: CHANNELS 3 & 4

It took an hour to warm the early cameras and we had only enough crew time for one schedule of programs. Union contracts called for a break – otherwise, we would have had to work technicians for eight hours straight; and the contracts also called for live cameras whenever there was any live action before the lens.

We wanted people to leave their sets on – it took time to warm them up and adjust them, too – so we thought we had a solution: We locked a camera down in front of a gold fish bowl with the fish swimming gaily back and forth – your TV screen under water! That lasted a week before the union won the jurisdictional dispute: the fish were a live act and required a manned camera![130]

BRETA GRIEM

On February 28, 1949 WTMJ-TV added ten hours per week to its daytime programming. The shows were aimed primarily at women and children.[131] The following day, what would become one of the station's most popular programs made its debut: "What's New in the Kitchen." Its host was home economist Breta Griem.

Breta Griem (left) was WTMJ-TV's home economist from 1949-1962. Connie Daniell (right) was one of her assistants over the years. (UWM Libraries, Archives Department, Milw MSS 203)

Griem had worked for numerous companies, and had been the home economist for WTMJ radio before starting her television show. Former WTMJ-TV program director Sprague Vonier remembered:

She was a well-known woman in the culinary field in Milwaukee. She was frequently featured in the Journal, and was apparently someone Walter Damm knew. She was presented to us as a fait accompli. *"Here she is; put her on television!" Nobody knew anything about television and how to do it, so we made it up as we went along!*[132]

Griem won numerous awards during her thirteen years on the air. The show was never scripted, and required her to ad-lib on occasion. Jim Robertson recalled one particular incident:

> I remember we had a kitchen program – as almost every early television station did, I guess, and the kitchen was not a fully-equipped kitchen. We had an arrangement of rolling platforms on which to put the essentials of a set for a given show such as a kitchen. When we didn't need it, we rolled it into the corner of the studio and brought in something else.
>
> As a result, the sink was not equipped with running water. There were pans of water underneath [the counter]. And Breta Griem, who was a fabulous character – a predecessor to Julia Child in that she was superb in knowing what she was doing, also very entertaining and very natural – was doing her kitchen show one day, and she got a frog in her throat.
>
> She just reached underneath for a glass of water, and realized that it was the soapy dishwater that she had washed the dishes in. But nobody knew that until after the program. She didn't miss a syllable. She didn't grimace or make any face.[133]

At first the show ran on Tuesdays and Thursdays. It was eventually expanded to first four and then six days a week.[134] In the fall of 1961, it was merged with Beulah Donohue's "The Woman's World." Griem's final broadcast was on Friday, June 29, 1962.

On July 11, 1949, WTMJ-TV became the twelfth television station to receive a permanent license. It had operated under temporary authorization until then.[135] On July 28, WTMJ-TV entered into an agreement with the Du Mont Network to carry its programming.[136] On October 16, the station finally turned a profit.[137]

The station got into trouble in February of 1950 after NBC announced a plan to tie together twenty-three affiliates for two and one-half hours every Saturday night for thirteen weeks. The FCC claimed that NBC violated its rules regarding networks, and that its proposed plan would restrain competition. WTMJ-TV had recently been granted a regular license. In reaction, the Commission set aside that license, and instead granted a temporary one.[138]

Radio and television manager Walter Damm filed a sworn affidavit saying that WTMJ-TV had not accepted NBC's offer, and as a consequence, the station was issued a regular license on February 21.[139]

Although Radio City had been built with television in mind, its planners had seriously underestimated the space needed for the storage of scenery and equipment, which was stored in the hallways. Art Olszyk remembered that the Milwaukee Fire Department condemned the practice as a fire hazard.[140] In response, on June 6, 1950, the Journal Co.'s board of directors approved plans for improvements to WTMJ-TV, including an addition to, and remodeling of, Radio City in order to provide more space. Also included in the improvements approved by the Journal Co. board were a new 500' tower and 20 kW transmitter. Although such improvements were put on hold by the FCC's television "freeze," an application was filed on June 23. In it the company also requested that WTMJ-TV be reclassified from "metropolitan" to "rural." Rural stations were allowed greater power and coverage area, but could cover only one metropolitan area – which the company admitted might be a problem if the tower was located within the city.[141] Two new studios – one with a model kitchen – were put into service on Monday, February 5, 1951. The

CHAPTER 2 ~ WTMJ-TV: CHANNELS 3 & 4   61

Radio City auditorium was remodeled for television use, and a new control room was put into operation.[142]

On March 9, 1951, WTMJ-TV withdrew its application for a new 500' tower, and instead applied for permission to erect a 1,000' version, as proposed FCC regulations were based upon them. Because of the "freeze," the station would have to reduce the output of its transmitter in order to maintain the same radiated power and coverage area with the taller tower. It was hoped that the Commission would grant quick approval so that steel – which might become hard to get because of Korean War priorities – would be available.[143]

On March 22, 1951, the FCC issued a proposed new frequency allocation and channel assignment plan.[144] In it, seventy UHF channels (14-83) were allocated, in addition to VHF channels 2-13. Approximately ten percent of the channels were reserved for noncommercial, educational use. Milwaukee was to be assigned VHF channels 4, 10 and 12, as well as UHF channels 19, 25 and 31. Channel 4 was assigned to WTMJ-TV, which would have to move from channel 3.

On April 6, 1951, FCC approved the proposed 1,000' tower. As expected, once erected, the transmitter's power would have to be reduced such that the effective radiated power (ERP) and hence the coverage area would not increase for the duration of the "freeze."[145]

On April 30, the station began morning programming by signing on at 9:30 a.m.[146] The move was a part of an expanded schedule that saw WTMJ-TV broadcast for 100 hours per week.

Popular WTMJ announcer Gordon Thomas (left) is shown with weatherman Bill Carlsen (center) and long-time news director Jack Krueger. Thomas began doing "Time Out with Thomas" on WTMJ-TV in 1951.
(UWM Libraries, Archives Department, Milw MSS 203)

That day, popular WTMJ radio announcer Gordon Thomas started "Time Out with Thomas" on WTMJ-TV. Sprague Vonier remembered that it was a challenge to fill time on that show:

> *Every morning, we killed 90 minutes (later, an hour) using only one camera, Gordon and an unused radio studio. (We were allotted no floor crew to move things around.)*
>
> *Gordy had a table and a chair and not much else. We went to Goodwill and found old serial stories – like 'Tom Brown's School Days' or Penny Dreadfuls in public domain and read 'a chapter a day' to the audience. Gordy had tropical fish we fed every day. We had indoor plants which we watered and groomed. We hatched baby chicks and baby turtles. Every morning Gordy pretended to sneak onto the set for Breta Griem's cooking show to raid her pantry and make himself a large, thick and weird sandwich, such as cucumbers, peanut butter and ham. She would always catch him of course, accuse him of sabotaging her show by eating the props and ridicule his sandwich – ten minutes gobbled up!*
>
> *We raised birds, grew corn in an outdoor garden, helped the Humane Society find homes for pets, and received visits from the zoo director accompanied by alligators and monkeys: all the stuff that later became mainstays of late night shows.*
>
> *By 1954 network morning soap operas had moved in and Gordy's Time Out was no more.*[147]

THE WEATHER

In early 1951, WTMJ-TV assistant station manager George Comte decided, as a part of plans to expand the station's programming, to start an afternoon weather segment called "TV Weatherman." He went looking for a weathercaster, and turned to a local insurance salesman for advice. The person he asked was Bill Carlsen.

Born in Clay Center, Kansas in 1904, Carlsen completed three years of chemistry studies before the lure of life as a musician and band leader caused him to quit college. He moved to Milwaukee in 1926, and became the leader of George Devine's Wisconsin Roof Orchestra, which played on the very first WTMJ radio broadcast in 1927.

He developed an interest in aviation in 1930, when he discovered that flying would allow him to get to from gig-to-gig easier. Like all aviators, he found that knowing about weather was a practical necessity, and began to take meteorology classes – although he never received a degree in that science.

In November of 1936, he and his orchestra joined the WTMJ musical staff.[148]

Carlsen quit music with the start of WWII, and became a civilian flight instructor in Chicago. After the war, he went into the insurance business, specializing in aviation risks. After Comte decided to start the weather program, he called Carlsen to ask if he could recommend anyone. Carlsen joked that he didn't know of anyone other than himself.[149] The next thing he knew, he was doing the weather at 12:45 p.m. Monday, Wednesday and Friday.

The weather show began on Monday, April 30, 1951. It was sponsored by Butter-Nut Coffee, who would stay with Carlsen for his entire run. It was later expanded and moved to 5:55 p.m. and 10:25 p.m. by 1954, and then to 5:25 p.m. and 9:25 p.m.

With the start of a new fall season on Monday, September 27, 1954, the station changed the approach to its news block. Carlsen and the weather ended the 5:45-6:00 p.m. newscast, but led the 10:00 p.m. version – something that was unheard of.

Bill Carlsen on an early WTMJ-TV weather set. (UWM Libraries, Archives Department, Milw MSS 203)

Longtime WTMJ-TV director, Budd Reth remembered Carlsen's sense of humor:

He would arrange stunts with the floor crew all the time. They would drop ice cubes on him if it was cold and we were maybe supposed to have some sleet. On occasion they would hit him on the head a little too hard, which would stagger him! He loved it.

He could do anything he wanted because he was so popular, and ButterNut went along with it. He did a live coffee commercial for a long time where he would step behind a table, pour himself a cup of coffee, take a sip, and say: 'Mmm…that's really good!'

Well, the crew did all kinds of things to him. One time they screwed the cup down to the table so he couldn't lift it up. So he bent over to take a sip. Another time they put some brandy in the cup! They would glue the cup to the saucer.

For quite awhile in the 1950s, he would do a thing where he had a spittoon over near the big thermometer he had on the set. At the end of his segment, he would make like he was spitting. The spittoon was wired, and there was a little bit of flash powder in it, so that a little puff of smoke would come out. Well, we had one guy there who was kind of rambunctious. I assigned him to take care of the powder. We had a bank of fluorescent lights above the set, and a boom microphone over Bill as he did the weather.

So this guy put a BIG charge in the spittoon. When Bill did his spitting routine, the thing blew up the whole area! It became so smoky that it obscured the news set. It also blew out a ribbon in the boom microphone and a couple of the fluorescent lights came crashing down! The following day, we got a memo from

management saying that: 'The exploding spittoon will no longer be used on the weather effective this day!'[150]
No matter what was done, no member of the crew – not even the director – ever heard from management. Bill was so popular with his audience and his sponsors that they treated him with kid gloves. When they did ask Bill about any of the gags, he would say it was all his idea.[151]

Judy Marks had done weather at WOKY-TV, WXIX and (briefly) at WITI-TV. In August of 1959, she joined the announcing staff at WTMJ-TV.[152] As she remembered:

When I was hired, I was told that I would NEVER do the weather. Well, Ted Moore was doing the weather at noon, but a sponsor asked that I do it, so they let me do it Fridays. Then the sponsor asked to have me do it five days-a-week.

The next thing I know, I was the substitute for Bill Carlsen, and then started doing the 6:00 and 10:00 p.m. weather on Saturdays. Ted would do it Sundays at 10:00 p.m., where he would also do the sports. He was also the voice of the Green Bay Packers on WTMJ radio. I would substitute for him if he was out-of-town for a game. Well, I was sitting at home one Sunday watching. Dave Adams was doing the news. I saw him moving from set-to-set doing news, weather and sports! Ted had overslept. So they took Sunday nights away from him and gave it to me.

They told me that I'd never do weather, but I wound up doing it seven days-a-week![153]

On August 24, 1959, WTMJ-TV became the first station in the city to install weather radar[154], which was used for the first time on a weathercast on November 3.[155] Judy Marks remembered that she had a lot to learn about it:

Bill Carlsen does a live commercial for ButterNut Coffee during his weathercast. (UWM Libraries, Archives Department, Milw MSS 203)

We were sitting in a meeting when they were talking about the radar. This shows how naive I was at the time, but it was so funny! They were talking about echoes. When you see something on the radar it's referred to as an echo. I didn't know that. So I said, "I don't hear anything!"[156]

Bill Carlsen and Judy Marks look over weather data, including the radar. (Milwaukee Journal photo, historic photo collection/Milwaukee Public Library, ©2008 Journal Sentinel, Inc., reproduced with permission.)

On June 29, 1970, Paul Joseph joined the WTMJ-TV staff. As a graduate meteorologist, he represented a major transition. Prior to his arrival, announcers had to learn about weather. Joseph knew about weather, but despite a year-long stint as a TV meteorologist while a graduate student in Utah, he still had a lot to learn about broadcasting. After being hired by WTMJ-TV, he wasn't allowed to do the weather! Paul Joseph:

> *They had told me when I was hired, that I would be taking over for Bill Carlsen, as he had told them that he was going to retire. They told me that it wasn't going to be easy, but that they wanted to take the route of using a meteorologist.*
>
> *I was ready, but the interesting thing was that I didn't do much weathercasting for awhile. They didn't have much for me to do. Bill hadn't announced his retirement yet and Judy was doing the weekends.*
>
> *I would work with Bill and help him prepare his forecast. They started a 5:00 p.m. newscast shortly after I arrived. In order to give me more to do they made me the science editor. I had to come up with story ideas related to science, go out with film photographers, and then they taught me how to edit the film! Then I did the science segments at 5:00 p.m.*
>
> *Late in 1970, Phil Laeser [who was now operations manager] walked into the weather office one day and said: 'Paul, how are you doin'? How do you like it here?'*

An approaching storm as seen on WTMJ-TV's first weather radar. (WTMJ-TV photo)

I must've been in a cranky mood, and sort of laid into him. I said: 'You guys hired me and moved me all the way from Utah, and I haven't even done a weathercast yet!'

He looked kind of surprised. That got things moving around the station[157]

In December, Joseph took over the weather slots done by Judy Marks, who subsequently left the station in February of 1971.[158]

By that time, station management had recognized that Carlsen was getting near retirement, and Joseph was slated to replace him. Paul Joseph:

Bill Carlsen still hadn't announced his retirement. I was still doing the science reports as well as the weekend weathercasts. I was also doing weekdays when Bill was on vacation. I remember asking news director Don Loose what was going on. He told me that Bill had changed his mind, and that he wasn't quite ready [to retire].

Art Olszyk recalled that Executive Producer Norb Tatro liked the fact that Joseph could do a tight, three and one-half minute weather segment, while Carlsen wanted five.[159]

After twenty-one years as WTMJ-TV's weatherman, Bill Carlsen retired on May 1, 1972, and Joseph took over. He remembered:

Bill Carlsen and Paul Joseph (UWM Libraries, Archives Department, Milw MSS 203)

I knew I wasn't very good when I started. I really didn't have a lot of experience in broadcasting. It was a struggle for the first few years. As I understand it, I was hired in a bit of controversy. There was a division at the station as to whether they should have a trained meteorologist or an entertainer, as 'Albert the Alley Cat' was very popular in the market at that time. As I understand it, top management wanted a meteorologist, but programming wanted more of an entertainer."

I wasn't an entertainer and I wasn't very funny, so if I was going to be successful I had to sell weather and its importance. I love changeable and interesting weather and always got excited when the big storms were approaching.[160]

Sprague Vonier remembered that it wasn't programming that wanted an entertainer:

I was always a strong advocate for a weather person, and was well aware that we beat the other guys with Bill Carlsen, not only because of his personality but because of his weather credentials. I also believed that the way to compete was to offer a solid, credible alternative to what the competition offered, rather than imitate what they were doing: provide something better.

Our sales people were strongly interested in a showbiz type, who would have a commercial impact and make for an easy sell. Carlsen probably had more commercial impact than any other person on our team, and there was always a waiting list to sponsor his program. However, with a new format, in which the news-weather-sports segments would no longer be individually sponsored, the new weather person would not be available for commercials.[161]

Joseph presided over many changes in weather forecasting at the station:

As soon as Bill retired, my first request to them was to get a facsimile machine that allowed me to bring in all of the National Weather Service maps and

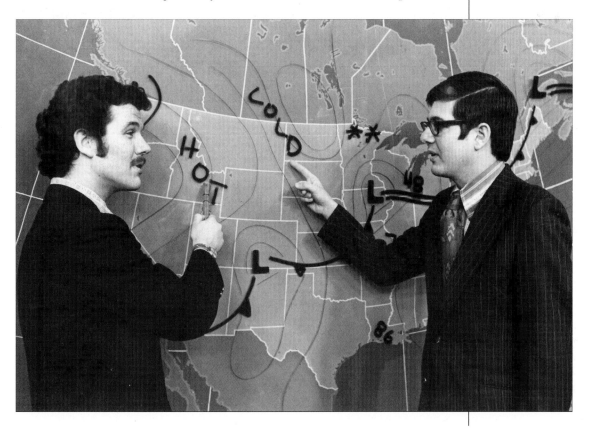

Dr. Walt Lyons (L) did the weather with Paul Joseph in the early 1970s. (WTMJ-TV photo)

computer models, that I had been trained to use in college. Bill had never been trained on computer models and drew all his maps by hand.

I remember using satellite pictures, and the only place I could get them was from the Journal downtown. I used to get a glossy picture in the middle of the afternoon that was delivered by someone from the newspaper. To show it, I would have to put it on a music stand, and a camera would take a close-up. I would use a pen to point out important features on the satellite picture. Then I thought I would get really advanced and draw weather features on it such as fronts and pressure systems."

I had known about Chroma-Key, but we didn't use it on the weather. We had one whole side of the round studio dedicated to weather. There was a huge map of the United States with plexiglass over it. I said, 'Couldn't I stand out in the ocean, and we could Chroma-Key the satellite picture over where I was?'

In the early 1980s we evolved into using computer graphics. What the viewers didn't see was that we used the computers to start analyzing weather data. It used to be we took raw data like, temperature, dew point, wind direction and speed, and hand plotted it on the maps. You would draw isobars – lines of equal pressure – on the map to determine where your central areas of areas of high and low pressure were located, and then locate your wind, temperature, and dew point fields to show where your frontal systems were. That took a LONG time. At first the computers just plotted the data. Then they got a bit more sophisticated, and if you asked for an analysis of whatever field you were looking for, they would do that for you.

Then color satellite images came into being, followed by color radar, where you could see more intense areas of rainfall with different colors. As the graphics became more and more advanced, the on-air look became more sophisticated. We eventually got one of the first Doppler radar systems that allowed us to not only see the location of precipitation, but also how fast it was moving, and generally in what direction. That helped in detecting severe thunderstorms and possible tornados.[162]

Joseph retired in 2006 after thirty-six years with the station, and the weather center in Radio City was subsequently named after him. John Malan, who had been hired away from WISN-TV to do the 10:00 p.m. weathercast and fill-in during Joseph's vacations, replaced him as chief meteorologist.

Milwaukee County granted the station an easement so that one of the guy wire anchors for the new tower could be located in Estabrook Parkway. Excavation for the foundations was begun in early November. It was hoped that the tower might become operational the following year.[163]

Live TV had its real dangers. Quick thinking saved what could've been a disastrous incident on "The Handy Workshop." Budd Reth:

On a day when a guest expert was demonstrating some fancy cutting at a table saw, two of his boys, around ten years old, were his guests. He was cutting pieces off a board: the sound was roar, ding, roar ding, when suddenly, it was roar, ding ding, ouch...and a muffled comment. I was in the control room about 30 ft above looking down on the studio. This was a week-end early morning show and we were all half asleep. I looked down for the floor director and said, "What was that, Cliff? It sounded like he said Jesus, I cut my finger off!"

Cliff replied with a hand sign holding up three of his fingers. I couldn't believe it. THREE FINGERS? Cliff got on the studio phone and said, 'If you get on a close-up, I'll crawl in and pick up the tops.' This we did. Meanwhile,

A simple wood and cardboard graphic used to open "The Handy Workshop." The piece of wood at the left was pulled to simulate its running through a table saw, revealing the name of the host. A guest expert once accidentally cut the tips off of three fingers on the show! (UWM Libraries, Archives Department, Milw MSS 203)

"The Woman's World" with Beulah Donahue made its debut on October 1, 1951. It featured crafts, interviews with celebrities, and other topics of interest to women. Donahue won a number of awards during the show's run. The show ran through December 29, 1961. (UWM Libraries, Archives Department, Milw MSS 203)

Marvin Moran and the Malone Sisters (Janice with accordion and Marilyn) hosted "Let's Remember" in 1951. They later did other shows on WTMJ-TV, and appeared on the first locally-produced color program. (WTMJ-TV photo)

immediately after he mumbled his comment, the expert coolly standing there with his mutilated fingers in his good hand, said, 'A little accident, I cut myself.' Fortunately, he had another 'expert' with him who he called on to take over. The show was over in about ten minutes. He was still in the studio holding the wounded hand. Cliff said he was taking him to the emergency room. He handed the man the tips, wrapped in some Kleenex and, believe it or not, the man put them in his jacket pocket, gave the pocket a couple pats with his good hand and said, "Sure, they'll sew those babies right back on."[164]

Sprague Vonier remembered:

Fortunately, the microphone had been turned off while the saw was in action, so we didn't hear his outcry. We had no desire to thrust several thousand viewers into a state of shock and distress.

One must be astonished at how quickly good people act in such a crisis. [Budd Reth] immediately swung the camera away. The announcer, who acted as straight-man, stepped in with reassuring words and a change of subject. But the most resourceful of all was the floor director, Cliff Lemke, who turned out to be an eagle scout and scout master, quickly found the severed fingers, wrapped them in a clean handkerchief, tucked them under his arm to keep them at body temperature, and hurried the expert and his fingers to the emergency room.[165]

Although the tips were sewn back on the expert's fingers, they didn't "take" and he lost them.[166]

An outdoor studio was constructed just west of Radio City starting in February of 1952. It was used for the first time on July 15 when "Time Out with Thomas" was broadcast from it.[167] Included were a small shelter and an outdoor grill, which is shown here, being used by Breta Griem. Long-time WTMJ/WTMJ-TV announcer Gordon Hinkley can also be seen. (UWM Libraries, Archives Department, Milw MSS 203)

MOVIE HOSTING

When WTMJ-TV began broadcasting, few feature films had been released to television. The Hollywood studios estimated at the time that TV revenue was less than half that they received from the reissue of their films to theaters. They considered developing theater and pay-TV, but the FCC consistently blocked such schemes during the 1950s. In addition, federal anti-trust rulings beginning in 1948, forced the studios to divest themselves of their theaters. Television was still considered a competitor to movie theaters, and the independent owners threatened to boycott the product of any studios which produced telefilms, or released their features to the medium.

In 1947, the Screen Actors Guild negotiated agreements with the studios which provided that should a producer permit television use of its films made for the theaters, which were completed after August 1, 1948, SAG could notify its members not to work for him. The studios came to residual payment agreements with the unions for films made after that date, but only after they had abandoned all monetary claims to the pre-1948 features. With the advent of Technicolor, Cinemascope, and 3-D technologies, the studios saw TV as a way to market their older, black & white films.

Judy Marks Joined WTMJ-TV in 1959 as a staff announcer, as well as to host "Theater at 4." (WTMJ-TV photo)

Bob Knutzen hosted "Star Award Theater." (WTMJ-TV photo)

The networks did not want Hollywood's product. This was the so-called "Golden Age" of live television drama and variety shows. NBC and CBS (The two dominant networks) thought their shows were of a high quality and feared dilution by Hollywood. NBC in particular, opposed the non-network distribution of programming. It anticipated broadcasting its live shows in color, and was opposed to showing black & white films. In addition, the networks had fears (founded) that the studios would package the less popular with popular features, forcing them to take the entire package.

The first trickle of films to television came from foreign studios, which had no agreements with the Screen Actors Guild. Republic Pictures withdrew from the production of feature films, and no longer fearing retaliation by SAG, released its films to TV. A 1954 decision by the U.S. Court of Appeals (Ninth District) established that the studio had the right to release a group of Roy Rogers and Gene Autry films to TV.[168] Other smaller (the so-called "poverty row") studios did so as well, as they feared that the advent of color broadcasting would diminish the value to TV.

The major break came when Howard Hughes sold RKO to General TeleRadio (a division of General Tire) in July of 1955. The RKO library included 740 feature films. In December of 1955, the television rights were sold to C&C Television. (General TeleRadio retained the right to show the films on its own stations.) C&C Television was a division of C&C Super Corporation, which made soft drinks and other products.

Since the networks had no interest in showing feature films, C&C began a series of single-market sales in June of 1956. C&C received advertising spots from the stations as partial payment. It also offered a deal in which in exchange for purchasing the entire package of 740 films, a station would receive the right to telecast the films as often as they wished, in perpetuity.[169] By that time, four other studios began releasing their films to individual stations in single markets, and in 1958 the last three studios followed.

Thus the showing of feature films during non-network hours or by independent stations became a local phenomenon. (There were a few exceptions, such as CBS' annual showing of *The Wizard of Oz*.) By the late 1950s feature films were accepted as just another programming source.

The broadcast quality of NTSC television was equivalent to that of 16mm film, and as such, that was the format chosen for films released to the medium. They were shown using a film chain ("telecine") or flying-spot scanner that converted them to NTSC video. In order to show commercials on film, a station had to edit them in or own more than one film chain.

CHAPTER 2 ~ WTMJ-TV: CHANNELS 3 & 4   73

To introduce the films and/or do live commercials, the stations needed someone to act as a host. All stations used a booth announcer, and it was easiest simply to have that individual perform those functions over a slide or film introduction. Most went a step further and used an on-camera host or hostess. WTMJ-TV had a number of them over the years.

In the 1960s, some stations began running franchised cash give-aways, such as "Dialing for Dollars" during movie shows. WTMJ-TV ran its own version called "Cash on the Line" in 1968-1969 during its afternoon movie. Judy Marks was the hostess, and broke up her floor crew one day:

> *There was also a similar show on the radio. On that one, the listener had to give the dollar amount if they were called. We asked our viewers to tell us a "mystery word" if we called them. So one day I called this lady who gave me a dollar amount. So I said, "Oh this is Judy Marks your television virgin – I mean version of the game!" It broke up the floor directors!*[170]

Judy Marks hosted "Cash on the Line" during "Three-Thirty Theater" and later "Movie 4." (WTMJ-TV photo)

Feature films continued to be a staple for local stations through the 1970s, although beginning in the 1960s the major networks began programming many popular ones. After much development and regulatory wrangling, cable TV began to grow during the 1980s. By the 1990s, the cable networks had obtained the rights to many feature films, and they were no longer available to local stations. First VCRs and later DVD players made it easy for viewers to own their own copies and watch them anytime they wanted to. With the switch to videotape distribution of films, there was no longer the need to use a host, and the stations simply had an announcer pre-record the introductions. Thus, the local movie host went the way of the film chain.

On April 14, 1952, the FCC issued its Sixth Report and General Order, which lifted the freeze on new television licenses as of July 1, and provided for 617 VHF and 1436 UHF licenses, 242 of which were reserved for noncommercial educational use. Twelve of the latter were assigned to Wisconsin: two VHF and ten UHF. The Commission adopted a policy of intermixing VHF and UHF channels in the same markets. Milwaukee received VHF channels 4, 10 and 12, and UHF channels 19, 25 and 31.[171] WTMJ-TV and WKZO-TV (now WWMT-TV) in Kalamazoo, Michigan interfered with each other – although it was outside of the area protected by each station's license. As such, WTMJ-TV was ordered to shift from channel 3 to channel 4, and the FCC authorized the shift on July 11.

Beginning in January of 1951, the station had begun showing Sunday services live from various churches in the area. The programs were the idea of the station's director of public affairs programs, Bruce Wallace, who worked with a group of local religious groups.[172] On July 13, 1952, it took a chance on a remote from Washington County. Sprague Vonier:

> *Our engineering crew, led by Henry Goeden and Nick Brauer, found a way to set up transmission from Holy Hill back to the studio and broadcast towers, and treated our audience to gorgeous live pictures of dawn rising over the misty woods and meadows of Erin township. Today it would be an unremarkable cliché; then it was a first.*[173]

WTMJ-TV began broadcasting local church services in 1951. Here is the 1959 Christmas Midnight Mass from Christ King Church. (WTMJ-TV photo)

A steel strike had delayed shipments, but the first carloads arrived for the new tower on September 1. In a ceremony on Friday, September 19, Walter Damm tightened a gold-painted bolt with a gold-painted wrench to begin erection of the first column. A gallon bottle of milk was broken against that column as a part of the dedication ceremony.[174]

On Tuesday, September 30, WTMJ-TV began a series of thirteen weekly, fifteen-minute film programs, amplifying editorials in the *Milwaukee Journal* dealing with

CHAPTER 2 ~ WTMJ-TV: CHANNELS 3 & 4   75

civic issues. Believed to be the first series of its kind in the nation, the first program focused on litter.[175] Called "The Milwaukee Editorial in Pictures," the segments were penned by editorial writer John Reddin, and narrated by Paul Skinner.[176]

On October 16, the new tower became the tallest structure in Wisconsin, when it passed the 420' level. Milwaukee's City Hall had been the tallest at 397'.[177] Sadly, one worker perished in a fall from the 400' level.

THE HOT SHOTS

With the end of the 1952 college football season, WTMJ-TV needed Saturday afternoon programming. At 3:00 p.m. on December 6, it began a new music show called the "Hot Shots Review." It featured Joe Szot and other Radio City musicians in a country-western music format. Long-time WTMJ radio personality Gordon Hinkley was tapped to emcee the show:

> *I had a little bit of a musical background. I played piano – although I didn't play on that show too often. So, I guess I just fit in.*
>
> *The other guys* [studio musicians] *had to switch from playing polkas* [on The Grenadiers] *to country music. They had to go out and buy some new music.*[178]

After "The Grenadiers" ended its long run as a noon show, it was replaced by "The Hot Shots." Like most shows of that era, it was done live, which always made for some interesting moments. Gordon Hinkley:

> *So I'm emceeing the show and I used to bring people up on the stage to participate in it. I had this girl – a teenager. She was a little reluctant to get up on the stage, but she finally came up. So I did a little interview with her, and she was so nervous that she fell over! I caught her! It scared me to have that happen while we were on the air!*[179]

The show continued until Friday, May 5, 1961. The following day, a new variety show, "Carousel" made its debut, and the Hot Shots were featured. The weekday

Joe Szot and the "Hot Shots." At the right is WTMJ's Gordon Hinkley, who emceed the show for many years. (UWM Libraries, Archives Department, Milw MSS 203)

version of "Carousel" ran until Friday, September 22, 1961. Thereafter, it was replaced by "Mid-Day." The Saturday show ran through March 24, 1962.

It was one of the last shows to be broadcast live from the auditorium studio. That facility was demolished in the 1980s, and new studios for AM and FM radio, as well as other offices were built in the space as a part of a major renovation. Gordon Hinkley missed the old studio:

> *It was sad to see what they did, since they weren't doing live shows anymore. I know that I wasn't the only one. We'd go in there when they were tearing it down, and it bothered me because that was a beautiful room – with good acoustics.*
>
> *During the 'Hot Shots', I don't believe that it was filled during the week, but on Saturday we always had a full house. It was sad when they got rid of it, but I guess they had to do something with the space.*[180]

Some were concerned that the new tower might pose a hazard. A station neighbor, The Milprint Co., asked Mayor Frank Zeidler for assurance that the tower was safe. The mayor asked city officials to study the matter, and in a memo dated January 5, 1953, such assurance was given by an expediter in the city's housing and annexation services department.[181] The tower was completed on March 27, with a height of 1,017'.[182] On April 20, the structure reached its final height of 1,035' after the antenna and beacon were installed.

When the Boston Braves announced that they were moving to Milwaukee in late March, Journal Co. management thought so highly of the move, that they characterized broadcasts of the games to be a public service! WTMJ-TV formulated plans to record NBC programs displaced by baseball telecasts for rebroadcast at a later date, while NBC considered placing some programs with other Milwaukee stations after they began broadcasting.[183] In the end, no home, and only a handful of away games were televised.

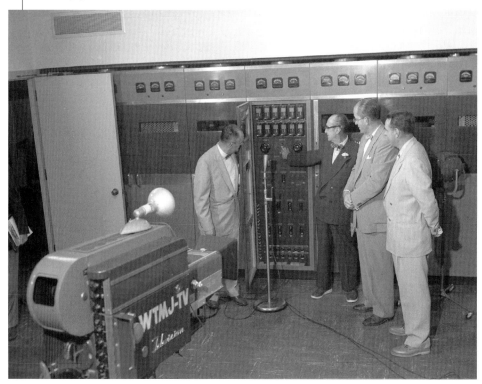

Walter Damm throws the switch that turned off the station's old transmitter. WTMJ-TV then began broadcasting on channel 4. At the left is Phil Laeser; at the right are WTMJ/WTMJ-TV Stations Manager Russ Winnie, and Promotions Director Sprague Vonier. (WTMJ-TV photo)

Holding up WTMJ-TV's switch to channel 4 was litigation involving the Zenith Corp. Zenith had broadcast over experimental station, KS2XBS on channel 2 in Chicago since 1939. In 1951, it had used the station to test its "Phonevision" pay-TV system. (See chapter 9.) It had a commercial construction permit for the channel in 1946, but was one of the many applicants who asked the Commission to dismiss it during the color TV hearings in 1946-1947. In 1948, it filed a new application for the channel, but that was frozen. Meanwhile, ABC had merged with Paramount Pictures, and as a condition, the FCC ordered Paramount to sell WBKB-TV, which broadcast on channel 4. CBS purchased the station and on February 11 changed the call letters to WBBM-TV. In its Sixth General Order and Report, the Commission ordered WBBM-TV to shift to channel 2 "as soon as practical." Zenith appealed, but the FCC denied it, and dismissed its application for channel 2 on February 9. In May, Zenith took the matter to the District of Columbia Circuit Court of Appeals, asking it to force the FCC to grant it a competitive hearing with CBS.[184, 185]

Wisconsin Governor Walter Kohler, Jr. (left) took part in the channel switch ceremony. He and Walter Damm look on as Russ Winnie (right) speaks to the audience. (WTMJ-TV photo)

Nonetheless, WTMJ-TV began broadcasting a visual and aural test pattern on channel 4 beginning on Monday, June 22, 1953. The tests took place one hour after the last station signed off, and between 5:30-7:30 a.m. They used the new 1,035' tower and 50 kW transmitter. July 11 was set as the date for the switchover.[186]

The following day, the FCC took what it thought was final action on the matter, and authorized WBBM-TV to shift to channel 2.[187] It did so on July 5.[188]

On Saturday night, July 11, 1953, WTMJ-TV made the switch to channel 4. At that time it began using the new tower and more powerful transmitter. The switch took place in a special show broadcast between 7-7:30 p.m. Included were tours of the new transmitter facility and film of the tower being erected. At 7:20:40 p.m. Walter Damm hit a switch that turned off the old transmitter. Less than thirty seconds later, WTMJ-TV began broadcasting on channel 4. The first person seen on that channel was Wisconsin Governor Walter J. Kohler, Jr., who spoke from the WTMJ-TV transmitter building. The new tower and more power increased the station's coverage to a radius of ninety miles – up from the forty-five to fifty it had previously.[189]

Since 1948, WTMJ-TV was able to receive network programming from Chicago via a one-way microwave relay system. It could not originate programming for the networks. That changed in 1953 with the completion of a $5M radio relay system between Chicago and Minneapolis that included a branch to Milwaukee. The first event originated in Milwaukee televised via a network (CBS) was the Kid Gavilan –

A WTMJ-TV cameraman pans up to show the new 1,035' tower during the ceremony. (WTMJ-TV photo)

The new WTMJ-TV color control room. In the foreground is the audio man. (UWM Libraries, Archives Department, Milw MSS 203)

Ramon Fuentes boxing match, held at the Milwaukee Arena as a part of a weekly series sponsored by the Pabst Brewing Co.[190] The program was cleared by sixty-nine stations and seen by an estimated 40-60 million viewers.[191]

In January of 1950, the Radio Manufacturers Association (RMA) proposed a second NTSC to study the color problem and propose standards. The FCC had participated in the first committee, but declined to do so in the second.[192] The FCC approved the CBS field-sequential color system and authorized commercial color broadcasting to begin as of November 20.[193] On October 19, the Office of Defense Mobilization announced that it was halting the production of color television sets, as some of the components would be needed for the Korean War effort.[194] After much litigation, CBS began color telecasts on June 25, 1951.[195] The network stopped color telecasting on October 19, 1951, due to the lack of receivers. (See chapter 3.) After thirty-two months of deliberations, the NTSC passed new color standards based on the RCA dot-sequential system in January of 1953.[196]

The FCC had not yet approved commercial color broadcasting using that system. It did allow testing to take place, and gave NBC special permission to broadcast *The Colgate Comedy Hour* in color on Sunday, November 22, 1953.[197] WTMJ-TV carried it, but viewers received it in black and white. A single RCA color receiver was set up in a Radio City lounge. It had been flown to Milwaukee the previous day. It was the first time a color receiver was used outside of NBC's studios or test locations.[198]

On December 17, the FCC approved the RCA electronic color TV system.[199] NBC claimed to have had the first color telecast (a bulletin with a colored insignia) at 5:59 p.m. EST that day, and a complete telecast at 6:30. CBS showed its first col-

or program at 6:15 p.m. EST. NBC and CBS planned to broadcast some programs in color. ABC had no plans, but said that it would begin formulating them now that the system had been approved. Du Mont said that it planned to show color programs, but had not developed a schedule. The *Milwaukee Journal* stated that there were only two color receivers in the Milwaukee area at the time! Nonetheless, WTMJ-TV had begun installing color transmitting equipment, in order to televise the Tournament of Roses parade on January 1, 1954.[200]

On December 20, 1953, WTMJ-TV broadcast its first color program from NBC: Menotti's Christmas operetta, *Amahl and the Night Visitors*.[201]

On New Years' Day, 500 people swamped the American Appliance and TV store at 2743 North Teutonia Avenue, to watch NBC's broadcast of the Tournament of Roses parade on WTMJ-TV. The store used a Hallicrafter color set which was equipped with a 12.5 inch RCA picture tube. Four police officers were needed to keep order.[202] The Blatz Brewing Co. signed on later that month as the first sponsor of color programs on WTMJ-TV.[203]

In late April, *Broadcasting Telecasting* magazine reported that a survey of distributors conducted by WTMJ-TV showed that there were fifty-five color receivers in use in the area.[204] Meanwhile, station engineers continued to receive, install, and test color equipment. On May 10, the station began broadcasting a color test pattern. Later that month, it announced that it would begin broadcasting some local shows in color beginning sometime around July 1. For the rest of the year, one sponsored show would be broadcast in color approximately once-a-week. Advertisers would not be charged extra, but the following year, the station planned to do so.[205]

On June 16 and 17, an NBC crew originated the first color telecasts from the Milwaukee area. The network's mobile unit visited ten cities as a part of the "America in Color" series. On June 16, two, eight-minute segments showing the flower gardens in Whitnall Park were aired on the *Home* show. The following day, two

RCA Chairman David Sarnoff (left) visits with Walter Damm in front of one of the station's color cameras. (UWM Libraries, Archives Department, Milw MSS 203)

segments were carried from the park on both the *Today* and *Home* shows. Outdoor fashions and German cuisine were featured in the segments, which used the park's rose garden as a background.[206]

On Sunday, July 18, 1954, WTMJ-TV televised "The Grenadiers" at 2:00 p.m. It was the first locally-produced program televised in color. Mayor Frank Zeidler made an appearance, as did the singing group Marvin Moran and the Malone Sisters.[207] The first commercially sponsored color program ran on July 20, when the Blatz Brewing Company's "Triangle Theater" presented a program titled "The Layton Art Story," a tribute to the Layton School of Art.[208] On August 26, a network color broadcast originated from Radio City, when a ten minute segment of the *Home* program featured arts and crafts from the Wisconsin State Fair, hosted by announcer Bob Heiss. Visitors to the fair were able to watch the program on a color receiver set up at the Journal's Communications Center there.[209]

In order to provide more color capability, WTMJ-TV took delivery of a second RCA color camera, and converted two studios to a single, larger one for color. They went online on October 29. The new color studio became the largest in the state, and featured more lighting, as required for color. To compensate for the additional heat generated, the air conditioning level was increased. All live, local programs broadcast between 11:00 a.m. and 6:30 p.m. were broadcast in color.[210] Beginning on November 1, 1956, all locally-originated programs were.

CBS purchased WOKY-TV on October 22, 1954 – shortly after the FCC changed its multiple-ownership rules to allow an individual entity to own two UHF in addition to five VHF stations.[211] Rumors began to surface indicating that NBC was looking to purchase a station in the city. They were quelled in a telegram from RCA Chairman David Sarnoff to Walter Damm on October 28. In it, Sarnoff said: "Any rumors to the effect that NBC contemplates buying or erecting its own station in Milwaukee are completely unfounded. I am very pleased with the progress of our present association with the *Milwaukee Journal* and you as reported to me by the boys at NBC."[212]

"BOWLING WITH THE CHAMPS"

Bowling has long been a Milwaukee staple. WTVW/WISN-TV began running a local bowling show in early 1955. (See chapter 6.) At noon on December 4 of that year, WTMJ-TV began its own. Named "Bowling with the Champs," the show would last for almost forty years.

Originally broadcast live from a different local alley each week, the show derived its name from the format, in which a nationally prominent bowler would roll a three-game match against one from the area. The first host was long-time WTMJ-TV sports announcer Larry Clark. *Milwaukee Journal* bowling writer Billy Sixty provided commentary. Sixty hand-picked the local bowlers. The first show was broadcast from Mitchell Recreation on the city's south side. In that match, Jimmy Miller defeated Ray Eklund.[213] Most of the best area bowlers competed on the show, and it became a Sunday staple for many viewers.

WTMJ-TV sports director Blaine Walsh later took over the hosting duties. Dick Johnson later hosted the show until he left the station for WISN-TV, at which time he was replaced by Bob Beasley.

In 1958, the show moved to its first permanent location, Serb Memorial Hall on the south side, and then to the Eagles Club in 1962. With the debut of the Professional Bowlers' Tour, national bowlers were hard to recruit. As a consequence,

"Champs" evolved into a showcase for state competitors. In 1964, the first qualifying tournament was held.[214]

In 1966, Dick Richards, who managed Red Carpet Leisure Industries for the Sampson brothers, convinced WTMJ-TV management to move the show to the Red Carpet Bowlero. Richards had to agree to pay $150 per show to cover the cost of moving the remote equipment to the facility, and also had to erect a microwave tower, so that the signal could be beamed back to Radio City.[215]

Hank Stoddard began hosting "Bowling with the Champs" in 1969, with Billy Sixty continuing to provide color commentary. Dennis Wright, who won the "Champs" title in 1956-'57 later replaced Sixty as color commentator. As Hank Stoddard remembered:

For almost forty years, WTMJ-TV presented "Bowling with the Champs" Sunday mornings. (UWM Libraries, Archives Department, Milw MSS 203)

Gerry McGrath was the program manager at WTMJ-TV at the time. Billy kept talking about Ned Day and Hank Marino and all of the great bowlers of decades earlier. Gerry decided that we needed someone who could relate more to present-day bowlers, so he brought in Dennis Wright as the color guy.[216]

Madison bowler Jeff Richgels, another show champion, was the last color commentator.

At first the show was done live, but it was later taped for rebroadcast. Women began competing in 1968, and the show was telecast in color beginning in 1972. In 1975, slow-motion was added.[217]

In 1977, the show moved to the Red Carpet Celebrity Lanes on Milwaukee's south side. The format changed in 1991. Hank Stoddard:

> *It used to be a head-to-head, three-game match. The total of the three games decided the winner, who would advance to the next round. Towards the end, we went to the stepladder format used by the 'Pro Bowlers Tour' on ABC. It became a one-game elimination situation, rather than the total of the three games.*[218]

In its heyday, the show was exceptionally popular. In a 1977 column, *Milwaukee Journal* sports writer Bob Wolf called it "the greatest phenomenon in Milwaukee television" – pointing out that the show had more viewers than Milwaukee Brewers', Milwaukee Bucks', Wisconsin Badgers', or Marquette Warriors' games.[219] Hank Stoddard:

> *It was enormously popular. I think as many people recognized me out on the street from 'Bowling with the Champs' than did people who knew I was the sports anchor. People might watch other channels during the week, but every Sunday morning, they would watch 'Bowling with the Champs'.*
>
> *Leo Pack who ran the Bowlero would do a commercial interview with me that we would run between games. I would ask him what he had coming up, and he would tell the viewers all about the tournaments at the Bowlero. I would always end it by saying: '…and if you want to learn more about this call Leo at…', and he'd always say: '258-9000; Thank you Hank!'*
>
> *I would have people on the street just walk by me and say: '258-9000; Thank you Hank!'*[220]

Stoddard continued to host the show, even after his retirement in June of 1994. By the 1990s, the television culture had changed, and the station had some decisions to make. The show was losing money, and the remote equipment used needed replacement. As a consequence, it elected to change the focus of its Sunday morning programming, and channel its resources into news. "Bowling with the Champs" was cancelled. After almost forty years of presenting the areas top bowlers, the last WTMJ-TV show was broadcast on April 9, 1995.[221]

On June 26, 1959, President Eisenhower and Britain's Queen Elizabeth formally opened the St. Lawrence Seaway. NBC provided live coverage of the ceremony at noon. WTMJ-TV originated part of the coverage, which resulted in yet another first for the station. Sprague Vonier:

> *WTMJ-TV Milwaukee was to provide the title shot of an ocean-going class of vessel, its prow rising over the horizon and coming toward the camera, looming larger and larger, until it filled the screen.*
>
> *The ship was the newly-commissioned Aquaramma – the largest passenger ship and the first of its kind on the Great Lakes – on its shakedown cruise from the ship yards in Michigan, where it was built, to Milwaukee. On board were students from Marquette University with a gala party in progress."*[222]

Vonier remembered that WTMJ-TV engineers Henry Goeden and Nick Brauer again came up with an innovative method to transmit the signal – this time from a moving ship:

> *They went out and found a surplus Army mount for a machine gun. They set one of their [microwave] dishes on it, so it could swivel. It had a powerful sight on it, so they could sight the dish that was on the ship. We experimented with the fire department's fire tug, "The Deluge." They let us mount a dish on it. We also had one on the top of a grain elevator. We took that tug all the way up the [Milwaukee] river, and were able to follow it all the way from its mouth to Gimbel's on Wisconsin Avenue.*[223]

CHAPTER 2 ~ WTMJ-TV: CHANNELS 3 & 4   83

NBC had GE College Bowl, but WTMJ-TV had a similar show for high school students. Here the author's alma mater takes on Wauwatosa West. (UWM Libraries, Archives Department, Milw MSS 203)

Even then, there were problems:

> It all had to be timed to the second. The ship itself, with a turn-around radius of 15 miles, had to be set to appear in the horizon at the precise moment when the show opened. For this, we stationed cameras atop waterfront grain elevators and on the decks of the lighthouse, one mile out at the harbor entrance. Just as the ship passed, the camera placed on the one-mile lighthouse was, also to take shots of the party in progress.
> Perfect timing. Everything went off without a hitch.
> Today, after pictures from space and the surface of the moon, such video seems routine; it was magic then. If we missed, we would have had national egg on our chins.[224]

"MID-DAY"

On September 25, 1961 "Mid-Day" replaced "Carousel." Beulah Donahue hosted the show, which opened with Judy Marks and the weather. Rod Synnes did the news, and Bob Heiss delivered an editorial and then read viewers' letters on those delivered previously. The second half of the show was filled with features such as interviews with visiting celebrities, previews of upcoming area events, or some facet of Milwaukee life. The last show was on February 10, 1967.

Thereafter, the weekday version of "Kids Klub" came to an end (See section on children's shows.). To replace it, WTMJ-TV started a new show on Monday, February 13, 1967. Called the "Noon Show," it featured host Bob Knudzen, Bunny Raasch, Jayne Whalen and long-time Journal Co. studio musician Grant Krueger in a variety format, featuring music, games, interviews, cooking segments, and participation by viewers. It ran for forty-five minutes, Monday-Friday, and was followed by a fifteen minute newscast. It ended on Friday, October 27, 1967.

In 1952, WTMJ-TV had broadcast programming which amplified editorials run in the *Milwaukee Journal*. The broadcasting division of the company had not formulated its own. That changed on August 16, 1962, WTMJ-TV when announced

Beulah Donahue hosted "Mid-Day." (UWM Libraries, Archives Department, Milw MSS 203)

that it would begin running them Monday-Friday at 10:15 p.m. beginning on September 3. Long-time announcer Bob Heiss was the first to deliver them.[225]

L-R: Bob Knudzen, Bunny Raasch and Jayne Whalen on the premiere of the "Noon Show." (WTMJ-TV photo)

"TODAY FOR WOMEN"

Beulah Donahue and "Woman's World" left the air at the end of 1961, leaving WTMJ-TV without a women's show. That changed on September 2, 1962 when "Today for Women" made its debut. Venerable WTMJ/WTMJ-TV announcer Gordon Thomas was the show's first host. Jayne Whalen served as the home economist. Beulah Donahue hosted the occasional segment, Debbie Drake gave fitness advice, and Ern Westmore gave make-up tips.

Thomas later left the show, and Donahue took over hosting responsibility. Bunny Raasch, who had joined the station as a continuity writer in 1964, later replaced Donahue as the hostess. Because the Playboy Clubs and their bunnies were all the rage, the station decided that Bunny had to use the name "Bea" to avoid any association with them. Judy Marks later joined as well. When the round studio was put into operation at Radio City in 1966, it included a new kitchen set for Whalen.

Home economist Jayne Whalen cooks in the WTMJ-TV kitchen studio. (UWM Libraries, Archives Department, Milw MSS 203)

Bunny remembered that even on a cooking show, live television could have its moments:

> One day we had a fellow on who was teaching us how to do fish. He was a chef, and he started out with a live trout. The idea was that he would start out with a live trout and show us how to prepare it. Microwaves were relatively new then, and we had one. Well, Jayne would open the door at every break and have this big grin on her face, ready to show it off, but the fish was flopping around. It was still alive!
>
> We had another instance where we had a singing quartet on the show. They were monks, who had recorded their music but did not play publicly. They wanted to do the show, but we had a tough time convincing the hierarchy within the order to let them appear. We promised to keep it very dignified, so we set them up on a stage in the middle of the studio on a low rise – very simple and

Bunny Raasch later joined "Today for Women" as a hostess. (UWM Libraries, Archives Department, Milw MSS 203)

far away from the kitchen and set action. We would interview them from a distance but mainly have them sing, because they did beautiful, beautiful harmonies.

Jayne had a brand new bread mixer. She was left handed, and she didn't know it was a right handed mixer. She put all of this flour into it. It was one of those deals where she said that we were going to break, and when we returned the brothers were going to sing. She then turned the thing on, and the flour shot all the way across the studio, all over their black suits and clerical collars just as the camera cut to the close-up of them! It was unbelievable![226]

Carol Cotter later joined the show to host various segments. The last show aired on Friday, June 2, 1967.

"MURL DEUSING SAFARI"

Between 1952 and 1958, Murl Deusing had been first the assistant and then the curator for education at the Milwaukee Public Museum.[227] While there, he hosted "Museum Explorers Club" on WTMJ-TV (See special section.), and had been involved in a number of shoots for Hollywood films, as well as for Walt Disney's *Disneyland* television program. He was instrumental in the founding of WMVS-TV, and later became a regular contributor to National Educational Television's *What's New?* series. (See chapter 8.)

In 1963, he approached WTMJ-TV with an idea for a weekly series of travelogues. The station bought the idea, and "Murl Deusing Presents" made its debut at 5:30 p.m. on Sunday, September 15, 1963. At first, it ran three Sundays a month, but that was soon changed to every Sunday, and the name changed to "Murl Deusing Safari."

Each show was hosted by Deusing, who either described footage he had shot, or introduced other noted travel photographers, who showed their own. It was a weekly trip to many exotic locations, which was eventually sold in syndication to other cities around the country.

Murl Deusing (UWM Libraries, Archives Department, Milw MSS 203)

In an unprecedented move, WTMJ-TV decided not to clear NBC's *The Virginian* and instead ran a second episode of "Safari" on Wednesday nights at 6:30 p.m. beginning on September 16, 1964. In the fall of 1965, the station began showing AFL football games on Sunday afternoons. The Sunday show's first run ended on September 12. It was so popular, however, WTMJ-TV decided not to clear NBC's shows scheduled for 6:30-7:30 p.m. on Fridays, and ran "Safari" instead. The first show began on September 17, 1965.[228] The two-nights-a week, prime-time broadcasts continued through September 6, 1967. The show was then shifted back to Sundays at 5:30 p.m. On January 25, 1968, a Thursday evening show was added. The Sunday show ended on May 19 of that year, but the Thursday version continued until June 11, 1970. It was then shifted back to Sunday afternoons in various timeslots – often pre-empted by sports – until September 3, 1972. The show was later picked up by WMVS-TV. (See chapter 8.)

On June 7, 1964, the Journal Co. announced plans to add a new wing to the west side of Radio City. The $1.5M addition, would house a circular television studio, and WTMJ-TV would become the first regular station to use one.[229] The new studio was sixty-nine feet in diameter. Also included in the modernization program was an upgrading of broadcast facilities within the building, including a new control

WTMJ-TV's 10:00 p.m. team in the early-to-mid 1960s. L-R: Blaine Walsh (sports), Tom Lueders (news) and Bill Carlsen (weather). (UWM Libraries, Archives Department, Milw MSS 203)

room. The new studio was formally dedicated on a special show that aired at 6:30 p.m. on Friday, August 26, 1966.[230]

In the mid-to-late 1960s, a number of Green Bay stations applied for, and received construction permits for translator stations in Wisconsin's Fox River Valley in order to improve their signal quality there. WTMJ-TV received a construction permit for one in Sheboygan on June 28, 1967[231], but the station was never constructed.

When the station's 1,035' tower was built in the 1950s, both the TV and FM antennas were side-mounted on it. Most television stations mount their antennas at the very top of their towers. WTMJ-TV decided to upgrade its antenna, and

WTMJ-TV dedicated its round studio in 1966. (UWM Libraries, Archives Department, Milw MSS 203)

CHAPTER 2 ~ WTMJ-TV: CHANNELS 3 & 4

A new antenna is readied for installation on the WTMJ-TV tower in 1967. (UWM Libraries, Archives Department, Milw MSS 203)

mounted a new one atop the tower, raising its total height to 1,096'.[232] The station began broadcasting from the new facilities on October 11, 1967.[233]

MAYOR HENRY MAIER & THE JOURNAL CO.

Henry W. Maier (1918-1994) served as Mayor of Milwaukee from 1960-1988. During his tenure he showed a great insight into the city and its problems, and fought tenaciously for federal funding of cities. Unfortunately, he was also thin-skinned, tolerated no criticism of his policies, and had a propensity for trying to manipulate his public image. His favorite target was the Journal Co.

The origins of the feud are obscure, but WTMJ-TV's Ed Hinshaw, who became a frequent foil for Maier, was given one opinion as to how it started:

> *John Reddin, a long-time editorial writer for the newspaper, told me that the State Democratic Convention was in Superior [Wisconsin] one year. Henry was up there – he was a state senator at the time – and he had toyed with the idea of running for mayor. In fact, there had been an event at the Milwaukee Auditorium called 'Draft Henry', meant to look like he had nothing to do with it, but, of course, it was pretty obvious that he had.*
>
> *So, the 'Journal' had run an editorial saying: 'Henry, why don't you just admit that you're running?' Henry ran into the editorial editor [at the convention] and quoted the whole editorial verbatim in a vicious anger. It was also probably smart politics for him to have an opponent, and it was the newspaper.[234]*

Whenever Maier had a bone to pick with the *Milwaukee Journal* or (after 1962) the *Milwaukee Sentinel*, he would go to the broadcast media to complain. The real trouble started in 1967. On July 31, tensions in the inner city came to the boiling point, and the city was plunged into what was politely called a "civil disturbance." The mayor was under pressure, and it spilled over into his relationship with the Journal Co.'s broadcast outlet. Ed Hinshaw:

> I tried to be straight with him for a very long time – even after I had started writing editorials as well as anchoring. But after the riots of 1967 had started, he held a news conference in his office, and I raised my hand and said, 'Would you be willing to meet with the head of the NAACP?'
>
> He said, 'Yes. If the national president of the NAACP wants to come here, I'll meet him.'
>
> I said, 'No, the local president'. He didn't answer and went on.
>
> We took our gear down and were packing it up outside City Hall. Henry came out of the door and said, 'You son-of-a-bitch', and just blew his stack at me.[235]

After the riots, Maier met with local leaders, and developed what he termed his "39 Points," a plan to deal with urban problems – particularly in the inner city. They were released on August 7.[236] In his 1993 self-published autobiography, he claimed that: "Both newspapers published the 39-Point Program. However, both then ignored the 39 points in order to magnify their major point and singular aim: central-city-only open housing."[237]

Shortly thereafter, Father James Groppi and members of the NAACP Youth Council began a series of open housing marches to the city's predominantly white south side, prompting angry reaction from residents of that neighborhood. Maier was not happy with the amount of media attention the marches – and the reaction – were given.

On September 19, he asked the city attorney for an opinion as to whether it was possible for him to sue the news media for damages because of what he claimed were distortions in their coverage of the riots.[238] On November 28, the city attorney issued an opinion saying that the news media had the right to criticize the government, and that the U.S. Supreme Court had, just the year before, affirmed that right.[239] Five days later, he went on WISN-TV to attack the two newspapers.[240] He gave a second televised speech On December 16 on WITI-TV, and a third on December 27 on WTMJ-TV.[241]

Things escalated in 1969. On March 3, Maier announced that the top priority of his administration was the establishment of a third newspaper.[242] On April 11, he asked the city attorney to file anti-trust complaints against the Journal Co. with both the federal justice department's anti-trust division and the state attorney general's office. In his complaint, he alleged that both newspapers fostered what he termed "synthetic conflict" over controversial issues in the community. On April 30, he gave a thirty-minute television address called "The Hidden Issue: The Fight Against the Journal Monopoly" live on WISN-TV. It was repeated later that night on WVTV and WTMJ-TV, and two days later on WMVS-TV.[243]

The *Milwaukee Journal* responded to all of the points made by Maier and his guests in a series of full-page editorials that

Advertisement for Mayor Henry Maier's television speech on the Journal Co., first shown on April 30, 1969.

ran May 21-23. WITI-TV, which had not carried the mayor's address, ran a news special on the conflict May 29.[244]

On May 16, Maier began a series of live, Friday morning news conferences on WISN-TV.[245] He refused to answer questions at any other time during the week.

During the news conference of August 15, the Mayor announced that he had filed a petition with the U.S. attorney general asking that the Journal Co. be investigated as a possible monopoly. He admitted that he had "no quarrel with Journal radio or TV," but thought that they should be separated because their profits contributed to the overall financial position of the company.[246]

The justice department announced on August 28, that they had replied to the mayor's petition in a letter, but did not disclose its contents. The mayor's office announced that he would answer all questions on the matter at his next regularly-scheduled news conference on September 12.[247] On August 30, the *Milwaukee Journal* ran a story disclosing the contents, which it said had been confirmed that day. It revealed that the justice department had rejected Maier's claims, saying that it had investigated the company's acquisition of the *Milwaukee Sentinel* in 1962, and had decided not to take action. Regarding the broadcast entities, the department suggested that Maier refer the matter to the FCC for investigation.[248]

The conflict continued to ferment. A glimmer of hope emerged on March 14, 1972 when Maier attended a meeting of the Milwaukee Area Broadcast News Association. In a confidential report to the Journal Broadcasting Editorial Board, Art Olszyk and Ed Hinshaw described how upon questioning, Maier explained that his problems with the Journal Co. were due to:

Mayor Henry Maier at his weekly televised news conference of June 12, 1969. (Milwaukee Journal photo, historic photo collection/ Milwaukee Public Library, ©2008 Journal Sentinel, Inc., reproduced with permission.)

1. The editorial editor of the Journal ignoring his 39-Points on the grounds that they were "too long range."
2. The Journal Co.'s Irwin Maier's setting up a confrontation between the mayor and Governor Warren Knowles over the issue of calling out the National Guard during the 1967 riot.
3. His feeling that the coverage and support of the open housing marches was a false and misleading issue.[249]

Despite that glimmer of hope, the trouble escalated. The Friday morning news conferences on WISN-TV had ended prior to the April elections. Radio news conferences replaced them, held in the studios of WISN, WOKY, WEMP and WRIT – but not WTMJ. In May, Maier requested that all of the television stations provide time for a monthly news conference.

Since December of 1971, Maier had refused to answer questions from any Journal Co. reporter – with rare exceptions. Beginning in December of 1970, the Journal had printed a weekly opinion column written by Maier without any editing or notations. However, the December 19 column was printed with a deletion and editor's note explaining that the paper thought the material was potentially libelous to reporter Joel McNally. Because of the threat of a lawsuit, his personal attorney advised Maier not to answer questions from Journal Co. reporters, until the company issued either an apology or a guarantee that they would not sue him.[250] Dick Leonard, the paper's editor, sent him a letter with such a guarantee dated May 25.[251]

The first television news conference under the new format was held on September 15. One requirement the stations insisted upon before agreeing to cover them was that the mayor answer questions from WTMJ-TV. He refused, and challenged the station to prove "their broadcasting independence" by launching an investigation "into what he called the company's "lies" involving the libel suit matter."[252] The American Civil Liberties Union asked the stations to end the news conferences, pointing out that: "In a dictatorship, the head of the government can silence the press for criticizing him."[253] Former Mayor Frank Zeidler joined in the battle when he wrote letters to the FCC complaining about Maier's refusal to answer questions from WTMJ-TV – although the Commission responded by saying that they had "no regulatory authority over the Mayor of the City of Milwaukee, and cannot direct him as to the manner in which he handles his relations with the press or with broadcasters."[254] Maier also received letters encouraging him to make peace with the Journal Co. and halt his attack on an independent press from the Associated Press Managing Editors Association, the Freedom of Information Committee, Sigma Delta Chi, the American Society of Newspaper Editors, and the Radio and Television News Directors Association.

WITI-TV gave the mayor time on "TV6 Report" that month to explain his battle with the Journal Co. In his address, he suggested that a televised debate be held between himself and the company's chairman, and that the moderators of the debate form a permanent "press review board to monitor the conduct of the press in Milwaukee." In an editorial delivered on October 17, WITI-TV Vice President and General Manager Roger Le Grand rejected the idea, as undue control over the free press.[255]

In February of 1973, the stations ended the mayor's monthly news conferences because of his refusal to answer questions from WTMJ-TV reporters.[256]

In early November of 1973, the justice department asked the FCC to delay the renewal of the licenses for the Journal Company's television and radio stations in Milwaukee because of "substantial problems of concentration." It was an early salvo

in the anti-trust division's desire to challenge the ownership of broadcast stations by newspapers.[257]

On November 15, the Commission rejected the request, stating that the justice department had not provided adequate reasons for the delay.[258] On November 28, the justice department filed a new request, and the Commission agreed to hold up the license renewals, which were slated for December 1.[259] In an editorial, WISN radio urged the FCC to renew the Journal Co.'s licenses, stating that Mayor Maier was behind the anti-trust complaint, and that freedom of the press was at stake.[260] Maier called on the FCC to hold the hearing in Milwaukee, so that the opinions of the city's citizens could be heard.[261]

The matter dragged on. In early 1975, the FCC adopted new rules allowing those newspapers that already owned broadcasting stations to continue to do so, and consequently the Journal Co. licenses were finally renewed on October 21, 1976.[262]

Maier continued to do battle, and on October 5, 1979 he said at a press conference that he would not speak with reporters from the *Milwaukee Journal* until he received a reply to a letter he wrote to the newspaper's managing editor that took exception to an article in the paper.[263] The mayor asked for free time on October 10 for a televised news conference to explain his position on the Common Council's resolution asking the U.S. Justice Dept. to investigate shootings in the city since 1968. He used most of the time to attack the newspaper. Both WTMJ-TV and WITI-TV carried the mayor's remarks live, and both chastised him for using the time provided for something other than what he stated in his request.[264]

Maier's greatest salvo was yet to be fired. Between 1940 and 1949, the FCC had forbidden broadcast stations to editorialize on the air. That changed with the adoption of the "Fairness Doctrine," which required licensees to devote a reasonable percentage of broadcast time to the coverage of controversial issues of public importance and to provide a reasonable opportunity for presentation of conflicting views regarding such issues.[265] The doctrine also codified what became known as the "personal attack rule" and the "editorial rule." The personal attack rule required broadcasters to notify those personally attacked on-the-air, and to then provide them with an opportunity to respond. The editorial rule allowed political candidates to respond either to criticisms or station endorsements of another candidate.

In March, April and May, 1981, editorials were broadcast over WTMJ, WKTI and WTMJ-TV critical of the mayor's policies on a firefighter's strike, contract negotiations between the city and the police and firefighters union and the city's garbage collection system. On April 8, the Journal published a letter to the editor from a Brookfield resident critical of some energy-saving recommendations.[266]

Maier demanded that the paper print a retraction. Because it was a letter from a reader and not an editorial, it refused. On June 3, he filed a Fairness Doctrine complaint against the Journal Co. with the FCC. He announced the fact in a news conference on June 10. In his autobiography, he stated that: "I contended that WTMJ, Inc., not only had acted unfairly, but also had viciously attacked me both personally, and by innuendo in broadcasting a series of 15 editorials critical of me, my administration and officials linked to me."[267]

On August 24, the FCC rejected the complaint citing procedural grounds. In a letter to the mayor, it outlined that he had failed to provide any evidence that the editorials were deliberately false, that no opportunity to present his point of view was made available, and that issues for which he was personally criticized were controversial and of public importance to the city.[268]

In his autobiography, Maier later stated: "It mattered not to the FCC that by virtue of the editorials' being broadcast, the station itself considered the issues controversial and of public importance.[269]

Maier filed an amended complaint on September 15[270], and the Journal Co. filed a response. On August 2, 1982, the complaints and compliance division of the FCC broadcast bureau rejected it, saying that he had been given time to respond to the editorials, but had not taken advantage of it.[271] Maier appealed to the full commission, which rejected the complaint in a 7-0 vote on February 18, 1983.[272]

Undaunted, he filed an appeal with the 7th U.S. Circuit Court of Appeals in Chicago on April 26[273], and on November 10, the court took it under advisement.[274]

Meanwhile, a bill to repeal the Fairness Doctrine was introduced in U.S. Senate. One of the bill's sponsors was Wisconsin Senator William Proxmire. WTMJ-TV's Ed Hinshaw testified in favor of its repeal before the Senate Commerce Committee on February 1, 1984, and outlined the Journal Co.'s experience with the mayor's complaint.[275] Maier was invited to testify[276], and one of his aides did so in favor of not only retaining, but strengthening the doctrine a week later.[277]

On May 8, a three-judge panel of the Court of Appeals upheld the FCC's decision, saying that Maier had been given adequate opportunity to respond, but had not taken advantage of it.[278] It did take exception to one suggestion, made by the FCC in its decision, when it stated: "Thus, we cannot conclude that WTMJ made a reasonable effort to inform the public about the issues addressed in its editorials simply by giving the petitioner invitations to respond to those editorials, at least where, as here, those invitations were declined."[279]

In his autobiography, Maier pointed out that in its decision the Court also stated that the stations' routine practice of inviting responses at the conclusion of each editorial did little or nothing to fulfill its obligations under the Fairness Doctrine, that it was also troubled that the stations did not offer the sanitation workers' union time to respond, and that none of the Journal Co.'s outlets reported those elements of the opinion.[280]

On May 22, the City Attorney announced that Maier asked the full court to reconsider the decision of the three-judge panel.[281] That appeal was filed two days later, but was rejected by the Court on June 7.[282]

The Fairness Doctrine was repealed in 1987.

In 1972, John Gardner was hired as the city's first African-American news anchor by WITI-TV. He had worked at WTMJ as an intern, and claimed that he was let go because he was "too ambitious."[283] Shortly thereafter, Affirmative Action began to drive all businesses to hire minorities and women. Jack Lee was radio program manager and sports network director for WTMJ and WTMJ-FM at the time. He remembered:

> We were in our Wednesday morning managers' meeting, and had just been advised by George Comte, the vice president and general manager for WTMJ-TV and Radio, that we needed to get very serious about affirmative action, and be looking for good hirable, qualifiable, minority candidates – more than just for the jobs that we might have open in our own departments. If we had such an applicant, we were told to look at how they might fit-in to some other job elsewhere in the building, and we were to share that information with each other.

June 7, 1967: John McCullough interviewed Fr. James Groppi. (WTMJ-TV photo)

Bill Taylor came to WTMJ looking for a job as a D.J., and got one as a news reporter. He later became an anchor, and popular personality. (J. Shimon and J. Lindemann photo, courtesy of UWM Libraries, Archives Department, Milw MSS 203)

The WTMJ-TV News/Weather/Sports team in the late 1960s. In the back row L-R: Lionel Aldridge (sports), Don Parcher (news) Bill Carlsen (weather), and Jim Irwin (sports). Center, L-R: Bunny Raasch (features), and Ed Hinshaw (news/editorials). Front row, L-R: Hank Stoddard (sports), Judy Marks (weather) and John McCullough (news). (UWM Libraries, Archives Department, Milw MSS 203)

So, coincidentally, I had a friend of mine in Milwaukee, who had been on one of the R&B stations – a guy named Bill Taylor – who came into the station looking for a job as a D.J. I didn't have an opening at WTMJ, but I knew Bill was very good. So, I asked him if he would have any objection to reading news, and I walked him over to our news director, Don Loose, gave him a recommendation, and told him that he ought to consider him.

About a week later, Don came over to me and said, 'Thank you for that lead; I hired Bill Taylor!'[284]

Flush with that victory, Lee made another recommendation:

"A couple of weeks later, I was taking a vacation visiting my family in Tennessee. My stepmother was watching WSM-TV in the kitchen, and I heard this great voice. She was standing up in front of a court house ad libbing. She had a serious afro hair-do – not the kind of thing you would expect to see on TV – with bad lighting. It was hard to get an idea of how she looked, but she had a fantastic presence and intelligence.

I asked my stepmother who she was, and she said that the gal was new. I wrote down a name as best my stepmother could remember it.

When I got back, I wrote a glowing recommendation to every department head in the building, saying that she was the strongest candidate for an anchor I'd ever seen. She was an ad libber, intelligent, and had a great voice. She wasn't your typical light-skinned black person – she was definitely black – and that was her strength. She needed some help with make-up and appearance, but that could be taken care of.

Ed Allen hosted "Hot Line" beginning on Monday, September 8, 1969. The show featured chats with visiting celebrities and dignitaries in which viewers could call in. Allen's last show was on May 29, 1970. On August 31, Jim Peck, who had joined the station after stints at WISN-TV and WVTV began hosting the program. Here Peck is shown with South Dakota Senator and 1972 Democratic Presidential candidate George McGovern. (UWM Libraries, Archives Department, Milw MSS 203)

I went on to say that she was in Nashville now, but that we should nab her before someone else did. She was a potential superstar.

I thought that I'd done a wonderful thing, but in retrospect, I was pushing too hard. For the next week, all of the other managers would avert their eyes when they passed me in the hall. I never received an answer to my recommendation.

Her name was Oprah Winfrey. Years later, after she became nationally syndicated, I would say: 'That's her! That's the girl from Nashville!'[285]

The news team had enjoyed the reputation of taking a serious, professional approach. Things expanded in the early 1970s, when Bob Sherwood joined, and became the city's first investigative reporter. He recalled:

I was recruited by Don Loose and Art Olszyk. To be fair, it was all very new and I'm sure none of us realized all of what was involved. It takes a great deal of time and effort to put together an investigative series that will stand up under close scrutiny. A good series will make a number of enemies and they won't forget you. It also is a positive boon for the community if they care to watch and learn from it; so I guess it balances out in the long run.[286]

One of his first series caused quite a stir:

I had gone to a news director's meeting in Minneapolis when I was still at WOKY [radio]. It was a short hop from here to Minneapolis and back – no stops – and the airline…lost my luggage. I couldn't image how that could happen.

I remembered that, and when I went to channel 4 and they wanted me to do these investigative pieces, I though: 'You know, I do wonder what happens back

The WTMJ-TV News/Weather/Sports team in the early 1970s stands around the "4" news set. L-R: Hank Stoddard, Jim Irwin and Lionel Aldridge (sports); Ed Hinshaw, Don Parcher and John McCullough (news/editorials); Bill Carlsen and Paul Joseph (weather). (UWM Libraries, Archives Department, Milw MSS 203)

there behind the scenes at an airport, and how something like that can happen so often.'

So I started nosing around, and I found that I could walk anywhere in the airport – where people shouldn't be allowed to walk – without anyone questioning me. At the time, I was not a well-known figure – in fact very few people even knew what I looked like.

At that point I decided to get my cameraman, and I took him with me behind the scenes, and had him film me doing various things. For instance, I walked into the luggage area, picked up a suitcase at-random and walked out-of-frame with it, as if I were taking it somewhere.

In another instance, I went into the air freight area where there is something called a 'valuables cage' where all of the expensive, valuable items are kept – allegedly under lock-and-key. Well, they weren't. You could easily just open the door and walk in. I recall one small package the size of a watch box with a De Beers label on it, valued at $500,000. Again, we got a shot of me taking it.

We did another one when I took my 1972 Cadillac Coup de Ville, drove it onto the airport grounds, and up to an airliner that was parked. I walked up the stairs into the airliner carrying a briefcase, and then walked back down without it. In other words, I'd left it on the airplane.

Eugene Grobschmidt was the chairman of the Airport Commission. We did an interview with him, wherein I told him what we had done. He didn't miss a beat. He said: 'Oh…Well…We knew that was you. We just allowed you to have free run of the airport. We didn't see any particular harm.'

So I said to myself: 'There goes my story.' Then I went to the head of security at the airport, and asked him: 'Are you aware of all of these things that I've done?' He virtually grabbed his chest and said: 'My God! You did what?! If we had known, you would've been jailed!'

CHAPTER 2 ~ WTMJ-TV: CHANNELS 3 & 4

L-R: Paul Joseph, Jim Peck and Bob Sherwood did "Newsweek 4" in the early 1970s. Sherwood was the city's first television investigative reporter. (UWM Libraries, Archives Department, Milw MSS 203)

That gave us the story. It was the first, as far as I know, story on the lack of security at a major airport."[287]

After Sherwood found ground pork in packages labeled "ground beef" at a Kohl's food store in Shorewood, Herb Kohl and his marketing director tried to get the station to kill the piece:

We had a major meeting. [General Manager for radio and television] George [Comte] was there. So were news director Don Loose, news editor, Art Olszyk, my cameraman, and a few others. It was a crowd. Herb was ranting and raving.

George Comte took all of this in. He just looked at me at one point and said: 'Well Bob, what can you tell me about all of this? Is your story solid? Do you have all the evidence that you say you have, and is this something that will stand up?'

I said: 'Yes Mr. Comte. I have all of the records. I have all of the reports from the Department of Agriculture [who tested the meat]. This is a straight story.'

He looked at Herb Kohl and said: 'We're going with it.'

Here was a man of such integrity. He was ready to blow the Kohl's account out of channel 4, rather than take a good story off the air.[288]

Sherwood wound up leaving that position as he realized that he was carrying a great deal of responsibility as an individual reporter:

I realized by the time I had done the work for a few years that it was something that was too much for one person; too big a responsibility that called for an enormous amount of effort. I could only sustain it for as long as I did because I had tremendous energy and I was too naive to realize just how immense a job it was. I'm very proud of what I accomplished over those years and I believe we provided a real service to the community.[289]

On September 3, 1989, "Sunday Night" made its debut after the 10:00 p.m. news. Hosted by Mike Gousha, the show featured one-on-one interviews with interesting

The Crown Room atop the Pfister Hotel, would book stars that were either just past their prime or on their way up, to perform. WTMJ-TV aired performances by and interviews with those appearing on "Crown Room Tonight." The first show, broadcast Sunday night at 9:30, was on February 11, 1973. Here host Hank Stoddard (left) interviews Soupy Sales. The last show aired on February 17, 1974. (UWM Libraries, Archives Department, Milw MSS 203)

"The Making of…" replaced "Crown Room Tonight," and made its debut on Sunday, March 3, 1974 at 9:30 p.m. Hosted by Pete Wilson, the show featured interviews with celebrities and other noteworthy individuals, which took place before a studio audience. Here Wilson (left) interviews Milwaukee native Tom Snyder on May 5 of that year. The show ran through September 7, 1975. (UWM Libraries, Archives Department, Milw MSS 203)

personalities. The show ended on July 30, 2006, after which Gousha left the station for a position with Marquette University.

As cable and satellite television made inroads during the 1980s, traditional over-the-air television stations searched for ways to attract younger viewers. WTMJ-TV had long been known for solid journalism and a serious approach to the news. However, station management began to be concerned about attracting younger

CHAPTER 2 ~ WTMJ-TV: CHANNELS 3 & 4

The news and weather team in the 1980s. Standing L-R: Jim Ott and Paul Joseph (weather); Seated L-R: Mike Jacobs, Melodie Wilson and John McCullough. (WTMJ-TV photo)

Two Mikes: Gousha and Jacobs anchored WTMJ-TV's newscasts after the departure of John McCullough in 1988. (UWM Libraries, Archives Department, Milw MSS 203)

viewers. As a result, the station fired reporter/anchor Melodie Wilson on September 11, 1991. Wilson told the *Milwaukee Sentinel* that she was told that she "skewed old."[290] In a prepared statement, news director Jim Prather said that Wilson "was not the person who could help move our newscast to the next level." He admitted

WTMJ-TV was a long-time supporter of the Milwaukee Athletes Against Childhood Cancer. Here is the 1989 telethon. (UWM Libraries, Archives Department, Milw MSS 203)

Melodie Wilson joined WTMJ-TV as a reporter in 1974, and she began anchoring in 1983. In September of 1991, she was let go by station management because her audience "skewed old." (J. Shimon and J. Lindemann photo, courtesy of UWM Libraries, Archives Department, Milw MSS 203)

to the *Milwaukee Journal* that the decision had nothing to do with journalism, but rather that it was a subjective, management decision.[291] Carole Meekins was hired as her replacement, and Wilson later moved to WITI-TV.

CHAPTER 2 ~ WTMJ-TV: CHANNELS 3 & 4   103

WTMJ-TV master control in 2007. (Courtesy of Garrett Wollman)

Alison de Castro (left) and Molly Fay hosted "The Morning Blend." (WTMJ-TV photo)

In 1990, Jill Carlson began working for WTMJ-TV as its first female sports reporter. She lasted about a year. In 1994, the station hired Jesse Garcia as both a sports reporter and the first female sports anchor.[292]

News Corporation, the parent company of Fox, acquired a 20% interest in New World Communications. As a consequence, all New World stations, including WITI, affiliated with the Fox Network. The switch was announced in May

A 2007 set. (Courtesy of Garrett Wollman)

L-R: John Malan (weather), Mike Jacobs, Carole Meekins, and Lance Allan (sports) made up the 10:00 p.m. team. (WTMJ-TV photo)

L-R: The 2008 weather team consisted of Scott Steele, Brian Gotter, Chief Meteorologist John Malan, Craig Koplien and Michael Fish. (WTMJ-TV photo)

of 1994.[293] WITI-TV had been the CBS affiliate, and that network began looking for a home in the city. One of the consequences was that WTMJ-TV (which had been an affiliate since 1948) announced a new seven-year agreement with the NBC network in August of that year.[294]

NBC acquired a stake in Paxson Communications, and began time-shifting some of its programming on Pax stations, including WPXE in the Milwaukee area. In a compromise with its affiliates, NBC "encouraged" them to enter into joint sales agreements with Paxson stations in their area. On May 12, 2000, Journal Broadcasting Group revealed that it had entered into such an agreement with WPXE in which WTMJ-TV would take over all operational responsibility, save for programming, on July 3. WTMJ-TV split advertising revenue with WPXE.[295] WTMJ-TV's newscasts were repeated on WPXE, as were some pre-season Green Bay Packer games. During the 2004 Summer Olympics, those games were shown on the Paxson station. The arrangement continued through June 30, 2005.

In November of 2000, WTMJ-TV became the second station in the city to begin broadcasting digitally.[296] Milwaukee Public Television had been the first.

Local production except for news/weather/sports disappeared from most commercial television stations during the 1990s. On September 12, 2006, WTMJ-TV began a hybrid show called "The Morning Blend." Co-hosted by Alison de Castro and Molly Fay, the lifestyle show was designed to appeal to female viewers in the desirable 25-54 age bracket. The "blend" in the name came from the fact that the show included both paid and unpaid segments. For a fee, someone promoting a product or event could become a guest on the show.[297]

Rating pressures and the desire to appeal to younger viewers continued to dominate management decisions in the new millennium. The decision to add more entertainment to the newscasts, as well as the fact that many of the on-air staff was older led to retirements or resignations. Those included long-time meteorologists Paul Joseph, and Jim Ott as well as anchor Mike Gousha.

Vince Vitrano and Susan Kim anchored "Live at Daybreak" in 2008. (WTMJ-TV photo)

Courtny Garrish and George Mallet anchored the 4:00 p.m. news in 2008. (WTMJ-TV photo)

L-R: The 2008 sports team of Rod Burns, Sports Director Lance Allan and Jessie Garcia. (WTMJ-TV photo)

The Journal Co. was a leader in both the city and the state in the field of television. For years it was the leader in news as well. As the twentieth century drew to a close, it began to add more entertainment in its newscasts. The transition was complete as we entered the new millennium. With the digital television transition, the station will face new challenges as it adapts to a rapidly changing media culture, and tries to attract younger viewers.

THE CHILDREN'S SHOWS

Larry Clark hosted "Little Amateurs." (WTMJ-TV photo)

On March 15, 1948, WTMJ-TV began its weekday programming an hour later – 3:00 p.m. – to make it easier for school children to watch its programming. It then started several shows aimed at them.

"Children's Corner" made its debut on Wednesday, March 17. A fifteen-minute show, it ran Wednesday, Thursday and Friday at 4:00 p.m. The following day at 4:15, "Little Amateurs" made its debut, hosted by Larry Clark. A third show, "Hi Kids" made its debut at 4:15 on Friday, March 19. One of the "little amateurs" found herself in the middle of a labor dispute at the station. Sprague Vonier:

> There was a jurisdictional battle between the janitors and the stagehands' union regarding our television studio. The janitors cleaned all the studios in the rest of the building, along with everything else. The stagehands claimed that the janitors were not permitted to do that in Studio D, because that was their jurisdiction. However, they wouldn't do that as part of their regular duties, they wanted overtime. Walter Damm said, 'No overtime!'
>
> So the floor got worse and worse. Things got dirtier and dirtier in there. So, along came a couple of these little tykes, and they're dancing around the dirty floor in bare feet, which then turned black.
>
> Larry Clark was hosting, and right in the middle of the show, when they'd finished their little dance, he says: 'Honey, come over here. Sit in my lap a minute.' So he reached down, picked up her little foot, and stuck it up in the camera lens.
>
> He said, 'I want you to see this. We can't get this floor cleaned because of the union! It's a disgrace, and somebody should do something about it!'
>
> The stagehands' union backed down, and the janitorial staff was able to get in there after midnight and clean.[298]

When WTMJ-TV expanded its programming to seven days a week in September of 1948, it also started a new children's show. It was called "Museum Explorer's Club," and the first show was on Friday September 24.

It was hosted by Murl Deusing. Like most of the station's shows, it was done live, and back-to-back with another. Sprague Vonier remembered that one of Deusing's "guests" caused quite a bit of commotion:

> There was another little show called 'The Dance Club' that had little girls doing their dance routines. Murl Deusing was back-to-back with it. We couldn't rehearse it, because it was always busy, and you might be in a position, as I was, where you might be directing 'Museum Explorers Club' and then Vi and Jerry Wagner's musical show right afterwards.
>
> So, Murl used to come up to the control room and drop a bunch of slides on my desk. Then he'd go down to the studio, to where we'd set-up a big mock-up of a woods, with a rustic log to sit on, and some fake grass in the front where the kids could sit. They would sit at his feet, and he would tell them a story and show them things.
>
> So, at the opening of the show, he had a sack in his hand, and all the titling would run over it. Then he would take the sack, as we gradually pulled the camera back, and he'd say, 'Hey kids! What do you think I have in the sack?' Then they would all try and guess what he had in it. Then he'd pull out a rock, or whatever it happened to be.

Murl Deusing hosted "Museum Explorers Club."

Staff announcers began reading the comics to young viewers on "Sunday Journal Comic Time" every Sunday morning beginning on May 6, 1951. It was a help to children who could not yet read. The show continued through September 5, 1965. (WTMJ-TV)

Cliff Robedeaux is surrounded by fans during "Foreman Tom" Day at Wisconsin State Fair Park. (UWM Libraries, Archives Department, Milw MSS 203)

CHAPTER 2 ~ WTMJ-TV: CHANNELS 3 & 4   109

Well, this particular day, all of the girls were dancing 'round on the stage on one end of the studio, and at a right angle to them was Murl preparing for the next show. Deusing's show had just gone on the air, and all of the little girls were picking up their stuff, as he asked, 'Hey kids. What do you think I have in the sack?' Out comes a nice big boa constrictor! The little girls started SCREAMING! I had them all over the studio![299]

Cliff Robedeaux was an attorney working in real estate in 1951. He was married to Janice Malone, who along with her sister Marilyn, performed as the "Malone Sisters." WTMJ-TV hired them to perform on a variety show, "Let's Remember" in 1951. Robedeaux started playing bit parts on that show.

Gene Autry appeared on the "Foreman Tom" show on January 20, 1956. (WTMJ-TV photo)

Later that year, he was asked to host an afternoon children's show. Some of the "poverty row" studios in Hollywood had begun releasing feature films to television. Many were westerns. WTMJ-TV tapped Robedeaux to play a character named "Foreman Tom." "Foreman Tom's B-Square Ranch" made its debut on July 30, 1951. The show was only thirty minutes long, so a film might be shown over three-four days.

Kids could join his B-Square Ranch Club, and become one of his "cowpokes." By November of 1953, it had enrolled its 25,000[th] member! The official pledge was: "Be happy, be healthy, be friendly, fair, helpful, handy, trusty, and square."

The show was extremely popular. Robedeaux made public appearances around the area, and held a special "Foreman Tom" day at Wisconsin State Fair Park. In July of 1953, more than 6,500 kids attended.

The last show was on Friday, October 26, 1956.

At 3:15 p.m. on Saturday, July 6, 1957, the station ran the first of eight programs designed to teach children how to do art. Called "Cappy Presents Miss Chris," the fifteen minute show was hosted by teacher "Miss Chris" (Joan Christopherson) under the auspices of the Milwaukee Junior League's Children's Art Program (CAP). "Cappy" was a costumed character played by children or adults wherever the program was featured. On the show, "Cappy" became a puppet who lived in a paint pot.[300] "Miss Chris" showed children how everyday materials could be used to produce art. Projects included making houses out of toothpicks, mobiles out of household items, etc.[301] Director Sprague Vonier's children, Thomas and Victoria, were regulars on the show. A special children's art exhibit featuring works produced by audience members was held at the Milwaukee Art Museum. The work was not judged; rather various samples were selected to show how artistic imagination and ingenuity could be encouraged at home.[302] "Miss Chris" would go on to be a hostess on WMVS-TV's "Children's Fair." (See chapter 8.)

On Labor Day, 1962 WTMJ-TV began a new children's show. In various incarnations, it would run for the next nine years. Called "Kids' Klub," the show was hosted by staff announcer Chuck Faber as "Mr. Chuck." The eyepatch-wearing Faber showed Mr. Magoo cartoons, and locally produced how-to segments, such as how to care for pets. WTMJ-TV crews had gone to the newly completed Milwaukee County Zoo that summer, and pointed film cameras at various animals. That footage was shown on segments such as "A Day on Monkey Island."[303] The thirty minute show ran Monday-Friday at noon, and Saturdays at 11:00 a.m.

Chuck Faber was the first host of "Kid's Klub"

Faber was soon joined by "Tobo" the clown, played by Pat Tobin. "Tobo" always entered the set by jumping out of a box. Tobin also played the characters "Hole-in-the-Head Fred" (a gold prospector), "Professor Sing Sing" (a con man), "Elrod Potter" (a seedy hick), and "Ling Tong" (a Chinese telephone operator). He also provided the voices for six puppets.[304]

Faber left the station in the spring of 1963 and was replaced by Bob Knutzen as "Mr. Bob." "Funny Company" cartoons were later added. Pat Tobin left, and was replaced by Bill Hirst, who played "Hat-O" the clown, whose name came from the variety of hats he wore. They were joined by singer Cherie Lee. She remembered:

CHAPTER 2 ~ WTMJ-TV: CHANNELS 3 & 4

I had been singing at WTMJ-TV on the 'Noon Show', 'The Executives' and the 'Hot Shots'. I had also sung on WTMJ radio. I had this wonderful opportunity to do a kids' show.

Grant Krueger was backing us up. He was a marvelous pianist. I would have a song that I would do each time that we were on. They would make a beauti-

"Mr. Bob" (Bob Knutzen) took over hosting in May of 1963. He was later joined by singer Cherie Lee and "Hat-O" the clown (Bill Hirst). (WTMJ-TV photo, courtesy of Cherie Lee Parcher)

ful setting for me. If I sang 'It Might As Well Be Spring' they'd have me on a swing, swinging among branches and flowers, making it look like I was really on a swing in the spring someplace.

The other thing that was cute was that we were always trying to find homes for all the puppies at the Wisconsin Humane Society. We would hold the puppies up and say, 'This guy's too cute not to have a home!' Kids would have their parents call in, and we found a lot of homes for a lot of lucky little puppies![305]

"Mr. Bob" would sing, or recite a list of names of youngsters with birthdays. The "Splendiferous Prize Machine," a contraption complete with dials, wheels and different noises, would deposit a prize in his hands.

The station purchased a twenty-four passenger bus, which it converted into a circus wagon it called "Kids' Klub Karavan," which was used for remote appearances at the Wisconsin State Fair, various county fairs, or other events.

The show was done in front of a live studio audience of kids. It was originally produced by Budd Reth, who remembered that made for some interesting moments:

I had a contact with a guy from United Artists. In those days they'd come into town and have some star that they would bring down to promote some film. This one time he was promoting some sort of 'gorilla' movie. So he had some guy in a gorilla suit that was going to come on, and we would give the movie a plug.

So, on Kids' Klub, the set we had was like a room, and then there was a door where the guests would come in. There was a big opening on the right side of the old auditorium stage. We had some risers up there, and we would put fifteen to twenty, three-to-six year-olds up there – the littlest ones. On this one show, we had the gorilla guy coming on. He really looked real, and I thought that he might scare the heck out of these little kids, you know? So I was talking to some guys about it, and they suggested that he take his head off, and take a little stroll through the stage without it. He did.

So, when we got to that part in the show, there was a knock on the door, and the host says just as he's about to open the door, 'I wonder who that is kids?'. Well, one little kid yelled out, 'Maybe it's the guy in the gorilla suit!'[306]

"Mr. Pete" (Bob Petrie) and "Miss Julie" (Julia Ellis) took over hosting on May 20, 1968. (Ad: Dick Golembiewski collection; Photo therein: UWM Libraries, Archives Department, Milw MSS 203)

Look Forward to
KIDS' KLUB KARAVAN

Visiting supermarket parking lots with an entertaining show for children. Watch KIDS' KLUB, Saturdays and Sundays, for the Karavan schedule.

"Kids' Klub" included a live studio audience. Animals, usually from the Wisconsin Humane Society, were held in the cages at the left. The puppet show stage is in the center, and the "Splendiferous Prize Machine" can be seen at the right. (UWM Libraries, Archives Department, Milw MSS 203)

CHAPTER 2 ~ WTMJ-TV: CHANNELS 3 & 4   113

After Hirth left the show, he was replaced by "Ronald McDonald," played by Aye Jaye. The weekday show ended on Friday, February 10, 1967, but the Saturday show continued.

Knutzen left the show in 1967 after suffering a heart attack.[307] Cherie Lee also left the show. They were replaced by the station's program manager, Bob Petrie, as "Mr. Pete" and Julia Ellis as "Miss Julie." The first show in the new format began on Sunday May 20, 1968. The Sunday shows were repeated the following Saturday. The two began an extensive series of remote visits to Kroger food store parking lots, playgrounds, and parks in the Kids' Klub Karavan.[308]

Petrie left the show in early 1969, and was replaced by broadcasting veteran Ken Vogt. Vogt had been the original "Fritz the Plumber" on WMIL radio, and had worked at a number of other local stations before joining the *Milwaukee Journal* stations in 1968. On "Kids' Klub" he played "Uncle Otto," using his German accent.[309]

A "King and Queen for the day" segment was added. They sat on two thrones on

L-R: Ronald McDonald (Aye Jaye), "Miss Julie" (Julia Ellis) and "Uncle Otto" (Ken Vogt), who replaced Bob Petrie. (UWM Libraries, Archives Department, Milw MSS 203)

either side of the puppet show. Aye Jaye:

> We would do an interview with them, and they would assist in a trick.
> They were picked at random. I was the one who suggested that, because every time you got a 'ringer': someone's kid, or a friend of someone, they were the worst king or queen. They had sad looks on their face. They were anticipating this, as they were told that they would be picked ahead of time. I had two ringers who were so upset that they wet themselves and had to be excused.
> The best were the kids who WANTED to be king or queen. They would WILDLY raise their hands and try to get picked, yelling: 'Pick me! Pick me!'"[310]

Charlene Piasecki and Farmer Vic joined "Kids' Klub" at the end of its run. (UWM Libraries, Archives Department, Milw MSS 203)

After Ellis left the show, Aye Jaye brought in Charlene Piasecki, a Marquette University student, who sang, and who had been employed by the newly-arrived Milwaukee Brewers as a cheerleader.[311] When Vogt left, he recruited "Farmer Vic" (Hellman), who ran a facility for mentally handicapped children called "The Ranch."

Just before the show's end, the Ronald McDonald character was removed. McDonalds bought spots on the show, but federal regulators now looked closely at characters, toys and other items that were used in children's programming. If they could be interpreted as promoting a product, they were considered an advertisement, and Ronald was deemed to be one.

The Saturday show ended on December 19, 1970, while the Sunday version continued until February 14, 1971.

NOTES

1 Earle M. Terry, letter to Birge, February 2, 1922 (copy), WHA Radio and Television Records 1915-84 (series 41/6/2/4), University of Wisconsin Archives. Provided by Randall Davidson.

2 Earle M. Terry, letter to Grant, February 8, 1922 (copy), WHA Radio and Television Records 1915-84 (series 41/6/2/4), University of Wisconsin Archives. Provided by Randall Davidson.

3 Harry J. Grant, letter to Terry, February 14, 1922, WHA Radio and Television Records 1915-84 (series 41/6/2/4), University of Wisconsin Archives. Provided by Randall Davidson.
4 Lewis W. Herzog, "The Beginnings of Radio in Milwaukee," *Historical Messenger*, The Milwaukee County Historical Society, Vol. 11, No. 4, December, 1953, 11.
5 "Journal Presents First City Radio Concert Monday," *Milwaukee Journal*, April 30, 1922. Also see: "Radio Tunes to Be Sent From Gimbels: Journal Concert Will Be Heard in Three Public Places. Stars Are Booked," Milwaukee *Journal*, May 1, 1922.
6 Will C. Conrad, Kathleen Wilson, and Dale Wilson, *The Milwaukee Journal: The First Eighty Years*. (Madison: University of Wisconsin Press, 1964), 147.
7 In the early days of radio, the wavelength rather than the frequency was commonly used. The two are related by a constant – the speed of light. Thus the product of the frequency (in Hz) and the wavelength (in meters) is equal to the speed of light in meters per second. The Bureau of Standards recommended that the frequency rather than the wavelength be used to identify a station's position on the dial, and effective with its General Order 11, which took effect on June 15, 1927, the FRC began using it, along with 10 kHz channel bandwidths for radio broadcasting.
8 The Radio Editor, "The Wave Meter," *Milwaukee Journal*, June 16, 1922.
9 "The Beginnings of Radio in Milwaukee," 12.
10 Marquette University Board of Governors, letter to Hon. Edward E. Browne, Wisconsin Congressman, January 20, 1930. Marquette University Archives, A-1.1, Series 3, Box 8.
11 The Radio Editor, "The Wave Meter," *Milwaukee Journal*, September 26, 1922.
12 "The Beginnings of Radio in Milwaukee," 12.
13 "New Station to Be Opened for Radio Fans," *Wisconsin News/Milwaukee Telegram*, October 22, 1922.
14 "Fight News to be Broadcast By Radio," *Wisconsin News*, January 24, 1924.
15 Gellerup would later become the chief engineer at WTMJ.
16 "The Beginnings of Radio in Milwaukee," 13.
17 "New Antlers Hotel Station to Open Monday Night: Mayor Hoan Scheduled for Address on Dedication of WCAY," *Milwaukee Journal*, June 8, 1924.
18 "The Beginnings of Radio in Milwaukee," 14.
19 "WIAO Changes to New Call Letters: WSOE to Designate Lake Front Station; More Power Added," *Milwaukee Sentinel and Milwaukee Telegram*, August 17, 1924.
20 "News Now Has Own Radio Studio," *Wisconsin News*, October 3, 1924.
21 Gaston, W. Grignon, "Close Big Deal for WCBD: School of Engineering Announces Purchase of Powerful Outfit," *Wisconsin News*, December 31, 1924.
22 Agreement Between Marquette University and The Journal Co., January 23, 1925. *Milwaukee Journal* Stations. 1922-1969. Milwaukee Manuscript Collection 203. Wisconsin Historical Society. Milwaukee Area Research Center. UWM Libraries. University of Wisconsin-Milwaukee (Box 6, folder 1).
23 "Open New WSOE Air Station July 7: Dedication to Last 7 Hours: New Equipment to be Most Powerful in State; May Reach Europe," *Wisconsin News*, June 26, 1925.
24 It was last listed in *Wisconsin News* on Friday, May 15, 1925.
25 "The Beginnings of Radio in Milwaukee," 14-15.
26 "Milwaukee Super Station Completed: Opening Program Tuesday Night," *Wisconsin News*, October 16, 1925. Also see: BCL, "The Listener In," *Milwaukee Journal*, October 18, 1925.
27 , "The Beginnings of Radio in Milwaukee," 15.
28 *Radio & Television Chronology*. (undated), 3. Krueger, Jack, 1914-2000. Papers: 1922-1978. Milwaukee Manuscript Collection 205. Wisconsin Historical Society. Milwaukee Area Research Center. UWM Libraries. University of Wisconsin-Milwaukee (Box 1, folder 43).
29 *Milwaukee Journal's Broadcast Service to Wisconsin, Part I & II*. (undated), 5. *Milwaukee Journal* Stations. 1922-1969. Milwaukee Manuscript Collection 203. Wisconsin Historical Society. Milwaukee Area Research Center. UWM Libraries. University of Wisconsin-Milwaukee (Box 3, folder 4).
30 Erik Barnouw, *A Tower In Babel: A History of Broadcasting in the United States to 1933*. (New York: Oxford University Press, 1966), 201.
31 *The Milwaukee Journal: The First Eighty Years*, 148.

32 *Milwaukee Journal's Broadcast Service to Wisconsin, Part I & II*, 5. Also see: Rev. John B., Kramer, memo to Rev. A. C. Fox, Marquette University Archives, A-1.1 (Series 3, Box 8).

33 *Milwaukee Journal's Broadcast Service to Wisconsin, Part I & II*, 11-12.

34 *Annual Report of the Federal Radio Commission for the Fiscal Year Ending June 30, 1927*. July 1, 1927, 5.

35 *Milwaukee Journal's Broadcast Service to Wisconsin, Part I & II*, 5.

36 Ibid., 13.

37 *Annual Report of the Federal Radio Commission for the Fiscal Year Ending June 30, 1927*, 9.

38 Ibid.

39 "WTMJ On Air Monday Night: Initial Broadcast of Journal's New Station at 7:30 P.M. *Milwaukee Journal*, July 25, 1927.

40 "WTMJ Will Broadcast Opening Program Monday Night," *Milwaukee Journal*, July 24, 1927.

41 "Chain Feature Over WTMJ: First Network Hook-Up Comes Sooner Than Expected," *Milwaukee Journal*, July 25, 1927. Also see: "Chain Feature On Air Tuesday: WTMJ to Broadcast First Network Program at 8:30 M.," *Milwaukee Journal*, July 26, 1927.

42 "Chain Features Over WTMJ: First Regular Network Broadcast on Local Station Monday," *Milwaukee Journal*, August 15, 1927.

43 "Three Locals Affected by Wave Change," *The Sunday Sentinel and Milwaukee Telegram*. September 25, 1927.

44 S.E. Frost. Jr., PhD, *Education's Own Stations: The History of Broadcast Licenses Issued to Educational Institutions*. (Chicago: University of Chicago Press, 1937), 212.

45 *The Milwaukee Journal's Broadcast Service to Wisconsin, Part I & II*, 18.

46 Ibid., 19

47 In 1941, the city's other two AM stations, WISN and WEMP had their frequencies shifted slightly as a part of the North American Radio Broadcasting Agreement (Havana Treaty), but WTMJ remained on 620 kHz.

48 *The Milwaukee Journal: The First Eighty Years*, 149.

49 Will C. Conrad., "State's Radio Fate at Stake," *Milwaukee Journal*, September 23, 1930.

50 "WTMJ Loses Opening Round: Radio Expert Praises Station but Opposes Increased Power," *Milwaukee Journal*, December 15, 1930.

51 "WTMJ-TV Notes 15th Anniversary," *Milwaukee Journal*, December 4, 1962.

52 "Open Station for Television: W9XD of The Journal Assures Wisconsin Place in New Field," *Milwaukee Journal*, September 9, 1931.

53 The Journal Co. would lease that space for various uses through sometime in 1967.

54 Christopher Sterling and John Kittross, *Stay Tuned: A Concise History of American Broadcasting*. (East Windsor: Wadsworth Press, 1990), 150.

55 "RCA Ready to Sell Visual Transmitters," *Broadcasting*, October 15, 1938, 11.

56 "Journal Makes Application to Use Television: Is First to Ask Commission for Permit to Transmit Radio Pictures to Public on Scheduled Programs," *Milwaukee Journal*, November 6, 1938. Also see: "WTMJ Seeks Television," *Broadcasting*, November 15, 1938, 20.

57 "Journal Is Given Praise as Pioneer in Television: Head of Radio Corporation Congratulated Newspaper on Its Enterprise, Aiding Service Improvement," *Milwaukee Journal*, November 10, 1938.

58 *Broadcasting*, January 15, 1939, 80.

59 "Hint of Commercial Television Noted in FCC License Grants," *Broadcasting*, July 1, 1940, 28, 68.

60 *Broadcasting*, October 29, 1940, 104. Also see: "Journal Ready to Build a Wisconsin 'Radio City': New Ventures Boosted Here: Commercial FM Station, Television Set Granted Permits by FCC," *Milwaukee Journal*, November 3, 1940.

61 "Radio Here Headed for a New Miracle: Poles Grow Atop Tower; Herald FM Station to Perfect Sound Quality and End Static," *Milwaukee Journal*, January 7, 1940.

62 The FCC used the alpha-numeric call letters between 1940 and 1943. FM had been allocated to 42-50 MHz in 1940. In the FCC's scheme, "55" meant 45.5 MHz, and "M" was used to mean Milwaukee.

63 "Journal Ready to Build a Wisconsin 'Radio City.'"

64 "Work to Start on 'Radio City' at River Park: The Journal's New Plant to Be Built on Tract Near Capitol Dr. and Humboldt Blvd.," *Milwaukee Journal*, February 23, 1941.

65 "Work to Begin on 'Radio City': The Journal's New Center Is to Be Completed in the Spring, 1942," *Milwaukee Journal*, June 24, 1941.
66 Lewie V. Gilpin, "Television Authorized by FCC on a Full Commercial Basis," *Broadcasting*, May 5, 1941, 12.
67 At the time, the FCC required each broadcasting station to use unique call letters, without suffixes to designate FM and/or TV stations owned by the same company.
68 "Journal Lays the Stone for Its Radio City: Crowd Sees Ceremony; Public Officials Praise Latest Step in Progress for Public Service," Milwaukee *Journal*, September 28, 1941.
69 "Freeze Order Leaves Room for Flexibility: Individual Facts to Guide FCC in Grants," *Broadcasting*, March 2, 1942, 9-10.
70 *Stay Tuned*, 209.
71 "Await Move to Radio City: WTMJ, W55M Ready to Settle In New Plant on Wednesday," *Milwaukee Journal*, August 4, 1942.
72 "4,500 Persons at Dedication of Radio City: Development Praised by Visitors; Crowd Watches Programs in large Auditorium," *Milwaukee Journal*, August 24, 1942.
73 Arthur L. Olszyk, *Live…At the Scene*, (Milwaukee: self-published, 1993), 20.
74 Ibid.
75 "Wait for Word on Television: Radio City Has Facilities for New Medium; Peace Is Seen as 'Go' Sign," *Milwaukee Journal*, August 23, 1942.
76 "TV Rules and Regulations" *Broadcasting*, September 24, 1945, 79-80.
77 "Rules Governing Television Broadcast Stations," *Broadcasting*, December 3, 1945, 76.
78 Lewis W. Herzog., "Television Report: Whither Television?" February 11, 1946. Krueger, Jack, 1914-2000. Papers: 1922-1978. Milwaukee Manuscript Collection 205. Wisconsin Historical Society. Milwaukee Area Research Center. UWM Libraries. University of Wisconsin-Milwaukee (Box 1, folder 33).
79 "WISN Asks TV," *Broadcasting*, July 2, 1945, 32.
80 "Television Report."
81 Federal Communications Commission, *12th Annual Report (1946)*. February 8, 1947, 17.
82 Walter J. Damm., "Television Plan Realignment Announced by The Journal Co. *Broadcasting Telecasting*, May 13, 1946, 25, 29.
83 "FCC to Hear CBS Color Case Dec. 9: Order Implies Complete Probe of UHF Video to be Held," *Broadcasting Telecasting*, October 14, 1946, 20, 82.
84 "'*Milwaukee Journal*' Plans to Reapply for Black-and-White Video Station," *Broadcasting Telecasting*, December 16, 1946, 83.
85 Walter J. Damm, "Radio and Television Progress Report as of February 28, 1947," *Milwaukee Journal* Stations. 1922-1969. Milwaukee Manuscript Collection 203. Wisconsin Historical Society. Milwaukee Area Research Center. UWM Libraries. University of Wisconsin-Milwaukee (Box 6, folder 4).
86 "CBS Petition for Color TV Denied: Performance Under Plan Cited As Not Adequate In Reasonable Time," *Broadcasting Telecasting*, March 24, 1947, 14, 74.
87 "Journal Plans Video Shows in Milwaukee," *Broadcasting Telecasting*, February 17, 1947, 30.
88 Walter J. Damm, "Radio and Television Progress Report as of April 30, 1947," *Milwaukee Journal* Stations. 1922-1969. Milwaukee Manuscript Collection 203. Wisconsin Historical Society. Milwaukee Area Research Center. UWM Libraries. University of Wisconsin-Milwaukee (Box 6, folder 4).
89 Walter J. Damm, "Radio and Television Progress Report as of May 31, 1947," *Milwaukee Journal* Stations. 1922-1969. Milwaukee Manuscript Collection 203. Wisconsin Historical Society. Milwaukee Area Research Center. UWM Libraries. University of Wisconsin-Milwaukee (Box 6, folder 4).
90 Walter J. Damm, "Radio and Television Progress Report as of June 30, 1947," *Milwaukee Journal* Stations. 1922-1969. Milwaukee Manuscript Collection 203. Wisconsin Historical Society. Milwaukee Area Research Center. UWM Libraries. University of Wisconsin-Milwaukee (Box 6, folder 4).
91 Walter J. Damm, "Radio and Television Progress Report as of July 31, 1947," *Milwaukee Journal* Stations. 1922-1969. Milwaukee Manuscript Collection 203. Wisconsin Historical Society. Milwaukee Area Research Center. UWM Libraries. University of Wisconsin-Milwaukee (Box 6, folder 4).

92 "Television Due Around Dec. 1: 20 Hours Weekly," *Milwaukee Journal*, August 17, 1947.

93 *Live…At the Scene*, 21.

94 "Television Show Planned in Store," *Milwaukee Journal*, September 24, 1947.

95 "Set Television Test Displays: WTMJ-TV Is Readied," *Milwaukee Journal*, October 30, 1947.

96 Walter J. Damm, "Radio and Television Progress Report as of October 31, 1947," *Milwaukee Journal* Stations. 1922-1969. Milwaukee Manuscript Collection 203. Wisconsin Historical Society. Milwaukee Area Research Center. UWM Libraries. University of Wisconsin-Milwaukee (Box 6, folder 4).

97 Sprague Vonier, email to the author, August 19, 2007.

98 "Television Pact for Schuster's: Firm Plans Program," *Milwaukee Journal*, October 12, 1947. Also see: "First WTMJ-TV Sponsor Contract is Signed," *Broadcasting Telecasting*, October 20, 1947, 67.

99 Walter J. Damm, "Planning Pays Off for New WTMJ-TV: Journal Co. Television Begins Commercially Next Wednesday," *Broadcasting Telecasting*, December 1, 1947, 30.

100 "Pictures on Air 'Equal to Best': WTMJ-TV is Praised," *Milwaukee Journal*, November 12, 1947.

101 "City's T-Day Is Tomorrow: Program Set: Ceremony Marks Start of Regular Television Broadcasts; City Leaders to Attend Debut," *The Milwaukee Journal*, December 2, 1947.

102 "Television Becomes Part of Community: Regular Broadcasts Are Inaugurated by WTMJ-TV; Thousands See Start," *Milwaukee Journal*, December 4, 1947.

103 *Live…At the Scene*, 24.

104 Robertson would go on to a distinguished career in educational/public broadcasting, and would write the oral history of public television, *TeleVisionaries*.

105 Jim Robertson, interview with author, August 18, 2007.

106 Jim Robertson, *Televisionaries: In Their Own Words Public Television's Founders Tell How It All Began* (Charlotte Harbor: Tabby House Books, 1993), 48. (Used with permission)

107 "Add Cameras for Television: WTMJ-TV Is Gainer," *Milwaukee Journal*, January 11, 1948.

108 "Truck to Aid TV Mobility: $10,000 Vehicle Arrives for Journal's Out of Studio Broadcasts," *Milwaukee Journal*, February 9, 1948.

109 R. G. Lynch, "Maybe I'm Wrong: Smart Promoters Take Long View of Television," *Milwaukee Journal*, February `5, 1948.

110 "No TV Charge: Milwaukee Ball Team Gives Services," *Broadcasting Telecasting*, March 8, 1948, 88.

111 "WTMJ-TV Cuts Baseball," *Broadcasting Telecasting*, May 1, 1950, 50.

112 "Change Hour of Television: WTMJ-TV Lists Shows," *Milwaukee Journal*, March 14, 1948.

113 "More Sets Installed," *Milwaukee Journal*, March 14, 1948.

114 "Milwaukee TV Sets," *Broadcasting Telecasting*, April 19, 1948, 46.

115 "Television Put Into Network: WTMJ-TV Signs Pact With National Group; Shows in October," *Milwaukee Journal*, May 17, 1948.

116 "Telestatus: Midwest Networks," *Broadcasting Telecasting*, August 30, 1948, 18.

117 Robertson, August 18, 2007.

118 "ABC TV Network to Begin Sept. 20: Date to Mark Start Programs From WENR-TV Chicago," *Broadcasting Telecasting*, August 23, 1948, 27.

119 "Videos in Midwest to Use Kinescopes," *Broadcasting Telecasting*, August 30, 1948, 63.

120 "List Television Feast for Fans: WTMJ-TV Will Have Broadcasts from 3 Major Networks," *Milwaukee Journal*, September 12, 1948.

121 "Television Net Has Its Debut: WTMJ-TV Presents a Program Showing ABC and NBC Fare," *Milwaukee Journal*, September 21, 1948. Also see: "Midwest TV: ABC and NBC Air First in Area," *Broadcasting Telecasting*, September 27, 1948, 34.

122 "Add Programs for Television: WTMJ-TV to Operate Seven Nights a Week Beginning Sept. 20," *Milwaukee Journal*, August 24, 1948.

123 Rufus Crater, "TV Faces Crisis: Channel Realignment Possible," *Broadcasting Telecasting*, September 13, 1948, 21, 74.

124 Rufus Crater, and Larry Christopher, "TV Expansion: Move Appears Imminent After FCC Hearing," *Broadcasting Telecasting*, September 27, 1948, 21, 70-72, 89.
125 Rufus Crater, "Television Freeze: FCC Action Halted pending Definite Policy," *Broadcasting Telecasting*, October 4, 1948, 22A.
126 "Order Freeze in TV Stations: FCC Holds Up Approval of Applications; Seeks to 'Polish' Service," *Milwaukee Journal*, September 30, 1948.
127 "WTMJ-TV Covers the Packer-Bear Game Today," *Milwaukee Journal*, November 14, 1948.
128 "Eastern Link for Television: Coast Broadcast Are Slated on WTMJ-TV Beginning Jan. 12," *Milwaukee Journal*, October 31, 1948.
129 Bea J. Pepan, "WTMJ-TV Eyes Given First Look at New York: Milton Berle Is Linked to Mississippi Valley Over Sight Waves," *Milwaukee Journal*, January 12, 1949.
130 Sprague Vonier, email to author, August 15, 2007.
131 "Add 10 Hours on WTMJ-TV: Offer More Afternoon Programs, Especially for Women, Children," *Milwaukee Journal*, February 20, 1949.
132 Sprague Vonier, interview with author, July 27, 2007.
133 *Televisionaries*, 48-49. (Used with permission)
134 Clarice Rowlands, "Home Economist's Own Home program: Breta Luther Griem Signing Off the Air to Enjoy Serene Lake View," *Milwaukee Journal*, June 28, 1962.
135 "WTMJ-TV is Permanent," *Milwaukee Journal*, July 12, 1949.
136 Mortimer W. Loewi, director, Du Mont Television Network, Letter to the Journal Co., July 22, 1949 (Agreement accepted by Walter J. Damm, July 28, 1949.) *Milwaukee Journal* Stations. 1922-1969. Milwaukee Manuscript Collection 203. Wisconsin Historical Society. Milwaukee Area Research Center. UWM Libraries. University of Wisconsin-Milwaukee (Box 32, folder 9.).
137 Raymond E. McBride, "The First 10 Years Were the Hardest," *Milwaukee Journal*, October 6, 1957.
138 "FCC Hits NBC Sat. Plan: Says Network Rules Violated," *Broadcasting Telecasting*, February 20, 1950, 68.
139 "Renew Permit for WTMJ-TV: FCC Acts on License," *Milwaukee Journal*, February 22, 1950. Also see: "TV Renewals: Previous Order Set Aside," *Broadcasting Telecasting*, February 27, 1950, 64.
140 *Live…At the Scene*, 7.
141 Walter J. Damm, "Questions and Answers About Journal Radio and Television Operations," The Unit Holders Council, December, 1950, 4.
142 "Improve TV at Radio City: Two New Studios Put Into Service; One Has a Model Kitchen," *Milwaukee Journal*, February 6, 1951.
143 "Journal Seeks Tall TV Tower: FCC Permit to Build 1,000 Foot Structure Applied For," *Milwaukee Journal*, March 11, 1951.
144 Larry Christopher, "FCC Plans 2,000 TV Outlets: 10% to Educators," *Broadcasting Telecasting*, March 26, 1951.
145 "Taller Tower for Television: 1,000 Foot Structure Is Authorized for Radio City's WTMJ-TV," *Milwaukee Journal*, April 8, 1951.
146 "Morning TV Shows to Start: New Schedule Will Add 15 Hours Each Week; Time Changes Set," *Milwaukee Journal*, April 22, 1951.
147 Vonier, August 15, 2007.
148 "Bill Carlsen's Orchestra Signed by WTMJ: Musical Staff Increased to Total 31 Men," *Milwaukee Journal*, November 8, 1936.
149 Bea Pepan, "It's Always Fair Weather: When TV Meteorologist Bill Carlsen Tells Viewers About Changes in the Temperature," *Milwaukee Journal*, October 7, 1951.
150 Budd Reth, interview with author, October 4, 2007.
151 Budd Reth, interview with author, December 13, 2007.
152 "Judy Marks Joins WTMJ-TV Staff," *Milwaukee Journal*.
153 Judy Marks, interview with author, October 11, 2006.
154 "You Will Be Able to Watch Approaching Storms on TV," *Milwaukee Journal*, August 24, 1959.
155 "TV Weather Uses Radar: Shown by WTMJ-TV," *Milwaukee Journal*, November 4, 1959.
156 Marks, October 11, 2006.
157 Paul Joseph, interview with author, December 20, 2007.

158 "Judy Marks Will Leave Radio City," *Milwaukee Journal*, February 20, 1971.
159 *Live…At the Scene*, 209.
160 Joseph, December 20, 2007.
161 Sprague Vonier, email to author, December 22, 2007.
162 Joseph, December 20, 2007.
163 "New Television Tower on Way Up at WTMJ: Excavations Made for 1,017 foot High Structure, to Be One of highest in U.S.," *Milwaukee Journal*, November 4, 1951.
164 Budd Reth, email to author, October 3, 2007.
165 Vonier, August 15, 2007.
166 Reth, December 13, 2007.
167 "Outdoor TV Studio Ready: WTMJ-TV Programs Will Begin Using It on Tuesday," *Milwaukee Journal*, July 13, 1952.
168 Kerry Segrave, *Movies at Home: How Hollywood Came to Television*, (Jefferson, NC: McFarland, 1999), 15.
169 Ibid., 41.
170 Marks, October 11, 2006.
171 "State Granted 51 Channels for Television: Delay in Starting of New Stations Seen; WTMJ-TV Will Move to Channel 4," *Milwaukee Journal*, April 14, 1952.
172 Jim Robertson, letter to author, January 17, 2008.
173 Vonier, August 15, 2007.
174 "Work Started on TV Tower: Gallon Bottle of Milk Is Shattered Against first Column," *Milwaukee Journal*, September 19, 1952.
175 "Editorials Go on TV Today: Weekly Programs Will Depict Milwaukee's Civic Problems," *Milwaukee Journal*, September 30, 1952.
176 Bea Pepan, "Editorial on Television: Milwaukee Scores another 'First' With Unique Show," *Milwaukee Journal*, November 23, 1952.
177 "New TV Tower sets Height Mark for State: WTMJ Structure Is at the 420 Foot Level; Passes City Hall and to Continue Upward," *Milwaukee Journal*, October 17, 1952.
178 Gordon Hinkley, interview with author, December 11, 2007.
179 Ibid.
180 Ibid.
181 Ray J. Sheehan, Memo to Mayor Frank Zeidler, January 5, 1953. WTMJ-TV: 1944-1989, Clipping file. Milwaukee Public Library.
182 "WTMJ-TV Tower Up to 1,017 Feet," *Milwaukee Journal*, March 27, 1953.
183 "Closed Circuit," *Broadcasting Telecasting*, April 6, 1953, 5.
184 "TV Channel Rule Studied: WTMJ-TV Affected," *Milwaukee Journal*, May 15, 1953.
185 Although it denied Zenith a temporary stay, the Court of Appeals would eventually force the FCC to reverse its decision and hold a competitive hearing. As such, the shift of WBBM to channel 2 and WTMJ-TV's to Ch. 4 were changed to temporary authorizations, and CBS was required to formally request a channel shift. The matter was not settled until November of 1954, after Zenith entered into an agreement with CBS, in which the latter agreed to purchase Zenith's transmitter and other equipment for $575,000. Zenith, in turn, agreed to buy a quarter segment of CBS' *Omnibus* program for about the same amount.
186 "Telecasts Set on Channel 4: WTMJ-TV Will Send Patterns Preparatory to Switchover," *Milwaukee Journal*, June 22, 1953.
187 "Clear Channel for WTMJ-TV: FCC Rules Finally on Shift of WBBM-TV From Channel 4," *Milwaukee Journal*, June 23, 1953.
188 "WBBM-TV on Ch. 2, WTMJ-TV Move Set," *Broadcasting Telecasting*, July 13, 1953, 70.
189 "TV Now on Channel 4; New Viewers Welcomed," *Milwaukee Journal*, July 12, 1953.
190 "Fight Telecast Facilities Set: Will use WTMJ-TV," *Milwaukee Journal*, July 1, 1953.
191 "Fight Telecast Is Smooth Job: Millions in Nation See First Live TV Show to Originate here," *Milwaukee Journal*, July 16, 1953.
192 "RMA Group Plan: FCC Declines Participation," *Broadcasting Telecasting*, January 9, 1950, 13.
193 "CBS Wins Color Battle: Standards Effective Nov. 20," *Broadcasting Telecasting*, October 16, 1950, 177, 192-193.
194 "Color TV Has Gone to War – Industry Gets 'Greetings,'" *Broadcasting Telecasting*, October 22, 1950, 5-6.

195 "CBS Color TV 'Premiere': 16 Sponsors Signed at Start," *Broadcasting Telecasting*, June 25, 1951, 25.
196 "Compatible Color Specifications Approved by NTSC at IRE Meet," *Broadcasting Telecasting*, January 19, 1953, 72.
197 "Comedy Hour in Color Test," Milwaukee *Journal*, November 22, 1953.
198 Raymond E. McBride, "First Color TV Here a Many Hued Success," *Milwaukee Journal*, November 23, 1953.
199 "FCC Approval Clears Way for Compatible TV Color," *Broadcasting Telecasting*, December 21, 1953, 27.
200 "FCC Okays Color TV; Journal Station Ready," Milwaukee *Journal*, December 18, 1953.
201 Ibid.
202 "5,000 Swamp Store, See Floats on Color TV," *Milwaukee Journal*, January 2, 1954.
203 "First Sponsor for Color TV: Local Shows Planned," *Milwaukee Journal*, January 17, 1954.
204 "55 Color Sets in Milwaukee," *Broadcasting Telecasting*, April 26, 1954, 9.
205 "WTMJ-TV to Begin Local Color Telecasts," *Milwaukee Journal*, May 23, 1954.
206 "TV to Show City in Color: NBC to Turn Cameras on Whitnall Park in June Programs," *Milwaukee Journal*, May 26, 1954.
207 Harry Hill, "First TV Color Cast Here Is Big Success: WTMJ's New Camera Put on Grenadiers; Hour Long Show Hailed as Milestone," *Milwaukee Journal*, July 19, 1954.
208 "Art in Color Taken Into Homes by Television," *Milwaukee Journal*, July 21, 1954.
209 "State Fair Casts Its Colors Over National TV Network," *Milwaukee Journal*, August 26, 1954.
210 "WTMJ-TV to Up Color: New Studio to Open," *Milwaukee Journal*, October 28, 1954.
211 "FCC Boosts TV Ownership Limits: Seven Allowed, Five VHF, Two UHF," *Broadcasting Telecasting*, September 20, 1954, 7.
212 David Sarnoff, telegram to Walter Damm. October 28, 1954. Marquette University Archives, Arthur Olszyk Collection (Box 16, folder 2). Also see: "Gen. Sarnoff Says NBC Not Buying Station Here," *Milwaukee Journal*, October 29, 1954.
213 "Miller Wins on TV," *Milwaukee Journal*, December 5, 1955.
214 Doug Schmidt, *They Came to Bowl: How Milwaukee Became America's Tenpin Capital*," (Madison: Wisconsin Historical Society Press, 2007), p 182-183.
215 Ibid. 165.
216 Hank Stoddard, interview with author, November 28, 2007.
217 Hank Stoddard, "Rolling with 'The Champs' Over Four Decades," *Milwaukee Journal Sentinel*, April 9, 1995.
218 Stoddard, November 28, 2007.
219 Bob Wolf, "Brewers Down, Ratings Up," *Milwaukee Journal*, August 14, 1977.
220 Stoddard, November 28, 2007.
221 Tim Cuprisin, "Show Not Spared: WTMJ Cancels Bowling Program After 40 years," Milwaukee *Journal*, February 7, 1995.
222 Vonier, August 15, 2007.
223 Vonier, July 27, 2007.
224 Vonier, August 15, 2007.
225 "TV Editorial Comment Set: WTMJ-TV, WTMJ to Begin Program on Controversial Issues," *Milwaukee Journal*, August 16, 1962.
226 Harvian Raasch-Hooten, interview with author, August 8, 2007.
227 Michael H. Drew, "Television Safaris: Murl Deusing Plans Another Season of Exciting TV Trips," *Milwaukee Journal*, June 14, 1964.
228 A special section in chapter 5 discusses how WUHF picked up the network shows not cleared by WTMJ-TV.
229 "WTMJ-TV to Build Circular TV Studio," *Milwaukee Journal*, June 7, 1964.
230 "Round Studio Will Receive TV Spotlight," *Milwaukee Journal*.
231 "For the Record," *Broadcasting*, November 6, 1967, 85.
232 "Journal's TV Tower Will Be Modernized," *Milwaukee Journal*, June 28, 1967.
233 "WTMJ-TV Begins Using New Antenna," *Milwaukee Journal*, October 11, 1967.
234 Ed Hinshaw, interview with author, July 2, 2007.
235 Ibid.

236 "Maier Lists 39 Point Foundation for Bias Fight," *Milwaukee Journal*, August 7, 1967.
237 Henry W Maier., *The Mayor That Made Milwaukee Famous* (Lanham: Madison Books, 1993), 83.
238 "Mayor Asks About Suing News Media," *Milwaukee Journal*, September 19, 1967.
239 "Mayor Given Advice Not to Sue for Libel" *Milwaukee Journal*, November 28, 1967. Also see: "Mayor Advised Not to Sue News Media," *Milwaukee Sentinel*, November 30, 1967.
240 Lawrence C. Lohman, "Maier Blasts City's Papers" *Milwaukee Journal*, December 4, 1967. Also see: "Maier Complains of 'Paper Barrier,'" *Milwaukee Sentinel*, December 4, 1967.
241 "Mayor Sets 2nd TV Talk for Saturday," *Milwaukee Journal*, December 15, 1967.
242 "Maier Hints at Plans for New Newspaper," *Milwaukee Journal*, March 4, 1969.
243 "Maier Again Rips News Coverage" *Milwaukee Sentinel*, May 1, 1969. Also see: "Attacks on Journal Renewed by Maier," *Milwaukee Journal*, May 1, 1969.
244 "'Maier vs. Press' Subject of Show," *Milwaukee Sentinel*, May 30, 1969.
245 "Mayor Slates TV Conferences," *Milwaukee Journal*, May 15, 1969. Also see: "Maier Plans Weekly Press Sessions," *Milwaukee Sentinel*, May 15, 1969.
246 "Maier Asks US to Probe Journal Co." *Milwaukee Journal*, August 15, 1969. Also see: "Maier Asks Probe of Journal Co." *Milwaukee Sentinel*, August 16, 1969.
247 "Justice Officials Reply to Mayor," *Milwaukee Journal*, August 28, 1969.
248 "US Rejects Proposal to Investigate Journal," *Milwaukee Journal*, August 30, 1969.
249 Art Olszyk and Ed Hinshaw, "Report to Editorial Board – Henry Maier MABNA Appearance," Krueger, Jack, 1914-2000. Papers: 1922-1978. Milwaukee Manuscript Collection 205. Wisconsin Historical Society. Milwaukee Area Research Center. UWM Libraries. University of Wisconsin-Milwaukee (Box 1, folder 15).
250 Henry W. Maier, "A Case of Libel?" (brochure), 1972. Krueger, Jack, 1914-2000. Papers: 1922-1978. Milwaukee Manuscript Collection 205. Wisconsin Historical Society. Milwaukee Area Research Center. UWM Libraries. University of Wisconsin-Milwaukee (Box 1, folder 15).
251 Richard H. Leonard, letter to Henry W. Maier (copy), May 25, 1972. Krueger, Jack, 1914-2000. Papers: 1922-1978. Milwaukee Manuscript Collection 205. Wisconsin Historical Society. Milwaukee Area Research Center. UWM Libraries. University of Wisconsin-Milwaukee (Box 1, folder 15).
252 Jack Krueger, letter to William Small, CBS News, September 25, 1972 (copy). Krueger, Jack, 1914-2000. Papers: 1922-1978. Milwaukee Manuscript Collection 205. Wisconsin Historical Society. Milwaukee Area Research Center. UWM Libraries. University of Wisconsin-Milwaukee (Box 1, folder 15).
253 "Plea to TV: Cut Maier Off," *Milwaukee Journal*, October 5, 1972. Also see: "TV Stations Rapped on WTMJ Exclusion," *Milwaukee Sentinel*, October 5, 1972.
254 William B. Ray, letter to Frank Zeidler (undated). Frank Zeidler paper Collection, Milwaukee Public Library, Public Enterprise Committee Editorial Statements and Correspondence 1949-1972 (Box 323, folder 4). Also see: "News Policy Up to Mayor, FCC Replies," *Milwaukee Sentinel*, November 22, 1972.
255 "Mayor's Proposal Would Be First Step Toward Censorship," TV6 Editorial No. 3063, October 17, 1972. Krueger, Jack, 1914-2000. Papers: 1922-1978. Milwaukee Manuscript Collection 205. Wisconsin Historical Society. Milwaukee Area Research Center. UWM Libraries. University of Wisconsin-Milwaukee (Box 1, folder 15).
256 "TV Channels End Maier Press Series," *Milwaukee Journal*, February 20, 1973.
257 "Delay Requested on WTMJ License" *Milwaukee Journal*, November 8, 1973.
258 "FCC Rejects Delay on WTMJ Licenses," *Milwaukee Journal*, November 15, 1973. Also see: "FCC Refuses Delay in WTMJ License," *Milwaukee Sentinel*, November 16, 1973.
259 "WTMJ Licenses Held Up by Antitrust Hearing Request," *Milwaukee Journal*, November 30, 1973.
260 "WTMJ Backed on License Issue," *Milwaukee Journal*, December 5, 1973.
261 "Maier Asks FCC to Hold Hearing Here," *Milwaukee Sentinel*, December 1, 1973.
262 "FCC Rejects Challenge, Renews WTMJ Licenses," *Milwaukee Journal*, October 22, 1976.
263 "Maier Stops Talking to Journal," *Milwaukee Journal*, October 6, 1979.
264 "TV Officials Rap Maier," *Milwaukee Journal*, October 12, 1979.
265 Red Lion Broadcasting Co. v. FCC, 395 U.S. at 377

266 Ron Elving, "WTMJ and Journal Criticized by Mayor," *Milwaukee Journal*, June 11, 1981. Also see: "Mayor Files FCC Complaint," *Milwaukee Sentinel*, June 11, 1981.
267 *The Mayor That Made Milwaukee Famous*, 171.
268 Elving, Ron, "FCC Rejects Maier Complaint," *Milwaukee Journal*, August 24, 1981, Part 2, p 1, 3.
269 *The Mayor That Made Milwaukee Famous*, 171.
270 Ibid., 174.
271 "FCC Again Rejects Complaint on WTMJ," *Milwaukee Journal*, August 3, 1982. Also see: "Panel Rejects Complaint," *Milwaukee Sentinel*, August 3, 1982.
272 "Maier's Complaint Rejected by FCC," *Milwaukee Sentinel*, February 19, 1983. Also see: "FCC Rejects Maier Complaint Against WTMJ," *Milwaukee Journal*, February 19, 1983.
273 "Maier to Appeal Decision by FCC," *Milwaukee Sentinel*, April 26, 1983. Also see: "Maier Appeals on Complaint," *Milwaukee Journal*, April 26, 1983.
274 "Court Has Maier Request," *Milwaukee Sentinel*, November 11, 1983.
275 "WTMJ Official to Testify," *Milwaukee Sentinel*, February 1, 1984.
276 "Maier Invited to testify on TV Fairness Rule," *Milwaukee Journal*, February 2, 1984.
277 "WTMJ Editorial Unfair to Maier, Aide Tell Panel," *Milwaukee Journal*, February 9, 1984.
278 "Maier Loses WTMJ Challenge" *Milwaukee Journal*, May 9, 1984. Also see: "Maier Loses His Appeal of Ruling in WTMJ Case," *Milwaukee Sentinel*, May 9, 1984.
279 *Henry W. Maier v. Federal Communications Commission*. United States Court of Appeals for the Seventh Circuit, No. 83-1737.
280 *The Mayor That Made Milwaukee Famous*, 190, 197.
281 "TV Ruling Not Dead Yet," *Milwaukee Journal*, May 23, 1984. Also see: "Maier Appeals FCC Case," *Milwaukee Sentinel*, May 23, 1984.
282 "Court Rejects Maier Appeal," *Milwaukee Journal*, June 14, 1984.
283 Nate Grimm, "Anchoring His Life," *Wisconsin People and Ideas*, Winter, 2007, p 62-68.
284 Jack Lee, interview with author, November 28, 2007.
285 Ibid.
286 Robert Sherwood, email to the author, December 11, 2007.
287 Robert Sherwood, interview with author, December 11, 2007.
288 Ibid.
289 Robert Sherwood, email to the author, December 13, 2007.
290 Jan Uebelherr, "WTMJ Fires Melodie Wilson," *Milwaukee Sentinel*, September 11, 1991.
291 Michael Zahn, "Wilson's Firing Didn't Follow the Script Provided by WTMJ," *Milwaukee Journal*, September 12, 1991.
292 Bob Wolfley, "Garcia Steps Up to the Mike, Breaks Down a Barrier," *Milwaukee Journal*, August 5, 1994.
293 Duane Dudek, "WITI Flips to Fox; CBS Left Looking," *Milwaukee Sentinel*, May 24, 1994.
294 Duane Dudek, "NBC, WTMJ-TV Reach 7-Year Agreement," *Milwaukee Sentinel*, August 10, 1994.
295 Rich Kirchen, "Journal Communications Adds a TV Station in Milwaukee – Sort Of," *Business Journal of Milwaukee*, May 19, 2000.
296 Tim Cuprisin, "Next After Channel 58: Windy City," *Milwaukee Journal Sentinel*, November 29, 2000.
297 Tim Cuprisin, "Channel 4 Brews a New, Local 'Blend,'" *Milwaukee Journal Sentinel*, August 10, 2006.
298 Sprague Vonier, interview with author, July 27, 2007.
299 Ibid.
300 Concept for "Cappy Presents Miss Chris," provided by Joan Christopherson-Schmidt.
301 Donald H. Dooley., "Cappy Brightens TV Picture," *Milwaukee Journal*, August 24, 1957.
302 Concept for "Cappy Presents Miss Chris."
303 Donald H. Dooley., "Milwaukee Studio Notes," *Milwaukee Journal*, August 12, 1962.
304 Michael H. Drew, "Kids' Klub's Funny Face," *Milwaukee Journal*, October 11, 1964.
305 Cherie Lee Parcher, interview with author, September 13, 2007.

306 Reth, October 4, 2007.
307 "Funeral Today in Winona for Knutzen," *Milwaukee Sentinel*, December 14, 1976.
308 Michael H. Drew, "Milwaukee Studio Notes," *Milwaukee Journal*, June 16, 1968, TV Screen, 24.
309 Michael H. Drew, "Milwaukee Studio Notes," *Milwaukee Journal*, March 2, 1969, TV Screen, 20.
310 Aye Jaye, interview with author, November 20, 2007.
311 Aye Jaye, interview with author, December 17, 2007.

CHAPTER 3
THE "FREEZE" AND UHF

In March of 1947, the FCC rejected CBS' petition to set standards for color television, which would have used the untested UHF portion of the spectrum between 480 and 920 MHz. In doing so, the Commission gave the go-ahead to monochrome, VHF television.

The problem was that there weren't enough VHF channels to develop a "truly nationwide, competitive television system," the way the Commission had envisioned – a fact it admitted. On November 21, 1945, it had issued its Rules Governing Television Broadcast Stations, in which it included a Table of Channel Assignments for major cities. Post-WWII interest in the new medium was high. The FCC's channel assignments were insufficient to give every community at least one station. Network operations had begun, and the four – NBC, CBS, Du Mont and ABC – had soon bought the maximum number of five stations FCC regulations allowed them to own. Radio stations, and other entities, had begun to apply for television construction permits, and in cities where only one or two channels had been assigned, lengthy license hearings were anticipated. Those that were successful in getting a channel hoped to affiliate with a network, and the networks hoped to show their programming throughout the country – even if at the time, it was primarily distributed via kinescopes.

Edwin Armstrong had objected to the FCC's 1945 decision to shift FM upward in the spectrum. Doing so had made all existing FM receivers obsolete. In addition, his Yankee Network made use of relay stations, instead of AT&T's co-axial cable system. That relay network only worked at the lower frequencies previously assigned, and FM spokesmen had pleaded with the Commission to allow them to use a portion of TV channel 1 (which had been previously allocated to FM) for that use.[1]

In addition, mobile services, such as dispatch, and other business uses of radio, needed more spectrum. Under the rules then in force, they were allowed to share time with television stations. The pressure on the FCC was strong.

One solution was to use the UHF band of frequencies, but there were objections to that. UHF was untried. Dr. Allan Du Mont said that: "The suggestion that television should utilize some of the higher frequencies between 500 and 900 mc seems to me to be premature."[2] He pointed out that the propagation characteristics of UHF – as then known – were inferior to VHF, that UHF transmitters then available were incapable of producing the same radiated power as their VHF counterparts, and that sets capable of receiving both signals would cost more.[3]

Broadcasters would have preferred to have many more channels in major cities on the east coast, as well as Chicago and Los Angeles. In that way, they would have a presence in the country's largest markets. In particular, New York City wanted seven full-power channels.

In reaction, the FCC took the following action on May 6, 1948:
1. Abolished the sharing of TV channels for non-broadcasting use.
2. Refused FM's plea for a portion of TV channel 1.

3. Re-assigned TV channel 1 strictly for non-governmental service use as of June 14, 1948.
4. Gave FM stations operating in the old band until the end of the year to move to the 88-108 MHz band.
5. Proposed a new and revised Table of Channel Assignments, which included many more cities, and added more channels to some major cities.
6. Called for a hearing starting on June 14 to discuss the proposed revisions to the Table of Channel Assignments.
7. Called for hearing starting on September 20, 1948 on the feasibility of using the UHF band.[4]

The 1945 channel assignments covered 405 stations in the largest 140 markets. In its new proposal, the FCC increased the number of channels to 900 in 461 markets. How, one might ask, could the Commission increase the number of assignments while eliminating one television channel? The 1945 television rules specified that stations on the same channel had to be at least two hundred miles apart, while those on adjacent channels had to be at least eighty-five miles away from each other. When it released its proposed new Table of Channel Assignments, the Commission also quietly reduced those requirements to one hundred fifty and seventy-five miles respectively. Doing so went against the recommendations of its own engineers.[5] The Commission based its separation distances solely on groundwave propagation, and ignored the effects of tropospheric ducting or thermal inversion.[6]

One of the goals of the new plan was to give New York City seven full-power channels. To do so, the Commission reassigned two of that city's low-power, community channels to full-power. That had the potential to cause interference with other stations on the east coast.

Channel 1 had been assigned to Racine-Kenosha, but the proposed revisions gave those communities channel 13 instead. The Johnson-Kennedy Radio Corporation had petitioned the FCC to delete it from Racine-Kenosha, and assign it to Chicago.[7]

Once WTMJ-TV started broadcasting, Milwaukee-area residents began purchasing television receivers. *Broadcasting Telecasting* reported that by April of 1948, 2,050 sets had been installed – of which seventy-four percent were in private homes.[8] Radio stations, not knowing if television would replace them as primary broadcast outlets, jumped on the bandwagon. The Wisconsin Broadcasting System, Inc. (owners of WFOX radio) applied for a construction permit for channel 8 on March 16, 1948. Hearst Radio, Inc. (which had filed an application for what was then channel 4 in June of 1945, but later rescinded it) filed an application for channel 10 on March 24. The Kapital City Broadcasting Co. of Des Moines, Iowa applied for channel 6 on April 13th. (One of the company's principals had a construction permit for an FM station in Milwaukee, WMIL, and transferred it to Kapital.) WEXT, Inc. (Owned by the Bartell Brothers, who later changed the frequency and the call letters to WOKY – See chapter 5) also applied for channel 6 that same day. Finally, Milwaukee Broadcasting Co. (WEMP) applied for channel 6 on May 21. All the applicants were scheduled for a consolidated hearing beginning on July 29.

The hearing on the proposed revision to the Table of Channel Assignments was scheduled to begin on June 7, but the Commission was inundated with briefs and comments. As a result, it was postponed until June 29.[9]

In the meantime, Dr. Allan Du Mont proposed his own channel allocation plan. His engineers presented field test data that showed that tropospheric ducting was likely to produce adjacent or co-channel interference – especially as more stations began broadcasting – if the FCC's proposed channel assignments were adopted. It was recommended that stations on the same channel be at least 180 miles apart.[10]

Du Mont had already spoken out against the premature use of the UHF band. His proposed plan called for the addition of eight additional VHF channels. He proposed two alternative allocation plans, with the additional eight channels coming from frequencies used for government services. In addition, he proposed that channels be assigned on a sliding scale based upon population. Areas with less than 25,000 people within their 500 microvolt contour would not receive a channel, while those with 5,000,000 or more, would receive seven.[11] Milwaukee's channel assignments would not have changed under the plan. The government was loath to give up spectrum, and the plan went nowhere.

At the same time, remarks by the FCC's acting chief engineer, John A. Willoughby, produced more uncertainty as to the short-term future of television. Willoughby opined that: color television would be available in less than two years, channels 2-6 would be taken away from television and given to fixed and mobile services, and channels 7-13 would be used for low-definition television, while the UHF band would be used for high-definition – monochrome and color.[12]

Confidence amongst broadcasters was shattered. Attorneys whose clients had applications for channels 2-6 said that they would ask the FCC to postpone them until decisions had been reached. Others suggested that the hearing on the proposed channel assignments should be adjourned until after the Commission held hearings on the UHF band.[13]

On July 7, 1948, Kapital Broadcasting amended its application to change the name of the applicant to the Majestic Broadcasting Co. Since there were three applicants for channel 6, Milwaukee Broadcasting petitioned the FCC "for leave to amend its application to specify channel 6 or such other channel as may be available for assignment in area in lieu of request for channel 6 only."[14] That petition was denied on July 23. Also denied that day was a petition by the Midwest Broadcasting Co. (owner of WMAW – later WCAN – radio; see chapter 4) asking for a continuance of the hearings. It is likely that this was because Midwest intended to apply for one of the available channels. Also that same day, Majestic Broadcasting asked the FCC to dismiss its application for channel 6. That the Commission did without prejudice.

On August 27, the FCC called for a joint FCC-industry conference to study the technical problems associated with UHF. At the conference, a schedule of technical sessions was set up for November – December, in which the topics included: tropospheric ducting, the use of directional antennas, increased power, and whether the 150 and 75 mile separation distances should be increased as a consequence.[15]

After the first round of Milwaukee hearings, several petitions were filed with the FCC: WEXT Inc. asked the FCC to dismiss its application for channel 6. The FCC granted that petition on September 10. That left three channels and three unopposed applicants. All three were granted a joint petition on September 7 – the day before the second round of hearings were to begin – for an indefinite continuance. The three asked the Commission to immediately grant them construction permits.

Unfortunately, that same week, the FCC passed over six applications, and indicated that it would not make any further grants unless at least two hundred miles separated the proposed station from another on the same channel. The Commission indicated that it would continue that policy until after propagation studies had concluded.[16]

Dr. Allen Du Mont submitted a new channel allocation/assignment plan that used UHF. That plan would have assigned four channels in the country's largest markets, and as such, would have insured that programming from all four networks – NBC, CBS, ABC, and Du Mont – could be seen in them. VHF and UHF were not inter-mixed in any market, and the proposed standards were the same for both. Du Mont's plan applied to monochrome TV, and he proposed that new frequencies be allocated for color, when it became available.[17]

Just prior to the UHF hearing, the FCC denied the petition of Edwin Armstrong and other FM broadcasters, which sought reallocation of a portion of the 44-50 MHz band for use by FM relay stations. The Commission in its decision stated that safety and special services were more important.[18]

The hearing on UHF began on September 20, and lasted for three days. At the end of those hearings, the Commission concluded that the matter was more complex than it had originally thought, and that more study was needed. There was a consensus that the UHF band would have to be used, but none as to how.[19] As a result, on September 30, it announced that all television applications would be put in pending files, that no hearings would be scheduled, and that no decisions would be made on cases already heard, until after the questions on channel allocations and assignments were settled.[20] At a news conference held to announce the freeze, FCC chairman Wayne Coy said that he expected the freeze to last "possibly six months."[21]

At the time of the "freeze," thirty-seven television stations were on the air, and another eighty-six construction permits had been issued. Three hundred three television applications were pending, and nine hearings were awaiting decisions. Stations with construction permits were allowed to begin broadcasting, but applications for modifications to those permits[22] or to licensed facilities were to be decided on a case-by-case basis, depending upon whether or not those modifications would be affected by possible changes in standards.

One of the nine cases awaiting a decision was for Milwaukee. The three remaining applicants for the three available channels were confident that they would receive grants. The freeze changed all of that. It would lead to battles after the freeze was lifted.

Another affect of the freeze was to make WTMJ-TV the only television station in the city – and the state. It would enjoy a *de facto* monopoly for over five years, and as such, would consolidate its position. It would take many years for any other station to challenge its dominance.

The FCC estimated that the freeze would only last six to nine months. Unfortunately, it would drag on for almost four years, as the Commission first considered color and educational reservations. Many broadcasters were upset, as in doing so, the FCC held up monochrome television.

On May 9, 1949, the FCC granted NBC a construction permit for an experimental UHF television station in Bridgeport, Connecticut. The call letters KC2XAK were later assigned to it.

On July 11, 1949, the Commission announced a draft channel allocation plan.[23] In it, 42 new channels were allocated in the UHF band.

The first issue to be considered was that of color television. Hearings began on September 26, 1949 – almost a year after the FCC announced the freeze. RCA had been working on a fully-electronic, dot-sequential color system that was compatible with the existing NTSC standards. CBS by that time had dropped its idea for high-definition color broadcasting using 16 MHz channels. The main issue was compatibility. The CBS system was not compatible with the NTSC standards, and used only 405 lines of resolution in order to get the necessary color information in a 6 MHz channel. In addition, receivers would still have to use a rotating color wheel.

In January of 1950, the Radio Manufacturers Association (RMA) proposed a second NTSC to study the color problem and develop standards. The FCC had participated in the first committee, but declined to do so in the second.[24]

Early tests were conducted on systems submitted by CBS, RCA and a line-sequential system developed by Color Technology, Inc. (CTI). Others submitted systems which they asked the FCC to consider, but all were turned down. A Milwaukee resident, Theodore A. Wetzel (who worked for Kearney and Trecker, and was an amateur radio enthusiast) claimed to have developed an NTSC-compatible system, and petitioned the FCC to consider it in early January.[25] He claimed that his system could be adapted to either field (CBS), line (CTI) or dot (RCA) sequential systems, and that receivers could be constructed to selectively receive signals from transmitters using any of those methods.[26] The Commission rejected his petition the following month, stating that "a *prima facie* showing has not been made that your proposed system can be used as a basis for the promulgation of color television standards."[27] It further stated that "…it appears from your petition that your proposed system has not progressed beyond the theoretical stage; that the amount of research and development which your system has undergone does not appear to be sufficient to permit you to determine fundamentals and to explore basic problems; and that no transmitting or receiving apparatus has been constructed by you which would be suitable for either laboratory or field testing."[28]

The CBS system performed the best in the trials, but most engineers thought that the NTSC-compatible systems could be improved with more development time. The FCC however, was under pressure to lift the freeze, and to do so, it needed to make a decision as to whether or not to include color standards.

That same month, KC2XAK began experimental broadcasting on 529-535 MHz. It rebroadcast programming from NBC's New York station, WNBT.[29]

In April, FCC Chairman Coy intimated that all television might be moved to the UHF portion of the spectrum, because of pressures to provide bandwidth for other uses. He opined that television broadcasters might be given six years in which to make the switch.[30]

The color hearings concluded on May 26, and on September 1, the Commission issued its First Report on color. It favored the CBS color system as being ready for immediate use, while holding the door open for NTSC-compatible systems. As such, it stated that it was prepared to approve the CBS field-sequential system, unless receiver manufacturers would guarantee by September 29, that they would be prepared to go into production of sets capable of receiving both the CBS and RCA systems in early November. If the set makers would agree to make sets to "bracket standards," the Commission would agree to hold off on making a decision until more development had been completed on NTSC-compatible systems.[31]

The timeframe took receiver manufacturers by surprise.[32] They had less than a month to reply to the FCC's challenge, and then ramp up for production less than two months after that. Most felt that they weren't given enough time.[33] At the deadline, many submitted replies – most of which said that they would not be able to manufacture sets to "bracket standards" in early November.[34]

On October 10, 1950, the FCC issued its Second Report on color. As expected, it approved the CBS field-sequential color system and authorized commercial color broadcasting to begin as of November 20.[35] The reaction from broadcasters and set manufacturers was negative.[36] On October 17, RCA and the Pilot Radio

Corporation filed separate lawsuits in which they asked the courts to issue temporary restraining orders preventing the FCC's order from becoming effective on the grounds that doing so was against the "public interest."[37]

On October 16, 1950, the FCC opened hearings on general issues related to the allocation of spectrum, the assignment of channels, and the issuance of standards.[38]

CBS faced the prospect of being able to broadcast commercially in color, but the general public was unlikely to receive those shows, as most set manufacturers refused to make receivers, and the lack of compatibility meant that they could not be received on those made to NTSC monochrome standards. CBS got a formal reprieve of sorts, in the form of the Korean War. On October 19, the Office of Defense Mobilization announced that it was halting the production of color television sets, as some of the components would be needed for the war effort.[39] The shortages threatened to affect the production of monochrome television receivers as well, and the prospect of the freeze ending soon looked dim.[40]

During the FCC allocation hearings, an RCA engineer, while reporting on the findings it had made after broadcasting on the NBC experimental UHF station in Bridgeport, Connecticut, stated that: "…It would be most unfortunate if the television expansion has to go into the UHF band."[41] Nonetheless, the tests showed that UHF signals were not subject to interference from automobile ignition systems and neon signs the way VHF signals were. Although the experimental station's signal could be received over longer distances than originally thought possible, it was thought that UHF would be most suitable for lower-powered, community stations.[42]

On November 16, a three-judge federal court in Chicago issued a temporary restraining order against the FCC's decision to allow commercial color broadcasting to begin using the CBS system.[43] Most television set makers approved of the decision.[44] However, after further study, the court, on December 22, decided to rescind part of its restraining order, and upheld the FCC's authority to issue its decision. The three-judge panel, however, continued to ban commercial color broadcasting.[45] The latter was a moot point, as no one would be able to receive such broadcasts, because no color receivers were available!

The Milwaukee Common Council passed a resolution on November 24, asking the FCC for at least three more television channels.[46] Meanwhile, at the urging of Commissioner Frieda Hennock, the FCC had decided to hold hearings on whether to reserve some television channels for educational use. Those hearings began on November 27. (See chapter 8.)

Speaking to members of the Wisconsin Radio, Refrigeration and Appliance Association on November 29, the Journal Co.'s manager for radio and television, Walter Damm, assured residents that WTMJ-TV would not begin full time color broadcasting unless residents could also receive the shows in black-and-white. If the CBS method was adopted, they would broadcast in color before or after regular telecasts, until the majority of sets in the Milwaukee area could receive a color signal. If the RCA method were adopted, Damm indicated that WTMJ-TV would begin full time color broadcasting ASAP, as those shows could also be received in monochrome.[47]

The Milwaukee Common Council reiterated its desire for more television service, when on January 16, 1951 it passed yet another resolution asking the FCC to assign at least three more channels to the city.[48]

On March 22, 1951, the FCC issued a proposed new frequency allocation and channel assignment plan.[49] In it, seventy UHF channels (14-83) were allocated, in addition to VHF channels 2-13. Approximately ten percent of the channels were reserved for noncommercial, educational use. Milwaukee was to be assigned VHF channels 4, 10 and 12, as well as UHF channels 19, 25 and 31. Channel 4 was assigned to WTMJ-TV, which would have to move from channel 3. Channel 10 was reserved for noncommercial, educational use. The Commission sought input, and requested that statements of interest be filed by May 7, 1951.[50]

In Milwaukee, the debate over the reservation of channel 10 for noncommercial, educational use was heated. The Milwaukee Broadcasting Co. (WEMP), Wisconsin Broadcasting System, Inc. (WFOX) and Hearst Radio, Inc. (WISN) had expected to receive grants just before the FCC froze the processing of all applications in 1948, and advocated that channel 10 be released for commercial use, and that one of the UHF channels be reserved for education.[51]

In order to push the color matter, on February 5, 1951, CBS, the FCC and the Justice Department jointly asked the United States Supreme Court to uphold the lower court's decision, and to remove its restraint on commercialization.[52] Oral arguments were held March 26-27, and the Court issued its opinion on May 28. In an 8-0 vote, the Court ruled that the FCC had the authority to approve the CBS system, and allow commercial color broadcasting using it to begin.[53]

On June 25, 1951, CBS began color telecasts on its stations in New York, Boston, Philadelphia, Baltimore, and Washington, D.C. The premiere aired between 4:30 and 5:30 p.m. In New York, fifteen color receivers were located around the city – most in CBS' studios. Three receivers were set up in Washington, D.C., two in Boston and Baltimore, and one in Philadelphia.[54] The network stopped color telecasting on October 19, due to the lack of color receivers.[55]

The Wisconsin Broadcasting System, Inc. (WFOX) and Hearst (WISN) filed a joint counter-proposal in which VHF channel 6 would have been deleted from Green Bay's assignment and given to Milwaukee. They also proposed that channel 10 be reserved for commercial use, and that instead, one of the UHF channels be reserved for noncommercial, educational use.[56] The counter-proposal would have given Milwaukee three available VHF channels, all of which would have been available for commercial use.

The Milwaukee Broadcasting Co. (WEMP) filed the first request for an amendment to a pre-freeze application on February 29.[57] (1952 was a leap year.) They proposed to have studios at 525 West Wells Street, and would erect a 1,000' tower. They also asked permission to mount their antenna on their 460' radio tower in the event that they couldn't get steel for the taller one[58] because of Korean War priorities. In that application, they also requested that the FCC take channel 6 from Green Bay, and assign it to Milwaukee.

The Wisconsin Broadcasting System, Inc., filed an objection to the WEMP application on March 7, stating that it constituted a new application, rather than an amendment, and that FCC rules forbade such applications twenty days after the start of hearings.[59] Those hearings had begun in 1948.

On April 14, 1952, the FCC issued its Sixth Report and General Order, which lifted the freeze on new television licenses as of July 1, and provided for 617 VHF and 1436 UHF licenses, 242 of which were reserved for noncommercial educational use. Twelve of the latter were assigned to Wisconsin: two VHF and ten UHF. The Commission adopted a policy of intermixing VHF and UHF channels in the same markets. Milwaukee received VHF channels 4, 10 and 12, and UHF channels 19, 25 and 31. Channel 10 was reserved for educational use, leaving channel 12 as the only VHF channel available for commercial stations, as channel 4 was assigned to WTMJ-TV.[60] New applications were to be filed by July 1.

A Mallory TV101 set-top UHF converter. This unit was also private-labeled to other manufacturers. (Courtesy of Mark Nelson)

In the Report and Order, the FCC rejected the counter-proposals which would have assigned VHF channel 6 to Milwaukee. The Commission's new regulations required that 170 miles separate stations on the same channel. Opposition to the proposal came from WJIM-TV in Lansing, Michigan and WOC-TV in Davenport, Iowa. WJIM-TV was already operating on channel 6, while WOC-TV was scheduled to move from channel 5 to channel 6. In the case of the former, the distance between Lansing and Milwaukee was determined to be 171 miles, while the distance from the station's transmitter site to Milwaukee was 173 – both met the FCC's separation requirements. In the case of WOC-TV, the distance between Davenport and Milwaukee was determined to be 170 miles, but that between Milwaukee and the WOC-TV transmitter site was only 167.[61] The Commission, in rejecting the counter-proposals, pointed out that to accept them would require a deviation from its own rules and standards.[62] It also stated that "the record did not support adding a fourth VHF channel to Milwaukee by deleting it from Green Bay," as the latter city was large enough to warrant a second VHF channel.[63] The Commission also reaffirmed its belief that channel 10 should be reserved for educational use, and rejected the idea that a UHF channel be substituted.

On September 18, 1952, KPTV in Portland, Oregon began broadcasting on channel 27. It was the first commercial UHF television station in the country.

In the plan Dr. Allen Du Mont had proposed to the FCC four years earlier, there was no intermixture of VHF and UHF stations in the same cities. The Commission in issuing its Sixth Report and General Order chose to do so. That was a mistake. UHF transmitters were not yet as powerful as their VHF counterparts, meaning that their coverage area was smaller. Even when more powerful transmitters became available, using them in the higher frequencies would mean that the electrical power requirements – and expense – would be prohibitive.

In addition, there was no requirement that manufacturers produce sets capable of receiving both bands, and those who already owned sets would have to purchase UHF converters. Early UHF tuners were continuous like a radio dial, and weren't very sensitive – effectively reducing the range of UHF stations.[64]

Further, early UHF receivers were susceptible to false images when there were nearby stations on various combinations of video and aural frequencies. They weren't capable of rejecting those images (it would have required at least two more circuits to switch in the tuner), which caused "herringbone" and other video anomalies. In response, the FCC published a list of "taboo" combinations that persisted long past the time that much better receivers became available.[65]

That meant that UHF stations were at a disadvantage in markets which had strong VHF competitors. In order to attract advertisers, the UHF stations had to get their signal to as many viewers as possible, and that meant that they needed more powerful transmitters. It also meant that they had to convince viewers to purchase UHF converters or all-channel sets.

UHF broadcasters were in trouble. In May of 1954, the U.S. Senate held hearings on the matter. The Ultra High Frequency Television Association (UHFTA) proposed that the FCC freeze all new applications for VHF channels until after the Senate committee had taken testimony, studied it, and made recommendations to the Commission.[66] It also made several suggestions to aid UHF broadcasters, which included:

- Freeze new VHF license applications for a minimum of 90-120 days
- The transfer of all VHF television to UHF, with a first step of eliminating intermixture of the two in the same markets
- Require all networks to provide programming to UHF
- Mandate that all sets be capable of receiving a UHF signal
- Speed up the depreciation of UHF equipment for tax purposes
- Provide federal contracts for UHF transmission and receiving tube research.[67]

In Milwaukee the reservation of channel 10 for noncommercial, educational use helped those who eventually sought UHF licenses. Since channel 4 was reserved for WTMJ-TV, channel 12 was the only VHF channel available for commercial use. That meant that the prospect for long hearings before the FCC might delay anyone getting a grant for at least two years. By contrast, Madison had only one VHF channel assigned to it (3), and initially, some applicants petitioned the FCC for rule making to change its status to noncommercial and educational, and assign UHF channel 21 for commercial use. In that way, all of the commercial channels would be in the UHF band (21, 27 and 33). That proposal was rejected by the Commission on November 1, 1954.

Milwaukee's UHF channels were granted rather quickly. The owners of two of them went on the air with network affiliations, with the hope that they would be strong enough to survive once channel 12 was granted. Hearst fought the reservation of channel 10 for noncommercial, educational use, and lost. It then dug up its old plan to assign another VHF channel (6) to the area. Rather than delete it from Green Bay, as it had proposed in 1952, it convinced the FCC to swap channels in Green Bay and Marquette, Michigan. To comply with the Commission's separation rules, Hearst proposed that the channel be assigned to the Village of Whitefish Bay rather than to Milwaukee. In that way, it was located more than 170 miles from WOC-TV.

The Commission assigned channel 6 to the area, as per Hearst's plan, in 1953, and that contributed to WCAN-TV's decision to go dark. (See chapter 4.) It would be many years before another station went on the air in Milwaukee – despite the fact that construction permits were issued.

That scenario was repeated throughout the country. Many UHF stations in intermixed cities either turned in their construction permits after never going on the air, or went dark within a short period of time. Milwaukee was cited as a prime UHF testing area.[68] Despite the Congressional hearings, no action was ever taken, and much of the UHF spectrum went unused. UHF broadcasters thought that pay-TV might offer revenue opportunities, but efforts to get it approved would drag on until 1970. (See chapter 9.) In early August of 1953, four UHF grantees petitioned the FCC for quick action on pay-TV proposals[69], and along with other UHF station owners formed a committee the following month to push the matter.[70]

From 1952-1962, the FCC would propose various plans to de-intermix a number of cities. In 1955, Commissioner Frieda Hennock floated a proposal to shift all television to UHF over a ten-year period. The Commission's staff proposed freezing all applications for new VHF stations that would lie within a fifty mile radius of a UHF station, as well as all modifications to existing VHF stations within that radius – including those requesting an increase in the effective radiated power. At the same time, it proposed to de-intermix Madison. The motion was not seconded, and it died.[71] In 1956, the FCC considered a plan to shift all television east of the Mississippi River to UHF, while the West would be predominantly VHF.[72] The VHF stations in Milwaukee reacted negatively[73], and the plan was never implemented.

While it deliberated, the Commission extended the date by which all UHF construction permit holders had to begin construction from January 16 to July 16, 1956.[74] Another three-month extension was later granted, pushing the date to October 16.[75]

In November of that year, the Commission adopted a "get tough" policy with those who held UHF construction permits, but who had not yet gone on the air. Eighty-three permit holders, who had filed for extensions, were given until February 15, 1957 to submit additional materials showing that they were making progress. Failure to comply would result in the dismissal of their applications, and the loss of their CP's. The FCC had granted extensions in January, but had provided warning that it would take a closer look at applications in the future. Both WCAN-TV (Ch. 25) and WFOX-TV (Ch. 31) in Milwaukee were among the eighty-three.[76]

In February of 1957, the FCC de-intermixed Fresno, California and Evansville, Indiana, but in a 4-3 vote, decided not to do the same to Madison.[77] Sixty holders of UHF construction permits responded to the Commission's order for more information. Most responded that they were uncertain of UHF's future, and were unable to compete against VHF stations. In addition, they were awaiting the outcome of the FCC's discussions on de-intermixture.[78] Ten stations had their construction permits deleted.[79]

The Communications Act of 1934 placed control of civilian broadcasting under the FCC, but the President had authority in matters of national security. In September of 1957, the military submitted a request to President Eisenhower for TV channels 2-6.[80] The request was denied.

In February of 1960, the Commission sent letters to fifty-four holders of UHF construction permits who had again filed for extensions. In that letter, the Commission stated:

> It appears that delay in construction has been due…to your voluntary decision to postpone construction because of your belief that the proposed station

could not succeed financially under present economic conditions. On this basis, the Commission is unable to find that you have been diligent in proceeding with the construction...Therefore, the Commission has concluded that a grant of your application would not be warranted.[81]

Those permitees were given thirty days to respond. In March, five permits were deleted at the request of their holders. Another sixteen were deleted in late April.[82] In November, the FCC denied the extension applications and deleted the construction permits of twenty-six stations. WFOX-TV (which was now channel 30) was one of them. Two commissioners dissented, saying that the FCC should decide on an allocation plan for UHF first.[83]

In 1961, the FCC proposed another plan to de-intermix selected markets, and again, Madison was one of them. Rural groups near Madison protested – with one sending a petition with 32,000 signatures to the Commission.[84]

In multi-path distortion, the signal is picked up by the receiver normally, but the same signal is also reflected off of a tall building or mountain. The reflected signal is received slightly later, resulting in "ghosting."

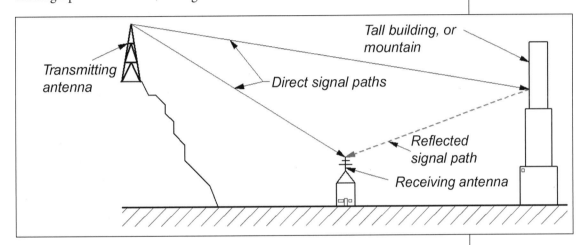

FCC Chairman Newton Minow then took another approach. Speaking at a meeting of the National Association of Educational Broadcasters on October 23, 1961, he called for a lobbying effort to require that all television receivers be capable of receiving both VHF and UHF signals.[85] (The Commission had suggested the same thing the previous year.) The proposals to de-intermix several markets were then dropped.

There had been no comprehensive study comparing UHF to VHF propagation characteristics in a major city. In 1962, the FCC received a $2 million appropriation to conduct such a study. A station, WUHF[86], was put on the air from the Empire State Building on channel 31 beginning on November 1, 1961. Tests were run into 1962. Finally, the industry had some data. It showed that ghosting could be a problem due to multi-path distortion in large cities, but that in open-terrain, the signal would be quite clear for long distances.[87] Later experience refuted those conclusions, and showed that UHF was in fact less susceptible to ghosting than VHF, and any that did occur was easily eliminated with proper antenna design.[88]

As of June 30, 1962, 508 VHF stations were in operation, but only 104 UHF, of which 44 were educational. Since 1952, approximately 100 more UHF stations had gone dark.[89]

Minow made the passage of an all-channel receiver bill the number one legislative priority of the FCC for 1962. The proposal to de-intermix some cities was used as leverage to get the law passed.[90] Congress did so, and on July 10, 1962, President Kennedy signed into law the All-Channel Receiver Act. The law affected all sets manufactured after April 30, 1964, and required that all sets shipped via interstate commerce (or imported) include the capability of receiving a UHF signal.[91]

However, the all-channel law did not drive up interest in UHF. Much of the spectrum still went unused. In 1963, channel 37 was allocated to radio astronomy, and no stations were allowed to use it as of January 1, 1974. (No over-the-air television station had ever done so. In 2000, it was allocated for use by low-power medical telemetry equipment, in addition to radio astronomy.)

Since 1945, the FCC was under pressure from land-mobile and emergency service users for more spectrum space. In July of 1968, it proposed rulemaking which would have allowed land-mobile users to operate on UHF channels 14-20 in the top twenty-five markets, if they were not being used by television (channel sharing). It also proposed that TV channels 70-83 be reallocated for land-mobile use. Comments were requested by December 2 of that year, and replies to those comments by January 31, 1969.[92] On March 20, 1970, they voted down that part of the proposal that would have allowed the sharing of channels 14-20.[93] In May of that year, the Commission finally resolved the issue, by passing a modification to their proposal, which allowed land-mobile users to share one or two of channels 14-20 in the top ten markets. It also voted to reallocate channels 70-83 for common carrier and private land-mobile use. Since that would displace television translators, it proposed opening up channels 14-69 for that use.[94]

It wasn't until the 1970s that UHF tuners were developed by Japanese manufacturers that could "lock-in" a UHF signal the way VHF tuners could. As a result, interest in UHF increased. Milwaukee's available channels were finally taken, and the FCC added channel 58 to the city's channel assignment. For the first time in years, a contest developed for a new TV channel. Next came digital tuners, and with the growth in cable and satellite distribution of television signals, most consumers treat the UHF portion of the spectrum the same way they do VHF.

Meanwhile, technology progressed such that the UHF band could finally be accessed by land-mobile users. Channels 70-72 are now used by pocket pagers and Nextel's SMR band. Channels 73-77 are used by cellular and mobile telephones. Channels 77-80 are used by public safety and channels 80-83 by cellular telephones and base stations.

On September 1, 1981, the Los Angeles County Sheriff's Department filed a request with the FCC which would have reallocated TV channels 14-20 for public safety and other land-mobile uses. Several law-enforcement and state agencies later joined in the request, including the Florida Division of Communications, which recommended that the Commission relieve potential congestion by "allowing land-mobile radio operations on unlicensed television channels 14 through 20 nationwide, on a noninterference basis with existing television stations."[95] The National Association of Broadcasters, the Association of Maximum Service Telecasters, and the National Association of Public Television Stations opposed the request.

Normally, when the FCC granted a broadcaster a construction permit, they were given the channel for free. After the Commission took UHF channels away from TV, they were auctioned off, resulting in billions of dollars in revenue for the federal government. In the mid-1980s, the FCC threatened to do the same with more of the UHF spectrum, which was still unused. Television broadcasters were loath to give up more of their spectrum, and they responded by digging up an argument from the past – the need for more bandwidth for high-definition television.

As a result, studies were conducted during the 1980s and 1990s. Finally, a set of standards was developed which called for digital, rather than analog television broadcasting. Digital broadcasting had a number of advantages, one of which was that stations in the same market could now be on adjacent channels. Analog signals required that such stations be separated by either two (VHF) or six (UHF) channels. As a consequence, spectrum could be taken away from television and reallocated for other uses.

After Congress passed the Telecommunications Act of 1996, the FCC promulgated a licensing regime for digital TV (DTV). The act provided that the FCC should restrict the issuance of DTV licenses to existing broadcasters – either licensees or those holding construction permits (effectively freezing new DTV applications). The digital signals were compressed into the old 6 MHz channel bandwidths. In an unprecedented move, television stations were given a second channel on which to broadcast digital signals during the analog-digital transition period. Once DTV was fully established, those existing analog broadcasters would have to surrender one of their licenses. The Balanced Budget Act of 1997 ordered that at the end of the transition period, four of the channels between 60 and 69 were to be allocated to public safety, while the others were to be auctioned for commercial use.[96]

In much the same way that sets equipped to receive UHF signals weren't popular outside of major UHF markets, sets equipped to receive a digital over-the-air signal did not sell well. The date on which the transition was to occur was to have been December 31, 2006, but the law establishing it had a loophole which allowed analog transmission to continue if not enough consumers in a given market (85%) were able to receive a digital signal from some source: over-the-air, cable or satellite. Pressure mounted. The September 11th Commission in its final report recommended that: "Congress should support pending legislation which provides for the expedited and increased assignment of radio spectrum for public safety purposes."[97]

Additional spectrum for that use would have to come from the unused UHF channels. The Deficit Reduction Act of 2005 required all analog television broadcasting to switch to digital by February 17, 2009, and expanded the number of channels to be "recovered." On December 20, 2005, the U.S. Senate passed a version of the bill, after Vice President Dick Cheney flew back from a Middle East trip to break a 50-50 tie. On February 1, 2006, the House of Representatives passed the bill[98], and it was signed into law by President George W. Bush on February 8, 2006. As a result, channels 52-69 will be given to emergency services, or auctioned after the transition to digital TV is completed.

All receivers with a screen size of thirteen inches or more, as well as VCRs, DVD-Rs, etc. were required to have DTV tuners by July 1, 2007.

Ironically, UHF is more desirable for broadcasting a digital signal, and most Milwaukee television stations will shift to that portion of the spectrum. Most viewers receive their signal via cable or satellite, but those who still want over-the-air television will have to purchase receivers with digital tuners, or converters.

NOTES

1 Rufus Crater, "More TV Channels: FCC Acts to Widen Availabilies," *Broadcasting Telecasting*, May 10, 1948, 21.
2 "500-900 MC: Idea for TV Premature Says Du Mont," *Broadcasting Telecasting*, April 5, 1948, 43.
3 Ibid.
4 "More TV Channels: FCC Acts to Widen Availabilies."
5 William Boddy, *Fifties Television: The Industry and Its Critics*. (Champaign-Urbana: University of Illinois Press, 1990), 50.
6 Channels 1-3 have very little ground wave.
7 "Telestatus Report," *Broadcasting Telecasting*, June 7, 1948, 14.
8 "Milwaukee TV Sets," *Broadcasting Telecasting*, April 19, 1948, 46.

9 "TV Channels: Allocation Hearing Postponed," *Broadcasting Telecasting*, June 14, 1948, 30.
10 "Telestatus: Du Mont's Allocation Plan," *Broadcasting Telecasting*, July 5, 1948, 14.
11 Ibid.
12 Rufus Crater, "TV Upheaval? Willoughby Talk Creates Stir," *Broadcasting Telecasting*, July 5, 1948, 21, 50.
13 "TV Crisis: Channels 2-6 at Issue; Border Allocations Listed," *Broadcasting Telecasting*, July 12, 1948, 21, 67.
14 "Actions of the FCC," *Broadcasting Telecasting*, August 2, 1948, 84.
15 Rufus Crater, "Television Freeze: FCC Action Halted Pending Definite Policy," *Broadcasting Telecasting*, October 4, 1948, p 22A, 57.
16 Rufus Crater, "TV Faces Crisis: Channel Realignment Possible," *Broadcasting Telecasting*, September 13, 1948, 21, 74.
17 Rufus Crater, "TV Processing: Shutdown Looms Til Standards Are Set," *Broadcasting Telecasting*, September 20, 1948, 21 & 74.
18 "FCC Affirms FM Low Band Ruling: Commission Denies the Request of Maj. Armstrong, FMA," *Broadcasting Telecasting*, September 20, 1948, 28.
19 Rufus Crater, and Larry Christopher, "TV Expansion: Move Appears Imminent After FCC Hearing," *Broadcasting Telecasting*, September 27, 1948, 21, 70-72, 89.
20 "Television Freeze."
21 "Order Freeze in TV Stations: FCC Holds Up Approval of Applications; Seeks to 'Polish' Service," *Milwaukee Journal*, September 30, 1948.
22 "Television Freeze."
23 Federal Communications Commission, *Notice of Further Proposed Rule Making*. FCC 49-948, July 11, 1949.
24 "RMA Group Plan: FCC Declines Participation," *Broadcasting Telecasting*, January 9, 1950, 13.
25 "FCC Actions," *Proceedings of the I.R.E.*, Vol. 38, No. 3, March, 1950, 317.
26 "Color Tests: Fourth System Seeks Hearing," *Broadcasting Telecasting*, January 9, 1950, 10.
27 "Color Hearings: Three-Day Week Set for Resumption," *Broadcasting Telecasting*, February 27, 1950, 53.
28 Ibid.
29 "UHF Video: NBC Opens Test Station," *Broadcasting Telecasting*, January 9, 1950, 12.
30 "VHF Move to UHF?" *Broadcasting Telecasting*, April 17, 1950, 2, 56-57, 69.
31 "FCC Favors CBS Color: Splits on Time; Delays Finale," *Broadcasting Telecasting*, September 4, 1950, 4, 85.
32 "Set Makers Puzzle: Time Need Felt," *Broadcasting Telecasting*, September 11, 1950, 61 & 75.
33 "Set Makers' Dilemma: Sept. 29 Answer said Impossible," *Broadcasting Telecasting*, September 25, 1950, 69, 72.
34 "Bracket Deadline Stumps TV Set Makers," *Broadcasting Telecasting*, October 2, 1950, 4, 94. For the full text of the manufacturers' responses, see: "Set Manufacturers' Replies to FCC Proposal for Production of 'Bracket Sets'," *Broadcasting Telecasting*, October 9, 1950, 57-59.
35 "CBS Wins Color Battle: Standards Effective Nov. 20," *Broadcasting Telecasting*, October 16, 1950, 177, 192-193.
36 "Violent Reactions to FCC Order: For CBS Color," *Broadcasting Telecasting*, October 16, 1950, 23, 30.
37 "Court Color Test: RCA, Pilot Seek Restraining Orders," *Broadcasting Telecasting*, October 23, 1950, 53, 64.
38 "TV Allocations: General hearings Opening," *Broadcasting Telecasting*, October 23, 1950, 56, 61.
39 "Color TV Has Gone to War – Industry Gets 'Greetings'," *Broadcasting Telecasting*, October 22, 1950, 5-6.
40 "Roadblocks to Freeze Lifting: Shortages Loom," *Broadcasting Telecasting*, December 4, 1950, 53 & 94.
41 "Bridgeport UHF: RCA-NBC Report Stirs FCC Hearing," *Broadcasting Telecasting*, October 30, 1950, 57-61, 65.

42 Richard W. Davis, "UHF Success: RCA and NBC's Connecticut Test Indicates Greater Vistas," *Broadcasting Telecasting*, February 6, 1950, 40, 47.
43 "Round One: RCA: Chicago Stay Stops CBS Commercial Color," *Broadcasting Telecasting*, November 20, 1950, 55, 82-83.
44 "Reaction to Order: Most Set Makers Laud," *Broadcasting Telecasting*, November 20, 1950, 56.
45 "Court Upholds FCC: Approves Color Order, Bans Commercialism," *Broadcasting Telecasting*, December 25, 1950, 61 & 66.
46 "Council Asks for More TV: Request to FCC," *Milwaukee Journal*, January 17, 1951.
47 "WTMJ-TV Tells Color TV 'Ifs': Sets Should Be Able to Get Black and White Too, Is View," *Milwaukee Journal*, November 30, 1950.
48 Ibid.
49 Larry Christopher, "FCC Plans 2,000 TV Outlets: 10% to Educators," *Broadcasting Telecasting*, March 26, 1951, 19, 27-30.
50 "Revised Proposed TV Channel Allocations," *Broadcasting Telecasting*, March 26, 1951, 58c.
51 "Give Up TV City is Urged," *Milwaukee Journal*, May 8, 1951.
52 "Color TV Progress: Court Ruling Nearer," *Broadcasting Telecasting*, February 12, 1951, 55, 62.
53 "CBS Color Stands: But Other Systems Have Chance If Good," *Broadcasting Telecasting*, June 4, 1951, 23, 62, 70-72.
54 "CBS Color TV 'Premiere': 16 Sponsors Signed at Start," *Broadcasting Telecasting*, June 25, 1951, 25.
55 After 32 months of deliberations, the NTSC passed new color standards based on the RCA dot-sequential system in January of 1953. The FCC later authorized their use as of December 23 of that year. The CBS field-sequential system was later used for the Apollo color broadcasts from the moon.
56 Federal Communications Commission, *Sixth General Report and Order*, Section 572(l). Washington, D.C., April 14, 1952.
57 "TV Applicants Ask for Revisions," *Broadcasting Telecasting*, March 3, 1952, 6.
58 "WEMP Seeks a TV License: Channel 6 Requested," *Milwaukee Journal*, March 6, 1952.
59 "WEMP Amendment Opposed," *Broadcasting Telecasting*, March 10, 1952, 94.
60 "State Granted 51 Channels for Television: Delay in Starting of New Stations Seen; WTMJ-TV Will Move to Channel 4," *Milwaukee Journal*, April 14, 1952.
61 *Sixth General Report and Order*, Section 572(i).
62 *Sixth General Report and Order*, Section 575.
63 *Sixth General Report and Order*, Section 574.
64 Ralph Evans, III, email to author, April 29, 2008.
65 Ibid.
66 "Freeze on new VHF's Asked by UHF Stations," *Broadcasting Telecasting*, May 24, 1954. 117-118, 120, 122, 124-125, 127.
67 "UHFTA Lists Suggestions to UHF Aid," *Broadcasting Telecasting*, May 24, 1954, 130.
68 "City is a TV Testing Area: Hearings Show This," *Milwaukee Journal*, May 23, 1954.
69 "'We Need Subscription TV,' Four UHF Grantees Tell FCC," *Broadcasting Telecasting*, August 10, 1953, 31-32.
70 "Committee Formed to Push Pay-See: UHF Grantees Call for Immediate FCC Action to Establish Subscription TV at Philadelphia Meeting," *Broadcasting Telecasting*, September 21, 1953, 46-48.
71 "Another TV Freeze?" *Broadcasting Telecasting*, March 14, 1955, 27-29.
72 "FCC Studies Plan to Split U.S. Into U and V Regions," *Broadcasting Telecasting*, May 7, 1956, 27.
73 "Proposed Shift to UHF Eyed With Skepticism: Local Television Men Point Out Problems of VHF Investments in Stations and Sets," *Milwaukee Journal*, July 27, 1956.
74 "UHFs Get Extension," *Broadcasting Telecasting*, February 13, 1956, 86.
75 "UHF CPs Extended," *Broadcasting Telecasting*, July 23, 1956, 50.
76 "UHF Permitees Get Ultimatum to Justify Extension Requests," *Broadcasting Telecasting*, November 26, 1956, 74.

77 "FCC Deintermixes Another Two: Fresno, Evansville May Lose Single VHF Channels; Commission Votes Down Deintermixture of Madison. *Broadcasting Telecasting*, February 11, 1957, 64-65.

78 "Sixty U's Tell Commission Why They Aren't on Air" *Broadcasting Telecasting*, February 18, 1957, 9.

79 "Build or Quit, 54 UHF Permitees Are Told," *Broadcasting*, February 22, 1960, 9-10.

80 "Military Seeks VHF Channels 2-6," *Broadcasting-Telecasting*, April 1, 1957, 31-33.

81 Ibid.

82 "Dormant UHF's Eliminated: FCC Cancels 16 Construction Permits," *Broadcasting*, May 2, 1960, 68.

83 "FCC Deletes 26 UHF Construction permits: Failure to Construct Cited; Dead UHF's Total 234," *Broadcasting*, November 28, 1960, 62.

84 "Channel 3 in Madison to Stay a VHF Station: FCC Agrees to Drop Proposal for Switch to UHF; All-Channel Sets Sought," *Milwaukee Journal*, March 18, 1962.

85 "UHF Urged for All Sets: Minow Seeks Law," *Milwaukee Journal*, October 24, 1961.

86 The call letters would later be used by Channel 18 in Milwaukee from 1963-66.

87 Donald W. Peterson., "Comparative Study of Low VHF, High VHF, and UHF Television Broadcasting in New York Area," *Broadcast News*, February, 1963, 6-20.

88 Ralph Evans, III, email to author, April 29, 2008.

89 Federal Communications Commission, 28th Annual Report, 1962, 59.

90 "All-Channel Sets Minow's Goal," *Broadcasting*, January 15, 1962, 27-30.

91 "All-Channel Law in Effect," *Milwaukee Journal*, May 1, 1964.

92 "FCC Reveals a UHF-Sharing Plan," *Broadcasting*, July 22, 1968, 25-26.

93 "Setback for Land-Mobile Users," *Broadcasting*, April 6, 1970, 82.

94 "Land Mobile Moves Into the UHF Band," *Broadcasting*, May 25, 1970, 62.

95 "Petitioners Want Lower UHF Channels for Land Mobile Use," *Broadcasting*, November 2, 1981, 76-77.

96 Paige Albiniak, "Budget Bill Brings Broadcasters Benefits," *Broadcasting & Cable*, August 4, 1997, 14.

97 *Final Report of the National Commission on Terrorist Attacks Upon the United States*. United States Government, Superintendent of Documents, 2004, 397.

98 "House Barely Passes Cuts in Entitlement," *Milwaukee Journal Sentinel*, February 2, 2006.

CHAPTER 4
WCAN-TV
CHANNEL 25

The Midwest Broadcasting Co. began as the idea of George E. Inghram. While working in sales at WEMP (then 1340 AM) in 1944, Inghram approached Herbert E. Uihlein, a director of the Schlitz Brewing Co., with the idea of starting another radio station in Milwaukee. Uihlein's wife Myrtle thought the idea a good one, as it would give her husband something to do.[1]

Inghram later claimed that Uihlein had promised to supply the capital for the new station, and in exchange he would supply his services to run it. They would each share half of the profits.[2]

On October 27, 1944 The Midwest Broadcasting Co., filed an application for a standard broadcasting (as AM was then known) license on 1250 kHz. The call letters reserved were "WMAW." Although the War Production Board had not frozen new radio station construction, applications were handled on a case-by-case basis. War production had priority for electronic components, and few new station construction permits were granted. In January of 1945, the FCC and the War Production Board froze new radio construction.

With the end of WWII, the FCC announced that they would begin processing the hundreds of new radio and television applications in its pending files as of October 7, 1945.[3] FM broadcasting in Milwaukee had begun in 1940 by the Journal Co., and broadcasters began to embrace the new technology. Midwest Broadcasting filed an application for a metropolitan FM station on February 5, 1946. The frequency and call letters were to be assigned by the FCC, but the calls "WPAW" were reserved for the station. The owners of Midwest were:

- Clifford A. Randall (16%), president
- George E. Inghram (21%), vice-president
- Oliver J. Vivian (21%), treasurer
- Herbert E. Uihlein (21%)
- John A. Fleissner (21%)

Inghram had become the owner of a *Radio Times* sales agency. Fleissner was the Postmaster of Milwaukee and a part owner of the Taylor Electric Co. Randall was a local attorney.

A hearing was held before the FCC on February 22, 1946. Uihlein made a poor impression as a witness, and had become upset while giving testimony. Since there were doubts that the group would get a construction permit if he remained, it was decided based on the advice of their Washington attorney, to drop him from the ownership group.

Nonetheless, on February 28, Midwest was granted a construction permit for a metropolitan FM station on 102.1 MHz. On March 14, the FCC granted Midwest's request to show R. C. Borchert as a stockholder in place of Uihlein. Vivian later testified that Randall's stock was really owned by Uihlein.[4]

Uihlein and his wife had formed an investment firm, the Hemdu Co. In February of 1947, it loaned Randall, Inghram, Fleissner, and Borchert $30,000 each. The loans were never reported to the FCC. Uihlein's health had declined and he was represented by Randall, who arranged the loans.[5] The attorney later arranged for an additional $75,000 loan from Hemdu.[6] Herbert Uihlein passed away later that year, but Randall went into the county court and enforced the loan agreement.[7]

On May 1, 1947, the FCC granted Midwest Broadcasting a construction permit for an AM station on 1250 kHz. That same month, Mrs. Uihlein asked for Midwest's books, and had them kept by accountant Marvin Dagen. Dagen later testified that Mrs. Uihlein was "vitally interested in WMAW" until her death later that year.[8]

With the large number of applications for radio and television stations, the FCC decided to assign those stations that either owned or held a construction permit for an AM station, call letters with the suffixes –FM or –TV for FM and television stations. As such, Midwest broadcasting was assigned the call letters WMAW and WMAW-FM in July of 1947.

Herbert Uihlein died on September 16, 1947. His wife Myrtle passed away on December 25 of the same year.

Midwest constructed a transmitter and AM antenna array on West Grange Avenue in Hales Corners. It also purchased a self-supporting tower for its FM antenna, which it planned to erect at the same location, and foundations were poured for it. The studios were located in leased space in the Towne Hotel on North 3rd Street.

WMAW began broadcasting at 11:30 a.m. on March 24, 1948,[9] and it applied for a license to cover on April 5. That same month, it joined the ABC radio network, as a partial affiliate. It became a full affiliate in September.[10]

WMAW-FM later began broadcasting, using a temporary antenna stuck through a second-story window of the transmitter building. It rebroadcast programming from WMAW, but was only on the air for around 40 hours before the decision was made not to proceed further with FM broadcasting. The self-supporting tower purchased for it lay on the ground in weeds at the transmitter facility.[11]

In July of 1948, an application was filed with the FCC for the involuntary transfer of control of WMAW and WMAW-FM from the late Myrtle Uihlein to the co-executors of her estate, Midwest president Clifford Randall and Wilke M. Zimmers.

CHAPTER 4 ~ WCAN-TV: CHANNEL 25

Those were not Midwest's only problems. George Inghram, who served as WMAW's vice-president and general manager, had been dismissed for incompetence, and making "adverse claims" against the company.[12] Inghram sued the Uihlein estate for $500,000.[13] No written agreement was produced at the time the lawsuit was filed, but Randall disclosed "that Uihlein had advanced an undisclosed amount of money to the Midwest Broadcasting Co."[14]

Without a license, the station had operated under temporary authorization, which was renewed monthly. From April 24-27, 1949, a hearing was held before an FCC examiner. The point of contention was whether or not Clifford Randall and the Uihleins had engaged in a conspiracy to deceive the FCC as to who the real owners were. Randall had served as an executor of the Uihleins estate. During the hearing, Oliver Vivian admitted that he had lied during the license hearing before the FCC in February of 1946.[15] Despite that, the examiner found that: "The officers and stockholders have not complied with all of the Commission's rules and regulations, but the noncompliance cannot be attributed to an intent to deceive the Commission or conceal material facts."[16] The station was given a temporary license on April 5, 1950.

However, later that year, a Commission attorney sought to overturn the examiner's recommendation. Besides concealing Uihlein's role, he claimed that Randall had arranged the loans while Uihlein was incompetent, and that while he was no longer a co-executor of the estate, serving as such had been a conflict of interest while he was the president of Midwest.[17]

On December 21, 1950, a hearing was held before the FCC. In a 3-1 decision, the Commission overturned its examiner's recommendation, and found Midwest unqualified to hold a broadcasting license. It sharply criticized Randall, finding that he had engaged in deliberate deception, and gave Midwest 90 days to wind up business and stop broadcasting.[18] Particularly damaging was Randall's testimony:

> **Q.** *But if you informed the commission that Mr. Uihlein was financing the station, you thought that they probably would not approve it, is that correct?*
> **A.** Yes.
> **Q.** *That is why you did it in this way, to keep the Commission from knowing what the facts were, is that not correct?*
> **A.** *That is right.*[19]

In addition, the Commission questioned the ownership status of two employees of WEMP, who had an interest in Vivian's stock.

Randall did not give up without a fight. He argued that since there were seven members of the Commission and only three had voted against issuing WMAW a license, a majority had not ruled. (Three members had not participated in the hearing.)[20] The FCC attorney that had sought to overturn the examiner's original ruling argued that nonetheless, a quorum had been present, and the Commission had ruled properly.[21]

On March 30, the full Commission heard Midwest's arguments.[22] On June 12, 1951, it reversed itself, and voted 5-0 to issue a license to WMAW. Two of the commissioners who voted to deny the license after the previous hearing did not vote, but the majority was moved by the fact that Uihlein had not acquired any Midwest stock, but had only supplied funds. They stated that their rule "...did not in its express terms during the period in question, provide for filing by permitees as distinguished from licensees."[23] The Commission found nothing improper with interest held by two employees of WEMP, agreeing with Randall that the fact wasn't disclosed in order to protect them, should their employer find out.

Despite finally receiving a license, WMAW was still in trouble. The station was losing money. By November 1, 1951, it reported a net loss of $269,134.83, and the owners were looking to sell.

On July 13, 1946, Lou Poller applied for an AM station in Chester, Pennsylvania. On September 16, he was granted a construction permit with the call letters WPWA. Poller had started as a sportscaster at a radio station in Scranton, Pennsylvania, and had built station WARM in that city in 1942. He enlisted in the Marine Corps that year, and served until the end of WWII.[24] (At WPWA he hired a struggling singer named Bill Haley as a D.J. and program director!) In partnership with his brother-in-law, Cy Blumenthal, he owned and operated WARL (and later

WCAN-TV
will be
Milwaukee's *NEW* Television Station

The F.C.C. (Federal Communications Commission) has granted permission to Midwest Broadcasting Company . . . present operators of radio station WCAN . . . to build and operate a new television station in Milwaukee . . . WCAN-TV, Channel 25, UHF.

You have been enjoying the wonders of television for 5 years. Now, even greater entertainment will be coming into your home!

The management of this new station will call upon the vast knowledge and experience gained through years of TV and Radio direction. Now they will channel this vast experience into a plan and operation that will give you the kind of programs that will make WCAN-TV the station of your choice!

Construction will commence immediately in order to give you greater entertainment at the earliest possible moment.

WARL-FM) in Arlington, Virginia. They were joined by Alex Rosenman, formerly executive vice president of WCAU in Philadelphia, and later with Official Films, Inc. The trio made an offer to buy WMAW for $235,000, which was accepted in December of 1951.[25] Rosenman received 50% of Midwest's stock, while the partnership of Poller and Blumenthal received the other half.

The Commission approved the sale in June of 1952, and the group took over the operations and changed the call letters to WCAN on the fifth of that month.[26] Poller and Blumenthal later bought out Rosenman, with Poller becoming the majority owner.

The FCC lifted the freeze on new television licenses the following month. On October 14, Midwest Broadcasting filed an application for VHF channel 12.[27] On November 17, they amended their application to specify UHF channel 25 instead. Poller's rationale was that because there was only one VHF channel available for commercial use – and license hearings before the FCC could take years – amending his application to specify one of the three available UHF channels, might allow Midwest to get on the air quickly, obtain a network affiliation, and build a strong audience before channel 12 went on the air.[28] The Wisconsin Broadcasting System (owner of WFOX radio) amended its application from channel 12 to channel 25 the following day.[29]

In late November, the Northwest Television Corp., which was owned by H & E Balaban Corp., (whose principals, Harry and Elmer Balaban and Otto Zeman were Chicago theater owners) applied for channel 25.[30] They owned 50 percent of WTVO (at the time Ch. 39) in Rockford, IL. In mid-December, they amended their application from channel 25 to channel 19.

The FCC had a policy of dealing with uncontested applications first. Milwaukee's applications came up for discussion on January 9, 1953, but since all of the available channels had more than one applicant, the Commission passed them over.[31]

Thereafter, Bartell Broadcasters, Inc., which owned WOKY radio in Milwaukee, received a construction permit for channel 33 in Madison. The Wisconsin Broadcasting System, Inc. thought that would disqualify Bartell from receiving one for channel 19 in Milwaukee, under the mistaken assumption that Madison was a part of the same market.[32] As such, they amended their application from channel 25 to channel 19 on January 31, 1953. That left Midwest's application for channel 25 unopposed, and the FCC issued them a construction permit on February 5.[33]

Planning began immediately. Midwest's original application as well as the construction permit specified that the transmitter and tower would be located at the Grange Avenue facility[34], and their engineering consultant, Adler Communications Labs, advised them that there was no terrain which would cause shadows for a UHF signal, and as a consequence "ghosting." The FCC granted the station special temporary authority to operate commercially between July 9-19, 1953[35], but the station never went on the air.

Adler recommended that Midwest locate the tower atop the highest point in the city. In order to get on the air quickly, they elected to use the self-supporting tower originally planned for WMAW-FM, which sat rusting on the ground at their transmitter site. The tallest building in the city was then the Schroeder Hotel (later the Sheraton-Schroeder, Marc Plaza, and now the Hilton), which had been the site of The Journal Co.'s experimental laboratories in the 1930s. On July 15, the station announced that it would erect the tower there, with the transmitter located in the north penthouse.[36] The FCC approved the change on July 27. Midwest paid $43,000 to have the hotel roof reinforced, and another $21,000 to erect the tower there.[37]

Midwest Broadcasting erected the self-supporting tower it had purchased for WMAW-FM atop the Schroeder hotel in downtown Milwaukee. The tower is still there.

The radio studios were moved to the transmitter facility, and television studios were constructed in the Towne Hotel.[38]

Irv Miller was a DJ on WCAN radio, who also did voice work for WCAN-TV:

> This was in the days before the expressway system was built. I would get off the air at 9:00 p.m. and had thirty minutes to drive from the radio studios in Hales Corners to the Towne Hotel. Believe me, it wasn't easy. I was stopped more than once by the police. After a while they knew who I was and they just waved me through. I don't think that I was ever late, but there were times when I would burst through the door with a minute or two to spare for my shift at the TV station![39]

Midwest signed an affiliation contract with CBS, which would give it network programming. WTMJ-TV still had a contract to carry selected CBS programs, but WCAN-TV would become the primary affiliate.

In the meantime, Poller acquired an additional 28⅓% of Midwest Broadcasting from Rosenman, who maintained a minority interest (5%) in the company, and became the station's advertising representative in NYC. That gave Poller 61⅔%, and he became general manager of WCAN and WCAN-TV.[40] The FCC approved the transfer on August 5.

A big challenge was to get the owners of the estimated 450,000 television sets in the greater Milwaukee area to purchase UHF converters or all-channel sets. To do so, Midwest started an aggressive promotional campaign. It hired an airplane to tow a banner around the city, bought billboard, newspaper and magazine ads, and held a giant rally shortly after receiving its construction permit. It entertained television set distributors, dealers and servicemen, and converted the sets owned by advertising agency executives and potential advertisers. Executives regularly appeared on WCAN radio, and before civic organizations, businessmen's clubs, and trade associations.[41] As a result, the station estimated that by the time it went on the air, some 70,000 sets had been converted to receive UHF.[42] The conversion rate was undoubtedly helped by the fact that WOKY-TV was scheduled to go on the air using channel 19 at around the same time, while WMIL-TV hoped to begin broadcasting at the end of the year on channel 31.

(This posed some problems, as UHF is more directional than VHF, making it even more important that antennas be pointed at the transmitting tower. This could have necessitated the purchase of antenna rotors by many Milwaukee TV set owners. One manufacturer of such rotors had been looking for a place to market them. Milwaukee proved to be ideal, as two UHF stations went on the air at almost the same time, while plans were still being developed for additional VHF stations. Some suggested local ordinances requiring that all TV transmitting towers be located within a one mile radius of each other.)[43]

CHAPTER 4 ~ WCAN-TV: CHANNEL 25   147

Erection of the tower began on August 16, 1953 and the station hoped to get on the air with a test pattern on Friday, September 4. It missed that target. It wasn't until Sunday, September 6, that the antenna was hoisted atop the tower. It was secured by 1:00 p.m., and the last task was the connection of the coaxial cable between the antenna and the transmitter. Thirty-five mile-per-hour winds, and darkness almost forced postponement of the task, but the workers persevered.[44] The first broadcasts were made at 11:25 p.m., and consisted of a 10 minute test pattern, followed by a station I.D. slide, over which an audio tape of "The Star Spangled Banner" was played. Hal Walker interviewed the workers who had installed the antenna atop the tower, and a series of films were shown. The station signed off the air at 1:30 a.m. Despite having no advance publicity, the station claimed to have received 1,800 calls from viewers who saw the initial broadcast.[45]

On Monday, September 7, 1953, WCAN-TV officially began broadcasting. The following day, the station became the city's primary CBS affiliate. Local news, sports, and cooking shows were featured.[46] Dr. Adolph Suppan, of the Wisconsin State Teachers' College (now UWM), served as the station's educational consultant, and did the initial newscasts. Housewife Mary Jane Jung, a former model and charm school teacher, served as the station's weather girl on a show called "The Weather Vane with Mary Jane." The two announcers were Ted Clark, who did "Fetchin' Food" twice weekly, and Lan Singer from WCAN radio. The two cooking experts were Pat Thompson and Trudy Beilfuss.[47]

The WCAN-TV studio in the Towne Hotel.

The following Saturday, Red Barber, who was in town to broadcast the game between the Milwaukee Braves and the Brooklyn Dodgers, originated his *Peak of Sports* program on CBS from WCAN-TV.[48]

Lou Poller claimed that it had cost Midwest $700,000 to put the station on the air.[49] It did so with a crew of 44, and had two live cameras, two film chains and two slide projectors. It used one large studio on the second floor of the Towne Hotel. Budde Marino was a producer/director for the station, and he remembered:

> We were on the second floor of the Towne Hotel. We had one studio, one large arena office, a manager's office, and a control room – just the bare essentials.
>
> In those days, anything you would've done locally would've been done live. Blatz beer sponsored our 6 o'clock and 10 o'clock newscasts. It required the pouring of a pilsner glass of beer just as you got the cue to go on-the-air. You prayed a lot that the head would be the proper consistency! You opened on a tight shot of the pilsner glass on a tray and a hand pouring the beer and setting down the bottle next to it, and then cut away quickly![50]

Since it now had a primary affiliate, CBS ended its affiliation with WTMJ-TV on September 26, 1953. WCAN-TV was an "optional basic" affiliate, meaning that it had to sell individual CBS advertisers on the advantages of buying time on CBS shows in Milwaukee.[51] As such, it occasionally found itself with holes in its schedule when it could not sell network shows. To fill the time, it relied heavily on film programming. The prevailing rates were based upon WTMJ-TV's $950/hour basic rate, but as a UHF station with less coverage, WCAN-TV couldn't command that much. After negotiating with film program distributors, it purchased many packages based upon a basic hourly rate of only $200/hour, although its first rate card called for $300/hour for Class A time.[52]

After less than two months on the air, Midwest Broadcasting estimated that 150,000 sets in the Milwaukee area had been converted to receive UHF. It started broadcasting seventeen hours a day, Monday through Friday, from 7:00 a.m. until midnight. Saturday broadcasting ran from 10:00 a.m. until 1:00 a.m., and Sundays, the station was on the air from 11:30 a.m. until midnight.

Despite the early success, all was not well. Midwest's decision to amend its application to specify UHF channel 25 instead of channel 12, was based upon the assumption that the latter would be the only commercial VHF channel available. In October of 1953, The Hearst Corp. successfully petitioned the FCC to assign VHF channel 6 to the Village of Whitefish Bay. (See chapter 7.) Hearst had reapplied for channel 10 after the freeze was lifted – despite the fact that the FCC had reserved the channel for educational use. (See chapters 7 and 8.) Dropping another VHF channel into the market would upset the balance that had made Midwest's decision to pursue a UHF channel viable.

That same month, the Ultra High Frequency Television Association was incorporated[53], and Lou Poller was elected its first president. Both the UHFTA[54] and Poller would tenaciously struggle to prevent the addition of channel 6.[55] The UHFTA argued that the assignment of another VHF channel to a city defeated the Commission's original purpose in intermixing UHF and VHF channels in the same markets, and had the potential to destroy the investment made by UHF station owners – without the benefit of a public hearing.[56] Poller claimed that the assignment of the channel to Whitefish Bay was a ruse, which was being used to get around the FCC's 170-mile separation rule, and that Hearst intended to locate the station in Milwaukee. He also claimed to have lost money because advertisers either cancelled or had not renewed contracts because Hearst (WISN) salesmen had told them that they would receive the assignment and would begin broadcasting on VHF within 60 days. On January 7, 1954, WCAN-TV asked the U.S. Court of Appeals in Washington to order the FCC to revoke its assignment of channel 6 to Whitefish Bay.[57] It also asked the court to issue a temporary injunction preventing the FCC from assigning channel 6 to the area.[58]

On January 20, 1954, the District of Columbia circuit court of appeals denied WCAN-TV's motion for a temporary injunction restraining the FCC from allocating channel 6 to Whitefish Bay.[59] The FCC proceeded with plans to hold hearings on the applications from Hearst, Cream City Broadcasting, Inc., and Independent Television, Inc. Such hearings were contingent on the court of appeals' final ruling on the matter. At the same time, WCAN-TV asked the FCC to dismiss Hearst's application for channel 6, claiming that it did not intend to locate the station in Whitefish Bay, but rather would locate its studios in Milwaukee, and its transmitter and tower on land it recently acquired in the town of Granville. Lou Poller also claimed that if Hearst was granted channel 6, his station would lose its CBS affiliation, as WISN had a clause in its contract which gave it the right of first refusal should it operate a television station in the area. He also opined that antitrust laws might be violated as Hearst owned WISN and the *Milwaukee Sentinel*. In addition, he complained that the assignment of another VHF station to the area would cost his station advertising revenue.[60]

In February of 1954, a 12 kW transmitter was put into operation[62], which gave the station an effective radiated power (ERP) of 212 kW, and pushed its signal out to a claimed 60-mile radius. The station also ordered a set of remote camera chains, a new antenna, waveguide, color equipment and a 60 kW transmitter. It also completed a second studio.[63] Those investments represented a commitment of an additional $600,000.

That same month, the station found itself in a bit of a controversy, as a contest it started resulted in so many calls

On Monday, January 11, 1954, WCAN-TV began a cartoon show called "Kids Karnival." It was hosted by announcer Lan Singer, who played "Uncle Natco." In December of 1954, the station held a contest in which young viewers suggested new names for the host. The winning name was "Commander Kimban." The last show aired on Friday, February 25, 1955.

When WCAN-TV began offering its "Movie Quick Quiz" in early 1954, the ready reference department at the Milwaukee Public Library was swamped with callers looking for the answers. As a consequence, the library asked the station to provide it with the questions and answers ahead of time![61])

to the station that telephone lines were tied up. The police chief sought an injunction, as emergency calls couldn't get through.[64] The station responded by making it harder for viewers to win.[65]

Irv Miller:

It was sponsored by the Rexall drug stores. It was bingo, and they would play it every Saturday night. It was mostly a call-in, and the stations were very well known for the game. It became very popular.[66]

On March 9, 1954, Edward R. Murrow denounced Senator Joseph McCarthy on *See It Now*. WCAN-TV was the only Wisconsin CBS affiliate to carry the show.

In its March 15 issue, *Broadcasting Telecasting* reported that WCAN-TV was grossing $100,000 a month and that its revenue was still increasing after six months on the air.[67]

The last week of April, 1954, the FCC agreed to allow WCAN-TV to participate in hearings on channel 6.[68]

A 12 kW General Electric UHF transmitter became operational in February of 1954. It was later used by the CBS-owned and the independent WXIX, as well as WUHF and WVTV. (Courtesy of Dennis Brechlin)

The following month, the U.S. Senate held hearings regarding UHF broadcasting. WCAN-TV president Lou Poller testified, and argued that all television broadcasting be shifted to UHF. In addition, the FCC and the Senate subcommittee endorsed plans to require that new color TV sets be capable of receiving both UHF as well as VHF.[69] The Ultra High Frequency Television Association proposed a multi-point plan that would allow them to compete with their VHF counterparts.

That same month, Midwest Broadcasting offered five hours per week of free on-air time to the Wisconsin Association for Vocational Education.[70]

In early May of 1954, the four applicants for channel 12 made public the fact that they had been holding merger discussions in order to avoid prolonged license hearings. In response, on May 19, 1954, Midwest Broadcasting filed a petition with the FCC to modify its construction permit to specify VHF channel 12. Poller proposed that WCAN-TV simulcast on both channels, "pending public choice of the best service."[71] That same day, the application was refused on the grounds that none may be accepted thirty days before hearings begin, and that the Commission's rules forbade stations from changing channels, except if the channel assignments for the city were changed.[72] As a consequence, that same day a FCC hearing examiner recommended granting a construction per-

mit for channel 12 to the Milwaukee Area Telecasting Corp. The merger agreement gave the other parties the option to purchase stock in the new corporation that was to be formed to operate the station. One of the applicants also received also received $30,000 as a reimbursement for expenses associated with its application.[73] (See chapter 6.)

On June 1, WCAN-TV resubmitted its application to switch from channel 25 to channel 12, but the FCC returned it.

On July 13, 1954, Midwest Broadcasting asked the FCC to reverse its grant to the Milwaukee Area Telecasting Co. Midwest charged that the cash payment to one of the applicants was a "payoff".[74] The Commission denied the petition. Midwest then filed an appeal with the U.S. Court of Appeals in Washington re: the FCC's return of its application to switch from channel 25 to 12.[75] It also filed a petition for a temporary injunction to prevent construction of a station on channel 12 until the court could hear the station's suit to force the FCC to reconsider its application to switch channels. Milwaukee Area Telecasting responded by charging that WCAN-TV was trying to stifle competition by preventing additional TV service from being started in the city.[76]

On July 22, Lou Poller announced that he was going to build a new $250,000 "Television Capitol" in the vicinity of North 60th Street and West Capitol Drive.[77] The new 15,000 square foot facility was to include color broadcasting equipment.[78]

Sponsor Omar Bakery had its products delivered to customers' doors by the "Omar Man." They sponsored the weather segment on WCAN-TV, and as a tie-in wanted a man to do it[79], so the station replaced Mary Jane Jung with Joe Kenny.

On August 10, 1954, WCAN-TV lost its petition before the U.S. Circuit Court of Appeals seeking a temporary injunction to prevent construction of a station on channel 12 until the court could hear the station's suit to force the FCC to reconsider its application to switch channels.[80]

In September of 1954, Lou Poller announced that instead of building the new studio facilities announced previously, he would instead convert a warehouse at 5445 N. 27 Street. The new building contained 3 studios, and color broadcasting equipment.

In mid-October, the FCC filed a brief with the U.S. Court of Appeals responding to WCAN-TV's appeal of its decision to assign channel 6 to Whitefish Bay. It denied all of WCAN-TV's allegations, saying that: the assignment met all of the separation requirements set fourth in its Sixth General Report and Order, that its previous rejection of assigning Ch. 6 to the area was based solely upon the separation requirements, that the Table of Channel Assignments had some flexibility, that there was no protection guaranteed to UHF stations, and that WCAN-TV's injury claims were private.[81]

Bartell Broadcasting sold WOKY-TV (channel 19) to CBS on October 22, 1954. This was shortly after the FCC changed its multiple-ownership rules to allow an individual entity to own two UHF stations in addition to five VHF.[82]

Disgusted with broadcasting, Lou Poller sold WPWA, and applied to the FCC for transfer of control on October 25.

On October 27, WTVW, owned and operated by the Milwaukee Area Telecasting Co., began broadcasting on channel 12. It became the ABC affiliate, and also carried Du Mont network shows.

WCAN-TV continued to use its studios in the Towne Hotel on North 3rd Street. During one show, 200 teenagers overcrowded the second floor studio, which had a

CHAPTER 4 ~ WCAN-TV: CHANNEL 25

capacity of ten.[83] The hotel filed suit to have the station declared a public nuisance, and asked for $10,000 in damages. It also asked for a temporary injunction, which it received. The injunction barred the station from: doing anything that would result in an increase in the hotel's insurance rates, rearranging the premises, using two rest rooms as dressing rooms, blocking the stairway between the first and second floors, and interfering with the entry or exit of hotel guests.[84]

In one year, Lou Poller had built WCAN-TV into what some thought was the most successful UHF station in the country, but by the end of 1954 he was about to lose his network affiliation. No other network was available, as WTMJ-TV was a long-time NBC affiliate, and ABC (along with Du Mont) had affiliated with WTVW. In addition, his efforts to prevent another VHF station from being assigned to the area had been unsuccessful. It was commonly held that without a network affiliation, a UHF station would not survive. CBS offered to purchase WCAN-TV's facilities, and Poller accepted on November 13.[85] WCAN-TV did occupy the new building in December.[86] Budde Marino:

That was Shangri-La compared to the Towne Hotel! It was ideal.[87]

Poller received $500,000 and the WOKY-TV facilities so that he could continue broadcasting as an independent. He then dropped his petition before the U.S. Court of Appeals regarding the FCC's assignment of channel 6 to the area.

Poller failed to file a brief re: his appeal on the channel 12 merger by the January 3, 1955 deadline, and it was subsequently dismissed.[88]

On January 14, 1955, the FCC approved the sale of WOKY-TV to CBS. Commissioner Frieda Hennock, who had led the fight to have channels reserved for noncommercial educational use (See chapter 8), dissented, citing both her opposition to the relaxation of the Commission's multiple-ownership rules, which had allowed the sale to take place, and her empathy for the fate of WCAN-TV.[89]

Midwest then sold WCAN radio to Milwaukee Broadcasting, who owned WEMP radio.[90] WEMP then shifted from 1340 to 1250 kHz, and sold its license and facilities to Texan Gordon McClendon's Foster and Holmes, Inc., who started WRIT on 1340 kHz.[91] The sales were approved by the FCC on March 2 – ironically, the same day the Commission approved the sale of WTVW to Hearst. (See chapter 6.)

Poller announced that he was moving from Milwaukee to Washington, D.C., and asked the FCC for permission to suspend television broadcasting for six months so that he could "appraise market and business conditions."[92] The last broadcast day for WCAN-TV was February 26, 1955. It then went dark. Some of the WOKY-TV facilities he had received in exchange for his own were donated to Marquette University on March 3, and others, including the transmitter, were acquired by the Milwaukee Vocational School, who used them to put WMVT-TV on the air in 1963. (See chapter 8.)

Broadcasting Telecasting reported in April of 1955 that Poller was being considered as a possible replacement for Commissioner Frieda Hennock, when her term on the FCC ran out later that year. He confirmed that he had been approached about the job, but denied that he was a candidate.[93] In October of that year, he and communications attorney William Roberts opened an office in Washington, D.C. in anticipation of a presidential run by Tennessee Senator Estes Kefauver, whom the pair supported.[94]

However, Poller still held the construction permit for channel 25 (which became channel 24, after the FCC shifted UHF channels in Milwaukee in 1958[95]), and was involved in litigation for many years.

National Telefilm Associates of New York sued Midwest Broadcasting, claiming that it had agreed to buy 500 hours of television films for $50,000. They claimed that the films were used, and that Midwest also owed them for other material.[96] Argyle Television Films and Hygo Television Films, Inc. also sued. Both cases were later settled and dismissed.[97]

The Towne Hotel filed suit against Midwest Broadcasting claiming that the station had moved before the expiration of its lease, and that it cost $8,000 to return the premises to a usable condition, after WCAN-TV personnel had pounded a hole in a wall in order to install air conditioning equipment. Midwest countersued, claiming that the hotel had forced it out.[98]

Midwest was later found to have negligently caused damage, and the hotel was awarded compensation, back rent, and attorney's fees. Midwest was awarded compensation for the loss of the use of equipment it had left behind.[99]

Poller, like many UHF broadcasters, saw pay-TV as a potential way to save his station. He formed a new corporation, TV Exhibitors of America, and on June 14, 1956 applied to the FCC for permission to transfer the license of WCAN-TV to it. As a part of that request, he also asked the FCC for permission to operate the station on a part-time, pay-TV basis.[100] On June 29, he filed an application to transfer ownership of WOPT (TV) in Chicago (Ch. 44) to the new company. Poller stated that he expected to operate both stations on a pay-TV basis twenty-five percent of the time.[101] Unfortunately, the FCC had not yet approved pay-TV (See Chapter 9.) and the Commission returned both applications on July 11, saying that they were unacceptable for filing.[102]

In September of that year, Poller filed suit against CBS, Bartell Broadcasters Inc., and Thad Holt, the consultant that CBS had hired to obtain the option on WOKY-TV. The suit alleged that CBS had conspired with Holt and the Bartells to drive him out of business. Poller claimed that CBS dissuaded the Storer Broadcasting Co., which eventually bought WITI-TV (See chapter 7.) from negotiating to buy WCAN-TV for $2 million. He also claimed that CBS assured him that he would continue to operate as the CBS affiliate, and as such he invested in his new facilities and equipment. Poller subtracted the $50,000 he estimated the WOKY-TV equipment he received from CBS was worth, as well as the $500,000 cash payment from that figure to come up with $1.45 million. Because the action was brought under anti-trust laws, treble damages were claimed, for a total of $4,350,000.[103] Poller later claimed that CBS intended to eliminate UHF broadcasting in Milwaukee – and possibly in the U.S.[104]

The trial judge awarded CBS a summary judgment against Poller, and that decision was upheld by the U.S. Court of Appeals. Poller then appealed to the U.S. Supreme Court, who overturned the summary judgment, and remanded the case back for trial.[105] The case set a precedent in the use of summary judgments in anti-trust cases. Poller and CBS later came to a settlement.

Poller continued to hold a construction permit for channel 24. In 1966 he sold it to the Field Communications Corp. (who had recently put WFLD-TV on the air in Chicago) for $35,000. Field acquired an option to purchase 40 acres of land on West Highland Boulevard, west of Highway 57 in Mequon, and planned on erecting studios as well as a 999' tower on the tract.[106] Although the tower location was approved by the Federal Aviation Administration (FAA), the operators of Timmerman Field in Milwaukee objected, and the Wisconsin State Astronautics Commission decided to hold a hearing on the matter.[107]

The FCC approved the station's sale on December 21, 1966. However, eight Mequon residents opposed the proposed tower location.[108] Despite those objections, the city's planning commission endorsed Field's plans on February 6, 1967, and its common council gave its initial approval on February 15.[109] The land was zoned for residential use, but the common council passed a resolution allowing its use as a tower site early the following month.[110] Field hoped to begin construction that spring, with a target on-air date of April 1, 1968.[111] It expected that seventy-five percent of the station's programming would originate in Chicago; the balance locally. It also expected to lose money during the first three years of operations.[112]

On May 11, 1967 the State Astronautics Commission approved the tower – over the objection of its director.[113] That should have ended the matter, but on May 23, two area residents – who lived within 600' of the proposed tower site – filed suit challenging the common council's ability to permit the commercial use of an area zoned residential.[114] The suit thwarted the station's plans to be on the air in April of 1968. Field finally decided to give up. In a letter to Mequon's mayor that was read to the common council on March 12, 1968, Field's chairman asked the city to suspend all litigation regarding the zoning of the site. He cited unnamed other problems that were also a cause of the delay.[115] The construction permit was later returned to the FCC, who deleted it.

Lou Poller was a true UHF pioneer. His decision to amend his application from VHF channel 12 to UHF channel 25 was a calculated risk, undertaken with the understanding that the Table of Channel Assignments for Milwaukee wouldn't be changed, and that a UHF station might have a chance if it could get on the air quickly with a network affiliation. Within a year of going on the air, he had built WCAN-TV into what was arguably the most successful UHF station in the country. Two unforeseen events – the FCC's assignment of VHF channel 6 to Whitefish Bay, as well as the surprise merger of the four applicants, which allowed channel 12 to go on the air earlier than expected – changed those initial assumptions. After battling tenaciously, WCAN-TV became one of the many UHF stations to go dark during the mid-1950s. Its facilities were used by four different stations, and although dead, it spawned a precedent-setting decision from the Supreme Court. Poller truly had an impact.

NOTES

1 "Probe Radio Stock Deals," *Milwaukee Sentinel*, October 25, 1949.
2 Ibid.
3 "New Radio Construction Begins October 7," *Broadcasting*, August 13, 1945, 18, 65.
4 "'Not a Front' Randall Says," *Milwaukee Journal*, October 27, 1949.
5 "FCC Looks at WMAW," Milwaukee *Sentinel*, September 17, 1950.
6 "Probe Radio Stock Deals."
7 "'Not a Front' Randall Says."
8 Ibid.
9 "Station Starts Wednesday," *Milwaukee Journal*, March 23, 1948.
10 "WMAW Special Show to Mark ABC Affiliation," *Broadcasting Telecasting*, August 23, 1948, 87.
11 Jack Krause, interview by author, April 6, 2006.
12 "Probe Radio Stock Deals."
13 "Ingram Sues Uihlein Estate," *Milwaukee Sentinel*, March 23, 1948.
14 "H.E. Uihlein's Estate is Sued: $500,000 Sought," *Milwaukee Journal*, March 23, 1948.
15 "'Not a Front' Randall Says."
16 "WMAW Gets License Okay," *Milwaukee Journal*, April 13, 1950.
17 "FCC Looks at WMAW."
18 WMAW Is Ordered to Get Off the Air," *Milwaukee Journal*, December 22, 1950.
19 Ibid.

20 "Court Fight on Edict is Predicted by Officers of Station; Minority of Board Criticized," *Milwaukee Journal*, December 22, 1950.
21 "FCC Counsel Hits WMAW," *Milwaukee Journal*, January 17, 1951.
22 "Hear WMAW License Pleas," *Milwaukee Journal*, March 31, 1951.
23 "WMAW is Given Permit as Board Reverses Itself," *Milwaukee Journal*, June 12, 1951.
24 "From Seminary to TV Boss – That's WCAN Chief," *Milwaukee Sentinel*, September 20, 1953.
25 "WMAW Sold to Easterners," *Milwaukee Journal*, December 28, 1951.
26 "Radio Station WMAW is Changed to WCAN," *Milwaukee Journal*, June 5, 1952.
27 "WCAN Asks '12,'" *Milwaukee Journal*, October 15, 1952.
28 "UHF on Trial," *Broadcasting Telecasting*, April 26, 1954, 76-79.
29 "WFOX Seeking a UHF Channel," *Milwaukee Journal*, November 19, 1952.
30 "Chicagoans File for Channel Here," *Milwaukee Journal*, November 25, 1952.
31 "Action Suspended on TV Bids Here," *Milwaukee Journal*, January 10, 1953.
32 "TV Application Channel Changed," *Milwaukee Journal*, January 31, 1953.
33 "City Will Get 2nd TV Outlet," Milwaukee *Journal*, February 5, 1953.
34 "Plan New TV Station Here by Summer," *Milwaukee Sentinel*, February 6, 1953.
35 "For the Record" *Broadcasting Telecasting*, July 20, 1953, 117.
36 "Tower for TV on Hotel Roof: WCAN Tells Plans," *Milwaukee Journal*, July 16, 1953.
37 Ibid.
38 "Start Planned By TV Station," *Milwaukee Journal*, June 18, 1953.
39 Irv Miller, interview with author, September 6, 2006.
40 "FCC Asked to OK Radio Stock Transfer," *Milwaukee Journal*, July 1, 1953. Also see: "Poller Will Buy Stock Control of WCAN-TV," *Milwaukee Sentinel*, July 1, 1953.
41 "UHF on Trial."
42 Ibid.
43 "Costly Aerial Need is Seen," *Milwaukee Journal*, September 4, 1953.
44 "WCAN-TV Makes 'Airsbreadth' Debut," *Milwaukee Sentinel*, September 20, 1953.
45 "WCAN-TV" Makes Initial Broadcast," *Milwaukee Sentinel*, September 7, 1953.
46 "WCAN-TV Is On the Air," *Milwaukee Journal*, September 8, 1953.
47 "Second TV Station," *Milwaukee Journal*, September 27, 1953.
48 "WCAN-TV Is On the Air."
49 "UHF on Trial."
50 Budde Marino, interview with author, November 5, 2007.
51 "UHF on Trial."
52 Ibid.
53 "UHF Operators Establish Own Trade Association," *Broadcasting Telecasting*, October 19, 1953, 3.
54 "TV Channel Plan Fought," *Milwaukee Journal*, October 14, 1953.
55 "Plan for New Channel Hit," *Milwaukee Journal*, October 8, 1953.
56 "UHFTA Protests VHF Allocation," *Broadcasting Telecasting*, December 28, 1953, 44-45.
57 "WCAN-TV Asks Court to Bar Ch. 6 Bids," *Broadcasting Telecasting*, January 11, 1954, 58. Also see: "Asks Hearing on Channel 6: WCAN-TV protests," *Milwaukee Journal*, January 8, 1954.
58 "WCAN-TV Asks Court to Prevent FCC Action on Whitefish Bay," *Broadcasting Telecasting*, January 18, 1954, 50.
59 "Ban Refused on Channel 6," *Milwaukee Journal*, January 20, 1954.
60 "Opposes Plea for Channel 6," *Milwaukee Journal*, January 22, 1954. Also see: "WCAN-TV Requests FCC Dismiss Hearst Bid," *Broadcasting Telecasting*, January 25, 1954, 54.
61 Wisconsin Dateline," *TV Guide* (Wisconsin Edition), February 19-25 1954, A-1.
62 "WCAN-TV Ups Station's Power," *Milwaukee Journal*, February 15, 1954.
63 "UHF on Trial."
64 "Seeks a Halt to TV Bingo," *Milwaukee Journal*, February 15, 1954.
65 "Map Change in TV Game," *Milwaukee Journal*, February 16, 1954.
66 Miller, September 6, 2006.
67 "Closed Circuit," *Broadcasting Telecasting*, March 15, 1954, 5.
68 "FCC Admits WCAN-TV Bid for Whitefish Bay," *Broadcasting Telecasting*, May 3, 1954, 59.
69 "Wisconsin Dateline," *TV Guide* (Wisconsin Edition), May 28 – June 3, 1954, A-1.

CHAPTER 4 ~ WCAN-TV: CHANNEL 25   157

70 "WCAN-TV Offers Free Time," *Broadcasting Telecasting*, May 11, 1954, 98.
71 "Milwaukee Merger," *Broadcasting Telecasting*, May 24, 1954, 9.
72 "WCAN's Plea for TV Denied: Midwest's Application Was Filed Too Late FCC Asserts," *Milwaukee Journal*, May 20, 1954.
73 "FCC Grants Channel 12: Goes to Telecast Corp," *Milwaukee Journal*, June 12, 1954.
74 "Dispute Arises on TV Grant: Channel 12 Involved," *Milwaukee Journal*, July 13, 1954.
75 "Two WCAN-TV Attacks Hit Milwaukee Merger," *Broadcasting Telecasting*, July 19, 1954.
76 "WCAN-TV Due to File for Stay of Rival Ch. 12," *Broadcasting Telecasting*, July 26, 1954, 9.
77 "WCAN-TV Plans to Build $250,000 'Television Capitol,'" *Milwaukee Journal*, July 23, 1954.
78 "Wisconsin Dateline," *TV Guide* (Wisconsin Edition), July 31 – August 6, 1954, A-1.
79 Judy Marks, interview with author, October 11, 2006.
80 "WCAN Loses a TV Protest: Channel 12 is Issue," *Milwaukee Journal*, August 11, 1954. Also see: "Two Stay Requests Denied By Court," *Broadcasting Telecasting*, August 16, 1954, 54.
81 "FCC Brief Defends Whitefish Bay Ch. 6," *Broadcasting Telecasting*, October 18, 1954, 58.
82 "FCC Boosts TV Ownership Limits: Seven Allowed, Five VHF, Two UHF," *Broadcasting Telecasting*, September 20, 1954, 7.
83 "Crowds at TV Result in Suit: Towne Hotel Seeks a Writ Against Its Tenant, WCAN," *Milwaukee Journal*, November 5, 1954.
84 "Judge Enjoins Video Station," *Milwaukee Journal*, November 6, 1954.
85 "Facilities Sold by WCAN-TV: Purchased by CBS," *Milwaukee Journal*, November 13, 1954.
86 "Columbia's First U," *Broadcasting Telecasting*, November 22, 1954, 37.
87 Marino, November 5, 2007.
88 Hearst Acquires WTVW(TV) Milwaukee; NBC Buys WKNB-TV New Britain, Conn.," *Broadcasting Telecasting*, January 10, 1955, 7.
89 "Sale of WOKY-TV Milwaukee to CBS-TV Gets FCC Approval," *Broadcasting Telecasting*, January 17, 1955, 7.
90 "WEMP Negotiates to Buy WCAN: Sale price $250,000," *Broadcasting Telecasting*, September 13, 1954, 9.
91 "Bitners Buy Two Minneapolis TV's; WTVW (TV) Sale Snags, WTAP (TV) Sold," *Broadcasting Telecasting*, January 31, 1955, 71-73.
92 "Closed Circuit," *Broadcasting Telecasting*, February 28, 1954, 5.
93 "Closed Circuit," *Broadcasting Telecasting*, April 25, 1955, 5.
94 "Two Radio-TV Men Open Shop, Back Kefauver for President," *Broadcasting Telecasting*, October 17, 1955, 90.
95 "Propose Change in UHF Channels," *Milwaukee Journal*, June 13, 1958.
96 "WCAN-TV Suit Seeks $53,660," *Milwaukee Sentinel*, October 18, 1956.
97 "Court Dismisses Suits on Bill for TV Films," *Milwaukee Journal*, August 25, 1958.
98 "WCAN Hurt Hotel, Claim," *Milwaukee Journal*, January 10, 1957.
99 "Hotel – TV Suit Award Made," *Milwaukee Journal*, January 19, 1957.
100 "Milwaukee UHF Wants Pay-TV Authorization From FCC," *Broadcasting Telecasting*, June 18, 1956, 95.
101 "Poller Would Buy WOPT (TV) As Subscription TV Station," *Broadcasting Telecasting*, July 2, 1956, 9.
102 "FCC Returns Poller Bids For Partial Pay TV Plan," *Broadcasting Telecasting*, July 16, 1956, 84. Also see: "'Pay as See' TV for Area Denied," *Milwaukee Journal*, July 13, 1956.
103 "CBS Is Sued by Lou Poller for $4,350,000," *Milwaukee Journal*, September 19, 1956.
104 *Poller v. Columbia Broadcasting*, 368 U.S. 464 (1962)
105 "Trial is OK'd in TV Dispute," *Milwaukee Journal*, February 20, 1962.
106 "OK to Be Asked for UHF Tower," *Milwaukee Journal*, September 1, 1966.
107 "State Hearing Planned on Mequon TV Tower," *Milwaukee Journal*, September 24, 1966.
108 "TV Tower in Mequon is Opposed," *Milwaukee Journal*, January 10, 1967.
109 "Tall Tower for TV Gets Mequon OK," *Milwaukee Journal*, February 16, 1967.
110 "Mequon Gives Final Approval to Video Tower," *Milwaukee Journal*, March 2, 1967.

111 Ibid.
112 *Milwaukee Journal*, February 16, 1967.
113 "State Aviation Board OK's Mequon Tower," *Milwaukee Journal*, May 12, 1967.
114 "Suit Fights TV Tower in Mequon," *Milwaukee Journal*, May 23, 1967.
115 "TV Tower Plan Killed in Mequon," *Milwaukee Journal*, March 13, 1968.

CHAPTER 5
WOKY-TV/WXIX/WUHF/WVTV
CHANNELS 19 & 18

THE CW 18
WVTV MILWAUKEE

(WVTV photo)

Milwaukee's third television station also began as an expansion of a local radio operation. Save for a few months in 1959, it would operate continuously, making it the city's second-oldest station, and would, for a time, be one of the most successful independent television stations in the country.

The Bartell family of Milwaukee would go on to make broadcasting history, and it all began after WWII. Lee and David graduated from the University of Wisconsin law school in the 1940s. Gerald (Jerry) Bartell was on the faculty of the University of Wisconsin, where he taught radio production, and served as the production director at WHA.[1] Mel was an opera singer. Their sister Rosa was a part-time singer and librarian at WHA. She met and married an electrical engineering student, Ralph Evans, and the two, along with Jerry Bartell helped run that station. In that team, they had all of the necessary expertise to successfully enter the broadcasting business.

Lee Bartell had a friend, classmate and colleague named Sam Miller. Miller became an attorney for the FCC right out of law school, probably because his brother-in-law Bill Lipman had become excited about the potential for radio broadcasting after WWII. Miller later opened his own practice in Washington D.C., specializing in commercial broadcasting law. Sam's first client was Bill Lipman, and the new Racine-area AM station WLIP was one of the first facilities to go on the air after the end of WWII. It was Miller who planted the seed in Lee Bartell's mind that radio might

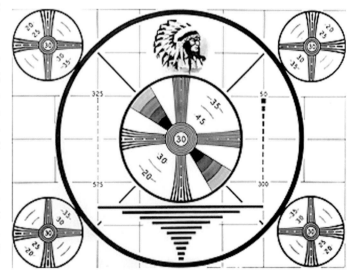

offer profit potential in Wisconsin. Lee went to his brother David, who had been in practice longer than he had, and represented various projectionist union locals. The two formed a company, AnDave, and decided to apply for an AM construction permit for Madison. David put up $20,000, and Lee contributed $5,000. Sam Miller advised them to get an engineer, and they convinced their brother-in-law, Ralph Evans, to join their company – and invest $5,000.[2]

The Bartell Brothers in a 1976 photo L-R: Mel, David, Lee and Gerald. (Courtesy of Ralph Evans, III)

After WWII, getting a license to operate a broadcast facility was a very competitive process. The AnDave (later Bartell) group unsuccessfully applied for a construction permit for 1010 kHz in Madison, and their application for a station in Gary, Indiana was also unsuccessful. They then turned their attention to the Milwaukee area, and filed an application for a radio station on 1430 kHz in October of 1946. The FCC granted them a construction permit for station WEXT on March 28, 1947. Thereafter, Lee wrote to his brother Gerald, asking him if he was going to take a role in the company. Gerald had tenure at the university, and took a leave of absence – just in case the station proved to be unsuccessful![3]

WEXT began broadcasting on August 31, 1947, and the FCC granted the group a license on November 25. It featured a typical blend of polka and other ethnic music, which was popular in Milwaukee at the time, and used the tag line "Your Neighbor on the Air." Most of the programming was live. John Reddy, Milwaukee's "polka king," featured a segment on his show called "Here Comes the Bride," in which he aired interviews with couples recorded at weddings using an old Webcor wire recorder.[4] Gerald Bartell pioneered the singing commercial. He, his sister Rosa, and Mel sang on commercials for Colders' Furniture and Weber Beer. Mel's wife played the piano and organ on the commercials, and provided background music.[5]

CHAPTER 5 ~ WOKY-TV/WXIX/WUHF/WVTV: CHANNELS 19 & 18   161

On December 3, 1947, WTMJ-TV began broadcasting. Radio stations were concerned that television might replace them, and began filing applications for the three other channels that were available. The Wisconsin Broadcasting System, Inc. (owners of WFOX radio) applied for a construction permit for channel 8 on March 16, 1948. Hearst Radio, Inc. (which had filed an application for channel 4 in June of 1945, which it later withdrew) filed an application for channel 10 on March 24. The Kapital City Broadcasting Co. of Des Moines, Iowa applied for channel 6 on April 12. (One of the company's principals had a construction permit for an FM station in Milwaukee, WMIL, and later transferred it to Kapital.)

WEXT applied for channel 6 on April 12, and for awhile it looked as if they might be the only local applicant. Then on May 21, the Milwaukee Broadcasting Co. (owners of WEMP) also applied for the channel.

Consolidated hearings were scheduled by the FCC for July 29. Prior to the hearings, Kapital Broadcasting amended its application to change the name of the applicant to the Majestic Broadcasting Co., and just prior to their start, asked the FCC to dismiss its application for channel 6. After the first round of hearings, WEXT, Inc. asked the FCC to dismiss its application. The FCC granted that petition on September 10, 1948. The group had determined that it had little chance against WEMP, which had been broadcasting since 1935, and was an established part of the city's radio scene.

That left three channels and three unopposed applicants. All three were granted a joint petition for an indefinite continuance of the consolidated TV hearings, which had been scheduled for September 8, and asked that the FCC immediately grant them construction permits. The Commission was considering the request when it froze all new television license applications on September 30, 1948.

WEXT continued to broadcast an eclectic mix of ethnic and community interest programming. However, it was licensed only for daytime operation, and as such was limited in its ability to reach listeners. While the station was paying its bills, it wasn't turning much of a profit.

It was Jerry Bartell who had the inspiration to switch to a new programming format called "Top 40." The family speculates that he had heard that format on WJJD in Chicago, and decided that it was where radio's future lay.[6]

The other critical piece of the plan required that they switch to another frequency that would allow them to broadcast twenty-four hours per day. Ralph Evans and John Mullany, a Washington D.C. consulting engineer, together determined that the only fulltime frequency that could theoretically be put into Milwaukee (using procedures and maps extant at the time) was 910 kHz, two channels (20 kHz) removed from clear channel station WLS on 890 kHz in Chicago. WLS shared that frequency with WENR, also in Chicago. Sam Miller advised the group that if they applied for 910 kHz, they could expect an objection by WLS/WENR seeking to protect its service area. Because it had significantly more resources, prevailing in a hearing against them would have been unlikely, but Miller had formulated an ingenious plan that would allow the Bartell Group to obtain a fulltime license without being exposed to the competitive process – and that would simultaneously satisfy WLS/WENR.

On April 22, 1949, Bartell Broadcasters, Inc. (as the group was now known) submitted an application for a construction

Sam Miller, Bartell Broadcasting's attorney in Washington, D.C. formulated a plan that allowed them to move from 1430 to 920 kHz. (Courtesy of Jane Bartell)

permit on 910 kHz to the FCC. As a condition of the grant, 1430 kHz would be vacated. However, Lee Bartell located another radio entrepreneur who was willing to apply for the same frequency in Beaver Dam, Wisconsin, thereby eliminating a competitor from the Milwaukee market. As predicted, WLS/WENR filed an immediate objection to the Bartell application, and they were joined by WSUI in Iowa City, Iowa (which broadcast on 910 kHz), Metropolitan Broadcasting of Milwaukee and Rock River Broadcasting of Watertown. The latter two petitioners had applied for other frequencies in the area. On April 29, the FCC designated the entire matter for a consolidated hearing.

At that time, the FCC's hearing calendar was full. Hearings were expensive and time consuming for both the litigants and the government. Consequently, if the major issues could be resolved prior to their start, the FCC would order that the resolution plan be implemented without re-opening the frequency assignments to new applicants. Sam asked Ralph if there was any other frequency that could work in Milwaukee. Ralph found that, because of low-conductivity soil conditions in Indiana and Illinois, the Purdue University station WBAA in Lafayette, Indiana, operating on 920 kHz, had a considerably smaller service area than the FCC charts anticipated. Ralph spent nearly a month measuring the strength of WBAA's signal in directions toward Milwaukee using a field strength meter recently introduced by a new radio equipment company called Nems-Clarke. Previous AM measurement equipment (such as the Federal Corporation meter) was cumbersome and inaccurate, and readings taken with them were suspect at FCC hearings.

Based on Evans' measurements, Bartell modified its application to 920 kHz on June 22, 1949. The timing was critical, and had been a part of Sam Miller's plan.[7] The amendment gave the FCC a way to avoid a lengthy hearing. As a result, Metropolitan petitioned the Commission to amend its application to specify 1470 kHz,

Ralph Evans, Sr., taking field strength readings. (Courtesy of Ralph Evans, III)

which was granted on June 3. On July 8, Rock River amended its own application for 920 kHz to 1580, and the FCC removed the matter from its hearing docket. On January 5, 1950, the Commission accepted the Bartell's amended application, dismissed the others' objections, and issued a construction permit specifying 920 kHz with full-time operation using a 3-tower directional pattern to protect WBAA.

The new station, renamed WOKY (Jerry came up with the call letters and the tag line "WOKY in Milwaukee"), began broadcasting on September 5, 1950, with a format that included ethnic programming and top 40 hits. The station became a powerhouse in the area.

By 1951, Bartell Broadcasters was in a stronger position to apply for a television construction permit than it had been in 1948. In addition, the FCC's policy of intermixing VHF and UHF channels in the same markets meant that it was likely that the less desirable UHF channels might go uncontested. Despite the FCC's freeze on television applications, Bartell applied for channel 19 in Milwaukee in October of 1951. It was the first application for a UHF channel in the city.[8] The Milwaukee application specified the location of the studio and transmitter as 2439 West Hopkins Street. In a December, 1991 interview with Wayne Hawk and Andrew Stone, Ralph Evans, Sr. recalled:

> *We looked at the situation and decided that maybe this was a good time to get into television because there weren't any applications for the two or three UHF channels that were allocated to Milwaukee, but there were three, as I recall, applications for the only VHF channel – 12.*
>
> *So, we thought that we could get a station on the air and get it established before anybody got on channel 12, because these hearing for the channels took a long time. So we applied for channel 19 in Milwaukee.*[9]

The FCC lifted its freeze on new television applications as of July 1, 1952. Milwaukee received VHF channels 4 (which was assigned to WTMJ-TV), 10 and 12, as well as UHF channels 19, 25 and 31. Channel 10 was reserved for educational use. Madison had received a single VHF channel, 3, as well as UHF channels 21, 27 and 33. Channel 21 was reserved for educational use. The Bartells already had an application on file for channel 19 in Milwaukee, and they also applied for Channel 33 in Madison in July of 1952. It too, was the first application for a UHF channel in that city.[10]

The Madison battle was very contentious, as there was a single VHF channel available. Radio Wisconsin, Inc., the owner of WISC, and an applicant for channel 27, petitioned the FCC for rule making to amend Madison's Table of Channel Assignments to reserve channel 3 for educational use. If approved, all commercial channels would have been on UHF.

In late August, Earl M. Fessler, the owner of WMFM (FM) in Madison, applied for channel 33.

The FCC had a policy of processing uncontested applications first, and as such, maneuvering had begun in many cities – including Milwaukee and Madison. In mid-December of 1952, the Northwest Television Corp. amended its application from channel 25 to channel 19. Northwest was owned by H & E Balaban Corp. (whose principals, Harry and Elmer Balaban and Otto Zeman, were Chicago theater owners), and had applied for channel 25 only a few weeks earlier.[11]

That same week, WIBA radio of Madison and Television of Wisconsin, Inc., merged to form the Badger Television Co. Both had been applicants for channel 3, and it was hoped that the merger would result in an immediate grant from the FCC. As a result, Radio Wisconsin, Inc. (WISC) amended its applications from channel 27 to channel 3. That left Monona Broadcasting as the only applicant for channel 27.

In response, Bartell Broadcasters Inc., and Earl Fessler merged to form a new entity, the Bartell Television Corp., which filed a new application for channel 33 in late December of 1952. At the same time, the Bartells reached an agreement with Northwest Television, in which the latter would withdraw their application for channel 19 in Milwaukee, in exchange for an option to purchase an interest in the station, should WOKY receive the grant.[12]

In early January of 1953, Monona Broadcasting was granted a construction permit for channel 27 in Madison[13], and on January 23, the Bartell Television Corp. was granted a CP for channel 33.[14] In late February, it was assigned the call letters WMTV.

As a consequence, on January 31 The Wisconsin Broadcasting System (WFOX) – which had first applied for channel 12 before amending its application to specify channel 25 – again amended its application to specify channel 19. They were under the mistaken assumption that Milwaukee and Madison were considered to be in the same market, and because the FCC had awarded Bartell a construction permit for channel 33 in Madison, that would disqualify them from receiving channel 19 in Milwaukee.[15]

The maneuvering continued, and on June 2, 1953, the Wisconsin Broadcasting System, Inc. amended its application from channel 19 to channel 12.[16] Their rationale was that if they had to go through a competitive hearing, they would do so for a VHF channel. The following day, the FCC granted Bartell Broadcasters, Inc. a construction permit for channel 19.[17] The call letters WOKY-TV were later assigned to the facility.

In its application, Bartell Broadcasters had specified the WOKY building as the location of its studio and transmitter. It later applied to the FCC for permission to modify its construction permit to show the studios in the Welch Building at 704 West Wisconsin Avenue, with the tower and transmitter atop the Tower Hotel (now the M. Carpenter Tower, a Marquette University residence hall).

The Bartells were able to affiliate the new station with both ABC and Du Mont, and had set a target date of September 30 for the first broadcast.[18] Meanwhile, Ralph Evans continued to search for a way to meet that target date. Rather than erect its own tower, Bartell Broadcasting entered into an agreement to lease space at the WEMP facility at 5407 West Martin Drive for their transmitter, as well as the ability to mount their TV antenna on that station's self-supporting tower.

The station went on the air with test patterns on September 26, 1953, and WOKY-TV officially began broadcasting on October 3. Besides network program-

(Courtesy of Ralph Evans, III)

ming from ABC and Du Mont, it also produced many of its own shows.

Production was crude at first. As program director Gene Harrison, remembered in a 1991 interview with Andrew Stone and Wayne Hawk:

> I had come from an NBC owned-and-operated station in Cleveland. There we had a technical director, a switcher, an audio man, and sometimes two shad-

> **WOKY-TV's First Day Programming**
> **October 3, 1953**
> * 5:00 p.m.   Roundup Time
> * 5:30 p.m.   News, Sports, Weather
> * 5:45 p.m.   Variety Time
> * 6:00 p.m.   Paul Whiteman Teen Club
> * 7:00 p.m.   NFL Football: New York Giants vs. Pittsburgh Steelers
> * 10:00 p.m.   Feature Movie: *Take it Big*

ers. I came to an operation that had two engineers: one to shade and one to do audio. The shader also did the switching. I guess we also had someone to operate the film room with slides, but we only had one film chain.

We had a two-person elevator. If you had a third person it was really close. We had a studio, a control room, a reception room, an announce booth, and a hallway. The floor in the studio slanted to the west, and the camera operators had to hang on to the camera, because if they let go it would roll down and hit the wall! Sometimes that happened. The other thing it had was an elevator to bring in cars and big props, and occasionally in the middle of a program someone would be banging on the door trying to get into the studio. They were really exciting times, because when you opened the door, you never knew what you were going to find there! [19]

Pat Buckett, who played "Chief White Buck" (See special section.), remembered that:

It was bare bones initially. The first microphone, was hung from a cord, which was wrapped around plumbing pipes overhead just off-camera. Then we graduated to a more sophisticated table microphone, and then a boom microphone as we slowly upgraded to better equipment. Eventually, we installed a rear projection screen which allowed us to expand into some special effects. That was an enormous step in the right direction. [20]

Live television had its share of interesting moments. Judy Marks had auditioned for the role of the weather girl at WCAN-TV, but the job was given to Mary Jane Jung. Marks was doing modeling work for Littman Furs, and was doing a live fashion show, "Milwaukee Style Theater," for them on WOKY-TV, when she was tapped to be the station's weather girl. She also played other roles, and did live commercials. Those triggered some interesting memories, and she remembered that things were not always what they seemed to be:

There were two that I remember: One was for Hide-a-Bed. I would say, 'It's so easy, a child can handle it.' Then with one or two fingers, I would open up the bed, which was folded in the sofa.

Well, there were two floor men on either side of me – off-camera – helping to open it, but it would look like I was just going zip, zip, zoop and it would open without much work.

Another commercial I did was for a mattress. I had something like a waffle maker that I would use to show how the rubber mattress was made. Then what they would have me do on camera was to show the viewers a light bulb that I would put under the mattress – between it and the box springs. Then I would sit down on the mattress. At the end of the commercial I would reach in and pull out the bulb to show how comfortable the mattress was, and how it didn't break the bulb. Well, we always hid two bulbs! I never came out with a bloody hand! [21]

Gene Harrison got a surprise one day:

> *I happened to be directing that night. As a program director, you're always filling in working the times other people either aren't available, or have a problem.*
>
> *We were watching the Paul Whiteman Show on the network. The control room was very dark, except for the monitors and some lights on desks. A woman walked in with a mink coat. She said that she was Hildegarde! I really didn't know who Hildegarde was at the time.*
>
> *She told me that she was going to be a judge on the Paul Whiteman Show, and that Paul Whiteman was going to call her at the end of this presentation – which happened to be a talent presentation – and ask for her opinion.*

> *That's what happened. She judged the show! That was the first time I worked with Hildegarde!*[22]

WOKY radio announcers Van Calligan and Wally Scott also served as booth announcers for the television station. Calligan also did news, and a music show. John Reddy came over to do sports. Trudy Beilfuss later came over from WCAN-TV to do a cooking show.

The station originated broadcasts of Milwaukee Hawks' basketball games for ABC. The new WOKY TV team was inexperienced, and ran afoul of the network on occasion. As Ralph Evans, Sr. remembered:

> *The first time we did a basketball game for ABC, the game ended, and John Reddy, who was announcing it, said something like: 'Well, that's it folks. That's the end of the game.'*
>
> *At that point we cut it off. ABC was left hanging there. We heard about that later! They asked: 'Why in the world didn't you throw it back to us? Why didn't you put up an ABC logo or something? Don't leave us hanging there!'*[23]

WOKY-TV didn't have remote equipment, but Ralph Evans was able to adapt:

> We had a source in Chicago. It was a school – a television school – that we rented the remote equipment from. There were two RCA remote cameras, a switcher, a sync-generator, and everything we needed to do remotes. We had a little Nash station wagon, and I would go down there. All of the equipment would just fit inside – if I packed it right! I would drive it back to Milwaukee, set it up, take it down after the event, and the next day haul it back down to Chicago. The phone company would provide the link from the remote location to our studio via a co-axial cable.[24]

Jim Lawler played "Shamus O'Hara" on WOKY radio, and he came over to do a variety show Friday nights called "Here's O'Hara." It featured teenagers, and students from Marquette University. As Gene Harrison remembered:

> He always opened the show by saying, 'Hey you kids! Get off that roof!' It was a Friday night show which, now that I think about it, was not unlike 'Saturday Night Live'. Most of the music was lip-synced. We had some campus humor, and a full studio of students and people participating.[25]

Marquette University student Jack Crowley, who started as a floor director, and went on to play "Red O'Rourke" (See special section.), ran afoul of the time constraints of live TV while doing some shtick on that show:

> I had just come off of doing 'Varsity Varieties' for Marquette, and I thought that I was a hit – the greatest comedian ever. Jim said, 'Hey! Do that bit for me!' It was (in a lisp) The Horse by Percy Griffiths.
> Well, I got halfway through the damned thing, when the floor director said, 'cut!' There was no punch line! I had gone as fast as I could, but they went black! I was never so embarrassed in my life, and I was almost close to quitting! I thought that everyone would come up to me and tell me about how I'd bombed![26]

When the Army-McCarthy hearings took place between April 22 and June 17, of 1954, only ABC carried them live and uninterrupted. WOKY-TV claimed that during one week in May they received 15,000 phone calls, letters, telegrams, and even people who came to the station offices to personally congratulate station executives for showing the hearings.[27] Ralph Evans, Sr. recalled that those broadcasts helped build an audience for the station:

> No one else in town wanted to touch it. I think there were a lot of people who went out and bought converters so they could get it.[28]

The station also worked with ad agencies, which used the facilities to train their personnel. The Milwaukee Broadcasting Co. (WEMP), provided space for the station's transmit-

The Milwaukee Station for the CBS television network.

Judy Marks went along as the weather girl when WOKY-TV became WXIX. (Courtesy of Hal Erickson)

ter and allowed its antenna to be mounted on their tower, also used the facilities. They were involved in a very competitive hearing for channel 12, and hoped to show the FCC that they were capable of producing television shows. (See chapter 6.) Marquette University also used the facilities in their new television production courses.

In September of 1954, WEMP announced that it was looking to buy the facilities of WCAN radio, and move from 1340 to 1250 kHz. *Broadcasting Telecasting* announced that since its transmitter and tower were located there, WOKY-TV would purchase the WEMP facilities.[29] That proved to be premature, and WEMP sold its license and facilities to Texas radio chain operator Harold McLendon's Foster & Holmes, Inc., who started WRIT on 1340 kHz.[30]

Although the station was holding its own, it was not as successful as its counterpart in Madison. CBS was affiliated with WCAN-TV in Milwaukee, but was actively seeking to buy a station in the city. It retained Thad Holt to obtain an option and then purchase WOKY-TV.[31] The sale was consummated on October 22, 1954, at a price of $350,000.[32] This was shortly after the FCC changed its multiple-ownership rules to allow an individual entity to own two UHF in addition to five VHF stations.[33] As a result of the sale, negotiations to purchase the WEMP facilities were dropped.

In their announcement, CBS stated that they had no plans to change the station's call letters, but they eventually changed their mind, and requested WXIX (the Roman numerals for "19"). They invoked the clause in their contract with WCAN-TV, which required them to give six-months notice before canceling their affiliation. Without a network affiliation, WCAN-TV owner Lou Poller sold his new facilities to CBS. In return, he received the WOKY-TV facilities, so that he might continue broadcasting as an independent station.[34] He never did.

On January 14, 1955, the FCC approved the sale of WOKY-TV to CBS. Commissioner Frieda Hennock, who had led the fight to have channels reserved for noncommercial educational use (See chapter 8), dissented, citing both her opposition to the relaxation of the Commission's multiple-ownership rules, which had allowed the sale to take place, and her empathy for the fate of WCAN-TV.[35] The original target date for the switch was February 20, but that was changed to February 27.[36]

The last broadcast day for WCAN-TV was February 26, 1955. It then went dark. The following day, CBS began broadcasting as WXIX from the former WCAN-TV studios at 5445 North 27th Street, using its former transmitter and tower atop the Schroeder Hotel.[37] It broadcast with an effective radiated power of 50 kW for its first two weeks.[38]

Some of the WOKY-TV facilities Lou Poller received in exchange for his own were donated to Marquette University on March 3, and others, including the trans-

CHAPTER 5 ~ WOKY-TV/WXIX/WUHF/WVTV: CHANNELS 19 & 18

mitter, were acquired by the Milwaukee Vocational School, who used them to put WMVT-TV on the air in 1963. (See chapter 8.)

In 1956, Poller sued CBS, the Bartells, and Thad Holt claiming that they had conspired to force him out of business.[39] (See chapter 4.)

Some WOKY-TV personnel such as Judy Marks and Trudy Beilfuss were hired by CBS. Others, such as Hal Walker, came from WCAN-TV. Guy Runnion served as the first news director. Budde Marino came over from WCAN-TV as a producer/director:

> It was initially exciting because we had decent budgets to work with, and we were challenged with coming up with creative sets.[40]

On Sunday, March 13, 1955, WXIX finished the installation of a new antenna, which allowed it to increase its effective radiated power to 263 kW.[41] The following month, it began a promotional campaign encouraging residents to purchase UHF converters. The campaign, which consisted of 2,000 spots on WEMP and WOKY radio, also described the CBS programming on the station.[42]

CBS took over the new WCAN-TV facilities on North 27th Street. Here the "Captain Jet" show is being broadcast. (Historic photo collection/ Milwaukee Public Library)

One of the popular, locally-produced shows was "On the Record," a live musical panel show that featured the latest records. A panel voted on whether each record was a hit or not. The show ran for an hour Saturday nights at 9:00 p.m. At first Bob Grant, a member of CBS' Chicago staff hosted the show.[43] He was later replaced by Hal Walker.

(Courtesy of Hal Erickson)

Guy Runnion decided to head home to the west coast, and was replaced as news director by Jerry Dunphy in May of 1955.[44] Dunphy later went to CBS' WBBM in Chicago, and was replaced by Roger Grimsby. Both would go on to distinguished careers in Los Angeles and New York.[45]

At first the late night version was called the "11th Hour News" – running at 11:00 p.m. It was later shifted to 10:30, and then to 10:00 p.m. like its competitors. Before *The Tonight Show* changed viewer's habits, the shift turned out to be necessary. As Judy Marks remembered:

My future colleague at WTMJ-TV, Bill Carlsen, led with the weather at 10:00 p.m. We had data from the electric company that showed that the power usage dropped at 10:05! Everyone watched the weather, and then they went to bed! By the time we started our news, fewer people were watching.[46]

In 1958, station manager Frank Shakespeare announced that CBS had inaugurated special air service from both New York and Washington D.C., which would allow WXIX to show news film the same day it was shot.[47]

Some viewers were experiencing problems with their reception of channel 19 – a combination of squiggly lines and a herringbone pattern. CBS engineers discovered that the problem only occurred in heavily populated areas of the city, where many sets were tuned to channel 12. Harmonic interference between the channels was causing the problem, but only if those sets were within 100 feet of each other.[48]

To counter the problem, CBS proposed that the FCC shift UHF channels in Milwaukee. The city would receive channels 18, 24 and 30 instead of 19, 25 and 31.[49] To avoid interference problems, the proposal also required that: Ludington, Michigan shift from channel 18 to 33; Beaver Dam, Wisconsin shift from channel 37 to channel 51; and Chilton, Wisconsin from channel 24 to channel 31.[50] The FCC gave notice of proposed rule making and asked WXIX, WCAN-TV (which had gone dark) and WFOX-TV (which was not yet on the air) to show cause why the switch should not be made.[51] The switch was announced on August 1, 1958, and formally took place as of August 15. The station shifted to channel 18 on August 27.[52]

CBS was still not happy. It was generally acknowledged that Storer Broadcasting's purchase of WITI-TV was motivated by its desire to affiliate with the network. (See chapter 7.) CBS denied the rumor[53], despite the fact that it announced

CHAPTER 5 ~ WOKY-TV/WXIX/WUHF/WVTV: CHANNELS 19 & 18 171

on August 9, that it was abandoning UHF station WHCT in Hartford, Connecticut, and affiliating with an independent VHF station there.[54]

Despite the denial, on February 27, 1959, CBS announced that it would sell WXIX and affiliate with WITI-TV.[55] The affiliation took place on April 1, 1959. Local stores were upset, as without a UHF channel, there was no longer a demand for UHF converters or all-channel sets.[56]

Broadcasting reported that Zenith might purchase the station, and seek the ability to test its Phonevision pay-TV system on it.[57] Zenith had conducted tests on the system in Chicago in 1951. (See chapter 9.)

On March 27 however, CBS sold the station to WXIX, Inc., headed up by Cream City Broadcasting owner Gene Posner.[58] Cream City operated WMIL radio, and had held a construction permit for channel 31, but had turned it in and was the first to apply for channel 6. It pulled out of that contest, after receiving consideration from Independent Television, Inc. (See chapter 7.) As a part of the purchase, WXIX, Inc. received the tower and transmitter atop the Schroeder Hotel, as well as other equipment. Storer Broadcasting purchased the WXIX studios on North 27th Street, so the decision was made to locate those of the new station in the hotel penthouse that housed the transmitter.[59]

The station would go dark while awaiting FCC approval of the purchase, and Milwaukee became an all-VHF city for a time. The new owners filed an application for the transfer on April 15. In that application it disclosed that the stockholders in WXIX, Inc. were Posner and his wife Ruth, Harold and Bernard Sampson, and Herbert Wilk. The latter three owned Sampson's appliance stores.[60] CBS asked the Commission to approve the transfer on April 20[61], and WXIX, Inc. was granted a construction permit on May 7.[62] Permission was granted to broadcast a test pattern on May

(Courtesy of Hal Erickson)

The staff of the CBS-owned WXIX gathered for one final picture on the station's last broadcast day.
(Courtesy of B.J. Rafenstein)

(Courtesy of Hal Erickson)

27.[63] and those tests began on June 8 between 4:00 and 6:00 p.m.[64] The tests went well, and the station announced that it would resume broadcasting at 4:00 p.m. on Monday, July 20.[65]

With the slogan "We Love Milwaukee," WXIX went back on-the-air July 20, 1959 as an independent station.[66] Bruce Kanitz did one minute of news every thirty minutes, as well as "Bruce Kanitz reports" from 6:30-6:45 p.m. The latter show included a three-minute editorial on local affairs.[67] Operations Director Larry Turet came from WITI-TV, and he brought Bob Hersh over to play his character on "The Advisor's Mystery Theater," Friday and Saturday nights.

Bruce Kanitz did the news and commentary on the independent WXIX. (Courtesy of Hal Erickson)

In October of that year, the station announced that it was negotiating with Zenith for the potential use of its "Phonevision" pay TV system, via an over-the-air signal transmitted on channel 18, or via cable.[68] The FCC had announced its inten-

The independent WXIX operation in the north penthouse of the Schroeder Hotel had a single camera. The zoom lens had a control on the handle, which was operated by an engineer who sat at the right. That engineer also did the switching between video sources! There was no room in the 12'x14' studio for the camera, so it shot through the window. (WVTV photo)

The 12'x14' studio in the Schroeder Hotel penthouse. All talent sat behind the desk. The curtain could be drawn back to show a photograph of Milwaukee's skyline shot from the hotel's roof. (WVTV photo)

Master control for the independent WXIX, as seen through the studio doorway. At the right is the film chain and slide unit. (WVTV photo)

All of Gene Posner's stations shared a common feature: The news teletype was located in the bathroom! It can be seen through the doorway at the right. The refrigerator held employees' lunches, and the room's mirror was used by on-air talent when applying make-up. (WVTV photo)

tion to allow tests of pay TV in March. Zenith would later use a station in Hartford Connecticut. (See chapter 9.)

The station's tower was originally purchased for WMAW-FM and was erected atop the Schroeder Hotel as an expedient way to get WCAN-TV on the air in 1953. (See chapter 4.) Gene Posner wanted a new tower for the station, and sought to make it a city landmark. The "Space Needle" was under construction in Seattle, and served as one inspiration. Germany's Fernsehturm Stuttgart, which opened in February of 1956, was another. Both of those towers included observation decks and restaurants. On June 24, 1960, he proposed that Milwaukee County fund the construction of a similar reinforced concrete tower. Posner estimated that it would take $2 million to build, and suggested that the county fund the project by issuing bonds, and then leasing it to him. Alternatively, he offered to form a consortium to build it.[69]

CHAPTER 5 ~ WOKY-TV/WXIX/WUHF/WVTV: CHANNELS 19 & 18   175

He suggested that the County sell or lease one of three tracts of land which were parts of: Washington Park (from where the zoo had just moved), the Emergency Hospital on North 24th Street and West Wisconsin Avenue, or the new Zoo on

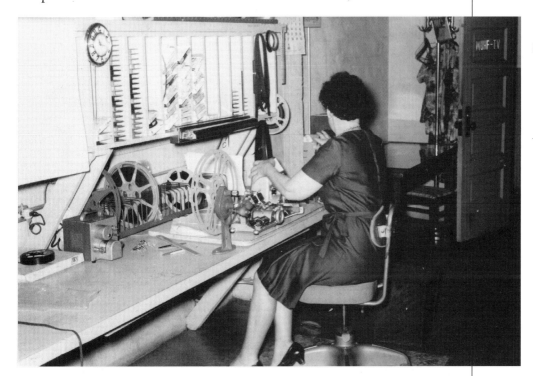

Lydia Zielsdorf works in the film room in 1966. (WVTV photo)

Hwy 100 and West Blue Mound Road. He would also use the tower for WMIL radio, and would offer antenna space to other broadcasting stations – especially the new educational station on channel 36.[70] The Milwaukee County Park Commission denied his request on August 3[71], and as a result Posner announced that he would seek private funding.[72]

(Courtesy of Hal Erickson)

Instead, he formulated another plan. The FCC had de-intermixed Fresno, California, and had given KFRE-TV permission to broadcast on both UHF and VHF during the transition period. Posner saw that as a precedent, and on March 14, 1961, WXIX, Inc. filed an application to amend the Table of Channel Assignments for Milwaukee to add VHF channel 8. It also requested permission to operate the station on both channels from a common transmitter facility. He promised to program ten hours a day separately on each station.[73] Posner announced that if his petition was accepted, he would erect a new 1,000 foot tower for the two stations.[74]

On December 23, 1959, the FCC approved a plan to broadcast educational programming to a number of states using an airborne antenna.[75] Called the Midwest Program on Airborne Television Instruction (MPATI), the program was headquartered at Purdue University, and utilized aircraft circling above Montpelier, Indiana at 23,000 feet. The idea of using an airborne antenna was not new. Westinghouse had proposed such a system, which it called "Stratovision" in 1944. Tests were run, but the idea was shelved when the FCC froze all TV license applications in 1948. After successfully testing the idea, the MPATI was put into operation in 1961 with funding from a grant by the Ford Foundation.

As a part of its sales pitch to operate both VHF and UHF channels, WXIX offered to provide the service on a free, experimental basis during the summer of 1961, during the hours it was not normally on the air. If the experiment proved successful, the station offered to continue the telecasts on channel 18, and charge only for its operating costs. The MPATI turned down the request in late June, saying that copyright and royalty provisions in its contracts required that its programming be broadcast on a noncommercial basis. WXIX offered to run no commercials during the educational telecasts, but the idea was still rejected.[76]

In late July of 1961, the FCC rejected the petition to have channel 8 added to the city, saying that it was within 170 miles from a station in Michigan. On September 6, the station renewed its request, and asked the Commission to assign it channel 8 until it formulated a long-range plan to de-intermix cities like Milwaukee. In that way, said Posner, the station could be competitive in the market. Another argument was that the Commission had reduced the separation distance required for stations on the same channel to 120 miles if one broadcast at a lower radiated power level.[77]

The station's logo was changed to include a dachshund when the call letters were changed to WUHF! (Courtesy of WVTV)

That petition was also rejected.

The station was not profitable, however. As a result, Gene Posner announced on June 18, 1962, that he would sell his fifty-one percent interest in the station to his partners, the Sampson brothers. In doing so, he stated that he wanted to devote more time to his two radio stations, WMIL and WMIL-FM, as well as his real estate interests.[78]

CHAPTER 5 ~ WOKY-TV/WXIX/WUHF/WVTV: CHANNELS 19 & 18

In the center is the RCA TRT-2B videotape unit used by WUHF. At right is a color monitor left by CBS. (WVTV photo)

The details of the sale were announced ten days later. Posner agreed to sell his majority interest for $1.00, with the understanding that he would not have to provide any more funds for the station. Under the agreement, the two Sampsons would each own forty-five and one-half percent. Their cousin, Herbert Wilk, would continue to own nine percent. Harold Sampson would become the company's president, while his brother Bernard would become its secretary and treasurer. The firm would continue to be known as WXIX, Inc. Posner was given the option of repurchasing twenty-five of his 255 shares within three years of the sale.[79]

The sale came at the time that Congress was contemplating an all-channel receiver bill. It later passed and was signed into law by President Kennedy. (See chapter 3.) After FCC approval, the call letters were changed to WUHF at midnight on December 31, 1962.[80] Those call letters had been used previously by an experimental station used to conduct propagation studies in New York.

One of the first things the station did was to increase its power to 440,000 watts starting in January of 1963. The station also purchased a videotape recorder.[81]

The station acquired a package of foreign and American "art" films with adult themes. The Jos. Schlitz Brewing Co. sponsored the program, called "Award Theater." The films were shown without commercial interruption. A panel consisting of four station and two Schlitz personnel previewed the films, and recommended cuts as necessary to make them suitable for TV. The films were shown Friday nights at 10:30 starting on June 7, 1963.[82]

On July 13, 1964, WISN-TV dropped *Captain Kangaroo* from its weekday morning schedule. (It continued to carry it Saturdays.) That prompted parents to complain.[83] The Milwaukee Radio and Television Council passed a resolution asking WISN-TV to return the show. After receiving permission from CBS, WUHF picked-up the weekday show as of August 31.[84] As such, it changed its schedule: It had been beginning its broadcast day in the afternoon. Instead, it began broadcasting from 8:00-10:30 a.m., signed off and then resumed at 4:00 p.m.[85]

(Courtesy of Hal Erickson)

In 1961, WXIX carried several NBA basketball games that local NBC affiliate WTMJ-TV elected not to clear. That was the first of many network programs the station would later clear. (Courtesy of Hal Erickson)

NETWORK SHOWS

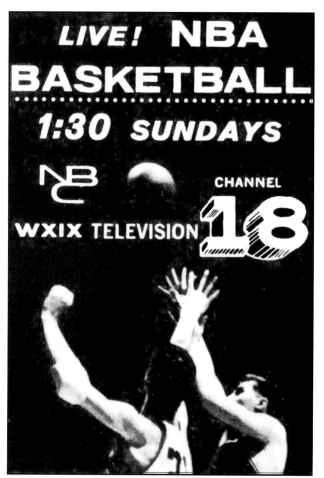

In late 1959, WXIX asked CBS if it could clear two network shows, *Camera Three* and *UN in Action*, that were not carried by local affiliate WITI-TV. The network turned them down because the shows were sustaining (not sponsored), and as such they could only be carried by affiliates. The station also made inquires regarding some other network shows, but was turned down.

In 1961, WTMJ-TV elected not to carry several NBA basketball games broadcast by NBC. WXIX received permission to clear those games. It would be the start of a strategy that would continue for three decades.

After it began clearing programs, the station occasionally ran afoul of the network's wishes. Such was the case with *The Dick Cavett Show*. WITI-TV ran its own "Late Show" film at 10:30 p.m. weeknights, and did not carry the ABC show. WVTV picked it up in. When the station began running its short-lived, fifteen-minute newscast at 10:00 p.m. in September of 1971, it wanted to carry Cavett at 10:15 instead of 10:30, but ABC refused. Nonetheless, clearing network programs the local affiliates dropped was a big part of the station's programming for many years.

TV/Film historian Hal Erickson provided the following summary of the station's history of doing so:

> As WXIX, the station picked up "The Benefactor," a very controversial episode of the old courtroom series *The Defenders*. The episode dealt with abortion, and because of that it was blacked out by the then-CBS affiliate, WISN-TV. The original telecast of that episode was April 28, 1962, but WISN-TV

scheduled a movie in its stead. WXIX delayed its "special" broadcast of the episode until Saturday, May 12, 1962, at 10:00 p.m. (Two and one-half hours later than the series' normal timeslot).

Some of the network shows carried by Channel 18 were daytime reruns. In Prime Time, the local affiliates often elected to run their own movie packages instead of either the networks' movies or a network show. For example, WUHF ran CBS's Route 66 for several months while WISN-TV carried an MGM movie package.

Occasionally, a locally-produced show proved more popular, as was the case with "Murl Deusing Safari" on WTMJ-TV. They elected not to clear The Virginian because of that show, and it was on WUHF/WVTV for 3 full seasons, from the fall of 1964 until the fall of 1967. Over the years, the station cleared a lot of network shows, including (in chronological order):

- American Bandstand (ABC) 1963 (Daytime); Saturday version 1964, then again in 1965-66)
- Chet Huntley Reporting (NBC) 1963
- Eyewitness (CBS) 1963
- Route 66 (CBS) 1963
- ABC Evening News with Ron Cochran (ABC) (1963-1964)
- CBS Sunday News with Harry Reasoner (CBS) 1963
- The Virginian (NBC) 1964-1967
- That Was the Week That Was (NBC) 1964-1965
- Make Room for Daddy (NBC) 1964
- Word for Word (NBC) 1964
- What's This Song? (NBC) 1964
- Captain Kangaroo (CBS) 1964-65
- Real McCoys (CBS) 1964
- Moment of Fear (NBC) 1965
- Cloak of Mystery (NBC) 1965
- Hullabaloo (NBC) 1965
- ABC Nightlife 1965
- The Young Set (ABC) 1965
- CBS Evening News with Walter Cronkite 1965
- Jack Benny Program (CBS) 1965
- Famous Adventures of Mr. Magoo (NBC) 1965
- Celebrity Game (CBS) 1965
- Love of Life (CBS) 1965
- Concentration (NBC) 1965
- Green Acres (CBS) 1965
- Frank McGee Report (NBC) 1966
- Some NBC AFL telecasts 1966-1967
- The Monkees (NBC) 1966
- Dark Shadows (ABC) 1967
- The Joey Bishop Show (ABC) 1968-1969
- Rowan and Martin's Laugh-In (NBC) 1968
- The Dick Cavett Show (ABC) 1969-1971
- CBS Late Movie/CBS Late Reruns at various times 1970s-1980s
- NBC Saturday Night at the Movies (1972-73)
- Jeopardy (NBC) 1980
- David Letterman Daytime Show (NBC) 1980
- The Tonight Show with Johnny Carson (NBC) 1983-1989

WAWA DJ "Dr. Bop" (Hoyt Locke) began a thirty-minute dance show Sunday afternoons at 5:30 on September 26, 1965.[87] It was later expanded to an hour. The "Dr." had to work inside the station's small studio! George Liberatore directed the show, and he remembered:

> It was always quite interesting because Dr. Bop always had live entertainment. Twistin' Harvey and the Seven Sounds is the band that comes to mind. It was a hot band at the time, and hot bands always have people that follow them around. They also have people who help set-up and help run the equipment. They were all there! It was such a tiny, tiny space. Twistin' Harvey had eight members. They were all in that small studio along with the doctor and on occasion his sidekick, 'The White Raven'!

Harvey Scales was "Twistin' Harvey." He recalled:

> I think that it was one of our first TV experiences. Oh man, I don't know how we got the whole band in there! You know we had these props up, and I was doin' my twistin' and dancin' and I knocked the whole set down! We had to set it up and shoot it all over again.[88]

All those people in that confined area occasionally caused another problem. George Liberatore:

> One day someone opened the door to the transmitter – which was located in the same penthouse as the studio – and knocked us off the air! That caused a lot of people to be scurrying around. At that time, you couldn't just close the door, hit a switch, and you were back on the air. The transmitter took some time to recycle. After you got back on the air, you had to make some sort of announcement telling folks that you had been knocked off the air because of technical difficulties!
>
> The Dr. always wore a white smock and reflector. The latter played havoc with the camera tubes, as it would reflect light right into it, burning a spot that would persist for a week after the show![89]

WUHF broke with the NAB Television Code when it accepted liquor advertisements.

The Dr. Bop show also became the first in the city to have a unique (for the time) sponsor. George Liberatore:

> The National Association of Broadcasters had a Code of Ethics that told you, among other things, what you could and could not advertise. One of them was liquor. Given the financial situation the station was in, we didn't really care about that code, because one of the things it did was to restrict your revenue stream.

So, *our sales staff got a hold of a liquor store, Keller's Beverage Center, that wanted to be on TV. They were happy, as they couldn't get on previously. We did a couple of spots, and they were very successful. We sold a lot of whisky on the Dr. Bop show! We also ran spots on some of our more upscale shows, featuring a wine, or whatever they had that was special.*[90]

The last Dr. Bop show was on April 10, 1966.

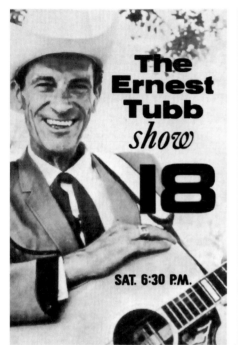

During the ownership transition, ads showed no call letters. (Courtesy of Hal Erickson)

At the time of the sale to Oklahoma Publishing, the station's operations, program, and promotions departments were still located in a suite in the Sheraton-Schroeder Hotel. Standing at the left is new production manager Dave Togie, who came from WTVT in Tampa. Standing at the rear is promotion assistant Adrienne Alm. Seated at the center desk is Chuck Olson, who was the station's manager at the time of the sale. (WVTV photo)

The station was still not making money. The Oklahoma Publishing Co. operated radio and television stations under its WKY Television subsidiary. They saw an opportunity for the little station, and purchased it on November 8, 1965. The new owners promised to expand the station's operations, and double the staff.[91]

While awaiting FCC approval of the sale, the station was like a lame duck. George Liberatore:

> *To save money, we had like six movies that we ran every night at ten o'clock. They would rotate and you would really get tired of them. One of them had aerial dogfights in it. So the audio guy would occasionally get a sound effects record and insert a couple of extra shots into the film while it was on the air – just so you wouldn't get so bored watching it!*[92]

The FCC approved the sale on March 24, 1966. The final sale price was $550,000. The officers of WXIX, Inc. were also paid $150,000 for agreeing not to operate another TV station within 75 miles of the station's transmitter.[93] Oklahoma Publishing took over operations on April 1.

Besides WKY radio and WKY-TV in Oklahoma City, the new owners, also owned WTVT in Tampa-St. Petersburg, KTVT in Dallas-Fort Worth, and KHTV in Houston. Since most of its stations had "TV" in their call letters, they applied to the FCC for permission to change WUHF to WVTV. The change was made on June 7, 1966.

Joe Loughlin joined the station as administrative assistant to Station Manager John Haberlan and later served as GM from 1968-1981. He remembered that a famous visitor was not impressed with the studio facility atop the hotel:

(Courtesy of WVTV)

WVTV received its new remote truck in time to cover the Schlitz Circus Parade on July 4, 1966. The station used four cameras with the truck: two at and two above ground level. A fifth camera was located atop the Sheraton-Schroeder Hotel, and was equipped with a long telephoto lens that sister station WTVT used to track launches from Cape Kennedy. The parade was covered live, and replayed on videotape in prime time the following evening. (WVTV photo)

Robert Kennedy was up there one time to be interviewed. He looked at the studio and said: 'You've got to be kidding!'[94]

WKY also began a massive investment in the station's plant and equipment. A remote truck with three monochrome cameras and a transistorized video tape recorder was ordered, as were three monochrome studio cameras, two color film chains, and two new studio videotape recorders with electronic editors.[95] They also purchased a building at 4041 N 35th Street, which they planned on remodeling for new offices and studios.[96] AT&T prepared microwave facilities so that programs originating in the new building could be sent to the transmitter atop the hotel.[97]

That wasn't all they invested in. George Liberatore:

> *When they came in, they brought professionals. Their station in Tampa was a CBS affiliate that was wildly successful. They brought in Ed Herbert and Joe Loughlin, who had been with CBS News in New York. So we got some really top-notch people.*
>
> *I think they knew when they came in that the transition would be difficult, but I don't think they fully understood how difficult it would be. The first thing they had to bring in was a sales staff that really knew how to sell a television station. Also, they had to promote the station. They brought in Jayne Boyd as the program director, and she started to buy programs like syndicated shows and decent movies. It was all based — as all successful independents were at the time — on counter-programming. We really concentrated on the times when our competition had their local news shows, and ran our most powerful syndicated shows against them so that people had an entertainment alternative.*[98]

Joe Loughlin:

> *When we took over our sign-on to sign-off share was two percent. We thought we had to get up to around ten percent to make the station economically viable. The first two years was like ten years of college education under John Haberlan. He had been sales manager at the Tampa station [WTVT, also owned by WKY]. John was just a very smart guy and a real leader. He assembled a really good group of people. In fact, our first program director was a gal named Jayne Boyd. As far as I know she was the first female program director of any major market television station in the United States.*
>
> *John started what we call the 'building block' theory, which in those days was radical, 'though it's routine now: Go for kids in the afternoon. Go for young adults in early fringe (5 – 6:30 pm) with situation comedies, and then movies during prime time.*
>
> *The station had such a terrible reputation, and we had a signal problem because of the location of our antenna. We really had a metro signal for the first few years. It was a long and difficult process of putting the right program mix together, buying things at the right price, and then learning how to promote it and make ourselves known.*[99]

Years later, Loughlin was questioned by a reporter about the station's turnaround. He remembered:

The tower atop the Sheraton-Schroeder Hotel was lit in July of 1966. (Milwaukee Journal photo, ©2008 Journal Sentinel, Inc., reproduced with permission.)

In 1967, WVTV carried both Chicago Cubs and Minnesota Twins baseball games. (Courtesy of Hal Erickson)

> MON. TWINS vs ORIOLES 7pm
> TUE. CUBS vs PIRATES 7pm
> WED. TWINS vs TIGERS 8pm
> in color/live
> WVTV 18 MILWAUKEE
> your major league station

As an independent station, high school and college sports made up a big part of WVTV's programming. (Courtesy of Hal Erickson)

> FRIDAY 7:30
> (DEBUT) AL MC GUIRE SHOW
> 8:00 LIVE
> KING VS LINCOLN 66 CHAMPS
> GREAT FOR SPORTS AND GROWING GREATER CHANNEL 18

He said: 'So you had to crawl before you walked?' I said, 'No, first we had to dig it up and stick electrodes in its neck. THEN we crawled. Later, we walked!'[100]

The tower got a facelift in early July when it received a new coat of paint, but that wasn't all. In 1964, WITI-TV had installed lights on its 1,078 foot self-supporting tower. WVTV did the same, and installed 326, 125-watt light bulbs. Automatic controls turned the lights on at dusk, and off at dawn. The station's promotions director stated that the tower could be seen from forty-four miles away at night![101] The lights would prove problematic, however. Dennis Brechlin began with the station as an engineer in 1962, eventually becoming chief engineer. He remembered:

> Winter was always hard on the bulbs. The fixtures were mounted along the outside faces of the tower legs and the bulbs were installed in the sockets without any enclosure around them. When ice would fall from the tower, the tendency was for it to slide along the legs for a distance which would sometimes wipe out 20 to 30 lamps in a row. It didn't take long for the tower to have numerous lamps out and in the winter, they usually could not be replaced immediately due to weather conditions and ice accumulation on the tower legs."[102]

The station hoped to erect a new 1,000 foot tower, and considered a number of different locations. They even considered mounting their antenna on a competitor's tower.

Joe Loughlin:

> We knew that we had a problem with the tower. John [Haberlan] was still the GM, and he talked to WTMJ-TV about sharing space on their tower. They were all in favor of it, but they said that they had to do an engineering survey that we would have to pay for. We were fine with that.
>
> Everything was going fine. Then some 'genius' at WTMJ-TV decided that what they would do was put a syndicated show on instead of some new show from the network that they thought would be a flop. It was called 'Laugh-In'!
>
> So we cleared it. Along came our first rating book, and there in a sea of ones was an eleven rating. That was the end of our space on the 'TMJ tower![103]

It would be fourteen years before the station would get a new tower.

By March of 1967, the WVTV reported that it had a net weekly circulation of 152,000 homes – an increase of sixty-three percent over a year earlier. That same year, it applied to the FCC for permission to increase its power to 1,892,000 watts. That made it the most powerful station in the state, with coverage from Sheboygan to the north to Waukegan, Illinois to the south. Baseball had left Milwaukee with the Braves after the 1965 season, but residents longed for it. WVTV carried fifteen Chicago Cubs games start-

CHAPTER 5 ~ WOKY-TV/WXIX/WUHF/WVTV: CHANNELS 19 & 18   185

The new 35th Street Building included a microwave tower similar to that at WTVT in Tampa. The station's calls were mounted on it in six foot-high letters, which were lit at night. (WVTV photo)

ing on Sunday, May 7.[104] It also carried Minnesota Twins' games, and a July 2 game against the Chicago White Sox generated higher ratings than Milwaukee's network affiliates.[105]

THE BOWLING SHOWS

Bowling shows had been a regular feature on Milwaukee TV since the 1950s. By 1967, one survived: "Bowling with the Champs" on WTMJ-TV. That show featured professional and semi-professional bowlers.

In 1967, WVTV returned to a format that was seen on early bowling shows: matches by amateurs. "Kings and Queens Bowling" was the idea of Carol Herbert, whose husband, Ed, was the station's news director. It featured average bowlers – male and female. Representatives from forty different lanes competed each week, and the top four were selected for the show, which was taped at a different lane each week, and aired at 6:30 p.m. Sundays. In June, the weekly winners competed for the top prizes: two color TVs. The show was hosted by popular WRIT DJ Lee Rothman, with color commentary by the executive secretary of the Bowling Proprietors Association of Milwaukee, Peter Pugal.[106] The show ran through January 21, 1968.

"Bowling for Dollars" was a franchised program offered to local markets. On May 4, 1970, the FCC issued a Report and Order on Network Television in which it promulgated a prime time access rule. As a consequence, in 1971, the FCC opened up the 6:30 p.m. time slot for local stations to fill, and WVTV elected to run the show. It was built around the idea of having a local bowler compete for a cash prize. Viewers could send in postcards, and if they were selected in a random drawing by the bowler, they became their "pin pal," and shared in the prize. Local TV veteran Dick Johnson hosted the show, which was taped at the Red Carpet Lanes - North. It first ran on Monday, September 13, 1971, and ended its run on March 15, 1974.

Dick Johnson welcomes a contestant on "Bowling for Dollars." (WVTV photo)

Rather than continue with the franchise, WVTV elected to run its own show, "The Bowling Game" from 7:00-8:00 p.m., beginning on Monday, August 26, 1974. The show was taped at the Red Carpet Regency Lanes, and Johnson continued as the host. Joe Loughlin:

> 'Bowling for Dollars' didn't work for us. It was too expensive. It was ok, but it didn't hit a homerun. Another guy at Gaylord Broadcasting, Crawford Rice, came up with the idea at one of our regular programming meetings. He said: 'Why don't you just do four frames of a regular bowling game?'
>
> Bill Franks was our program director at the time, so I said: 'Bill, you know bowling. Let's do it!'
>
> Back in those days, the Journal Co. did an annual survey of the Milwaukee market. Their survey said that the number one form of winter entertainment for men and women, 18-49 was watching television. The second was bowling. Well, you didn't have to be a genius to figure out that if you put the two together, that would work in Milwaukee.[107]

On October 13, 1975, Johnson was involved in a traffic accident in which two women were killed. He was convicted of two counts of homicide by intoxicated use of a motor vehicle.[108] As a consequence, he lost his job at WVTV. As his replacement, the station again turned to Lee Rothman, who had served as Johnson's substitute. Rothman was joined by color commentator Tom Kohl.

Like its predecessor, the show allowed viewers the opportunity to share in the prizes, by becoming what were now called "bowling buddies." The bowlers also had a "secret frame," in which they could win another prize if they rolled a strike.

CHAPTER 5 ~ WOKY-TV/WXIX/WUHF/WVTV: CHANNELS 19 & 18

"The Bowling Game" proved to be immensely popular. In 1985, station management called the show its "biggest merchandiser." At one point, it drew a fifteen share. Joe Loughlin:

> *It took about two years for the show to take hold, but once it did the thing was very strong. Charlie Edwards, our sales manager, said: 'Don't fool with the Bowling Game! That's my news department.' It was a great success! As far as I know it was the only regularly scheduled prime time local show on any television station in the country.*[109]

Lee Rothman (L) and Tom Kohl hosted "The Bowling Game." (WVTV photo)

After an eleven and one-half year run, the show drew only a five share. Its demographic was said to be age 65+, and as such, the station no longer felt that it was an appropriate lead-in for its 8:00 p.m. movie.[110] The last show was on Friday, January 2, 1987. It would later be picked up by WDJT-TV. (See chapter 12.)

On October 5, 1975, WVTV started yet another bowling show: "Pins Over." The show differed from "The Bowling Game" in that it was a tournament in which league bowlers from around the area were invited to compete. The show ran at noon on Sundays, and ended on May 6, 1976.

After dropping "The Bowling Game," the station started a new show, "Alley 18," which like its predecessors featured local bowlers, who competed for prizes. The new hosts were Tom Luczak, a DJ at WKLH-FM and Playboy model Sharon Kay, a student at the University of Wisconsin – Whitewater. The show made its debut at 9:00 p.m. on Saturday, February 14, 1987.[111] It was ill-conceived, and was not accepted by local bowlers. It ended on March 21 after only six weeks.

On Monday, June 3, 1968, WVTV began signing on at noon. A week later, it began broadcasting at 1,892,000 watts of power, and formally became the most powerful TV station in the state.[112] It was quite a change from the early days of UHF!

The station prided itself on counter-programming against its network-affiliate competition. Up against a drama, it might run a romance. Against a situation comedy, it might run a police drama. Over the years on Saturday nights it might run the country music shows: *Ernest Tubb*, *Bill Anderson*, *The Stoneman Family*, *Porter Wagoner*, or *The Grand Ole Opry*. Irv Kupcinet's *Kup's Show* ran Saturday nights for many years, and was eventually cut down from three hours to ninety minutes and moved to Sunday nights. Weekdays, the station ran various syndicated shows against local news programs – often leading the time slot. It also ran a variety of sports programming.

(Courtesy of Hal Erickson)

CHAPTER 5 ~ WOKY-TV/WXIX/WUHF/WVTV: CHANNELS 19 & 18

A shot of the control room in the new building on North 35 Street during a live telecast of "Romper Room." (WVTV photo)

"UWM NEWS FOCUS"

On March 31, 1969, WVTV began a long relationship with the University of Wisconsin – Milwaukee when a new news show made its debut at 11:30 a.m. – right after the station signed on, and before "Romper Room." The show was called "UWM News Focus."

It was the brainchild of nineteen year-old Scott Shuster, a junior majoring in journalism at UWM. As "Scott Davis," Shuster had started as a disk jockey at Gene Posner's WMIL at age fifteen after he had come to the station to play the banjo on a country music show a few times. At sixteen, he moved to WRIT to become a newscaster, where he was still working while going to UWM. It was during a broadcasting law class with lecturer Jay Sykes that Shuster got his inspiration:

Thomas Jones (left) and Scott Shuster on the set of "UWM News Focus." (WVTV photo)

We were studying broadcast law. At that time before President Reagan changed things, there was a requirement that broadcasting stations had to devote a certain percentage of their time on-the-air to news and public affairs. As I recall, I realized right then and there in the class that WVTV could not be in compliance with that requirement.

So I went to Professor Sykes and said, 'Look, they're in violation of the law!' I was really, really excited about it! I said, 'Why don't we go to them and tell them that we can make them legal! We can bring them within the bounds of this law – if they'll put us on the air!'

Jay looked at me seriously and said, 'That's a really terrific idea. Go ahead; make it happen.'

My immediate reaction was, 'Me? I have to do it?' I was really young.

So I made a call to the station and talked with Jayne Boyd. Jayne was extremely kind to me on the phone and arranged a meeting with Operations Manager Ed Herbert. He saw the potential in News Focus right away, but it was kind of funny how it actually started.

I came in for the appointment that Jayne arranged, and was ushered into Ed's office. He heard me out, and then said, 'First of all, you're wrong. Sports counts as news, and we carry Chicago White Sox games, which puts us way over the limit of that requirement.'

I was crestfallen, until Ed said, 'But I love the idea; let's see if we can do it"

Triumphantly, I drove down Capitol Drive, back to UWM, and reported what had happened to Professor Sykes.[113]

CHAPTER 5 ~ WOKY-TV/WXIX/WUHF/WVTV: CHANNELS 19 & 18

Sykes met with Dr. Ruane Hill, of the Mass Communications Department at UWM. The two of them then met with Joe Loughlin and finalized the arrangement. Loughlin remembered:

> "I think when Scott and Ed Herbert were talking; Scott may have confused news and public affairs. Back in those days, each station, as part of its license application – or license transfer in the case of WVTV – submitted a proposed public service/public affairs schedule to the FCC. If the Commission okayed it, those were the standards you had to hit, NOT – standards proposed by the FCC.
>
> Part of our public affairs commitment came in a couple of thirty-minute public affairs shows which Ed Herbert and/or I hosted, and, later, Jim Peck. We also, in the early days, did a series of "Minute Memos," in which we invited local community leaders we'd interviewed as part of the license transfer process, to talk about whatever they perceived as community problems and potential answers. We'd tape them and run them as a spot schedule throughout the broadcast day.[114]
>
> It [the idea for "News Focus"] was a combination of Ruane Hill and our operations manager, Ed Herbert. The two of them cooked it up and came to me with the idea. I said: 'Let's try it. We'll give it thirteen weeks'. It took off and stayed there.
>
> A lot of good people came through that program. One of the other great things that came out of it was the number of them who said: 'You know, I thought I wanted to be in television news. I didn't realize how hard it was. I don't want any part of that!' I figure that saved these kids years of working in the vineyard, and finding out that they hated it.
>
> I decreed that there would be no commercials in it, only public service announcements, because those students were working gratis.[115]

Jay Sykes assigned Shuster to go ahead and launch the show. He recalled:

> I didn't quite know what to do – although I had been doing news on WRIT radio since I was sixteen. I knew how to rip and rewrite, do man-in-the-streets for radio, and get news out of the police to create a newscast, but I'd never done television. That, of course, was the point: Real, on-air TV experience for UWM students. It was a spectacular learning opportunity[116]

Jay Sykes also assigned a few other students to create the show with Shuster: John Severson, Thomas Jones, and a young woman were the start-up team.

Shuster was the principal anchorman, while Severson was named news director. Tom Jones and the young woman were the first to join Shuster on camera for the show. The students prepared the entire newscast, but because of the station's union contracts, were not able to serve as cameramen or in other operational positions. At first, the team decided not to use any police or fire news – and no sports. Emphasis was placed on national and international news.[117] Scott Shuster:

> ...this, of course, is what we could get from the UPI machine. It was not fancy at the start...but that was just the start – and it was a great start for us.[118]

After WVTV cancelled its 10:00 p.m. news in 1972, "UWM News Focus" became its sign-off newscast. It remained on the air for many, many years thereafter.

Joe Loughlin was a member of Variety, and was the chief barker for one term. He had the idea of doing a fund raiser on the station. Beginning in 1970, The Variety Club of Wisconsin began hosting telethons on WVTV to support the epilepsy

Gathered together at the end of the 1971 Variety Club Telethon are L-R: The Steve Swedish Orchestra, Jack Lee, Bob Crane, Angela Cartwright, Ronald McDonald, Lee Rothman and Karen Caldwell of Talent Central, who coordinated the talent. Behind Rothman is "Farmer Vic" (Hellman). Next to him (at rear) is Roy Schroeder, the Variety Club's executive director. Holding the microphone at the far right is Ralph Barnes. In the foreground at the right is Robert Clary. (Milwaukee Journal photo, ©2008 Journal Sentinel, Inc., reproduced with permission.)

clinic at Mt. Sinai Hospital. Over the years, a variety of visiting celebrities, including Angela Cartwright, Robert Clary, Bob Crane, Arte Johnson, Maureen McCormick, Barbara McNair and others, along with local celebrities including the Steve Swedish Orchestra and Berkley Fudge, joined together to raise money for the charity.

WUHF had begun carrying Verne Gagne's *All-Star Wrestling* in 1966, and it became very popular. Local professional wrestler Reggie "Da Crusher" Lisowski made appearances, and danced to the polka music of "Concertina Millie" (Kaminski). Veteran TV and radio personality Lee Rothman told the *Milwaukee Journal* that Lisowski raised $7,000-8,000 while he was there.[119] In 1975, Henry Winkler, who played "Arthur Fonzerelli – the Fonz," on ABC's *Happy Days* appeared, and caused such a commotion that he had to be escorted from the Mayfair Mall Ice Chalet location ninety minutes early![120]

Jack Lee had done television early in his career, but was better known in Milwaukee for his radio work on a number of stations. He was often called upon to help:

> Joe Loughlin was the general manager of the station. I was on the Variety Club board, as was Aye Jaye, who was the original Ronald McDonald.
>
> Some local talent agencies volunteered to produce the talent and decide who was on at what time. For about five or six of the telethons, I acted as an off-camera floor director in addition to WVTV's personnel. I lined up the visiting national stars, briefed them as to what they were going to say, and if they needed a script or forgot what city they were in [laughs] always had a suit on, so I could go on-camera with them as the token board member who could explain some of our history and get them out of a bind.
>
> Some of the talent – people like Arte Johnson – did very well. Some of the new people like Henry Winkler, who'd never done a telethon before, or Bob Crane from Hogan's Heroes, were uncomfortable carrying a show, other than

just waving at people and asking them to send their money in. I think we had the misconception that we could just hand them a mic and tell them to fill the next three hours by holding up a cue card telling them who was going to come on next so that they could introduce them.

Most of the big stars didn't really want to be on the air in Milwaukee at 2:00 a.m., so come around 12:30, they would head to their hotel, freshen-up and get some sleep before the big Sunday morning push. So after that, Aye Jaye and I would run the telethon. We didn't have a lot of acts that late at night, but we had to ad lib and introduce pre-recorded clips that were recorded earlier. Most of the staff had gone home, so we would have to direct. I really enjoyed that, as it reminded me of my days doing a live kids' show early in my career."[121]

The telethons proved to be very successful. Joe Loughlin remembered:

I remember the first year we had a fishbowl where people could come in and dump nickels, dimes and dollars. At the end of the day we had $20,000 in cash in that thing! It was an incredible turnout. We had a lot of fun doing it![122]

Tom Lueders (bottom – news), Judy Marks (weather), and Ted Moore (sports) hosted the short-lived 10:00 p.m. news on WVTV in 1971-72. (WVTV photo)

The last telethon was held in 1976.

WVTV executives Ed Herbert and Joe Loughlin had both worked at CBS News. National advertisers were always looking for news ratings. So, on September 6, 1971, the station started a 10:00 p.m. newscast. It turned to three WTMJ-TV alumni: Tom Lueders (News), Judy Marks (Weather), and Ted Moore (Sports). Marks came full-circle, as she began her TV career at WOKY-TV in 1953. The station had no news gathering staff, so the three were limited to a 15-minute "rip-

and-read" format. The show didn't do well, and only ran through March 31, 1972. It was replaced with "UWM News Focus." Joe Loughlin:

> What we called it internally was the 'no bullshit news'. I wish we could've promoted it that way, because that's precisely what it was. The concept was that if you wanted to find out what happened today – minus the commercials and the feature stories and the weather in Timbuktu – this is the place to do it. With those three people fronting it, the credibility was automatically there.
>
> It didn't work. We couldn't get the commercial support for it that we thought we could. It was too radical an idea. It would probably work today![123]

The station was still not turning a profit, and as a result, some changes were made in January of 1972 in order to cut costs. They included the shifting the weekday sign-on to 1:45 p.m. from 7:00 a.m., which resulted in the elimination or moving of a number of programs. Several staffers were also laid off.[124] That year was not profitable, but 1973 was.[125]

Throughout the 1970s, WVTV continued to grow. By the end of the decade, it had established itself as one of the top independent stations in the country. Its policy of counter-programming against its competition paid off. It also continued to clear network programs that the local affiliates chose to drop. Joe Loughlin:

> The big turnaround year was 1976. That was a presidential election year, and there was too much money chasing too few commercial spots. So, a lot of advertisers, who would never touch independent, UHF stations, had to in order to meet their rating goals. 'Lo and behold they found that what we had been telling them for years and years was true – that it worked! We really started to fly from around 1976 on, but it was a long struggle getting there. Once we made our mark, we were always in the top four independent stations in the country in terms of audience share – particularly prime time share.[126]

During that period, the radio and TV holdings of the Oklahoma Publishing Co. were consolidated as a subsidiary: Gaylord Broadcasting.

For the 1977 season, WVTV won the right to broadcast Milwaukee Bucks' games.[127]

At the time of the purchase in 1966, the new owners began a search for a new tower location. Although they had become the most powerful station in the state back in 1968, the old tower atop what was now the Marc Plaza Hotel was limiting. WMVS/WMVT faced a similar challenge. New tower rules meant that the WITI-TV tower their antennas were mounted on was overloaded, and they were also looking for a new location. They had acquired property in the "blue hole" section of the city, just north of East Capitol Drive and just west of the Milwaukee River, which was near the WTMJ-TV and WITI-TV towers.

On December 27, 1979, Gaylord broadcasting and the Milwaukee District Board of Vocational, Technical, and Adult Education (MATC), the licensee of the city's two public television stations, announced that they had entered into a unique public-private partnership, in which WVTV would erect a 1,100' guyed tower and construct a new transmitter building on the land owned by MATC. In exchange for the use of the land, WMVS/WMVT would be able to mount their antennas on the new tower, and relocate their transmitters to the new building.[128]

The new facilities went into operation in 1981.[129] The investment gave the station a coverage area that was competitive with its VHF competitors. The Milwaukee Brewers were looking for a way to expand the number of games broadcast in the city. WTMJ-TV had been broadcasting about forty games a season – a limit imposed by their network programming. With its expanded coverage area, WVTV

was able to win the rights to broadcast the Brewers' games beginning with the 1981 season. At first the decision almost backfired, as a baseball strike halted all play for a time. The station only lost eight of its sixty games, but had to scramble to fill unsold time after play resumed.[130]

In 1963, the station experimented with showing films with "mature" themes on its "Award Theater." On Friday, January 9, 1987, it elected to run uncut "R" rated films at 11:30 p.m.[131] The public's reaction was negative, and the experiment was short-lived. Viewers who tuned in to see the R-rated *My Tutor* on February 13 found that it had been replaced with *Pirates of Penzance* at the last minute.[132]

In 1988, WCGV-TV outbid WVTV for the rights to show both Milwaukee Bucks and Brewers games.

WVTV quit offering a locally-produced newscast in 1972. On Monday, August 22, 1988, it started another. Called the "Nine O'Clock Nightly News," the new show featured co-anchors Liz Talbot and Duane Gay, weatherman Marlon McGhee, and sports director Bob Bach. In 1971, the newscast suffered from the lack of reporting team, and the new show suffered from the same handicap. Instead it emphasized national news, with footage provided by the INDEX News Service from WPIX-TV in New York. The on-air team tried to provide a local slant on those national stories.[133] Bob Bach remembered the start:

> *It was such a humble beginning! The news department was to occupy a space that had been a sales office. It was like Household Finance in the 1950s. It had the wavy glass partitions between the offices, and cubicles that were used by the sales department.*
>
> *So, until the news department was remodeled, Duane, Liz and I shared a table, which was maybe six feet long by three feet wide. There were three computer terminals there. Marlon McGhee was about three feet behind us on a card table. That was the weather office! There was one cameraman who shot primarily for news. If he had some extra time – which there never was – he might get some sort of sports coverage.*
>
> *For about three nights before we started we had rehearsals. There was a sixty-second open to the newscast. It took three and one-half hours to produce the sixty-second open. There were that many false starts and mistakes. I was doing the math and saying to myself: 'If it takes you three and one-half hours to do a one-minute open, this doesn't look good!'"*[134]

The following year, the show was expanded to an hour, as the station developed a limited local reporting capability. They also purchased state-of-the-art script writing software that was eventually adopted by other local stations.

Bob Bach remembered that Gay and Talbot were often at odds – but in a respectful way:

> *I think when they hired Duane Gay they got some of the edginess that they were looking for. Liz was an attractive woman, who was a skillful news reporter, but didn't have the harder edge that Duane did when it came to [asking] what was news, what was newsworthy, and what are trends. Duane had this kind of blank canvas on which to work his news magic and together with Liz it was a very successful tandem.*
>
> *They were kind of a 'point – counterpoint', and would get into arguments – heated discussions – about news coverage of various events almost every day when they were assembling the newscast. You'd hear the first distant salvos about ten after five. By seven it was point blank! They were just blasting each other! By that time, they had cheering sections. You'd have the producer on*

The "Nine O'Clock Nightly News" team L-R: Bob Bach, Mike Hegan, Duane Gay, Liz Talbot, and Marlon McGhee. (WVTV photo)

Duane's side, and the director would be on Liz's side. Marlon would lob in a few things, because he was extremely well-read.

I didn't know how they were going to get that script done, but they eventually did – even though there were some nights, when I swear, Duane was still putting his make-up on during the open! Then he'd look calm, and cool and ready to go!"

I think that it was Duane's personality to be assertive with his points of view, and to practice his communications skills on other people by trying to make his point. Liz had opinions of her own, and for the most part enjoyed the give-and-take. It drove her a little crazy once and awhile because as they got closer and closer to deadline, she began to worry. Like me, Liz liked to have things ready to go ahead of time with a little padding, while Duane – and there are a lot of those people in broadcasting – worked best when he was under time-pressure.[135]

Bach took a medical leave of absence in June of 1989, and was temporarily replaced as sports anchor by Dwayne Mosley. Former Milwaukee Brewer, Mike Hegan took over the position in August[136], after Bach requested that he be shifted from anchoring to reporting. By September of 1991, the news staff had grown to twenty-four full-time and three part-time employees.[137] The ratings, while not high enough to challenge the city's three network affiliates' newscasts, were steadily improving.

That same year, Gaylord Broadcasting was combined with some of the parent corporation's other holdings, including the Grand Ole Opry and The Nashville Network, into the Gaylord Entertainment Co.[138]

Deregulation of broadcasting had begun during the 1980s, and continued into the following decade. By January of 1993, the FCC was considering a change to its multiple-ownership rules that would allow a single entity to own more than one broadcast outlet in a single market. As a result, ABRY Communications, who owned Fox affiliate WCGV-TV at the time, entered into a lease management agreement (LMA) with Gaylord Broadcasting in which they agreed to provide the promotion, billing, production, and other administrative functions for WVTV. In return, ABRY received an option to purchase the station, if the Commission relaxed its rules.[139] ABRY took over operations in March.

As a consequence, on February 26, all seventy-five WVTV employees were told that their jobs were to be terminated, but that some might be rehired as needed. Because it had a stronger signal, Milwaukee Brewers' games were to be moved to WVTV. Since those games, and other sports broadcasts would often air between 9:00 and 10:00 p.m., the station dropped its "Nine O'Clock Nightly News." The last show was on Friday, March 12, 1993, and all members of the news staff were let go as of March 15.[140]

The timing of the LMA was interesting. ABRY Communications was negotiating the sale of WCGV-TV to the Sinclair Broadcast Group of Baltimore. The sale was later consummated, and approved by the FCC, and Sinclair took over on May 25, 1994.[141] As a part of the sale, Sinclair received the LMA for, as well as the option to purchase WVTV. In August, ABRY announced that Eddie Edwards, Sr., the owner of Glencairn Broadcasting, had agreed to purchase its option on WVTV. Edwards had been the general manager of WPTT in Pittsburgh, which was owned by the Sinclair Broadcast Group. Sinclair also owned WPGH in the same city, and sold WPTT to Glencairn – financing the purchase.[142] As a part of the deal, Glencairn also agreed to buy Baltimore station WNUV-TV from ABRY.

Scripps Howard Broadcasting, the owner of WMAR-TV in Baltimore, filed an objection to the sale of WNUV-TV with the FCC, and as a consequence, Glencairn – for the time – withdrew both its application to acquire the Baltimore station and its offer to purchase the option on WVTV.[143]

On July 26, Paramount Communications, Inc. announced that WVTV would join its new United Paramount Network. At the same time, four other stations – all associated with Sinclair – also signed affiliation agreements.[144]

In October, Sinclair confirmed that it had assigned its option to purchase WVTV to Glencairn, fueling speculation that CBS might affiliate with that station.[145] Opposition to the sale was again expressed by Scripps Howard, with the contention that Sinclair had *de facto* control over Glencairn, and that it would violate the FCC's rules against one entity owning more than one station in a single market.[146]

As a consequence, Sinclair decided to affiliate WCGV-TV with UPN, rather than WVTV, and programming began on Monday, January 16, 1995.[147] No Milwaukee station chose to affiliate with the new Warner Bros. Network (WB), which also started in January of 1995.

Despite the objections, the FCC approved the sale of WVTV to Glencairn on June 20, 1995, and the sale was consummated on July 24. Glencairn then entered into an LMA with Sinclair for WVTV.

Since Gene Posner and WXIX, Inc. purchased the station in 1959, the station had no network affiliation. Under Gaylord's ownership, it had become one of the top independent stations in the in the country. That all changed on Sunday, March 2, 1997, when WVTV became a WB affiliate.[148]

With the passage of the Telecommunications Act of 1996, the FCC began to relax its multiple-ownership rules, and as a result, consolidation through merger began to take place in the industry. In 1999, the Commission lifted its restriction against an entity owning more than one station in a given market, and in November,

Sinclair filed applications with the FCC to acquire WVTV and four other stations from Glencairn.¹⁴⁹

However, the sale was opposed by Jesse Jackson's Rainbow/PUSH Coalition, which contended that minority-controlled Glencairn was a front for Sinclair. Glencairn had restructured itself to give Edwards 100 percent of the voting stock – despite the fact that he only owned three percent of the common stock. The balance was owned by Carolyn Smith, the mother of Sinclair's CEO David Smith and a trust for her grandchildren.¹⁵⁰ Edwards denied the allegations.

In December of 2001, the FCC finally approved the sale of WVTV to the Sinclair Broadcast Group.¹⁵¹

WVTV ran a 9:00 p.m. newscast between 1988 and 1993. While it had grown steadily in the ratings, it never really challenged the city's network affiliates. On Monday, August 11, 2003, the station began running yet another hour-long, 9:00 p.m. newscast. Called "WB 18 News at Nine," the national news and commentary were picked up from Sinclair's News Central in Baltimore, whose stations had all started similar newscasts. All featured a local anchor, who would segue to the Sinclair feed, and report local news. WVTV's was Lisa Fielding.¹⁵² Tammie Hughes later replaced Fielding. WVTV's version never made a dent in the ratings, and the show was cut to thirty minutes on Monday, August 22, 2005.

By January of 2006, Sinclair stations around the country were opting to shut down their news operations. Some entered into agreements with other stations to produce their newscasts.¹⁵³ WVTV followed suit, and the last "WB 18 News at

Lisa Fielding was the first anchor of "WB 18 News at Nine." (WVTV screen grab)

Nine" ran on Friday, March 31, 2006.¹⁵⁴

On January 24, 2006, CBS (which now owned UPN), and Warner Bros. Entertainment (by then a division of Time-Warner), jointly announced that UPN and WB would merge to become a new network called CW. The move caught observers

by surprise. Since Sinclair owned the two local stations affiliated with the two networks, it had to decide which, if any, would affiliate with the new network.[155]

By early March, Sinclair announced that WCGV-TV would affiliate with the new MyNetwork TV, which Fox decided to launch in the fall of that year.[156] That meant that WVTV would become the CW affiliate, and that affiliation began on Monday, September 18, 2006.

After beginning as a network affiliate and then a CBS-owned station in the early days of UHF broadcasting, the station endured a period of very slow growth as a locally-owned independent. The injection of capital and expertise by Oklahoma Publishing helped it become the state's most powerful television station for a time, as well as one of the country's strongest independents. It then became the city's first commercial duopoly, and has once again become a network affiliate. The digital television transition will test the staying power of stations like WVTV. It has risen to challenges before; will it do so now?

THE CHILDREN'S SHOWS

Jerry Bartell had started "Playtime for Children" while at WHA. The thirty minute program featured stories for children. He later recorded the series, and ran them on the stations owned by Bartell Broadcasters. The show was quite successful, and won a number of awards from the Milwaukee County Radio and Television Council.

(Dick Golembiewski collection; photo therein Jane Bartell)

In 1952, he produced thirteen stories as a film series, each fifteen minutes long. It was syndicated as "Jerry Bartell's Playtime," and played on stations around the country. Bartell then brought the show to WOKY-TV. It took place before a live studio audience.

Westerns were the rage in the 1950s, and WOKY-TV jumped on the bandwagon. Cliff Robedeaux had played "Foreman Tom" on WTMJ-TV since 1951. To counter him, WOKY-TV turned to a twenty year-old Marquette University student, Pat Buckett. Buckett had become interested in Native American culture while a high school student. W. Ben Hunt of Hales Corners was a writer for *Boy's Life* magazine, and had a group of adults called the Mila Scopa (a Sioux word for "crooked knife" which was used for carving wood) Club. The club met monthly to discuss Native American culture. Buckett joined them, and had become an accomplished Native American dancer – in particular the hoop dance.

One of the students in Marquette's School of Speech was working as a floor director at WOKY-TV. He spoke to someone at the station, who in turn asked Buckett to come in for an audition. He was hired, and "Chief White Buck" was born.

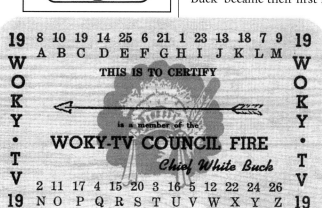

(Courtesy of Pat Buckett)

The first show was on January 4, 1954. All of the shows were done live. On the show, a western film would be run – stretched out over several days. To fill the rest of the time (The station had only one film chain.), Buckett would show his viewers various elements of Native American culture, including how to sew moccasins, do beadwork, and dance. He was also given quite an honor, by being adopted as a son of "Gogeweosh" and made an honorary member of the Bad River Ojibwe tribe. The adoption ceremony was performed live on the "Chief White Buck" show. Pat Buckett:

> Gogeweosh was an important member of the Ojibwe (Chippewa) tribe. He was originally from the Bad River Reservation at Odanah, Wisconsin. He was not a chief...more like a medicine man, or elder, and was living in Milwaukee. I met him through my affiliation with Ben Hunt and the Mila Scopa group which met monthly at Ben's log cabin in Hales Corners. Gogeweosh, a.k.a. Frank Smart attended many of the Mila Scopa meetings to impart knowledge of the Ojibwe people.[157]

The show's popularity continued to grow, and on April 17, 1954, an hour-long Saturday show, called "Chief White Buck's Council Fires" was added. No film was shown, but rather "Chief White Buck" entertained visiting children's groups – especially scouts – and told stories, interviewed the guests, and demonstrated various aspects of Native American culture. The Saturday show only ran for five weeks, and ended on May 15. The main reason for discontinuing the Saturday show was the lack of room for a live audience in the small studio area. The fact that one of the guests accidentally fell through and ruined the new, very expensive, rear projection screen didn't help![158]

While hosting the show, Buckett convinced Marquette University to change the name of their sports teams from "the Hilltoppers" to "the Warriors." "Chief White Buck" became their first mascot. He was named Milwaukee's 1954 "Local TV Personality Most Worthy of Network Recognition" by *TV Guide*. The daily show ended on June 10, 1954.

Like Buckett, Jack Crowley was a Marquette University student. He wanted to break into television and heard about an opening at WOKY-TV. He was interviewed by Mel Bartell and the station's general manager Don Mann, who hired him as a floor director. Program director Gene Harrison was looking to add more programming, and had purchased a package of Flash Gordon and Buck Rogers serials.[159] The "Chief White Buck" show was successful, and Harrison wanted to do something similar with the space films. The station obtained a cut-away of an F4U Corsair from the Navy, and began auditioning talent to host the films.

Crowley was working as a floor director when the auditions took place. He was not impressed with what he saw:

> So I've got my headset on, and Gene Harrison was on the other end. I had been in a Marine Corps Air Wing before going to Marquette, and I would say to Gene, 'This guy sucks! He doesn't know diddly! This is an actor who's trying to con you!'
> So Harrison finally says to me through the headset, 'Well if you think you're so god damned good, get out there!'
> I did – and I got the job!

Jack Crowley played "Red O'Rourke" on WOKY-TV. (Courtesy of Jack Crowley)

I had lots of red hair back then. I thought Crowley was pretty darned Irish, but they decided to call me 'Red O'Rourke'. I had my blue gabardine flight suit from the Marine Corps, and they added a helmet.

I would sit in that Corsair cutaway and call in to the control tower. Gene Harrison insisted that I say 'WOKY tower' instead of Milwaukee tower. So, I would call in by saying, 'WOKY tower, WOKY tower, this is Red O'Rourke over Franksville marker!'[160]

"Red O'Rourke, Space Adventures" premiered on March 15, 1954, and ran Monday through Friday. Flash Gordon, Buck Rogers, Don Winslow, Red Barry, *Radio Patrol*, *Lost City*, Tim Tyler and Ace Drummond serials were shown.

Crowley found that playing the role had some side benefits. Miller Brewing Co. owner Fred Miller called the station to tell Crowley how much he appreciated how he promoted flying. After Crowley told him how little he made per show, Miller invited him down to the brewery, and Bernie Strachota hired him as a tour guide. Miller also used him to represent the brewery at flying shows at local airports.[161]

Hi Kids!
IT'S SOOOO NICE YOU'RE LOOKING IN!

UNCLE HUGO
AFTER SCHOOL AT 4:00
MONDAY THRU FRIDAY
WOKY-TV
CHANNEL 19

After the sale to CBS, "Red O'Rourke, Space Adventures" was cancelled. The last show was on January 14, 1955. Gene Harrison went to WMTV in Madison, which was also owned by the Bartells, and Crowley went with him.

Racine native Hugh O. Rowlands was Marquette University's first television production instructor. Pat Buckett and Jack Crowley were both Marquette students, and Rowlands decided to audition at WOKY-TV. Program director Gene Harrison finally found a spot for him.

"After School with Hugo" made its debut at 4:00 p.m. on February 8, 1954, and ran Monday through Friday. Rowlands' "Uncle Hugo" character was a janitor, who was harassed by his boss "Oswald," as well as his wife. After a thirteen week run, the last show aired on May 7. Rowlands would later take the show to WTVW (See chapter 6.)

One of the first kids' shows on the CBS-owned WXIX was hosted by Robert March, who played a character named "Captain Jet's Space Funnies." Little Rascals shorts and "Oswald the Rabbit" cartoons were shown. The show ran Monday – Friday at 5:30 p.m. beginning on Monday, March 1, 1955. It was shifted to 4:30 p.m. on Monday, April 27, to 4:15 p.m. a week later and finally to 4:00 p.m. on Monday, September 12. "Captain Jet" made numerous personal appearances[162], and held a contest in which viewers were to make a drawing of what they thought a "Man from Mars" would look like.[163] In September of 1955, the how added a quiz, in which one of the animated cartoons posed a question, and kids called in with their answers.[164] The show's run ended on Friday, April 27, 1956.

When WXIX went back on the air as an independent station on July 20, 1959, it turned to eleven year-old Steve Hildebrandt to play a character named "Cooky." At first, the show ran Monday through Friday from 4:00-5:30 p.m., and was the first show on the reconstituted station. "Cooky" showed Laurel and Hardy comedies, Krazy Kat cartoons, *African Patrol* and Tim McCoy westerns.[165] The show was shifted to 4:30-6:00 p.m. on September 14, as the station picked up the syndicated *Ding Dong School*, which it showed at 4:00 p.m. The last show was on December 25 of that year.

Ward Chase (Wardwell Chase Rosenberg) played a character named "Mac the Mailman" on WITI-TV. On Saturday, October 3, 1959, he moved to WXIX, and hosted the "Scrappy" cartoons and western film beginning at 4:00 p.m.

Chase also served as an announcer, and did short newscasts. On December 28, 1959, he replaced "Cooky" Monday – Friday. The weekly show shifted to 4:00-5:00 p.m. on Monday, August 1, 1961. Over time, George Pal's "Puppetoons," as well as *Cowboy G-Men*, *Sheena: Queen of the Jungle*, *Ramar of the Jungle*, *Jungle Jim*, *Sgt. Preston*, *Western Marshall*, *Three Musketeers*, *Judge Roy Bean*, and *Junior Science* films were added.

"Mac" proved to be very popular. Contests – which were tied in with a sponsor's product – drew thousands of entries. Live segments included such things as "Clean-Up and Pick-Up Time," wherein "Mac" would look through a telescope, and mention the first names

HOWDY BUCKEROOS!

JOIN THE BIG ROUND-UP WITH TRUDY ON

"GOLDEN G. RANCH"
5:00-5:30 P. M. • Saturday
— LEARN HOW TO HELP MOM IN THE KITCHEN

WOKY Channel 19 Milwaukee

After "Chief White Buck's Council Fires" ended on Saturday afternoons, WOKY-TV turned to their cooking expert, Trudy Beilfuss to host a kids' cooking show called "Golden G Ranch." The first show aired on May 22, 1954; the last on February 12, 1955.

of youngsters (often sent in by parents), who had to tidy up their rooms or pick-up toys.

The Saturday show shifted to 3:30 p.m. on October 6, 1962, and then a half hour earlier on December 29. The last Saturday show was on February 13, 1965. The weekday show ended on Friday, July 2, 1965.

Jane Gibbons joined WVTV in the spring of 1968. She hosted "Pick a Pet," which gave children tips on handling animals. She also hosted the station's daily "Kids' Contest."[166]

Both WISN-TV and WITI-TV had carried the franchised "Romper Room" in various formats and time slots from 1955-1965. WISN-TV dropped the show in 1965 because of low ratings.

At noon on Monday, September 1, 1968, WVTV began its own version of the show. It was hosted by Baltimore native "Miss Diane" (Gangler).[167]

At first it ran for thirty minutes, but was expanded to an hour on January 20, 1969. Its starting time was shifted to 11:30 on September 22 of that year, and to 11:00 p.m. on

"Mac the Mailman" presents a certificate of merit to Joanne Seriol "for work published on the Contributors' Pages of Jack and Jill Magazine." The certificate is dated June, 1962. (Courtesy of John & Kathleen Retzlaff; all rights reserved)

WVTV began carrying the syndicated Marvel Superheroes cartoons in 1966. In early 1967, it held a six-week coloring contest for children. In that period, the station received approximately 7,500 entries! Here, Shari Joyce, an administrative assistant in programming, views some of the entries. (WVTV photo)

(Courtesy of Hal Erickson)

CHAPTER 5 ~ WOKY-TV/WXIX/WUHF/WVTV: CHANNELS 19 & 18

January 19, 1970. The following Monday, it was cut from an hour to forty-five minutes.

The show was done live. George Liberatore directed it at times, and remembered:

> Live television was always a challenge – especially when you had kids! You never knew what they were going to say, or what they were going to do. Sometimes they would tell "Miss Diane" that they had to go pee! It was unbelievable, but Diane was a pro. She handled every situation![168]

The last franchised show was on Friday, August 21, 1970. The following Monday, the station dropped "Miss Diane" for the thirty-minute syndicated version out of Baltimore, and shifted the show to 9:00 a.m.. It ran until December 31, 1971. Thereafter, the station decided to end its morning programming, and signed-on at 1:45 p.m. "Romper Room" was one of the shows that was cut.

In August of 1990, WVTV began a hosted block of kids' programming that featured *Super Mario Brothers*, *Merrie Melodies* and *Tiny Toon Adventures*. Rather than broadcast a single show, it tried something different. A set of bumpers and station IDs ran between a series of shows, which was called "Super 18 Superkids Club." Included were educational and informational public service announcements about reading, immunizations, bike safety, health, nutrition, etc.

Amy Hastert

(WVTV photo, courtesy of Amy Hansmann)

As a host, the station turned to a senior at Carroll College majoring in theater arts, Amy Hastert. She was joined by a costumed character, "Dudley the Dragon," which during studio sessions was played by various people at the station who could fit in the costume! For remote events, it was played by John Hattori, the brother-in-law of the station's public relations manager.[169]

"Super 18 Superkids Club" ended in September of 1995, when sister station WCGV-TV began hosting "Take 1." (See chapter 9.)

HORROR MOVIES

After it became an independent station, films made up a big part of the programming. Operations manager Larry Turet came from WITI-TV, where he'd purchased the *Shock!* and *Son of Shock* packages of horror films, and had Bob Hersh host them as "The Advisor." WITI-TV cancelled the shows after affiliating with CBS on April 1, 1959, and Turet later asked Hersh to reprise his role at the newly-independent WXIX. Instead of horror films, Hersh hosted "The Advisor's Mystery Theater," Friday and Saturday nights at 9:30. The shows made their debut on July 24/25, 1959

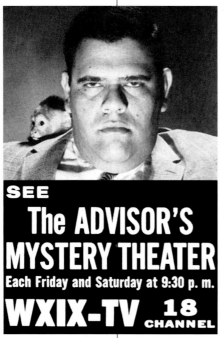

Veteran broadcaster Tom Snyder, who knew Hersh, was out of work at the time, and selling advertising for WXIX. He wrote a number of scripts for the show. Hersh left the program at the end of January 1960.

After WXIX restructured its ownership and changed its call letters to WUHF, it acquired the *Shock!* and *Son of Shock!* packages, and began showing its own version of "Shock Theater" Saturday evenings, beginning on September 7, 1963. (A number of the films had already been shown on "The 9:30 Mystery.") The opening and commercial graphics featured a photograph of Glenn Strange as Frankenstein's monster. The time slot varied quite a bit. Initially, the films were shown in the 9:30 -10:00 p.m. slot. Later, they were shifted to 8:30 p.m. In the summer of 1964, WUHF showed Langsdorf Baseball League games at 8:00 p.m., pre-empting "Shock Theater." However, those nights when no game was shown, saw the show expanded to a double feature. That fall, it was again shown as a single feature at 8:00 p.m. It ran through September 11, 1965.

Although WITI-TV was showing the "choice" Universal films, WVTV acquired another package of the "lesser" films, and also showed some from Republic Pictures, which came from a package it acquired in 1964. It showed them as "Shock Theater" Friday nights at 10:00 p.m. beginning on October 21, 1966. The old graphic of Glenn Strange as Frankenstein's monster was used again.

In April of 1967, WITI chose not to carry ABC's "The Joey Bishop Show," preferring to run its "Late Show" instead. WVTV picked up the show as of April 17, 1967, and dropped horror films on Friday nights.

From January 16 through May 29, 1970 WVTV occasionally showed one of the "lesser" Universal horror films which was not being shown on WITI-TV's "Nightmare Theatre" as "Shock Theater", utilizing the old graphic of Glenn Strange as Frankenstein's monster, and featuring voice-over by announcer Bob Beringer. The show ran on Friday nights at 10:30 p.m.

When WVTV began looking for programming for its new season in the fall of 1971, it again turned to the venerable Universal horror film packages (as well as others), when it began running "Shock Theater" Saturday nights beginning on September 4, 1971. The opening sequence was made up of clips from various films, and utilized a voice-over by announcer Bob Beringer. The old graphic of Glenn Strange was again used at the commercial breaks. The first show ran at 8:30 p.m., but it was shifted to 10:00 p.m. the following week. It continued in that format until January 1, 1972, when it was shifted to a double feature beginning at 8:00 p.m. That continued until September 16. With the new season, WTMJ-TV elected not to carry the *NBC Saturday Night Movie*, but rather ran its own film at 8:00 p.m. WVTV picked up the NBC film, bumping "Shock Theater" to a single feature at 10:00 p.m. This continued through April 6, 1974.

At that time, WTMJ-TV elected to again carry the NBC film, so WVTV turned back to a horror film double feature beginning at 8:00 p.m. It purchased many films, and changed the opening sequence. A dusty book, with the title "Saturday Night at the Movies" sat on a table top, which was illuminated by a candle. WVTV's 1970s logo (a cube with "WVTV Milwaukee" on one face and "18" on another) rested behind it. A rope was coiled to the book's left. Lightning flashed through a background window, while thunder could be heard crashing. "Shirley," a tarantula

CHAPTER 5 ~ WOKY-TV/WXIX/WUHF/WVTV: CHANNELS 19 & 18

"Shirley" the tarantula leaves the hand of her keeper, the Milwaukee County Zoo's Ken Schoenrock, during the taping of the opening for WVTV's "Saturday Night at the Movies." (WVTV photo)

provided by the Milwaukee County Zoo, crawled over the book[170], while announcer Bob Beringer intoned the film's title. (The spider was named after its keeper's wife![171]) The ubiquitous graphic of Glenn Strange was again used at the commercial breaks! It ran in this format until September 3, 1977, when it was shifted back to a single feature. It continued as such until August 29, 1979.

WVTV showed many of the same films Saturday afternoons in various time slots between 1970 and 1980. It ran Charlie Chan films on Sunday afternoons, and showed horror films as the second feature in 1977. It showed them Friday nights in 1979-1980 and Saturday nights in 1980-1982 as "Late Movie 18."

The station had so many horror films in its library that it chose to bring them back as a regular feature on November 30, 1985. They ran first as "Movie 18" and then as "Late Movie 18" in various time slots as either a single or double feature through October 12, 1991. From 1970-1991, no station got as much mileage out of its horror and science-fiction films as did WVTV!

NOTES

1 "Our Respects: Gerald Aron Bartell," *Broadcasting Telecasting*, April 9, 1956, 26
2 Evans, Ralph, III, interview with author, June 7, 2006.
3 Ibid.
4 Ibid.
5 Ibid.
6 Ibid.
7 Ibid.
8 "UHF TV Channel Sought by WOKY," *Milwaukee Journal*, October 22, 1951.
9 Ralph Evans, Sr., interview with Andrew Stone and Wayne Hawk, December 18, 1991.
10 "File Application for UHF Channel Here," *The Capital Times*, July 24, 1952.
11 "Chicagoans File for Channel Here," *Milwaukee Journal*, November 25, 1952.
12 "TV Application Channel Changed," *Milwaukee Journal*, January 31, 1953.
13 "Madison TV Station OK'd: UHF Channel 27 Permit is First Granted in That City," *Milwaukee Journal*, January 8, 1953

14 "Madison Gets a Second TV: UHF Channel 33 Goes to Bartell Corp.; City Still Minus Station," *Milwaukee Journal*, January 24, 1953.
15 TV Application Channel Changed."
16 "WFOX Shifts Channel Plea: Asks VHF 12 for TV," *Milwaukee Journal*, June 2, 1953.
17 "WOKY Gets TV Channel: Station Hopes to Be on Air With UHF by Labor Day," *Milwaukee Journal*, June 4, 1954. Also see: "WOKY Wins TV Channel 19, Hopes to Operate by Sept. 7," *Milwaukee Sentinel*, June 4, 1954.
18 "WOKY-TV Sets 'Target': Sept. 30 is TV Goal," *Milwaukee Journal*, August 27, 1953.
19 Gene Harrison, interview with Andrew Stone and Wayne Hawk, September 25, 1991.
20 Pat Bucket, interview with author, October 14, 2006.
21 Judy Marks, interview with author, October 11, 2006.
22 Harrison, September 25, 1991.
23 Evans, December 18, 1991.
24 Ibid
25 Harrison, September 25, 1991.
26 Jack Crowley, interview with author, October 13, 2006.
27 "Wisconsin Dateline," *TV Guide* (Wisconsin Edition), May 14-20, 1954, A-1.
28 Evans, December 18, 1991.
29 "WEMP Negotiates to Buy WCAN; Sale price $250,000," *Broadcasting Telecasting*, September 13, 1954, 9.
30 "Bitners Buy Two Minneapolis TV's; WTVW (TV) Sale Snags, WTAP (TV) Sold," *Broadcasting Telecasting*, January 31, 1955, 71-73. Also see: "Physical Assets Sold, Station WEMP Says," *Milwaukee Journal*, January 20, 1955.
31 Poller v. Columbia Broadcasting, et. al., 368 U.S. 464 (1962)
32 "Reveals Price of WOKY-TV: CBS Pays $350,000," *Milwaukee Journal*, October 24, 1954.
33 "FCC Boosts TV Ownership Limits: Seven Allowed, Five VHF, Two UHF," *Broadcasting Telecasting*, September 20, 1954, 7.
34 "Columbia's First U," *Broadcasting Telecasting*, November 22, 1954, 37.
35 "Sale of WOKY-TV Milwaukee to CBS-TV Gets FCC Approval," *Broadcasting Telecasting*, January 17, 1955, 7.
36 "WOKY-TV Switch Delayed," *Broadcasting Telecasting*, February 7, 1955, 94.
37 "WXIX Start Set Thursday: CBS to Take Station," *Milwaukee Journal*, February 15, 1955.
38 "WXIX(TV) Begins As CBS' First UHF," *Broadcasting Telecasting*, February 28, 1955, 86.
39 "CBS Is Sued by Lou Poller for $4,350,000," *Milwaukee Journal*, September 19, 1956.
40 Budde Marino, interview with author, November 5, 2007.
41 "WXIX(TV) Ups Power From New Antenna Rig," *Broadcasting Telecasting*, March 14, 1955, 95.
42 "WXIX(TV) Turns to Radio Spot Saturation," *Broadcasting Telecasting*, April 18, 1955, 88.
43 "Wisconsin Dateline," *TV Guide* (Wisconsin Edition), July 9-16, 1955, A-1.
44 "Wisconsin Dateline," *TV Guide* (Wisconsin Edition), May 7-13, 1955, A-1.
45 Tom Snyder, email to the author, April 24, 2002.
46 Marks, October 11, 2006.
47 "Shakespearean Success Story," *Milwaukee Sentinel*, June 15, 1958.
48 "WXIX Gets Channel 18: To Cut Interference," *Milwaukee Journal*, August 1, 1958.
49 "Propose Change in UHF Channels," *Milwaukee Journal*, June 13, 1958.
50 "FCC Re-Shuffles Ch. 8 in Carolinas," *Broadcasting*, August 4, 1958, 63.
51 "For the record," *Broadcasting*, June 23, 1958, 91.
52 "WXIX to Shift To Channel 18 Starting Today," *Milwaukee Sentinel*, August 27, 1958.
53 "WXIX Chief Denies CBS Moving to WITI," *Milwaukee Sentinel*, August 10, 1958.
54 "CBS to Keep WXIX in City: Drops One in East," *Milwaukee Journal*, October 9, 1958.
55 "CBS-TV Will Move to WITI on April 1," *Milwaukee Sentinel*, February 28, 1959. Also see: "CBS to Shift to Channel 6," *Milwaukee Journal*, February 27, 1959.
56 "UHF Action hurts stores: Converters Obsolete," *Milwaukee Journal*, March 1, 1959.
57 "Closed Circuit," *Broadcasting*, March 16, 1959, 5.
58 "UHF Station Here is Sold: WXIX is Purchased," *Milwaukee Journal*, March 28, 1959.

59 "New Firm to Keep WXIX on the Air," *Milwaukee Sentinel*, March 28, 1959.
60 "Firm Asks FCC for '18' Approval," *Milwaukee Journal*, April 16, 1959. Also see: "WXIX Seeks Transfer to Channel 18," *Milwaukee Sentinel*, April 16, 1959.
61 "FCC Asked to OK Sale of Channel 18," *Milwaukee Journal*, April 21, 1959.
62 "Channel 18 to Go on Air: FCC Grants a Permit to Posner to resume WXIX Telecasts," *Milwaukee Journal*, May 7, 1959, Part 2, 1.
63 "WXIX-TV Test OK'd," *Milwaukee Sentinel*, May 28, 1959. Also see: "WXIX Is Authorized to Return to the Air," *Milwaukee Journal*, May 28, 1959.
64 "Channel 18 Test Pattern to Start," *Milwaukee Sentinel*, June 8, 1959.
65 "WXIX to return to Air July 20," *Milwaukee Journal*, June 23, 1959. Also see: "WXIX to Resume On July 20," *Milwaukee Sentinel*, June 25, 1959.
66 The effects of all the changes were that all of the city's network affiliates were on VHF, while the sole independent station was on UHF.
67 Donald H. Dooley, "WXIX Lights Up Again Monday: UHF Station to Stress Sports and Films," *Milwaukee Journal*, July 19, 1959.
68 Lawrence C Ecklund, "What's Happening with Pay TV?" *Milwaukee Journal*, October 4, 1959.
69 "Park Land Sought as Site for New WXIX-TV Tower," *Milwaukee Journal*, June 23, 1960.
70 "WXIX Seeks OK to Build 650-Ft. Tower," *Milwaukee Sentinel*, June 24, 1960.
71 "WXIX Denied Use of Park Land for Tower," *Milwaukee Sentinel*, August 4, 1960.
72 "WXIX to Push Private Land Tower Project," *Milwaukee Sentinel*, August 5, 1960.
73 "Two UHF Stations Ask for VHF Assignments," *Broadcasting*, March 20, 1961, 77.
74 "Petition is Made for Channel 8," *Milwaukee Journal*, March 15, 1961.
75 "FCC Okays TV By Plane: Wisconsin Included," *Milwaukee Journal*, December 24, 1959.
76 "Airborne Group Refuses WXIX-TV's ETV Offer," *Broadcasting*, July 3, 1961, 62.
77 "WXIX Renews Request for VHF Channel," *Milwaukee Sentinel*, September 7, 1961. Also see: "WXIX-TV Resubmits Channel 8 Petition," *Milwaukee Journal*, September 7, 1961.
78 "Posner Agrees to Sell His Television Stock," *Milwaukee Journal*, June 19, 1962.
79 "Posner OK's Selling for $1: 51% of WXIX-TV," *Milwaukee Journal*, June 29, 1962.
80 "WXIX-TV Will Become WUHF," *Milwaukee Sentinel*, December 13, 1962. Also see: "UHF Channel Here to Alter Call Letters," *Milwaukee Journal*, December 13, 1962.
81 Michael H. Drew, "Milwaukee Studio Notes," *Milwaukee Journal*, April 14, 1963.
82 Michael H. Drew, "Milwaukee Studio Notes," *Milwaukee Journal*, June 2, 1963.
83 As they would in 1977. See chapter 7.
84 "Channel 18 to Broadcast Captain Kangaroo Show," *Milwaukee Journal*, August 20, 1964.
85 Captain Kangaroo returned to WISN-TV on November 19, 1965.
86 Donald H. Dooley, "Operatic Afternoon on Radio," *Milwaukee Journal*, December 6, 1959.
87 Michael H. Drew, "Milwaukee Studio Notes," *Milwaukee Journal*, September 26, 1965.
88 Harvey Scales interview with author, December 17, 2007.
89 George Liberatore, interview with author, June 21, 2007.
90 Ibid.
91 "WUHF-TV Sold to Oklahoma Publishers," *Milwaukee Sentinel*, November 9, 1965. Also see: "WUHF-TV Sold to Oklahomans," *Milwaukee Journal*, November 9, 1965.
92 Liberatore, June 21, 2007.
93 "Us Approves WUHF Sale," *Milwaukee Journal*, March 25, 1966.
94 Joe Loughlin, interview with author, January 15, 2008.
95 Tony Bachman, letter to Mike Drew, August 16, 1966, provided by WVTV.
96 N. 35th St. Building Acquired by WVTV," *Milwaukee Journal*, July 11, 1966.
97 Bachman, August 16, 1966.
98 Liberatore, June 21, 2007.
99 Loughlin, January 15, 2008.
100 Joe Loughlin, email to author, January 19, 2008.
101 Michael H. Drew "Milwaukee Studio Notes," *Milwaukee Journal*, July 17, 1966.
102 Dennis Brechlin, email to author, March 23, 2007.
103 Loughlin, January 15, 2008.

104 "WVTV to Carry 15 Cub Games Starting Sunday," *Milwaukee Sentinel*, May 4, 1967.
105 Michael H. Drew "Milwaukee Studio Notes," *Milwaukee Journal*, September 17, 1967.
106 Behling, James P., "Bowling With the Duffers," *Milwaukee Journal*, February 5, 1967.
107 Loughlin, January 15, 2008.
108 After serving a work-release sentence, Johnson would spend the rest of his life speaking against drinking and driving. He died on October 11, 2003 at the age of 76.
109 Loughlin, January 15, 2008.
110 Michael H. Drew "The Ratings Game Leads 18 to Cancel Bowling Show," *Milwaukee Journal*, December 19, 1986.
111 "Channel 18 Reracks Bowling," *Milwaukee Journal*, February 3, 1987.
112 Michael H. Drew "Milwaukee Studio Notes," *Milwaukee Journal*, June 9, 1968.
113 Scott Shuster, interview with author, July 2, 2007.
114 Loughlin, January 19, 2008.
115 Loughlin, January 15, 2008.
116 Scott Shuster, interview with author, July 2, 2007.
117 Keith Spore, "UWM News Crew Scores Hit on TV," *Milwaukee Sentinel*, April 19, 1969, Part 1, 13.
118 Scott Shuster, email to author, July 9, 2007.
119 Richard Vonier, "What Do You Do When You Turn On the Teevee and See a Girl in a Bikini Dancing Wildly on the Screen?" *Milwaukee Journal*, April 30, 1972.
120 "Variety Club Gets $85,629 in 1st Count," *Milwaukee Journal*, February 3, 1975.
121 Jack Lee, interview with author, November 28, 2007.
122 Loughlin, January 15, 2008.
123 Ibid.
124 Michael H. Drew "On the Milwaukee Scene," *Milwaukee Journal*, January 2, 1972.
125 Michael H. Drew "The Switch is On at Channel 18," *Milwaukee Journal*, August 14, 1981.
126 Loughlin, January 15, 2008.
127 Jeff Pryor, "Milwaukee's WVTV: 18 and Anxious," *Milwaukee Journal*, March 25, 1984.
128 "Gaylord Broadcasting Company to Construct Television Tower and Transmission Facility," WVTV press release, December 27, 1979, provided by WVTV.
129 Michael H. Drew "Stronger Signals: New Antennas Should Boost 10/36 Audience," *Milwaukee Journal*, April 29, 1981.
130 Drew, August 14, 1981.
131 Melita Marie Garza, "Channel 18's Uncut R Films Getting Unfavorable Ratings," *Milwaukee Journal*, January 15, 1987.
132 Michael H. Drew "A Reel Switch: Channel 18 Ends Showings of Unedited R-Rated Movies," *Milwaukee Journal*, February 14, 1987.
133 Duane Dudek, "Channel 18 to produce Nightly News Show with Local Slant," *Milwaukee Sentinel*, August 19, 1988.
134 Bob Bach, interview with author, December 3, 2007.
135 Ibid.
136 "WVTV Expected to Name Hegan Sports Anchor," *Milwaukee Sentinel*, July 28, 1989.
137 Michael Zahn, "Channel 18 News: Feisty Station is Gaining Ground," *Milwaukee Journal*, September 1, 1991.
138 "Gaylord Firm Seeking Combination," *Milwaukee Journal*, August 29, 1991.
139 David I. Bednarek, "Channels 18, 24 to Combine Some Operations," *Milwaukee Journal*, January 14, 1993.
140 Crocker Stephenson, "WVTV Drops Nine O'Clock News Show: 25 Will Lose Their Jobs After March 12 Finale," *Milwaukee Sentinel*, February 27, 1993. Also see: Michael H. Drew "WVTV Drops 9 O'Clock News, Dismisses Staff in Merger with WCGV," *Milwaukee Journal*, February 27, 1993.
141 Joel Dresang, "Channel 24 Sale Brings Shake-Up: With Loss of Fox, Its Status is Unclear," *Milwaukee Journal*, May 25, 1994.
142 Mildred Freese, "Pittsburgh Broadcaster May Buy Channel 18," *Milwaukee Journal*, August 20, 1993.
143 Duane Dudek, "Protest by Baltimore Station Stops Purchase of WVTV," *Milwaukee Sentinel*, April 20, 1994.

144 "Channel 18 Joins New Network," *Milwaukee Sentinel*, July 27, 1994. Also see: "Paramount Signs WVTV, Other for New Network," *Milwaukee Journal*, July 27, 1994.
145 Duane Dudek "Will Likely Sale of Channel 18 Lead to CBS Affiliation Here?" *Milwaukee Sentinel*, October 31, 1994.
146 Rich Kirchen "Edwards Pushes Back as Jesse Jackson's Group Challenges Channel 18 Sale," *The Business Journal* of *Milwaukee*, April 13, 2001.
147 Tim Cuprisin "UPN Network Debuts With 'Star Trek' Classics," *Milwaukee Journal*, January 12, 1995.
148 Tim Cuprisin "Channel 18 to Broadcast WB Network," *Milwaukee Journal Sentinel*, January 15, 1997.
149 "Sinclair Files to Acquire WVTV License," *The Business Journal* of *Milwaukee*, November 17, 1999.
150 "Edwards Pushes Back as Jesse Jackson's Group Challenges Channel 18 Sale."
151 Rich Kirchen "FCC Approves Channel 18 Sale," *The Business Journal* of *Milwaukee*, December 12, 2001.
152 Tim Cuprisin "Program 'Tweaking' Splits Stouts," *Milwaukee Journal Sentinel*, April 3, 2006.
153 Tim Cuprisin "Channel 18's 9 p.m. News Might Sign Off," *Milwaukee Journal Sentinel*, August 12, 2003.
154 Tim Cuprisin "WB's 9 O'Clock Newscast Bids Final Farewell," *Milwaukee Journal Sentinel*, January 17, 2006.
155 Joanne Weintraub, "A Fresh New TV Merger: TV's Youngest Networks Will Become One," *Milwaukee Journal Sentinel*, January 25, 2006.
156 Tim Cuprisin "Wisconsin Native Extends Sitcom Stay," *Milwaukee Journal Sentinel*, March 3, 2006.
157 Pat Buckett, email to author, February 2, 2007.
158 Ibid.
159 "Wisconsin Dateline," *TV Guide* (Wisconsin Edition), March 12-18, 1954, A-1.
160 Crowley, October 13, 2006.
161 Ibid.
162 "Wisconsin Dateline," *TV Guide* (Wisconsin Edition), April 30-May 6, 1955, A-1.
163 "Wisconsin Dateline," *TV Guide* (Wisconsin Edition), May 21-27, 1955, A-1.
164 "Wisconsin Dateline," *TV Guide* (Wisconsin Edition), September 3-9, 1955, A-1.
165 Dooley, July 19, 1959.
166 Michael H. Drew "Milwaukee Studio Notes," *Milwaukee Journal*, September 8, 1968.
167 Michael H. Drew "Milwaukee Studio Notes," *Milwaukee Journal*, October 13, 1968.
168 Liberatore, June 21, 2007.
169 Amy Hansmann, email to author, November 7, 2007.
170 Alicia Armstrong, "ZooPerstars: The Not So Itsy-Bitsy Spider," *Milwaukee Journal*, May 9, 1974.
171 Adine Mikolajczak, email to author, October 20, 2005.

CHAPTER 6
WTVW/WISN-TV
CHANNEL 12

WISN-TV photo

When the FCC issued its Sixth Report and General Order on April 14, 1952, only one VHF channel assigned to Milwaukee was still available for commercial use. That was channel 12.

When the freeze was lifted on July 1, the Wisconsin Broadcasting System, Inc. (WFOX) filed an application for the channel. The following week, The Milwaukee Broadcasting Co. (WEMP) also did so. Both had filed applications in 1948 and after the first round of hearings before the FCC, there were only three applicants for the three available channels. WEMP expected to receive a grant for channel 6, while WFOX expected the same for channel 8. Then the FCC froze all license applications. Both stations, along with the Hearst Corp. (WISN) had filed objections to the FCC's proposed allocation plan, and suggested that the FCC reassign channel 10 for commercial use, while assigning one of the available UHF channels for educational television. They also proposed that the Commission take channel 6 from Green Bay and assign it to Milwaukee. (See chapters 3 & 8.) That would've given the city three VHF channels – all of which would've been available for commercial use.

WISN-TV photo

The FCC rejected the argument that the applications of the three radio stations had precedent because they had applied for them before the freeze. It stated unequivocally, that they "had no legal right or preference because of their past participation in a hearing" regarding VHF channels, and that the Commission had the legal right to change the Table of Channel Assignments as it saw fit.[1]

WEMP had been working on its application for almost a year. Program Director Tom Shanahan had taken a leave from his duties, and he and Carl Zimmermann drafted it.[2] Zimmermann had been recalled to active duty with the Army during the Korean War, and started in television, producing *The Big Picture*. When he returned to Milwaukee, he was one of the few people outside of WTMJ-TV who had any television experience.[3]

Before the freeze was lifted, WEMP had once again asked that channel 6 be taken from Green Bay and given to Milwaukee, and filed a new application for that channel. The application stated that new studios would be located at 525 W Wells Street, and that it would use its 460' radio tower (which had been erected after WWII with television in mind) if it couldn't get steel for a 1,000' tower because of Korean War priorities.[4] They were so confident that they would get a channel, that they purchased land for a tower site. At first, they attempted to have thirty-five acres of land in Glendale north of West Silver Spring Drive, between the Milwaukee River Parkway and North Green Bay Road rezoned for a 1,083' tower. When that request was denied, they purchased six acres just north of Lincoln Park, and asked the County for an easement, so that one of the guy wires for the proposed tower could be anchored in the park. In consideration, they offered to make five acres of the property along West Villard Avenue available for park use, provided that they were allowed access to their tower site.[5]

WEMP's application for channel 6 was denied by the FCC, so they then filed their application for channel 12. On July 18, 1952, the Milwaukee Area Telecasting Corp., headed up by theater owner L.F. Gran applied for the channel. On October 14, the Midwest Broadcasting Co., (WCAN) filed an application for VHF channel 12[6], but on November 17, they amended their application to specify UHF channel 25 instead. The Wisconsin Broadcasting System (WFOX) amended its application from channel 12 to channel 25 the following day.[7]

In late January of 1953, Bartell Broadcasters, Inc., which owned WOKY radio in Milwaukee, received a construction permit for channel 33 in Madison. The Wisconsin Broadcasting System thought that would disqualify Bartell from receiving one for channel 19 in Milwaukee, under the mistaken assumption that Madison was a part of the same market. As such, they amended their application from channel 25 to channel 19 on January 31, 1953.[8]

As there were now three applicants for channel 19 in Milwaukee, the process took longer, as the FCC had a policy of hearing uncontested applications first. The maneuvering continued, and on June 2, 1953, the Wisconsin Broadcasting System again amended its application from channel 19 back to channel 12.[9] Its rationale was that if it was to be involved in a competitive hearing, it would prefer to do so for a VHF channel.

On November 3, 1953, Kolero Telecasting Corp., owned by local businessmen (as well as Catholic Knights Insurance) filed an application for channel 12. It proposed to broadcast from facilities in, and with a tower mounted atop, the Tower Hotel at 716 North 11th Street (now the M. Carpenter Tower, a Marquette University residence hall). The hotel was owned by Catholic Knights Insurance, and had been one site proposed for the WOKY-TV tower.

With four applicants, the hearings promised to be contentious. WEMP allowed WOKY-TV to mount its antenna on their tower, and in return, they were allowed to use the television facilities for testing and demonstration purposes. Tom Shanahan remembered:

> We thought that if we could demonstrate our ability to produce TV programs – even though we weren't on the air yet – it would work in our favor before the FCC.[10]

The Commission set December 31, 1953 as the starting date for the consolidated hearing in Washington, D.C. Kolero asked the Commission for conditional authority to construct a station, pending the outcome of the hearing. In its application, it claimed that it was the only applicant with the financial means to construct a station.[11]

On December 29, two days before the hearings were scheduled to begin; several petitions were filed with the FCC by the Milwaukee Area Telecasting Corp. They asked the Commission to:

Carl Zimmermann and Earl Gillespie, who both worked for WEMP at the time, participated in a series of tests using the WOKY-TV facilities. (Courtesy of Bob Wundrock)

• Dismiss the application of the Kolero Telecasting Corp., as two of that company's stockholders held notes of the Midwest Broadcasting Co., which owned WCAN-TV, and that violated FCC rules against a party owning an interest in more than one television station in a given city. The same concern was expressed by the Milwaukee Broadcasting Co.

• Determine whether the other applicants had the funds to fulfill their promises – although all four applicants had been found financially able to construct and operate a television station.

• Investigate the coverage area proposed by the other three applicants. It claimed that because its proposed tower location was at 6600 West Capitol Drive, its location further west would provide greater coverage, as that proposed by two of the other applicants was primarily over Lake Michigan.

• Dismiss the application of the Milwaukee Broadcasting Co. on the grounds that granting it a license would violate the rule prohibiting any entity from owning more than five VHF stations. It offered as evidence a complicated chart showing that CBS had ownership positions in five stations, and that one of Milwaukee Broadcasting's proposed stockholders had an interest in a company, which had an interest in another company, which was partially owned by CBS.[12]

On January 6, 1954, the FCC rejected Kolero's petition for an immediate, conditional grant.[13]

As the hearings began, Milwaukee Area Telecasting and the Milwaukee Broadcasting Co. reacted vigorously to the Kolero's allegation that they weren't in a financial position to construct a television station. In addition, the FCC had to determine whether the towers proposed by both Kolero and the Wisconsin Broadcasting System would pose hazards to air navigation.[14] On February 19, 1954, the FCC denied the motion by Milwaukee Area Telecasting to dismiss Kolero's application.

The four applicants for channel 12 began to discuss the idea of merging their applications, so that they could avoid a lengthy hearing and get on the air quickly, and they made the fact public in early May of 1954.[15]

In response, on May 19, Midwest Broadcasting filed a petition with the FCC to modify its construction permit to specify VHF channel 12. Owner Lou Poller proposed that WCAN-TV simulcast on both channels, "pending public choice of the best service."[16] The Commission refused WCAN-TV's application the grounds that none may be accepted thirty days before hearings begin, and that the Commission's rules forbade stations from changing channels, except if the channel assignments for the city were changed.[17] That same day an FCC hearing examiner recommended granting a construction permit for channel 12 to the Milwaukee Area Telecasting Corp., around whose application the others had agreed to merge.

On June 11, 1954, the FCC granted a construction permit for channel 12 to the Milwaukee Area Telecasting Corp. The merger agreement gave the other parties the option to purchase stock in the new corporation that was to be formed to operate the station. Kolero Telecasting Corp. received ten percent; the others, thirty percent each.[18] Kolero also received also received $30,000 as a reimbursement for expenses associated with its application. The call letters requested were WTVW, which stood for "Wisconsin's Television Window." Its principals were:

- Paul A. Pratt (3%), president
- Loren E. Thurwachter (10%), vice president
- J. Martin Klotsche (3%), general manager
- Rolando F. (known as L. F.) Gran (50%), treasurer
- Joseph M. Baisch, secretary
- Maxwell H. Herriott (2%)
- Thomas E. Allen (7%)
- Eliot C. Fitch (7.5%)
- R. P. Herzfeld (5%)
- W. A. Roberts (4%)
- Peter T. Shoeman (2.5%)
- O. W. Carpenter (2%)
- Edmund Fitzgerald (2%)
- Louis Quarles (2%)

On July 13, 1954, Midwest Broadcasting asked the FCC to reverse its grant to the Milwaukee Area Telecasting Co. Midwest charged that the cash payment to Kolero was a "payoff".[19] The Commission denied the petition. Midwest then filed an appeal with the U.S. Court of Appeals in Washington regarding the FCC's return of its application to switch from channel 25 to 12.[20] It also filed a petition for a temporary injunction to prevent construction of a station on channel 12 until the court could hear the station's suit to force the FCC to reconsider its application to switch channels. Milwaukee Area Telecasting responded by charging that WCAN-TV was trying to stifle competition by preventing additional TV service from being started in the city.[21] On August 10, the appeals court turned down WCAN-TV's request for a temporary stay.[22]

CHAPTER 6 ~ WTVW/WISN-TV: CHANNEL 12   217

CBS had begun negotiations to purchase WOKY-TV, and as a result, on August 31, 1954 it was announced that WOKY radio and WOKY-TV had cancelled their affiliations with the ABC network. The television cancellation became effective on October 1; the radio December 31. The same day, The Milwaukee Area Telecasting Corp., announced that it would become the ABC outlet.[23] The station would also affiliate with Du Mont.[24]

The ABC affiliation gave the station's technical staff a tough deadline to meet. The inaugural broadcast of Walt Disney's *Disneyland* was scheduled for October 27, and that was set as the target date to have the station up and running.[25] Milwaukee Area Telecasting purchased WEMP's land near Lincoln Park, and the FCC approved the location on September 8.[26] Two days later – just seven weeks before the deadline – ground was broken for a small building, which would house the transmitter and temporary studio facilities.[27] When rains threatened to delay work, a 3,500 square foot tent was erected over the site, and the building erected under it.[28] Bob Truscott was the assistant chief engineer at the time, and he remembered:

> *In the summer of 1954 Lionel "Witty" Wittenberg, the chief engineer, assigned me, along with Marty Johnson, Warren Schlaugat, and Herb Nowicki (Al Schaefer may also have been there.) to pre-wire the control room equipment racks so that we could load them up and haul them to the transmitter site and just 'plug them in' when the building was far enough along to allow us to do that. This was one of the relatively unconventional things we had to do to meet the 'impossible' air date that management set for Witty in order to meet their network commitment. We did this job at the old Gueder, Pesky and Frey warehouse somewhere in Milwaukee, I don't remember where. While all this was happening the building contractor was doing his best to get the transmitter building ready, but when it became apparent that he could not, we decided*

The building which housed both the temporary studios and transmitter for WTVW is still used for the latter purpose. At the right is the temporary "hut" that housed the news, production and film departments. The tent was used for live car commercials. (Historic photo collection/ Milwaukee Public Library)

to erect a large circus tent at the site and build the building underneath it. As soon as the floor slab was completed we moved the racks in and began the final installation. At the same time, Ed Welcome, the transmitter supervisor, and his crew, were installing the transmitter. So while we all did these things the construction crew built the walls around us and the roof over our heads. Those were fun days. Not recommended, but we got the job done and met the deadline.[29]

A prefabricated metal "hut" was attached to the building to temporarily provide more space. Bob Truscott:

It was built on a concrete slab on the east side of the transmitter building, which housed the film projection equipment and a minimum control room facility, in addition to the transmitter. The news, production, and film departments were in the hut.[30]

A temporary 300' tower was erected, from which the station planned to start broadcasting with 100,000 watts of power. Later that year, they planned on increasing the power, and the following year erecting a 1,105' tower, which would be the tallest in the state. New studios would also be built at an unspecified location.[31] The station's offices, like WEMP's were located in the Empire Building on the northeast corner of North Plankinton and West Wisconsin Avenues in downtown Milwaukee.

Veteran WEMP announcers Carl Zimmermann and Bill Bramhall were tapped as film/news director[32] and weatherman[33] respectively. Carl Zimmermann remembered:

The antenna is hoisted atop WTVW's original 300' tower. (WISN-TV photo)

CHAPTER 6 ~ WTVW/WISN-TV: CHANNEL 12   219

We were pioneers, really. We were editing negative film because that's the way it came out of the lab. We made a few mistakes (chuckling), but we got it on the air![34]

Executives enjoy a cake that was sent by TV Guide for their debut celebration at the Milwaukee Athletic Club. L-R: An unidentified executive, Ernest Lee Uahnke – assistant to the president of ABC, Loren F. Thurwachter – executive vice president of Milwaukee Area Telecasting, Charles Lamphier – general manager of WFOX, and Andrew Spheeris – president and general manager of WEMP. (WISN-TV photo)

As a service to viewers and repairmen, the station showed a test pattern at regular times throughout the day. Monday - Friday it began showing one at 9:00 a.m. – even though it didn't begin programming until 4:30 p.m. Saturdays and Sundays, it ran it for fifteen minutes before the start of programming, which began at 9:30 a.m., and 12:30 p.m. respectively.[35]

The first program was a dedication film containing addresses by Milwaukee Mayor Frank Zeidler, Wisconsin Governor Walter Kohler, Jr., station officials and staff.[36] According to WTVW's Duke Larson, an estimated seventy percent (400,000) of the area's television sets were tuned to *Disneyland* that night.[37]

The rush to get the station on the air led to some technical problems. Some viewers had good reception, while others had trouble with the picture quality. Others reported receiving the picture on one channel and the sound on another.[38] The problems were resolved by the end of the first week of broadcasting.

Because of the small studio space, and the fact that neither ABC nor Du Mont provided a lot of network programming, the station did a lot of remote broadcasting. Included were Milwaukee Braves' games from County Stadium, commercials from car dealerships, wrestling from the South Side Armory, and a bowling show.[39] Tom Shanahan:

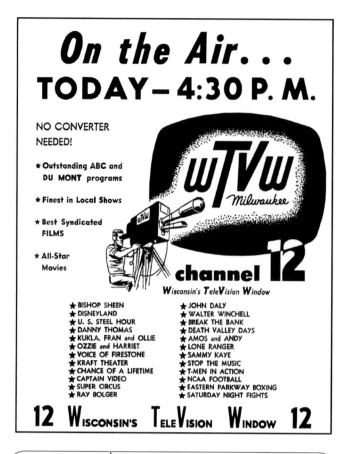

WTVW'S FIRST DAY PROGRAMMING:

OCTOBER 27, 1954

•	4:00 p.m.	Sign-on and Test Pattern
•	4:30 p.m.	Dedication Film
•	4:45 p.m.	Roundup Time (Cowboy Films)
•	5:15 p.m.	Dr. Eon's Lab (Serial)
•	5:45 p.m.	Captain Video
•	6:00 p.m.	Kukla, Fran, and Ollie
•	6:15 p.m.	News with John Daly
•	6:30 p.m.	Disneyland
•	7:30 p.m.	Stu Erwin
•	8:00 p.m.	Masquerade Party
•	8:30 p.m.	Bulldog Drummond
•	9:30 p.m.	The Stranger
•	10:00 p.m.	Weather
•	10:05 p.m.	News
•	10:10 p.m.	Sports
•	10:15 p.m.	Movie
•	1:00 a.m.	Late News
•	1:05 a.m.	Evening Prayer

The bowling show with Carl was the only TV show I ever did. It was live, and we opened every one with me throwing a ball down the alley. Nowadays, I'd keep trying until I rolled a strike, and then they'd run that tape every week, but we were live. In thirteen weeks, I think had four gutter balls, and two splits,

Electrician Marvin Cox working in the original control room located in the transmitter building in Lincoln Park in 1955. (Marvin Cox photo)

Electrician John Gill works on the Du Mont color "Multi-Scanner" flying-spot scanner unit located inside the WTVW transmitter building in 1955. The unit allowed the station to show 16mm film or 35mm slides. (Marvin Cox photo)

but not one strike! I don't know why they picked me to throw the ball, because I was the wrong guy![40]

However, the merger which allowed the station to get on the air was a marriage of convenience, and the joint corporation that was to have run the station was never formed. Andrew Spheeris, who owned WEMP at the time, told Art Olszyk in 1990 that L.F. Gran, who owned the company, that the others had merged behind, had sixty-six stockholders. While he was trying to get the station on the air with a tight deadline, he would get calls from relatives of Gran and his stockholders who were looking for jobs. In addition, Gran tried to micromanage the day-to-day operations of the company.[41]

The Hearst Corporation was still struggling to establish a television presence in the city. On July 22, 1922, its evening newspaper, the *Wisconsin News*, was issued a license jointly with the School of Engineering (now the Milwaukee School of Engineering) for radio station, WIAO. That station began broadcasting on 833.3 kHz on October 23, 1922.[42] Subsequent licenses were issued only to the school. The newspaper began programming some shows on WIAO in January of 1924.[43] The frequency was changed to 1220 kHz on June 9[44], and the call letters to WSOE on August 18 of that year.[45] The newspaper opened its own studio from which it could broadcast over the station that October.[46] At the end of 1924, the School of Engineering announced that it had purchased all of the equipment from WCBD in Zion, Illinois (one of the nation's first religious broadcasters, and the "flat earth" station). That gave the station one of the most powerful transmitters in the nation,

---

HERE'S THE STORY ON

WTVW RECEPTION

WTVW is now transmitting its programs to the maximum degree of effectiveness under its present 100,000 watts of power and its 300-foot tower.

Speed in getting the station on the air by the promised October 27 date was responsible for some reception problems during the first week of operation, but all major technical difficulties have now been corrected.

Within the station's present 40-mile coverage area, you should be able to receive a good picture and sound.

IF YOU ARE NOT, IT IS BECAUSE:

1. A minor channel adjustment may be necessary since almost all TV sets manufactured require a separate adjustment of each channel to receive the best possible picture.

2. UHF converter strips presently located on channel 12 must be removed and channel 12 VHF strips reinstalled in order to receive WTVW.

3. In the fringe areas of WTVW's 40-mile radius coverage, some sets may require high band antennas to receive a perfect picture. Since this is the first high band (channels 7 to 13) station in this area, all antennas presently in use are low band (channels 2 to 6) antennas or UHF antennas.

These are the only possible reasons why you may not be able to receive WTVW satisfactorily. If you have encountered these problems, we suggest you contact a reliable serviceman and have them corrected.

WTVW Channel 12
WISCONSIN'S TELEVISION WINDOW

CHAPTER 6 ~ WTVW/WISN-TV: CHANNEL 12   223

as well as two transmitting towers. The *Wisconsin News* announced at that time that it "would 'cooperate' with operation of the station."[47] The new, more powerful, WSOE was dedicated on July 8, 1925[48], and the newspaper took over programming responsibility. On June 15, 1927, the frequency was changed to 1120 kHz by the new Federal Radio Commission (FRC).[49] In September of that year, the FRC ordered WSOE to share time with WHAD, Marquette University's station. The following month, the FRC cut the station's power from 500 to 250 watts because of interference complaints from WTMJ.

The Journal Co. had programmed Marquette University's station, WHAD, since January of 1925. (See chapter 2.) In 1927, it purchased WKAF, and changed its call letters to WTMJ on July 25 of that year.[50] To compete, the *Wisconsin News* entered into a lease arrangement with the School of Engineering on November 15, 1927. The lease was for a minimum of three years. The agreement specified that the newspaper was to "operate the station and furnish all financial support while its ownership and technical supervision was to remain in the hands of the school."[51] The call letters were changed to WISN on January 23, 1928.

Tom Shanahan and Carl Zimmermann did a live bowling show. The station's Native American mascot was named "Little Moose."

The School of Engineering continued to handle the technical operation of the station, and the transmitter and towers were still at its facility. The station was sold to the *Wisconsin News* in November of 1930.[52] In 1932, the School of Engineering reorganized itself as a non-profit corporation, and changed its name to the Milwaukee School of Engineering (MSOE). It moved from the Oneida Street building after purchasing the German-English Academy on North Broadway Street. In April of that year, the WISN studios were moved to the *Milwaukee Sentinel* building (Hearst had purchased that newspaper in 1924.) building at 123 West Michigan Avenue, and the towers and transmitter to the top of the Milwaukee Electric Railway & Light Co.'s Public Service Building at North 2nd and West Michigan Streets. In 1934, Hearst purchased WHAD, and WISN was able to broadcast full time.[53] The *Wisconsin News* became the *Milwaukee News* in 1937, and closed two years later. WISN then became the *Milwaukee Sentinel* station.

Hearst had begun broadcasting in competition with the *Milwaukee Journal*. It desperately wanted to compete with WTMJ-TV. Despite the fact that new television construction was frozen because of WWII, on June 13, 1945 it applied for VHF channel 4 (then 78-84 MHz).[54] Because of the post-war uncertainty as to whether TV would be moved to the UHF portion of the spectrum, Hearst asked the FCC to return its application on March 22, 1946.

It was the only applicant for channel 10 in 1948, and had purchased property at 3720 West Wisconsin Avenue for new TV and radio studios[55], which went unused. Unfortunately, the FCC froze new television license applications before a grant could be made. Hearst then fought a losing battle to have that channel reassigned for commercial use. (See chapter 8.) In June of 1952 it purchased the old Norris property on North 19th Street and West Wisconsin Avenue, which it planned on using for new studios.[56]

Shown atop the School of Engineering's Oneida (now Wells) Street building are the towers it purchased from WCBD. As WISN, the station continued to broadcast from this building until 1932. (Milwaukee School of Engineering photo)

Construction permits for all three UHF channels had been granted, but Hearst was only interested in a VHF. With four applicants for channel 12, the hearings promised to be lengthy. Undaunted, Hearst revisited the idea of assigning VHF channel 6 to Milwaukee. The FCC had rejected the idea previously, but a change in the Commission's membership made the idea appealing. Instead of deleting channel 6 from Green Bay, as their previous proposal had done, Hearst proposed that the FCC swap channel 6 from that city and channel 5 in Marquette Michigan, which would allow it to assign channel 6 to the Milwaukee area. In its rejection of the earlier proposal, the FCC pointed out that WOC-TV of Davenport, Iowa (Now KWQC) was 167 miles from Milwaukee – three miles within its minimum radius of 170 miles that had to separate stations on the same channel. To counter that argument, Hearst proposed that the channel be assigned to the Village of Whitefish Bay instead. The FCC proposed rule making, and despite objections from the Ultra High Frequency Television Association and WCAN-TV in Milwaukee, the Commission assigned channel 6 to Whitefish Bay on December 4, 1953.[57] Hearst then filed an application for the channel. The following month, it purchased forty-three acres of property at North Range Line and West Good Hope Roads in the Town of Granville for a transmitter and tower.[58]

To show the FCC what kind of public service shows it would provide to the community, Hearst put together a team consisting of personnel from WISN as well as its television station WBAL-TV in Baltimore. On January 4, 1954, the team set-up a temporary, closed-circuit studio in a second floor suite of the Loyalty Building at 611 North Broadway. There, in cooperation with local civic and educational groups including The Milwaukee Public Schools, The Milwaukee Public Museum, Civil Defense and city officials, and others, a series of programs was shown beginning on January 7. Through January 25, the team produced thirty-seven programs, includ-

ing television versions of WISN radio programming and original programs developed by that station's staff.[59]

On January 12, 1954, Hearst announced that it had purchased forty-three acres of land in the Town of Granville at North Range Line and West Good Hope Roads for a tower and transmitter site.[60]

The hearings for channel 6 were every bit as contentious as those for channel 12, as Hearst, Cream City Broadcasting, Inc. (WMIL), and Independent Television, Inc. battled for the grant. (See chapters 7 and 8 for further information.) On November 5, 1954, the three applicants announced that they were attempting to negotiate a merger agreement. They were granted a continuance from the FCC until December 7.[61] The negotiations snagged, and they were granted another continuance until January 11, 1955.[62] Hearst then began negotiations to purchase WTVW.[63]

In reaction, L.F. Gran made an offer to purchase the station in a meeting of the Milwaukee Area Telecasting Corp. held on December 17, at which an offer from Hearst was being considered. Gran claimed that he wanted to keep the station locally owned and operated.[64]

On November 27-28, WTVW conducted a telethon to benefit United Cerebral Palsy. Participating personalities included film and TV star Preston Foster, singers Tommy Leonnetti, Bobby Wayne, and Roberta Quinlan, and Al Markin, who played "Astro" on *Tom Corbett, Space Cadet*.[65]

Hearst announced on January 7, 1955 that it had purchased WTVW for $2 million. The price included more than $1 million for the assumption of contracts for a more powerful transmitter and new 1,105' tower. WCAN-TV owner Lou Poller had sold his facilities to CBS, and began divesting himself of his broadcast holdings. He failed to file a brief regarding his appeal on the channel 12 merger by a January 3 deadline, and it was subsequently dismissed.[66] On January 23, Hearst formally withdrew its application for channel 6.[67]

On January 27, 1955, L.F. Gran, through a Washington attorney, filed a letter with the FCC in which he objected to the sale of WTVW to Hearst, and stated that he had offered to purchase the station himself. In the same letter, he advised the FCC that he was preparing an application for channel 12, and asked for a hearing on the sale. He claimed that the Milwaukee Area Telecasting board was motivated to sell by the understanding that they might lose their ABC affiliation, and that Hearst might merge with another applicant for channel 6. At the December 17 meeting to discuss Hearst's offer, Gran said he offered to buy the station and pay all of the stockholders. At a subsequent meeting on January 4, 1955, he presented a second proposal. He also said that he voted to sell the station to Hearst, but that he had done so "under protest."[68] Gran resigned as chairman of Milwaukee Area Telecasting on January 26.[69]

Andrew Spheeris told a different story. He told Art Olszyk that Gran had no real money on the table, and that when pressed for details on his financing, he responded with "I'm good for it."[70]

Despite the controversy surrounding the possible sale, in late January of 1955, the station increased its power to 316,000 watts.

On February 2, L.F. Gran filed an application for channel 12[71], but on February 4, the FCC dismissed it on the grounds that it violated its rule prohibiting the filing of more than one application for the same channel by the same applicant, as he still held a 38.5% interest in Milwaukee Area Telecasting. Gran had hoped to force a competitive hearing, but in its response, the Commission stated that five years earlier, Congress had abolished a rule permitting the consideration of competitive offers.[72] In response, on February 7 he asked the U.S. Court of Appeals to grant him a stay preventing the sale of the station to Hearst, and for an injunction to force the Commission to accept his application and hold a hearing.[73]

Opposition to the Hearst purchase came from Milwaukee labor organizations, as both the AFL Milwaukee Federated Trades Council[74] and the Milwaukee County CIO Council[75] went on record with letters to the FCC. The former had discussed the matter in December, and its membership authorized its leadership to notify the FCC of its opposition "at the appropriate time."[76] It decided to do so in mid-February. Both organizations favored local ownership, and voiced concerns about the concentration of communications companies by a few large interests.

The Court of Appeals heard Gran's argument for a temporary stay in mid-February.[77] Late that month, it denied his request, without giving a reason.[78]

Because the temporary studio facilities were so small another tent was erected in front of the transmitter building's entrance. It was used for live commercials featuring automobiles, and worked fine until it collapsed in February of 1955 during a heavy snowstorm – just as they were about to go on the air from it![79]

In a 5-2 vote, the FCC approved the sale of WTVW to Hearst – subject to any action taken by the Court of Appeals – on March 2, 1955. Hearst then applied

---

THE HEARST CORPORATION

announces

that on March 8, 1955

it assumed operation of

Television Station **WTVW,**

Channel 12, Milwaukee, Wisconsin

WTVW will be operated at the same high standard of service to its community and its advertisers as are other Hearst Corporation stations.

WBAL	NBC Affiliate
WBAL-TV	NBC Affiliate
WISN	CBS Affiliate

316,000 watts   **W T V W**   ABC Affiliate

I. E. Showerman, Manager

Nationally Represented by Edward Petry & Co.

CHAPTER 6 ~ WTVW/WISN-TV: CHANNEL 12

to have the call letters changed to WISN-TV.[80] Dissenting opinions were filed by commissioners Hennock and Bartley. Frieda Hennock objected to the fact that approval of the sale meant that the issue of Hearst's media control would no longer be evaluated, as it would have been in a hearing on channel 6.[81]

Hearst assumed ownership of WTVW on Match 8, 1955. It announced plans to begin the broadcast day earlier – at noon, as well as for new studio facilities to be built at an undisclosed location.[82] That same month, the station announced that it had purchased a $100,000 remote truck.[83] When problems developed with

WTVW's first remote truck. With limited studio space, it got a lot of use! Operating the camera is Jerry Robinson. (WISN-TV photo)

equipment at the transmitter building, the truck was used to keep the station on the air.[84]

In May of 1955, Hearst moved the studio facilities to the coach house on the old Norris property. Bob Truscott:

> *Impossible deadlines were rather common in the early days. For example, in the summer of 1955 after Hearst took over the station, it was decided to build a temporary studio facility on West Wisconsin Ave. in what had been the coach house of one of the early mansions in the area. The completion date was set to coincide with the start of a new live show. I believe it was The Romper Room, a kids show. We were behind schedule, of course, so Bob Behee, later Asst. Chief Engineer at WITI, and I started work at 8:00 a.m. to put the finishing touches on the technical installation a day before the first program was to air. We ran into problems and ended up working until 10:00 a.m. the next day. And after the 26 hour work day we decided to celebrate a bit before going home. We played 18 holes of golf, but skipped the 'nineteenth' hole and the beverages which usually went with it. Behee always claimed it was 36 holes, but I don't think so. If it was, I slept through the last 18. The program went on the air right on schedule!*[85]

Before constructing its current facility, WISN-TV used the old coach house on the Norris property at North 19th Street and West Wisconsin Avenue. (Historic photo collection/ Milwaukee Public Library)

With limited studio facilities, (WTVW and later WISN-TV) did a lot of remote broadcasts. The weekly wrestling matches at the South Side Armory proved popular.

On June 17, the FCC approved the station's request to change its call letters to WISN-TV.[86]

Construction continued on the new 1,105' tower, and the station held a contest for viewers, who had to guess the exact date and time that it would be completed. At the time, it became the tallest structure in the state. Mrs. Irene Kocjan guessed that it would be finished on July 24, at 6:02 p.m. She was off by only eight minutes, and won a new Plymouth Plaza sedan.

Christened "Operation Switchover," the new tower went online at 11:30 a.m. the following day. The call letters were changed to WISN-TV, and a special program marking the changes was held at 7:00 p.m.[87]

In September of 1955, a polio outbreak in the city delayed

The new 1,105' tower under construction. Electrician John Gill stands atop an enclosure housing the controller for the tower's elevator. The original 300' tower is in the background. (Marvin Cox photo)

the start of the school year. WISN-TV, along with WTMJ-TV and WXIX broadcast special, educational programming for students who stayed home. WISN-TV called its program "Operation Three-R." The first broadcast was on September 7. For the Milwaukee Lutheran Schools, WISN-TV broadcast a program of religious education called "In the Shadow of the Cross" at 10:00 a.m., followed by music instruction at 10:45. At 1:30 p.m., it broadcast a program for the Milwaukee Public Schools aimed at the lower grades, that featured scratch coloring and how to make cardboard clock cut-outs.[88] The special shows ran through Monday, September 19, after which all area schools returned to their normal schedules. The programs earned praise from Milwaukee Public School Superintendent Harold Vincent.[89]

In March of 1956, Hearst announced that it had sold the Norris property, but would continue to lease the coach house for its television studios. On April 21, it announced that it would build a new building for its television studios and facilities on the southwest corner of North 19th and West Wells Streets.[90] Ground was broken on July 16.[91]

Gretchen Colnik had begun hosting a show for women on WTMJ-TV. Produced by Sid Stone and his wife Shanah for sponsor Mrs. Karl's Bread (the only sponsor the show would ever have), it featured cooking, entertaining, and decorating tips for the housewife. In 1955, the Stones shifted the show to WTVW. It ran on WISN-TV through 1961. (WISN-TV and the Dick Golembiewski collection)

In April of 1956, Ampex demonstrated the first practical video tape recorder at the NAB show in Chicago. WISN-TV became the first Milwaukee station to order one that June,[92] although it was never received.

On Monday, October 20, 1957, WISN-TV moved into new studios at North 19th and West Wells Streets. A portion of the dedication ceremony was broadcast by the station at 6:30 p.m. that evening.[93]

In January of 1958, WISN-TV joined the Badger Television Network. It consisted of WISN-TV, WFRV-TV (Ch. 5) in Green Bay, and WKOW-TV (Ch. 27) in Madison. The first two shows were "Homemakers' Holiday," a comedy/quiz show hosted by Charlie Hanson at 1:00 p.m., and "Good Housekeeping," which was hosted by Trudy Beilfuss at 1:30 p.m. weekdays.[94] Hanson had joined WISN radio, and Beilfuss had done a similar show on WOKY-TV. The following month, a third show, "Pretzel Party," hosted by Larry Clark was added at 12:30 p.m. Clark also hosted "Saturday Night Theater" on WTMJ-TV.[95] He was later replaced

"It's a Draw," produced by local cartoonist Sid Stone, debuted on WCAN-TV. It moved briefly to WTMJ-TV, and then to WTVW in 1955. The show featured a moderator, who gave clues to the phrase Stone was illustrating to a panel that tried to guess what it was. That panel usually included visiting celebrities. Shown here are: L-R: Milwaukee native and author Robert Bloch, Carolyn Lawrence, and Boston Pops conductor Arthur Fiedler. Later, CBS wanted to produce the show in New York, but Stone declined. It ran on WISN-TV until 1959. (WISN-TV photo)

by local comedian Tommy Richards (who would later play "Pops" – see special section.). "Pretzel Party" was presented before a live studio audience, which was served lunch. It featured music by the "Pretzel Benders" band, community singing, interviews and variety acts. All three shows originated from the WISN-TV studios.[96] In March, the network broadcast one-hour film highlights of the Kohler Co. - UAW hearings of the Senate Investigating Committee each night at 11:00 p.m.[97] In August of that year, long-time WISN-TV staff announcer Charlie LaForce replaced Richards as host of "Pretzel Party."[98] The network lasted less than a year, its last broadcast taking place on August 8.

The new WISN-TV studios were dedicated in October of 1957. (WISN-TV photo)

THE OTHER 98

A TV Show
by and for Teen Agers

SPECIAL GUEST TODAY
ANN HAWKINS

Shorewood High School Junior who plays the leading role in "Annie Get Your Gun."

3:00 P. M.

WISN-TV 12

WISN-TV finally took delivery of its first videotape recorder in 1960. The 2" RCA unit had serial number 00001. (WISN-TV photo)

On April 1, 1959, WISN-TV broadcast its first color program. Produced by the Miller Brewing Co., *Pride of the Braves*, a film program, was shown at 8:30 p.m. To mark the occasion, "Weather in the Weather" was broadcast from home plate at Milwaukee County Stadium that evening.[99]

Teenagers made up a big part of television's audience. In the 1950s, juvenile delinquency was a major issue. Experts liked to say that only two-percent of teenagers engaged in such behavior.[100] To showcase those who spent their time constructively, WISN-TV began showing a public service series called "The Other 98" on Saturday, June 20, 1959. Hosted by Gertrude Puelicher, the show featured teenagers from around the area. Both the show and its host won numerous awards, including a resolution honoring her passed by the Milwaukee Common Council.[101]

In those days, many commercials were done live, which led to some interesting moments. As Jerry Robinson remembered:

During rehearsals our stage crew would use lard as a substitute for ice cream because of the hot studio lights. Just before air time the lard was to be replaced. Well during one live commercial for Sealtest, Charlie LaForce was to eat a large spoonful of ice cream and show with facial expressions how good it tasted. The stage crew forgot to make the switch! Charlie put the spoonful of lard in his mouth, and immediately knew that it wasn't right. He was trying his best to pretend he liked it, while also trying to swallow. After many seconds he said with pained expression, 'This is good ice cream!'

Roger Krupp did a commercial for a furrier which used live chinchillas. It required him to reach into a cage and take one chinchilla out to hold and pet in order to show how soft the fur was. On occasion Roger would be bitten and finished the commercial in pain. The crew suggested that if Roger would feed the chinchillas before each commercial this wouldn't happen. Each day Roger would come to work with a large shopping bag filled lettuce, carrots and celery. It worked – most of the time![102]

On January 27, 1961, WISN-TV announced that it would be switching its network affiliation to CBS.[103] WISN radio was a CBS affiliate, and the station had wanted the television affiliation. WITI-TV wound up as the ABC affiliate, and the switch took place on Sunday, April 2.[104]

In July of 1962, Hearst announced that it would sell The *Milwaukee Sentinel* to The Journal Co. The move followed a strike by Milwaukee Newspaper Guild members that began on May 27. The Journal formally began publishing the morning paper on July 23. The sale did not include WISN or WISN-TV.[106]

CHAPTER 6 ~ WTVW/WISN-TV: CHANNEL 12

In 1960, "Open House 12" debuted. The first co-hosts were Fred Niedermeyer and Lynn Honeck, who was later replaced by Barbara Orteig. Niedermeyer was later replaced by Bill Plante. A live band was included. The show lasted until 1962. (WISN-TV photo)

"Milwaukee Reports" had been a feature on the CBS-owned WXIX. It moved to WISN-TV in 1960. The show, which ran at 10:30 p.m. Sundays, featured moderator Robert Herzog, and a panel of reporters and attorneys, who questioned a single guest. Featured guests included Arizona Senator Barry Goldwater, Teamsters President Jimmy Hoffa, Minnesota Senator Hubert Humphrey (shown here), actor Pat O'Brien, and Michigan Governor George Romney. The show ended in 1963. (WISN-TV photo)

WTVW/WISN-TV began holding annual telethons for the March of Dimes in 1955. Here in 1961, Charlie Hanson interviews special guest Nick Adams, who played "Johnny Yuma" in *The Rebel*. (WISN-TV photo)

Popular sportscaster Dick Johnson moved from WTMJ-TV to WISN-TV in 1959. (WISN-TV photo)

To compete with popular weathercasts on other stations, WISN-TV started "Weather in the Weather." In the segment, members of the station's staff did the weather from North 19th Street and West Wisconsin Avenue. After local youths threw snowballs at them during the winter months, the weathercasts were moved to the roof of the WISN-TV studios. Here Bill Plante does a segment. Preceding Plante were Tommy Richards, Jerry Sundt and Chuck Arnold105, who started the segment on Monday, December 15, 1958. (WISN-TV photo)

WISN-TV's Wisconsin News team in the early 1960s. Standing L-R: Sportscaster Dick Johnson, Bill Plante, who did news mornings and "Weather in the Weather" for a time, and Charlie LaForce, who did weather. Seated L-R: News Anchor Bob Herzog, Barbara Orteig, who did women's news, and her father Patt Barnes, who did special features. After Orteig was widowed, she married Plante, who would go on to work for CBS. (WISN-TV photo)

During the folk music craze of the early 1960s, WISN-TV produced its own version of *Hootenanny*. On Saturday, June 27, 1964, "Singin' Here Tonight" made its debut at 6:00 p.m. The show featured "The Hitchhikers" from Marquette University, including Keith Clow, Patsy Johnston, James Murtaugh, and Dennis Gray. Murtaugh served as the emcee.[107] The show featured a local or visiting folk group each week, and was taped before a studio audience made up of high school and/or college students. One of the featured groups was the Smothers Brothers! In 1965, the show was voted the best locally produced entertainment show by the Milwaukee County Television and Radio Council. The last show was on June 4, 1966. (WISN-TV photo)

On March 15, 1965 the station elected to drop the CBS Evening News with Walter Cronkite. In its place at 5:30 p.m., it ran "Sumthin' Else"; a rock 'n' roll show it produced featuring local bands.[108] "Danny Peil and the Tigers" was the first house band. They were later replaced by "The Saints Five" (shown). It ran through Friday, November 5, 1965. (WISN-TV photo)

CHAPTER 6 ~ WTVW/WISN-TV: CHANNEL 12

HOWARD AND ROSEMARY GERNETTE

"Dialing for Dollars" was a franchised show that became popular in the mid-1960s. On the show, a name would be picked from the telephone book, and that person called. If they knew the jackpot amount (and later a "count" such as "four up"), they won. On Monday, December 11, 1967, the show began on WISN-TV at 12:05 p.m., and ran until 12:30 p.m. The first hosts were the station's new weatherman, Howard Gernette, and long-time station puppeteer and announcer Bob Trent. Gernette's name was Gernetzke, but WISN-TV management decided to change it. Howard's wife Rosemary recalled:

> [WISN-TV general manager] *Jim Butler insisted that we change our last name. What we couldn't understand was that we were in ethnic Milwaukee, and it shouldn't have been a problem. At first it wasn't an issue, but they came closer to signing a contract, it became one. It bothered Howard, and it bothered me. It bothered Howard so much that he turned the job down at first. Then we got a call which said that it wasn't a big deal. We assumed that that was all there was to it. Well, when we got down to Milwaukee, it was a big deal.*
>
> *We got back to Wausau, and we were worried because we had our house on the market. Howard went to talk to his mother who blew it off by saying, 'Well,*

Howard Gernetzke replaced John Coleman (who went on to found The Weather Channel) as the station's weatherman in February of 1967. (WISN-TV photo, courtesy of Rosemary Gernetzke)

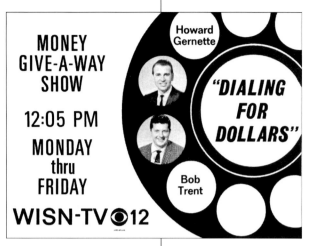

Howard Gernette was joined by his wife Rosemary in August of 1968. (WISN-TV photo)

doesn't everybody in the business change their name?' That made him feel better!

She also remembered that Howard was surprised on his first show:

> The station paid some big bucks for the franchise. They were told when they bought it that it would take a good six months to build an audience, and have a winner. They had a winner on the first call![109]

Bob Trent left the station on August 2, 1968.[110] As a co-host, the station turned to Gernette's wife Rosemary. However, they first called her "Rosemary Ross" rather than Gernette, which confused viewers. As Rosemary remembered:

> When I joined him on 'Dialing for Dollars', they made me change my last name. 'Rosemary Ross' is about as phony as you can get. I was doing commercials for a supermarket chain, and they were being shown on many stations. They didn't want the person doing the commercials to be identified with the station, so they came up with the idea of giving me a phony name. So they gave me a choice of using either 'Ross' or 'Dickson'. So I told them, 'You pick it; they're both phony.' So, I became 'Rosemary Ross'.
>
> People would yell the name from across the street, and I would ignore them because I wasn't used to the name at all. It would be confusing for people.

Howard once got a letter from a woman who was just irate. She said, 'How dare you carry on with that blond while your wife is at home with those eight children!'[111]

The show was done live. In addition to the contest, the pair interviewed visiting celebrities. Rosemary remembered that they met one famous celebrity in an interesting manner:

> A guest that never made it into the studio was Bob Hope. I was so upset, because our co-producer told us that his driver came in and said that he was so sorry that they missed our show. Channel 6 had held him over. So I ran out on Wells Street. The limo was still there, and Bob was sitting next to the limo driver. He rolled the window down, and said, 'Oh honey, what can I do for you?'
> I said, 'Could you just come in so we can get a picture?'
> He said, 'I can't right now, because I have to be out at State Fair Park, and we have to do a rehearsal.' It just so happened that Howard and I were going to be out there later that afternoon doing some things for the station. He said, 'You come backstage, and I'll do anything you want.'
> Well, we did. We took away the 'Fairest of the Fair's' golf cart, and put Bob in it. He was so cute! He was a wonderful man![112]

The couple took over responsibility for promoting the Muscular Dystrophy Association backyard carnivals from children's show host, "Pops." On August 23, 1971, the show was expanded to an hour, and Chef Sophie Kay joined the show to do a cooking segment.

In 1980, the show was transformed into "At Twelve with Howard and Rosemary." (WISN-TV photo)

On Monday, September 8, 1980, the show's name was changed to "At Twelve with Howard and Rosemary."[113] Ratings were high enough that the station no longer wanted to pay the franchise fee or the prize money, so the show focused strictly on interviews. Rosemary Gernetzke:

> *We thought it wasn't necessary to be 'Dialing for Dollars' anymore. Either we could have our own show and give a bigger prize, or just have guests.*
>
> *The show was on in a lot of different formats around the country, and some of our guests didn't want to come on because it was 'Dialing for Dollars'. We had to convince them. Once they saw the ratings, it was different. A lot of stars who would be appearing at the Crown Room at the Pfister Hotel, or at The Melody Top Theater wanted to be on the show.*[114]

On Friday, October 24, 1980, Howard ended his long stint as the station's head weatherman.[115] The station bowed to pressures to use a meteorologist, but he continued to do "At Twelve with Howard and Rosemary."

In September of 1983, it was announced that because of low ratings, and an aging audience, the Gernettes were going to be replaced as the show's hosts.[116] After sixteen years on the air together, Howard and Rosemary Gernette paid a tearful goodbye to their audience on Friday, December 31, 1983.[117]

In 2007 Howard and Rosemary Gernetzke were inducted into the Milwaukee Press Club Media Hall of Fame.

In the mid-to-late 1960s, a number of Green Bay stations applied for, and received construction permits for translator stations in Wisconsin's Fox River Valley in order to improve their signal quality there. WISN-TV also applied for one, and W70AO went on the air in May of 1968. It broadcast with 100 watts of power. A license to cover was granted by the FCC on August 1 of that year. Jerry Robinson:

> *Because channel 12 was right on Lake Michigan, we tried to direct our signal to the West, North and South. As such, we had some dead spots in the Fond du Lac area. We had a little transmitter building and a 300' tower. It would receive channel 12's signal directly off the air, and transpose it to channel 70.*
>
> *In the beginning, we were not sure if it would solve the problem, and as it turned out, I don't think it really did. We found that we never had a big viewership on channel 70. The people were still trying to get channel 12, and would put up with a weaker signal.*[118]

The FCC stripped channels 70-83 from television in 1970 (See chapters 3 and 15.), and W70AO broadcast through the mid-1970s.

Green Bay Packer defensive end Lionel Aldridge had been doing sportscasts on WTMJ-TV. On August 23, 1968, WISN-TV announced that it had hired his counterpart, Willie Davis, to do the same. He also did "Packer Preview" shows with sportscaster Dick Johnson.[119] Davis would go on to found his own broadcasting empire – including stations in Milwaukee.

When the Braves left after the 1965 season, Milwaukee was without baseball. To give residents a "fix," WISN-TV announced in February of 1969 that it would televise thirty-seven Chicago Cubs games that season.[120]

Milwaukee Mayor Henry Maier had a stormy relationship with the *Milwaukee Journal*. (See chapter 2.) In 1969, he found a home for a weekly news conference on WISN-TV. It was broadcast at 10:00 a.m. Fridays, and began with one or more statements by the mayor, followed by questions from other reporters. The first was on May 16.[121]

CHAPTER 6 ~ WTVW/WISN-TV: CHANNEL 12   241

In 1971, several aldermen complained that because of the television coverage the mayor had an advantage when expressing his views, and in a letter to station management, asked for "equal time." General Manager James T. Butler replied that in his opinion the "equal time" provisions of the Communications Act of 1934 (as amended) did not apply. Rather, argued Butler, what applied was the Act's "Fairness Doctrine," which since 1949 had required broadcasters to provide the opportunity for presenting contrasting viewpoints on issues of public importance.[122] Although there was some discussion of broadcasting a half hour, monthly program for aldermen, it never happened. The mayor's weekly, televised press conference ended in 1972.

Since April of 1961, WISN-TV had been a CBS affiliate. However, by the mid-1970s, ABC was not happy with WITI-TV's parent, Storer Broadcasting.[124] In addition, CBS was not happy with WISN-TV, as ratings for its programming were lower in Milwaukee than the national average. In September of 1976, it was announced that WITI-TV would switch its network affiliation from ABC to CBS.[125] As a consequence, WISN-TV announced that it was holding discussions with ABC.[126] The changes took place on Sunday, March 27, 1977, reversing the affiliation swap both stations had made sixteen years earlier.

In 1979, the station decided to replace the show it was running at 6:30 p.m. with a syndicated program, "P.M. Magazine." Developed by Westinghouse, the show was a bit different in that approximately sixty percent consisted of segments produced by other stations that carried it. The other forty percent was produced locally. The first show was on Monday, September 10, 1979, and the first co-hosts were Donna Jordan and Ken Bell.[127] WISN-TV claimed that it cost $400,000 to start up their version. Besides the co-hosts, it hired five additional people, and new equipment, including a new remote truck, two new mini-cameras, and additional editing facilities.[128] Bobby Rivers later joined the show as its movie critic.

In 1982, Bell and Jordan resigned and were replaced by Nancy Christopher and Jim Mika. Both had hosted the show in other cities. The show was revamped at

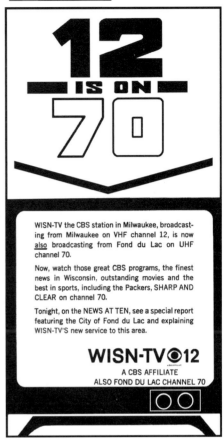

From 1969-1972, WISN-TV broadcast Mayor Maier's weekly news conference Friday mornings. (WISN-TV photo)

WVTV had run the franchised "Bowling for Dollars" from 1971-1974 before replacing it with its own "The Bowling Game." In 1976, WISN-TV, which was running local news at 5:00 p.m., elected to counter-program against the other stations' news, and began running "Bowling for Dollars" at 6:00 p.m. Their version was hosted by weatherman/announcer Bruce Bennett (shown here), and featured local bowlers who rolled in alleys built in the station's studios.[123] The show debuted on Monday, September 13, 1976, and ran through Friday, January 6, 1978. (WISN-TV photo)

the same time, and featured more, shorter segments.[129] The show ended on July 27, 1984.

On Thursday, May 17, 1979, WISN-TV and WMVS-TV cooperated in a program called "Milwaukee: Behind the Headlines," that gave viewers a behind-the-scenes look at the making of channel 12's newscast. Beginning at 9:00 p.m., WMVS-TV examined what went into a newscast, using interviews with WISN-TV personnel, including producers, reporters, editors, directors, camera operators, engineers and technicians. The newscast was then simulcast on both stations – although WMVS-TV's cameras provided a behind-the-scenes look. At 10:30 p.m., program host, Marquette University journalism professor Larry Lorenz, and commentator, former CBS news correspondent Daniel Schorr joined WISN-TV staff members for a critique.[130]

When WISN-TV switched back to an ABC affiliation on March 27, 1977, it used a graphic depicting a bloodshot CBS "eye" closing, and then reopening to become an ABC logo (WISN-TV photo)

In 1978, Jill Geisler became the first female news director of a major market affiliate, when she was appointed at WITI-TV. Milwaukee got a second in late August of 1981, when WISN-TV named Bunny Raasch as its news director.[131] Raasch had come to the station in 1971 from WTMJ-TV. She became the city's first female prime-time news anchor in 1974. Geisler attempted to lure her to channel 6 as a reporter/anchor, and in response WISN-TV named her as assistant news director in 1978.[132] Channel 12's 10:00 p.m. news had ranked third among the city's three network affiliates for many years, but in July, it had climbed into first place.[133]

CHAPTER 6 ~ WTVW/WISN-TV: CHANNEL 12

Ken Bell (left) and Donna Jordan hosted WISN-TV's version of PM Magazine from 1979-1982. (WISN-TV photo)

Jim Mika (Left) and Nancy Christopher hosted PM Magazine in its last year. (WISN-TV photo)

In 1979, WISN-TV became the first Milwaukee TV station to use a helicopter – just beating WITI-TV. (WISN-TV photo)

The "Action News" team in September of 1976. L-R: John Gillespie (sports), former Milwaukee County Executive John Doyne, Barry Judge, Bunny Raasch, and Howard Gernette. Raasch would go on to become first assistant and then news director. (WISN-TV photo)

Raasch had moved to WISN-TV to do hard news, and wanted to get into management. She threw herself into the role. As she remembered:

We were able to affect such a major change in the market. It was a wonderful feeling. I'm not talking only about finally becoming number one at ten o'clock, but actually taking a more in-depth approach to news. It was much more serious – and by serious, I mean interesting and meaningful.

> *Our approach to developing the news was very methodical. Channel 4 was the historic leader. They had serious, very well educated anchors and intelligent people running the newsroom. But the product was flat. They did not attempt to go 'outside of the box' to cover the news in Milwaukee. They followed a traditional approach.*
>
> *One of the first things Mickey Hooten did was to hire a non-traditional consultant. We learned about psychographic research. We used it in both our broad research and in our focus groups, because we knew that you weren't suddenly going to put a new product on the air and whisk everyone away from WTMJ or WITI.*
>
> *What we began to learn was that you could no longer look at demographics the same way. Milwaukee was always under-rated. It was an extremely savvy news market. The audience was very, very interested in what was going on in the city and the country and why. By taking this approach we were able to target certain segments of the audience by developing things that would have particular appeal to the informational needs of that type of viewer.*
>
> *One of the things we did was to start an investigative team. It was an extremely committed group, and they researched and produced two to three projects a year. It represented a major financial commitment, and we were fortunate to get corporate support.*
>
> *More important, after I became news director, we began to look at issues that were crucially important to this area. We developed what we called 'impact' weeks and months. Everyone else was doing series during the rating periods. We decided that our impact periods didn't have to be only during those times. We weren't just going to do two-minute segments during the ten o'clock news. What we did was to cover an issue every way possible. That meant morning, early afternoon, evening and late news programming. We would weave it into our noontime talk show. If necessary, we would expand our newscast. If we had to we would dump a game show at 6:30, and go on with our news for an hour.*
>
> *We set up a consortium of people who were involved in various aspects of the community and held weekly meetings with them. We used them as the sounding board, rather than superimposing our views as news people or station people.*[134]

The first successful program of the type was "Take Back the Night," which dealt with violence against women. According to Raasch, the rewards were immediate:

> *For our whole team it was incredibly rewarding, because in January – our series ran in November – the Wisconsin Legislature called a special session and changed the sexual assault laws.*
>
> *Some mocked what we did, saying that journalists were just supposed to report what was happening, but we felt it was critical to put major issues into context and provide enough information that others would advocate for solutions and changes. We knew that there were problems in this city and state that needed addressing. It wasn't done for sex-appeal purposes.*
>
> *It was fun! It was so exciting! We did another impact month on health issues and at the end presented a 'Family Health Fair' downtown. Everyone in that newsroom could be proud, knowing that they did something really important, and made a difference. It was a great time to be in television!"*[135]

On July 5, 1982, WISN-TV began broadcasting twenty-four hours a day, seven days a week.[136] The move was made because cable television had begun providing service around the clock, and the station wanted to serve that need.[137]

In September of 1988, WISN-TV was chosen over six other competitors to receive a contract to establish a state-wide network for lottery broad-

On January 9, 1984, WISN-TV debuted a live, local afternoon interview show. Named "More," the show was hosted by Liz Ayers and Bobby Rivers. At first the hour-long show ran at 3:00 p.m., but after the Summer Olympics, it was shifted to an hour later, swapping slots with the syndicated "Hour Magazine." After almost a year on the air, the show succumbed to low ratings, and ended its run on December 14. (WISN-TV photo)

casts.[138] Included was "The Money Game," a show that ran Saturday evenings at 6:30. Its run ended in 2003, when it succumbed to budget cuts within the lottery agency. As a part of the same cuts, the daily drawings were moved to the lottery offices in Madison.

News Corporation, the parent company of Fox, acquired a 20% interest in New World Communications. As a consequence, all New World stations, including WITI, affiliated with the Fox Network. The switch was announced in May of 1994.[139] WITI-TV had been the CBS affiliate, and that network began looking for a home in the city. One of the consequences was that Hearst Corporation signed ten-year contracts with ABC extending the affiliations of five of its television stations – including WISN-TV.[140] The station began a new promotional campaign based upon The Turtles' song "Happy Together" – which was sung by the original Turtles, Howard Kaylan ("Flo") and Mark Volman ("Eddie").[141] It proclaimed that WISN-TV and ABC were "Happy Together."

One of the results of the Fox affiliation with WITI was that CBS had to find a new home in the city. It finally affiliated with WDJT-TV, whose parent, Weigel Broadcasting, began making improvements. One of those was to erect a new tower, and Lincoln Park – next to WISN-TV's tower – was the most desirable location. (See chapter 12.) As a result, on February 14, 1995 WISN-TV sued to prevent Weigel from erecting a tower, citing potential interference with its signal to viewers, as well as microwave signals to and from its studios and remote trucks.[142] A Milwaukee County Circuit Court judge issued a temporary injunction on February 27, saying that the new tower would violate a 1984 land-use agreement between WISN-TV and Milwaukee County.[143]

CHAPTER 6 ~ WTVW/WISN-TV: CHANNEL 12   247

In 1989, WISN-TV began an hour-long talk show called "Milwaukee's Talking." Each show ran at 10:00 a.m. and was based upon a single topic. Mark Siegrist hosted the show before a live studio audience. Viewers were also encouraged to call-in with questions. In 1992, the show was shortened to thirty minutes, and moved to 12:30 p.m., and Siegrist was replaced with Shaun Robinson. The show ended in 1993. (WISN-TV photo)

Hearst filed a petition to deny with the FCC, but in May of 1996, the Commission ruled against it.[144] As a consequence, the City Planning Commission unanimously approved WDJT-TV's plan.[145] WISN-TV then made an offer which would have allowed WDJT-TV to hang its antenna on the Hearst station's tower.[146] That offer was given careful consideration, but rejected. After reportedly spending $500,000 in legal bills to fight the new tower, WISN-TV threw in the towel.[147]

WDJT-TV subsequently erected a new tower and transmitter facility in Lincoln Park. In what became a "tower war," WISN-TV denied its new neighbor the ability to access its facility via a road running through its property, forcing WDJT-TV to build a bridge over nearby Lincoln Creek. After Congress mandated a switch from analog to digital television broadcasting in 1996, local stations began plan-

Jerry Taff came to WISN-TV in 1979 and retired in 2005. He's shown here with another long-time news anchor, Kathy Mykleby. (WISN-TV photo)

ning. Channels 10 and 36 elected to build a new digital tower in partnership with a private tower firm, and hoped to lease the other stations space on it. Most, including WISN-TV, elected to mount their digital antennas on their existing towers. Its engineers proposed to extend its 1,105' tower by 115 feet. That idea was opposed by channels 10 and 36, as well as WDJT-TV. On July 29, 1999, the Milwaukee Board of Zoning Appeals turned down the station's request.[148]

Hearst-Argyle Stations, Inc. filed suit in Milwaukee Circuit Court that September in an attempt to force the Board of Zoning Appeals to allow the station to extend its tower. The suit accused the board of trying to force WISN-TV to mount its antenna on the new tower built by MATC for channels 10 and 36.[149] The court eventually ruled against WISN-TV. In December of 1999, WDJT-TV offered a deal in which WISN-TV could share its tower. The idea was rejected.[150] In a counter-proposal, WISN-TV proposed a new ordinance which would allow extensions to existing towers of up to 150'. In exchange for its support, the station offered WDJT-TV the use of its road, which would have allowed the latter station to remove its bridge over Lincoln Creek.

The Milwaukee Common Council's Zoning, Neighborhoods and Development Committee voted to reject the station's request to extend its tower, sent it to the full common council for a vote, then pulled it back for another hearing, and again voted against the idea on January 11, 2000.[151] The matter went to the full Common Council, which approved the proposed ordinance in a 10-7 vote.[152] Mayor John Norquist then vetoed the measure, saying that it would violate the city's policy of encouraging TV stations to consolidate their antennas onto fewer towers.[153]

There the matter sat until July 30, 2002, when the Common Council's Zoning, Neighborhoods and Development Committee reversed its two year-old decision, and voted 4-1 to allow the extension.[154] On August 1, the full Council voted 12-5 to approve the station's request.[155] Mayor Norquist vetoed the measure a week later[156], and after a series of procedural errors and shifting votes, the full Common Council failed to override the mayor's veto on September 4.[157]

The Communications Act of 1996 allowed the FCC to relax its multiple-ownership rules. As a result, consolidation through merger began to take place in the in-

The remodeled WISN-TV studio entrance as seen in the evening. (WISN-TV photo)

A new "Chopper 12" made its debut in 2002. (WISN-TV photo)

dustry. In August of 1997, the broadcast group of the Hearst Corporation merged with Argyle Television, Inc., to form Hearst-Argyle, Inc. WISN-TV came under this new ownership.

In December of 2001, the station's news helicopter crashed near the intersection of I-43 and Highway 164 in Waukesha County. Poor visibility was the cause of the crash, which killed the pilot.[158]

Clear Channel Communications acquired WISN and WLTQ(FM), leaving empty space in the North 19th street building occupied by WISN-TV since 1957. With the station's fiftieth anniversary scheduled for October of 2004, Hearst embarked on a multi-million dollar upgrade to it, which included renovation of both the interior and exterior, as well as new equipment.[159] Included in the remodeled lobby was a timeline of the station's history featuring a look at many of the events, shows and on-air personalities that had been seen over the years.

In October of 2006, the station named Lori Waldon as its news director – the first African-American to hold the position in the city.[160]

In 2006 WISN-TV became the first commercial station in the city to broadcast a locally-originated program in high-definition, when it showed the annual July 3 fireworks using Milwaukee Public Television's HDTV remote truck. (WISN-TV)

The 2008 WISN-TV News team at 10:00 p.m. L-R: Dan Needles (sports), Kathy Mykleby (news), Toya Washington (news) and Mark Baden (weather). (WISN-TV)

After going on the air as a marriage of convenience between the four applicants, the station underwent a turbulent first two decades under Hearst ownership. Starting in the 1980s, it began to emerge from its status as Milwaukee's third commercial VHF station, and began to challenge its competitors for leadership in news and other programming. It, like all the city's stations, faced the challenge of cable and

Long-time anchor Mike Gousha returned to television on a part-time basis to host "UPFRONT with Mike Gousha" Sunday mornings at 9:00. The show made its debut on January 27, 2008, and featured interviews and analysis of political news. (WISN-TV)

satellite competition, which diluted the available revenue stream. As it enters the digital television age, WISN-TV faces a whole new way of transmitting video information. That will open up yet another chapter in its long and storied history.

THE CHILDREN'S SHOWS

Both WTVW and WISN-TV broadcast many children's shows during their first dozen years. Until the debut of *The Mickey Mouse Club* in 1955, ABC didn't provide its affiliates with programming until the evening hours, and it didn't provide daytime programming until the late 1950s. As such, the station was forced to produce most of its own morning and afternoon programming, and the children's shows were prominent.

The first broadcast day, Michael W. Klein, Jr. showed western films as "Cowboy Mike" on "Roundup Time." It was designed to compete with WTMJ-TV's "Foreman Tom," and ran Monday through Friday at 4:45 p.m. For the first two weeks the station was on the air it was also shown on Saturday at 4:15 p.m. The last show was Friday, June 17, 1955.

Following "Roundup Time" that first broadcast day, Marquette University student Jerry Sundt showed serials as "Dr. Eon" on "Dr. Eon's Lab." Jerry Sundt:

> I went to Marquette to the School of Speech to study broadcasting. In my second year, I decided that I ought to get a job in the business in order to gain some experience. I went to Channel 12, which was signing on at the time in the fall of 1954. What I hoped to do was to get a job doing whatever I could to get into the business. When I interviewed with the program director, Elden Anspach, he said, 'We're looking for some on-air personalities – one of which would be a cowboy – but you don't look like a cowboy.' The other was to be a scientist – that would be Dr. Eon. He said, 'You look like you could do that.'
>
> I went home, and didn't hear anything for two weeks. Then I got a call from Elden two days before the station went on the air. He told me that I got the role. There was no second interview or audition. I was told to show up at the transmitter site in Lincoln Park!
>
> The concept was that Dr. Eon was a scientist that developed a pill that dissolves in water, and takes us to a time and place in space that we determined. That was the segue to an episode of one of the old cowboy serials we were showing. The camera would dolly-in on the pill that was dissolving in water, and we would go into the serial. Usually we had more time, so we would go into a cartoon to fill it."
>
> The Dr. Eon's Lab role grew into my doing experiments on the air. I used to have to go down to the library and scour around to try and find something that was both simple enough and visual on the black-and-white picture we were broadcasting. I didn't know what I was doing, but in those days I guess we all faked it a little bit!¹⁶¹

There were four different types of pills: the "regular" which transported the viewers to the time and place in space corresponding to the serial shown; the "24-hour," which kept the show's continuity intact overnight; the "72-hour," which did the same over the weekend; and the "comic," which was used before cartoons.¹⁶²

The show ran weekday afternoons, as well as on Saturdays. Jerry Sundt was a Navy ROTC student, and during the summer of 1955, he was ordered on a two month, European training cruise. While on it, he shot film in every port-of-call, and later showed the footage on his show.¹⁶³ The last weekday show was on Friday, August 12, 1955, after which WISN-TV revamped its afternoon schedule to include *The Mickey Mouse Club*. "Dr. Eon" was tapped to host "Children's Hour" at noon weekdays. The show featured cartoons, comedies, games and stories. One contest, which required children to write an essay on "What Christmas Means to Me," received hundreds of entries.¹⁶⁴ The last show was on Friday, March 23, 1956. Jerry Sundt:

> I ate lunch with the kiddies. I was trying to give them some nutritional knowledge. The

Jerry Sundt played "Dr. Eon," and showed serials on "Dr. Eon's Lab." He later hosted "Children's Hour." (Courtesy of Jerry Sundt)

funny thing was, I was a student at Marquette, and I didn't eat very nutritiously! I knew nothing about this stuff when I started![165]

Sundt and Jerry Robinson became personal friends, and the engineer helped "Dr. Eon" out of tight spots common during the early days of live television. Jerry Robinson:

Everything was either live or on film in those days. If a film would break, we would fill the time by opening up the side of the camera and 'Dr. Eon' explained to the audience how the camera worked![166]

WEMP personalities played a role in WTVW's programming. One was Bob "Coffeehead" Larsen, who did a show called "Half-Pint Party" Saturday mornings at 11:00. Larsen was joined by cartoonist Sid Stone, who produced the show.[167] Like all of Stone's shows, it was produced for a sponsor, in this case the Gehl Dairy, and the time was purchased from the station. As always, live shows with kids produced some interesting moments, as Sid's son John remembered:

It was a party for the kids where they would play games and other things. They would wind it up with an auction. Milk bottles at the time had cardboard tops that you could save. The idea behind the auction was that the kids would save the tops from Gehl milk bottles, and then use them like cash to bid on prizes.

They had something like three prizes. The first might be a paint set, and the second a little wagon. The grand prize this one time was a Schwinn bike. So, the kids were bidding, fifteen, twenty, twenty-five bottle tops. Then one kid bet several thousand! Well the auction stopped.

My dad had noticed that when he came in, he'd brought all of these milk caps in a little briefcase! The other kids had a few caps in their pockets, but this kid had a briefcase! He was the son of an employee, and he'd gotten them at the dairy. They stopped doing the auctions after that!"[168]

The first "Half-Pint Patty" aired on January 1, 1955; the last, on May 25, 1957.

"Romper Room" was offered to stations as either a syndicated (filmed in Baltimore), or a franchised pre-school program. The franchised programs used their own teachers – who had often taught kindergarten. WTVW chose the latter option, and its version made its debut on Monday, May 2, 1955. Ruth Scheidecker played "Miss Ruth" on the show, which ran from noon until 1:00 p.m. weekdays. The show taught children various lessons – especially safety. A line of branded merchandise was used on the show, and marketed in toy stores.

At the end of each show, the hostess would look through her "magic mirror," and say, "Romper, bomper, stomper boo. Tell me, tell me, tell me, do. Magic mirror, tell me today. Have all my friends had fun at play?" After which, she would call out a list of first names of all the children she saw.

"Romper Room" with teacher "Miss Ruth" made its debut on WTVW on 1955.

"Miss Barbara" was Milwaukee's third "Romper Room" teacher. (WISN-TV photo)

The show was shifted to 11:00-noon on September 26, 1955, after WISN-TV began its broadcasting day earlier. When the station revamped its morning schedule on September 17, 1956, "Romper Room" was cut to thirty minutes. "Miss Pat" (Oliver) replaced "Miss Ruth" in March of 1957[169], and the show was shifted to afternoons at 3:30 p.m. on May 27 of that year. The last show was on Friday, July 26.

The following Monday, the show moved to WITI-TV (Ch. 6)[170], where it ran in three different time slots until July 24, 1959. In January of that year, "Miss Barbara" (Gresser) had replaced "Miss Pat"[171] after she was chosen from ninety-eight applicants.[172] "Romper Room" returned to WISN-TV on Monday, July 27, 1959, when it was expanded back to an hour between 9:00-10:00 a.m.

In 1962, Gresser had a child, and was replaced by "Miss Jane" (Woods)[173] until "Miss Barbara" returned the following year. In April of 1963, the show was cut to thirty minutes. The station was under pressure from CBS to show *I Love Lucy* reruns, and because it had so many children's shows, it decided to cut "Romper Room," and use the time to show them.[174] On Monday, July 13, 1964, the show's time slot was shifted earlier – to 7:30 a.m. "Miss Maureen" replaced Barbara Gresser in January of 1965, and the show's long run on WISN-TV came to an end on Friday, April 23 of that year.

Hugh Rowlands had begun playing his "Uncle Hugo" character on WOKY-TV. After a thirteen-week run, the show ended. He then brought the character to WTVW to host "Looney Tunes" cartoons. The first show was on Monday, June 20, 1955, and it ran through Friday, June 28, 1957.

"Uncle Hugo" was the station's janitor, and occupied the "second sub-basement."[175] As he had been at WOKY-TV, he was harassed by his boss "Oswald," and spent a lot of time eating sponsor Mrs. Howe's Potato Chips product!

"Miss Jane" temporarily took over the show in 1962-63 during the pregnancy of "Miss Barbara." (WISN-TV photo)

The station then purchased a package of Max Fleischer Popeye cartoons, and the title was changed to "Uncle Hugo and Popeye" on Monday, July 1, 1957, and ran until replaced by "The Three Stooges and Pops" in 1959.

Mary Schmidt had started at WTVW as an announcer. She later became an on-air talent, and one of the first shows she did was "Magic House." It was a part of a new morning line-up introduced in March of 1956, after the station began signing-on at 9:00 a.m. Supposedly set in a Victorian-style home (a model was used), the show featured Schmidt as "Melody." Joining her was a puppet named "Teddy." Schmidt did how-to demonstrations between the requisite cartoons.[176] The first show was at 9:30 a.m. on Monday, March 26, 1956, and it ran through Friday, May 24, 1957.

When "Romper Room" moved to WITI-TV, it was replaced in 1959 by "Chuck Wagon." Chuck Bruce played "Curley," and introduced western films. He was a singer in the chorus and danced in a production of *Brigadoon* that had played in Chicago. He had also appeared in two Roy Rogers TV shows.[177] Besides introducing the films, "Curley" entertained the children with "tall Texas tales" and songs. The first show was on Monday, July 29, 1957, and the show ran through Friday, March 7, 1958.

CHAPTER 6 ~ WTVW/WISN-TV: CHANNEL 12   255

On Monday, April 28, 1958, the station started another kid's show. It was called "Fun House" and featured slapstick shorts by Leon Errol, W.C. Fields, Ned Sparks, Clark and McCullough, and Billy Gilbert.[178] The show ran Monday-Friday at 11:30 a.m. In October of that year, it was shifted to 9:00 a.m., and in April of 1959, to 10:00 a.m. By that time, the show featured cartoons, as well as two clown hosts: "Stubby" and "Tubby," played by announcers Lee Murray and Art Jones respectively. It was shifted to 8:30 a.m. on October 3, 1960, and cut to thirty minutes. The show's run came to an end on Friday March 31, 1961, as the station affiliated with CBS that weekend, and picked up that network's daytime programming.

At 6:00 p.m. on Monday, December 1, 1958, WISN-TV began a new show called "Punky and His Pals." The show featured hostess "Miss Melody" (Wiken) and puppeteer "Ci-Ci" (Cynthia Shove). Wiken was a freshman at Shorewood High School. Her father, Dick, was a sculptor, who helped give the puppets their look. Shove was a sophomore at the University of Wisconsin – Milwaukee, majoring in education. The puppets included: "Punky," "Chico," "Porky," "Grandma," "Grandpa," "Baby Teddy," "Grandma Cricket," "Sim Sala Bim" and "The Giurk."[179]

On Monday, August 28, 1961, Punky was shifted to 4:00 p.m. and ran there through Friday, 24 August 1962. It then went off the air for a time, and "Pops Theater" moved into the 4:30 p.m. time slot. The puppets returned when they joined "Pops" on Monday, October 8, 1962. That ran through Friday, December 27, 1963. The show was very popular and won an award as the "Best TV Program for Young Children" from the Milwaukee Radio and Television Council in 1960.[180]

After the Three Stooges shorts were released to television in 1958, stations around the country began running them. In Milwaukee, WTMJ-TV turned down the package when it was offered to them. Sprague Vonier was the program director there at the time:

> I refused to put on the Three Stooges because of the eye-poking, which I felt was rather dangerous because kids would then think that you could do that and it wouldn't hurt – or that you could recover right away. So they took it over to WISN, and beat the hell out of us with it![181]

To host the show, WISN-TV turned to comedian Tommy Richards (Thomas R. Joho). Richards portrayed "Pops," the assistant manager at the mythical "Bijou" Theater. The first show was at 5:00 p.m. on Monday, August 31, 1959, and ran for thirty minutes.[182] It ran in that time slot Mondays and Fridays, and also from noon until 1:00 p.m. Saturdays and Sundays.

When it came time to run the film, "Pops" would always yell, "Roll 'em Lester!" The show's theme song was "Miss Trombone," a.k.a. "The Slippery Rag," written by Henry Fillmore, "father of the trombone smear."[183]

Richards had been a risqué comedian when playing nightclubs[184], and the name "Pops" came from that background. As he recalled in a 2004 interview with author Steve Cox:

> The name 'Pops' comes from Burlesque," explained Richards. "Pops was the guy who used to keep the Johns away from the women and the dancers in the back of the theater. It's kind of an old showbiz title.[185]

Puppeteer "Ci-Ci" (at left) and hostess "Miss Melody" (holding "Punky") with the menagerie of puppets seen on "Punky and His Pals." (WISN-TV photo)

"Pops" was the assistant manager of the "Bijou Theater." (WISN-TV photo)

On Monday, September 5, 1960, the show expanded to Monday through Friday in the same time slot (the weekend shows remained unchanged). After WISN-TV became a CBS affiliate, the weekday shows expanded to an hour. That took place on April 3, 1961.

The weekday show was shifted to 4:30-5:30 p.m. on August 28, 1961. On August 27, 1962, it was shifted back to the 4:00-5:00 p.m. "Pops" was joined by puppet "Punky" on October 8, 1962, at which time the show was renamed "Pops Theater and Punky." On December 30, 1963, the show began showing "Rocky and Bullwinkle" cartoons, and the name was changed to "Pops Theater and Rocky."

The show was cut to 30 minutes, beginning at 4:30 p.m. on August 23, 1965. The show was shifted to 5:00 p.m. on January 3, 1966. On January 24, 1966, it was again renamed as "Pops Theater and Popeye," and featured the made-for-TV "Popeye" cartoons. By that time, Bob Trent's puppets: "Lippy Lucy," "Nasal," "Finius T. Badnick" (a gloved hand), as well as "Fielding Mouse" and his friends the "Rodent Sisters," had joined the show[186], residing in a store across the alley from the Bijou Theater. The last Pops show aired on April 22, 1966. It was replaced by "Lippy

Lucy" featuring Bob Trent's puppets on the following Monday, April 25. That show ran through Friday, December 8, 1967.

"Pops" proved to be extremely popular. He made appearances around the city, cut a record for sponsor Johnston's Cookies, and was the spokesman for the station's "Backyard Carnivals" for the Muscular Dystrophy Association.[187]

In 1960, producers Nick Nicholson and Roger Muir produced 130 ten-minute shorts named *Funny Manns*. The segments featured comic actor Cliff Norton, who

The Three Stooges visit "Pops Theater," and sample a sponsor's product. (WISN-TV photo)

At the end of its run, Bob Trent's puppets, including "Lippy Lucy," joined the show. (WISN-TV photo)

played various members of the "Mann" family: "Con Mann," "Poor Mann," "Milk Mann," etc.[188] Norton told viewers "that everything he'd learned in life, he'd learned from his uncles," and then provided comic narration to silent film footage.[189] WISN-TV bought the package, and tapped staff announcer Lee Murray to host them as "Stubby" the clown. Murray had played the character on the station's 'Fun House" program. A thirty-minute show, "Funny Manns and Stubby" made its debut at 5:30 p.m. on Monday April 2, 1961, and ran weekdays. The show also ran Saturdays at 5:00 p.m. and Sundays at 11:00 a.m. The Sunday show was moved to 11:30 a.m. on May 21; the Saturday show on June 23. Bob Trent's puppets: "Darwin" (a monkey) and "Koo-Jee-Boo" (a crow)[190] later joined "Stubby."

On September 10, the Sunday show ended. The weekday version was cut to Thursday-Friday on September 14. On September 30, the Saturday version ended, and the weekday version followed on Friday, October 6.

"Stubby" the clown (Lee Murray) is shown with Bob Trent's puppets "Koo-Jee-Boo" (left) and "Darwin." (WISN-TV photo)

Staff announcer Lee Murray played "Sergeant Lee" on WISN-TV's version of The Dick Tracy Show. An old Du Mont console was used as a prop.[193] (WISN-TV photo)

CHAPTER 6 ~ WTVW/WISN-TV: CHANNEL 12   259

Bob Trent and "Skip" hosted the second incarnation of The Mickey Mouse Club on WISN-TV. Here they're shown with Disney characters "Pluto" and "Goofy." (WISN-TV photo)

In 1959, Larry Harmon Productions, in cooperation with Jayark Films, produced a series of 156 five-minute, color cartoons, based upon the popular "Bozo the Clown" character.[191] WISN-TV bought the package, and replaced "Funny Manns and Stubby" with "Bozo and Stubby." The first show was on Sunday, October 1, 1961. Like its predecessor, the new show also ran on Thursday and Friday afternoons at 5:30 p.m., and Saturday mornings at 11:30 a.m. All versions ended Sunday, October 9, 1962, when they were replaced by yet another cartoon package.

In the late summer of 1961, United Productions of America (UPA) produced 130, five-minute cartoons based on Chester Gould's "Dick Tracy" character. The shows were designed to tie in with a local host. After the animated opening credits were shown, the station dissolved to a mock police station. Each host would call Tracy over a microphone or intercom. At the start of each cartoon, the Dick Tracy character would respond by saying, "OK, Chief, I'll get on it right away." UPA also produced thirty-second "Crime Stoppers" features, which were used as bumpers between cartoons. Commercials for Mattel Toys and American Character tie-in products were often shown.[192]

Membership card issued to WISN-TV Mickey Mouse Club members. (WISN-TV)

Staff announcer Lee Murray played "Sergeant Lee" on WISN-TV's version of the show, which ran Thursdays, Fridays, Saturdays, and Sundays in the same time slots "Bozo and Stubby" had been seen. Often, Sergeant Lee would talk about crime fighting techniques, or interview a guest law-enforcement officer.[194] The weekday show shifted to 5:00 p.m. on Thursday, October 4, 1963, when the station shifted its afternoon programming thirty minutes earlier after picking up the CBS Evening News with Walter Cronkite. The Friday afternoon version ended on January 10, 1964; the Thursday version on September 10. The Sunday version's last show was on September 16, while Saturday's lasted a bit longer – until November 28.

As an ABC affiliate, WISN-TV had carried *The Mickey Mouse Club* weekday afternoons between 1955 and 1959. In 1962, the show went into syndication, and since each episode was only eighteen minutes long, stations around the country used local hosts to fill the remaining time. At WISN-TV, resident puppeteer and ventriloquist, Bob Trent, was again tapped for the role. Trent was joined by his ventriloquist's dummy "Skip." Once again the show ran weekday afternoons, beginning on August 27, 1962. On September 30, 1963, the time slot was shifted thirty minutes earlier, and the last show was seen on Friday, August 20, 1965.

"TOLOUSE NONECK"

Horror films on television had become the rage with the release of the Universal versions in October of 1957. In 1962, WISN-TV decided to jump on the horror/sci-fi bandwagon when it began showing such films on its "Big Movie" show Friday nights at 10:20 p.m. beginning on September 21, 1962, and running through June

CHAPTER 6 ~ WTVW/WISN-TV: CHANNEL 12   261

14, 1963. The station took a break from showing those films that summer, but they returned on September 4, and ran through September 25 of the following year.

To get even more air time (in a time slot more suitable for younger viewers) it began running the same films as "Movies From Tomorrow" Saturday afternoons beginning on January 4, 1964. These ran as a single feature through July 11 of the same year. The opening sequence featured a clock that ran backwards, slowly at first, gaining speed until it overheated. Simultaneously, long-time WISN-TV announcer Charlie LaForce introduced the film.[195] For its theme, the show used the synthesized opening music from *Forbidden Planet*, which the station had acquired along with dozens of other post-1948 MGM titles.[196]

By 1964, television was in the midst of the second "horror boom." The networks featured *Bewitched*, *The Addams Family*, and *The Munsters*. With the new season that fall, the station decided to expand the format Friday nights into a double feature, and change the name to "Movies From Tomorrow." It ran in that format from October 2, 1964 through September 10, 1965, when it was replaced by "Movies From the Combat Zone."

Beginning on January 8, 1966, the station showed many of the same films on "The Saturday Afternoon Movie." It ran them off-and-on through September 7, 1968.

On September 15, 1972, WISN-TV began running horror/sci-fi films again. It called the show "Time for Terror", which ran Friday nights/Saturday mornings at approximately 12:35 a.m. The show's opening graphic showed drops of blood appearing against a black background until they spelled the title of the show. Howard Gernette did an echo-plex voice-over announcing the title of the film, which was followed by a blood curdling scream. During the commercial breaks title cards sporting the show's title and that of the movie being shown were seen, done in yellow or orange art-nouveau letterings against a black background.[197] The show ran through March 30, 1973.

(Courtesy of Hal Erickson)

(Courtesy of Hal Erickson)

"Tolouse NoNeck" with sidekick "Dr. Feeleystein." (WISN-TV photo)

In late 1979, the station decided to again run a package of horror/science-fiction films. This time, it elected to use a host. Chicago native Rick Felski had come to the station after having been a theater supervisor at Great America. He had also performed with the Second City Children's Program in Chicago.[198] Felski was in the staging department, when one day he got a surprise:

> One day, one of the other fellows told me that he was going to be designing a horror set. I said, 'That sounds cool. Is that a project we have coming up?'
> He said to me, 'Well, yeah. Don't you know you're involved?'
> I said, 'I am?'
> He said, 'I'm doing the set and [unnamed staff member]'s doing the lighting plot, and you're developing the character. Didn't they tell you that?'
> I was the last one to know that they were going to start running some horror movie packages!'[199]

Felski turned to Bill Scherbarth at the Miller-Armstrong Costume Company for help. Scherbarth developed Felski's look, which featured a top hat and tails, spiked teeth, and aviator sunglasses. Scherbarth said that after he and Rick first met, he conceived the basic approach: Felski had a long face with large teeth and a beard. As such, he covered the beard with hair. Rather than use fangs, he opted to paint the teeth as "spiked." They had a white, yak hair, Santa Claus wig from the 1920-30s lying around, which they dyed and used. The top hat happened to be at the com-

pany as well, so they elected to use it. Rather than the usual clown white make-up, Scherbarth decided to use a grey tone. Felski picked out his own tuxedo.[200]

The character's name came serendipitously. Rick Felski:

> "The day we did the make-up I went back to the studio to see how people liked it. One of my daily responsibilities was that I was in charge of the staging for 'Dialing for Dollars'. They would have a guest on to help them give away some money. So, I had my make-up on, and the producer said, 'Let's have Rick do this section. It'll be a good way to promote the new horror show we have coming up in a few weeks.'
>
> It was a great idea, but this character had no name. Literally it was a couple of minutes before air time. Everybody's in the back of the studio thinking about what we could call this character. One guy came up with 'Gravedigger', and other bizarre names. I don't know why, but Toulouse-Lautrec went into my mind, and just like that it became Toulouse-NoNeck. Then, boom, we were on."[201]

The station called the show "Shock Theater," and as it had in the mid-60s, it elected to show the films Saturday afternoons – this time at 12:30. The first show was on January 5, 1980.

The station changed the spelling of the character's name to "Tolouse NoNeck." The opening sequence was shot at night in the graveyard at St. Francis Seminary. The first show only had a 30 second open and close, but the station received enough positive feedback, so that each was lengthened and a mid-break added. The theme music was "Do You Think I'm Sexy" by Rod Stewart. Felski was joined by his sidekick "Uncle Geek," played by WISN-TV staffer Jim Mathews. Other characters made regular appearances including Tolouse's girlfriend "Betty" (played by Jim Feeley), as well as "Dr. Feeleystein" (also Feeley). Over the years the character changed a bit. Originally Tolouse had a hump, which was offset to one side, as well as a bird

Tolouse making "ghoul-ash" with Chef Sophie Kay on "Dialing for Dollars." (Courtesy of Rick Felski)

on his shoulder. Those were eventually eliminated, and the character became a "wild and crazy zombie."

For the summer of 1980, the show was shifted to a double feature starting at 10:30 p.m. As was the norm throughout much of its run, it was pre-empted during the fall by college football or other sports programming. Tolouse became quite popular, and undoubtedly prompted WITI-TV to bring back the "Dr. Cadaverino" character for Halloween 1980. Tolouse had a "Shock Theater Double Feature" the same evening!

He later did a radio show "Tolouse NoNeck and the Zombie Zone Radio Hour" on what was then WISN-TV's sister station, WLPX radio. He made numerous public appearances for the station, and began booking gigs with the band "The Lucky Stiffs."[202] Felski often featured local bands on "Shock Theater", including The X-Cleavers, The Balloons, and Pat McCurdy and the Men About Town, who later did the theme "Welcome Zombies." Badfinger lived in town for a short period of time. They appeared on the show, and Felski co-promoted their appearance at the Eagle's Club.

The show continued through 29 December 1984. The station continued to run the films Sunday mornings, through the end of 1986.

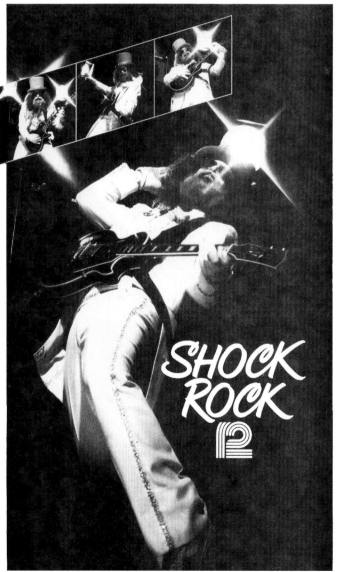

In 1985, Tolouse hosted "Shock Rock" (WISN-TV photo)

Felski had argued for some time that the station should run a music video show. Given his background he was tapped to host one in 1985. It ran in various time slots, and featured 60-90 minutes of music videos along with the antics of "Tolouse NoNeck" and guests.

In 1989, Rick Felski was the owner of a video company specializing in real estate shows. Having some extra time on his hands, as well as a studio and equipment, he decided to produce some programming based on his old character. Cassandra Peterson had syndicated her "Elvira" character, and Felski thought he would try to do the same. To avoid any conflicts with WISN-TV, he changed the character's name to "TooLoose NoNeck." He and his cohorts – executive producer Ken George, director Paul Johnson (who had worked on WITI-TV's "Nightmare Theatre"), writers John Bierman, Jim Feeley and Bob Robinson, and others like Ken Behan – purchased a public domain film, the classic *Night of the Living Dead*, produced the intro's and wraps, and marketed it in thirteen cities as "The 1989 TooLoose & Company Halloween Special." It was shown on WISN-TV on October 28.

CHAPTER 6 ~ WTVW/WISN-TV: CHANNEL 12　　　　　　　　　　　　　265

Since WISN-TV had a few more horror films, it contracted with Felski to produce "TooLoose & Company" in early 1990.²⁰³ Felski and his crew would produce the intros, breaks and wraps, and simply insert the name of the film to be shown. They would then drop the tape off at WISN-TV. The first show was on January 6 and the last on May 19, 1990.

NOTES

1 Federal Communications Commission, *Sixth General Report and Order*, April 14, 1952, Section 573.
2 Tom Shanahan, interview with author, November 14, 2006.
3 Carl Zimmermann, email to author, October 10, 2006.
4 "WEMP Seeks a TV License: Channel 6 Requested," *Milwaukee Journal*, March 6, 1952.
5 "Radio Station Buys TV Land," *Milwaukee Journal*, May 24, 1952.
6 "WCAN Asks '12,'" *Milwaukee Journal*, October 15, 1952.
7 "WFOX Seeking a UHF Channel," *Milwaukee Journal*, November 19, 1952.
8 "TV Application Channel Changed," *Milwaukee Journal*, January 31, 1953.
9 "WFOX Shifts Channel Plea: Asks VHF 12 for TV," *Milwaukee Journal*, June 2, 1953.
10 Shanahan, November 14, 2006.
11 "FCC Study Set on Channel 12" Hearing to Be Dec. 31," *Milwaukee Journal*, December 3, 1953.
12 Laurence C. Eklund, "Battle Looms on Channel 12: Petitions for Use of TV Outlet Promise a Hard Fight at Hearing," *Milwaukee Journal*, December 29, 1953.
13 "FCC Rejects Kolero TV Plea," *Milwaukee Journal*, January 7, 1954.
14 "Milwaukee Firms Argue Financing Plans for TV: Two Companies Angry About Kolero's Views on Their Ability to Build Stations," *Milwaukee Journal*, January 3, 1954.
15 "TV Merger is Discussed: Four Applicants Talk of Joint Application for Channel 12," *Milwaukee Journal*, May 6, 1954.
16 "Milwaukee Merger," *Broadcasting Telecasting*, May 24, 1954, 9.
17 "WCAN's Plea for TV Denied: Midwest's Application Was Filed Too Late FCC Asserts," *Milwaukee Journal*, May 20, 1954.
18 "FCC Grants Channel 12: Goes to Telecast Corp," *Milwaukee Journal*, June 12, 1954.
19 "Dispute Arises on TV Grant: Channel 12 Involved," *Milwaukee Journal*, July 13, 1954.
20 "Two WCAN-TV Attacks Hit Milwaukee Merger," *Broadcasting Telecasting*, July 19, 1954.
21 "WCAN-TV Due to File for Stay of Rival Ch. 12," *Broadcasting Telecasting*, July 26, 1954, 9.
22 "WCAN Loses a TV Protest: Channel 12 is Issue," *Milwaukee Journal*, August 11, 1954. Also see: "Two Stay Requests Denied By Court," *Broadcasting Telecasting*, August 16, 1954, 54.
23 "New TV Outlet to Be ABC Link," *Milwaukee Sentinel*, September 1, 1954.
24 "WTVW(TV) Joins Du Mont," *Broadcasting Telecasting*, September 27, 1954, 9.
25 Gerald R. Robinson, interview with Andrew Stone and Wayne Hawk, November 20, 1991.
26 "TV Station Given Towers Site OK," *Milwaukee Journal*, September 8, 1954.
27 "TV Station Arises in Month and a Half," *Milwaukee Sentinel*, October 27, 1954. Also see: "Two TV Stations Begin Operations," *Broadcasting Telecasting*, September 20, 1954, 68.
28 "Tent to Provide Cover Against Rain in Building of WTVW by Oct. 27," *Milwaukee Sentinel*, October 7, 1954. Also see: "Tent Enabled Workmen to Complete Building," *Milwaukee Sentinel*, October 27, 1954.
29 Robert Truscott, email to the author, February 21, 2007.
30 Robert Truscott, email to the author, November 30, 2006.
31 "WTVW Will Join TV List: Starts Wednesday," *Milwaukee Journal*, October 24, 1954.
32 "Veteran Film Director on New Station," *Milwaukee Journal*, October 27, 1954.
33 "Bill Bramhall to Be on WTVW," *Milwaukee Sentinel*, October 27, 1954.
34 Carl Zimmermann, interview with author, March 31, 2006.

35 "Plan Test Patterns as TV Service," *Milwaukee Sentinel*, October 27, 1954.
36 "WTVW Will Join TV List: Starts Wednesday."
37 Herzog, Buck, "Look 'N Listen," *Milwaukee Sentinel*, October 31, 1954, Sunday Magazine, 6.
38 "VHF Station Makes Debut: Telecasts by WTVW," *Milwaukee Journal*, October 28, 1954, Part 2, 4.
39 Robinson, November 20, 1991.
40 Shanahan, November 14, 2006.
41 Arthur L., Olszyk, *Live…At the Scene* (Milwaukee: self-published, 1993), 54.
42 "New Station to Be Opened for Radio Fans," *Wisconsin News/ Milwaukee Telegram*, October 22, 1922.
43 "Fight News to be Broadcast By Radio," *Wisconsin News*, January 24, 1924.
44 "Wave Length is Changed by WIAO," *Wisconsin News & Evening Sentinel*, June 9, 1924.
45 "WIAO Changes to New Call Letters: WSOE to Designate Lake Front Station; More Power Added," *Milwaukee Sentinel and Milwaukee Telegram*, August 17, 1924.
46 "News Now Has Own Radio Studio," *Wisconsin News*, October 3, 1924.
47 Gaston, W. Grignon, "Close Big Deal for WCBD: School of Engineering Announces Purchase of Powerful Outfit," *Wisconsin News*, December 31, 1924.
48 "Open New WSOE Air Station July 7: Dedication to Last 7 Hours: New Equipment to be Most Powerful in State; May Reach Europe," *Wisconsin News*, June 26, 1925.
49 "Stations Will Changes Waves Tomorrow," *Wisconsin News*, June 14, 1927.
50 "WTMJ On Air Monday Night: Initial Broadcast of Journal's New Station at 7:30 p.m.," *Milwaukee Journal*, July 25, 1927.
51 S.E. Frost. Jr., PhD, *Education's Own Stations: The History of Broadcast Licenses Issued to Educational Institutions*. (Chicago: University of Chicago Press, 1937), 212.
52 This is based upon the fact that the initial lease was for three years, as well as that according to Frost (213) in its license application of December 30, 1930 WISN stated that the newspaper was the owner.
53 Lewis W. Herzog, "Radio in Milwaukee: 1929-1955," *Historical Messenger*, March 1956, 9-12.
54 "WISN Asks TV," *Broadcasting*, July 2, 1945, 32.
55 "WISN Asking for Television: New Studios Planned," *Milwaukee Journal*, March 23, 1948.
56 "WISN To Build Radio Center: Buys Norris Home," *Milwaukee Journal*, June 12, 1952.
57 "TV Channel 6 Given to 'Bay'," *Milwaukee Journal*, December 4, 1953.
58 "Station WISN Buys Site for VHF Channel 6," *Milwaukee Sentinel*, January 13, 1954. Also see: "Tract Purchased as TV Tower Site," *Milwaukee Journal*, January 13, 1954.
59 Robert J. Riordan, "Television Preview," *Milwaukee Sentinel*, March 20, 1955.
60 "Station WISN Buys Site for VHF Channel 6," *Milwaukee Sentinel*, January 13, 1954. Also see: "Tract Purchased as TV Tower Site," *Milwaukee Journal*, January 13, 1954.
61 "Seek to Unite on Channel 6," *Milwaukee Journal*, November 4, 1954. Also see: "3 Channel 6 Applicants Study Merger," *Milwaukee Sentinel*, November 5, 1954.
62 "Channel 6 Merger Talks Snag," *Milwaukee Journal*, December 7, 1954. Also see: "Merger Talks on Channel 6 to Continue," *Milwaukee Sentinel*, December 8, 1954.
63 "Hearst's Firm Seeks WTVW: Negotiations Are On," *Milwaukee Journal*, December 15, 1954. Also see: "Milwaukee Revisited," *Broadcasting Telecasting*, December 13, 1954, 5.
64 "Gran in Offer to Buy WTVW: Would Block Hearst," *Milwaukee Journal*, December 19, 1954.
65 "Wisconsin Dateline," *TV Guide* (Wisconsin Edition), November 20-26, 1954, 1954, A-1.
66 Hearst Acquires WTVW(TV) Milwaukee; NBC Buys WKNB-TV New Britain, Conn.," *Broadcasting Telecasting*, January 10, 1955, 7.
67 "Petition for Channel 6 Withdrawn by Hearst," *Milwaukee Journal*, January 25, 1955.
68 "Bitners Buy Two Minneapolis TV's; WTVW(TV) Sale Snags; WTAP (TV) Sold," *Broadcasting Telecasting*, January 31, 1955, 71.
69 "Gran Battles WTVW Sale: Appeals to the FCC," *Milwaukee Journal*, January 28, 1955.
70 *Live…At the Scene*, 54.

71 "Gran Files Application for Milwaukee's Ch. 12," *Broadcasting Telecasting*, February 7, 1955, 86. Also see: "Gran Applies for Channel 12: Contests Hearst," *Milwaukee Journal*, February 3, 1955.
72 "Gran Denied His TV Plea: Appeal Is Planned," *Milwaukee Journal*, February 6, 1955. Also see: "Milwaukee Plea Dropped," *Broadcasting Telecasting*, February 7, 1955, 9.
73 "Gran Seeks to Block Action on WTVW(TV) Sale to Hearst," *Broadcasting Telecasting*, February 14, 1955, 72. Also see: "Gran Appeals FCC Decision: Channel 12 Issue," *Milwaukee Journal*, February 8, 1955.
74 "Labor Hits WTVW Sale: Hearst is Target," *Milwaukee Journal*, February 16, 1955.
75 "CIO Opposing TV for Hearst: Will Protest to FCC," *Milwaukee Journal*, February 17, 1955.
76 "Labor Hits WTVW Sale: Hearst is Target."
77 "Stay of Ch. 12 Milwaukee Is Argued Before Judges," *Broadcasting Telecasting*, February 21, 1955, 85.
78 "Gran Denied Stay Order of Hearst Ch. 12 Purchase," *Broadcasting Telecasting*, February 28, 1955, 76. Also see: "Court rejects Stay on WTVW Action," *Milwaukee Journal*, February 22, 1955.
79 Gerald R. Robinson, interview with author, April 2, 2007.
80 "FCC Approves Hearst Bid on WTVW Here: Apply for Change to WISN-TV," *Milwaukee Sentinel*, March 4, 1955.
81 "FCC Okays WTVW Sale: Hearst is Buyer," *Milwaukee Journal*, March 4, 1955.
82 "Hearst Corp. Assumes Ownership of WTVW," *Milwaukee Sentinel*, March 9, 1955. Also see: "TV Station's Operations Taken Over by Hearst," *Milwaukee Journal*, March 9, 1955.
83 "Wisconsin Dateline," *TV Guide* (Wisconsin Edition), March 5-11, 1955, A-1.
84 Gerald R. Robinson, interview with author, July 13, 2007.
85 Truscott, February 21, 2007,
86 "It's WISN-TV Milwaukee," *Broadcasting Telecasting*, June 20, 1955, 7.
87 "WSIN-TV (sic) Tower On Air Today," *Milwaukee Sentinel*, July 25, 1955.
88 "Pupils Kept Home Learn 3 R's Via TV," *Milwaukee Sentinel*, September 8, 1955.
89 "TV Graduates With High Honors From Teacher Role" *Milwaukee Sentinel*, September 21, 1955.
90 "Radio Television Building Planned," *Milwaukee Journal*, April 22, 1956. Also see: "WISN Plans New Building," *Milwaukee Sentinel*, April 22, 1956.
91 "Start WISN, WISN-TV Center," *Milwaukee Sentinel*, July 16, 1956.
92 "WISN-TV Adds Video Recorder" *Milwaukee Sentinel*, June 3, 1956.
93 "WISN-TV Center Dedication Today," *Milwaukee Sentinel*, October 20, 1957.
94 "WISN-TV Joins 'Badger' Net," *Milwaukee Sentinel*, January 26, 1958.
95 Donald H. Dooley, "Who Are Carmen La Rosa and Richard Weidenbruch?" *Milwaukee Journal*, February 9, 1958.
96 "Local…and Timely," *TV Guide* (Wisconsin Edition), February, 8-14, 1958, A-1.
97 "Local…and Timely," *TV Guide* (Wisconsin Edition), March, 22-28, 1958, A-1.
98 "Local…and Timely," *TV Guide* (Wisconsin Edition), August, 2-8, 1958, A-1.
99 Janet Kern, "WISN-TV Will Add Color Next Wednesday," *Milwaukee Sentinel*, March 28, 1959.
100 Newspapers, Radio, TV Air Youth News, Views," *Milwaukee Sentinel*, October 16, 1966.
101 "Miss Puelicher Wins Praise From Council," *Milwaukee Journal*, April 23, 1963.
102 Gerald R. Robinson, email to author, July 13, 2007.
103 "WISN-TV Switches to CBS Net," *Milwaukee Sentinel*, January 28, 1961.
104 "WISN-TV to Shift to CBS on Sunday," *Milwaukee Sentinel*, March 30, 1961.
105 "Local…and Timely," *TV Guide* (Wisconsin Edition), January 24-30, 1959, A-1.
106 "125 Year Old Sentinel Starts New Era Monday," *Milwaukee Sentinel*, July 23, 1962.
107 Michael H. Drew, "Milwaukee Studio Notes," *Milwaukee Journal*, June 21, 1964.
108 Michael H. Drew, "Milwaukee Studio Notes," *Milwaukee Journal*, March 21, 1965.
109 Rosemary Gernetzke, interview with author, April 27, 2007.
110 "Bits of Show Business," *Milwaukee Journal*, August 1, 1968.
111 Gernetzke, April 27, 2007,
112 Ibid.
113 Greg Moody, "TV Today" *Milwaukee Sentinel*, August 26, 1980.

114 Gernetzke, April 27, 2007,

115 Michael H. Drew, "Gernette's Forte: Credibility," *Milwaukee Journal*, October 24, 1980.

116 Michael H. Drew, "WISN to Replace Gernettes as Hosts," *Milwaukee Journal*, September 14, 1983.

117 Paul Bargren, "Teary Signoff: TV's Gernettes Say Goodby," *Milwaukee Journal*, December 31, 1983.

118 Robinson, April 2, 2007,

119 "Channel 12 Signs Packer of Its Own," *Milwaukee Journal*, August 23, 1968. Also see: "Sign Willie Davis as TV Sportscaster," *Milwaukee Sentinel*, August 24, 1968.

120 "Channel 12 to Show 37 Cubs Contests," *Milwaukee Journal*, February 8, 1969. Also see: "37 Cubs Tilts On WISN-TV," *Milwaukee Sentinel*.

121 "Mayor Slates TV Conferences," *Milwaukee Journal*, May 15, 1969. Also see: "Maier Plans Weekly Press Sessions," *Milwaukee Sentinel*, May 15, 1969.

122 "'Equal Time' Doesn't Apply: Channel 12," *Milwaukee Journal*, March 27, 1971.

123 In the July 13, 2007 interview, Jerry Robinson mentioned that they had been doing a bowling show from a local alley every week prior to the launch of "Bowling for Dollars," General Manager Mickey Hooten asked if there was some way to cut down on the expense, and Robinson suggested building the lanes in the studio. The equipment was borrowed from Bunswick, and returned after the show's run.

124 Michael H. Drew, "On the Milwaukee Scene," *Milwaukee Journal*, October 3, 1976.

125 Chris Stoehr, "Channel 6 Gets CBS and Everybody's Happy (They Say)," *Milwaukee Sentinel*, September 25, 1976.

126 Michael H. Drew, "Channel 12 Woos ABC-TV, Clients," *Milwaukee Journal*, September 27, 1976.

127 Greg Moody, "TV Today: Channel 12 to Open Its 'P.M. Magazine' Monday," *Milwaukee Sentinel*, September 8, 1979.

128 "Michael H. Drew, "Those Whirled Series," *Milwaukee Journal*, April 17, 1979.

129 Michael H. Drew. "Remodeled 'PM' is Strictly Showbiz," *Milwaukee Journal*, September 14, 1983.

130 "TV Critique to Focus on Channel 12," *Milwaukee Journal*, May 17, 1979.

131 "Miss Raasch Picked for News Director," *Milwaukee Sentinel*, August 27, 1981.

132 Jill Geisler, email to author, August 11, 2007.

133 "Raasch Named News Director," *Milwaukee Journal*, August 27, 1981.

134 Harvian Raasch-Hooten, interview with author, August 8, 2007.

135 Ibid.

136 "2 TV Stations to Begin 24-Hour Formats," *Milwaukee Journal*, June 11, 1982.

137 "24-Hour TV a Response to Cable," *Milwaukee Sentinel*, June 12, 1982.

138 "The Winner Is…: Channel 12 Chosen for Contract to Establish Lottery Show Network," *Milwaukee Journal*, September 26, 1988.

139 Duane Dudek, "WITI Flips to Fox; CBS Left Looking," *Milwaukee Sentinel*, May 24, 1994.

140 Duane Dudek, "Channel 12, ABC Sign a Long-Term Contract," *Milwaukee Sentinel*, July 26, 1994.

141 Tim Cuprisin, "Channel 12 replies to Change with Stability," *Milwaukee Journal*, December 5, 1994.

142 "WISN-TV Sues to Block Tower," *Milwaukee Sentinel*, February 15, 1995. Also see: "WISN is Suing to Stop WDJT Antenna Project: Station Claims That Plan of New CBS Affiliate Would Cause Problems," *Milwaukee Journal*, February 15, 1995.

143 Michael R Zahn, "Channel 12 Can Block WDJT Tower," *Milwaukee Journal*, March 2, 1995.

144 Tim Cuprisin, "Channel 58 is Helped by FCC Ruling," *Milwaukee Journal Sentinel*, May 20, 1996.

145 "Panel OK's Plan to Erect WDJT-TV Tower in Park," *Milwaukee Journal Sentinel*, May 21, 1996.

146 Tim Cuprisin, "Channel 12 Makes Move in Tower War," *Milwaukee Journal Sentinel*, June 4, 1996.

147 Tim Cuprisin, "TV Tower Battle Finally May Be Over," *Milwaukee Journal Sentinel*, August 22, 1996.

148 Rich Kirchen, "WISN Loses Tower Case," *Business Journal of Milwaukee*, August 6, 1999.
149 Doris Hajewski, "Hearst Sues Zoning Appeals Board Over Its Denial for WISN-TV Tower Extension," *Milwaukee Journal Sentinel*, September 27, 1999.
150 Greg J. Borowski, "Channel 58 Suggests Deal to Share Tower with Channel 12," *Milwaukee Journal Sentinel*, December 17, 1999.
151 Greg J. Borowski, "City Panel Rejects Taller Station Tower: Channel 12's Bid for New Antenna for Digital Signal Will Go to Common Council," *Milwaukee Journal Sentinel*, January 12, 2000.
152 Greg J. Borowski, "Council Approves Liquor License for Planned Capitol Drive Nightclub – Johnson-Odom Implores Peers to Give Matrix a Chance, Despite Their Concerns About large, Uncontrollable Crowds," *Milwaukee Journal Sentinel*, January 19, 2000.
153 Greg J. Borowski, "TV Tower Plan Vetoed by Norquist: Aldermen had Approved Ordinance to let Channel 12 Increase tower's height," *Milwaukee Journal Sentinel*, January 28, 2000.
154 Greg J. Borowski, "Panel OKs Higher WISN-TV Tower: Supporters Hope to Move Beyond Norquist's Earlier Veto of Measure," *Milwaukee Journal Sentinel*, July 31, 2002.
155 Greg J. Borowski, "Council Approves Taller Tower for Channel 12: 12-5 Vote May Withstand Mayor Veto," *Milwaukee Journal Sentinel*, August 2, 2002.
156 "Norquist Vetoes Taller Channel 12 Tower," *Milwaukee Journal Sentinel*, August 9, 2002.
157 Greg J. Borowski, "Tower Veto Stands After Series of Shifting Votes, Procedural Missteps," *Milwaukee Journal Sentinel*, September 5, 2002.
158 Meg Jones, and Rick Barrett, "News Chopper Crashes Onto I-43; Pilot Dies," *Milwaukee Journal Sentinel*, December 13, 2001.
159 Rich Kirchen, "WISN-TV Invests Millions In First Renovation in 25 Years," *Business Journal of Milwaukee*, November 7, 2003.
160 Rich Kirchen, "In the Latest of Her Firsts, Waldon Leads WISN-TV News," *Business Journal of Milwaukee*, January 5, 2007.
161 Jerry Sundt, interview with author, March 1, 2007.
162 Carl Schrank, "Marquette Junior Stars on Own Television Show," *The Marquette Tribune*, December 10, 1954.
163 "Wisconsin Dateline," *TV Guide* (Wisconsin Edition), August 13-19, 1955, A-1.
164 "Wisconsin Dateline," *TV Guide* (Wisconsin Edition), December 10-16, 1955, A-1.
165 Sundt, March 1, 2007.
166 Robinson, July 13, 2007,
167 Buck Herzog, "Look 'N Listen," *Milwaukee Sentinel*, September 11, 1955.
168 John Stone, interview with author, June 24, 2007.
169 "Wisconsin Dateline," *TV Guide* (Wisconsin Edition), March 30-April 5, 1957, A-1.
170 "Wisconsin Dateline," *TV Guide* (Wisconsin Edition), July 27 – August 2, 1957, A-1.
171 Donald H. Dooley, "Milwaukee Radio and TV Studio Notes," *Milwaukee Journal*, January 26, 1958.
172 Dooley, Donald, H., "TV Kindergarten," *Milwaukee Journal*, May 3, 1959.
173 Dooley, Donald, H., "Milwaukee Studio Notes," *Milwaukee Journal*, July 8, 1962.
174 Michael H. Drew, "Milwaukee Studio Notes," *Milwaukee Journal*, April 7, 1963.
175 Tim Cuprisin, "Glory Days in Milwaukee: Kids' TV Shows Reined in '50s, '60s," *Milwaukee Journal Sentinel*, August 21, 2001.
176 "Forenoon 'New Look': WISN-TV Makes Six Changes in Schedule," *Milwaukee Sentinel*, March 25, 1958.
177 Donald H. Dooley, "It's La Rosa Under the Stars Tuesday," *Milwaukee Journal*, August 4, 1957.
178 "Cream Pies, Funny Guys in TV Series," *Milwaukee Sentinel*, May 4, 1958.
179 "Punky and His Pals Start Puppet Skit Show Monday," *Milwaukee Sentinel*, November 30, 1958.
180 "Win TV Award," *Milwaukee Sentinel*, May 12, 1960.
181 Sprague Vonier, interview with author, July 27, 2007.
182 "Coming to WISN-TV…Have Fun! See the Stooges," *Milwaukee Sentinel*, August 30, 1959.
183 Hal Erickson, email to author, February 18, 2007.

184 Michael H. Drew, "Popular Pops: Comic Tommy Richards Is Happy in Kiddie Video," *Milwaukee Journal*, January 12, 1964.

185 Steve Cox, *One Fine Stooge: A Frizzy Life in Pictures*. (Nashville: Cumberland House Publishing, 2006), 119.

186 Michael H. Drew, "Mouseketeers' First family: Puppeteer Bob Trent of the Mickey Mouse Club Has a Critical Tryout Audience at Home," *Milwaukee Journal*, December 27, 1964.

187 "Entertainer to Head Drive on Dystrophy," *Milwaukee Journal*, October 25, 1964.

188 "'Mann' of Many Faces and Forms," *Milwaukee Sentinel*, April 1, 1961.

189 Hal Erickson, *Syndicated Television: The First Forty Years 1947-1987*. (Jefferson: McFarland & Co., 1989), 121-122.

190 Hal Erickson, email to author, February 14, 2007.

191 Hal Erickson, *Television Cartoon Shows: An Illustrated Encyclopedia, 1949-2003*, Second Edition, Vol. 1, (Jefferson: McFarland & Co., 2005), 153-155.

192 Ibid., 245-247.

193 Robinson, April 13, 2007,

194 Hal Erickson, email to author, February 14, 2007.

195 Larry Widen, "Late Night Horror in Milwaukee," *Scary Monsters Magazine* #8 (September 1993), 14-15.

196 Hal Erickson, email to author, May 9, 2002.

197 John Scott, email to author, June 13, 2002.

198 Dick Nitelinger, "Shock (With Rock) Milwaukee's Last horror Host...An Interview with TooLoose No-Neck," *Scary Monsters Magazine* #30 (March 1999), 70-75.

199 Rick Felski, interview with author, October 1, 1998.

200 William Scherbarth, interview with author, February 13, 2003.

201 Rick Felski, October 1, 1998,

202 Joe Cannariato, "NoNeck Shakes Loose with Ghoulish Live Show," *Milwaukee Sentinel*, April 15, 1983.

203 Jackie Loohauis, "Gallows Humor: NoNeck is back With the Bad, the Ugly." *Milwaukee Journal*, February 16, 1990.

CHAPTER 7
WITI
CHANNEL 6

(WITI photo)

Channel 6 was not among the channels assigned to Milwaukee in the FCC's Sixth General Report and Order. Its existence was due to the efforts of a long-time competitor to have the Commission assign another VHF channel to the city.

The Hearst Corp., the owner of WISN radio, had applied for channel 10 on March 24, 1948.[1] After consolidated hearings, three applicants remained for the available VHF channels (6, 8, & 10), and they petitioned the Commission for immediate construction permit grants. Before they could be made, the FCC froze all TV applications.

Hearst was one of the parties that had suggested to the FCC that it delete channel 6 from Green Bay's channel assignments, and add it to Milwaukee. The FCC rejected that idea, stating that Milwaukee was 167 miles from the transmitter site of WOC-TV in Davenport, Iowa, which was scheduled to shift from channel 5 to 6. That was within the 170 mile minimum required between stations on the same channel.[2] The Commission also rejected the proposal that channel 10 be reassigned for commercial use and that one of the UHF channels assigned be reserved for noncommercial educational use.

Nonetheless, Hearst purchased property on North 19th Street and West Wisconsin Avenue, on which it intended to build a new studios for both radio and television.[3]

When the freeze was lifted, channel 10 was reserved for noncommercial, educational use. Nonetheless, Hearst immediately reapplied for the channel, and asked the FCC to reconsider its reservation. It and the Wisconsin Broadcasting System, Inc. (the owner of WFOX radio) asked the FCC to assign other VHF channels to the area. The FCC rejected both requests on November 13, 1952[4], and Hearst asked the FCC to reconsider its decision.[5]

For the first time, the FCC heard oral arguments in a license matter, when it heard Hearst's petition to have channel 10 assigned for commercial rather than educational use on February 16, 1953. On March 31, the FCC denied Hearst's petition for a rehearing, and dismissed its application for channel 10. Wisconsin Senator Joseph McCarthy then tried to prevent the FCC from taking action on the vocational school's application. Hearst then filed yet another request for a rehearing on April 14, and submitted supplementary materials on April 20.[6] The FCC said that oral arguments would again be heard on Hearst's petition for yet another rehearing. On June 30, the FCC rejected that petition in a 4-1 vote. (See chapter 8 for a detailed discussion of Hearst's bid for channel 10.)

As a result, Hearst appealed to the U.S. Court of Appeals in Washington on the grounds that the FCC could not "arbitrarily" impose a reservation on a channel unless it was a part of a master plan.[7]

Meanwhile, Hearst engineers reviewed the FCC's table of channel assignments and concluded that by swapping channels in Green Bay and Marquette, Michigan, channel 6 could be assigned to the Village of Whitefish Bay. On September 30, 1953, they asked the FCC to do just that.[8] A resolution supporting the plan was introduced the following day[9], and the plan was endorsed by the Milwaukee Common Council on October 6.[10] Mayor Frank Zeidler vetoed that resolution three days later, saying that it was inappropriate for the city to take a stand on an FCC matter, and that the addition of another VHF channel to the city's Table of Channel Assignments would hurt WCAN-TV and WOKY-TV.[11]

Green Bay had been assigned channel 6, and had two applicants, while Marquette had been assigned channel 5, but had no applicants. In Hearst's proposal, Green Bay would receive channel 5, and Marquette channel 6. Whitefish Bay was chosen, as assigning the channel there would meet the FCC's requirement that stations on the same channel be at least 170 miles apart. WJIM-TV of Lansing, Michigan (now WLNS) was on channel 6. WOC-TV of Davenport, Iowa (Now KWQC) was on channel 5, but scheduled to move to channel 6. Both filed objections to Hearst's plan.[12] Objections were also filed by both WCAN-TV and WOKY-TV in letters to Milwaukee Mayor Frank Zeidler.[13]

Within a week after receiving Hearst's proposal, the FCC proposed rule making to amend its channel assignments and add channel 6 to Whitefish Bay.[14] Hearst indicated that if the channel was assigned to the area it would drop its appeal of the FCC's decision to reserve channel 10 for educational use, and requested a continuance of its case before the U.S. Court of Appeals while it waited for the FCC's decision.[15]

WCAN-TV President Lou Poller, fearing that the assignment of another VHF channel to the area would render his station uncompetitive, was a driving force in the formation of a new trade organization. The Ultra High Frequency Television Association was incorporated in October of 1953, specifically to lobby for such stations.[16] Poller became the association's president, and their first effort was to block the assignment of channel 6 to Milwaukee. Poller also filed a formal objection as president of WCAN-TV.[17]

Hearst formally replied to the objections filed to its proposal on channel 6 on November 21, 1953.[18]

On December 4, 1953, the FCC assigned channel 6 to the Village of Whitefish Bay. Per Hearst's plan, it also assigned channel 5 to Green Bay and channel 6 to Marquette, Michigan.[19] In doing so, it rejected objections both WJIM-TV and WOC-TV, as the location of the new station would comply with its regulations on adjacent and co-channel separation. It also rejected arguments by WCAN-TV and

The Ultra High Frequency Television Association that the table of channel assignments couldn't be changed.[20]

The same day, Cream City Broadcasting, Inc., which had received a construction permit for UHF channel 31, turned it in and filed an application for channel 6.[21] On December 7, Hearst filed an application for the same channel.[22]

The Ultra High Frequency Television Association filed a protest with the FCC asking it to reconsider its assignment of channel 6 to Milwaukee. The UHFTA argued that the assignment of another VHF channel to a city defeated the Commission's original purpose in intermixing UHF and VHF channels in the same markets, and had the potential to destroy the investment made by UHF station owners – without the benefit of a public hearing.[23]

Lou Poller complained that the FCC had made its assignment decision without giving those objecting a chance to be heard. He also claimed that the assignment of the channel to Whitefish Bay was a ruse that was being used to get around the 170-mile separation rule, and that Hearst intended to locate the station in Milwaukee. He also claimed to have lost money because advertisers either cancelled or had not renewed contracts because Hearst (WISN) salesmen had told them that they would receive the assignment and would begin broadcasting on VHF within 60 days. On January 7, 1954, WCAN-TV asked the U.S. Court of Appeals in Washington to order the FCC to revoke its assignment of channel 6 to Whitefish Bay[24], and asked the court to issue a temporary injunction preventing the FCC from assigning channel 6 to the area.[25] Hearst and Cream City Broadcasting, Inc. both objected.

On January 8, 1954, Independent Television, Inc., headed up by Holeproof Hosiery Co. Vice-President Jack Kahn, applied for channel 6. Kahn (25%) served as the corporation's president. Other officers and owners were:
- Richard G. Fried (14%), vice-president
- Lawrence Fleischman (10%), secretary-treasurer
- Blair Moody, Sr. (10%)
- Max Straus (10%)
- Max Osnos (9%)
- Others

Fried was formerly the president of the Fried Osterman Co., a manufacturer of gloves, mittens and outdoor clothing. Fleischman was involved in advertising and real estate, and had a 15% interest in Leader Newspapers, Inc. He also owned the Fleischman Rug and Carpet Co. of Detroit with his father, Arthur. Moody was a former U.S. senator from Michigan. Straus owned 1/3 of Omnibook, Inc., and Osnos owned 95% of the Woodward Broadcasting Co., and was the president of Sam's, Inc., the second largest department store in Detroit. Sol Kahn (no relation to Jack) was a local attorney.

On January 12, 1954, Hearst announced that it had purchased forty-three acres of land in the Town of Granville at North Range Line and West Good Hope Roads for a tower and transmitter site.[26]

On January 20, 1954, the District of Columbia circuit court of appeals denied WCAN-TV's motion for a temporary injunction restraining the FCC from allocating channel 6 to Whitefish Bay.[27] The FCC proceeded with plans to hold hearings on the applications from Hearst, Cream City Broadcasting, Inc., and Independent Television, Inc. Such hearings were contingent on the Court of Appeals' final ruling on the matter. At the same time, WCAN-TV asked the FCC to dismiss Hearst's application for channel 6, claiming that it did not intend to locate the station in Whitefish Bay, but rather would locate its studios in Milwaukee, and its transmitter and tower on land it recently acquired in the town of Granville. Lou Poller also claimed that if Hearst was granted channel 6, his station would lose its CBS affiliation, as WISN had a clause in its contract which gave it the right of first refusal should it operate a television station in the area. He also claimed that antitrust laws might be violated as Hearst owned WISN and the *Milwaukee Sentinel*. In addition, he claimed that the assignment of another VHF channel to the area would cost his station advertising revenue.[28]

The last week of April, 1954, the FCC agreed to allow WCAN-TV to participate in hearings on channel 6. However, it refused to dismiss Hearst's application. At the same time, it questioned the engineering qualifications of Cream City Broadcasting.[29]

In late May of 1954, the FCC delayed hearing the applications for channel 6, while it considered various motions. Cream City Broadcasting, Inc. and Independent Television, Inc. asked for more information regarding Hearst's broadcasting activities. At the same time, Hearst sought to have the Midwest Broadcasting Co. (WCAN-TV) removed from the hearings. Cream City and Independent countercharged that each had filed applications in bad faith: Independent's attorney had also represented the Ultra High Frequency Television Association, and as such Cream City suggested that its late application might have been designed to obstruct the proceedings. A stockholder in Cream City had been an administrative assistant to Wisconsin Senator Joseph McCarthy (who had actively urged the FCC to adopt Hearst's proposal to assign another VHF channel to the area). As such, Independent suggested that Cream City's application (which had been submitted without adequate details regarding its financing) would be withdrawn in order to allow Hearst an immediate grant. (Two weeks earlier, Cream City had asked the FCC to dismiss Independent's application, as it had been notarized by a party with an interest in the matter. Independent claimed that the Wisconsin law cited by Cream City only applied to banks.)[30]

On June 9, 1954, the FCC's broadcast bureau filed objections to Midwest Broadcasting's petition to broaden the hearings for channel 6 to include Hearst's affiliation contract with CBS, as well as Cream City Broadcasting's petitions regarding Independent Television Inc.'s application. The Bureau asked that the petitions be dismissed.[31]

On July 29, 1954, the FCC rejected Cream City Broadcasting's petition to dismiss the application of Independent Television, Inc. on the grounds that its application was improperly notarized. The Commission ordered that the documents be notarized a second time. The FCC also rejected Cream City's request for an inquiry into whether Independent had filed its application in "good faith." At the same time, it denied a motion by Midwest Broadcasting which proposed that it investigate whether the three applicants for channel 6 intended to primarily serve Whitefish Bay or Milwaukee. It also denied Hearst's petition that it reconsider its decision to allow Midwest to intervene in the hearings.[32]

In mid-October, the FCC filed a brief with the U.S. Court of Appeals responding to WCAN-TV's appeal of its decision to assign channel 6 to Whitefish Bay. It denied all of WCAN-TV's allegations, saying that: the assignment met all of the separation requirements set fourth in its Sixth General Report and Order, that its previous rejection of assigning Ch. 6 to the area was based solely upon the separation requirements, that the Table of Channel Assignments had some flexibility, that there was no protection guaranteed to UHF stations, and that WCAN-TV's injury claims were private.[33]

After CBS purchased WOKY-TV in October of 1954, it offered to buy WCAN-TV's facilities. Faced with more VHF competition and the loss of his network affiliation, Lou Poller accepted the offer. He then dropped his petition before the U.S. Court of Appeals re: the FCC's assignment of channel 6 to the area. (See chapter 4.)

CHAPTER 7 ~ WITI: CHANNEL 6   275

On November 5, 1954, the three applicants for channel 6 announced that they were attempting to negotiate a merger in order to avoid lengthy hearings, and the three were granted a continuance until December 7.[34] When the hearing continued, the three conceded that the negotiations had stalled, and they were granted another continuance until January 11, 1955.[35] Hearst then entered into negotiations to purchase WTVW (Ch.12).[36] The deal was made on January 7, 1955[37], and as they had promised, Hearst then asked that the FCC dismiss their application for channel 6. That petition was filed on January 23[38], and the Commission formally dismissed the application on February 1. The sale was approved by the FCC on March 4. (See chapter 6 for more details.)

On April 22, 1955, Cream City Broadcasting, Inc. asked the FCC to dismiss its application for channel 6 after reaching an agreement with Independent Television, Inc. Posner had concluded that Independent had "stronger financial resources" and that continuing the matter would mean an unnecessary delay in the establishment of service on channel 6.[39] In consideration, Independent agreed to reimburse Cream City for a portion of its engineering and legal expenses once a construction permit was granted.[40] As a result, on June 11, 1955 an FCC examiner recommended that a construction permit be granted to Independent Television, Inc. The FCC did so on June 29[41], and the call letters WITI-TV were later assigned to it.

Independent opened offices at 212 W Wisconsin Ave., and set up a temporary facility in the Bay Shore shopping center. Ground was broken for studio and transmitter facilities near the intersection of N Port Washington and W Donges Bay Roads in Mequon on October 11, 1955 – although construction had already started.[42] A 1,046 foot-tall guyed tower was erected at the site.

WITI-TV elected to broadcast in color, and rather than invest in the more expensive RCA color cameras, it became the first station to use the Du Mont Vitascan color system (See special section.). In early March of 1956, WITI-TV gave a

The WITI-TV Facilities in Mequon. Under construction is the transmitter building for WMVS-TV. (MPTV photo, courtesy of Paul K. Taff)

closed-circuit demonstration of the system to 200 representatives from local advertising agencies, and executives from other stations in the area.[43]

At 7:55 p.m. on April 22, 1956, WITI turned on its transmitter for the first time[44] and broadcast a test pattern. It continued to do so at intermittent intervals, with a target starting date of May 21.[45] On May 4, it requested and received permission from the FCC to begin commercial operation on a limited (four hours per day) basis.[46]

At 4:30 p.m. on May 21, 1956, WITI-TV began broadcasting with an effective radiated power of 100,000 watts. The first program was "Afternoon Edition," a

The WITI-TV staff rehearses for their first broadcasts in the master control room of the Mequon facility. In the center of the photo in the dark suit and bowtie is Independent's first president Jack Kahn. Standing behind him is announcer John Anthony. Standing in front of Anthony is Roger Cotey. Leaning over the table is staff director Richard Christensen, standing next to him wearing a headset is staff director Edward Dittloff, and leaning on the table wearing a white shirt is program director Dean McCarthy. Standing at the far left is promotions manager Lee Dolnick. Bending over the console is staff engineer Mark Ingerson, and seated to his left, looking back toward the directors, is staff engineer John Holmes. In the foreground at the right is staff engineer Bob Behee. (Milwaukee Sentinel photo, ©2008 Journal Sentinel, Inc., reproduced with permission.)

CHAPTER 7 ~ WITI: CHANNEL 6

15 minute newscast featuring Stu Armstrong, who served as the station's first news director.

Copying an idea used in other cities, "Cinema 6" ran the same film Monday-Wednesday and Thursday-Saturday, giving viewers multiple chances to see the offerings. On Sundays, comedies were featured.

> **WITI-TV's First Day Programming**
> **May 21, 1956**
> - 4:30 p.m. Afternoon Edition (News)
> - 4:45 p.m. Billy Bounce and Witi (Kids)
> - 5:55 p.m. Weather
> - 6:00 p.m. Sheena Queen of the Jungle
> - 6:30 p.m. Family Affair
>   (A live official dedication program featuring previews of things to come on channel 6)
> - 7:30 p.m. Cinema 6 (First film: *The Captain's Paradise*)
> - 9:25 p.m. Weather
> - 9:30 p.m. I Spy (Not to be confused with the later NBC series)
> - 10:00 p.m. The Passerby
> - 10:15 p.m. The Six Million Dollar Movie (First film: *The Bandit*)
> - 11:45 p.m. Night Final (Night)

YOUR INVITATION TO THE GREAT MIDWEST **color Premiere** OF THE WORLD'S FIRST VITA SCAN TV STATION, BRINGING A NEW CONCEPT TO TELEVISION ENTERTAINMENT

keep your eyes on **witi** serving greater milwaukee with greater family fare

TODAY!
fabulous COLOR premiere
→ Channel 6 is on the air —

WORLD'S FIRST VITASCAN COLOR STATION—SEE IT IN COLOR OR BLACK AND WHITE

Pioneered by Du Mont and WITI-TV, the Vitascan Color system is the most astounding advancement in the television industry. All the brilliance of full natural color is picked up by an electronic device which transmits the image, unchanged, to be received by both color and black and white sets. Even conventional sets will pick-up the clarity, depth, and beauty that is characteristic of the Vitascan system, and there's no dial-fumbling once you've tuned in Channel 6. If your set is operating correctly, one setting will permit you to enjoy WITI-TV all evening long, because OUR signal will never change. For more than one reason we'll be well received in Greater Milwaukee Homes.

AN ENTIRELY NEW CONCEPT IN PROGRAMMING—NO NEED TO MISS YOUR FAVORITE SHOW

Bridge date tonight? Alec Guinness will be back on WITI-TV tomorrow night at the same time. And if you're busy then, you can still catch the show on Wednesday evening . . . but see it from the beginning. Because Channel 6 has picked the best in first-run television entertainment, we know you won't want to miss a single full length feature. That's why we decided to run Cinema 6, our mid-evening movies, three days in a row, with a complete change every Monday and Thursday. Naturally, all the other programs will change nightly . . . but our feature movies will run long enough to give everyone a chance to see them.

EVERY SHOW A TELEVISION PREMIERE—ALL-NEW FAMILY FUN AND ENTERTAINMENT

Comedy, mystery, love and adventure . . . variety is the spice of WITI-TV. Every program telecast on Channel 6 has been carefully screened to provide the best in family entertainment. And every show is brand new . . . you'll see the great Selznick classics during the Six Million Dollar Shows . . . top name comedians on the Sunday Comedy Theater . . . and there's the nightly adventure series featuring "Orient Express," "I Spy," "Fu Manchu," "The Falcon" and others. Expect the best and get it . . . on Channel 6.

See a good movie tonight . . . on Channel 6

THE DU MONT VITASCAN COLOR SYSTEM

(The author wishes to express his sincere gratitude to former WITI-TV engineer Ron Yokes for providing most of the technical details in this section.)
WITI-TV was the first of two stations to use the Du Mont Vitascan system for broadcasting its locally-produced programs. (The other was a station in Minnesota.[47])

Introduced at the National Association of Radio and Television Broadcasters (NARTB) convention in May of 1955, it was conceived as a low-cost alternative to RCA's color cameras. Du Mont had introduced its own color "flying-spot scanner" (called the "Multi-Scanner") in 1954.[48] (See photo on p. 221.) A beam of light from a cathode-ray tube (CRT) was used to scan objects. The light was reflected off of the object being scanned and picked up by separate photo-multiplier tubes, each fitted with an appropriate red, blue or green filter. The highest level was green, which was suitable for use alone as a monochrome signal. The output from the tubes was then processed, leveled (color balanced), combined, and distributed to a device which encoded the signal to an NTSC compatible color signal.[49] The scanner could be used for slides or opaque images. When used for film, the scanning beam was directed through one of two modified Bell & Howell 16mm film projectors. It passed through a 24-sided prism assembly, which effectively "stopped" an individual frame for scanning. It then passed through a dichroic prism, which split the light into its colors. Red, green and blue photo-multiplier cells picked up the primary colors. The output was then converted into the 29.97 frames/sec. used for NTSC color video.

The Vitascan system utilized the Multi-Scanner to scan live action inside an enclosed studio. Light from CRTs in portable scanning units, known as "studio scan-

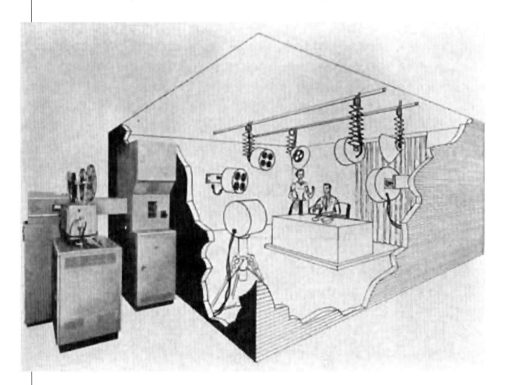

Du Mont Vitascan Studio.

ners," was directed at the studio by a lens and mirror system. Instead of lights, the studio was equipped with a series of photo-multiplier tubes arranged within fixtures called "scoops" or "buckets." Colors were differentiated by the placement of color transparent gels in front of each respective photo tube.⁵⁰ Each scoop contained four photo tubes: one for green, one for blue, and two for red. Two were used for red because the light source was deficient in that part of the spectrum, and the photo-multiplier tubes weren't as sensitive to that color. The most sensitive of the cells were selected for the red.⁵¹ Bundles of coaxial cables from each "scoop" carried the RGB signals to Master Control where they were processed, balanced, combined, and converted to NTSC color. Special display oscilloscopes, used for those purposes, were console mounted next to the RGB and composite signal mixing/matching controls.⁵² Five oscilloscopes were utilized: one for each color, one for the composite signal, and a spare.

The "scoops" picked up reflected light from the front, side and top of the set and were repositioned for various "lighting" effects⁵³. Unlike a normal studio, which contains numerous lights, the system's complexity did not allow for an over-abundance of scoops. The smaller number led to the use of large diameter, floor level "turntables" which were divided into sets for different purposes (e.g., news, weather and sports).⁵⁴ Each was rotated into the field covered by the stationary ceiling scoops. At its original Mequon location, WITI-TV had two studios: Studio "A" measured 53 ft. x 35 ft., contained an 18 ft dia. turntable, and was used for live programs. Studio "B" measured 26 ft x 24 ft., contained a 16 ft. dia. turntable, and was primarily used for production work and effects.⁵⁵

Set rotation took place during commercial (film/slide) breaks. The turntable was motor driven and operated by a floor director using a control in the studio. Other locations, i.e. automobile display, could be located in another section of the studio. Since this required the movement of the ceiling mounted scoops, a track-mounted (to the ceiling) scoop fixture support system allowed the limited number of scoops to be moved to a scene set-up anywhere within the four walls of studio "A." The system was designed by Elden Anspach, and allowed the scoops to be rotated as well.⁵⁶

Considerable pre-planning was required for each studio session. Each studio had two scanners, each with four rack-mounted lenses. The scanning light was turned off when the lenses were changed. If both were "on" and aimed at a scene, the two pictures would be superimposed. Therefore, switching from one scanner to another was accomplished either as a lap, lap-dissolve or a fade to black from one scanner to another.

Control of the scanner light sources took place in the control room. Each light source required 37,000 volts to operate. That voltage was generated in the master control room and transported out to the camera via a special high-voltage capacity coaxial-type cable. Any dampness in the studio would be cause for a bit of high-voltage arcing inside the scanner. Internal adjustments were also a bit tricky and very carefully attempted.⁵⁷

System maintenance had its own peculiar difficulties. The high-voltage rectifiers in the power supply were immersed in a bath of silicone oil to provide the dielectric insulation necessary to prevent arcing. Whenever maintenance of the power supply required its removal from its bath, some of the oil would unavoidably be transferred to the hands of the person doing the maintenance. If that person touched their eyes, some of the oil would be transferred. This resulted in a very uncomfortable "sandy" feeling in the eyeball sockets, which eventually washed away with tears.⁵⁸

If one looked directly at the surface of the scanning tube while adjusting/aligning them, the whites of the eyeballs could become discolored by X-Ray exposure. The 7" tube in the 16mm film scanner was viewed through a small lead-glass window to eliminate X-Ray exposure, but the portable scanning units had no such feature.⁵⁹

Du Mont Vitascan "scoop" with its cluster of photo-multiplier tubes.

The component (RGB) video made possible the first use of video effects such as horizontal and vertical wipes. Combined with the fixed location, scanned light source, it was capable of being used to generate a studio image cut-out that simulates the Chroma-Key (studio-image-shadow) effect that allowed studio talent to be superimposed upon an image from a 35mm color slide, or 16mm film.[60]

At WITI-TV, a translucent rear-projection screen was mounted along one wall in studio "B." Behind it, an array of photo cells sufficient to "scoop" light from the entire screen, were mounted. All the photo cells were mounted on a frame so as to function as a single unit. They were not covered with gels, and as such produced a green signal.[61] (In that way, they functioned in the same way as a "green screen" does with the "Chroma-Key" process.) The opposite wall separated the studio from the Master Control room. The Multi-Scanner unit used for slides and film was located in Master Control along that wall. The output from that unit could be directed toward one of the two modified Bell and Howell film projectors, via mirrors, or directly into the slide projector.[62]

To superimpose a second image or live person on that background, the scanner output could also be directed into the studio through an opening in the wall, via a mirror and fixed lens. On the studio side of the wall was mounted a very large, light-tight bellows, not unlike those used for early still cameras. If talent stepped in front of the screen, their shadow was cast on it, creating a cut-out silhouette. By mixing the video, that image was superimposed on that from either a slide or film projector.[63]

After the effect was achieved, the RGB component video was encoded to NTSC for transmission. When not used for effects, studio "B" could be used in the same manner as "A" by wheeling in one of the portable scanning units.[64]

So as not to interfere with the scanning process, the studio had to be completely dark, and sealed so that extraneous light could not enter. Any light would produce random noise (snow) in the picture. As such, the system could not be used outdoors.

Since the light from the flying-spot scanner was insufficient, some method had to be devised to illuminate the studio so that talent could read, and otherwise function. As such, stroboscopic lights were utilized in a system Du Mont called "Sync-Lite"[65], which operated only during the vertical blanking period. (As per the NTSC standards, the flying-spot scanner scanned 525 lines per frame, but only used 483 of them for the picture. The others allowed the scanned light beam to retrace itself back to the upper, left-hand corner of the frame.) The lights decayed to zero before the beginning of the next active picture scan line. The result was an "eerie glow"[66] inside the studio, which not all talent was able to adapt to.

At WITI-TV, entry into the darkened studio was by means of a "double-door" light-lock system – similar to a film darkroom.[67]

Since it "worked in the dark," the Vitascan system did not require the heavy lighting loads[68] necessary to produce a color picture using conventional color cameras. As a result, the talent was much more comfortable (if they could get used to the stroboscopic lighting) and the air conditioning requirements were significantly lower.

Color registration was not a problem as scanning occurred before the light was split into the three primary colors. In addition, no long "warm up" was necessary. Color cameras of the period required hours to warm up, and still tended to drift, requiring frequent adjustment.

Du Mont initially priced a complete one-studio system, with Multi-Scanner, at $32,570. Once a station had a Multi-Scanner, an additional studio could be

CHAPTER 7 ~ WITI: CHANNEL 6   281

equipped for $15,692. By comparison, Du Mont estimated that a single color camera cost between $60-80,000.[69]

WITI-TV would later donate the flying-spot scanner to WMVS, who would use it for the first regular, color, educational TV broadcasts in the U.S. (See chapter 8.)

Stu Armstrong, who was the first person to appear on the air, remembers working with Vitascan:

> *Not many of us knew about the type of color system WITI was going to use, other than it wasn't RCA. I was working in Minneapolis at the time, and drove in for my final interview at WITI, which took place at the newly completed studio in Mequon. So, I met the station's program director Dean McCarthy, who showed me the studio and told me to go in, sit down and start my audition.*
>
> *So, I sat there, and sat there, and finally Dean said, "Well, any time Stu."*
> *I said, "Well aren't you going to turn on the lights?"*
> *He said, "Oh, I didn't tell you. We have a new system. We don't use lights!" It was the craziest thing I ever saw.*
>
> *The only light in the studio was a strobe light that pulsed in sequence with the flying-spot scanner. After a while you got used to it, but working under those conditions was unbelievable. Sometimes the strobe light would go out. I would just ad-lib and tell folks that, "I know it's hard to believe, but I'm in a totally black studio." They probably thought that I was drunk or something!*
>
> *If you were doing the news and moved the copy, the lines would converge under the strobe light. You'd have to wait until things settled down and your eyes focused again. I'm sure that went over big with the viewers.*
>
> *If it was difficult for me, it was tougher on guests. People would come in and not know what they were getting into. I had a talk show called "Around the Town," and I had to explain to my guests that they were coming into a totally dark studio. They were expecting to come onto a brightly-lit set. I would tell them to just look at me, and talk.*
>
> *It was terrible to work under those conditions. I remember going home many nights, and feeling like my eyeballs were way down by my legs. We were happy when they finally got rid of the system.*[70]

(Courtesy of Hal Erickson)

In October of 1956, the NTA Television Network began operations, and WITI-TV became an affiliate. Spearheaded by producer Ely Landau from its flagship station, WNTA-TV, Channel 13, New York, NTA was a hook-up of independent stations which allowed them to share film and "live" programs with each other. It began with fifty-two first-run 20th Century Fox features, as well as most of the non-Popeye and non-Superman Fleischer/Famous Studios cartoons and the George Pal "Puppetoons." It also released a number of syndicated anthologies, including Landau's fifteen-minute *The Passerby*. In 1958, it released *This is Alice*, *How to Marry a Millionaire*, and *Man Without a Gun*.[71]

After WITI-TV became profitable, Independent Television, Inc. formulated plans for expansion. On February 13, 1958 it applied for a 1,000 watt, daytime-only AM radio station on 1030 kHz.[72] The plans were later dropped.

The station did well enough to attract suitors, the strongest of which was The Meredith Publishing Co. of Des Moines, Iowa.[73] However, those offers were rejected[74]. (By this time, Jack Kahn had retired to Florida where he ran the Far Horizons resort on Longboat Key[75], but still retained an ownership interest in WITI-TV. Sol Kahn [no relation] was now the president.)

Before there was "American Bandstand," there was "Dance Party" on WITI-TV. Hosted by announcer John Anthony and former Conover model Barbara McNeil (Others would later replace McNeil.), the show featured top 10 records, which the live studio audience danced to. The show proved very popular and continued until 1960, when it was dropped during the "payola" scandal that hit radio.

However, there was one suitor that WITI-TV ownership took much more seriously. Since 1955, CBS had owned and operated WXIX on channel 19. It was the only UHF station in the city, and as such did not reach the same number of potential viewers that its VHF competitors did. Storer Broadcasting of Miami owned five VHF stations – the maximum then allowed by FCC regulations. However, it intended to sell WVUE in Wilmington, Delaware, and it purchased WITI-TV for $4,462,500 on August 8, 1958.[76] Both Storer and CBS denied that the sale was in anticipation of the network affiliating with the station[77], but most observers thought that the motivation.

FCC approval was not immediate however. In a letter to Storer management, the Commission asked if they intended to set advertising rates for WITI-TV in combination with its other stations. Storer had operated WVUE as an independent station, but had discontinued operations for financial reasons. The FCC wanted to know how Storer intended to operate WITI as an independent station if they couldn't make WVUE work.[78]

In its response, Storer indicated that it would not set its advertising rates for WITI in combination with its other radio and TV stations, unless forced to do so by its competition (Hearst and CBS). It also stated that although it had failed to operate both WVUE and WGBS-TV successfully as independents, it had learned from those experiences. It also pointed out that the competitive situation was different in those markets than it was in Milwaukee.[79]

After receiving Storer's response, the FCC voted 3-1 to approve the sale on November 13, 1958.[80] Storer took over operations on December 22.

Shortly thereafter, CBS announced that it would sell WXIX and affiliate with WITI-TV.[81] The affiliation took place on April 1, 1959.

CBS sold the license, transmitter and tower atop the Schroeder Hotel to WXIX, Inc., whose majority owner was Gene Posner of Cream City Broadcasting, Inc. Cream City had held a construction permit for channel 31, but had turned it in and was the first to apply for channel 6. CBS sold its studios and equipment at 5445 N 27th St. to Storer.

When it first went on the air in 1956, WITI heavily promoted its use of the Du Mont Vitascan system. However, the public did not rush out and buy color receivers, and it took another ten years for sales to increase significantly enough to warrant further investment in color broadcasting equipment. In addition, those early receivers had a great deal of difficulty reproducing color consistently. It wasn't until the late 1970s that the tuner technology advanced sufficiently.

WTMJ-TV had started studio color broadcasting in 1954. In 1957, it had completely converted its studio operations to color. It used RCA cameras and other

equipment, and the color produced was thought by some to be superior to that produced by the Vitascan system. By October of 1957, WITI-TV was only broadcasting 17 hours a month in color; while in contrast, WTMJ-TV was doing so 24 hours a week.[82] Even so, many thought the contrast of monochrome was preferable to the color picture then available – no matter which system was used. Given the lack of color receiver sales, and the troubles with its Du Mont Vitascan system, WITI-TV decided to convert to black-and-white for its studio operations. Included in the purchase of the 27th Street facility were image orthicon, monochrome cameras and other equipment. It took a few months, but eventually all of the station's operations were shifted to their new facility, and at that time color telecasting using the Vitascan system was discontinued.

Carl Zimmermann, who had been the film and news director at WTVW and the manager of WISN radio, was on the news staff of WEMP radio in early 1959, and was hired to be station's new news director. Hal Walker and Judy Marks came over from WXIX to serve as sports director and weather girl.

TEN O'CLOCK REPORT

Monday thru Friday — 10-10:15 PM

•

Judy as Miss Fairweather
Carl Zimmerman with the News
Hal Walker on Sports

6 CBS

WITI-TV
The New Address for CBS

WITI-TV took over the old WCAN-TV/WXIX building at 5445 N 27th St. on April 1, 1959, and remained in it until 1978. (WITI photo)

Besides investing in studios, equipment and personnel, Storer also purchased more films. As an independent station, WITI-TV depended heavily on feature films. The station had about 1,800 films in its library, including an RKO package, and the *Shock!* and *Son of Shock* packages of Universal horror films. The day of the CBS affiliation, WITI-TV began showing a package of 720 Paramount feature films. That gave the station the largest film library in the city – if not the state.[83]

In addition, WITI-TV ordered a videotape recorder, and was the first station in the state to broadcast programs it taped earlier. One of those programs was "Big Time Wrestling," which was taped Wednesdays at the station (probably as the wrestlers were in town for matches at the old South Side Armory), and broadcast the following Saturday.

WITI-TV had been licensed to the village of Whitefish Bay. The station wanted to be listed in Milwaukee in trade publications, and petitioned the FCC to change its city of license. The shift was approved by the Commission on July 30, 1959.[84]

WITI-TV chief engineer Bob Truscott (L) and assistant chief engineer Ron Yokes (R) examine the new Ampex videotape recorder.(WITI photo)

In addition, Storer (in consultation with ABC[85]) sought to move the WITI-TV tower closer to those of WTMJ-TV and WISN-TV. Doing so would make it easier for viewers, as they could orient their VHF antennas in the same general direction. As such, the station optioned an acre of land at the rear of the "Pig 'N' Whistle" drive-in on East Capitol Drive – just down the street from The Journal Co.'s "Radio

CHAPTER 7 ~ WITI: CHANNEL 6

City." The Shorewood Village Board approved the plan on August 1, 1960, and in the process waived its 50 foot height limitation on structures.[86]

In January of 1961, Storer named Roger Le Grand as general manager of WITI-TV. Le Grand had been the vice-president for radio and TV at the Cramer-Kasselt advertising agency – the largest in town. The choice of Le Grand was inspired. According to former WTMJ-TV news editor Arthur Olszyk:

> *I knew him well, and remember him as one of those rare individuals who kept saying to anyone who would listen, "If I were running a television station…" and then proceed to do exactly those things when he got the chance.*
>
> *Not only did Le Grand bring channel 6 into a fully competitive position, but he changed the balance for the next two decades, with the momentum rolling on even after his early death.*[87]

Carl Zimmermann was at the station when Le Grand joined:

> *He came in and he didn't know a damned thing about operating a station, but boy did he take over! It was a big success because Roger loved what he was doing; he loved the station, and he promoted it every chance he could. He really knew how to promote something, and he helped us build ratings.*[88]

Ward Allen joined the station as a staff announcer in 1962. He remembered:

"Roger said to us, 'You do what you're supposed to do. I'm a PR man. I'm good at that. You know television and I don't. You do that stuff.'"[89]

On April 2, 1961, WISN-TV and WITI-TV swapped affiliations, with WITI-TV becoming the ABC affiliate, and WISN-TV the CBS. CBS had WISN radio as its local outlet, and had wanted to affiliate with WISN-TV as well.

Originally, the station had planned to build only a tower on the land it had acquired in Shorewood, and the FCC approved the plan on March 30, 1961.[90] However, as the station studied its future needs, it was obvious that the facilities on North 27th Street were inadequate. As such, it optioned another parcel of land, across the street[91], which was adjacent to Estabrook Parkway. Many thought that the land, which had been a private residence, would complete the parkway, but the Shorewood Village Board, having no room to expand its border, and therefore its tax base, approved rezoning of the site on April 3, 1961.[92] The two acres was thought to be large enough for WITI-TV to construct not only a new tower, but also new studio and office facilities.

Roger Le Grand, shown here with the WITI-TV "Tower of Light," led the station from 1961 until his untimely death in 1973. (WITI photo)

Roger Le Grand (L) examines the architect's drawing of the proposed new WITI-TV studios and offices along with George B. Storer, Jr., president of Storer Broadcasting, and chairman, George B. Storer. (WITI photo)

THE "TOWER OF LIGHT"

When WITI-TV announced its plans to erect a new tower, it faced a problem, as there was no room for guy wires on the property it had purchased. As such, it elected to construct a self-supporting tower. In order to make it a landmark, it selected a height, 1,078 feet, which would make it the world's tallest, surpassing the 1056 foot-tall Tokyo Tower, which had been completed in 1958.

Dresser-Ideco was selected to engineer and manufacture the new tower. Thomas Bentley & Sons of Milwaukee was selected as the foundation and grading contractor and the Seago Construction Co. of Dallas was chosen to do the erection work. Construction began in August of 1961[93]. On May 25, 1962, the tower had reached 868 feet when the only accident occurred. A gin pole, which was being used to raise a pre-fabricated section, snapped. The section fell approximately 400 feet down the north side of the tower, and embedded itself 5-1/2 feet into the ground. No one was hurt, but several construction workers were narrowly missed by the falling steel.[94]

Also constructed was a new building which housed the transmitters for both WITI-TV and WMVS (Ch. 10). The educational station's antenna was on WITI-TV's old tower, and that arrangement continued. The new facilities were

Artist's conception of the self-supporting tower and the area in Estabrook Parkway. (Courtesy of WITI)

CHAPTER 7 ~ WITI: CHANNEL 6

(Courtesy of WITI)

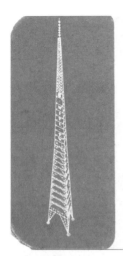

The WITI-TV "Tower of Light"
(WITI photo)

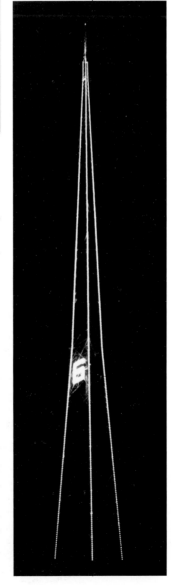

used for regular broadcasting as of sign-on at 7:19 a.m. on Monday, September 17, 1962. On Tuesday, October 9, more than 400 civic, business, and broadcasting leaders gathered for the tower's formal dedication. Milwaukee Mayor Henry Maier dedicated one leg of the tower to "community affairs." ABC television network vice-president Tom Moore dedicated the second leg to "entertainment." Finally, Storer Broadcasting president George Storer dedicated the third leg of the new tower to "news and editorials."

However, the station could no longer claim that the structure was the tallest self-supporting tower in the world. Additional members had been added to the Tokyo Tower, raising it to 1,091 ft., and allowing it to reclaim the title. Nonetheless, the WITI-TV tower was the tallest in the United States, and would remain so for many years.

Seeking to make the tower a Milwaukee landmark, in October of 1963 the station received permission from the Shorewood village board to install lights on it. Shortly thereafter, approximately 2000 25 watt lights were installed at 30 inch intervals along the tower's legs. Spotlights shone on the 90 ft. antenna atop the tower. The original plan was to install both a lighted "6" and a time/temperature unit, but only the former was installed. Station manager Roger Le Grand coined the phrase "Milwaukee's Tower of Light," and in a special ceremony broadcast on February 6, 1964, the lights were turned on at 6:00 p.m.[95]

However, all were not happy with the idea. Shorewood officials indicated that the lighting was under a "trial period."[96] The station had tested the lights shortly before the official lighting ceremony, and several area residents voiced complaints.[97] Although the lights were only on from dusk until midnight, an architect who lived 1400 ft. north of the tower filed an objection, citing Shorewood's illuminated sign ordinance, which prohibited such signs over fifty square feet. He also argued that the lighted tower was an infringement on the "aesthetic rights" of Shorewood residents who lived nearby.[98] Other residents also objected, and on March 25, 1964 the Shorewood village attorney stated that he thought that the illuminated "6" on the sign might indeed violate rules pertaining to illuminated signs, but that the lights did not violate any ordinances.[99] Later that month, he opined that objectors had not presented sufficient evidence to have the lights declared a public nuisance.[100] On March 18, the village board granted WITI permission to use the lighted "6" provided that it was backed with reflectors so that it shined only toward the southwest.[101]

In October of 1973, the second Arab-Israeli war and the U.S. support of Israel caused O.P.E.C. to embargo oil, which plunged the country into an "energy crisis." A viewer, Stephen Dearholt, wrote a letter to the station suggesting that it turn off the lights as a way to save energy.[102] Several other viewers made the same suggestion. In response, the station turned off the lights attached to the tower's legs at dusk, on Wednesday, November 14, 1973, and they were not turned on again.[103] (The illuminated "6" remained on, but it too was eventually removed in the 1990s.) In 2003, the lights were finally removed as part of the station's effort to reinforce the tower and make it ready for the installation of a new digital TV antenna.

The proposed new studio/office facilities were never built. Priorities within the Storer company delayed the project, and by the time resources were allocated, it was determined that larger facilities would be required and that there was not enough room on the property. (Constructing a larger building would mean that the park-

On February 5, 1962, WITI-TV began presenting a daily editorial. (Bruce Kanitz at WXIX began doing so in 1959.[106]) The station's consultants, and Storer management expressed concern about Zimmermann writing and delivering the news, as well as editorials, but viewers never complained.[107] (WITI photo)

CHAPTER 7 ~ WITI: CHANNEL 6

The WITI-TV on-air team in 1965: Standing L-R: Tom Hooper, John Anthony, Earl Gillespie, Larry Ebert, Jack DuBlon, and WOKY radio's Bob Barry, who was hosting the "Early Show" movie[109] at the time. Seated L-R: Ward Allen, Carl Zimmermann, Barbara Becker and Jim Major. (WITI photo)

ing lot would have to been expanded right up to the base of the tower, thus putting employees, visitors, and their cars at greater risk from falling ice.[104])

In 1959, WITI-TV had stopped broadcasting in color. That changed on Sunday, September 23, 1962, when it broadcast "The Jetsons."[105] The station relayed color shows from ABC, and did yet not broadcast its locally-originated shows in color.

At 1:30 p.m. on March 5, 1963, WITI experimented with a process developed in Austria called Telcon, which produced a "color effect" on black & white sets. For 60 seconds a "channel 6" identification card was shown surrounded by pulsating diagonal lines. Some viewers reported seeing yellow, purple and green lines on their sets.[108] The station continued the experiment the rest of the week.

Le Grand, news director Carl Zimmermann, and Fred Cowley steadily grew WITI-TV's news operation. By the mid-1960s, it was shooting more news film than its competitors. Zimmermann remembered that as the news department grew, they began changing their philosophy toward stories:

> We started out doing what everyone else was doing at the time: If we didn't have a good picture or didn't have film of it, we would say, "The hell with it; we don't need that story." That was WRONG! We knew it when we were doing it, and we CHANGED it.
>
> We never had a written code on how to conduct the news on a television station. It developed by itself. I remember when a guy came in with a story one day about two kids drowning in the Milwaukee River. The mother was there, and they stayed on that mother (with the camera) for I don't know how long while she cried. I said, "This is WRONG! If that was your family, you wouldn't want that to happen, right?" They said no. So I said, "Well, then DON'T DO IT!" We sort of developed a little bit of integrity of our own. It wasn't written, but it was there.[110]

Besides the sports, Earl Gillespie also did a series of "Earl Goes Fishing" specials. Here he's shown with sponsor Maury Marasco, owner of M&M Sporting Goods. (Courtesy of Bruce Nason)

In 1963, the station hired the Milwaukee Braves' radio play-by-play announcer Earl Gillespie as its sports director. Zimmermann remembered that the timing was perfect:

I remember sitting down and talking with Earl, and he said: "You guys must've been talking to my wife, because she wanted me to get off that baseball circuit!" So he came with us. God, what an important part of that team he was![111]

He also remembered Le Grand's support for growing the news department:

"I was asking all of the time for more money so I could hire more staff. Roger would say, "Carl, I'd love to do it, but I can't. I can't make the budget; I don't have the money for it."

I said, "I'm letting you know that I'm going to keep asking for more money for more staff, for a good reason."

He said, "OK, and I'll let you know something; when I can afford it, I'll let you know."

One day, about a month later, he came to me and said, "You know, I figured it out. Go get your people." That's the way the guy was. He was fun to work with.[112]

WITI-TV shot a lot of news film as it grew during the 1960s. Here cameraman Jim Pluta and John Drilling head out to cover a story sometime in 1968. (WITI photo)

CHAPTER 7 ~ WITI: CHANNEL 6

One of the first announcers hired by the station in 1956 was John Anthony. He hosted the wildly popular "Dance Party," as well as various movie programs. He's shown here in the announcer's booth in the 27th Street studios. Booth announcers did station I.D.'s, read commercial copy, and kept the programming logs. If a problem occurred, they were the ones who intoned: "Please stand by!" (WITI photo)

A 1965 survey commissioned by WTMJ-TV and conducted by Frank Magid showed that Carl Zimmermann was the "best liked local television personality," beating out long-time WTMJ-TV weatherman Bill Carlsen.[113]

Although they had started out broadcasting their local, studio programs in color, the station made the decision to convert its studio operations to monochrome when they moved to the 27th Street building. In 1966, the sales of color television sets had reached the point where it made sense to switch back to color. WITI-TV purchased color studio cameras, transmitting and color film processing equipment and went to all-color studio operations on July 4, 1966.[114]

WARD ALLEN AND "ALBERT THE ALLEY CAT" WITH THE WEATHER

(Courtesy of Hal Erickson)

In the summer of 1965, Roger Le Grand took another chance. Barbara Becker had served as the station's weather girl since the departure of Judy Marks to WTMJ-TV in 1959. There she met and fell in love with Jim Major, who had joined the station as a floor director on the day the station affiliated with CBS in 1959, and had risen to become first a producer/director, then a newsman, and then production manager. They were married in late 1964, and a few months later Barbara elected to give up her daily role as weather girl. (She would continue to host "Cartoon Alley" and perform in specials.)[115] According to Art Olszyk, Le Grand then unsuccessfully attempted to lure long-time WTMJ-TV weatherman Bill Carlsen away from them.[116]

To compete, operations manager Bob Oliver suggested that they use staff announcer Ward Allen – who had done the weather on weekends – and add one of the Jack DuBlon puppets. It was classic counter-programming. Carlsen took a serious approach to the weather, but he and the WTMJ-TV production staff had fun

during his live commercials. (See chapter 2.) Allen would take a serious approach too, but the puppet would provide entertainment and comic relief. The initial response from viewers was negative. Ward Allen:

> *Jack DuBlon and myself, we thought: 'Why are they doing this?'*
> *We got so much bad mail. Oh man! People would write letters that would scorch you!"*
> *I call what happened next Divine intervention. It was the last part of September or early October. I was sitting at home drinking coffee and praying. I thought I was going to lose my job because the viewer reaction was so bad. A little girl knocked on my door. She said, 'Mr. Allen, can you tell me about the weather? My class (She was in the fifth grade) is doing a project on weather and I don't know anything about it. Could you tell me something about it?'*
> *I thought to myself, Bingo! I said, 'You tell your teacher to give me a call, and I'll come to your school next Tuesday at one o'clock, and talk to the whole class.'*[117]

Le Grand still wanted "Albert the Alley Cat," but DuBlon thought differently. As he told the *Milwaukee Journal*'s Jeff Pryor in 1982:

> *I thought Albert was too outlandish for the newscast, and I suggested they should use Waldo the Bear; the three W's – 'Ward Allen and Waldo with the Weather'. Waldo was this big, brown, stuffy bear I created, who was 'A BIG TALKER...AND JUST AN ALL 'ROUND FUNNY GUY'*
> *But Roger was bent on Albert's personality. He thought there was something smart-assed about Albert, and Waldo was 'too loving'.*[118]

Allen found a promotional inspiration in his first appearance at a school:

> *I had a cameraman come out to that first school I went to, and we ran film. I told all of the kids, 'Now, you watch Channel 6 tonight, because at 10:15 you're going to be on our weather program.' The kids watched, and so did their moms and dads, grandmas and grandpas, their aunts and uncles – they all watched."*[119]

After the success of that first weather class, Allen began going to two or three schools a week starting in January of 1966. He had found a way to make the segment succeed:

> *After that first night the phone lit up, and I went to another school two days later. I went to two or three schools a week after that.*[120] *I did it for two or three weeks before [Roger] Le Grand knew about it. Being that he was a promotional man, he thought that it was a great idea. Our ratings were so high! We had a seventy share and a twenty-seven percent rating. You don't hear numbers like that anymore!*[121]

Albert joined Allen in the weather classes a couple of years later, and the kids loved it. In 1968, the TV6 weather segment was named No. 1 weather show in the country by the National Association of Program Executives. The citation read: "For presenting information in an interesting, entertaining way."[122]

DuBlon had numerous job offers during this time period, but elected to remain at WITI-TV. It's possible that he and Ward Allen would not have succeeded anywhere else, but as Art Olszyk remembered:

> *They could and did in Milwaukee, because Roger Le Grand knew his audience to a degree most general broadcasting executives never do, no matter what they spend on surveys and consultants.*[123]

Carl Zimmermann concurred:

Roger did see all those things that we probably didn't. Boy did that [adding Albert to the weather] work![124]

Some of the many sweaters and hats viewers made and sent to "Albert the Alley Cat" displayed above the painting used during the opening of "Cartoon Alley." (WITI photo)

Albert proved immensely popular. DuBlon took advantage of that popularity and occasionally made comments he wouldn't ordinarily have gotten away with as himself, but could when he made them through the puppet. Milwaukeeans remember the weather cat regularly mispronouncing humidity as "humidery" while giving the "sadistics." However, he never joked during the actual weather presentation.

Viewers sent Albert hundreds of custom-made sweaters and hats. The station received so many inquiries that they commissioned patterns which they sent to those requesting them.

WTMJ-TV hired Paul Joseph as its first meteorologist in 1970. WITI-TV responded in 1975 by hiring Tom Skilling to do its 10:00 p.m. weather forecast, relegating Ward Allen to noon and 6:00 p.m. Skilling attended the University of Wisconsin, and had done the weather on WKOW-TV in Madison and another station in Jacksonville, Florida. He held the seal of approval from the American Meteorological Society, and under their rules, had to reapply for it after changing markets.[125] The AMS informed Skilling that he had to stop doing the weather with Albert within 90 days, or they would take away his seal of approval. Henry Davis, the station's vice president and general manager said that if it came down to the seal or Albert, the seal would go. They still had a two-year contract with Jack DuBlon.[126]

At the time, Skilling thought that Joseph had complained to the society about one of their members working with a puppet."[127] That turned out to be untrue. Paul Joseph:

CHAPTER 7 ~ WITI: CHANNEL 6

Since then, Tom and I have talked about it. I had absolutely nothing to do with Tom's seal one way or the other. I was on their broadcast board, and there was a three-year cycle where I was involved reviewing tapes [from those wanting the seal], but the whole issue of Tom never once came up with any of the proceedings I was involved with.

When Tom lost his seal, I contacted someone at AMS headquarters to find out what had happened. What I was told was that the president-elect of the AMS, UWM Chancellor Werner Baum, was upset that a seal-holder was working with a puppet. I was told that he was instrumental in denying Tom his seal. I was not sent anything [renewal materials]. I was not asked, and had nothing to do with it.[128]

When the story broke in the *Milwaukee Journal* that Albert might be on his way out, the station received 10,000 letters objecting.[129] Albert stayed on the weather segment, and Skilling lost his seal. In 1978, he quit in a dispute with WITI management[130] over the time he spent on his weather segment, and later wound up on WGN-TV in Chicago.

In mid-1981, the station finally bowed to suggestions from consultants, and pulled Albert from the weathercasts. He was moved to the Sports Quiz with Earl Gillespie. However, the handwriting was on the wall, and after 16 years as a regular member of WITI-TV's newscasts, Albert made his last appearance on December 7 of that year.[131]

"Albert the Alley Cat" and Jack DuBlon. (WITI photo)

Le Grand continued to aggressively attack the competition. In 1967, the station started what Art Olszyk called: "...their greatest promotional effort to date, perhaps in the history of the market..."[132] The campaign was the idea of promotions director Ron Polera, and was called "The Winners." At first it was just promotional hype based on a series of "...brilliantly executed on-air promos..."[133], but in the November ratings period, the campaign paid off, and they beat WTMJ-TV at 10:00 p.m.

"The Winners," arguably the most famous Milwaukee television team of the 1960s. L-R: Earl Gillespie, "Albert the Alley Cat," Ward Allen, Tom Hooper and news director/anchor Carl Zimmermann. (WITI photo)

Carl Zimmermann:

> *Roger was out to beat WTMJ-TV in the ratings – as we all were – and we did it! We did it for quite a while there and we held it. The night we did it, he came in after our 10 o'clock news and said, "You guys are number one; did you know that? Come on into the conference room." He had champagne set up and threw a party. That was Roger. He loved what he was doing, and he loved the people he worked with.*[134]

Station personalities were shown in newspaper and *TV Guide* ads, and the station's newsletter, *The Antenna*, featured monthly biographies of all the on-air staff. Carl Zimmermann thought it was all great:

> *When a guy was doing news, there was his name right under him on your screen. That paid off, because that name was identified with the station. They went together. It was great promotion. When one of our folks would be around town, folks would recognize him as being from the station. The personality was tied in with the call letters. Roger knew how to promote and he did it beautifully.*[135]

WHO KNOWS?

GE College Bowl on NBC spawned a number of imitations in which stations used a similar concept with local high school students. WTMJ-TV had produced "High School Bowl" in the early 1960s, and WITI-TV would later follow with its own versions.

Beginning in the fall of 1966, it produced a discussion show called "Viewpoint." The half-hour show made its debut on Sunday, September 25 at 11:30 a.m. Included was a high school quiz show for the Sodality Union of the Milwaukee Archdiocese (SUMA). Jack DuBlon served as the host. The quiz ended in December, but "Viewpoint" lasted until June 4, 1967.

Jack DuBlon hosted a high school quiz for the Sodality Union of the Milwaukee Archdiocese (SUMA) on "Viewpoint" in the fall of 1966. (Courtesy of Paul Johnson)

Tony Karr replaced DuBlon as the host of "Who Knows?" (WITI photo, courtesy of Tony Karr)

Station staffer Paul Johnson, who had built the set for the SUMA quiz show, recalled that an executive from the Wisconsin Electric Power Co. saw the show, and wanted to do something similar.[136] The station developed a different one based on a similar format. Called "Who Knows?" it made its debut on Saturday, April 8, 1967. Like its predecessor, it was hosted by Jack DuBlon. The first season ended on June 10.

Jack DuBlon grew a beard in 1968, and station management decided that wasn't appropriate for the host of "Who Knows?" He was replaced by announcer Tony Karr[137], who would remain with the show for the rest of its run. Tony remembered when the decision to use the set for an episode of "Nightmare Theatre" had repercussions:

> *One evening when Dr. Cadaverino was taping his show, the Who Knows? set had not been struck. So…it was Igor against the doctor with me as host. It was late on Saturday night when the segment aired and as I watched it in the booth that night [Karr was a booth announcer, and also did the "Late Show News" right before Nightmare aired.], I had the feeling that we should not have desecrated such a high brow show. I was right! Jim Major, who was program director at that time, was watching at home. We were all suspended for a time for pushing the envelope a bit too far.*[138]

Paul Johnson remembered another anecdote:

> *The director of the program, Bill LeMonds, used to bet his neighbor on the outcome of the program. It aired on Saturday, but we taped the show on the previous Thursday, so Bill knew who had won!*[139]

Wisconsin Electric picked up part of the production costs. The balance was covered by the station as a part of its public service programming. The student teams played for prizes that consisted of funds to be used for the purchase of books by the schools' libraries. The questions were researched and submitted by members of the Marquette University faculty. Dr. Roger Parr was the show's authority/judge for many years. New tournaments were held each spring, with the last running between February 2 and May 11, 1974.

During what were politely called the city's "civil disturbances" in 1967, photographer Bruce Nason found himself in the middle of the action while trying to cover a fire at North 1st and West Center Streets:

> *I arrived on that scene when the house was fully engulfed in fire. Cops were all around but they didn't pay much attention to me. I was basically lying at the curb near one's feet. About the time a volley of shots rang out Carl [Zimmermann] called on the handi-talkie to warn crews that shots were being fired at 1st and Center Streets. I keyed the mike about that time and all he heard was my voice and gun fire. It sort of freaked him out and we never went out alone again.*[140]

Carl Zimmermann:

> *He was talking to me on the radio, and suddenly he was off. I said, 'Where are you?' Nothing... We just heard a lot of noise, but we didn't know what was happening.*
>
> *I said, 'Are you alright?' There was no answer, so I said, 'If you're ok, give me a flick of the microphone three times.' He did it, and I said, 'OK buddy, when you're ready, call me.'*[141]

WITI-TV reporter Roy Meyer (center) and photographer Bruce Nason (right) covered the city's 1967 "civil disturbances." (Courtesy of Bruce Nason)

Barbara Becker began doing "Season's Greetings from Barbara Ann Becker" in the early 1960s, which became "Season's Greetings from TV6." (WITI photo, courtesy of Paul Johnson)

Long-time WITI-TV reporter/anchor John Drilling pounds out a story in the crowded newsroom in the 27th Street building. Assistant News Director Lil Kleiman is at the far left. The staff labored for years in inadequate facilities. Some thought the tight quarters had one advantage: a feeling of camaraderie. (WITI photo)

CHAPTER 7 ~ WITI: CHANNEL 6   301

In 1972, John Gardner was hired as the city's first African-American news anchor. Gardner would stay until the following year.[142]

On Monday, August 14, 1972, WITI-TV started the city's first hour-long, local newscast, which ran from 6-7:00 p.m. On that show, a new segment debuted, called "Contact 6," hosted by Tom Hooper.[143] It was the city's first consumer affairs and problem solving segment, in which viewers could call-in or write with problems, which Hooper would attempt to mediate or solve.

On May 10, 1973, vice president and general manager Roger Le Grand, who had led the station through a period of tremendous growth, suffered a fatal heart attack.[144]

Since 1959, the station had used the former warehouse building that had housed first (briefly) WCAN-TV and then the CBS-owned WXIX. Space was always at a premium, and after abandoning plans to build new studios/offices at its transmitter site in the 1960s, plans for new facilities were finally announced in December of 1973.[145] Construction started in July of 1976.[146]

That same year WITI-TV became the first station in the city to use a portable mini-cam for electronic news gathering. Until then, all television news footage was shot on film, which had to be returned to the studios, developed and edited. The use of the mini-cam allowed the station to react quickly to events, and go "live" with remotes. Its use led to a conflict with WTMJ-TV over the right to broadcast live from Milwaukee Brewer's games. The Journal station had the rights to broadcast the games at the time, and they objected to a competitor broadcasting live from Milwaukee County Stadium during its newscasts. The Brewers sided with WTMJ-TV and as a consequence, WITI-TV threatened to boycott all reporting of the team, save for the line score.[147] That decision backfired, and was reversed.

WITI-TV's mid '70s team: Back row L-R: Tom Skilling, Albert, Earl Gillespie, and Tom Hooper Front Row L-R: Jill Geisler, Ken Matz, and Carl Zimmermann (WITI photo)

Since April of 1961, WITI-TV had been an ABC affiliate. However, by the mid-1970s, ABC was not happy with Storer Broadcasting.[148] In addition, CBS was not happy with WISN-TV, as ratings for its programming were lower in Milwaukee than the national average. In September of 1976, it was announced that WITI-TV would switch its network affiliation from ABC to CBS.[149] As a consequence, ABC affiliated with WISN-TV. The changes took place on Sunday, March 27, 1977, reversing the affiliation swap both stations had made sixteen years earlier.

SUPER BAND

WITI-TV anchors Julie Roberts and Tom Hooper hosted the second "Super Band" show in 1978. (WITI photo, courtesy of Sue Riordan)

In 1977, WITI-TV began a prime time, public service program designed to increase season ticket sales for the Milwaukee Symphony Orchestra. The program was the brainchild of D. Andrew Moquin, the symphony's director of development and public relations, Audrey Baird, a member of their board and chief ticket seller, and Sue Riordan, the station's director of community relations. As Riordan remembered:

> I was approached by the two of them that year. I think it Audrey who with her contacts in other cities had come across the 'Super Band' idea, which had been done in Buffalo, and Oakland. They called me and wanted to go to lunch to see if we would be interested in doing this.
>
> We looked at the tapes, and decided that the show that they were showing me was pretty boring – although it had been successful. I thought there was a lot we could do with the concept. I got very excited about it, as what they were trying to do was to reach an audience that had not been exposed to symphony music before. We would do it on prime time, commercial television. I thought that it had real potential if we could package it right.

I gave it some thought and pitched it to the station. The first reaction was, 'That's a public television show. We're not a symphony-type audience.'

I said, 'Well, almost everybody has been exposed to classical music.' The first time I was exposed was watching cartoons. If you think about it, what is in the background of almost all those cartoons from the '40s and '50s is classical music.

I said, 'The key here is number one a short attention span for television watchers, so what we have to do is a show, but jazz it up and make it fun – only do two or four minute clips of familiar pieces from a symphony or a pops tune. Then we have to package it in a familiar context.' The one that was the most familiar was The William Tell Overture, which most people know as the theme from The Lone Ranger.

As we batted ideas around, we thought of Tom Hooper with his wonderful announcer voice introducing that piece as The Lone Ranger. Then somebody thought of 'Albert the Alley Cat' doing Carnival of the Animals. We just started throwing ideas around, and the more we did, the more people got excited about it.[150]

Riordan served as the first executive producer and Tom Koester directed the show. In what became its annual format, the two-hour show was broadcast live from Uihlein Hall at Milwaukee's Performing Arts Center – without an audience. There the symphony would play short segments of various pieces, which were introduced by station talent. Backstage, telephones were set up to take calls from viewers ordering season tickets. The phones were staffed by station and area celebrities.

The first year, the symphony originally requested thirty phones, but cut that to twenty before the show. After one piece, conductor Kenneth Schermerhorn was worried when he didn't hear any phones ringing. A musician peered backstage, and reported that they weren't ringing because they were all busy![151]

When the show was over, 1,157 season ticket packages were sold: 626 for classical and 531 for the pops series. Most were to people who had never attended the symphony – many from the city's working-class, South Side.

The station continued the concept, and then tweaked it the last few years by making it a battle between local celebrity conductors before a live audience at Uihlein

"Battle of the Conductors" – 1985: L-R: professional wrestler "Da Crusher" (Reggie Lisowski), Milwaukee police chief Robert Ziarnik, D.J. Larry "the Legend" Johnson, Milwaukee Brewers' owner Bud Selig, Wisconsin Gas Co. director of corporate and media relations, Sue Riordan, Green Bay Packer offensive tackle Tim Huffman, Phil Witliff of the Milwaukee Admirals, Milwaukee Bucks' center Paul Mokeski, and co-hosts Jill Geisler and Tom Hooper. Riordan and Huffman tied for first, Ziarnik was second, and "Da Crusher" third. (WITI photo, courtesy of Sue Riordan)

Hall. Riordan, who went on to become Governor Lee Dreyfus' press secretary, and then director of corporate and media relations for the Wisconsin Gas Co., returned as a guest conductor for the last two shows, tying for first in 1985 with Green Bay Packer offensive tackle Tim Huffman. The last show was in 1986.

In 1978, general manager Henry Davis named Jill Geisler as the station's news director. Geisler had started as a reporter in 1973 after graduating from the University of Wisconsin, and had co-anchored the short-lived 5:00 p.m. news with John Drilling in 1975. In 1976, she began co-anchoring first the noon, and then the 6:00 p.m. newscast. She was the first female news director of a major market network affiliate.[152]

Carl Zimmermann hired her as a reporter, and remembered that they had to sell Storer on the idea of promoting her to news director:

> *I got out of the news director position, and was strictly writing and delivering editorials. Henry Davis and I were on a conference call with our home office and we told them that we were going to promote a woman. There was a long pause, and then they asked us if we really wanted to do that. They were stunned! We said, 'Yeah we want to do it! We have great confidence in her.' Let me tell you, she didn't let us down!*[153]

Jill Geisler recalled:

> *Henry Davis told me they said 'Are you out of your mind?'*
> *When Mr. Davis talked with me about taking the job, he asked me if I thought there were people who'd have a problem with the fact that I was a woman.*
> *'Yes,' I replied, 'but as long as we think of it as THEIR problem, not mine, things will be fine.' He agreed."*[154]

Passing the torch: Carl Zimmermann and Jill Geisler. (WITI photo)

Beginning August 30, 1979, WITI-TV experimented with the use of a helicopter for news reporting. The concept was sound, but the technology had not yet caught up with the idea. The antenna systems available at the time made it difficult to get a stable signal. The receiving antenna was on the 1,078 foot tower. Getting a

CHAPTER 7 ~ WITI: CHANNEL 6

The WITI-TV master control room in the 27th Street building in the mid-1970s. (Courtesy of Ed Rosenthal)

The offices of the new building were built around a two-story high atrium, which has been used as another studio for telethons, etc. (WITI photo)

good signal from outside Milwaukee wasn't a problem, but the surrounding terrain made it difficult when the helicopter was near the tower.[155] WITI-TV stopped using "Skycamera 6" in February of 1981, and it took over a decade before the antenna technology made the use of helicopters viable.

Storer Broadcasting continued to own the station into the 1980s. In 1983, it changed its name to Storer Communications, Inc. (SCI). In May of 1986, Lorimar Pictures announced that it was buying six television stations from SCI, including

In March of 1978, WITI-TV moved into new studios located just north of the intersection of North Green Bay and West Brown Deer Roads. The office area is at the right, while the studios, engineering facilities, etc. are at the left. (WITI photo)

WITI-TV began experimenting with the use of a helicopter in 1979. (WITI photo)

WITI-TV[156]. The deal was signed on June 30[157], but collapsed in November due to the parties' failure to come to terms on some issues as well as softness in television revenues.[158]

However, another party was interested. Racine native George Gillette had built an empire using risky financing. Included were resorts, meat packing companies (including Peck Foods Corp. of Milwaukee) and interests in television stations. In partnership with Kohlberg, Kravis, Robert & Co. (KKR), Gillette purchased SCI (including WITI-TV) for $1.3 billion in 1987. Gillette held fifty-five percent, while KKR held the remainder. The stations were held by a new company, SCI Television, Inc.

The problem was that Gillette paid too much for the stations. In the economic frenzy of the mid-to-late 1980s, Drexel, Burnham, Lambert had put together the highly leveraged purchase based on junk bonds. Cable television had penetrated most markets, and advertising revenue dropped. By the end of 1989, Gillette and KKR could not pay their bond holders. A small group of those bond holders tried to force an involuntary bankruptcy, while Gillette and KKR tried to work out a deal to restructure their debt.[159]

Gillette's bondholders forced it into bankruptcy in 1992.[160] SCI Television was not a part of that action, but it nonetheless defaulted on its debt the previous year. New World Entertainment offered to purchase fifty-one percent of SCI Television as a part of its debt restructuring.[161] Instead, SCI Television merged with Wometco Broadcasting. They then merged with New World Entertainment to form New World Communications in December of 1993.

News Corporation, the parent company of Fox, acquired a 20% interest in New World Communications. As a consequence, all New World stations, including WITI-TV, affiliated with the Fox Network. The switch was announced in May of 1994[162], and took place on December 11 of that year. Since Fox had no national news department, WITI-TV responded by expanding its own local news program at 5:00 p.m. to a full hour. It also introduced an hour-long news program at 9:00 p.m.

Melodie Wilson moved to WITI-TV in 1992. Here she is in a "town hall meeting" with Democratic presidential candidate Bill Clinton, which was held in the station's atrium that year. (WITI photo, courtesy of Jill Geisler)

From 1971 - 1997, WITI-TV hosted the annual Jerry Lewis MDA telethon. Here Jill Geisler and Tom Hooper serve as co-hosts. (WITI photo, courtesy of Jill Geisler)

News Corporation acquired all of New World Communications in January of 1997, and as a result became the new owner of WITI. Fox then brought in a new general manger, Carol Rueppel, who took over on April 15, 1997.[163] She became the city's first female television GM. After four and one-half years, she left for Minneapolis and more responsibility in October of 2001.[164] Chuck Steinmetz replaced her.

On July 12, 1998, the station's call letters were changed from WITI-TV to WITI.

In 2006 WITI acquired a new helicopter. (WITI photo)

CHAPTER 7 ~ WITI: CHANNEL 6   309

"ASK GUS"

(WITI photo)

Gus Gnorski moved from WTMJ radio to WITI-TV. His "Ask Gus" program of home/workshop hints is a rarity nowadays – a local production. The first "Ask Gus" show" was broadcast live on Nov. 8, 1992. It was co-hosted by Gus Gnorski and Mark Concannon, who were both celebrating birthdays that day. Because the show was live, the pair took phone calls and answered questions on the fly. A second live show was broadcast that December. The response was such that the decision was made to tape shows which would air weekly. The first aired on January 2, 1993. To get questions for the first taped shows, Gus solicited questions at the annual Home Builders Expo.[165] The last show aired on November 24, 2007.[166] Gnorski continued to host segments during the news.

In the summer of 2005, WITI began converting all of its news gathering equipment to digital technology.

On June 13, 2007 News Corporation announced that it was putting nine of its owned-and-operated stations, including WITI on the market.[167] On December 22 of that year, it announced that it had agreed to sell eight of its Fox network-affiliated television stations in the U.S. – including WITI – to Oak Hill Capital Partners LP for about $1.1 billion in cash. The stations would become a part of its media arm, Local TV, LLC, and managed by the Tribune Co. The FCC approved the sale on June 9, 2008,[168] and the deal was consummated on July 14 of that year. WITI's license was formally held by Community Television of Wisconsin, LLC., which in turn was owned by Local TV.

The insertion of channel 6 into the area's channel assignments upset the delicate balance which gave UHF stations a chance to be competitive in an intermixed city. As a result, one UHF station went dark, and it took years before its frequency and the third assigned to the city would be used. In the 1960s WITI-TV underwent

WITI master control in 2008. (WITI photo)

Mark Concannon and Kim Murphy on the set of Wake Up. (WITI photo)

CHAPTER 7 ~ WITI: CHANNEL 6   311

Brad Hicks and Katrina Cravy of the afternoon news team. (WITI photo)

Ted Perry and Beverly Taylor anchor the 10:00 p.m. news. (WITI photo)

tremendous growth with the combination of Storer ownership and the leadership of Roger Le Grand. Since the 1970s the station has had many ups-and-downs, as it struggled in a changing environment which saw additional channels go on the air, and cable/satellite television dilute available advertising revenue. Under Fox ownership, those ups and downs continued. New owner Local TV, LLC will face challenges as the station makes the transition to digital broadcasting.

L-R: Sports anchors Tim Van Vooren and Tom Pipens. (WITI photo)

L-R: Meteorologists Rob Haswell and Vince Condella are shown on the weather deck during a snowstorm in early 2008. (WITI photo)

CHAPTER 7 ~ WITI: CHANNEL 6   313

In June of 2008, WITI introduced new sets for "Wake Up"... (WITI photo)

...and its news programming. (WITI photo)

THE CHILDREN'S SHOWS

Billy Bishop played "Billy Bounce." (Courtesy of Ann & Glenn Bishop)

Once a staple of local programming, kid's shows, all but disappeared from the airwaves by the mid-1980s. For those who grew up with them however, some of the warmest memories of WITI-TV are of those children's' shows.

WITI-TV broadcast a kids' show the first day it went on the air. Magician, Billy Bishop, who had appeared on *The Ed Sullivan Show*, *Bandstand Review* and other network shows[169], played "Billy Bounce." Billy appeared with his puppet friend, a rabbit named "Witi" (pronounced "Witty") who (appropriately) lived in Billy's hat. Witi didn't speak, but rather whispered to Billy, who would then say to the viewers: "Witi says…" The few viewers with color televisions could see that Billy often wore his trademark red jacket[170], as the show was broadcast using WITI-TV's Du Mont Vitascan system. "Billy Bounce and Witi" ran at 4:45 p.m. Monday through Friday. The show featured cartoons on film, including *Little Lulu*, George Pal's *Puppetoons*, and *Noveltoons* – all in color. WITI-TV ran the show from May 21 through December 24, 1956.

Thereafter, WITI-TV began showing films at 4:00 p.m. on a program called "Hollywood Matinee." A new kids' show made its debut on December 26, 1956. The show was called "Clubhouse Gang." Elden Anspach played a character named "Uncle Buck." Anspach was in charge of the floor crew[171], and had done shows in Rockford, Illinois and Omaha, Nebraska.[172] (Prior to the station's sale to Hearst, he had been the program director at WTVW.) It ran Monday through Saturday at 5:30 p.m. The M-F show switched to a 5:15 p.m. time slot as of March 1, 1957. The show ran through Saturday, May 18, 1957, after which Anspach left for WFRV-TV in Green Bay.[173]

WTVW/WISN-TV had run a franchised version of "Romper Room" since 1955. On Monday, July 29, 1957, the show and its teacher, "Miss Pat" (Oliver) moved to WITI-TV in its same time slot – 3:30-4:00 p.m. On Monday, January 26, 1958, "Miss Barbara" (Gresser) replaced "Miss Pat"[174] after she was chosen from ninety-eight applicants.[175] The show's time slot was shifted thirty minutes earlier on March 3. After the station affiliated with CBS, the show was shifted to 9:00 a.m. It stayed in that time slot through Friday, July 29, 1959, after which it returned to WISN-TV.

In early 1959, WITI started another kids' show. Named "Post Office Box 6," the show ran weekday afternoons from 4:00 to 5:00 p.m., and again featured *Little Lulu*, George Pal's *Puppetoons*, and *Noveltoons* – all in color. Also included were *Jungle Jim*, *Ramar of the Jungle*, Gene Autry, *Sir Lancelot* and *Johnny Jupiter* films. Staff announcer Ward Chase (Wardwell Chase Rosenberg) played a character named "Mac the Mailman," who wore an official postman's uniform supplied by the Milwaukee Post Office. The first show was on Monday, January 19, 1959; the last on Tuesday March 31, 1959.

After WITI affiliated with CBS, Chase was shifted to a new show called (appropriately) "Mac the Mailman," Saturday mornings from 11:00 a.m. until noon. A contest sponsored by a candy company in which the winner received a giant, cream-filled Easter egg, and could designate another for a charity, received 10,000 entries! The first show was on April 4, 1959; the last on September 12, 1959. Chase then moved to the newly independent WXIX (channel 18).

Thereafter, WITI-TV acquired a package of Popeye cartoons and elected to show them on a show with a nautical theme. "Captain WITI" (again, pronounced "Witty") made its debut on Monday, September 14, 1959 and ran through Friday, 26 February 1960, at 5:30 p.m. The captain was played by Russ Widoe, who had played "Colonel Caboose" on WBAY in Green Bay.[176] Widoe was a ventriloquist, teacher, musical expert and experienced showman.[177] The "Captain" was joined by an assortment of puppets and his talking parrot "Griselda." Widoe then elected to return to WBAY, reprising his role as "Colonel Caboose" there.

The show was replaced by one called "Roy the Cabin Boy," which kept the nautical theme. Roy was played by Bob Munn. His two puppet sidekicks were a 50 year-old parrot and a 2000 year-old genie. Like its predecessor, the show ran at 5:30 p.m. This show ran from Monday, February 29 through Friday, July 29, 1960.

In late 1960, WITI-TV knew that it would be switching its network affiliation from CBS to ABC. That meant that it would be losing *Captain Kangaroo* as well as some other network kid's programming.

(Courtesy of Hal Erickson)

Anticipating this, the station hired Jack DuBlon as a staff announcer in October of that year. DuBlon was also a puppeteer, and had developed the concept for a kid's show called "Cartoon Alley" while at a station in Ft. Worth Texas. DuBlon moved to Milwaukee in anticipation of WITI-TV running the show.

(Courtesy of Hal Erickson)

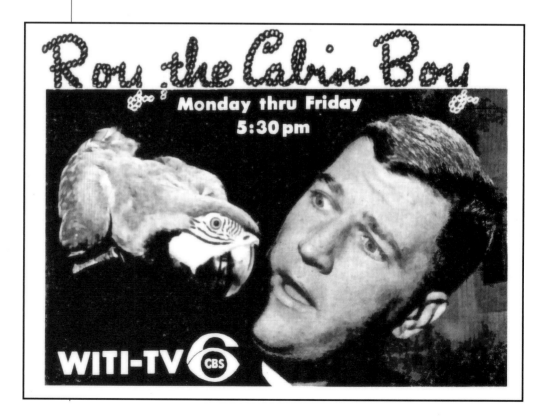

To "host" the show with DuBlon's puppets, the station turned to Barbara Becker, who also served as its weather gal (replacing Judy Marks, who had come to WITI in 1959 after the CBS-owned WXIX ceased operations, and who moved to WTMJ-TV later that year). Becker grew up in Iowa, and later moved to Whitefish Bay with her parents. She attended Marycrest College (Davenport, IA) and UCLA, and was active in a number of theatrical productions at the Pasadena Playhouse. Besides working as a model, she also sang with a number of big bands, including Ralph Flanagan, Les Brown, Paul Whiteman, and Fred Waring. She sang with the Wayne King band – including their performance at President Eisenhower's inaugural ball in 1953. She started her television career in Milwaukee with her own show

1961 promo card sent to kids who requested it. Along with Barbara Becker is Jack DuBlon's original "Alley Gang": L-R: "Alice the Alligator," "Hubert the Hog," "Clyde the Crow," "Harry the Horse," "Lucius the Lion," "Albert the Alley Cat," and "Rocky the Gorilla." (WITI photo)

"Barbara Becker Sings" on WTMJ-TV, and later moved the show to Chicago and Hollywood. Before coming to channel 6 she appeared on NBC-TV's "Club 60," which originated in Chicago.

"Cartoon Alley" made its debut on Saturday, April 1, 1961, at 10:30 a.m. At first it ran from 5:00-5:55 p.m. M-F, beginning on Monday, April 3, 1961. On April 8, the Saturday slot was shifted to 9:30-10:30 a.m. The show featured the Jack DuBlon puppets including Albert the Alley Cat, his brother Filbert (actually an old Albert), his nephew Floyd, Rocky (a cigar chomping gorilla), Lucius the Lion, Alice the Alligator, Waldo the Bear (His last name was "Bruinowski." He had a Polish accent, and was the local postmaster), Hubert the Hog, Harry the Horse, Hyde and Clyde (two crows), Sheldon (with a Jewish accent) and others.

Jack DuBlon with his puppets in the early 1960s. (WITI photo)

During the week, WITI-TV showed Popeye cartoons in the mornings. On January 8, 1962, the weekday version was shifted from the afternoon to 8:30 a.m., and continued through August 30, 1968.

At that time the station decided to change the concept. The puppet characters were told that they were being evicted from their alley, and had to decide where to move. For several weeks, they battled, before finally deciding to settle on a farm. "Funny Farm" made its debut on September 2, 1968. DuBlon was given a larger role. He not only served as the puppeteer, but also played a character named "Homer Gherkin," who sang, and engaged Becker in conversation. A new set was designed by Carol Milman Davis, and built by Paul Johnson.[178] Like "Cartoon Alley" the show ran Monday through Saturday. The Saturday show ran through August 30, 1969.

Barbara Becker had married Jim Major, who started as a floor director, and rose up through the ranks to eventually become the station's program director, and operations manager, after the death of Bob Oliver in 1968. When he was transferred to a new position as operations manager at WJBK-TV in Detroit during the summer of 1973, Becker naturally went with him.[179] For six months, she flew back to

The Cartoon Alley set included the "Shake Shop," in which visiting kids – especially scouting groups - were entertained. It disappeared in 1966, but returned in early March of 1968. (WITI photo, courtesy of Paul Johnson)

The "Shake Shop" welcomed Jack DuBlon as Santa Claus for an annual "Santa Claus Party" segment wherein children (usually employees') outlined what they wanted for Christmas. Santa had an earphone, and the children's parents were off-camera where they told Santa what the kids wanted – surprising them. (WITI photo)

Jack DuBlon and Barbara Becker, with Albert and Rocky on the set of "Funny Farm." (WITI photo)

Metric lesson – 1974. L-R: Jack DuBlon as "Mr. Letterbags," "Alice the Alligator" and Darlyne Berg. (WITI photo, courtesy of Darlyne Haertlein)

The "You and I" cast in 1977. L-R: Larry Grzegorek as "Jeremy the Jogger," Darlyne Berg, and Wally Dobiesz. (WITI photo, courtesy of Darlyne Haertlein)

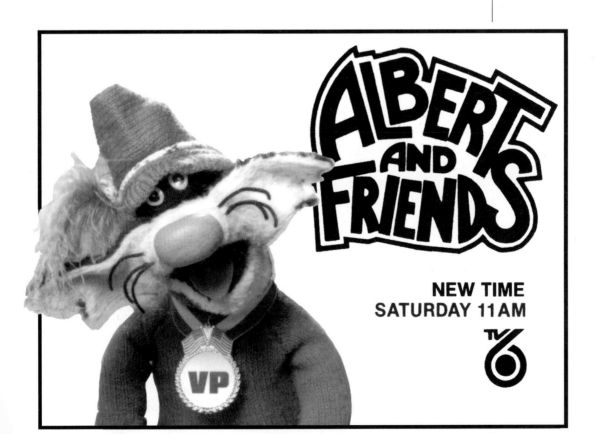

(WITI photo)

Milwaukee once a month to tape 4 weeks of the show, but elected to end her involvement at the end of January, 1974. The last show was on February 1, 1974[180], and featured a film clip from a "Cartoon Alley" show from 1963, as well as various still photos from over the years.

One of the reasons the shows were so successful was that Jack DuBlon instilled personality into his puppets. Barbara Becker commented that she never thought of "Albert" and the others as puppets, but rather as characters. To her (and others) they were very real.[181] So real, that her husband, Jim Major, once found himself on the weather set and noticed that he felt he was speaking to "Albert" and not to Jack.[182]

Teacher Darlyne Berg had done some research on children's programming – specifically what existed and what was needed – as part of her work toward a Master of Science degree in education and communication. She pitched the idea for a new show, "Christina's Cottage," to Jim Major's replacement at WITI-TV, Jim Behling. Behling liked the concept and script. Berg then did a pilot, and waited for the opportunity to surface. That happened when "Funny Farm's" run came to an end. Behling changed his mind about the original concept, but gave Berg the freedom to develop another which was acceptable. "You and I" made its debut on Monday, February 4, 1974.

Jack DuBlon performed as a mailman called, "Mr. Letterbags." Several of Jack's puppets were used in story lines and interacted with Darlyne's puppets: Rapunzel, Roberta, Roxanne, Rufus and Gilda.

On January 5, 1975, the show was switched to a weekly format. On Monday October 27, it was once again scheduled M-F at 7:00 a.m. During this time period, Jack DuBlon left the show.

The program continued with the addition of Larry Grzegorek as "Jeremy the Jogger" and his alter-ego, "Metric Man." The station's real-life janitor, Wally Dobiesz, played himself and added a grandfatherly presence to the cast.

During one summer, the "You and I" Show attracted more viewers for its time period than any other program on Milwaukee television. Like its two predecessors, "You and I" got better ratings than CBS's "Captain Kangaroo." That led to a confrontation.

In January of 1977, WISN-TV, knowing that on March 27 it would shift to ABC, stopped carrying "Captain Kangaroo," replacing it with ABC's "Good Morning America," which was not carried by WITI-TV. Parents petitioned WITI-TV to carry the show.[183] They met with station management, and threatened to boycott "You and I" if the station refused to carry the "Captain." All of that irritated WITI-TV's general manager Henry Davis, as it was WISN-TV's decision to drop the show early. (Stations in other cities had also wanted to drop the show because of low ratings.[184]) As a result, WITI-TV elected to carry both shows. However, later that year, the decision was made to drop "You and I." The show had only broken even[185] during its run, and although it was highly regarded, there was only room in the schedule for one kids' program. It ran through December 30, 1977.

In late 1981, the station decided to accept the advice of a consultant, and eliminated "Albert" from the weather forecasts. Jack DuBlon was given a Saturday morning kid's show, and Albert was made "vice president for important things kids should know." "Albert and Friends" made its debut on January 24, 1981. It ran through September 8, 1984. DuBlon left the station in 1985, and passed away on July 25, 1988.

CHAPTER 7 ~ WITI: CHANNEL 6

THE HORROR HOSTS

In October of 1957, Screen gems released a package of Universal horror and mystery films to television in a package it called *Shock!* The public ate them up, and ratings soared.[186] That touched off a boom in TV horror shows across the country. As was the norm in those days, many of the shows featured hosts, dressed in appropriate costumes, who would introduce the films and engage in antics.

WITI-TV already had many of the RKO horror films in its library. In late 1957, it purchased another package of such films, and elected to run them Saturday nights at 9:30 p.m. on a program called "Haunted."[187]

The show made its debut on January 11, 1958, and featured films from RKO and Monogram, such as *The Thing from Another World*, *King Kong*, and *Doomed to Die*. It ran through August 16, 1958.

In early 1958, WITI-TV purchased the *Shock!* and *Son of Shock* packages, and made plans to show them on Friday and Saturday nights. These made their debut on August 22, 1958.

Local actor Robert Hersh was appearing as Kobish in the stage version of "The Desperate Hours" with the Shorewood Players. Larry Turet, who was at the time the assistant program director for WITI-TV, saw the play on the recommendation of a floor man (the late Allan Winstrom), who also worked with the theater group. Turet saw in Hersh the person he wanted to host the shows. During their

Robert Hersh as "The Advisor" (George Brzesinski photo, courtesy of Artie Rickun)

first meeting, Hersh was noncommittal. He did not think it a worthy role. After some discussion, they settled on a character named "The Advisor," who would give gratuitous advice to his audience, based on current events, the movie being shown, etc.[188] Hersh was reluctant to play a horror host in the same way as others had done so, and did not use an elaborate set or make-up.

The show opened with him in a coffin which was standing on-end. The camera then came into a close-up (the "ugly shot"), which picked up the warts under his eyes.[189] During the breaks, he would be seated at a desk or table, with a sign that said "The Advisor," and give his spiel. A monkey named "Sancho" (real name "Doodles" – owned by Allan Winstrom) sat on his shoulder or ran around. "Shock" ran at 11:30 p.m. Friday nights, while "Double Shock" ran at 9:30 p.m. Saturday nights. Hersh was extremely popular at the time, and WITI received upwards of 1000 letters a week asking for its "Horror Club" membership cards. The shows continued through March 28, 1959, when WITI-TV affiliated with CBS, and changed its programming. Robert Hersh passed away on April 30, 2006.

WITI-TV later showed the same films in 1960-61, and another package including films from RKO and MGM in 1961-62.

By 1964, television was in the midst of the second "horror boom." The networks featured *Bewitched*, *The Addams Family*, and *The Munsters*. WUHF was showing the old Universal films on its own version of "Shock Theater." WISN-TV was running several packages of horror/sci-fi films on its "Movies From Tomorrow" program.

It was in that atmosphere that WITI-TV elected to jump on the bandwagon. It called its show "Nightmare Theatre." To differentiate itself from the two other Mil-

"Dr. Cadaverino" and "Igor" (played by the late Roger Cotey) in 1964. (WITI photo)

CHAPTER 7 ~ WITI: CHANNEL 6

waukee horror movie shows, it turned to DuBlon to create a character named "Dr. Cadaverino." The doctor was joined by his headless aide "Igor" (played by members of the floor crew), who got into all kinds of mischief. The show debuted on October 10, 1964.

The show developed a loyal following. So much so, that DuBlon dropped the make-up (He started wearing work gloves after reaching into a package sent in by a viewer and grabbed a handful of decomposing rat![190]), and morphed into a "hipster." The first set had been slapped together from items in the station's prop room (including the wooden coffin used to open "Shock" and "Double Shock") and was destroyed – on the air – by DuBlon in 1968. It was replaced by a new one built specifically for the show by Paul Johnson.[191]

The show ran through September 24, 1977, when DuBlon (who had become tired of the role and the difficulty doing the voice)[192] elected to end its 13 year run.

'Dr. Cadaverino" and "Igor" (Larry Grzegorek) in late 1968. (WITI photo)

(The last show he hosted was broadcast on July 16, 1977. Thereafter, horror films were still shown while the Dr. Cadaverino character was on hiatus.) On October 29, 1977, a special farewell show was aired. There was no film, but rather DuBlon and a multitude of guests reminisced about the show's run.

In January 1980, WISN-TV began running its own version of "Shock Theater," with Rick Felski as "Tolouse NoNeck." That character looked a great deal like DuBlon's. The station decided to bring DuBlon's character back, and aired "Dr. Cadaverino's Halloween Special" on October 31, 1980. It was the last appearance for the character.

"Farewell Nightmare Theatre," October 29, 1977: L-R: Ralph ("Gump") Gilmore and Hans Geyer of "Scud International," Illusionist David Seebach, Igor, Doc, and "Miss Nightmare – 1975," Mary Modrzyk. (WITI photo)

NOTES

1. "WISN Asking For Television: New Studios Planned," *Milwaukee Journal*, March 23, 1948. Also see: "WISN Applies for Television Permit," *Milwaukee Sentinel*, March 23, 1948.
2. Federal Communications Commission, *Sixth General Report and Order*, FCC 52-294 74219, April 11, 1952, Section 575.
3. "WISN to Build Radio Center: Buys Norris Home," *Milwaukee Journal*, June 12, 1952.
4. "TV Channels Plea Rejected: Decision by FCC," *Milwaukee Journal*, November 14, 1952.
5. "For The Record," *Broadcasting Telecasting*, March 30, 1953, 120.
6. Edward F. Ryan, "McCarthy Plays a Role in TV Channel 10 Fight," *Milwaukee Journal*, May 17, 1953. (Reprinted from *The Washington Post*)
7. "Hearst Ch. 10 Appeal Delay," *Broadcasting Telecasting*, October 19, 1953, 50.
8. "Hearst Asks Ch. 6," *Broadcasting Telecasting*, October 5, 1953, 33. Also see: "Seek Channel Shift for Extra TV Here," *Milwaukee Sentinel*, October 1, 1953.
9. Stanley J. Witkowski, Certified Copy of Resolution, File Number 53-1943, October 13, 1953. Frank P. Zeidler Papers, Milwaukee Public Library (Box 163, folder 2). Also see: "Text of Resolution Backing Hearst TV Plan," *Milwaukee Sentinel*, October 2, 1953. "Aldermen Back Hearst TV Plan," *Milwaukee Sentinel*, October 2, 1953.
10. "Council Backs New TV Plea," *Milwaukee Journal*, October 7, 1953.
11. Frank P. Zeidler, letter to Milwaukee Common Council, October 9, 1953, Frank P. Zeidler Papers, Milwaukee Public Library (Box 55, folder 10).
12. "May Oppose TV Proposal," *Milwaukee Journal*, October 2, 1953.
13. Lou Poller, letter to Hon. Frank Zeidler, October 7, 1953. Gerald A. Bartell, letter to Hon. Frank Zeidler, October 8, 1953. Lou Poller, letter to Mr. H.J. Van Valkenburg, Wisconsin Association for Vocational Education, May 4, 1953. Frank P. Zeidler Papers, Milwaukee Public Library (Box 163, folder 2). Also see: "Plan for New Channel Hit," *Milwaukee Journal*. October 8, 1953.
14. "Ch. 6 Proposal," *Broadcasting Telecasting*, October 12, 1953, 54.
15. "Hearst Ch. 10 Appeal Delay," *Broadcasting Telecasting*, October 19, 1953, 50.

16 "TV Channel Plan Fought," *Milwaukee Journal*, October 14, 1953.
17 "Duluth, Milwaukee Stations Protest New Assignments," *Broadcasting Telecasting*, November 16, 1953, 66.
18 "Hearst Argues for Channel 6," *Milwaukee Journal*, November 21, 1953.
19 "TV Channel 6 Given to 'Bay,'" *Milwaukee Journal*, December 4, 1953.
20 "FCC Denies Violating Rule," *Milwaukee Journal*, December 5, 1953.
21 "First to Apply for Channel 6," *Milwaukee Journal*, December 7, 1953.
22 "WISN to File For Channel 6," *Milwaukee Sentinel*, December 5, 1953.
23 "UHFTA Protests VHF Allocation," *Broadcasting Telecasting*, December 28, 1953, 44-45.
24 "WCAN-TV Asks Court to Bar Ch. 6 Bids," *Broadcasting Telecasting*, January 11, 1954, 58. Also see: "Asks Hearing on Channel 6: WCAN-TV protests," *Milwaukee Journal*, January 8, 1954.
25 "WCAN-TV Asks Court to Prevent FCC Action on Whitefish Bay," *Broadcasting Telecasting*, January 18, 1954, 50.
26 "Station WISN Buys Site for VHF Channel 6," *Milwaukee Sentinel*, January 13, 1954. Also see: "Tract Purchased as TV Tower Site," *Milwaukee Journal*, January 13, 1954.
27 "Ban Refused on Channel 6," *Milwaukee Journal*, January 20, 1954.
28 "Opposes Plea for Channel 6," *Milwaukee Journal*, January 22, 1954. Also see: "WCAN-TV Requests FCC Dismiss Hearst Bid," *Broadcasting Telecasting*, January 25, 1954, 54.
29 "FCC Admits WCAN-TV Bid for Whitefish Bay," *Broadcasting Telecasting*, May 3, 1954, 59.
30 "Whitefish Bay Ch. 6 Case Begins," *Broadcasting Telecasting*, May 31, 1954, 79.
31 "Oppose Wider TV Hearings," *Milwaukee Journal*, June 10, 1954.
32 "TV Petition Change OK's," *Milwaukee Journal*, July 30, 1954. Also see: "Independent, WCAN-TV Upheld in Ch. 6 Bid," *Broadcasting Telecasting*, August 2, 1954, 56.
33 "FCC Brief Defends Whitefish Bay Ch. 6," *Broadcasting Telecasting*, October 18, 1954, 58.
34 "Seek to Unite on Channel 6," *Milwaukee Journal*, November 4, 1954. Also see: "3 Channel 6 Applicants Study Merger," *Milwaukee Sentinel*, November 5, 1954.
35 "Channel 6 Merger Talks Snag," *Milwaukee Journal*, December 7, 1954. Also see: "Merger Talks on Channel 6 to Continue," *Milwaukee Sentinel*, December 8, 1954.
36 "Hearst's Firm Seeks WTVW: Negotiations Are On," *Milwaukee Journal*, December 15, 1954. Also see: "Milwaukee Revisited," *Broadcasting Telecasting*, December 13, 1954, 5.
37 "Hearst Acquires WTVW (TV) Milwaukee; NBC Buys WKNB-TV New Britain, Conn," *Broadcasting Telecasting*, January 10, 1955, 7.
38 "Petition for Channel 6 Withdrawn by Hearst," *Milwaukee Journal*, January 25, 1966.
39 "Independent TV Cleared for Milwaukee Ch. 6 Grant," *Broadcasting Telecasting*, April 25, 1955, 72.
40 "Seek to Push Video Station," *Milwaukee Journal*, April 22, 1955.
41 "Grant Permit to TV Station," *Milwaukee Journal*, June 30, 1955. Also see: "Whitefish Bay Ch. 6 Grant Made Effective by FCC," *Broadcasting Telecasting*, July 4, 1955, 66.
42 "Set Ground Breaking for New TV Station," *Milwaukee Journal*, October 8, 1955.
43 "Wisconsin Dateline," *TV Guide* Wisconsin Edition, March 10-16, 1956, A-1.
44 Robert Truscott, email to the author, January 29, 2006.
45 "Set WITI-TV Starting Day," *Milwaukee Journal*, May 18, 1956.
46 "Three get FCC Green Light," *Broadcasting Telecasting*, May 7, 1956, 9.
47 Truscott, January 29, 2006.
48 "Du Mont Shows 19" Color Tube for Sets, New Color Multi-Scanner for Stations," *Broadcasting Telecasting*, May 3, 1954, 92. Also see: "By Popular Demand...Local Live Color in a Single Unit: The Du Mont Multi-Scanner," *Broadcasting Telecasting*, May 23, 1955, 51-56.
49 Ron Yokes, email to the author, February 6, 2006.
50 Ibid.
51 Ron Yokes, email to the author, February 26, 2006.
52 Yokes, February 6, 2006,
53 "'Vitascan' for Color TV," *Color Television, Selection-Operation-Servicing*, (New York: Ziff-Davis, 1957), 134.
54 Yokes, February 6, 2006,
55 "Color Shows Galore Feature New Station," *Milwaukee Sentinel*, May 21, 1956.

56 Yokes, February 6, 2006,
57 Ibid.   58 Ibid.   59 Ibid.   60 Ibid.   61 Ibid.
62 Ibid.   63 Ibid.   64 Ibid.
65 "Scanner System Permits Pickup of Television Picture in Color," *Electrical Engineering*, July, 1955, 630.
66 "'Vitascan' for Color TV."
67 Yokes, February 6, 2006,
68 "'Vitascan' for Color TV."
69 "Du Mont Shows 'Vitascan' Color Plan," *Broadcasting Telecasting*, May 23, 1955, 122, 124.
70 Stu Armstrong, Interview with the author, March 9, 2006.
71 Hal Erickson, email to author, March 16, 2007.
72 "WITI-TV Is Asking Radio Station OK," *Milwaukee Journal*, February 14, 1958.
73 "WITI Owners Considering Sale," *Milwaukee Journal*, May 15, 1957.
74 "WITI Won't Sell, President Kahn Says," *Milwaukee Journal*, May 21, 1957.
75 Steve Richter, email to the author, September 16, 2005.
76 "TV Station WITI Sold," *Milwaukee Journal*, August 9, 1958. Also see: "Storer Buys WITI-TV Milwaukee, To Sell WVUE(TV) Wilmington," *Broadcasting*, August 11, 1958, 9.
77 "Denies Shift to WITI-TV: CBS Spiked Report," *Milwaukee Journal*, August 10, 1958.
78 "Storer Queried Further On Milwaukee VHF Plans," *Broadcasting*, October 20, 1958, 70, 72.
79 "WITI-TV Purchase Defended By Storer," *Broadcasting*, November 3, 1958, 70.
80 "WITI Transfer Step Approved," *Milwaukee Journal*, November 14, 1958.
81 "CBS-TV Will Move to WITI on April 1," *Milwaukee Sentinel*, February 28, 1959. Also see: "CBS to Shift to Channel 6," *Milwaukee Journal*, February 27, 1959.
82 Donald H. Dooley, "Where the Shows Come From," *Milwaukee Journal*, October 6, 1957.
83 "CBS Move Spells Big Movies," *Milwaukee Journal*, March 29, 1959.
84 "Whitefish Bay 'Loses' Its Television Station," *Milwaukee Journal*, July 31, 1959.
85 Robert Truscott, Interview with the author, August 8, 2002.
86 "OK 1000 Ft. Shorewood Tower," *Milwaukee Sentinel*, August 2, 1960.
87 Arthur L. Olszyk, *Live…At the Scene*, (Milwaukee: self-published, 1993), 77.
88 Carl Zimmermann, Interview with the author, March 31, 2006.
89 Ward Allen, interview with the author, March 30, 2007.
90 "FCC Okays TV Antenna," *Milwaukee Sentinel*, April 1, 1961.
91 "WITI-TV Plans for Shorewood Move Outlined," *Milwaukee Sentinel*, March 7, 1961.
92 "Shorewood OKs Zoning for WITI," *Milwaukee Sentinel*, April 4, 1961. Also see: "TV Station's Site Rezoned," *Milwaukee Journal*, April 4, 1961.
93 "WITI-TV Starts Work on Tower," *Milwaukee Journal*, August 12, 1961.
94 "Steel Plunges From Tower," *Milwaukee Journal*, May 26, 1962.
95 "Trustee Abramson Lights TV Tower; Tall Beacon New Landmark in Area," *The Herald*, February 6, 1964.
96 Ibid.
97 "Illuminated TV Tower Stirs Up Village Protest," *Milwaukee Sentinel*, January 21, 1964.
98 "2,000 Bulbs on TV Tower Make Neighbor See Red," *Milwaukee Journal*, January 21, 1964.
99 "TV Tower '6' Ruled Illegal in Shorewood," *Milwaukee Sentinel*, March 3, 1964.
100 "Backs lights on TV Tower," *Milwaukee Journal*, March 16, 1964.
101 "Channel 6 Sign to Glow Again," *Milwaukee Sentinel*, March 19, 1964.
102 Stephen M. Dearholt, Letter to WITI-TV, October 31, 1973.
103 "Lights Out on TV6 Tower" *Storer Story*, Vol. XX, No. 1 (January, 1974), 17.
104 Robert Truscott, email to the author, January 29, 2006.
105 Donald H. Dooley, "Milwaukee Studio Notes," *Milwaukee* Journal, September 23, 1962.
106 Donald H. Dooley, "WXIX Lights Up Again Monday," *Milwaukee* Journal, July 19, 1959.
107 Carl Zimmermann, email to the author, July 15, 2006.

108 "Regular TV Gets Color," *Milwaukee Sentinel*, March 6, 1963. Also see: "Color Effect on TV Seen by Some Viewers," *Milwaukee Journal*, March 6, 1963.
109 Jim Major, email to the author, March 1, 2006.
110 Ibid
111 Ibid.
112 Ibid.
113 Frank Magid, *Attitudes and Opinions Toward Television in the Milwaukee, Wisconsin Area*, 1965, 269. Milwaukee Journal Stations. 1922-1969. Milwaukee Manuscript Collection 203. Wisconsin Historical Society. Milwaukee Area Research Center. UWM Libraries. University of Wisconsin-Milwaukee. (Box 32, folder 7).
114 Michael H. Drew, "Milwaukee Studio Notes," July 3, 1966.
115 "Show Business," *Milwaukee Journal*, July 27, 1965.
116 *Live…At the Scene*, 99.
117 Allen, March 30, 2007.
118 Jeff Pryor, "Jack DuBlon: Looking Back at Those Years with Albert the Alleycat," *Milwaukee Journal*, TV Screen, February 21, 1982.
119 Allen, March 30, 2007.
120 Allen, Ward, email to the author, April 10, 2007.
121 Ibid.
122 "Jack DuBlon: Looking Back at Those Years with Albert the Alleycat."
123 *Live…At the Scene*, 99.
124 Zimmermann, March 31, 2006.
125 Beth Slocum, "Meteorological Society Wants to Yank Puppet," *Milwaukee Journal*, July 15, 1976.
126 Ibid.
127 Vic Ziegel, "When it Comes to the Weather, It's What's Up Front that Counts," *Milwaukee Journal*, January 8, 1984.
128 Paul Joseph, interview with author, December 20, 2007.
129 "When it Comes to the Weather, It's What's Up Front that Counts."
130 Greg Moody, "Skilling Quits in Dispute with Channel 6," *Milwaukee Sentinel*, July 4, 1978.
131 Michael H. Drew, "Albert Purrs a Farewell to Channel 6 News," *Milwaukee Journal*, December 30, 1981.
132 *Live…At the Scene*, 130.
133 Ibid, 131
134 Zimmermann, March 31, 2006,
135 Ibid.
136 Paul Johnson, email to author, June 4, 2008.
137 Tony Karr, conversation with author, December 19, 2007.
138 Tony Karr, email to author, June 7, 2008.
139 Paul Johnson, June 4, 2008.
140 Bruce Nason, email to the author, October 18, 2007.
141 Zimmermann, March 31, 2006,
142 Nate Grimm, "Anchoring His Life," *Wisconsin People and Ideas*, Winter, 2007, 62-68.
143 Michael H. Drew, "On the Milwaukee Scene" *Milwaukee Journal*, August 13, 1972.
144 "LeGrand Dies, Guided WITI-TV," *Milwaukee Sentinel*, May 11, 1973. Also see: "LeGrand Dies, WITI Manager," *Milwaukee Journal*, December 13, 1973.
145 "WITI Plans Studio Move to Brown Deer," *Milwaukee Sentinel*, November 13, 1986.
146 "New Studio Going Up for Channel 6," *Milwaukee Journal*, July 28, 1976.
147 *Live…At the Scene*, 247.
148 Michael H. Drew "On the Milwaukee Scene," *Milwaukee Journal*, October 3, 1976.
149 Chris Stoehr, "Channel 6 Gets CBS and Everybody's Happy (They Say)," *Milwaukee Sentinel*, September 25, 1976.
150 Sue Riordan, interview with author, April 25, 2007.
151 Lawrence B. Johnson, "Super Band! Super Show! Super Deal for Symphony!" *Milwaukee Sentinel*, June 10, 1977.
152 Vernon Stone, "Women Break Glass Ceiling in TV News," (Website) http://www.missouri.edu/~jourvs/tvfnds.html, University of Missouri, 1997.
153 Zimmermann, March 31, 2006,
154 Jill Geisler, email to the author, April 2, 2006.

155 Truscott, August 8, 2002.
156 "Lorimar Buying WITI-TV," *Milwaukee Journal*, May 21, 1986.
157 "WITI Sold to Lorimar," *Milwaukee Sentinel*, July 1, 1986.
158 "Deal for Channel 6 Collapses," *Milwaukee Sentinel*, November 13, 1986.
159 Geeta Sharma-Jensen, "Gillette Scrambles to Shore Up Empire," *Milwaukee Journal*, November 19, 1989.
160 "Bondholders Seek Gillette Bankruptcy," *Milwaukee Journal*, February 28, 1991.
161 "Bankruptcy Reorganization Sought for WITI Parent," *Milwaukee Journal*, March 3, 1993.
162 Duane Dudek, "WITI Flips to Fox; CBS Left Looking," *Milwaukee Sentinel*, May 24, 1994.
163 Tim Cuprisin, "Aggressive New Exec at Channel 6," *Milwaukee Journal Sentinel*, April 16, 1997.
164 Tim Cuprisin, "Limbaugh Admits He's Losing His Hearing," *Milwaukee Journal Sentinel*, October 9, 2001.
165 Kelly Skindzelewski, email to the author, March 29, 2006.
166 Tim Cuprisin, "'American Idol' Winner Gets Stage Legs on Tour of 'Heaven I Need a Hug,'" *Milwaukee Journal Sentinel*, November 21, 2007.
167 Tim Cuprisin, "TV's 'Mr. Wizard' Made Science Fun for Children Over Several Decades," *Milwaukee Journal Sentinel*, June 14, 2007.
168 Barbara A. Kreisman, letter to Foxco Acquisition Sub, LLC, June 9, 2008.
169 "Wisconsin Dateline," *TV Guide* Wisconsin Edition, May 26 – June 1, 1956, A-1.
170 "Fun For the Youngsters," *Milwaukee Sentinel*, May 21, 1956.
171 Fabian Campion, email to the author, August 4, 2004.
172 "Wisconsin Dateline," *TV Guide* Wisconsin Edition, January 19 – 25, 1957, A-1.
173 "Wisconsin Dateline," *TV Guide* Wisconsin Edition, June 29 – July 5, 1957, A-1
174 Donald H. Dooley, "Milwaukee Radio and TV Studio Notes," *Milwaukee Journal*, January 26, 1958.
175 Dooley, Donald, H., "TV Kindergarten," *Milwaukee Journal*, May 3, 1959.
176 Tim Hollis, *Hi There Boys and Girls!* University Press of Mississippi, 2001, 298-299.
177 "Local…and Timely," *TV Guide* Wisconsin Edition, September 12 - 18, 1959, A-1.
178 Paul Johnson, interview with author, November 23, 2003.
179 Michael H. Drew, "On the Milwaukee Scene," *Milwaukee Journal*, July 1, 1973.
180 "Funny Farm Hostess Says Goodby," *Milwaukee Sentinel*, February 1, 1974.
181 Barbara Becker, Interview on the "Reitman and Mueller Show," WKTI radio, Milwaukee, May 24, 2002.
182 Jim Major., Personal Interview, October 21, 2000.
183 Michael H. Drew, "Kangaroo Fans Hopping Mad," *Milwaukee Journal*, January 11, 1977.
184 Michael H. Drew, "'Hearts for Hank," *Milwaukee Journal*, February 9, 1977.
185 Michael H. Drew, "'Captain' Conflict Continues," *Milwaukee Journal*, January 18, 1977.
186 "Late Nite Chiller-Diller Ratings Open Up New Vistas for TV," *Variety*, October 16, 1957.
187 Don Dornbrook, "Invasion of the Monsters," *Milwaukee Journal*, January 5, 1958.
188 Dick Nitelinger, "A Consultation with the Advisor," *Scary Monsters Magazine* #36 (September 2000), 82-87.
189 Ibid.
190 Dick Nitelinger, "Dr. Cadaverino's Sidekick Igor Speaks!" *Scary Monsters Magazine* #40 (September 2001), pp. 84-89.
191 Johnson, November 23, 2003.
192 Maripat Gnabasik, "DuBlon Never Thought TV's Albert Would Make It." *Northwest Post*, January 10, 1979.

CHAPTER 8
WMVS/WMVT
CHANNELS 10 & 36

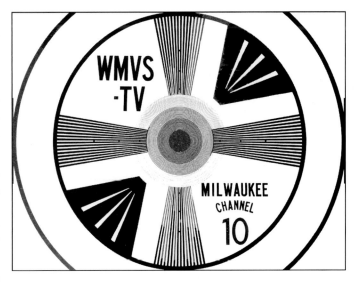

(MPTV photo)

Public television is taken for granted today, and the thought that a major metropolitan area would be without at least one public TV station is almost unthinkable. Nevertheless, the fight to reserve television channels for educational use was a long and arduous one. As it had been in the battle over VHF-UHF, Milwaukee was also in the forefront in the battle over educational/public television.

Broadcasting by educational institutions was not new. Many early radio stations were founded by schools, colleges and universities. On October 23, 1922, WIAO, owned and operated by the School of Engineering of Milwaukee (now MSOE), began broadcasting.[1] The station later became WSOE and then in 1928, WISN after being leased by The *Wisconsin News*, an evening newspaper owned by the Hearst Corp.[2] Hearst bought the station in 1930.[3] Marquette University had its own radio station, WHAD, which began broadcasting on September 27, 1922.[4] On January 23, 1925, Marquette entered into an agreement with the Journal Co. for the joint operation of WHAD.[5] That continued until 1927. Thereafter, it had to share time with WISN. WHAD was purchased by WISN in 1934. (See chapters 3 and 6.)

In August of 1928, the Federal Radio Commission (FRC) announced its General Order 40. That order, which took effect in November, shifted most station's frequencies throughout the country. A handful of stations were given sole use of a given frequency, and became known as "clear channel" stations. Smaller stations were forced to share the same frequencies, and had their power and hours of operation specified so as to avoid interfering with each other. FRC policy was to give preference to commercial stations as being the best to serve the "public interest, convenience, and necessity". Noncommercial broadcasters were considered to be "propaganda" stations, which were "more interested in spreading their particular viewpoint than in reaching the [broadest] possible audience with whatever programming was most attractive".[6] With limited spectrum space available, the Commission made it difficult for educational institutions to continue broadcasting.

In 1928, the FRC issued the State University of Iowa a construction permit for experimental television station W9XAZ. The university never met the operating requirements, and the CP was dropped, but its Electrical Engineering Dept. maintained an interest in television. In 1931, an alumnus, Clement Wade, heard of that interest. Wade was the president of The Western Television Corp.[7], and he agreed to provide the university with mechanical scanning equipment if it would provide the funds for the transmitter. Once again they applied to the FRC, which issued them a construction permit on January 8, 1932 for W9XK. William Parker and Ulises Sanabria[8] constructed a 100 watt transmitter and designed the studio facilities. On January 25, 1933, the station broadcast its first programming, with the visual signal transmitted over the 2-2.1 MHz channel, and the audio over the university's radio station WSUI. It was the first television station owned by an educational institution.

While educational institutions owned and operated broadcasting stations during this period, few broadcast instructional programming. Those institutions with electrical engineering programs were more likely to use their stations as a way to study the technical problems associated with broadcasting.

Because the FRC preferred to grant licenses to commercial interests, the idea of reserving some frequencies for educational use was proposed. No provision for such reservations was made in the standard broadcasting band (as AM radio was then known). In 1934 the National Committee for Education by Radio began lobbying for the reservation of frequencies exclusively for educational stations.[9] The Wagner-Hatfield Act proposed such reservations, but it received little support from Congress or the FCC, and was opposed by the radio networks. The bill subsequently failed to pass.[10]

New technologies were on the horizon, and educators sought frequencies in the bands used by them. In 1938, the National Association of Educational Broadcasters persuaded the Federal Communications Commission (FCC, which replaced the FRC) to reserve twenty-five channels in the experimental, high frequency AM ("Apex") band[11] for educational use. By 1940, "Apex" radio had given way to FM, and the FCC reserved for educational use, five of forty channels allocated. In 1945, when the Commission shifted FM from the 42-50 MHz band to that between 88-108 MHz, it reserved 20 of the 100 available channels for educational use.

On May 22, 1948, President Harry Truman nominated New York attorney Frieda Hennock to be the first female commissioner of the FCC. She faced opposition from many Republicans for her support of President Roosevelt, and *Broadcasting Telecasting* magazine described her subsequent confirmation as "tantamount to a legislative miracle".[12] She was sworn in on July 6, 1948.[13] Hennock later said that Truman was responsible for the reservation of television channels for educational use, as he once called Commission members to the White House to ask them to do so.[14] M. S. Novik, the head of New York's municipal radio station WNYC, planted the idea in Truman's mind by making the analogy between the land-grant colleges and educational television stations. Truman caught on to the idea of using television to educate the people, and called the FCC chair to ask Hennock to meet with

him while Novik was in the Oval Office.[15] It was Hennock who fought tenaciously for the reservations.

The FCC froze all television license applications as of September 30, 1948 in order to study the problems of creating a nationwide television system. On July 11, 1949, it announced a draft channel allocation plan.[16] In it, 42 new channels were allocated in the UHF band, but there was no mention of reserving channels for educational use. Hennock in her lone dissent asserted that the Notice "should include a provision for the reservation of a specified number of frequencies in the ultra-high frequency band for the establishment of a noncommercial educational television service."[17]

The Notice required that interested parties who wished to testify on the matter inform the FCC by August 8, 1949. Hennock embarked on a letter writing campaign in which she encouraged educators to do just that. As a result of her campaign, the Joint Committee on Educational Television was formed in August of that year. The JCET was comprised of seven educational organizations, including: the American Council on Education, the National Education Association, the National Association of Educational Broadcasters, the Association of Land Grant Colleges and Universities, and others.[18] Its purpose was to convince the FCC to reserve television channels for educational use. The Ford Foundation provided funding for legal expertise.[19]

In October of 1950, the nation's 100th TV station, WOI-TV, began broadcasting. Owned by Iowa State University, it was the first post-WWII television station owned by an educational institution – although it operated commercially.[20]

On October 16, 1950, the FCC began further hearings into the future of television broadcasting. In those hearings, broadcasters were not necessarily opposed to the reservation of channels for educational use, but nearly all of the witnesses who testified assumed that noncommercial broadcasters would be confined to UHF channels.[21] Du Mont submitted its own allocation plan, and in it channels reserved for educational use were allocated to the very highest UHF channels[22] – those thought unusable, or at best undesirable. When pressed by Hennock, Du Mont representative Thomas Goldsmith agreed that the educational channels could easily be moved.[23]

Commissioner Hennock made it clear that *she* didn't assume that all noncommercial stations would be confined to UHF. She believed that educational broadcasting

Frieda Hennock (Courtesy of the Schlesinger Library, Radcliffe Institute, Harvard University)

had as much right to the highly favored VHF as did the commercial licensees, a point she repeatedly stressed.[24]

Frank Keer of ABC professed support for the reservation of educational channels, but Hennock's continued questioning revealed his belief that such reservations should not be held "indefinitely."[25] It was his position that if unused by educators after a period of time, such channels should be made available for commercial broadcasting.

The Milwaukee Common Council passed a resolution on November 24, asking the FCC for at least three more television channels.[26]

As a direct consequence of Hennock's efforts to encourage educators to testify, the FCC began hearings specifically on educational television on November 27, 1950. At those hearings, some advocated that twenty-five percent of the available channels be reserved for educational use. Others advocated that all educational TV be allocated to the UHF band. Opponents argued that since UHF was untried, it would be prudent to reserve some VHF channels for educational use.[27] Hennock estimated at the time that a VHF license was worth approximately $5 million.[28] Since the FCC (at the time) couldn't force manufacturers to sell sets capable of receiving a UHF signal, educators were advised to not give up VHF television. The hearings concluded on January 31, 1951[29], and on March 22, the FCC reserved approximately ten percent of television channels for noncommercial educational use.[30] In that Report and Order, any community with one or two VHF stations in operation had a VHF educational television frequency reserved.[31] Milwaukee received VHF channels 4, 10 and 12, as well as UHF channels 19, 25 and 31.[32] VHF channel 10, which the Hearst Corp. had applied for before the "freeze," was reserved for educational use.

Although she had prevailed on the issue of educational channel reservations, Commissioner Hennock nevertheless dissented to the Report and Order because it only reserved ten percent of channels rather than twenty-five.[33]

During the hearings, the Milwaukee Common Council reiterated its desire for more television service, when on January 16, 1951 it passed yet another resolution asking the FCC to assign at least three more channels to the city.[34]

After announcing its proposed new channel allocation/assignment plan, the FCC sought input, and requested that comments be filed by April 23. Replies to those were to be filed by May 8. Hearings were scheduled to begin on May 23.[35]

The president of the U.S. Conference of Mayors, the Hon. David Lawrence, mayor of Pittsburgh, asked that the channels be reserved for a "reasonable and publicly accepted period before being made available for private commercial exploitation."[36] In a letter to all members, he pointed out that the channels reserved for educational use might be lost if the FCC did not give final approval to the proposed reservations, and encouraged his fellow mayors to express their interest. He encouraged them to:

> ...preserve this once-in-a-lifetime opportunity. In my opinion, an educational television station serving your community's educational, cultural, moral, industrial, and recreational needs will be an everlasting credit to the community which sponsors it. It is unthinkable that any city would allow this opportunity to slip by and permit a proposed reservation to be taken away.[37]

Educational television in Milwaukee began on March 13, 1951, when five members of the Common Council's Public Utilities Committee introduced a resolution directing its Special Committee on Radio to inquire into, and study the prospect of, a municipally-owned TV transmitter that would be available for use by any bona

fide educational agency in the city.[38] The resolution also went on-record in support of having twenty-five percent of television channels reserved for educational use.[39]

It was not the first time the city had considered owning a broadcasting station. In April of 1947, the Common Council's Finance Committee approved a resolution asking for a study on a city-operated radio station.[40] In his subsequent report, William L. Slayton, the city reference librarian, recommended that the city operate such a station, or sponsor a program on one of the commercial ones.[41] Time for such programming was offered by WTMJ, WISN, WEMP and WMLO.[42] Broadcasting started on September 20 on WEMP, and in October on WTMJ and WISN. WMLO carried the mayor's weekly address.[43] As a consequence, the idea of a city-owned radio station was dropped.

On March 30, 1951, the Milwaukee County Radio and Television Council passed a resolution urging the FCC to reserve twenty-five percent of television channels for educational use. The Council had been announced as the Milwaukee County Radio Council in October of 1946[44], and formed in January of 1947[45]. Members included women's clubs, Protestant, Catholic and Jewish groups, parent-teacher units, and the WTMJ, WISN, WEMP, WFOX and WMLO radio stations.[46] The goals of the organization were to: "...seek to enlarge the listener's horizon through education and discussion, promotion of programs of good listening value, to aid in utilization of radio in the classroom, and to co-ordinate civic interests through broadcasts."[47] The Council's name and charter were later changed to include television.

The FCC was flooded with comments, and pushed the deadline for filing comments back to May 7. (April 23 was still the deadline for filing general comments.) Replies to those comments had to be filed by May 22, and the hearing was pushed back to June 11.[48]

On April 2, the Milwaukee Common Council asked the city attorney for an opinion as to whether the city could expend funds to own and operate an educational television station. Ten days later, Assistant City Attorney Clyde E. Sheets replied that in his opinion the city could expend funds to conduct a study on the matter, but would have to ask the state for enabling legislation to actually own and operate such a station.[49]

On April 17, 1951, the Milwaukee Common Council's Public Utilities Committee held a public hearing on the matter. Representatives from schools, colleges, and labor groups all favored an educational television station.[50] There was some discussion on whether the committee was to recommend whether to express an interest in the reserved channel, or simply to study the matter further. It was pointed out that the FCC had asked for statements of interest by May 7, and that they were to recommend whether or not to express such an interest.[51] The following day, two officers of the Vocational School Board, President Otto A. Jirikowic and Secretary John J. Mutz, filed comments supportive of the idea with the FCC. In them, they offered office space for the proposed new station. The full Common Council unanimously adopted a resolution on April 24, 1951 that authorized its Special Committee on radio to "inquire and study the prospect of a municipally owned and operated television transmitter." It also supported the reservation of channel 10 for educational use, and asked the FCC to inform the city of any hearings on the matter.[52]

On May 1, The Public Utilities Committee discussed the matter further, and set a public hearing for May 7. Opposition was expressed by the counsel for The Affiliated Taxpayers' Committee, an alliance of real estate and property owners' groups, who said: "You don't need a study, and you don't need a city station, and you could vote today to stay out of that business. It's just too deep for you. It's a field in which you can't adequately qualify. Let the people who know the business take care of it."⁵³ That was only the first salvo from the group, which would oppose spending any tax dollars on an educational station for the next 5 years.

At the hearing on May 7, representatives from The Milwaukee Broadcasting Co. (WEMP), the Wisconsin Broadcasting System, Inc. (WFOX), and Hearst Radio, Inc. (WISN) spoke out against the plan, and advocated that the city give up its interest in channel 10. Instead, they suggested that one of the UHF channels the FCC proposed to assign to Milwaukee be reserved for educational use.⁵⁴ (After the first round of hearings before the FCC in 1948, the three were the only ones left in the contest for the three available channels, and had asked the FCC to immediately grant them construction permits. Before it acted on the matter, the Commission froze all license applications.) They offered the city fifteen percent of their broadcast time for educational use, if it would give up its interest in channel 10. William Rasche, director of the Milwaukee Vocational and Adult Schools, and Harold Vincent, superintendent of the Milwaukee Public Schools asked the committee to "keep the door open" for VHF, educational TV.⁵⁵ One alderman introduced a resolution supporting the alternative proposal, but it was referred to committee.⁵⁶

Milwaukee Mayor Frank Zeidler fought to establish an educational TV station in the city. (Historic photo collection/Milwaukee Public Library)

WFOX and WISN filed a joint comment and counter-proposal in which VHF channel 6 would have been deleted from Green Bay's assignment and given to Milwaukee. They also proposed that channel 10 be reserved for commercial use, and that instead, one of the UHF channels be reserved for noncommercial, educational use. WEMP filed one as well in which it suggested that channel 6 be assigned to Milwaukee and channel 2 to Green Bay.⁵⁷ The counter-proposals would have given Milwaukee four VHF channels, all of which would have been available for commercial use – although channel 4 was already assigned to WTMJ-TV.

The secretary of the Common Council's Special Radio Committee had just returned from the Institute for Education by Radio-TV at the Ohio State University, and he testified at the May 7 hearing, that he had asked three prominent FCC members:
- Brig. Gen. Telford Taylor (former chief counsel for the FCC, and the chief prosecutor at the Nuremburg trials)
- Paul Walker (FCC vice-chair)
- Benedict Cottone (FCC chief counsel)

about the relative value of VHF vs. UHF licenses. Each advised against being talked into giving up VHF channel 10⁵⁸, and Gen. Taylor said that the FCC had made the educational reservations indefinite, knowing that it would take time for educational groups to obtain the funding necessary to construct and operate a television station.

CHAPTER 8 ~ MPTV: CHANNELS 10 & 36

To study the matter further, the chair of the Common Council's Public Utilities Committee, after conferring with Mayor Zeidler, appointed the Special Committee on Educational Television.[59] The public utilities committee voted to appoint it on May 15.[60] The membership was drawn from the Public Utilities Committee, the Common Council's Special Radio Committee, leading educators, and representatives from the Milwaukee Public Library and the Milwaukee Public Museum. The members were:[61]

- Rev. Edward O'Donnell (president, Marquette University)
- Dr. J. Martin Klotsche (president, Wisconsin State Teacher's College (Milwaukee) – now UWM)
- Dr. William Rasche (director, Milwaukee Vocational and Adult Schools)
- Msgr. E. J. Goebel (superintendent, Milwaukee Catholic Schools)
- Dr. Edward Fitzpatrick (president, Mount Mary College)
- Miss Lucia Briggs (president, Milwaukee – Downer College)
- Dr. George Parkinson (director, University of Wisconsin, Milwaukee Extension)
- Harold S. Vincent (superintendent, Milwaukee Public Schools)
- Paul Pratt (president, Milwaukee Association of Commerce)
- W. C. McKern (director, Milwaukee Public Museum)
- Richard Krug (city librarian)
- Peter Schoemann (president, Milwaukee School Board)
- Frank Ranney (secretary, Affiliated Trades Council (AFL))
- Fred Erchul (secretary, Milwaukee County Industrial Union Council (CIO))
- Ben Schumacher (superintendent, Milwaukee Lutheran Schools)
- Public Utilities Committee:
  + Walter Koepke
  + Alfred Hass
  + Charles Quirk
  + Patrick Fass
  + Richard Nowakowski
- Special Radio Committee:
  + Fred Meyers
  + Martin Schreiber
  + James Mortier
  + Gerald Caffrey
  + Frank Birch
  + Mrs. Alvin Gross (citizen member)
  + George Senderhauf (citizen member)

The committee studied four areas:
- Administration
- Programming
- Costs

Its first meeting was on May 22 and the committee began public hearings on June 11. The FCC scheduled further hearings in September, and the *ad hoc* committee was ordered to report by then. Support for the reservation of channel 10 came from the State Radio Council.[62]

The previous day, the Milwaukee School Board expressed an interest, and voted unanimously to support the reservation of channel 10.[63] However, it did not have the finances to construct and operate a station.

Mayor Zeidler filed the first reply to the initial comments made on the FCC's proposed channel assignment plan, when on May 17 he argued against the joint counter-proposal of WFOX and WISN.[64]

Discussion was heated within the Special Committee on Educational Television. At its first meeting, one member asked that the city attorney provide an opinion as to whether it would be legal for the local parochial schools to use a municipally-owned educational station.[65] An inquiry was also made of the city attorney re: the city's ability to operate such a station.

In a letter to the Common Council on June 18, 1st Assistant City Attorney Harry G. Slater concluded that the use of such a station, paid for by city tax monies, by parochial or other schools within the city's limits, but not its jurisdiction, would be legal as it served the public interest.[66]

After its hearings were concluded, the committee filed reports with the Common Council. In its report to the council, the subcommittee on costs estimated that it would cost $886,525 to construct the station. The subcommittee on administration recommended that such a station be run by a commission "composed of persons of outstanding educational stature in the community."[67]

On July 25, Assistant City Attorney Carl F. Kinnel presented an opinion which stated that the vocational school had the needed authority to operate either a closed-circuit or over-the-air television station.[68] However, the public utilities committee did not support the establishment of a municipally-owned station. Instead, in a 4-1 vote the same day, it recommended that the full common council ask the FCC to reassign channel 10 for commercial use.[69] During heated debate on July 31, the full common council voted to postpone a vote on the matter. One alderman offered an amendment which would ask WISN, WFOX and WEMP for written guarantees that they would provide fifteen percent of their broadcast time for educational programming, if channel 10 was reassigned for commercial use.[70]

The pressure to make a decision mounted, as the Joint Committee on Educational Television informed the city attorney that if Milwaukee was interested in using channel 10 for educational use, it had to file sworn statements and exhibits with the FCC by September 24.[71]

The Milwaukee Board of Vocational and Adult Education decided to take action. At its meeting of August 21, 1951, it adopted a resolution in favor of an educational television station for the city. In that resolution, the board requested approval to construct an educational television station:

A. To broadcast educational programs originating from the cooperating educational institutions and organizations, including the city and its departments

B. To broadcast educational programs originating from its own departments and field services

C. To offer technical instruction in radio and electronics programming, broadcasting station operation, and maintenance, and in the acquisition of other allied technical skills which can be developed through such a project.[72]

Dr. William Rasche, director of the Milwaukee Vocational School, fought tenaciously to establish an educational television station in the city. (MATC photo)

Rasche proposed, and the board instructed him to file a sworn statement with the FCC in support of the reservation of channel 10 for educational use, and authorized the start of necessary studies.[73] Included in the sworn statement was a list of relevant Wisconsin statutes that the board believed authorized it to build and operate a television station.[74]

Rasche also asked Mayor Zeidler to form a new committee to conduct the studies.[75] Named the Milwaukee Educators' Committee on Television, the original members appointed were: Rasche, Zeidler, Klotsche, Parkinson, and Vincent, all of whom had served on the common council's *ad hoc* committee.

Rasche chaired the committee, which had as its purposes:
1. To support the reservation of channel 10 for educational use in the area
2. To study and plan as a group the best method of making a noncommercial educational station a reality in this community.[76]

Meanwhile, the public utilities committee continued to debate the issue. On September 5, the idea of requiring the three radio stations to provide fifteen percent of their broadcasting time – with five percent in the morning, afternoon and evening – was again raised. Some aldermen pointed out that the city had no legal authority to demand such a guarantee, and as such the FCC couldn't accept it as a requirement.[77] A week later, the Milwaukee Common Council declined to vote on the matter, and referred it back to its public utilities committee.[78] On September 18, the public utilities committee voted to recommend that the full common council adopt a resolution asking the FCC to assign four VHF channels to the city.[79]

On September 21, the Milwaukee Educators' Committee on Television filed a statement with the FCC in support of the reservation of channel 10 for educational use[80], and at the request of Mayor Zeidler, published a summary of relevant facts to support their statement.[81] The Milwaukee Board of Vocational and Adult Education also filed a statement of support with the FCC.[82]

The Milwaukee Common Council again postponed a vote on the matter, deciding to give itself two weeks to study the educators' committee report.[83] Finally, on October 9, it voted 20-3 against a municipally-owned educational television station. Instead, it passed a resolution asking the FCC to assign four VHF channels to the city, while reserving a UHF channel for noncommercial educational use. The resolution also asked the three radio stations whose TV applications were frozen by the FCC, to guarantee that they would provide fifteen percent of their broadcasting time for educational programming.[84]

Mayor Zeidler vetoed the resolution on October 16, saying that educational groups favored reserving the channel and that: "The only opposition to the reservation of such a channel was made by special tax organizations and those parties having a direct financial interest in promoting a commercial television channel."[85] The following day, the three radio stations gave city officials written statements guaranteeing that they would provide the requested fifteen percent of programming time.[86]

Mayor Zeidler spoke out against the resolution, and on October 23, the common council failed to override his veto.[87] Some aldermen called for another vote, but after the city attorney opined that the vote was final, the matter was dropped with no debate.[88]

Opposition mounted. At its meeting of November 21, the Milwaukee County Property Owners' Association passed a resolution opposing a city-owned, educational TV station.[89] Hearst argued that the Milwaukee Vocational School was not in a position financially or otherwise to construct or operate a TV station.[90]

The Milwaukee Broadcasting Co. (WEMP) filed the first request for an amendment to a pre-freeze application on February 29.[91] (1952 was a leap year.) They proposed to have studios at 525 West Wells Street, and would erect a 1,000' tower. They also asked permission to mount their antenna on their 460' radio tower in the event that they couldn't get steel for the taller tower[92] because of Korean War priorities. In that application, they also requested that the FCC take channel 6 from Green Bay, and assign it to Milwaukee.

The Wisconsin Broadcasting System, Inc., filed an objection to the WEMP application on March 7, stating that it constituted a new application, rather than an amendment, and that FCC rules forbade such applications twenty days after the start of hearings.[93] Those hearings had begun in 1948.

On April 14, 1952, the FCC issued its Sixth Report and General Order, which lifted the freeze on new television licenses as of July 1, and provided for 617 VHF and 1436 UHF licenses, 242 of which were reserved for noncommercial educational use. Twelve of the latter were assigned to Wisconsin: two VHF and ten UHF. The Commission adopted a policy of intermixing VHF and UHF channels in the same markets. Milwaukee received VHF channels 4, 10 and 12, and UHF channels 19, 25 and 31. Channel 10 was reserved for educational use, leaving channel 12 as the only VHF channel available for commercial stations, as channel 4 was assigned to WTMJ-TV.

In the Report and Order, the FCC rejected the counter-proposals which would have assigned VHF channel 6 to Milwaukee. The Commission's new regulations required that 170 miles separate stations on the same channel. Opposition to the proposals came from WJIM-TV in Lansing, Michigan and WOC-TV in Davenport, Iowa. WJIM-TV was already operating on channel 6, while WOC-TV was scheduled to move from channel 5 to channel 6. In the case of the former, the distance between Lansing and Milwaukee was determined to be 171 miles, while the distance from the station's transmitter site to Milwaukee was 173 – both met the FCC's separation requirements. In the case of WOC-TV, the distance between Davenport and Milwaukee was determined to be 170 miles, but that between Milwaukee and the WOC-TV transmitter site was only 167.[94] The Commission, in rejecting the counter-proposals, pointed out that to accept them would require a deviation from its own rules and standards.[95] It also stated that "the record did not support adding a fourth VHF channel to Milwaukee by deleting it from Green Bay," as the latter city was large enough to warrant a second VHF channel.[96]

The Commission also reaffirmed its belief that channel 10 should be reserved for educational use, and rejected the idea that a UHF channel be substituted. It cited the strong support from the Milwaukee Educators' Committee on Television, as well as from the Milwaukee Vocational School[97], and other educational interests. It also stated that the vocational school appeared to have the taxing power needed to finance the construction and operation of such a station. The Commission also rejected the notion that the applications of the three radio stations had precedent because they had applied for them before the freeze. It stated unequivocally that they "had no legal right or preference because of their past participation in a hearing" re: VHF channels, and that the FCC had the legal right to change the table of channel assignments as it saw fit.[98]

In the Report and Order, the FCC stated that:

> *The setting aside of channels for non-commercial, educational use is precisely the same type of reservation as channels as that provided by the assignment table for commercial stations in the various communities, and the two should be governed by the same rules. With respect to changes in the table, the Com-*

mission has provided for amendment of the assignment table by appropriate rule making proceedings in the rules herein adopted. Such proceedings will be required for changing the assignment of a channel from one community to another, and for changing the status of a channel reserved for non-commercial educational stations to a channel available for commercial applicants.[99]

Further, the Report and Order (referencing the language in the Third Notice of Further Proposed Rule Making) stated that:

…upon adoption in the instant proceedings of the Table of Assignments, said table shall not be subject to amendment on petition for a period of one year from the effective date of the Commission's final order amending said table. Upon the expiration of said one year period, the Commission will consider petitions filed during said period requesting changes in the table.[100]

The Commission did however reject the suggestion that it review the status of those channels reserved for noncommercial, educational channels every six months, with the intent of freeing up for commercial use those channels which went unapplied for, or for which the applicants had made insufficient progress.

Commissioner Hennock had filed a dissent to the Report and Order in which she expressed the opinion that more channels should have been reserved for educational use. In it she mentioned that the reservations were *indefinite*, but that was never explicitly stated.

In a speech on April 18 before the National Association of Educational Broadcasters (NAEB) held at the twenty-second Institute for Education by Radio and Television at the Ohio State University, FCC Chairman Paul Walker spoke out for the first time on the reservations. In that speech, he emphasized that: "Commercial TV stations must not let noncommercial outlets 'carry the burden of meeting educational needs.'" He also warned educators that, "Efforts are underway to 'initiate an organized campaign for the commercialization…of these noncommercial educational assignments. You have won only the first round. Do not…let these reservations of 1952 go by default.'"[101] Walker let it be known that if educational groups did not apply for the reserved channels within the one-year time period in which the Table of Channel Assignments could not be amended, they might be made available for commercial use.[102]

On May 6, a resolution was introduced in the Milwaukee Common Council which questioned the right of the vocational school to spend a portion of its budget to construct a television station, and asked the city attorney to provide an opinion. The resolution was adopted unanimously under suspension of the council's rules[103], and was vetoed on May 12 by Mayor Zeidler, who thought it appropriate that the vocational school ask for such an opinion if necessary.[104]

Nonetheless, the common council overrode the mayor's veto with a 20-7 vote on May 20. At the same time, two aldermen suggested a city-wide referendum on whether or not the vocational school should construct and operate a television station.[105] In response, the mayor wrote letters to teachers' organizations in southeastern Wisconsin, asking them to enlist support.[106] He also spoke at a symposium on city government at the Wisconsin State Teachers' College (Milwaukee).[107]

Hearst re-filed its application for channel 10 as soon as the freeze was lifted. It asked the FCC to reconsider its decision to reserve the channel for educational use. Hearst and the Wisconsin Broadcasting System, Inc. (WFOX) also asked that additional VHF channels be assigned to Milwaukee.[108]

The *Milwaukee Sentinel* ran a series of articles outlining its positions on how to get more television channels for the city. It questioned the vocational school's financing plan,[109] and argued that a UHF channel would be more appropriate for a tax-supported, educational station, as the reduced signal would cover less of the area, and non-residents in the suburbs wouldn't be able to take advantage of a service they hadn't paid for.[110]

The campaign described by FCC Chairman Walker began to take shape. It was designed to discourage educational institutions from applying for one of the reserved channels, as it would be difficult for them to secure financial support in such a short time period. If the channels went unapplied for, it would give support to the claims of commercial broadcasters that educational institutions were ill prepared to construct and operate television stations.[111] In reaction, Dr. William Rasche urged the Vocational School Board to apply for channel 10.[112]

Support for educational television came from one commercial broadcaster. Gerald Bartell started at WHA in Madison while on the faculty of the University of Wisconsin. He and his family owned WOKY in Milwaukee and had applications pending for commercial TV stations in both Milwaukee and Madison (which were eventually granted, see chapter 5). In a letter to the Wisconsin Broadcasters Association in 1952, Bartell stated:

> *We are convinced without question of the necessity for educational television operated under the direct supervision of educators. A businessman cannot – nor should he be expected to – plan, develop, and produce valid educational materials for television presentation on a regular basis. It is our conviction that the people of Wisconsin will demand, and rightly deserve, a well-rounded TV service.*[113]

In reaction to FCC Chairman Walker's statements, some behind-the-scenes maneuvering took place. C. Scott Fletcher, the president of the Ford Foundation's Fund for Adult Education held a dinner meeting at which members of the Fund met with the FCC. Fletcher insisted that the entire Commission be present, so that they might reach a decision. At that meeting, he laid out a plan by which they would guarantee the financing of thirty educational television stations, with the program set up by the Fund for the Advancement of Education (FAE), The Joint Committee on Educational television (JCET), and the National Citizens' Committee for Educational Television (NCCET). He then left the commissioners alone to discuss the matter. Because of the Fund's commitment, the Commission unanimously agreed NOT to mention the "grace period" any more, and it was "hushed up."[114]

The Milwaukee Broadcasting Co. (WEMP) made an offer to the Vocational School which would allow it to mount its antenna on its radio tower, and provide space for a transmitter. It also offered to do the same on a new 1,000' tower should it receive a construction permit for channel 12.[115]

On October 9, the Milwaukee Board of Vocational and Adult Education adopted four resolutions:[116]
1. Approved spending $131,055 to set-up a closed-circuit television laboratory
2. Approved entering into an agreement with WEMP radio, which would allow the school to locate a television transmitter at the station's facilities, and an antenna on its tower
3. Authorized director William Rasche to apply to the FCC for channel 10
4. Asked the Milwaukee County Board to contribute funds for the station

Glenn Koehler, an engineering and communications professor at the University of Wisconsin in Madison, was hired to consult on the development of the closed-circuit laboratory.[117]

In response, the chairman of the Affiliated Taxpayers' Committee filed, as a private taxpayer, a lawsuit against the vocational school. On October 15, a Milwaukee County Circuit Court judge, issued a temporary restraining order against the school, which required it to show why a permanent order preventing them from applying to the FCC, or spending tax monies on a television station shouldn't be issued. The taxpayers' group claimed that because the signal of such a station would go beyond the Milwaukee city limits, residents should not be required to fund a facility which non-residents would benefit from.[118]

The common council then passed a resolution which would have prevented the city attorney from representing the vocational school in the suit. Mayor Zeidler vetoed it, and in a stinging message to the council, doubted the validity of the resolution.[119] The resolution was not read into the record, and newspaper reporters later saw that it had been given Tally No. 197-½ – something the council's clerk never did. Newspaper reporters said that they had seen numbers 197 and 198, but not 197-½.[120]

FCC Commissioner Freida Hennock was on her way to visit friends in Appleton, and stopped in Milwaukee on the way. In a speech at city hall, she said that "Any talk that the educational reservation expires in a year is hokum. Your channel 10 assignment has no limit on it." She also stated that while the Commission normally didn't get involved in local court matters, she promised to consult with their legal counsel and inform city officials whether the FCC should intervene in the circuit court suit that was holding up educational TV in the city. She also said that the Commission would fight for the educational reservations in federal court – even up to the Supreme Court if necessary.[121]

That same month, a "trial balloon" bill was drafted for the State Legislative Council, which proposed a $5.00 surtax on all television receivers and a $1.00 annual use tax, both of which would be used to fund a state-wide educational television system. The bill proved too controversial and was tabled without debate on November 20.[122] The Wisconsin Citizen's Committee for Educational Television, a coalition of labor, farmers, PTAs, women's clubs, religious, professional, educational and civic groups, vowed to find a way to fund such a network.[123]

On October 29, a circuit court judge lifted the part of the temporary restraining order which prevented the vocational school from applying for a television license. However, he upheld the other parts of the order, which forbade the school from entering into any contracts or beginning actual operations until after the matter was tried. The judge also ruled that because of the mayor's veto, the city attorney could represent the vocational school.[124]

On November 5, the common council failed to override Mayor Zeidler's veto of their resolution which would've prevented the city attorney from representing the vocational school.[125]

On November 13, 1952, The FCC rejected the proposal to add more VHF channels to Milwaukee and dismissed Hearst's application for channel 10.[126] Two days later, the attorney for the Affiliated Taxpayers' Committee, and the city attorney, made public an agreement to dismiss the lawsuit which sought to prevent the vocational school from constructing and operating a TV station. Reasons cited included the belief that the 1953 state legislature would pass new laws giving vocational schools the right to operate such stations, the fact that the school already had $250,000 in its budget for such a station, that the proposed agreement with WEMP would not require the school to spend any significant taxpayer money, and that the school already had the right to operate a closed-circuit television station.[127] The suit was formally dropped on November 24.[128]

As a consequence, the Milwaukee Board of Vocational and Adult Education applied for channel 10 on November 25.[129]

Hearst, through WISN radio and the *Milwaukee Sentinel*, had supported Senator Joseph McCarthy in the general election earlier that month. On November 29, he announced that the FCC would come under the scrutiny of his Senate investigating committee in the new Congress, which three unnamed senators had suggested "look into wastefulness and 'favoritism' in granting new licenses to radio and TV stations."[130]

On December 17, Hearst petitioned the FCC for a new hearing.

On January 13, 1953, Senator McCarthy was named the chair of the Senate investigating committee, and the following day, he announced that he was doubling its investigating staff.[131] On January 28, the FCC granted Hearst a new hearing to begin on February 16. Precedent was set in that it was the first time the FCC allowed oral arguments in such a matter.[132] On February 6, the Milwaukee Board of Vocational and Adult Education filed a statement with the FCC supporting the reservation of channel 10 for educational use, and asked for a dismissal of Hearst's petition for a rehearing.[133]

In early February, the Wisconsin Citizen's Committee for Educational Television, proposed a new scheme for funding a state-wide educational TV network. It proposed that either a $0.01 surtax would be levied on all individual or corporate incomes, or the state would tax electrical power usage.[134] That same week, the vocational school board approved an agreement with the Milwaukee Broadcasting Co. wherein the school would lease space for its transmitter, and mount its antenna on the WEMP tower – each for $1.00 per year.[135]

Rumors continued to fly that the channels reserved for educational use would be made available to commercial applicants as of June 2, 1953,[136] and FCC chairman Paul Walker urged educators to mobilize and apply for the reserved channels, or else they would be "lost by default."[137]

The Joint Committee on Educational Television petitioned the FCC to become a party to the Hearst hearing, and that petition was granted, as was one from the Milwaukee Board of Vocational and Adult Education. On February 9, 1953, Wisconsin Senators McCarthy and Wiley (R) stated in a letter to the FCC that "We recommend that you reconsider your past decision…and that following such reconsideration, you make the channel available for commercial operation."[138] Wisconsin representative Kersten (R), in a letter signed by his colleagues Smith (R) and Zablocki (D)[139], argued that commercial stations in the city would provide all the educational air time that a publicly-owned channel 10 could promise – without charge, and that the vocational school would probably never get the taxing power to support such a station.[140]

FCC chairman Walker replied to all the letters by stating that the question raised by Hearst's motion did "not involve the issue of whether the public interest would or would not be served by the vocational school board's application," and "that oral arguments were limited to whether Hearst has any 'accrued procedural rights' for Ch. 10."[141]

At the hearing, Charles S. Rhyne of the vocational school board testified that Hearst thought that they could make more money with a VHF station, and that they had said that UHF was "good enough" for educational TV. He also stated that, "We don't agree that educational TV should have second class status."[142] Dr. William Rasche testified that the Vocational School's plan was backed by both the State Radio Board, and the State Board of Vocational and Adult Education, and

that they were in a better position to offer educational TV than the commercial stations.[143]

William Dempsey, an attorney for Hearst, said that they would provide more time for educational programming than any educational station could offer, and that if the FCC ruled adversely against their petition, they would take the matter to court.[144] He also stated that they were entitled to the channel as they had applied for it prior to the FCC's freeze on new television applications.[145]

The Wisconsin Broadcasting System, Inc. (WFOX) asked that it be permitted to apply for channel 10 if was reassigned for commercial use. Hearst opposed that request.[146]

The same day as the Hearst hearing, the Wisconsin Citizen's Committee for Educational Television proposed that the state fund two educational television stations at first: one in Madison and the other near Rib Mountain, and then expand to all 12 available channels as funding became available.[147] It also sponsored legislation that would give the Milwaukee Vocational School authority to construct and operate an educational TV station.[148] The bill gave specific permission to the state's vocational schools to employ "such means or media" as they "may determine to be best suited" for their courses of instruction, and to "enter into any agreements to co-ordinate any media facilities it may employ."[149]

The announcement came as the State Assembly Committee on Education was holding hearings in Madison. At that hearing, William Rasche testified that such authority was necessary as a taxpayers' group lawsuit had challenged the Vocational School's proposal to construct and operate an educational television station on the grounds that present state law didn't authorize vocational schools to go into TV.[150]

Opponents argued that adoption of the legislation would "create a monster" as there were "no brakes" on the vocational schools in the state. They were governed by boards which were not elected, and their taxing powers were independent.[151]

At the same hearing, twenty-two of twenty-seven Milwaukee Aldermen filed a petition with the Assembly committee opposing an educational television station run by the Vocational School.[152] Reasons cited included:
- All money available for educational purposes is needed for ordinary school expenditures such as building new schools, and repairing old ones.
- Commercial television stations can better provide educational programs without adding to the tax bill.
- Any money that educators spend for television can be better used to present educational programs on private stations.[153]

On March 19, 1953, Hearst filed a petition with the FCC for a rehearing and a vacating action charging that the Commission had "erroneously and improperly" dismissed their application. (The application had been reinstated earlier.)

The same day, the bill to give vocational schools authority to construct and operate television stations was introduced in the State Assembly.[154]

On March 31, the FCC denied Hearst's petition for a rehearing, and dismissed its application for channel 10.[155]

On April 5, William Rasche announced that the Ford Foundation had provided the Vocational School with a $100,000 gift to defray the costs of constructing an educational TV station.[156]

On April 13th, outgoing FCC chair Paul Walker was summoned by one of Senator McCarthy's aides to an executive session of the Senate Investigating Committee on the following Monday in the Senator's office. Walker protested, saying that he had a meeting of the full Commission that day. The aide said that he would check with the Senator, and would call Walker back. He did, indicating that McCarthy had said that they could meet at 9:30, that the business would only take a few minutes, and that Walker would be able to chair his meeting.[157]

McCarthy's motivation was that the FCC was in transition. Outgoing FCC Commissioner Eugene H. Merrill was forcing the issue[158], and McCarthy feared that it would have been possible to hold a quick session and grant channel 10 to the vocational school.[159]

Walker, Merrill and FCC General Counsel Benedict P. Cottone arrived in McCarthy's office at the time requested, only to be shunted to a different office and left to wait for over an hour. When McCarthy finally arrived, he told the trio that their business would take another six or seven hours. No other Senators were present for what was to have been a committee meeting.[160] Walker protested, and McCarthy suggested that they might meet later in the week. Walker pointed out that his last week as FCC chair was filled, and that they might as well stay and get it over with.[161]

McCarthy then started to question Merrill, suddenly stopped, and suggested that he be sworn in. A stenographer was called in, and both Merrill and Walker were sworn. McCarthy then berated the pair for allowing "a TV monopoly" in Milwaukee[162], and suggested that improper influences were being brought to bear against Hearst. He went on to demand assurances that in Walker's last week as chair, the Commission would not grant the vocational school a construction permit for channel 10. Walker later requested a transcript of the meeting, but McCarthy said that stenographer's notes were too garbled to produce one.[163]

Hearst then filed yet another request for a rehearing on April 14[164], and submitted supplementary materials on April 20.[165] In its petition, Hearst still contended that the reservation of channel 10 for educational use was illegal, and that in view of its long-standing application for channel 10, some other channel should be reserved for the schools.[166] McCarthy's investigators then demanded files which were normally kept in a locked safe in the FCC General Counsel's office.[167]

On April 20, the Milwaukee Common Council's Judiciary Committee voted unanimously to recommend to the council as a whole that it pass a resolution opposing two bills in the state legislature: The first was the assembly bill which would've broadened the powers of vocational schools to run educational television stations. The second would've changed the name of the State Radio Council to the State Radio and Television Council, and created a state educational television network.[168] Mayor Zeidler vetoed the resolution in early May of 1953, pointing out that the sponsors of the first bill had withdrawn it on April 29.[169] The council overrode the veto a week later.[170]

The Wisconsin Association for Vocational and Adult Education voted to support the bill which would have created a state-run educational television network,[171] and the Milwaukee School Board also did so two days later.[172]

On May 4, WCAN-TV president Lou Poller invited the Milwaukee Vocational School to send representatives to observe the construction of his facilities. At the same time, he offered the school five hours per week of time to develop educational programming.[173]

With the one-year period in which changes could not be made to the Table of Channel Assignments about to end, Commissioner Hennock testified before the Senate Foreign and Interstate Commerce Committee in favor of indefinite reservations for educational stations. Its chair, Senator Charles Tobey of New Hampshire later stated, "I shall keep a watchful eye on each and every one of these 242 channels and upon the slightest evidence that the FCC is about to weaken and to delete one

of them or substitute a substantially less valuable channel for one of them, I shall call for a full-scale investigation."[174]

As a result of those hearings, on May 11, 1953, the FCC issued a public notice in which it stated that: "While the Commission stated that such a reservation should not be for an excessively long period and should be surveyed from time to time, it placed no limit whatever on the duration of the assignment of channels for non-commercial educational operation."[175]

It clarified its position in no uncertain terms by stating: "A belief that the reservation of television channels for noncommercial educational use will expire on June 2, 1953" was "not the case; such reservations continue *indefinitely*."[176]

On May 12, 1953, the Wisconsin legislature adopted a surprise resolution calling for a two-year study by the legislative council on the feasibility of a state educational TV network.[177] It also asked the FCC to continue the channel reservations pending the outcome of the study, and expressed the "opinion" of the legislature that the channels should be used by the "highest educational authority in the state."[178] Commissioner Doerfer voiced his opposition to the application of the Milwaukee Vocational School, on the grounds that the state should have the first opportunity to get the channel. He said that he would "consider letting the vocational school go ahead with its station on condition that absolutely acquiesce in turning over complete control to the state if and when it gets into the picture."[179] In fact, the governor's office later stated that Doerfer had advised him to apply for the channels to show that the state was serious about educational TV.[180]

The Milwaukee Vocational School's Dr. William Rasche pointed out that no funds had been appropriated for a state network[181]

Mayor Zeidler protested the resolution in telegrams sent to both Governor Walter J. Kohler, Jr. (R) and the FCC. He pointed out that a two year delay would result in the loss of valuable experience and denied residents of southeastern Wisconsin "the desirable programs for which they have been clamoring."[182]

The same resolution directed Governor Kohler to apply for all of the channels reserved for educational use in the state, and two days later, his office made it clear that before any future hearings before the FCC, he would oppose granting the channel to the vocational school, until after the 1955 legislature decided whether it wanted to incorporate channel 10 into a state educational television network.[183] The same day, the state attorney general's office began preparing applications for the twelve channels. Kohler said that the vocational school's application "must be subordinated to that of the state" and that the legislature's resolution took precedent over the previous endorsement of the school's application by the State Radio Council.[184]

The Wisconsin Citizen's Committee for Educational Television voiced opposition to the resolution, stating that the state would likely lose $200,000 promised by the Ford Foundation to both the University of Wisconsin and the Milwaukee Vocational School. At that time, the bill which would have created a two-station educational television network was still in a state assembly committee, although the assembly's finance committee recommended that the bill be defeated.[185]

After receiving the governor's wire, the FCC passed over the vocational school's application. Commissioner Hennock dissented, and favored prompt action on the matter.[186]

Rasche feared that a two-year delay would increase the pressure to release channel 10 for commercial use and assign a UHF channel to education. He pointed out that Assembly Bill 710-A, which would create a state-wide educational television network was stalled in the taxation committee.[187]

On May 18, 1953, the State Radio Council applied to the FCC for Milwaukee's channel 10.

Another bill was introduced in the Wisconsin State Senate on May 19 that would have funded a state network with a $1.00 surtax on television sets.[188] On May 20, Governor Kohler proposed legislation to add $75,000 to the University of Wisconsin's budget so that work on a television station could be started that year.[189] It passed in the State Senate the following day.[190]

The Assembly Judiciary Committee recommended passage of a bill which would prohibit any city or county government or agency from owning or operating a television station.[191] That bill and other legislation specifically designed to prevent the Milwaukee Vocational School from operating an educational television station had been introduced in both houses of the legislature, but both bills failed to pass. Meanwhile, the school proposed to Governor Kohler that if it was granted channel 10, it would turn it over to the state should it decide to construct a state-wide network. The governor turned that proposal over to the State Radio Council. Alternatively, it was suggested that the state could contract with the vocational school to operate the channel.[192]

On May 25, 1953, the first noncommercial, educational television station in the U.S., KUHT, began broadcasting in Houston, Texas. The licensee was the University of Houston.

On June 1, the State of Wisconsin applied for channel 21 in Madison.[193]

The FCC again allowed oral arguments to be heard on Hearst's petition for yet another rehearing. On June 30, the FCC rejected that petition in a 4-1 vote.[194] Commissioner Rosel H. Hyde had held up the matter for weeks citing a need for further study. He was testifying before Congress the morning the matter came up on the Commission's agenda, and *Broadcasting Telecasting* wondered if it would have again been passed over had he been present. Hyde was present for the afternoon session, and cast the sole dissenting vote.[195] Commissioners Hennock and Doerfer abstained. The Commission in its opinion stated that: "No new facts had been presented which were not previously considered and disposed of in our memorandum opinion and order of April 1, 1953. Under these circumstances, no useful purpose would be served by developing further at this time, the merits of this matter, which have been set forth in detail in our previous decisions. We reaffirm our views as stated within."[196] Hearst then appealed to the District of Columbia Circuit Court of Appeals.[197] The State Radio Council opposed Hearst's appeal.[198]

Although the state legislature had called for a two-year study on the issue of a state-wide educational network, it reversed itself, and decided to allow the state to build an "experimental" television station on UHF channel 21 in Madison. John Doerfer, in an address before the National Institute of Municipal Law Officers in Washington, D.C. on September 15, said that, "The 242 channels reserved for educational television should continue to be reserved until such time as the legislatures of the states have acted and rejected the idea of engaging in educational television. If the states have not acted during two more legislative sessions that should give us some indication of whether they are interested. We on the Commission must also consider that it is a waste of a natural resource to have those channels lie dormant."[199]

Meanwhile, Hearst found itself in a dilemma. If its appeal was denied, there would be only one other VHF channel in Milwaukee (12) assigned for commercial use, and there were already four other applicants. Construction permits for the three UHF channels assigned to the city had already been granted. Hearst engineers searched for a way for the FCC to assign another VHF channel to the area, and they found

CHAPTER 8 ~ MPTV: CHANNELS 10 & 36   349

one. On September 30, they filed a proposal with the FCC to assign channel 6 to the Village of Whitefish Bay, and indicated that if that occurred, they would drop their appeal for channel 10.[200] The FCC quickly proposed rulemaking.[201] Hearst then requested a continuance of its case before the U.S. Court of Appeals.[202] The FCC assigned channel 6 to the Village of Whitefish Bay on December 4, 1953.[203] Hearst then dropped its appeal before the Court of Appeals. (See chapter 7.)

In March of 1954, Paul K. Taff was hired as the first faculty member in the vocational school's new television program. Taff had been the program director for a television station in Decatur, Illinois. On his recommendation, Jim Wulliman was hired as chief engineer and Nile Hunt as his assistant.[204]

In May of 1954, Otto Schlaak was named chairman of the vocational school's new television laboratory. Schlaak also served as the program coordinator for cooperating educational institutions in the Milwaukee area.[205]

On May 3, 1954, WHA-TV began broadcasting on UHF channel 21 in Madison, as Wisconsin's first educational station. In August, the State Radio Council withheld action on its application for channel 10. It still had an interest in making the channel a part of a state network, but had no funds appropriated to do so.[206]

In September, the first students began classes in the Milwaukee Vocational School Institute of Technology's television program. The students used a single studio on the school's sixth floor. Programs were broadcast via closed circuit to monitors located throughout the school.[207]

Legislators called for a state-wide advisory referendum on whether the state should run an educational TV network, and one was scheduled for the general elections on November 2, 1954.

Students in the first Introduction to Television class work in the original laboratory on the sixth floor of the Milwaukee Vocational School's Institute of Technology. (*Vocational School News* photo)

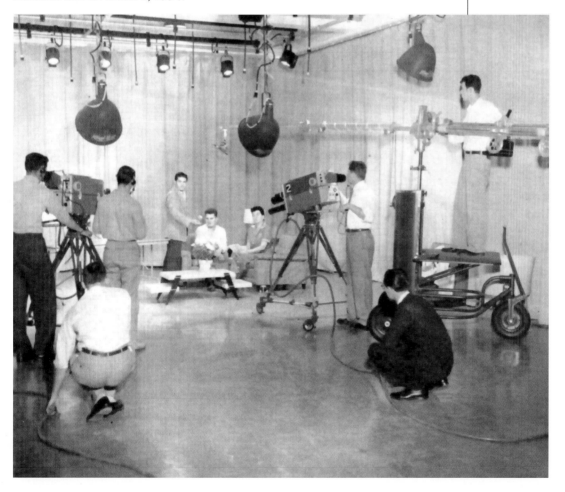

The referendum said:

> *Shall the state of Wisconsin provide a tax-supported, state-wide noncommercial educational television network?*

Groups lined up on both sides of the issue. The *Milwaukee Sentinel* and several taxpayers groups including The Wisconsin Committee on State-Owned, Tax Supported Television, and The Affiliated Taxpayers Committee[209], were against the network. The Wisconsin Citizen's Committee for Educational Television and The Citizens' Committee to Preserve Some Non-Commercial Television Channels were for it.

The League of Women Voters held a debate on the issue in Milwaukee on October 22. That debate mirrored public sentiment. Supporters of the network pointed out that without tax support, the network was doomed to failure, as it couldn't count on sufficient funding from other sources. Opponents argued that the state could not afford to spend money on such a network, and that the money would be better spent on teachers and schools. Opponents also argued that a state-run television network would become a "propaganda medium."[210]

Voters rejected the idea by a 2-1 margin. Only Dane County, where WHA-TV broadcast, voted in favor of the proposal. The Citizens Committee for Educational

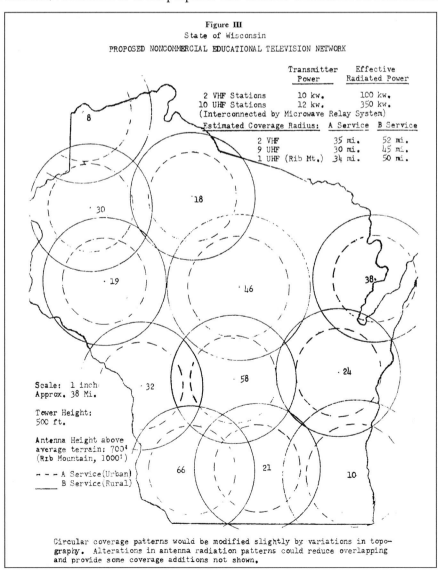

The State-Wide, Educational TV Network proposed in 1954.[208]

CHAPTER 8 ~ MPTV: CHANNELS 10 & 36

Television thought that placing the words "tax-supported" at the beginning of the referendum caused it to be rejected.[211]

Harold McCarty, who ran WHA and WHA-TV for many years, and who had been the president of the National Association of Educational Broadcasters (NAEB) in the 1930s, recalled that although WTMJ-TV was covering the greater Milwaukee area, and some state residents received the Minneapolis/St. Paul stations, vast areas in the interior of Wisconsin had no idea of what television was.[212] Although only advisory, the results killed off any chance that the 1955 legislature would take up the issue.

The Milwaukee Vocational School continued with its plans. On December 15, the vocational school board voted to renew its request with the FCC.[213] The Ford Foundation had set a deadline of January 31, 1956 in order to receive the $100,000 grant it had offered. In response, on December 20, the State Legislative Council's Education Committee adopted a resolution recommending that the State Radio Council withdraw its application for channel 10, and instead support the application of the Milwaukee Vocational School, but instead threw the matter back to the Council for action.[214]

Although it didn't have a construction permit to build an over-the-air television station, the vocational school's staff and students had begun to produce educational and public service programs for local commercial stations. They also produced experimental programs as a part of the television production classes. Some of the programs produced by the end of 1955 included:
- "Lifetime," a 13-week, 15-minute series on community health, broadcast on WISN-TV
- "Milwaukee on Camera," a 15-minute program produced in

Both sides took out ads prior to the advisory referendum on the state-wide, educational television network proposal.

cooperation with the Milwaukee Public Museum, which was also broadcast on WISN-TV
- "Sportsmanlike Driving," a 30-minute program series produced in cooperation with AAA and shown every other week on WTMJ-TV beginning in January of 1956
- "Photogram," a series produced by the University of Wisconsin-Milwaukee, which alternated with "Sportsmanlike Driving" on WTMJ-TV[215]
- "Discovery," an experimental series produced by the Milwaukee Public Museum.

Also produced were shows for the museum's "Let's Experiment" and "Explorer's Club" programs, and several experimental children's programs by the Milwaukee Art Institute.[216]

The State Radio Council had awaited legislative action in 1955, and still hadn't withdrawn its application. The contest delayed FCC action, and also the potential grant from the Ford Foundation. Finally, on January 11, 1956, the State Radio Council voted unanimously to withdraw its application for Milwaukee's channel 10, as no funds had been appropriated by the 1955 legislature.[217] It formally asked the FCC to dismiss its application for channel 10 and the Commission did so on February 13, 1956.

The Affiliated Taxpayers' Committee once again threatened to hold up plans. In letters sent to various officials, it charged that the vocational school board had disregarded the wishes of Milwaukee voters, since the 1954 state-wide referendum had rejected a tax supported educational TV network. It asked that a city-wide referendum be held in the April elections that year, and that the vocational school board hold a public hearing on the matter before it spent any money on a station.[218] Those charges and suggestions were rejected.

Opposition also existed on the Vocational School Board. Opponents argued that even though the school still had a promise from the Ford Foundation for $100,000, it would still cost too much.[219] On March 21, the Milwaukee Board of Vocational

An episode in the "Sportsmanlike Driving" series produced in cooperation with the AAA, which aired on WTMJ-TV. The GPL camera used a servo motor to change lenses, and the noise it made could be picked up by the studio microphones! (*Vocational School News* photo)

CHAPTER 8 ~ MPTV: CHANNELS 10 & 36   353

and Adult Education authorized the school to construct and operate a station in a 3-2 vote. It authorized an expenditure of $114,871 from its reserve fund, which when combined with the grant from the Ford Foundation, covered the $207,000 it was estimated would be needed to construct the station.[220]

After almost four years of political wrangling, the FCC finally granted the vocational school a construction permit for channel 10 on June 6, 1956.[221] The call letters WMVS-TV were later assigned to the station. (The letters stand for "Milwaukee Vocational School.")

WMVS-TV and WITI-TV personnel gather at the base of the WITI-TV tower in Mequon. L-R: Milwaukee Vocational School assistant director, Hy Barg, WITI-TV president Sol Kahn, WITI-TV promotions manager and assistant program director, Larry Turet, WMVS-TV station manager Paul K. Taff, WITI-TV program director Dean McCarthy, and WMVS-TV chief engineer, Jim Wulliman. (MPTV photo, courtesy of Paul K. Taff)

Planning began immediately. Milwaukee Broadcasting had purchased the old WCAN radio facilities, moved WEMP there, and sold its own to a Texas group that had started WRIT radio. (See chapter 4.) As such, the self-supporting tower once used by WOKY-TV was no longer available. As a result, the Vocational School originally planned to erect a 400' tower at the school and locate the transmitter there.[222] That would have required an expenditure. Instead, Dr. William Rasche and the Board negotiated a deal which allowed them to locate their transmitter at the Mequon facilities of WITI-TV, and to mount their antenna on that station's new tower.[223]

Station manager Paul K. Taff, was asked by the vocational school's assistant director, Hy Barg, to set-up a tour of a successful educational station. WQED in Pittsburgh had a strong reputation under Jack White (NET's first president), so Taff set-up a tour for Barg and himself. (There they met Fred Rogers and Josie Carrie who were doing "Children's Corner." Fred wasn't seen in those early shows – he was the puppeteer.)[224]

Contracts were issued in April of 1957 totaling $78,604[225], and testing began in October of that year.

Initially the station planned to broadcast from 5:00-8:30 p.m., Monday-Friday. For programming, WMVS-TV turned to the Educational Television and Radio Center. Founded in 1952, and sustained with grants from the Ford Foundation, the center started out as a means for educational stations to exchange programs they had produced. By 1954, it had begun airing five hours of programming daily from its headquarters in Ann Arbor, Michigan. WMVS-TV elected to run an hour of the center's programming. In addition, it would carry a live, 30 minute program produced by the NBC-Education Television project.[226]

The educational mission of the station went beyond the programming. Students from the school's television program helped operate it.[227]

On September 20, the station put a test pattern on the air for the first time. The Milwaukee Braves (who would go on to win the World Series) were in the middle of a pennant race, and played the Cubs in Chicago that day. Fans were often able to pick up WGN-TV's broadcasts of the games on channel 9, and were upset, as the adjacent channel interference from channel 10 prevented them from receiving the telecast. After only three minutes, the station began receiving calls from fans. To assuage them, the transmitter was turned off during the game![228]

Finally the big day arrived: October 28, 1957. In order to broadcast special shows to mark the occasion, the station began its day earlier. Seconds before 4:15 p.m. in an announcer's booth on the sixth floor of the vocational school, station manager Paul K. Taff, sat behind a microphone and said:

> *There's variety in programming for the entire family on Milwaukee's newest television station. So stay tuned to WMVS television, channel 10 as we make our television debut...*[229]

What followed was fifteen minutes of recorded music played from the booth, while a slide was shown. At 4:30 p.m., activity shifted to the station's single 50' x 30' studio, where a live dedication show began when a 22 year-old student floor director cued station manager Paul K. Taff, who welcomed viewers to "your community TV station."[230] Taff then introduced the guests who included:

October 28, 1957: station manager Paul K. Taff welcomed viewers to "your community station." (Screen grab from MPTV kinescope.)

Panel members who appeared on WMVS-TV's debut show. L-R: Dr. William Rasche, Dr. George Parkinson, Dr. J. Martin Klotsche, and Harold S. Vincent. (Screen grab from MPTV kinescope.)

Dr. William F. Rasche (director, Milwaukee Vocational and Adult Schools)
Dr. J. Martin Klotsche (Provost, University of Wisconsin – Milwaukee)
Dr. George Parkinson (Vice-Provost, University of Wisconsin, Milwaukee)
Harold S. Vincent (Superintendent, Milwaukee Public Schools)
The Very Rev. Edward J. O'Donnel, S.J. (president, Marquette University)
Richard E. Krug (City Librarian)
Murl Deusing (Educational Curator, Milwaukee Public Museum)
Mrs. Anita V. Webster (Administrator, Milwaukee Art Institute)

Other panel members, L-R: The Very Rev. Edward J. O'Donnel, S.J., Richard E. Krug, Murl Dusing, and Mrs. Anita Webster. (Screen grab from MPTV kinescope.)

Rasche had chaired the Milwaukee Educators' Committee on Television back in 1951, which included Klotsche, Parkinson and Vincent as members. Mayor Frank Zeidler was also a member, but couldn't make the show because of illness. Special guest Ralph Steetle, executive director of the Joint Council on Educational Television, was grounded by airplane difficulties in Cleveland, and also failed to appear.[231]

> **WMVS-TV'S FIRST DAY PROGRAMMING:**
> **OCTOBER 28, 1957**
>
> - 4:15 p.m.   Recorded Music
> - 4:30 p.m.   Dedication Ceremony (Live)
> - 5:00 p.m.   International Geophysical Year: A Planet Takes a Look at Itself*
> - 5:30 p.m.   Search on Delinquency
> - 6:00 p.m.   UN in Review
> - 6:15 p.m.   Friendly Giant (Children's show produced by WHA-TV)**
> - 6:30 p.m.   Children's Corner***
> - 7:00 p.m.   Our Nation's Roots
> - 7:30 p.m.   The Written Word
> - 8:00 p.m.   Vocational Schools
>
> * Produced by the NBC-Education Television Project
> ** Distributed by the Educational Television and Radio Center
> *** Fred Rogers was the puppeteer for this show, which was produced by WQED in Pittsburgh.

Robert Doerfler (right) started as a telecasting student, and later went on to great fame as "Bob Barry" on Milwaukee radio. (MPTV photo, courtesy of Bob Barry)

The student crew for the first telecast included studio manager Stanford Levy, Cameramen Robert Doerfler and Robert Johnson, and boom microphone operator Joseph Savage.[232] Donald Pinsker rounded out the crew.[233]

Stanford Levy went on to a career with KCET in Los Angeles, then to NET, and then to Connecticut Public Broadcasting.[234] Joseph Savage became a long-time producer for the station. Robert Doerfler became "Bob Barry" and a powerhouse on WOKY radio in the 1960s. His introduction of The Beatles during their 1964 Mil-

CHAPTER 8 ~ MPTV: CHANNELS 10 & 36   357

waukee appearance, and exclusive interview with the group, solidified his position as one of the city's most popular DJ's. Barry also appeared on WITI-TV during the 1960s, and later was heard on other radio stations in the area.

Bob Barry:

> I was in the class of '58. The Channel 10 TV school was a fabulous opportunity for young people to get into the communications business. There was nothing else available at the time. We could try our hand at all aspects of the TV business: directing, cameras, lighting and both booth and on-camera announcing. Class director Otto Schlaak, another speech professor, and others at the school, encouraged me to pursue a TV or radio announcing career.[235]

The Ford Foundation's Fund for the Advancement of Education funded a 25-city experiment utilizing television in the classroom, and the Milwaukee Public Schools developed a series of courses.[236] Teachers were selected in June of 1957. Elementary, junior high and high school students were all involved. The courses offered were:

- Elementary: An integrated program of 5th & 6th grade Science, Health & Safety
- Junior High: 7th grade Wisconsin Social Studies
                 9th grade General Science
- High School: 10th grade Biology
                 11th grade U.S. History

The courses were presented Monday through Thursday. The elementary school programs were fifteen minutes in length; the junior and senior high programs, thirty.

The experiment utilized the WMVS-TV facilities which included:

- A 30'x 50' studio with two (2) RCA Image Orthicon monochrome cameras
- A 3000 watt rear projector and a 9'x12' screen
- Two (2) 16mm film chains
- Two (2) 2"x2" slide projectors

One of the first WMVS-TV logos. (Courtesy of MPTV)

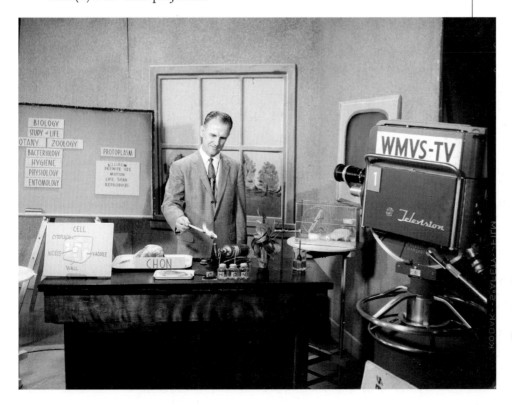

10th grade Biology, taught by Walter Olen, was one of the first telecourses produced with the Milwaukee Public Schools. (MPTV photo)

The original WMVS-TV studio on the 6th floor of The Milwaukee Vocational School. Seen in this photo are two RCA Image Orthicon monochrome cameras, a rear projection screen, boom microphone, and studio monitor. (MPTV photo)

Film Supervisor John Lemke uses WMVS-TV's kinescope recording unit. (MPTV photo)

- A Balopticon[237]
- A kinescope recording unit[238]

A rehearsal was held on January 3, 1958 in The WMVS-TV studios. In it, the instructors scheduled to teach the courses did so to an audience made up of those teachers who would use the telecourses in their classrooms via closed-circuit television.[239]

Station manager Paul K. Taff hired Al Binford to direct the shows at WMVS-TV.[240]

Telecasting began on February 3, 1958 and continued through June 5 of that year. As a control, other students received the same instruction in a traditional classroom environment, and the students who received their instruction via television were found to have achieved just as well, as measured by test scores.[241] After only three weeks one teacher, Ms. Wenonah Eis, who taught at Rufus King High School, commented that, "I don't kid myself – TV holds the attention I couldn't in class."[242]

That same February, WMVS-TV offered its first college credit course, in conjunction with Marquette University. "Heredity in Everyday Life" was offered by Dr. Eugene McDonough as a one semester-hour biology course. Instruction was telecast live from the WMVS studios, once each week. Each show was thirty minutes in length. Marquette had previously offered three other college credit courses on WXIX.[243]

The success of the experiment caused the Milwaukee Public Schools to extend the television in the classroom experiment to five more schools for the 1958-59 school year.[244]

Sister Gilmary Lemberg was one of the first School Sisters of Notre Dame to participate in a similar program later undertaken for the schools of the Milwaukee Archdiocese. Her experiences were typical of those of other teachers who served as the pioneers of instructional television:

> I taught a 15-20 minute program called "Designed for You," which taught teachers how to teach art. During the summer, I prepared the instruction manual, and worked out the details of each lesson. Director Al Binford was a great guy! I loved him! He was wonderful to work with! At first they gave me instruction on what was involved in producing a television program. I had to take a turn at trying each job on the production staff: floor director, camera operator, director, etc., so that I would know what would take place." That was very beneficial."
>
> In those days, of course, I was wearing the old habit, which was big, and had a lot of starch in it, so they had to use an overhead boom microphone."
>
> I was teaching at the time, and would have to take the bus to the Channel 10 studios. The shows were live back then, and if you made a mistake, it went out over the air, and there was nothing you could do about it. I learned how to have things passed to me under the camera's field of view, so people wouldn't see them. One time I spilled my glass of water, and they had to pass a new one to me."
>
> After the show, I would get a cab, and go to one of the schools that used my program. The students used to send me their work, and I would show it on my program. One time I took the wrong portfolio of art with me to the studio. It had the student-art that I wasn't going to show. I called one of my colleagues, and asked her to get a senior who had a car to bring the right one to me. When it came, they had to pass it to me under the camera!
>
> I later did a similar show once the Milwaukee Archdiocese began their instructional television system. It was a wonderful time in my life. I had about 500 shows under my belt when I stopped! It opened up a number of doors for me. Years later I would run into former students or teachers, who would ask me if I was on television![245]

Sister Gilmary's program was an example of how television could help provide instruction to students who otherwise might not be able to receive it. In an article in the *Catholic Herald Citizen*, "Designed for You" was described by Sister M. Jogues, O.P., the original program coordinator for the archdiocese, as "the best in-service program for teachers." She went on to explain that not everyone can teach art, and

The first college level course offered by the Milwaukee Vocational School on WMVS-TV was "Beginning Slide Rule" with Paul Witzke. (MPTV photo)

A second studio became operational in September of 1958. (MPTV photo)

CHAPTER 8 ~ MPTV: CHANNELS 10 & 36   361

that Sister Gilmary's programs enhanced the curriculum in the smaller schools – especially those outside Milwaukee County, where the archdiocesan shows had the most viewers.[246]

On Friday, June 6, 1958 the school's telecasting students took over operations of WMVS-TV for the first time. From 10:00 a.m. until 5:00 p.m., the station broadcast student productions.[247] All aspects of the operations: directing, producing, cameras, lights, master control, etc., were handled by the students.

On September 15, 1958, the Milwaukee Vocational School began offering its first college level course, "Beginning Slide Rule," with instructor Paul Witzke.[248] That same month, a second studio became operational. Since most programs were broadcast live at the time, the second studio helped to facilitate back-to-back shows.

On January 24, 1959, the Educational Television and Radio Center changed its name to the National Educational Television and Radio Center. It moved its headquarters from Ann Arbor to New York City that July. Rather than act strictly as a distributor of programs produced by educational TV stations, the organization – now being identified as National Educational Television (NET) – began producing its own shows. It also acquired high-quality shows from outside sources such as the BBC. In effect, it had become a "fourth network." At the same time, the NET began to move out of pure educational programming, and into the arts, culture and documentaries. Not all were happy with the transition.

Station manager Paul K. Taff and chief engineer/operations manager Jim Wulliman examine the new Ampex VR-1000B videotape recorder as well as reels of videotape. (MPTV photo)

That year, station manager Paul K. Taff and chief engineer Jim Wulliman wrote an application to the Ford Foundation for an AMPEX videotape recorder.[249] The foundation was making them available to all educational television stations. Each cost $55,000. The unit allowed WMVS-TV to expand its broadcast day – especially during the summer months, when many television students were off.[250]

Milwaukee had been assigned three UHF channels in 1952, channels 19, 25 and 31. WCAN-TV went dark in 1955, although Lou Poller still held a construction permit. Business Management Inc., which had purchased WFOX radio, had received a construction permit for channel 31 that same year, but never built the station. (See chapter 10.) The FCC reassigned UHF frequencies in Milwaukee in 1958, and the city had received channels

18, 24 and 30. In February of 1960, the FCC informed the holders of unused construction permits that they had 30 days to inform the FCC that the stations would be built or have their permits cancelled.[251]

During the 1959-60 school year, WMVS-TV began offering educational programming to seventy-four Catholic schools in the Milwaukee archdiocese. (Participation would grow to 206 schools during the 1963-64 school year.) The station found itself with a problem – a lack of time. It was now offering a variety of programming throughout the day and didn't have enough time to offer all that was requested of it. To solve the problem, the board of the Milwaukee Vocational and Adult Schools applied to the FCC for permission to construct a second station using either channel 24 or 30. Both of those UHF channels were assigned to commercial interests, but were not being used. Specifically, the board hoped to utilize the second channel to provide instructional television programming to local business and industry and to provide a laboratory for the students in its television and transmitter and communications courses. It asked the FCC to reassign one of the unused UHF channels to educational use. The school already had a UHF transmitter, having purchased the old WOKY-TV unit given to Lou Poller when he sold the facilities of WCAN-TV to CBS.[252]

The three-year experiment in the use of television in the classroom sponsored by the Ford Foundation ended in 1960. Milwaukee Public Schools Superintendent Harold Vincent declared the concept "proven," and asked the Milwaukee School Board to make the program permanent.[253]

In October of that year, station manager Paul K. Taff to become director of children's programming at NET. He was replaced by Dr. Otto Schlaak.

In late November of 1960, Business Management, Inc. lost its construction permit for channel 30. Rather than reassign it to educational use, the FCC added channel 36 to Milwaukee and reserved it for educational use in late January of 1961.[254] The vocational school filed an application with the FCC in early April.

Dr. Otto Schlaak, shown here with Vincent Price, became the station manager for WMVS-TV in late 1960, and led the station until his retirement in February of 1986. (MPTV photo)

CHAPTER 8 ~ MPTV: CHANNELS 10 & 36

Experiments with instructional television continued. During the 1960-61 school year, 600 fourth grade students watched a series of sixty-six, 15-minute lessons called "Patterns in Arithmetic." When compared to 400 students who received traditional classroom instruction, the students who watched the televised lessons had had higher test scores, and their attitude toward arithmetic was rated "higher than in previous years."[255]

In March of 1961, 128 representatives from 48 educational television stations and the NET met at a conference hosted by the Milwaukee Vocational School.[256]

In a speech before the National Association of Broadcasters (NAB) that May, Welfare Secretary Abraham Ribicoff revealed that the Kennedy Administration planned on asking Congress for funding which would promote educational TV on the national level.[257] In a speech given at the same meeting, FCC chairman Newton Minow declared television to be a "vast Wasteland."

That fall, WMVS-TV produced its first adult telecourse, "The Inquiring Mind," for NET. Dr. Otto Schlaak produced the show, which debuted on September 11th. The show was hosted by Dr. Cyril O. Houle, an adult educational specialist at the University of Chicago, and told stories of those who continued their education after graduating from a formal school.[258]

On February 21, 1962, The Milwaukee Board of Vocational and Adult Education received a construction permit for UHF channel 36.[259] In doing so, the FCC waived its multiple-ownership rules, which prohibited an entity from owning more than one station in a given market. The call letters WMVT-TV were later assigned to the facility. (The call letters stand for "Milwaukee Vocational Technical.")

The original plan was to locate the transmitter and a new tower near the vocational school, so that telecasting students might have easier access to them, but that idea was abandoned. Since 1957, WITI-TV had provided space for

In 1961, WMVS-TV acquired its first remote truck, which was used for its first live, remote broadcast from Wisconsin State Fair Park. The truck was purchased from WWJ-TV in Detroit. (MPTV photo)

The interior of MPTV's first remote truck. The truck was remodeled by station engineers with help from the school's auto body shop. At left is a compact videotape recorder which was installed in a short rack by station engineers. (MPTV photo)

WMVS-TV's transmitter, and had allowed the vocational school to mount the station's antenna on its tower. In 1962, WITI-TV constructed a new self-supporting tower on land near Estabrook Parkway, and space was provided in the transmitter building for both of the vocational school's stations, as both antennas would be mounted on the new tower. WMVS-TV went off the air on June 29, as the transmitter was moved to the new site and the antenna relocated. On September 7, broadcasting resumed from the new facilities.

The FCC was seeking to push the UHF band as a way of expanding television service. It urged Congress to pass a bill requiring all manufacturers of television sets shipped via interstate commerce (or imported) to include the capability of receiving a UHF signal. On July 10, 1962, President Kennedy signed into law the All-Channel Receiver Act. The law affected all sets manufactured after April 30, 1964, and would help provide an audience for WMVT-TV. Station manager Dr. Otto Schlaak stated that the new station would be used primarily for instructional purposes, and would free up time for WMVS-TV to broadcast programs of a non-school nature.[260]

On October 22, 1962, WMVS-TV began offering a special course designed to teach illiterate, unemployed welfare recipients how to read and write. Named "Operation Alphabet," the series of 100 lessons was produced by the Philadelphia Public Schools. The program was offered five days a week, with each lesson shown twice daily.[261] Eighty-eight persons on county relief were required to view the program

Transmitter Engineer Harold Wagner sits at the control console of the old WOKY-TV, UHF transmitter used by WMVT-TV. The transmitter was located in the WITI-TV transmitter building in Estabrook Parkway. Wagner later became the stations' chief engineer. (MPTV photo)

each morning in the vocational school's cafeteria. Eleven other viewing centers were set up around the area.[262] The program ended on March 8, 1963, and all eighty-eight who were required to participate finished.[263] However, despite selling about 500 manuals when the course started, not many of the others watching, who were not required to participate, sent in their final exams, and as such there didn't appear to be a demand for the program. It was not renewed.[264]

That year, Congress passed and President Kennedy signed the Educational Television Facilities Act. It authorized appropriations of up to thirty-two million federal

CHAPTER 8 ~ MPTV: CHANNELS 10 & 36   365

dollars for educational TV stations.[265] The appropriations were for five fiscal years, and provided for construction grants for educational television facilities. They were matching grants and covered up to fifty percent of the cost of new facilities, and up to an additional twenty-five percent of the cost of improving existing facilities, with a total cap of $1 million per state. The Milwaukee Vocational School applied for a grant of $167,475[266], so that it might boost channel 36's power from one to thirty kilowatts. The State Coordinating Committee for Educational Television recommended that the FCC only approve $154,000 of the request, as it wanted the balance to be used by other educational television stations in Wisconsin.[267] Despite that recommendation, the vocational school received a grant for the full amount requested the following year.[268]

On January 29, 1963, Milwaukee's second educational television station, WMVT-TV, began broadcasting on channel 36. A special dedication ceremony was broadcast at 8:30 p.m., which featured a talk by Jim Robertson, vice-president of NET. Robertson had been at WTMJ-TV when it went on the air in 1947.[269] At 9:00 p.m. NET Science Report was shown. It was a one-hour program which showed

The film room used by WMVS-TV and WMVT-TV. (MPTV photo)

the vehicles and equipment being developed for the moon landings. Originally, the new station broadcast only 10 hours per week.[270]

Using four cameras, WMVS-TV made the first live broadcast of The Great Circus Parade on July 4, 1963. Segments from the broadcast were shown later that month on NET's *What's New?* program.[271]

In 1964, the Ford Foundation decided to substantially increase their support of NET through a series of $6 million per year grants. Those grants allowed the network to produce a series of programs between 1964 and 1968, and initiated a period of creativity which had previously not been seen. Besides adult dramas like *NET Playhouse* and children's programming like *Mister Rogers' Neighborhood*, NET producers decided to try and plug a perceived gap in public affairs and documentary programming. They produced a series of hard-hitting documentaries under the series title *NET Journal*, programs like *The Poor Pay More*, *Black Like Me*, *Appalachia: Rich Land, Poor People*, and *Inside North Vietnam*.[272] For some stations, the public affairs programs "were considered too liberal, anti-establishment, and often

MPTV began showing "The Great Circus Parade" in 1963. The parade would later be broadcast in high-definition. (MPTV photo)

unbalanced; other programs raised questions of profanity, obscenity, and matters of taste."²⁷³

Milwaukee's two educational stations were undergoing their own evolution. In order to transform what was perceived by some as dull programming, the staff began using techniques which had been successful in commercial broadcasting. Rather than a straight lecture, the productions made better use of visual aids and on the scene activities in an attempt to make the programs more interesting.²⁷⁴

It had become obvious that the Ford Foundation could not, by itself, continue to support the continuous growth of NET. In early 1962, Hartford Gunn, the manager of WGBH in Boston (later the first president of PBS) proposed an FCC-appointed commission chaired by Eleanor Roosevelt to FCC Chairman Newton Minow. Minow thought that the idea was sound, but that it would be inappropriate for the Commission as a regulatory body to become involved. The idea died.

The problem did not go away. With funding from the Department of Health, Education and Welfare, the first NAEB conference on long-range financing for educational television was held December 7-8, 1964. The attendees agreed that federal money was needed, and that the best way was for a commission to be appointed to study the matter. Next, a letter was sent to Lyndon Johnson asking him to appoint a presidential commission. It was suggested that might cause problems as the use of presidential funds would also mean that Johnson would appoint the members of the proposed commission. So, the Carnegie Corporation was approached. With a recommendation from President Johnson, they agreed to fund the study, and set up a private commission to conduct it.²⁷⁵

In late 1964, WITI-TV donated its Du Mont flying-spot scanner to the vocational school. The equipment had been used to broadcast that station's color programs from the time it went on the air in 1956 until it completed a move to its 27th Street building in 1959. (See chapter 7.) WISN-TV also donated its old Du Mont color scanner. Originally, the thought was that students might get some benefit from studying the obsolete equipment, but the stations' engineers saw the donations as opportunities. Harold Wagner and Frederick Goll cannibalized both

CHAPTER 8 ~ MPTV: CHANNELS 10 & 36   367

systems, to produce one complete unit from the two, and added some circuitry and controls, in order to update it.[276] Using that equipment, WMVS-TV became the first educational station to broadcast in color on a regular schedule.[277, 278]

Former chief engineer Jim Wulliman recalled:

> Harold built some miniature preamps right at the base of the phototubes rather than the phototube having to feed a long co-axial cable to the amplifier unit. He could do this because technology had developed small components rather than regular sized tubes by this time. This improvement made the film scanner really work quite well, so WMVS was able to transmit very good quality color films and slides.[279]

Nels Harvey, another station engineer remembered:

> Before the station acquired an RCA TK-27 color film chain, the films were presented by switching from the studio microwave feed to the Du Mont unit at the transmitter. The transmitter engineer then became a projectionist. When I was there we used the Du Mont for a sign-on ID slide instead of color bars. There wasn't a color bar generator at the transmitter, and no way to insert an ID available.[280]

Color telecasting began in late December of 1964 on an unscheduled basis.[281] The first regularly scheduled color show was "Travelogue" on January 28, 1965. The other shows broadcast in color were "Sports-A-Rama," "Strictly for Women," and "Canada – Land of Color," All were free films, found by staff photographer and film supervisor John Lemke.

WITI-TV had combined the flying-spot scanner with Du Mont's Vitascan system to broadcast live studio action. WMVS-TV didn't receive any of that equipment, so the color telecasts were limited to film or slide shows.

At a meeting of the Public Relations Society of America at Marquette University that May, NAEB president William G. Harley "said he would support a study

MPTV Master Control in the 1960s. (MPTV photo)

In June of 1966, Channels 10 and 36 moved to their current home at 1036 North Eighth Street. (MPTV photo)

which might lead to a national commission to operate the educational outlets in a 'dual system' with commercial television."[282]

The Carnegie Corporation established the first Carnegie Commission on Educational Television on November 10, 1965. It was charged with studying the future of educational television in the United States. After study, it released its report on January 26, 1967. Some of the proposals included increasing the number of ETV stations, imposing an excise tax on all television sets sold, interconnection of stations for more efficient program exchange, and the creation of a "Corporation for Public Television."[283]

Changes took place in both stations' schedules in the fall of 1966. For the first time, viewers had a choice of two different program schedules each evening, with general information and cultural programming on Channel 10, and instructional programming on Channel 36.[284]

On February 5, 1967, Sunday programming began.

On May 10, 1967, the Milwaukee Radio and Television Council evolved into the Community Broadcast Council and took on the added role of seeking financial support for the city's educational television stations.[285] Dick Wenzel, who played "Barkey the Barker" on "Children's Fair" (See special section.) was the president of the Council at the time:

> The Council was a 'do-gooder' organization that evaluated radio and television programs and gave awards every year. I eventually became its president and Jane Bradley–Uihlein (later Petit) was vice-president. It became very time

CHAPTER 8 ~ MPTV: CHANNELS 10 & 36

consuming. In addition, a lot of the people judging the programs didn't have any background in the industry, so the awards became based more on popularity than production quality.

So, I met with Jane and Otto [Schlaak]. We talked about it and said, 'You know, this is a couple of hundred member organization – maybe more. It's a loose organization that's sort of struggling for survival. Why don't we just concentrate on doing something for you?'

The idea came from the Friends of the Museum. It was an independent organization that could do fund raising. It allowed for a bit more creative thinking.[286]

During 1966-67, the vocational school purchased more color equipment, using a grant from the Department of Health Education and Welfare[287], including that needed to originate live, studio programs. Included in the acquisitions were a color video tape recorder, a color film chain, and two studio cameras. On May 22 of that year, the first live color broadcast was made on Channel 10.

On November 5, 1967, the Ford Foundation started "Public Broadcasting Laboratory," a live, Sunday night magazine program. It was carried by WMVS-TV.[288]

Two days later, President Johnson signed the Public Broadcasting Act of 1967. It amended the Communications Act of 1934, and set up the Corporation for Public Broadcasting (CPB) to administer federal aid to educational television stations. In March of 1968, the CPB was incorporated.

Initially, the CPB supported NET in its role as the "fourth network." By 1969 however, a combination of factors led to its withdrawal of that support. First, there was a perceived conflict of interest between the network's production and distribution roles. Second, NET had alienated most of its affiliates. Third, the CPB, under pressure from the Nixon Administration and various affiliates, wanted to tone down the programming offered, while NET was still producing hard-hitting documentaries.[289] In response, the Public Broadcasting Service was incorporated

The first "Great TV Auction" was held in 1969. Shown (L-R): Station Manager Dr. Otto Schlaak, General Auction Chairman Orren Bradley, and emcee Lee Murray. (MPTV Friends photo)

on November 3, 1969. The CPB and the Ford Foundation threatened to cut NET's program grants unless it merged with WNDT in NYC. It did so in late 1970, and the station's call letters were changed to WNET-TV. That ended NET's role as a network.[290]

May 12-17, 1969, the first "Channel 10 Auction" was held with a goal of $50,000.[291] Co-sponsored by the Community Broadcast Council and the Gambrinus Society (which sponsored Milwaukee's 'Summerfest"), it featured local celebrities. The first few versions of the auction were a little different than they are today. Milwaukee radio personality Jack Lee was one of the many who helped:

> The first few years it was held at Wisconsin State Fair Park, and the idea was that we would get people to watch by having some local entertainment, and then getting some pitches in for the items being auctioned. It was a nightmare. In order to fill all of those hours, we had high school marching bands, drum and bugle corps, cub scouts twirling flags, and all kinds of groups lined up in the parking lot. You never knew what was going to come through the door!
>
> There was no rehearsal and no setting up of the groups. All of a sudden a sixty-piece drum and bugle corps would come marching in. You had to figure out how to get them in so that the camera could get a shot, and then clear out. You had to ad lib while all of it was going on.
>
> As they compared the results here with those around the country, they figured out that what it was really about was raising money, and that you had to get as many things as you could donated ahead of time, and not have things that took a lot of time to demonstrate. Those first few auctions, we might've had someone drive a garden tractor in and take ten minutes to show how it operated. Nowadays, it would be put on a 'super board' and at the end of an hour they would close it and raise $2,000.[292]

"Hatha Yoga," an MPTV production with yogini Kathleen Hitchcock premiered on WMVS-TV on October 5, 1970. In September of 1971, it went into national distribution on PBS. The show ran through 1986. (MPTV photo)

On September 17 of that same year, WMVS-TV broadcast the opening ceremonies of Milwaukee's new Performing Arts Center live.

In the late 1950s, the Milwaukee Vocational School had divided its educational mission into two distinct areas: vocational and adult education, and two-year college programs. The latter were offered through what it called the Milwaukee Institute of Technology (MIT). In 1964, the name was changed to The Milwaukee Vocational, Technical and Adult Schools.[293] A few years later, the name was changed to The Milwaukee Technical College (MTC). In 1969, plans were formulated to combine technical schools in Milwaukee, Cudahy, West Allis and West Milwaukee into a single vocational, technical school district. The change was to take place in 1970, and in anticipation, the name was changed again, this time to the Milwaukee Area Technical College (MATC).[294] As a con-

CHAPTER 8 ~ MPTV: CHANNELS 10 & 36

sequence, on June 17, 1970, the Milwaukee Board of Vocational and Adult Education voted to ask the FCC to change the call letters of WMVT-TV to WMTC.[295] The change was never made.

As a part of the effort to unify the vocational – technical school district, MATC formulated plans to offer some college classes via television in 1969.[296] The program, named the "College of the Air," made its debut in 1970.[297]

In early March of 1972, a survey of the top twenty-five public television markets conducted by the Corporation for Public Broadcasting showed that WMVS-TV ranked second in the number of television owners who watched public TV. Only Boston had a higher percentage.[298]

In a dispute over program content, President Richard Nixon vetoed a bill which would have funded the Corporation for Public Broadcasting for two years on June 30 of that year. A reduced one-year bill was later passed and signed into law. That same year MATC filed an application with the federal government in which it asked to use the abandoned Nike surface-to-air missile site in River Hills. The college hoped to obtain either a reduced price or a long-term lease for the facility, on which it hoped to erect a new tower and transmitter building for its two television stations.[299]

On May 15, 1973, Robert MacNeil and Jim Lehrer teamed up for coverage of the Senate Watergate hearings, presented by the National Public Affairs Center for television. Channel 36 carried complete coverage in prime time.

Since 1957, WITI-TV had provided space in its transmitter building, and allowed MATC to mount the antennas for its stations on its towers. However, the tower's rating had been changed from 100 MPH winds, **or** 2 inches of ice, to 100 MPH winds **with** 2 inches of ice.[300] As such, it was overloaded, and WITI informed the college that it would have to secure another facility. The Channel 10 antenna was only at 750 ft., while Channel 36's was only at 400 ft. As such, neither

One of the shows begun by WMVS-TV in 1964 to give the station's producers and directors a chance to experiment was "Showcase." It featured music, drama, documentary or any other subject the staff found to be creative. Here in a performance first broadcast on January 12, 1972, is the group "Woodbine." Shown L-R are: Bruce Riddiough on guitar and steel guitar, Bob Mueller on drums, singer/songwriter/guitarist Bill Camplin, and Ken Pfaff on bass. (MPTV photo)

station was covering the area it had the potential to. An application was filed, and in July of 1975, the Department of Health, Education and Welfare made a grant of $326,980 to the college for new antennas. B&F Broadcasting had received a construction permit for Channel 24 in June of 1973 (See chapter 9.), and planned to erect a new 1000' tower on the site of an old Sealtest ice cream plant at 505 East Capitol Drive.[301] The college planned on locating its antennas on that tower.

That same year, the first on-air membership campaign raised $23,000.

In 1965, a federal lawsuit was filed by Lloyd Barbie, charging that the Milwaukee Public Schools were racially segregated. The suit was amended in 1968, and after years of discovery, the matter went to trial in September of 1973, and concluded in January of 1974. No cameras were allowed inside the federal courtroom of Judge John Reynolds, but that February, WMVS-TV produced "Year of Decision: The Milwaukee School Desegregation Case From 1965-1974." In that program, Barbie and defense attorney Laurence Hammond reconstructed major arguments from the trial. In addition, the show included discussion of the issues facing the city.[302]

Reynolds found for the plaintiffs, and ordered that the schools be desegregated. Both sides attempted to reach a plan acceptable to each other and the court. In May of 1976, hearings were held by the special desegregation master appointed by the federal court. Cameras were allowed in the courtroom for those hearings, and Channel 36 provided live coverage.[303]

B&F Broadcasting took longer than expected to construct its transmitter facility and erect a new tower. As such, the Milwaukee Board of Vocational, Technical and Adult Education approved a resolution recommending the purchase of a new site for its own facilities in March of 1977.[304] The project was to be financed by a $1.9 million, 5-year loan. The college later received approval for the plan from the State

Murl Deusing in an early show on WMVS-TV. (MPTV photo)

CHAPTER 8 ~ MPTV: CHANNELS 10 & 36

Vocational, Technical and Adult Education Board, and the MATC board gave its final approval later that month.³⁰⁵ It entered into negotiations with the City of Milwaukee for eight acres of land along the Milwaukee River north of East Capitol Drive, and the transaction was later consummated.

One of the longest running programs in Milwaukee television history came to an end in September of that year, when "The Murl Deusing Safari" ended its run. Deusing, who had served as the educational curator for the Milwaukee Public Museum, had done "Museum Expeditions" on WMVS-TV starting in 1958. He began doing "Safari" on WTMJ-TV in 1963. It ran on that station until 1972, after which time it was picked up by WMVS-TV.³⁰⁶

The first program underwriting announcement was made in 1977.

On March 1, 1978, Public TV's satellite interconnection began operation. Channels 10 and 36 were the first Milwaukee TV operation to carry a regular schedule of programs via satellite.

Until 1978, cameras were not allowed in Wisconsin courtrooms. Courts around the country had been reluctant to allow televised proceedings ever since the United States Supreme Court overturned the 1962 conviction of Billie Sol Estes in 1965, ruling that he had not received a fair trial because of the coverage.³⁰⁷ The first experimental program since that ruling began in Florida In July of 1977, and ran through June of 1978.³⁰⁸

WTMJ-TV's Ed Hinshaw headed up an informal group of members of the Society of Professional Journalists, the Milwaukee Press Club, the First Amendment Congress and the National Press Photographers, who along with some judges, attorneys and other interested parties asked the Wisconsin Supreme Court to allow cameras in courtrooms. The group negotiated a set of guidelines and rules which the Court adopted. Part of the process was allowing photography in some mock trials at the Marquette University Law School.³⁰⁹

"Business of Wisconsin" with host Peter Banzhaf premiered in 1978. (MPTV photo)

The Wisconsin Supreme Court approved a one-year experiment which allowed television cameras and audio recording equipment in courtrooms as of April 1, 1978. It was the second state to allow their use.[310]

On June 21, 1978, Filemon Amaro, Jr. – who was on trial in Waukesha County – grabbed a deputy's gun, killed the deputy and a sergeant, and kidnapped two others. Waukesha County Circuit Judge Max Raskin agreed to allow WMVT-TV to televise the trial. Opponents argued that defendants and witnesses might become nervous if they knew they were on camera, and that lawyers and judges would be tempted to posture.[311] Hispanic groups in both Waukesha and Milwaukee Counties objected to the negative publicity that might be generated.[312] To assuage the concerns, Raskin set strict rules for the trial, which included allowing the camera to be located only in the rear of the courtroom, where it would not block the view of spectators, prohibiting camera shots of the jury, allowing the camera to focus on witnesses only momentarily, and prohibiting commentators from speaking into microphones in the courtroom.[313]

The trial began on November 30, 1978. Commentators used a conference room adjacent to the courtroom. The audio in the courtroom was picked up by the court's own sound system so that additional microphones and their cables would not clutter the room. Two witnesses objected to being shown on television, and Raskin ordered that the cameras be turned off during their testimony. One was an inmate at the state prison, who served as a prosecution witness, and the second was Amaro.[314] It was the first trial broadcast live in Wisconsin since the experimental period started, and the response was positive. The public saw all of the proceedings, including arguments made outside the presence of the jury. The experiment served to educate the public on how the court system worked.

On January 25, 1979 MPTV originated its first, live broadcast via satellite. Participating in the three-way "Satellite Forum on the Nation's Economy" were Wisconsin Rep. Henry Reuss in Washington, D.C., the presidents of the Milwaukee chapter of the NAACP and Wisconsin AFL-CIO, along with fifty of the congressman's constituents who were in Allen-Bradley's Milwaukee headquarters, and the director of the Milwaukee Urban League along with former Wisconsin Governor Warren Knowles, who were in the MPTV studios. Also that year, MPTV became the first television service in the state to offer closed-captioned programming.

Channel 10 began a month-long experiment with 24-hour a day broadcasts on March 1, 1980. Thousands phoned in during the night with positive responses.

On May 12, 1980, MPTV aired a controversial episode of the PBS news and public affairs series *World*. Featured was the docudrama "Death of a Princess." which recounted the 1977 public execution of a young Saudi Arabian princess and her lover, after their conviction for the crime of adultery. The Saudi government, and major PBS underwriter, Mobil Oil Corporation, asked the network not to air the program, because it reflected poorly on life within the kingdom. Some members of Congress did the same, fearing that the Saudis might cut off their oil shipments. Others supported the network's decision. The controversy was high before the program aired, but died out shortly thereafter.

Although it had looked for an alternative for a number of years, MPTV still had not vacated the WITI-TV tower. In 1980, it entered into an agreement with Gaylord Broadcasting. Gaylord owned and operated WVTV, (See Chapter 5.), and wanted to upgrade its own transmission facilities after using the old WCAN-TV/WXIX transmitter and tower atop the Marc Plaza hotel in downtown Milwaukee. A public-private partnership was formed to build a new tower owned by WVTV on the land MATC had purchased along the Milwaukee River. In return for a long-

CHAPTER 8 ~ MPTV: CHANNELS 10 & 36

term lease, both MPTV stations received transmitter space, and were allowed to mount their antennas on the new tower at no charge. The new facilities went into operation in 1981.[315]

On November 4 of that year, WMVT-TV changed its call letters to WMVT.

The Channel 10/36 Friends continued to look for new ways to raise funds, and they held their first wine tasting event outdoors at the MGIC building on August 20, 1981.

First Lady Nancy Reagan hosted two PBS programs designed to target pre-teens and teenagers, and warn them about drug and alcohol abuse. The programs aired on November 2, and 9, 1983. Over one hundred-fifty town hall meetings were held across southeastern Wisconsin to discuss the topic.

In another of a string of firsts in Wisconsin, MPTV began experimenting with full stereo audio in June of 1985. On July 4, it began broadcasting in stereo full-time.[316] On that same day, Channel 10 experimented for a second time with temporary, 24-hour a day broadcasts.

Federal support for the stations through the Corporation for Public Broadcasting had risen over the years, but it made up a smaller percentage of their overall budget. To study the matter, the college appointed a blue ribbon panel.

Dan Small has hosted "Outdoor Wisconsin" since its debut on November 1, 1984. (MPTV photo)

"Black and White in Milwaukee: the First Hundred Years," was an MPTV original production, which explored relationships between black and white Milwaukeeans between 1835 and 1940. Each episode was an hour-long docudrama. The first was shot on "The Streets of Old Milwaukee" exhibit at the Milwaukee Public Museum, and debuted on February 6, 1985. Subsequent episodes ran periodically through February 19, 1988. (MPTV photo)

In December of 1985, the panel released its report. In it, they recommended that MATC give up its license for Channel 36 to the State Educational Communications Board (as the State Radio and Television Council was now known), in exchange for a lump-sum payment or an annual state subsidy. Alternatively, it recommended that

"A Wok Through China" with Diane Lisko and Patrick Garland, was an MPTV-produced cooking show that started as a student production. The "pilot" ran at 6:30 p.m. on Wednesday, May 14, 1980 as a part of MPTV's annual student operations, named "Studentvision" that year. The reaction was such that a series was later produced for national distribution. (MPTV photo)

the MATC board consider creating a non-profit community licensee. It was also recommended that the stations look for ways to increase corporate underwriting, increase fund raising among viewers and foundations through challenge grants, the on-air auction, planned giving programs, and workplace giving. It recommended that an endowment be established. It also recommended that the college look for ways to increase tax support, such as giving the State Educational Communications Board more use of the stations' programming schedules, in exchange for an annual fee.[317]

The station was already considering the lease of the vertical blanking period to transmit stock ticker information or weather reports.[318] The recommendation to give up one of the licenses was not met with approval, as the MATC board preferred not to give up its autonomy.

Dr. Otto Schlaak had joined the vocational school in May of 1954 as chairman of its new television laboratory. In 1960, he was named station manger after Paul K. Taff left to become director of children's programming for NET. Schlaak retired in February of 1986, after many years of distinguished service. Anticipating the retirement, Tom Axtell, executive director of Channel 10/36 Friends, Inc, was named Station Manager on December 20, 1985.[319]

While leading the 10/36 Friends Axtell saw donations rise from $750,000 to $3 million per year. As station manager, he sought to diversify and increase the stations'

CHAPTER 8 ~ MPTV: CHANNELS 10 & 36   377

revenue streams, revitalize the technical college's television curriculum, upgrade the stations' technical systems, create local programming that reflected community issues, and expand channel 36 to a full-time station.[320]

The string of firsts continued in January of 1987; when Channel 10 joined nine other public TV stations in the nation, in an experiment with Descriptive Video Service (DVS), pioneering an audio service to help the visually impaired enjoy more TV. In 1990, the station received an Emmy Award for the development and implementation of DVS.

In June of 1987, "*Conciencia*" began offering a Spanish version on the Second Audio Program (SAP) channel.

Sony Corporation provided WMVS with high-definition television (HDTV) cameras, which were used to tape the Great Circus Parade in July of 1988. The production was later used to demonstrate the potential of the new technology to the United States Congress and other interested parties. The analog broadcast featured experimental, stereo-surround sound, which had first been used for the telecast of the City of Festivals Parade the previous month.[321]

Veteran WTMJ-TV newsman/anchor John McCullough ended his twenty-one year career there in November of 1988. He formed his own production company, and began producing "Emphasis Wisconsin" for WMVS. The first show aired in December of that year.[322] The show was supported by the Lynde and Harry Bradley Foundation, and allowed McCullough to devote more

"Homework Hotline" debuted on October 6, 1986. In order to help increase student success and retention, a panel of Milwaukee Public School teachers took questions, in the same way that the Milwaukee Public Library provided its "ready reference" service. Other MPS teachers took questions on the air. The show ran through the spring of 1988, when it succumbed to a lack of funding. In its prime, more than 300 questions per week were fielded by the participating teachers. (MPTV photo)

"Smith and Company" with host Joe Smith made its debut on October 5, 1987. The show featured guests who discussed topical issues, and viewers could call in with their questions. The last show was broadcast on May 26, 1994. (MPTV photo)

"Black Noveau" with host Keith Murphy is a magazine show focusing on the concerns of the local African-American community. The show premiered in November of 1988, with hosts Rodd Walker and Sharon Davis. (MPTV photo)

Veteran Milwaukee newsman/anchor John McCullough began doing "Emphasis Wisconsin" in 1988. (MPTV photo)

time to an in-depth examination of issues facing the area. The show ran through 2000.

In March of 1989, a fire in Channel 36's antenna forced it off the air for nearly a week. The station went back on with a temporary, low-power antenna[323] until full-power equipment was installed in September at a cost of more than $100,000.

MATC president Barbara Holmes fired sixteen college administrators and department chairs on February 8, 1991, including station manager Tom Axtell. Axtell had no warning, and told the *Milwaukee Sentinel*:

The president said she wanted to build a new administrative team and that she was terminating me."[324]

In defending her moves, Holmes told the *Milwaukee Journal* that the move did not suggest any problems at the stations, but rather that she "wanted someone who could build better relationships with the Educational Communications Board in Madison and with community leaders."[325] The 10/36 Friends later reported that 250 people refused to renew their support for the stations as long as Holmes remained the college's president.[326] In response, the MATC board revoked her authority to hire and fire senior administrators without their approval, and fired her in November of 1992.

Bryce Combs, who was the executive in charge of production, was named as the interim manager, and after a search, was given the job permanently. Combs told the author that he had expanded the stations' local productions, and during one year, twenty percent of the stations' programming originated in either the city or the state. The efforts were recognized when the stations were recognized with the third highest ranking among entities which impacted the quality of life in the area. No other public institutions were in the top ten.[327]

Development of HDTV continued, and proposals were floated which would not only increase picture definition, but would change the transmission standard from analog to digital. Five organizations were, by 1992, competing to develop a system which would become the standard in the United States. In the first round of tests, all had problems. One of the competitors was a partnership between Zenith Corp. and AT&T. They had corrected the problems uncovered during the first round, and had requested a retesting. While they waited for a decision, they decided to show-off their system in a public demonstration. Another competitor, General Instruments, had made an over-the-air, digital transmission of seven miles. Zenith-AT&T decided to top that. They wanted a UHF station (as most digital television would probably use that portion of the spectrum), which was near Zenith's facility in Glenview, Illinois. WMVT was selected to make the first

CHAPTER 8 ~ MPTV: CHANNELS 10 & 36   379

"Tracks Ahead," which explores railroading in all of its forms, has been produced by MPTV since 1990. Spencer Christian, former weatherman for ABC's "Good Morning America" hosts the show. (MPTV photo)

experimental, long-distance, digital, high-definition broadcasts. They took place May 26-29, 1992. A Chicago Bulls-New York Knicks game was taped using the new technology, and broadcast over the air to Zenith's facility.[328] At Channel 36, Zenith engineers had been sending test signals for hours before the demonstration, and the system was working well. As the demonstration began, they began to lose their signal. The engineers tried a number of solutions, but none worked. In desperation, one technician slapped one of the pieces of equipment, and the signal strength returned. The demonstration was a success![329]

Bryce Combs:

> We were able to do the test because of our relationship with Zenith, and the fact that we were near to their facility. They couldn't get on the Sears Tower to test, and we were able to use our UHF transmitter. The previous digital test had used a breadboard device, but this one used a real transmitter.
>
> The physicists and electronics people who were working with Zenith were Norwegian, and their English was limited. While we were doing the testing, one of them looked at the results and yelled, 'eureka!'
>
> "I said, 'I understand that word. What do you mean, eureka?'
>
> He said, 'We're not using all of the bandwidth.'

"DOLLAR SIGNS" with hosts Elizabeth Kay and Bob Landaas premiered on September 11, 1992, succeeding Business of Wisconsin. (MPTV photo)

I said, 'what do you mean, we're not using all of it?'

He said, 'We're only using about half of it, and we have a full-fidelity picture over here. There's something wrong!'

I said, 'There's nothing wrong! That means we can do something else with the extra bandwidth!'

That was a 'eureka' moment, and it happened in Milwaukee! No one had predicted that. No one at the FCC had thought that the compression algorithms would be that efficient. There were some lab tests that showed that it was efficient, but no one thought that once it went through a thirty year-old transmitter that had a new encoder attached to it, that it would be that efficient.[330]

In the early 1990s, financial troubles began to plague many public television stations, which struggled with finding new ways to finance their operations. MPTV was no different. In mid-February of 1994, word leaked that budget cuts might mean that many of MPTV's locally-produced shows might be cut.[331] Shows without underwriters were particularly susceptible. "Smith and Company," which started in October of 1987, was one of the first shows to be cut. It was broadcast for the last time on May 26, 1994.[332]

Despite the budget woes, MPTV continued to look for new opportunities. In October of 1994, WMVS and WTMJ-TV cooperated in a unique program in which a debate on proposals which would have banned handguns in several local communities was produced in Channel 4's studios, but broadcast over Channel 10.[333] That same month, both stations began an experimental, cooperative effort in which WTMJ-TV provided Channel 10 with a nightly newsbreak. The following month, WMVS broadcast WTMJ-TV's election night coverage.

After a viewer survey showed a preference for outdoor, nature, leisure, cooking and hobby shows, WMVS dropped its weekly "Milwaukee Tonight" program in 1995. Compounding the decision was anticipated federal funding cuts.[335]

Developed by station engineer Nolan Tobias, MPTV's web site went on-line with 65 pages on October 3, 1995. The launch was unannounced, but an ex-Milwaukee resident, living in Florida, was the first visitor just 3 hours later, simply by "surfing." By mid-November, the site had grown to 210 pages. It was formally launched with a series of on-air promotions during the first weekend of February, 1996.[336]

With the Communications Act of 1996, Congress mandated a conversion from analog to digital broadcasting. Anticipating that commercial stations might want to locate their antennas on a taller tower, and thus eliminate the "tower farms" along the Milwaukee River and Lincoln Creek, MATC requested proposals for a

"Classic Car Shop" with Roger Beavers and Jack Yaeger was an extremely popular MPTV production in the 1990s. (MPTV photo)

CHAPTER 8 ~ MPTV: CHANNELS 10 & 36   381

new, tall tower, which would be constructed on the same land on which the college had allowed WVTV to construct its. As it had previously, the new agreement allowed MPTV to locate its antennas on the new tower, and the college would receive a portion of any rental fees. Towercom Ltd. received the contract, which was later transferred to Omni America, and finally the American Tower Corp.

In early 1997, the Milwaukee Common Council approved a deed amendment necessary for the project to proceed.[337] WDJT-TV raised questions, which delayed approval by the Milwaukee Board of Zoning Appeals.[338] The Board finally approved the project on November 20[339], and ground was broken on March 16, 1998. The 1,220' tower was completed in June of 1999, and went on the air, using the WMVS analog transmitter and antenna for the first time at 1:48 a.m. on August 11, 1999 – twenty-two hours before the deadline set by the construction permit issued by the FCC.[340] At first, none of the major Milwaukee stations elected to locate their digital antennas on the new tower, and instead chose to use their existing units.[341] Later, several, including WCGV-DT, WVCY-DT, WPXE-DT and WVTV-DT did.

The first digital, HDTV broadcast in Milwaukee was made on October 29, 1998, when Channel 35, the digital channel assigned to WMVT, broadcast the launch of the space shuttle Discovery, with astronaut John Glenn. The station used a borrowed transmitter, and broadcast at low-power from the WVTV tower. (The station had gone on the air with a feed from the Kennedy Space Center the previous day.)[342]

Public television stations continued to struggle, as they tried to find new revenue sources. The switch to digital broadcasting would require significant expenditure of capital, which might tax available resources. In addition, the television environment was changing, and many cultural, scientific, and culinary shows, long-associated with public television, could now be seen on numerous cable channels. As a consequence, the Wisconsin legislature appointed a commission to study the future of public television in the state.[343]

Veteran Broadcaster Jim Peck returned to Milwaukee's airwaves on February 7, 1995, on the MPTV production "I Remember Milwaukee," an interview program featuring prominent residents of the area.[334] The first guest was former Milwaukee Mayor Frank Zeidler, who would return two more times. In the fall of 2001, the show's name was changed to "I Remember." While still featuring area residents, the show's guests now included prominent personalities from around the world who were visiting the area. (MPTV screen grab)

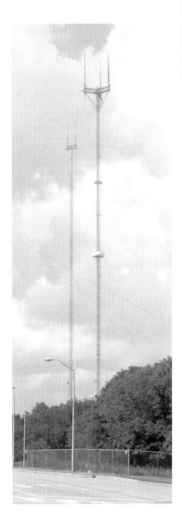

At the left is the WVTV tower completed in 1981. At the right is the new digital tower completed in 1999. Both are on land owned by MATC.

The commission issued its report on June 11, 1998. It recommended that that the state's eight public television stations be given the flexibility to create non-profit corporations to own them.[344] The idea was initially endorsed by MPTV manager Bryce Combs, and the Channel 10/36 friends offered to take the licenses if the state forced MATC to give them up. At a meeting of the MATC board on October 21, 1998, a passionate debate ensued. Former Milwaukee Mayor Frank Zeidler, who had battled for the city's educational reservation, was one of those who spoke against taking the licenses away from the college.[345]

The following day, the MATC board's Public Television Committee recommended that the college keep the licenses,[346] and the full board voted to do so on October 27.[347]

When Governor Tommy Thompson's state budget was released on February 16, 1999, it had no funds appropriated for public television. The governor indicated that if public television in the state was privatized, he would restore $2.6 million – 25 percent of which would go to MATC. He also proposed that that a community board be established made up of members he would appoint.[348]

The state continued to press the idea, and the Channel 10/36 Friends proposed that if that pressure continued, that control of the stations pass to a new, private, non-commercial organization in southeastern Wisconsin.[349] In that proposal, the Friends would have appointed eighty percent of the members of the proposed organization's new board.[350] The Republican-controlled State Assembly proposed that all public television stations be transferred to a new Wisconsin Public Broadcasting Corp., which would be controlled by a twenty-member board. The MATC president, and five persons nominated by the Channel 10/36 Friends, and approved by the governor would be members. The MATC board rejected that idea on June 23, 1999.[351]

The MATC board would have preferred that the Channel 10/36 Friends concur, so as to show solidarity in lieu if the state's proposal, but the fund raising group chose to keep its contingency proposal on the table, which angered college officials.[352]

The battle for control of the stations' licenses escalated in September when MATC president John Birkholz suspended – with pay – General Manager Bryce Combs and Director of Program Production Luise Fuzy. Officially, the suspensions were said to be because of a "personnel matter" involving a producer. Insiders (at the time) believed that both were suspended because of their perceived support for a plan to transfer the stations' licenses to a private entity, especially after Birkholz held a meeting in which he dramatically spelled out his opposition to such a proposal, and referred to the Channel 10/36 friends as "the enemy."[353]

Combs reached a settlement with the college, and on October 26, he announced his resignation. The same day, MATC President John Birkholz admitted that the personnel matter "...was related to philosophic differences related to the licenses..."[354]

Bryce Combs:

> The issue regarding the possible transfer of the licenses was that some within the stations wanted to preserve the status quo, involving a traditional public broadcasting service and the employment status of its staff. All public broadcasting stations are faced with fiscal challenges, and in Milwaukee as well, we were trying to anticipate and meet the future needs and interest of the viewers." [355]

Fuzy insisted that she had done nothing wrong, and that she wanted her job back.[356] However, she settled with MATC in December. Her settlement agreement did not

CHAPTER 8 ~ MPTV: CHANNELS 10 & 36   383

include a provision preventing her from speaking out on the license debate, and she insisted that the college was mismanaging the stations.[357]

On Tuesday, May 16, 2000, MATC dedicated its new 1,220 foot-tall digital television tower.[358] As they entered the digital age, channels 10 and 36 began rebranding themselves as "Milwaukee Public Television" (MPTV).

In June of 2000, Ellis Bromberg, who had run the University of Illinois' public television station WILL-TV, was named as general manager of MPTV.[359] He started on August 15.

On July 16, MPTV produced "The Great Circus Parade" as the first live, HDTV broadcast on PBS.[360]

After years of operating at less than its full, authorized power, WMVT finally boosted its signal in January of 2001. The antenna was mounted atop the new digital tower, which facilitated the power upgrade.[361]

Channel 10 and other public television stations broke with PBS in April of 2002, when they elected to rerun "Louis Rukeyser's Wall Street." Rukeyser had earlier been let go by PBS as the host of the long-running "Wall Street Week," and had been hired by MSNBC to host the new show. Viewer reaction to PBS' decision was negative, and prompted the stations to rerun Rukeyser's cable show.[362] (Rukeyser passed away in 2006.)

L-R: Kathleen Dunn, Joel McNally, moderator Dan Jones, Gerard Randall, and Kevin Fischer hold a lively discussion on "InterCHANGE." The show debuted on October 13, 1999 with Dunn, Fischer, McNally, and Eric Von as panelists. Mark Siegrist was the original moderator. Rick Horowitz provides commentary. (MPTV photo)

The new digital television technology gave stations the option to use the bandwidth to broadcast a single program in high-definition, or a number of programs in standard-definition on subchannels. WMVS-DT had broadcast on channel 8 since October of 1998. While it occasionally broadcast in high-definition, it usually multicast on five subchannels: one each for WMVS and WMVT and three others for various PBS feeds. On July 24, 2003, WMVT-DT made its debut on channel 35. It was the first, 24-hour, high-definition TV channel in Milwaukee.[363]

The Milwaukee County Historical Society published John Gurda's comprehensive book *The Making of Milwaukee* in 1999. Gurda then adapted the book into a television documentary – the most ambitious ever undertaken by MPTV. The three-part series ran October 9-11, 2006, and featured historical photographs, vintage film footage, animations, and re-enactments. All three nights, the shows drew

Patricia Gomez is the producer and hostess of "¡Adelente!," which explores issues of interest to the Hispanic community. The show made its debut in 1999. (MPTV photo)

the highest prime time ratings for any public TV station in the country.[364] The series helped to define MPTV's role as a public television affiliate that produced locally-oriented programming which commercial stations would not have attempted.

With the introduction of digital cable at the turn of the century, a certain amount of interactivity became possible, and viewers were able to order an increasing number of programs through their cable boxes. In April of 2007, "MPTV on Demand" was inaugurated in cooperation with Time-Warner Cable. The service allowed viewers to order MPTV-produced programs any time they wanted for a week after the shows first aired.

On May 5 of that year, MPTV launched "V-Me," public TV's first twenty-four hour, Spanish-language channel on one of its digital sub-channels. With a name taken from the Spanish for "see me," the service was a product of WNET-TV in New York, and private investors.[365]

After five years of almost constant battles, Milwaukee's first educational television station finally went on the air. Demand for instructional programming as well as an increase in the amount of cultural, art, and documentary programs obtained from NET, resulted in the start of a second educational station in the city. Both grew as NET gave way to PBS. Like all public television stations, MPTV has seen its share of

Melinda Myers hosted "Wisconsin's Lawn and Garden" on MPTV in 1996-99. In May of 2002, she began hosting a new show, "Great Lakes Gardener." (MPTV photo)

Produced in cooperation with the Milwaukee Turners, 4th Street Forum began in September of 2002, as a series of free, public discussions on that year's gubernatorial race. It later expanded to include other issues of interest to citizens of the area. (MPTV photo)

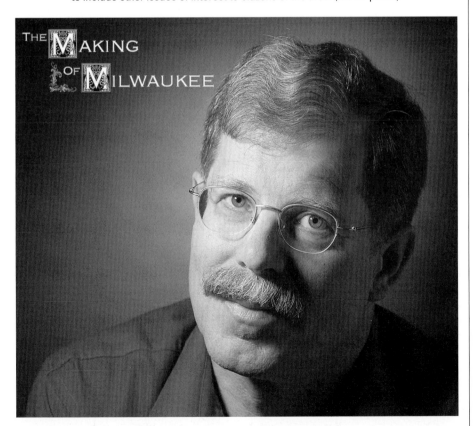

Local historian John Gurda's book *The Making of Milwaukee* was very successfully adapted into a series by MPTV in 2006. (MPTV photo)

Since 1958, MATC telecasting students have run one of the stations for a period of time each spring, as their final project. "Student Ops" have become a part of MPTV's educational legacy. (MPTV photo)

controversy, as new sources of financing had to be found. As television entered the digital age, MPTV emerged as a leader in the new technology. Despite a number of attempts to incorporate it into Wisconsin Public Television, it has remained independent – although it carries some of the state network's programming.

True to its educational mission, MPTV has trained thousands of telecasting students. As started in 1958, students continue to run one of the stations for most of a broadcast day as their final project. In an era where locally-produced shows on the commercial stations have been reduced to news/weather/sports, MPTV still manages to produce a number of shows – some of which are distributed nationally.

Had three local radio stations received grants in 1948, it is unlikely that Milwaukee would have had such a strong educational television history. All of the VHF channels would have been taken, and with the networks on them, there would've been little incentive for viewers to buy UHF converters or all-channel sets. In other cities where that occurred, educational television stations floundered on UHF. Milwaukee supported a station before New York, Los Angeles or Washington D.C. got theirs, and the demand was such that the city very quickly got a second educational channel.

In the same way that "educational television" gave way to "public television," the convergence of the internet with television may lead to a whole new way of looking at video – both for entertainment and education. That chapter will be written in the future…

FINE ARTS PROGRAMMING

Milwaukee Public Television has long supported the arts in the area. Performances by the Milwaukee Symphony Orchestra, the Milwaukee Ballet Company, the Florentine Opera, and the Milwaukee Repertory Theater are just some of the specials which have been featured over the years.

MPTV began airing live performances by the Milwaukee Symphony Orchestra in 1983. For a time, the audio was simulcast in stereo, on WHAD radio. (MPTV photo)

MPTV has also featured performances by the Milwaukee Ballet Company. Shown here are Jim Sutton and Susan O'Leary in "Coppelia." (MPTV photo)

"The Lunts: A Life in the Theatre" made its local debut on June 21, 1980, and was syndicated nationally by PBS. The documentary was shot at the couple's home, "Ten Chimneys" in Genesee Depot. Here the narrator/interviewer, renowned television director George Schaefer, is receiving a final touch-up to his make-up, while Lynn Fontanne waits at left. Schaefer had directed the Lunts in the Hallmark Hall of Fame production of "The Magnificent Yankee" in 1965, for which they received Emmy awards. Producer/Director Phillip Byrd is in the foreground. (MPTV photo)

CHILDREN'S PROGRAMMING

Children's programming began on WMVS-TV's first day on the air in 1957. Two of the programs shown were specifically aimed at children: "Friendly Giant" and "Children's Corner." The former was first produced by WHA-TV in Madison, and enjoyed a long run. The latter was produced by Fred Rogers at WQED in Pittsburgh, and featured Josie Carrie as host. Fred Rogers was the puppeteer, and wasn't seen on-camera![366]

Locally, telecasting students under the direction of Dr. Otto Schlaak produced "Wee Weekly," which followed the exploits of the staff of a mythical newspaper. The show was designed to teach children safety. The students handled all of the production duties, including the generation of program ideas, script writing, sound effects, cartoons, puppets, camera work, lighting, and direction.[367]

CHAPTER 8 ~ MPTV: CHANNELS 10 & 36   389

The cast of "Wee Weekly": (L-R) Wayne Gratton as "Doodles" the cartoonist, Mary Berndt as "Sandy Safety," and Rod Thole as editor "Jim Dandy." The puppets were (top) "Bear E. Tone," "Mr. Wise Owl," (bottom) "Frieda the Elephant" and "Beauregard Boo Boo." (Screen grab from MPTV kinescope)

Rod Thole played editor "Jim Dandy." Mary Berndt, a student at the University of Wisconsin – Milwaukee, portrayed "Sandy Safety," the feature editor. Wayne Gratton was "Doodles" the cartoonist. Gratton also designed and operated three pup-

Station manager Paul K. Taff (center) receives a public interest award from the National Safety Council recognizing the station's efforts to educate children about safety on the "Wee Weekly" show. Watching on the right is editor "Jim Dandy," who was played by telecasting student Rod Thole. (MPTV photo, courtesy of Paul K. Taff)

The original "Children's Fair" cast included (L-R): "Barkey the Barker" (Dick Wenzel), "Boo Boo" (manipulated by Wayne Gratton), "Miss Chris" (Joan Christopherson), "Frieda the Elephant" (manipulated by Alan Haushalter) and "Uncle Al" (Al Binford). At the bottom is Gratton's "Brownie Bear." (MPTV photo, courtesy of Joan Christopherson-Schmidt)

pets: "Mr. Wise Owl," "Beauregard Boo Boo," and "Bear E. Tone." The voice for the latter was provided by Henry Bartel, who was a student at the Milwaukee Institute of Technology, and UWM. Bartel also helped manipulate the puppets. The sound effects were produced by telecasting students Fred Grunert, Alan Haushalter, Walter Wilde, and Marcus Bodovinac.[368] Haushalter manipulated and provided the voice of "Frieda the Elephant."

Thole worked at WMVS after graduating, and later received a degree from the University of Wisconsin. He later served as production manager, and then program manager at Channels 10 and 36.

The first show ran on Tuesday, October 29, 1957; the last on May 31, 1961.

Another show produced by WMVS-TV was "Children's Fair." It was a variety show, featuring art, music and crafts. Al Binford, who was hired to direct the instructional programming for the Milwaukee Public Schools, served as the show's first host, "Uncle Al." Dick Wenzel of the MPS, played "Barkey the Barker," while Bayside art teacher Joan Christopherson, played "Miss Chris," who showed the youngsters art projects. Telecasting student Wayne Gratton manipulated his puppets, "Beauregard Boo Boo," and "Brownie Bear." The latter drew pictures for the children.[369] Gratton would go on to become the station's artist. His fellow telecasting student, Alan Haushalter, manipulated and provided the voice of "Frieda the Elephant." "Children's Fair" first ran on September 29, 1958. It later received awards from the Milwaukee Radio and Television Council, and was syndicated around the country by NET.

Dick Wenzel remembered:

> The first show I produced on Channel 10 was 'At Your Convenience'. It was a recreation-oriented thing. Then Otto [Schlaak] approached me one day and said, 'Would you be interested in doing a children's show? You'd be a lead character.'
>
> I said, 'Well, why not?'

We would literally find out what they [the writers] wanted to do and do it. It was strictly an ad lib situation. It was very much ahead of its time because it was open-concept shooting with no strings attached.³⁷⁰

The show was done live, and made for some interesting moments. As Joan Christopherson-Schmidt remembered:

Lemke and Gratton would write the script, and would usually hand it to me as I walked into the station. We'd often ad lib as we went along.

Sometimes we would sit on three stools and do the shows from them. The puppets would come over our shoulders, and we would be talking to them. I had the habit of taking my shoes off and curling my toes around one of the stool's cross-braces. Well, here over my shoulder comes 'Boo Boo', who says:

'Miss Chris! Miss Chris! Look what I found! Whose shoes are these? Do you know who they belong to? Maybe you want some!'

Then they panned down to my feet! So, I kept ad libbing:

'You know, I could use some shoes, because I lost mine someplace.'³⁷¹

She later found herself ad libbing a different scene while playing the "Story Princess":

After my son was born, I'd have to take him to the station with me once in awhile. Lois Robinson was at the front desk and she would hold him for a half hour while I did the show. This one time I had my son with me, but no one was there to watch him.

"Children's Fair" in its first incarnation. In the center (in cowboy hat) is host "Uncle Al" Binford. Kneeling and manipulating "Boo Boo" is Wayne Gratton. Joan Christopherson as "Miss Chris" is seated at the right. Kneeling at the far right, manipulating "Frieda the Elephant" is Alan Haushalter. (MPTV photo)

Leon Weissgerber hosted "No Doubt About It." (Screen grab from MPTV kinescope.)

So, I switched what I was going to do. I was the "Story Princess," and told the viewers that I had this wonderful little baby that had come to visit me in my castle in the clouds. Then I said:

'You can't tell a big, long story to a little baby. They wouldn't understand it. So, if nobody minds, I'm going to sing him some nursery rhymes, and if you know them out there, you sing along with me, ok? Because we have to entertain this little baby, and maybe teach him a few things.'

So I sang to him, 'Rock-a-Bye-Baby' and 'Twinkle, Twinkle Little Star'. This went fine until he got hungry. It was nursing time! That was one of the reasons I took him along, because I was going to nurse him. He started noodling. I did a few other things, and then said:

'It's kind of fun to have a baby on the show. We'll have to have him back again, but right now, I think I better take him to his mother! Bye boys and girls!'[372]

Leon Weissgerber of the Milwaukee Public Museum began hosting "No Doubt About It" on October 4, 1960. Aimed at older children and teenagers, the show was built around museum artifacts that Weissgerber would bring into the studio. The guests then tried to guess what the artifacts were. Viewers were also encouraged to call during the live program, and offer their guesses.[373] The last show was on December 19, 1966.

In the fall of 1958, Dr. Otto Schlaak was named to head up an NET study on programming for children 7-12 years old. Supported by the Ford Foundation, the study included the first broadcasts of an experimental program developed by the Educational Television Center called *What's New?* The segments of that program were designed to test the interests of the children participating in: the everyday world, their own bodies, the world unknown to them, appreciation, ethics and values.[374] Those segments which proved to be the most interesting to the children would then be shown by educational stations across the country. *What's New?* made its debut on October 26, 1959.[375]

WMVS-TV station manager Paul K. Taff, complained to NET at several affiliates' meetings about the lack of children's programs, as well as an inconsistency in their times. The quota of 45 minutes per day was sometimes met by three, fifteen-minute programs and at other times by a fifteen-minute program plus a half-hour program, making it difficult to schedule the shows and build an audience.

NET vice-president of programming, Bob Hudson, offered Taff the job, and the network's president, Jack White, came to Milwaukee and talked to him about it. Taff accepted, and became NET's first Director of Children's Programs.

One of his first missions was to find someone to host the revived and revised version of *What's New?*[376] Taff recruited Al Binford, who left WMVS-TV in June of 1963. Taff used a number of local affiliates to produce segments for the show, and both Leon Weissgerber and Murl Deusing of the Milwaukee Public Museum did so.

Leon Weissgerber replaced Binford as the host of "Children's Fair." Weissgerber, who hosted a number of other shows on Channel 10, played "Big Lee." Other characters who joined the show included "Cowboy Bill," a folk singer played by the station's continuity writer Bill Perrin, "Little Moonbeam," played by station secretary Noel Hildebrandt, "Halow Figley," the gumball concession operator, played in pantomime by Bill Hirst (who would later become "Hat-O" the clown on WTMJ-TV's "Kid's Klub"), and "King Louis," played by station manager Dr. Otto Schlaak. John Lemke, who joined the station as its film man and photographer, operated and provided the voices for the puppets "Ho Ho the Clown" and "Bernie Bear."[377] Wayne Gratton added "Grandma Boo Boo" (who always made her son peanut butter pie) to his menagerie of puppets. Besides doing art projects, Joan Christopherson-Schmidt also played the "Story Princess" in her castle in the clouds, and Rod Thole played "Ranger Don."

"Children's Fair" ended its long run on May 29, 1969. It impacted a generation, who still remembers. Joan Christopherson-Schmidt:

"The head of Milwaukee's Discovery World museum spoke at a Unitarian Forum that I attended. I walked in late, and sat down somewhere in the middle of the audience. You know how when someone recognizes another, how there's a gleam in their eye? Well, I sat down and his eyes lit up for a minute. I wondered where I might know him from.

He kept talking about Discovery World, and about how chil-

Al Binford left WMVS-TV to host *What's New?* (MPTV photo)

dren could learn about their world – now – with hands-on activities. Then he looked at me – pointed right at me – and said, "We want Discovery World to do for the kids – to inspire them to believe that they are somebody, and they can do something, the way "Miss Chris" inspired me when I was a little boy, watching her every day on channel 10.

I tell you my head went right up! That was my goal in television and for somebody to say that was very rewarding."[378]

NET affiliates were still asking for more children's programming. President Jack White asked them if they would each contribute $100 per week to fund it. Not all did. Nonetheless, enough funding was raised so that Paul K. Taff could buy the rights to *Friendly Giant* from the Canadian Broadcasting Corporation. The show had originated at WHA-TV in Madison, but co-creator Bob Homme had moved to Canada.[379]

Friendly Giant was a fifteen minute program. To fill a half-hour, Taff suggested to Fred Rogers, who was by that time doing *Mister Rogers' Neighborhood* at WQED in Pittsburgh, that he do a fifteen minute version for national distribution. Rogers declined, as he needed a half-hour to do his program. The NET Program Department wasn't interested in funding it, so Win Horton (NET Development Dept. and nephew of Hollywood's Edward Everett Horton) and Taff obtained a grant from the Sears Foundation.[380] *Mister Rogers' Neighborhood* went into national distribution with Taff as its first executive producer – and announcer!

With a grant from *McCall's* (through Norman Cousins) Taff later put a children's program study group together.[381] Many of the results of that study influenced the Children's Television Workshop, when it produced *Sesame Street*.

As first NET and then PBS offered affiliates more quality children's programming, local affiliates no longer chose to produce their own. The focus at MPTV shifted to community outreach projects, which tied into many of the PBS initiatives.

Darlyne Berg produced and hosted "You and I" on WITI-TV from 1974 to 1977. She was later hired by MPTV. In the summer of 1994, "Ready to Learn" was launched as a national effort by PBS, and Berg (now Haertlein) coordinated activities at MPTV. The program helps children – especially those from low-income families. The core of the program is a schedule of PBS programming. Locally, MPTV provides workshops, story times and other educational resources for families, teachers, and child care providers.

On-site "Ready to Learn" workshops are offered free to qualified groups, and include a basic workshop, as well as one in family literacy, anger management for children, writing, and diversity. Story times built around a theme are also offered

free and on-site for children aged four to seven. As a part of those programs, books are distributed to children who have little access to them.

"Vacation Station" is a summer project initiated in 1995. It too is based upon PBS programming, and encourages children aged six to twelve to make the best use of their summer vacation time. Included is a magazine, which is distributed at no-charge to local libraries, book review and art contests, and a club, which children are encouraged to join. The Milwaukee Art Museum also collaborates in the program by designing story times, art cart activities, and other programs tied to the magazine's theme.

Since 1995, MPTV has sponsored the "Reading Rainbow Young Writers and Illustrators Awards" program. Each January, a workshop is held at MPTV for adults and children who wish to enter the contest, but have no previous experience in writing or illustrating stories. Haertlein also does on-site writing workshops at schools, libraries, and community centers throughout the area, for children grades K-3. Approximately 1000 students participate in those workshops annually.[383] The children are then encouraged to enter an original, illustrated story in an appropriate age category. Locally, winners receive numerous prizes, while all receive a certificate of participation. The children's stories are narrated and edited with sound and music and air as their own program on both MPTV channels in June. The children's on-

The Milwaukee Public Museum's Leon Weissgerber replaced Al Binford as the host of "Children's Fair" in 1963. Here he's shown with "Bernie Bear" and "Boo Boo" (MPTV photo)

John Lemke manipulated "Bernie Bear" (MPTV photo)

"Ho Ho" and "Boo Boo" at the controls of a rocketship. (MPTV photo)

camera promo and stories air as interstitials for a year on MPTV. MPTV honors the winners, their families and teachers at an awards reception in May.

MPTV also produces "Kids in the Kitchen," a series of interstitials featuring children cooking food that is fresh and healthy. Taped in the MPTV studio in the kitchen set, each segment is one to six minutes long. Darlyne Haertlein works with the children, but all the recipes are simple enough for them to do with minimal adult intervention, and are easy to duplicate at home. The interstitials are designed to address the growing problem of childhood obesity in the United States.

In addition, MPTV conducts several drives tied-in to the children's programming:

For more than thirty years, Mister Rogers' familiar cardigan sweater represented the gentle spirit and warm nurturing environment of his neighborhood. Since 1998, MPTV sponsored a drive to collect new or freshly cleaned sweaters for families in

CHAPTER 8 ~ MPTV: CHANNELS 10 & 36   397

southeastern Wisconsin. 55,000 were given free of charge to families in need of a little extra warmth during Wisconsin's cold winters.

Clifford's Book Drive is held in November to coincide with "Children's Book Week." Its purpose is to collect new books for children who have very few, or none of their own. Fun activity sessions are offered for those donating new children's books at "Clifford's Day" at MPTV.[384]

MPTV started its "Letters to Santa" program as a project for MATC telecasting students, who produce, direct, and engineer the show.[382] (MPTV photo)

NOTES

1 "New Station to Be Opened for Radio Fans," *Wisconsin News/Milwaukee Telegram*, October 22, 1922.
2 S.E. Frost. Jr., PhD, Education's Own Stations: The History of Broadcast Licenses Issued to Educational Institutions. (Chicago: University of Chicago Press, 1937), 212.
3 This is based upon the fact that the initial lease was for three years, as well as that according to Frost (213) in its license application of December 30, 1930 WISN stated that the newspaper was the owner.
4 The Radio Editor, "The Wave Meter," *Milwaukee Journal*, September 26, 1922.
5 Agreement Between Marquette University and The Journal Co., January 23, 1925. *Milwaukee Journal* Stations. 1922-1969. Milwaukee Manuscript Collection 203. Wisconsin Historical Society. Milwaukee Area Research Center. UWM Libraries. University of Wisconsin-Milwaukee (Box 6, folder 1).
6 Robert McChesney, *Telecommunications, Mass Media, and Democracy: The Battle for Control of U.S. Broadcasting, 1928-1935.* (New York: Oxford University Press, 1994), 27.
7 Edwin B. Kurtz, *Pioneering in Educational Television*, (Ames: State University of Iowa Press, 1959) 10-11.
8 See Chapter 1 for more on Sanabria.
9 Christopher Sterling and John Kittross, *Stay Tuned: A Concise History of American Broadcasting* (East Windsor: Wadsworth Press, 1990), 159.
10 Section 307(a) of the Communications Act of 1934 nonetheless required the FCC to investigate the need for reserving radio frequencies for noncommercial, educational use. In response, in 1935 the Commission recommended against the reservation of frequen-

cies for educational use. Instead, it recommended greater cooperation between educators and the commercial stations and networks.

11 See Chapter 1 for further details on Apex radio.
12 "Lady Commissioner," *Broadcasting Telecasting*, June 28, 1948, 25, 62.
13 Federal Communications Commission, *Fourteenth Annual Report*. 1948, 12.
14 "Hints TV 'Monopoly' Got Her Out of FCC," *Milwaukee Journal*, April 4, 1958.
15 Jim Robertson, *Televisionaries: In Their Own Words Public Television's Founders Tell How It All Began* (Charlotte Harbor: Tabby House Books, 1993), 64.
16 Federal Communications Commission, *Notice of Further Proposed Rule Making*. FCC 49-948, July 11, 1949.
17 Ibid.
18 Telford Taylor, "Finding a Place for Education on TV," *The New York Times*, January 28, 1951.
19 Sharon Zechowski, *Educational Television*. The Museum of Broadcast Communications (website), http://www.museum.tv/archives/etv/E/htmlE/educationalt/educationalt.htm
20 *Televisionaries*, 57.
21 Susan L. Brinson, *Personal and Public Interests: Frieda B. Hennock and the Federal Communications Commission*. (Westport, CT/London: Praeger, 2002), 98.
22 U.S. Congress, Senate, *Official Report of Proceedings Before the Federal Communications Commission*, 82nd Congress, 1st session, October 24, 1950, Vol. 73, 13524-13525.
23 *Personal and Public Interests*, 97.
24 Ibid., 98.
25 Ibid., 97.
26 "Council Asks for More TV: Request to FCC," *Milwaukee Journal*, January 17, 1951.
27 Frank Zeidler, *Does Milwaukee Need a Non-Commercial, Educational Television Transmitter?* April 24, 1951, 2.
28 Ibid., 5.
29 "Educational Phase Ends: FCC to Start New Hearing," *Broadcasting Telecasting*, February 5, 1951, 57, 70.
30 Larry Christopher, "FCC Plans 2,000 TV Outlets: 10% to Educators," *Broadcasting Telecasting*, March 26, 1951, 19, 27-30.
31 Joan Stuller-Giglione, Allocation. The Museum of Broadcast Communications (website), http://www.museum.tv/archives/etv/A/htmlA/allocation/allocation.htm
32 "Revised Proposed TV Channel Allocations," *Broadcasting Telecasting*, March 26, 1951, 58c.
33 "FCC Plans 2,000 TV Outlets."
34 "Council Asks for More TV."
35 "Revised Proposed TV Channel Allocations."
36 Ibid.
37 David L. Lawrence, letter to Frank P. Zeidler, April 6, 1951, Frank P. Zeidler papers, Milwaukee Public Library, (Box 162, folder 2). Also see: *Does Milwaukee Need a Non-Commercial, Educational Television Transmitter?*, 7.
38 Ibid. Also see: "City Operated TV Station Proposed," *Milwaukee Journal*, March 13, 1951.
39 Ibid.
40 "City Radio Station Study is Ordered," *Milwaukee Journal*, April 8, 1947.
41 "City is Urged to Go On Air: Municipal Program Favored in Report by Librarian," *Milwaukee Journal*, May 23, 1947.
42 "Radio Time Offer is Given Okay," *Milwaukee Journal*, September 10, 1947.
43 "Series Opens Sept. 29," *Milwaukee Journal*, September 21, 1947
44 "County Radio Council to be Organized Here," *Milwaukee Journal*, October 23, 1946.
45 "Radio's Role Concern for New Council," *Milwaukee Journal*, January 5, 1947.
46 "County Radio Group is Set to Function," *Milwaukee Journal*, May 11, 1947.
47 "Radio's Role Concern for New Council."
48 Larry Christopher, "Allocation Delay: Hearing June 11; Deadlines Altered," *Broadcasting Telecasting*, April 16, 1951, 137, 146.
49 Clyde E. Sheets, letter to Milwaukee Common Council, April 12, 1951, Frank P. Zeidler papers, Milwaukee Public Library (Box 162, folder 2).
50 "Municipal TV Move Urged," *Milwaukee Journal*, April 17, 1951.
51 "Council's TV Talk Tangled," *Milwaukee Journal*, April 18, 1951.

52 Milwaukee Common Council Resolution, April 24, 1951, Frank P. Zeidler papers, Milwaukee Public Library (Box 162, folder 2). Also see: *Does Milwaukee Need a Non-Commercial, Educational Television Transmitter*, 3.
53 "Municipal TV Hearing is Set." *Milwaukee Journal*, May 2, 1951.
54 "Give Up TV City is Urged," *Milwaukee Journal*, May 8, 1951.
55 Ibid.
56 *Does Milwaukee Need a Non-Commercial, Educational Television Transmitter?*, 4.
57 "Comments on Proposed Allocations," *Broadcasting Telecasting*, May 14, 1951, 92.
58 *Does Milwaukee Need a Non-Commercial, Educational Television Transmitter?*, 5.
59 Ibid., 6.
60 "City to Appoint Group to Give It 'Picture' on TV," *Milwaukee Journal*, May 15, 1951.
61 "City Owned TV Study Set," *Milwaukee Journal*, May 17, 1951.
62 Harold B. McCarty, letter to Frank P. Zeidler, September 18, 1951, Frank P. Zeidler papers, Milwaukee Public Library (Box 162, folder 3).
63 "School Board Asks for TV," *Milwaukee Journal*, May 22, 1951.
64 Frank P. Zeidler, "Reply and Comments of the City of Milwaukee to the 'Appearance and Comments' Filed By Wisconsin Broadcasting System, Inc. (WFOX) and Hearst Radio, Inc. (WISN)," (submitted by City Attorney Walter J. Mattison), Frank P. Zeidler papers, Milwaukee Public Library (Box 162, folder 2). Also see: "'Partial' Freeze Lift? FCC Action Expected Soon," *Broadcasting Telecasting*, May 28, 1951, 59, 66.
65 "Group Argues City TV Value," *Milwaukee Journal*, May 23, 1951.
66 Harry G. Slater, letter to Milwaukee Common Council, June 18, 1951, 1951, Frank P. Zeidler papers, Milwaukee Public Library (Box 162, folder 2).
67 "City Owned TV Cost Told," *Milwaukee Journal*, June 20, 1951.
68 Carl F. Kinnel, letter to Milwaukee Common Council, July 25, 1951, Frank P. Zeidler papers, Milwaukee Public Library (Box 162, folder 4).
69 "City TV Plan is Set Back by Council Group Vote," *Milwaukee Journal*, July 24, 1951.
70 "TV Backers Win a Round," *Milwaukee Journal*, August 1, 1951.
71 "City's Position on TV Asked," *Milwaukee Journal*, August 5, 1951.
72 William Rasche, letter to Frank P. Zeidler, August 23, 1951, Frank P. Zeidler Papers, Milwaukee Public Library (Box 162, folder 2). Also see: *Sworn Statement of Milwaukee Vocational and Adult Schools*. August, 1951.
73 "Station Offered for School TV," *Milwaukee Journal*, August 24, 1951.
74 *Sworn Statement of Milwaukee Vocational and Adult Schools*.
75 Rasche, letter to Zeidler, August 23, 1951.
76 *Milwaukee Needs Educational Television: Sworn Statement of Milwaukee Educators' Committee on Television*, September 1951.
77 "Continue City TV Argument," *Milwaukee Journal*, September 5, 1951.
78 "Council Stalls Action on TV," *Milwaukee Journal*, September 12, 1951.
79 "City TV Plan Again Is Hit," *Milwaukee Journal*, September 19, 1951.
80 *Milwaukee Needs Educational Television: Sworn Statement of Milwaukee Educators' Committee on Television*.
81 Milwaukee Educators' Committee on Television, *Summary of Facts in Support of Non-Commercial Educational Television for Milwaukee on VHF Channel 10*.
82 "Groups Back Channel 10," *Milwaukee Journal*, September 22, 1951.
83 "Council Stalls TV Decision," *Milwaukee Journal*, September 26, 1951.
84 "Public Owned TV Rejected," *Milwaukee Journal*, October 10, 1951.
85 Frank P. Zeidler, letter to Milwaukee Common Council, October 16, 1951, Frank P. Zeidler Papers, Milwaukee Public Library (Box 55, folder 8). Also see: "Mayor Vetoes Action on TV," *Milwaukee Journal*, October 16, 1951.
86 "Stations Sign Pledge on TV," *Milwaukee Journal*, October 18, 1951.
87 "Mayor's Veto on TV Upheld," *Milwaukee Journal*, October 24, 1951.
88 "Council Ends Video Debate," *Milwaukee Journal*, November 7, 1951.
89 Alma Bartell, letter to Frank P. Zeidler, November 26, 1951, Frank P. Zeidler papers, Milwaukee Public Library (Box 162, folder 3).
90 Federal Communications Commission, *Sixth General Report and Order*, April 14, 1952, Section 572(l).
91 "TV Applicants Ask for Revisions," *Broadcasting Telecasting*, March 3, 1952, 6.
92 "WEMP Seeks a TV License: Channel 6 Requested," *Milwaukee Journal*, March 6, 1952.

93 "WEMP Amendment Opposed," *Broadcasting Telecasting*, March 10, 1952, 94.
94 *Sixth General Report and Order*, Section 572(i).
95 *Sixth General Report and Order*, Section 575.
96 *Sixth General Report and Order*, Section 574.
97 *Sixth General Report and Order*, Section 572 (h).
98 *Sixth General Report and Order*, Section 573.
99 *Sixth General Report and Order*, Section 214.
100 *Sixth General Report and Order*, Section 209.
101 Paul A. Walker, transcript of Address to NAEB, April 18, 1952, Frank P. Zeidler papers, Milwaukee Public Library (Box 162, folder 4). Also see: "Don't Lag in TV, Walker Tells Schools," *Broadcasting Telecasting*, April 21, 1952, 5.
102 "School Video Action Urged," *Milwaukee Journal*, April 20, 1952.
103 Resolution by Alderman LaBelle, File No. 52-316. Frank P. Zeidler Papers, Milwaukee Public Library (Box 163, folder 1).
104 Frank P. Zeidler, letter to Milwaukee Common Council, May 12, 1952, Frank P. Zeidler Papers, Milwaukee Public Library (Box 55, folder 9 & Box 162, folder 4), Also see: "Zeidler Tunes Out TV Quiz," *Milwaukee Journal*, May 9, 1952.
105 "Mayor's Veto on TV Loses," *Milwaukee Journal*, May 21, 1952.
106 "Asks Support for School TV," *Milwaukee Journal*, May 20, 1952.
107 "Carries Fight to Educators," *Milwaukee Journal*, May 20, 1952
108 "Hearing is Set on Channel 10," *Milwaukee Journal*, January 27, 1953.
109 Robert J. Riordan, "Milwaukee Can Have More Television: Vocational School Has a Plan, But Financing is Something Else," Milwaukee *Sentinel*, July 30, 1952.
110 Robert J. Riordan, "Milwaukee Can Have More Television: Bravoes Have Died Away Since FCC Reserved Channel for Education," Milwaukee *Sentinel*, July 31, 1952.
111 *Personal and Public Interests*, 134.
112 "Action Urged on School TV," *Milwaukee Journal*, June 6, 1952.
113 Wisconsin Citizen's Committee for Educational Television, *These Are the Facts About Educational Television in Wisconsin*, 1954. The entire letter was published in: Doudna, Bill, "Bill Doudna's Spotlight: TV for Education," *The Wisconsin State Journal*, September 22, 1952.
114 *Televisionaries*, 87-88.
115 Robert La Follette, Jr., letter to: Milwaukee Board of Vocational Education, Board of Regents of the University of Wisconsin & Wisconsin State Radio Council, August 20, 1952, Frank P. Zeidler papers, Milwaukee Public Library (Box 162, folder 5).
116 "Open Up Way for School TV," *Milwaukee Journal*, October 10, 1952.
117 "Board Rehires TV Consultant: School Plans Circuit," *Milwaukee Journal*, July 10, 1953.
118 "Judge Curbs Action on TV," *Milwaukee Journal*, October 15, 1952.
119 Frank P. Zeidler, letter to Milwaukee Common Council, October 27, 1952 Frank P. Zeidler Papers, Milwaukee Public Library (Box 55, folder 9 & Box 162, folder 5).
120 "Zeidler Veto Counters Educational TV Slap," *Milwaukee Journal*, October 26, 1952.
121 "Powerful Forces Seek to Block Channels for School Use, an FCC Member Says," *Milwaukee Journal*, October 26, 1952.
122 "TV Sales Tax Plan Shelved," *Milwaukee Journal*, November 21, 1952.
123 "Group to Draft State TV Bill: Network for Education," *Milwaukee Journal*, November 20, 1952.
124 "Judge Eases Writ Against TV at School," *Milwaukee Journal*, October 29, 1952.
125 "Zeidler Veto Upheld 14-12," *Milwaukee Journal*, November 6, 1952.
126 "TV Channels Plea Rejected: Decision by FCC," *Milwaukee Journal*, November 14, 1952.
127 "School Video Station Here Seen in 1953: Dismissal of Taxpayer Suit Expected; FCC Application Will Be Filed Monday," Milwaukee *Journal*, November 23, 1952. Also see: "Taxpayer Suit to Bar School TV Withdrawn," *Milwaukee Sentinel*, November 23, 1952.
128 Stipulation Re: State of Wisconsin, Milwaukee County Circuit Court, Edwin Zedler v. Milwaukee Board of Vocational Education et. al., November 24, 1952, Frank P. Zeidler Papers, Milwaukee Public Library (Box 162, folder 5). "Anti-TV Suit Dropped," *Milwaukee Journal*, November 25, 1952.

CHAPTER 8 ~ MPTV: CHANNELS 10 & 36

129 "FCC Gets Plea for School TV: Petition by Raasche," *Milwaukee Journal*, November 25, 1952, Part M, 21.
130 Edward F. Ryan, "McCarthy Plays a Role in TV Channel 10 Fight," *Milwaukee Journal*, May 17, 1953. (Reprinted from *The Washington Post*) Also see: Arthur L. Olszyk, *Live… At the Scene*, (Milwaukee: self-published, 1993), 50-51.
131 Ibid.
132 "Hearing is Set on Channel 10.
133 "For the Record," *Broadcasting Telecasting*, February 16, 1953, 113.
134 "Income, Power Tax Proposed for State TV," *Milwaukee Sentinel*, February 5, 1953. Also see: "Bill Will Propose State Owned TV," *Milwaukee Journal*, February 7, 1953.
135 "Okay Lease of TV Tower," *Milwaukee Journal*, February 6, 1953.
136 "Fate in Doubt for School TV," *Milwaukee Journal*, February 9, 1953.
137 "Teachers Get TV Warning," *Milwaukee Journal*, February 15, 1953. Also see: "Education TV Opportunity," *Milwaukee Journal*, February 21 1953.
138 "Station WISN TV is Asked: Congressmen Write," *Milwaukee Journal*, March 13, 1953.
139 Ibid.
140 *Live…At the Scene*, 50.
141 "Station WISN TV is Asked."
142 "McCarthy Plays a Role in TV Channel 10 Fight." Also see: *Live…At the Scene*, 50-51.
143 Ibid.
144 "Argue WISN Right to Channel 10," *Milwaukee Sentinel*, February 17, 1953.
145 "FCC Weighs Plea For TV," *Milwaukee Journal*, February 17, 1953.
146 Ibid.
147 "Urges Action on School TV," *Milwaukee Journal*, February 17, 1953.
148 "Seek Funds for 2 State TV Channels," *Milwaukee Sentinel*, February 17, 1953.
149 Robert J. Riordan, "Vocational TV Station Bill Debated at Hearing," *Milwaukee Sentinel*, March 18, 1953.
150 Ibid.
151 Ibid.
152 "22 Aldermen Oppose Voc TV Station," *Milwaukee Sentinel*, March 18, 1953.
153 "Alderman Hits School TV Bill: Circulates Petition," *Milwaukee Journal*, March 13, 1953.
154 "Bill Offered to Authorize School TV," *Milwaukee Sentinel*, March 20, 1953.
155 Federal Communications Commission, *Memorandum Opinion and Order*, FCC 53-359. April 1, 1953. Frank P. Zeidler Papers, Milwaukee Public Library (Box 163, folder 1). Also see: "Deny WISN Channel 10: Commissioners Say Band is Limited to Educational Use," *Milwaukee Journal*, April 1, 1953.
156 "Aid Promised to School TV," *Milwaukee Journal*, April 5, 1953.
157 "McCarthy Plays a Role in TV Channel 10 Fight." Also see: *Live…At the Scene*, 50-51
158 "Closed Circuit," *Broadcasting Telecasting*, April 13, 1953, 5.
159 "Closed Circuit," *Broadcasting Telecasting*, April 20, 1953, 5.
160 McCarthy called such meetings an "executive session,"
161 "McCarthy Plays a Role in TV Channel 10 Fight." Also see: *Live…At the Scene*, 50-51
162 McCarthy is speaking of The Journal Company's WTMJ-TV, which was at the time the only TV station on the air in the area. At the time, Hearst's *Milwaukee Sentinel*, and *Milwaukee Journal* were rival newspapers. The Journal Co. bought the morning paper from Hearst in 1962.
163 "McCarthy Plays a Role in TV Channel 10 Fight." Also see: *Live…At the Scene*, 50-51
164 Paul A. Walker, letter to Hon. Frank Zeidler, April 14, 1953. Frank P. Zeidler Papers, Milwaukee Public Library, (Box 163, folder 1).
165 "Hearst Asks Review of Ch. 10 Denial," *Broadcasting Telecasting*, April 20, 1953, 66.
166 "WISN TV Channel 10 Petition Denied Again By FCC," *Milwaukee Sentinel*, July 2, 1953.
167 "McCarthy Plays a Role in TV Channel 10 Fight." Also see: *Live…At the Scene*, 50-51
168 "School Video Bills Opposed," *Milwaukee Journal*, April 21, 1953.
169 "Mayor Vetoes TV Opposition," *Milwaukee Journal*, May 11, 1953.
170 "Council Raps Education TV: Overrides a Veto," *Milwaukee Journal*, May 21, 1953.
171 "Group Favors TV Network," *Milwaukee Journal*, May 3, 1953.

172 "State Owned TV is Backed," *Milwaukee Journal*, May 6, 1953.
173 Lou Poller, letter to Mr. H. J. Van Valkenburg, Wisconsin Association for Vocational Education, May 4, 1953. Frank P. Zeidler Papers, Milwaukee Public Library (Box 163, folder 1). Also see: "Offer to School," *Milwaukee Journal*, May 5, 1953.
174 "Statement of Senator Charles W. Tobey (R. N.H.), Chairman Senate Committee on Interstate and Foreign Commerce," May 11, 1953. Frank P. Zeidler Papers, Milwaukee Public Library (Box 163, folder 1). Also see:
"Tobey Warns FCC on Channels Issue," *Broadcasting Telecasting*, May 18, 1953, 47. "TV Channels Are Clarified: Rights Not Expiring," *Milwaukee Journal*, May 12, 1953.
175 Ibid.
176 Federal Communications Commission, "Educational Television Channel Reservations," FCC Public Notice 90136, May 11, 1953. Frank P. Zeidler Papers, Milwaukee Public Library (Box 163, folder 1).
177 Walter Kohler, telegram to FCC Chairman Rosel H. Hyde, May 12, 1953 (typed copy). Frank P. Zeidler Papers, Milwaukee Public Library Box 163, folder 1). Also see: "Favors State on TV Issue," *Milwaukee Journal*, May 14, 1953.
178 "Doerfer Advised Wisconsin to Seek Educational TV," *Broadcasting Telecasting*, July 13, 1953, 11.
179 : "Favors State on TV Issue."
180 "Doerfer Advised Wisconsin to Seek Educational TV."
181 "Channel 10 Contest Seen: Governor Directed to Apply for Educational TV Rights," *Milwaukee Journal*, May 13, 1953.
182 Frank Zeidler, telegram to Governor Walter Kohler, May 14, 1953 (copy). Frank P. Zeidler Papers, Milwaukee Public Library (Box 163, folder 1. Also see: "Favors State on TV Issue."
183 Ibid.
184 "State Applies to FCC for 12 TV Channels," *Milwaukee Journal*, May 19, 1953.
185 "State TV Bill Death Urged," *Milwaukee Journal*, May 20, 1953.
186 "Hennock Opposes Wisconsin Ch. 10 Bid," *Broadcasting Telecasting*, May 25, 1953, 66.
187 "Sees Pressure for Channel 10," *Milwaukee Journal*, May 17, 1953.
188 "State Applies to FCC for 12 TV Channels."
189 "Kohler Urges Start on School TV in Capital," *Milwaukee Journal*, May 21, 1953.
190 "School TV Bill Passes Senate," *Milwaukee Journal*, May 22, 1953.
191 "Vote is a Jolt to School TV," *Milwaukee Journal*, May 28, 1953.
192 "Planning Set on School TV," *Milwaukee Journal*, July 2, 1953.
193 "Channel 21 Asked for State," *Milwaukee Journal*, June 2, 1953.
194 "Hearst TV Bid Again Rejected," *Milwaukee Journal*, July 1, 1953.
195 "Closed Circuit," *Broadcasting Telecasting*, July 13, 1953, 5.
196 "Why State Democratic Chairman Among Five New TV Grantees: In Last Week's Grants, FCC Again Awards VHF Ch. 2 at Midland Tex., and Issues First Grant for Alaska. Hearst Corp.'s Plea for VHF Ch. 10 in Milwaukee is Turned Down," *Broadcasting Telecasting*, July 6, 1953, 56.
197 *The Hearst Corp. v FCC*. United States Court of Appeals for the District of Columbia. July 15, 1953. Frank P. Zeidler Papers, Milwaukee Public Library (Box 163, folder 2). Also see: "Hearst Appeals FCC Ch. 10 Denial," *Broadcasting Telecasting*, July 20, 1953, 52. "Plans Appeal of TV Ruling: WISN Seeks Channel," *Milwaukee Journal*, April 7, 1953.
198 "State Radio Body Fights TV Appeal," *Milwaukee Journal*, July 26, 1953.
199 "FCC to Delay Action on TV," *Milwaukee Journal*, September 16, 1953.
200 "Hearst Asks Ch. 6," *Broadcasting Telecasting*, October 5, 1953, 33. Also see: "Seek Channel Shift for Extra TV Here," *Milwaukee Sentinel*, October 1, 1953.
201 "Ch. 6 Proposal," *Broadcasting Telecasting*, October 12, 1953.
202 "Hearst Ch. 10 Appeal Delay," *Broadcasting Telecasting*, October 19, 1953, 50.
203 "TV Channel 6 Given to 'Bay,'" *Milwaukee Journal*, December 4, 1953.
204 Paul K. Taff, Facsimile correspondence to Ellis Bromberg, May 8, 2006.
205 "Four Join Faculty to Direct School's New TV Activities," *Vocational School News*, Vol. XXX, No. 5, March 24, 1954.
206 "State Defers Action on TV Channel 10," *Milwaukee Journal*, August 3, 1954.
207 *Vocational School News*, Vol. XXXI, No. 1, October 29, 1954.

208 Wisconsin Committee on State-Owned, Tax-Supported Television, Inc., *The Proposed Wisconsin State-Owned, Tax-Supported, Educational Television Network: A Report*. September, 1954.
209 "Group Backs 'No' Vote," *Milwaukee Journal*, October 23, 1954.
210 "Education TV Vote Debated," *Milwaukee Journal*, October 23, 1954.
211 "Educational TV Loses; Vote is More Than 2-1," *Milwaukee Journal*, November 3, 1954.
212 *Televisionaries*, 134.
213 "Plea Renewed for School TV," *Milwaukee Journal*, December 16, 1955. Also see: "Voc School Again Seeks TV Channel," *Milwaukee Sentinel*, December 16, 1955.
214 "School TV Given Start, Then Stalled By Group," *Milwaukee Journal*, December 21, 1955.
215 "School's First TV Program is Being Telecast on WTMJ-TV," *Vocational School News*, Vol. XXXII, No. 3, January 23, 1956.
216 *Vocational School News*, Vol. XXXII, No. 2, December 16, 1955.
217 "Path Cleared for School TV: Milwaukee Vocational Now Sole Applicant for Channel 10," *Milwaukee Journal*, January 12, 1956.
218 Start Dispute on School TV," *Milwaukee Journal*, January 15, 1956.
219 "Educational TV Station Will Start on Monday," *Milwaukee Journal*, October 25, 1957.
220 "Vocational School Vote Starts Educational TV: Institution Will Apply for Channel and Build Station Here; Has Aid of Ford Foundation." *Milwaukee Journal*, March 22, 1956. Also see: "Vocational Board Agrees on TV Outlay," *Milwaukee Sentinel*, March 22, 1956.
221 "FCC Approves Voc School TV Channel," *Milwaukee Sentinel*, June 7, 1956.
222 "School Pushes Educational TV Station Plans," *Milwaukee Journal*, June 7, 1956.
223 "Vocational School to use WITI Tower," *Milwaukee Journal*, April 3, 1957. Also see: "WMVS, Educational Channel 10, Next in Sight for TV Viewers," *Vocational School News*, Vol. XXXII, No. 1, October 18, 1956.
224 Paul K. Taff, email to the author, July 19, 2006.
225 "Contracts Let for School TV," *Milwaukee Journal*, April 12, 1957.
226 "WMVS-TV Program Gains with N.Y. Network's Aid," *Milwaukee Sentinel*, September 22, 1957.
227 "Voc Students to Learn by Helping ETV Teach," *Milwaukee Sentinel*, September 23, 1957.
228 "Educational TV Debut Riles Braves Fans Here," *Milwaukee Sentinel*, September 21, 1957.
229 Jerry Cahill, "Educational TV Starts Broadcasts," *Milwaukee Sentinel*, October 29, 1957.
230 "It's a Big Day, Rasche Exclaims as Educational TV Makes Debut," *Milwaukee Journal*, October 28, 1957.
231 Ibid.
232 Ibid.
233 "Educational TV Starts Broadcasts."
234 Taff, July 19, 2006.
235 Bob Barry, email to the author, July 21, 2006.
236 "List Courses for TV's Use: Lessons to be Given," *Milwaukee Journal*, January 4, 1958.
237 Balopticons were produced by Bausch and Lomb, and projected slide-like images called "Balops,"
238 Kinescopes captured the image sent to a television receiver on 16mm film. Prior to the development of videotape in 1956, they were the only way to record television programs.
239 "City 'TV School' Holds Trial Run," *Milwaukee Sentinel*, January 4, 1958.
240 Taff, July 19, 2006.
241 Robert R. Suchy, and Paul C. Baumann, *Milwaukee Experiment in Instructional Television: The Evaluation Report for the 1957-1958 School Year*. September, 1958, 47-48.
242 "TV Students Work More, Teacher Says," *Milwaukee Sentinel*, February 20, 1958.
243 "Channel 10 Offers College Credit Class," *Milwaukee Sentinel*, February 9, 1958.
244 "Extend Education TV to 5 Schools," *Milwaukee Sentinel*, June 1, 1958.
245 Sister Gilmary Lemberg, interview with the author, October 13, 2006.

246 Eugene Horn, "Archdiocesan Television Classes Enter Sixth Year; Technique Gains Acceptance," *Catholic Herald Citizen*, September 26, 1964.
247 "TV Students Take Over WMVS Friday," *Milwaukee Sentinel*, June 1, 1958.
248 "First TV Study Sessions Set for Sept. 15," *Milwaukee Sentinel*, September 3, 1958.
249 Taff, May 8, 2006.
250 Donald H. Dooley, "Videotape Goes to School," *Milwaukee Journal*, July 26, 1959.
251 "TV Applicants Face Deadline," *Milwaukee Journal*, February 21, 1960.
252 "School Unit OK's Bid for New TV Channel," *Milwaukee Journal*, June 17, 1960. Also see: Jerry Cahill, "Voc Board Seeks 2nd TV Outlet," *Milwaukee Sentinel*, June 17, 1960.
253 "Vincent Will Request Use of Classroom TV," *Milwaukee Journal*, March 27, 1960.
254 "UHF Channel Added for Educational TV," *Milwaukee Journal*, January 27, 1961.
255 "Pupils' Scores Up With TV Tests," *Milwaukee Sentinel*, March 28, 1962.
256 "TV Leaders to Convene: Educational Stations," *Milwaukee Journal*, March 12, 1961.
257 "US Will Seek Funds For Educational Video," *Milwaukee Journal*, May 10, 1961.
258 "'The Inquiring Mind' to begin on WMVS-TV," *Milwaukee Sentinel*, August 27, 1961.
259 "FCC Okays Channel 36: Educational Station," *Milwaukee Journal*, February 24, 1962. Also see: "FCC Grants UHF TV Channel to Voc," *Milwaukee Sentinel*, February 24, 1962.
260 "TV Station Aims Given," *Milwaukee Journal*, March 14, 1962.
261 "TV Class to Instruct Milwaukee Illiterates," *Milwaukee Journal*, July 16, 1962.
262 "TV Will Help Poor Readers," *Milwaukee Journal*, October 21, 1962.
263 "88 Finish 'Alphabet' Class on TV," *Milwaukee Journal*, March 15, 1963.
264 "WMVS-TV Plans to Write Off Class for Milwaukee Illiterates," *Milwaukee Journal*, February 3, 1963.
265 *Educational Television*.
266 "WMVT Wants $167,475 Grant," *Milwaukee Journal*, July 16, 1963.
267 "Trim urged for TV Funds: Plan for Schools," *Milwaukee Journal*, October 26, 1963.
268 "WMVT Given $167,475," *Milwaukee Journal*, April 24, 1964.
269 Robertson later wrote a history of early public television which is referenced in this chapter!
270 "Second Educational TV Station On Air," *Milwaukee Journal*, January 29, 1963.
271 "Circus Parade Telecast Slated," *Milwaukee Journal*, July 16, 1963.
272 Carolyn N. Brooks, *National Educational Television Center.*, The Museum of Broadcast Communications (website), http://www.museum.tv/archives/etv/N/htmlN/nationaleduc/nationaleduc.htm.
273 Robert Pepper, and Robert Avery, "The Interconnection-Connection: The Formation of PBS," *Public Telecommunications Review*, January/February, 1976, 9. Also see: Stone, David M., *Nixon and the Politics of Public Television* (New York: Garland, 1985), 17.
274 Mary Bader, "Educational TV Brightens Up. *Milwaukee Journal*, September 30, 1964.
275 For a discussion of the complete story on the commission's establishment, see: *Televisionaries*, chapter 23.
276 Jim Wulliman, email to the author, July 17, 2006.
277 "1st Educational Color Series by Channel 10," *Milwaukee Sentinel*, January 20, 1965. Also see: "Obsolete Equipment Puts WMVS on Air With Color," *Milwaukee Journal*, January 20, 1965.
278 A handful of educational TV stations had broadcast the occasional show in color, but none had done so on a regular basis.
279 Jim Wulliman,, email to the author, July 18, 2006.
280 Nels Harvey, email to the author, January 27, 2006.
281 "Bits of Show Business," *Milwaukee Journal*, January 29, 1965.
282 "Public Operation Proposed for ETV," *Milwaukee Sentinel*, May 19, 1965.
283 *Educational Television*.
284 WMVS and WMVT *Hi-Lites*, Vol. 8, Issue 2, October, 1966, 1.
285 "New Group to Push Educational TV Aims," *Milwaukee Journal*, May 11, 1967.
286 Dick Wenzel, interview with author, September 14, 2007.
287 "WMVS, WMVT Get Aid for Color," *Milwaukee Journal*, August 19, 1966.
288 Mary Kay Larson, "New Slant on the News From NET," *Milwaukee Journal*, November 5, 1967.
289 *National Educational Television Center*.
290 Ibid.

291 Ralph Dannheisser, "Celebrity Auction Will Aid Educational TV," *Milwaukee Sentinel*, January 7, 1969.
292 Jack Lee, interview with author, November 28, 2007.
293 "School Gets New Name," *Milwaukee Sentinel*, June 4, 1964.
294 "Name Change Disputed, but 'Area' Added to MTC," *Milwaukee Journal*, September 17, 1969. Also see: "Voc School Undergoes Fourth Name Change," *Milwaukee Sentinel*, September 22, 1969.
295 "Station WMVT Will Be WMTC," *Milwaukee Journal*, June 18, 1970.
296 "Education at the Flick of TV Dial Planned Here," *Milwaukee Journal*, July 13, 1969.
297 The name had been used in the early 1960s.
298 "Channel 10's Pull Ranked Among Best," *Milwaukee Journal*, March 11, 1972.
299 "MATC Seeks Nike Site in River Hills," *Milwaukee Sentinel*, July 20, 1972.
300 Harvey, January 27, 2006.
301 "Stations Get Grants for New Antennas," *Milwaukee Journal*, July 21, 1975.
302 "School Bias Suit Foes Meet on '10,'" *Milwaukee Sentinel*, February 22, 1974.
303 "School Hearing Aired Live," *Milwaukee Sentinel*, May 13, 1976.
304 "TV Tower Plan Receives Backing," *Milwaukee Sentinel*, March 10, 1977. Also see: "TV Tower Need, Board Says," *Milwaukee Journal*, March 11, 1977.
305 "Panel OKs Loan to Build TV Tower," *Milwaukee Sentinel*, March 24, 1977.
306 Michael H, Drew, "'Atlantis' Should Be Scuttled," *Milwaukee Journal*, September, 1977.
307 James Kilpatrick, "TV on Trial," *Milwaukee Journal*, November 17, 1978.
308 "California to Give TV a Court Test," *Milwaukee Journal*, December 13, 1978.
309 Ed Hinshaw, email to author, July 10, 2008.
310 "California to Give TV a Court Test."
311 "Courtroom TV Gets Real Test," *Milwaukee Journal*, November 17, 1978.
312 "Spanish Criticize TV Trial Coverage," *Milwaukee Journal*, November 27, 1978.
313 "TV Rules for Trial Issued," *Milwaukee Journal*, November 10, 1978.
314 Milo Bergo, "Most Seem Satisfied With Telecast of Trial," *Milwaukee Journal*, December 18, 1978.
315 Michael H, Drew, "Stronger Signals: New Antennas Should Boost 10/36 Audience," *Milwaukee Journal*, April 29, 1981.
316 "Channel 10 Goes Stereo," *Kenosha News*, June 30, 1985.
317 "Channel 36 Switch Seen As Fundraiser," *Milwaukee Journal*, December 19, 1985.
318 Ibid.
319 "Axtell Named Manager at 10/36," *Milwaukee Journal*, December 21, 1985.
320 Tom Axtell, email to the author, January 12, 2007.
321 Duane Dudek, "WMVS Brings Captain Kangaroo, Blimp, '3-D' Sound to Parade," *Milwaukee Sentinel*, July 14, 1988.
322 Duane Dudek, "McCullough Bows Out as Anchor Man," *Milwaukee Sentinel*, November 23, 1988. Also see: Michael H, Drew, "McCullough An Anchor of Stability," *Milwaukee Journal*, November 23, 1988.
323 Duane Dudek, "Antenna will help Channel 36 Return to Regular Schedule," *Milwaukee Sentinel*, March 15, 1989.
324 Gretchen Schuldt, "4 MATC Administrators Fired," *Milwaukee Sentinel*, February 9, 1991.
325 Jim Stingl, "Holmes Defends Stormy Firing of 4 MATC Officials," *Milwaukee Journal*, February 9, 1991.
326 Stan McCoy, "Controversy at MATC Cost Public TV $10,000, Report Says," *Milwaukee Journal*, November 9, 1993.
327 Bryce Combs, interview with author, November 24, 2006.
328 Duane Dudek, "City Will Have Starring Role with HDTV Documentary," *Milwaukee Sentinel*, May 25, 1992.
329 Joel Brinkley, *Defining Vision: The Battle For the Future of Television*. (New York: Harcourt Brace & Co., 1997), 212-213.
330 Combs, November 24, 2006.
331 Michael H, Drew, "Cutting Local Shows May Be First of Changes at Channels 10/36," *Milwaukee Journal*, February 18, 1994.
332 Tim Cuprisin, "Channel 10 Parts Company With Smith," *Milwaukee Journal*, October 5, 1994.

333 Tim Cuprisin, "Channels 4 and 10 Further a Partnership," *Milwaukee Journal*, October 26, 1994.
334 Michael H. Drew, "Roving Jim Peck is Back on Local TV," *Milwaukee Journal*, February 7, 1995.
335 Tim Cuprisin, "Programming Shift Ends 'Milwaukee Tonight,'" *Milwaukee Journal Sentinel*, June 29, 1995.
336 Tim Cuprisin, "Public Stations Spin Their Way Into the Web," *Milwaukee Journal Sentinel*, February 7, 1996.
337 Mike Nichols, "Television Stations Battle Over Tower: City Hall becomes Stage for Fight Over proposal by Public Channels," *Milwaukee Journal Sentinel*, October 27, 1997.
338 "CBS 58 Action Stalls College's 'Tall Tower,'" *The MATC Times*, November 13, 1997.
339 Mike Nichols, "Broadcast Tower Approved: 1,200-Foot Tower for Public TV Stations to Go Up on E. Capitol Drive," *Milwaukee Journal Sentinel*, November 21, 1997.
340 "Analog Transmitter Goes On Air for Test," *Milwaukee Journal Sentinel*, August 12, 1999.
341 Rich Kirchen, "Digital TV Tower Still Isn't feeling the Power," *Business Journal of Milwaukee*, March 2, 2001.
342 Douglas Armstrong, "Digital TV Makes City Debut for Shuttle's Blastoff," *Milwaukee Journal Sentinel*, October 30, 1998.
343 "State Panel Looking At Role of Public TV," *Milwaukee Journal Sentinel*, April 5, 1998.
344 Alan J. Borsuk, "Changes in Public TV Ownership Likely to Be Slow," *Milwaukee Journal Sentinel*, June 12, 1998.
345 Jack Norman, "MATC Likely to Back Keeping TV Licenses," *Milwaukee Journal Sentinel*, October 22, 1998.
346 "Panel Wants MATC TV Role to Continue," *Milwaukee Journal Sentinel*, October 23, 1998.
347 "MATC Board to Hold On to Public TV Licenses," *Milwaukee Journal Sentinel*, October 28, 1998.
348 Ken Kobylarz, "Governor Trying to Force PBS Into Privatization," *The Ozaukee Press*, Letter to the Editor, April 6, 1999.
349 Jack Norman, "Local TV Officials Wary of Assembly's 'Overture,'" *Milwaukee Journal Sentinel*, June 24, 1999.
350 Jack Norman, "Channel 10/36 Friends Hold Firm on Shifting Station Control," *Milwaukee Journal Sentinel*, June 22, 1999.
351 "Local TV Officials Wary of Assembly's 'Overture.'"
352 "Channel 10/36 Friends Hold Firm on Shifting Station Control."
353 Tim Cuprisin, "Public TV Manager, Director Suspended: Insider Links Decision to Debate Over License Change," *Milwaukee Journal Sentinel*, September 17, 1999.
354 Tim Cuprisin, "Combs Settles Dispute, Resigns Public TV Post," *Milwaukee Journal Sentinel*, October 27, 1999.
355 Bryce Combs, email to the author, November 30, 2006.
356 "Combs Settles Dispute, Resigns Public TV Post."
357 Tim Cuprisin, "Second 10/36 Official Reaches Settlement," *Milwaukee Journal Sentinel*, December 17, 1999.
358 Jason Gertzen, "MATC Dedicates Area's First Digital Television Tower," *Milwaukee Journal Sentinel*, May 17, 2000.
359 Tim Cuprisin, "Channels 10/36 Import New Leader From Illinois," *Milwaukee Journal Sentinel*, June 29, 2000, Part B, 2.
360 Tim Cuprisin, "Circus Wagons Look Sharp on HDTV Screen," *Milwaukee Journal Sentinel*, July 17, 2000.
361 "College's Channel 36 Signal Boosts Its Broadcast Range," *The MATC Times*, Vol. 42, No. 9, January 29, 2001.
362 Tim Cuprisin, "Channel 10 Disregards Letter, Reruns Rukeyser," *Milwaukee Journal Sentinel*, April 23, 2002.
363 Tim Cuprisin, "Public TV Launches First 24-Hour High-Definition Channel," *Milwaukee Journal Sentinel*, July 22, 2003.
364 Tim Cuprisin, "Elections Are Small Part of TV Newscasts," *Milwaukee Journal Sentinel*, October 13, 2006.
365 Tim Cuprisin, "Will 'Idol' Prediction Sing True? Sparks Apparent Leader of Show's 6-Pack," *Milwaukee Journal Sentinel*, April 25, 2007.

366 Taff, July 19, 2006.
367 David Breyer, "Wee Weekly's a Big Success," *Milwaukee Sentinel*, March 9, 1958.
368 Ibid.
369 Donald H. Dooley, "The Thinking Man's Television: Educational Station on New Fall Schedule," *Milwaukee Journal*, September 20, 1959.
370 Wenzel, September 14, 2007.
371 Joan Christopherson-Schmidt, interview with author, November 26, 2006.
372 Ibid.
373 Donald H. Dooley, "'No Doubt About It,' Quiz Is Tough," *Milwaukee Journal*, February 26, 1961.
374 "Children's TV Show Research Set: Otto Schlaak of Channel 10 Heads Project," *Milwaukee Sentinel*, October 25, 1958.
375 "Channel 10 to Start Children's Program," *Milwaukee Journal*, October 8, 1959.
376 Taff, July 19, 2006.
377 Michael H. Drew, "Milwaukee Studio Notes," *Milwaukee Journal*, December 8, 1963.
378 Christopherson-Schmidt, November 26, 2006.
379 Taff, July 19, 2006.
380 Ibid.
381 Ibid.
382 Duane Dudek, "'Letters to Santa' on TV: He Knows if You've Been Bad or Good," *Milwaukee Sentinel*, December 12, 1988.
383 Darlyne Haertlein, email to the author, September 1, 2006.
384 Darlyne Haertlein, email to the author, July 14, 2006.

CHAPTER 9
WCGV—TV
CHANNEL 24

(WCGV-TV photo)

Lou Poller held the construction permit for channel 24 for eleven years after WCAN-TV went dark. In 1956, he applied for permission to operate it on a part–time subscription basis, but was turned down, as the FCC had not yet approved pay-TV. In 1966, he sold the CP to the Field Communications Corp. of Chicago. Field announced plans to build a station, but after obtaining approval to locate studios, transmitter and tower in Mequon, its plans were thwarted by a lawsuit brought by area residents who objected to the location. Field abandoned its plans, and the CP was deleted by the Commission. (See chapter 4.) It would take FCC approval of over-the-air pay television and the vision of a local advertising executive to bring another commercial UHF station to the city.

The concept of charging for television had been around since the medium's early days. It wasn't until after WWII however, that the idea began to take hold. In the era before satellites, pay-TV took on one of two forms:

♦ Subscription Television (STV), also known as over-the-air scrambling, in which the signal was received normally, using an antenna, but which required some sort of device to unscramble the signal.

♦ Cable TV, in which programming was distributed via a closed-circuit system using a cable

The FCC had not approved pay-TV, but it had allowed limited testing of systems. On November 24, 1950, the FCC granted the Skiatron Electronic Corp. permission to test its "Subscriber-Vision" system over WOR-TV in New York. The thirty-day test could be conducted only between midnight and 10:00 a.m., and had to utilize only a test pattern or pictures of engineers working or explaining the system. The system did not require a connection to the phone lines.[1]

On August 21, 1951 the National Telemeter Corp., in which Paramount had a fifty-seven percent share, requested permission to conduct over-the-air tests of its pay-TV system over Paramount's KTLA in Los Angeles. The FCC requested more information on the system[2], and after receiving it, approved the test in early October. The Telemeter system used a box in which viewers dropped coins. The price varied depending upon the perceived value of the program being offered. The system made a record of shows ordered, allowing officials to determine which were popular. The tests took place twice weekly, between midnight and 9:00 a.m., with only six receivers – all in homes of Paramount executives – equipped with decoder boxes.[3] The test was only supposed to last ninety days, but the Commission extended it until May 10, 1952.[4]

The Commission next allowed a limited ninety-day test to take place in Chicago. The Zenith Radio Corporation had developed a system it called "Phonevision." Three hundred homes were wired for the system, which required the subscriber to have a telephone. A box was used to unscramble the over-the-air signal, which was broadcast over its experimental station KS2XBS (Ch. 2). Only movies were available, and all had been in theaters. When the subscriber wanted to see a film, they dialed a number, and the phone company sent a signal to the box which unscrambled the visual and aural signals.[5]

In February of 1952 Zenith petitioned the FCC for hearings which would establish a nationwide pay TV system.[6] Opponents – primarily theater owners, networks, and some over-the-air broadcasters – opposed the idea. The Commission filed Zenith's petition, and would not act upon it for a few years.

After its over-the-air test using KTLA, International Telemeter planned a more extensive one. It built a Community Antenna TV (CATV) system in Palm Springs, California. An antenna picked up the signal from KTLA, and distributed it to subscribers via a closed-circuit system using cables. The system made its debut on Thanksgiving Day, November 28, 1953, and featured the Notre Dame-USC football game. The system was shut down in early November of 1954.[7]

In September of that year, Skiatron had joined Zenith in asking the FCC to approve pay-TV.[8] After the conclusion of its Palm Springs test, International Telemeter did so as well. The Commission then agreed to act upon the matter.[9] UHF broadcasters, who were having trouble turning a profit, saw pay-TV as a potential way to solve their problems. (See Chapter 3.)

As a result, the FCC issued a notice of proposed rule-making on February 11, 1955, and invited comments, with a deadline for filing of September 9. At the same time, it rejected the petitions of two UHF stations which were not on-the-air to conduct pay TV experiments. The Commission held hearings on April 23-27, 1956. That same year, a draft report by the Senate Interstate and Foreign Commerce Committee's TV investigative staff recommended that the FCC act "at its earliest possible moment" on its pending rule-making proposal on pay TV.[10]

In 1957, another test took place in Bartlesville, Oklahoma. Because it was a cable system, it did not did not require FCC approval. Called "Telemovies," operations began on September 3. At first, subscribers were not charged, but on October 1, a flat fee of $9.50 a month was collected in exchange for thirteen first-run films, and the same number of reruns. After a short time, subscribers dropped the service. On June 6, 1958, the system went dark. Two lessons were learned from the experiment: The first was that significant investment would be needed to wire a major metropolitan area for a cable service. The second was that consumers were unwilling to pay a blanket fee for movies – they wanted to choose and pay only for those they wanted to see.[11]

That same year, Skiatron formulated plans to build a pay-cable system in Milwaukee. The plan called for the cable to be mounted on utility poles, but the Wisconsin Telephone Co. would not negotiate with them unless the Milwaukee Common Council gave the idea their approval. On September 26, the streets-zoning and public utilities committee recommended that the full Council give its permission to Skiatron to negotiate with any public utilities necessary to implement the plan, but not to grant permission, at that time, to use city streets for poles, etc.[12]

The following day, Milwaukee Mayor Frank Zeidler received a letter from the counsel for Tele-Movie Development Co., which had built the experimental cable system in Oklahoma, asking for the opportunity to meet with the Common Council regarding its obtaining a cable franchise. Mayor Zeidler wanted a public hearing on the matter.[13]

The Common Council approved the resolution on October 2.[14] Mayor Zeidler vetoed it two days later, saying that he was not opposed to the idea of subscription television, but that the matter needed more study.[15] On October 7, he asked the city's municipal reference librarian to prepare a summary of all the data available on the subject.[16] The mayor's veto was upheld on October 15.[17]

In a public hearing held on October 7, opposition to the plan was expressed by the local attorney for the American Federation of Television and Radio Artists (AFTRA), the chairman of the executive board of the Wisconsin Broadcast Engineers Local of the International Brotherhood of Electrical Workers (IBEW) and WISN-TV.[18] Mayor Zeidler received the study he requested the same day.[19]

On October 17, the FCC released its First Report on Pay Television. In it, the Commission concluded that it had the jurisdiction to authorize subscription television operations if they were found to be in the public interest. It also proposed limited trials under conditions that would not interfere with free-TV programming in the communities where the trials would be conducted.[20] Communities which had at least four stations would be eligible. The Commission saw pay-TV as a way generate interest in UHF.[21]

In response, Zenith sent telegrams to interested parties, including Mayor Zeidler, in which it expressed confidence that over-the-air subscription TV would be preferable to cable systems.[22]

On November 7, Milwaukee's deputy city attorney submitted a new ordinance which would've given the Common Council more control over pay-TV.[23]

The House Interstate and Foreign Commerce Committee had held hearings on subscription TV, and on February 6, 1958, it issued a report in which it stated that subscription TV should not be allowed unless the Communications Act of 1934 was amended to allow it. On February 19, the Senate's similar committee expressed the same opinion. As a consequence, on February 26, the FCC issued its Second Report on Pay Television and informed Congress that the status quo would be maintained until after the 85th Congress adjourned.[24] In July, the House Interstate and Foreign Commerce Committee informed the Commission that it would not be able to conduct hearings that session. As a consequence the FCC agreed to maintain the status quo until the following session of Congress.[25]

As a result, the companies seeking to build pay-TV systems withdrew their requests around the country – including Milwaukee. The city would not enact a cable TV ordinance until 1966.

On March 23, 1959, the FCC issued its Third Report on Pay Television, in which it announced that it would consider applications for a three-year experiment. It would allow five tests – one per city. The cities selected had to have at least four television stations. Those selected to conduct the tests had to provide decoders, and weren't allowed to sell them.[26] Besides International Telemeter Corp.'s coin box, and Skiatron Electronic Corp.'s "Subscriber Vision," systems then available included: "Bi-Tran" by Blonder-Tongue Laboratories (which used phone lines to provide the decoding "key" for both the visual and aural signals), and Teleglobe Pay-TV's, which at the time received the visual signal unscrambled, but scrambled the audio, the "key" for which was transmitted via phone lines.[27]

Between 1960 and 1965, International Telemeter tested its system in Etobicoke, Ontario, Canada, where FCC approval was not required. On June 22, 1960, Hartford Phonevision, Inc., a division of RKO General, applied to the FCC for permission to conduct pay TV tests. The Commission held hearings in October, and granted permission on February 23, 1961. Tests were supposed to commence within six months, but the Commission later extended the deadline to July 1, 1962.[28]

Testing began on Friday June 29. For $1.00, the 200 subscribers who initially signed up received two uninterrupted films. The scrambled signal was broadcast over UHF station WHCT in Hartford Connecticut, which was owned by RKO General. The signal was unscrambled using Zenith's Phonevision system.[29] The tests continued through 1969.

On July 14, 1967, a three-member FCC committee recommended that the full Commission approve pay TV. One of the committee's recommendations was that stations offering over-the-air subscription TV be required to broadcast twenty-eight hours per week of free programming.[30] Hearings were later set to begin on October 2.[31]

Despite opposition from the networks and theater owners, the FCC issued its Fourth Report and General Order on Pay TV on December 12, 1968, in which it approved its use on a nationwide basis.[32] The National Association of Theater Owners asked the U.S. Court of Appeals for the District of Columbia to overturn the Commission's decision. In early October of 1969, the Court of Appeals rejected all arguments made by the theater owners (and the Joint Committee Against Toll TV)[33], and in late February of 1970, the U.S. Supreme Court declined to hear the matter.[34]

In mid-1970, the FCC approved Zenith's Phonevision system – the first in the country. Blonder-Tongue's system was later approved, as was the Teleglobe 410, which by that time scrambled the video as well as the audio.

In Milwaukee, the profit-potential for pay-TV caught the attention of Robert S. Block. Block ran his own advertising agency, and had developed numerous TV commercials – including the singing Pontiac for Phil Tolkan. He had a friendship with Larry Turet, who had been at WITI-TV and later managed the

(Courtesy of Robert S. Block)

independent WXIX/WUHF. He then managed the stillborn plans of Field Communications to put channel 24 on the air. After that endeavor failed, Turet had moved to the San Francisco area.

On November 3, 1964, California voters had passed an initiative banning pay-TV, and it had been enacted into law. The ban was subsequently appealed and overturned by the courts. Turet told Block that the US Supreme Court had refused to hear the case, which had the effect of making pay-TV legal in California.

Block had developed a program to analyze television audiences. He used it to buy TV spots around the country. That led to a revelation:

> *I knew what advertisers could afford to pay for spots, and I realized that viewers could afford a lot more. If only 1,000 people bought a movie for $3.00 that was $3,000 per thousand – more than any advertiser or group of advertisers could afford to pay for the same time. That told me that there was a business opportunity, and I became focused on putting together a pay television industry. I testified before the Federal Communications Commission (FCC) and did all kinds of work to get pay television authorized.*[35]

In June of 1972, a survey of Milwaukee residents was conducted in which 284 people were asked if they would be willing to pay for certain programming not then available for free via over-the-air television. A majority indicated that they would pay for films and blacked-out sporting events.[36]

Block looked for financing, and partnered with Milwaukee real estate man Marvin Fishman, who was one of the owners of the Milwaukee Bucks. The pair obtained the licensing rights to the Teleglobe 410 system in all but three markets. Block then developed a business structure consisting of three parts:

* Telease developed the technology to operate pay-per-view and subscription television. The scrambling system was sourced by Telease from Teleglobe. Telease created and patented the billing and parental control systems, and then licensed the technology to various American Subscription Television companies.

* American Subscription Television (AST) operated the pay-TV services under the trade name SelecTV. AST purchased time from television stations, provided the pay-TV technology, purchased the programming, collected fees from subscribers, etc.

* The television stations broadcast the programs provided by AST. Some of the stations were owned by the owners of Telease and AST and some were not.

B & F Broadcasting, Inc. was formed to own a station in Milwaukee. Block and Fishman contracted to purchase WFAN-TV in Washington. On March 22, 1973, they applied for a construction permit for channel 24 in Milwaukee. Since no one was interested in UHF at the time, they received it less than three months later on June 13.[37] The call letters WCGV-TV (Wisconsin's Choice for Great Viewing) were later assigned to the station.

Block also developed several facets of pay-TV:

> *I believed that subscribers would prefer to pay for what they watch and not pay for what they don't watch. I also believed that we had to make it easy for subscribers to purchase programs on an impulse basis. The major challenge for impulse pay-per-view was how to bill subscribers only for programs they watched. To do that, we needed a way to collect information from the customer's set-top decoder box. I wanted to use the telephone network as the return path for that information.*
>
> *At the time, AT&T refused to allow anyone to attach any third-party device to their telephone network. The FCC did not agree with AT&T's policy so they enacted regulations that required AT&T to allow third-party connections*

> *to the telephone network. At that point, AT&T allowed the connections if a device provided by AT&T (what amounted to be a fuse) was connected between the third-party party device and the wall socket. AT&T charged $5.00 a month for the fuse. I invented a way to connect our set-top decoder to the subscriber's telephone that circumvented the fuse requirement. Instead, it required subscribers to place their telephone handset into a sleeve once a month.*
>
> *While we were developing the system, the FCC mandated that AT&T allow third-party party connections to their network if the device contained the equivalent fuse protection and met certain other standards. We quickly modified our system to provide the required isolation and meet the other standards. That allowed us to automate the system so no subscriber action was required.*
>
> *Well, everyone looked at pay-TV from the standpoint of scrambling a signal to deny access. I looked at it, and said, 'I'm not in the business of denying access; I'm in the business of granting access.' That slight difference in thinking made it possible to design a practical way to allow subscribers to select programs on an impulse and to charge them only for the programs they selected… just what impulse pay-per-view needed.*
>
> *Denying access to everyone that did not receive advance permission to view a program caused problems because everyone who wanted to watch a program wanted to order it a few minutes before it started. For major events such as a world championship heavyweight boxing match, blockbuster movies, etc., the phones would be jammed with many subscribers trying to place an order. Some people could never get through while others called in weeks in advance so they would not go through that hassle.*
>
> *My idea was to automatically grant qualified subscribers permission to watch the programming. Instead of requiring permission before the program, we designed the set-top decoder billing system to automatically report what they watched. The SelecTV system used a store-and-forward method. To watch a program, all subscribers had to do was tune in the station. The first ten minutes of programs were usually not scrambled to provide a preview for the viewer. Subscribers who decided to watch the program simply pushed a green button on the set-top decoder. The selected program information was stored within the box, and once a month the box would dial our central computer and report what was watched so we could bill for the service."*[38]

By May of 1974 Block had obtained a $30 million line of credit from the Kohl family (Block's agency had the Kohl's account), and had deals for franchises in both Los Angeles and Philadelphia.[39] Clarion Corp. made the decoder boxes, and they were an investor.

Block wanted to start the system in Milwaukee – with a target of 1975, but his investors thought differently:

> *Frankly, I wanted to start in Milwaukee not only because it was my hometown, but because I thought we would have an easier time managing things in a smaller market. Our investors thought differently. They wanted to start in Los Angeles – not only because it was a much larger market, but also because the major movie studios were there, and we would have a much larger influence over the future of pay television with them watching.*[40]

Marv Fishman remembered:

> *I thought: What a great area that [Los Angeles] would be – and if it worked, what a great money maker it would be, as opposed to the Milwaukee-Chicago area. It would be better than New York, Philadelphia, or many other big cities.*[41]

The new WCGV-TV transmitter was installed in what had previously been a Sealtest ice cream plant on East Capitol Drive. (VCY America photo)

By early 1976, American Subscription Television owned pay-TV operations in Milwaukee, Los Angeles, Minneapolis, and Washington, D.C. It later added stations in Kansas City and Miami, as well as minority interests in stations in Houston and Fort Worth.

One of the problems delaying the start of WCGV-TV was that, like Field Communications, Block found it difficult to find a place to erect a tower. Finally, he bought an old Sealtest ice cream plant across the street from the Journal Co.'s "Radio City." There he erected a 1,000' guyed tower, installed a transmitter, and built offices. The property had room for two of the three guy wire anchors. The third had to be poured on the adjacent Adelman Cleaners property. The location put the tower near those of WITI-TV and WTMJ-TV.

The tower location wasn't the primary delay, however. Bob Block:

> We didn't want to open a second operation until we had the first one running well in Los Angeles. It took us some time to raise the money, and we didn't get on the air in LA until mid 1978. In addition, we had technical, 'buzz and fuzz,' problems with the decoder box, which we had to get worked out. There was litigation with Teleglobe, but that didn't delay our going on the air.[42]

WITI-TV had built new studios, and WCGV-TV moved into the old WCAN-TV/WXIX/WITI-TV building on North 27th Street. Ed Rosenthal was an engineer at WITI-TV, and was one of the engineers hired in 1979 to build WCGV-TV. He would later become chief engineer. As he remembered:

> The four of us had the chance to design and build one of the most modern television facilities in the Midwest. We gutted out the old channel 6 building. It wasn't easy to do as there was a lot of history in that building, but when you have the ability to start from scratch, you do it.
>
> We used more microcontroller devices there than in any other facility that I know of. We ran our on-air services, and all of our routine, day-to-day activi-

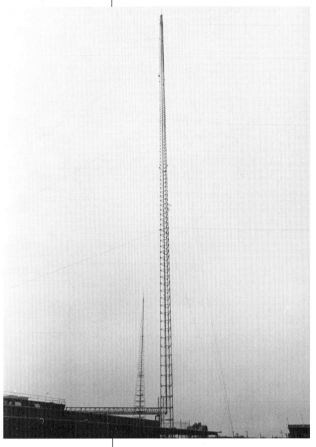

The WCGV-TV tower. (VCY America photo)

ties. *Anything that was predictable, we did via computer.*

Our initial signal was very powerful. My dad owned a business in Madison, and he was able to receive us out there. On the north side we had a regular audience in the Sheboygan area.[43]

Finally, broadcasting began on Monday, March 24, 1980. Programming consisted of films and syndicated reruns, as well as Pat Robertson's *PTL Club* – which bought time. A short newscast opened the day's programming. The pay-TV service was supposed to be the station's primary revenue source, as American Subscription television paid for the time.

On April 14, WCGV-TV premiered a two-hour daily call-in show. Called "Tempo 24," the show, which ran from 1:00-3:00 p.m., was co-hosted by Joe Thompson and B.J. Rabb. Thompson had been a sportscaster at WITI-TV, while Rabb had been on WTMJ-TV and WBCS radio. The executive producer for the show was former WTMJ-TV and WVTV anchor Tom Leuders.[44] The show repeated at 7:00 p.m. until SelecTV service began.

The show was cancelled in November of 1980. Rabb later sued the station for sexual discrimination, claiming that co-host Thompson was paid more than she was. A jury later found that the station did not discriminate against her, but that they did break promises it had made regarding salary and job security.[45]

The old WCAN-TV/WXIX/WITI-TV building on North 27th street was completely gutted and converted into a state-of-the-art facility for WCGV-TV. (Courtesy of Ed Rosenthal)

CHAPTER 9 ~ MCGV: CHANNEL 24   417

The state-of-the-art master control room for WCGV-TV. (Courtesy of Ed Rosenthal)

**WCGV-TV's First Day Programming
March 24, 1980**
- 9:25 a.m.   Tempo 24 News
- 9:30 a.m.   Journey to Adventure
- 10:00 a.m. The PTL Club
- Noon   New Zoo Review
- 12:30 p.m. Uncle Waldo
- 1:00 p.m.   Movie Matinee Double Feature:
    - *My Favorite Brunette*
    - *The Luck of the Irish*
- 5:00 p.m.   Chico and the Man
- 5:30 p.m.   Get Smart
- 6:00 p.m.   Bonanza

In late June, the SelecTV service began. Subscribers paid a one-time $49.95 installation fee, a refundable $50.00 security deposit, and a $19.95 (+ tax) monthly fee. For an additional $5.00 a month, subscribers could receive R-rated movies. The set-top decoder included impulse pay-per-view options and the parental control system.

SelecTV broadcast between 11:00 a.m.-1:00 p.m. weekdays, 2:30-4:00 p.m. Saturdays, 2:00-4:00 p.m. Sundays, and 7:00 p.m.-1:00 a.m. nightly.

Meanwhile, a competitive service, TVQ, had begun broadcasting HBO to area residents, but it required that subscribers purchase a small satellite dish, as well as a decoder.

TELEVISION'S NEWEST ALTERNATIVE
Tempo of the 80's
CHANNEL
24
WCGV-TV

See Our Program Schedule
Under TV Listings

"All Television sets CAN receive Channel 24. If your set is not programmed for Channel 24, please consult your TV repairman."

The WCGV-TV studio. (Courtesy of Ed Rosenthal)

Robert Block sold his interest in American Subscription Television to Clarion Corp. As he remembered:

"We had the 'fuzz and buzz' problems with the set-top decoder boxes so we couldn't charge customers. That resulted in a big debt to Clarion. We didn't want to pay them until they got the problem fixed. Rather than continue to fight over the cause of the techni-

When B.J. Rabb had cosmetic surgery, she was temporarily replaced on "Tempo 24" by Sue Riordan (foreground at left). Next to her is co-host Joe Thompson. At the rear are L-R: chief engineer Ed Rosenthal, Programming and operations manager Chuck Olson, engineer Karen Demos, and Tom Tomczak of the production crew. (WCGV-TV photo, courtesy of Sue Riordan)

cal problems, I sold my interest in American Subscription Television to Clarion."[46]

Marv Fishman soon sold his interest in B&F Broadcasting to Byron Lasky, and Robert Block eventually did the same. By March of 1983, a trade publication estimated that the number of SelecTV subscribers in Milwaukee had dropped from 36,000 to 24,000. As a consequence, the staff was trimmed, and the station cut fourteen hours from the weekly pay-TV schedule by cutting the afternoon movie shown on that service.[47] Ed Rosenthal:

When WCGV-TV made the transition to SelecTV programming, it displayed its original ID logo. (Courtesy of Hal Erickson)

> I think one issue, was when the [SelecTV] people out in California made us raise our rates. They asked us to raise them to $24.95. What was odd was that they didn't raise them in Los Angeles!
>
> We were looking at the technology available at the time. A major company had come out with system where we could've transmitted two scrambled signals on the same 6 MHz channel. That would've given our customers a choice. We ran out of time when cable came in – that killed SelecTV.[48]

The station was being run by its third general manger, and had a stormy first three years. Programming changes were frequent, and ad revenue was low. In May of 1983, it launched an ad campaign designed to build audience awareness. Jerry Mathers, the star of *Leave it to Beaver*, one of the station's most popular reruns, was featured in both radio and print ads.[49] It also added more shows to its afternoon line-up, replacing the SelecTV afternoon movie.

The transition was completed with an animated SelecTV logo. (Courtesy of Hal Erickson)

Although they had originated as distinct business entities with the same owners, B&F Broadcasting (WCGV-TV) and American Subscription Television (SelecTV) had, by 1984, come under separate ownership. The original franchise agreement was for twenty years, but relations between the two had become strained.

Since Lasky obtained control of the station in 1982, the two had tried to renegotiate their agreement. WCGV-TV objected to the explicit nature of some of the late night films shown on SelecTV. It often pre-empted the pay-TV service for sporting events, pageants and telethons. In addition, first suburbs and then the City of Milwaukee were wired for cable, and viewers lost interest in over-the-air pay-TV. As a result, the two severed their relationship, and WCGV-TV dropped SelecTV as of Sunday, July 8, 1984. The evening was filled with films from the station's library of 1,100+ films, as well as reruns, including two picked up from CBS' late night programming, which were not cleared by local affiliate WITI-TV.[50]

The FCC approved the sale of an additional 46 percent of WCGV-TV to the Arlington Broadcasting Group on 23 July 1984. Arlington had owned 20 percent of the station. The price was $1 million.

The station finally turned a profit in the fourth quarter of 1985. As a result, it became attractive to potential buyers.

Officers of Hal Roach Studios formed HR Broadcasting Corp. in 1986. Since Canadians owned fifty-five percent of the company, they were limited to a twenty-percent ownership in the new concern, so the officers needed to hold personal stakes. On May 14, 1986, they purchased WCGV-TV as well as WTTO-TV in Birmingham, Alabama from Arlington Broadcasting for $30.5 million.[51]

When the Fox network made its debut on October 9, 1986, Milwaukee was the only market in the top-30 not to have a station affiliated with it. The two independent stations, WVTV and WCGV-TV, were successfully carrying other shows. In the case of WCGV-TV, its back-to-back reruns of *The Bob Newhart Show* were a ratings hit. Fox had debuted *The Late Show with Joan Rivers* in October of 1986, but the show drew low ratings nationally, and the network would not allow either Milwaukee station to delay it.

With plans to expand its offerings to include quality prime time shows in April of 1987, and Saturday programming in June – all supported by national promotion – Fox wanted a Milwaukee affiliate. WVTV had sports commitments, which would've resulted in the pre-emption of network programming. So, Fox relented on its demand that WCGV-TV carry Joan Rivers' show, and the two announced that they had entered into a verbal agreement on March 11, 1987.[52] The affiliation began on Sunday, March 15.

In June of 1988, WCGV-TV announced that it had acquired the rights to broadcast both Milwaukee Brewers and Milwaukee Bucks games beginning in 1989. Both deals were for three years. In doing so, it outbid rival WVTV, who had the rights for three years.[53]

In the meantime, an Australian television production and distribution firm, Quintex Entertainment, Inc., had purchased convertible notes, which if exercised, would give it majority control of HR Broadcasting. Quintex filed for bankruptcy, and its assets were auctioned in May of 1990. The highest bidder was ABRY Communications, a Boston firm founded by a pair of Harvard alumni, Andrew Banks and Royce Yudkoff. ABRY was started in 1988 to buy independent stations, which could be had inexpensively. Included in the

assets were WTTO-TV in Birmingham and WCGV-TV in Milwaukee.[54] FCC approval came at the end of December.

Deregulation of broadcasting had begun during the 1980s, and continued into the following decade. By January of 1993, the FCC was considering a change to its multiple-ownership rules that would allow a single entity to own more than one broadcast outlet in a single market. As a result, ABRY Communications entered into a lease management agreement (LMA) with Gaylord Broadcasting in which they agreed to provide the promotion, billing, production, and other administrative functions for WVTV. In return, ABRY received an option to purchase the station, if the Commission relaxed its rules.[55] ABRY took over operations of WVTV in March, and moved WCGV-TV's operations to WVTV's building on North 35th Street.

Because it had a stronger signal, Milwaukee Brewers' games were to be moved to WVTV. The change also meant that Fox programming on WCGV-TV would not be pre-empted for the games.

The timing of the LMA was interesting. ABRY Communications was negotiating the sale of WCGV-TV to the Sinclair Broadcast Group of Baltimore. After FCC approval, the sale was consummated, and Sinclair took over on May 25, 1994.[56] As a part of the sale, Sinclair received the LMA for, as well as the option to purchase WVTV.

On July 26, Paramount Communications, Inc. announced that WVTV would join its new United Paramount Network (UPN). At the same time, four other stations – all associated with Sinclair – also signed affiliation agreements.[57]

In August, ABRY announced that Eddie Edwards, Sr., the owner of Glencairn Broadcasting, had agreed to purchase its option for WVTV. Opposition came from one of Sinclair's competitors, and Glencairn first withdrew both its application to acquire the Baltimore station and its offer to purchase the option on WVTV.[58]

News Corporation, the parent company of Fox, acquired a 20% interest in New World Communications. As a consequence, all New World stations, including WITI in Milwaukee, affiliated with the Fox Network. The switch was announced on May 23, 1994[59], and took place on December 11 of that year. That meant that WCGV-TV would no longer be a Fox affiliate. Fox had obtained the rights to broadcast NFC football games, and until the December switch, they were seen on WCGV-TV.

As a consequence, Sinclair decided to affiliate WCGV-TV with UPN, rather than WVTV, and programming began on Monday, January 16, 1995.[60]

Despite the objections, the FCC approved the sale of WVTV to Glencairn on June 20, 1995, and the sale was consummated on July 24. Glencairn then entered into an LMA with Sinclair for WVTV.

After WTMJ-TV dropped "Bowling with the Champs" in April of 1995 (See chapter 2.), American Red Carpet Lanes attempted to find new sponsors, and in October, they were able to sign the Miller Brewing Co. as well as some local pro shops. Eighty-four men and sixteen women competed in qualifying rounds. The finals were taped on January 7, 1996 and broadcast on WCGV-TV as "The American Red Carpet Lanes Bowling Championships."[61] The format was the same. Hank Stoddard hosted, and local bowler Joe Natoli provided color commentary. Instead of thirty weeks, the broadcasts were cut down to only two: the women's finals televised on January 21, and the men's on January 28.[62]

In January of 1995, Warner Bros. began its WB network. No Milwaukee station opted to affiliate with it. That changed on Sunday, March 2, 1997, when WVTV began carrying its programming.[63]

Sinclair had differences with UPN over ratings and other matters, and as a result many of its stations dropped their affiliations in January of 1998, and switched to the WB network. Since Milwaukee already had a WB affiliate (WVTV), WCGV-TV became an independent station again.[64] Reversing a move made in 1993, Sinclair shifted Milwaukee Brewers' games from WVTV to WCGV-TV, so that WB programming wouldn't be pre-empted on the former.[65]

UPN produced *Star Trek Voyager*, and fans of the show were upset with the decision. Sinclair settled its differences with UPN, and WCGV-TV re-affiliated with them on August 4, 1998.[66]

On January 24, 2006, CBS (which now owned UPN), and Warner Bros. Entertainment (by then a division of Time-Warner), jointly announced that UPN and WB would merge to become a new network called CW. The move caught observers by surprise. Since Sinclair owned the two local stations affiliated with the two networks, it had to decide which, if any, would affiliate with the new network.[67]

By early March, Sinclair announced that WCGV-TV would affiliate with the new MyNetwork TV, which Fox decided to launch in the fall of that year.[68]

After starting as an over-the-air subscription television channel, WCGV-TV grew to become the city's second strong independent station before affiliating with the fledgling Fox network. Just as that network's fortunes were on the rise the station lost the affiliation, and once again joined with another fledgling network – UPN. After briefly flirting with independence, it rejoined that network, and became part of a duopoly with WVTV. When UPN and the WB merged to become the CW network, WCGV-TV again found itself affiliating with a fledgling network, this time Fox's MyNetwork TV. It has weathered those ups-and-downs for over a quarter-century now, and it will be interesting to see how it weathers the transition to digital broadcasting.

THE CHILDREN'S SHOWS

Although it sold a lot of time to SelecTV, WCGV-TV still had to generate revenue from the hours it did not broadcast that service. Like many independent stations, it ran a number of children's shows. One of them would have an infamous, short-lived run.

Larry Harmon Productions owned the rights to the "Bozo" the clown character, and franchised the show to stations around the country. Potential "Bozos" had to attend training and be approved.

WCGV-TV bought a franchise, and began running *Bozo's Big Top Circus*, on which the old Bozo cartoons were shown. The show debuted at 8:00 a.m. on Monday, June 1, 1981.

Station manager Dick Weis had hired Howell Urich, who had played Bozo in El Paso to host WCGV-TV's version. However, Urich became upset with Weis, and abruptly quit. Racine-Kenosha theater owner Frank Carmichael published *Happenings* magazine, which featured celebrity interviews as well as the television listings. Frank's twenty-three year-old brother Kurt was a stand-up comedian, and had played "Bojangles the Clown" in appearances at Frank's theaters. The two were approached about taking over the role. As Frank remembered:

> The way Weis got Howell to come up here was to promise that his wife could do the weather. The problem was that the station didn't have news.
> Howell got disenchanted with the deal. They would tape the shows on a Saturday for the next week. They also had a week 'in the can' as a buffer. Well,

CHAPTER 9 ~ MCGV: CHANNEL 24

after he got done taping on Saturday, Howell left a note under Weis' door saying that he had quit.

Rick DeGraves was the sales manager. He knew that my brother was a stand-up comic. So he called me and asked if we might be interested in doing Bozo.

So we met and did a little audition with Kurt and one other person. They decided on Kurt.[69]

Larry Harmon didn't want to lose Milwaukee as a franchise, so he arranged for the Carmichaels to fly to Dallas one weekend for training. Unfortunately, Kurt Carmichael ran into trouble shortly after arriving there:

I got food poisoning and was sick the entire weekend! I showed the person who was supposed to teach me a tape of my audition, as well as tapes of my doing stand-up.

He told me, 'You'll do fine, you got it down.' He showed me a few things and kind of rubber-stamped the thing.[70]

The brothers returned to Milwaukee and had to face an excited station manager. Frank Carmichael:

Dick Weis was very enthusiastic about Bozo. He was all pumped-up. He had explained to us that WTMJ-TV had John McCullough, WISN-TV had Jerry Taff, and WITI-TV had Carl Zimmermann, but WCGV-TV was going to have Bozo! That was going to be the franchise. Kurt and I looked at each other, and I thought, 'He can't be serious?!'

We got back and had to meet with him. He wanted all the details about 'Bozo School'. So, Kurt just made something up to ease his mind.[71]

Kurt Carmichael started playing Bozo straight according to the Harmon formula on Monday, June 1, 1981. Beginning on Monday, September 14, the show was repeated at 4:00 p.m. The morning show shifted to 7:30 a.m. on Monday September 21, and the afternoon repeat to 3:30 p.m. on Monday, October 21. He ran the show according to that strict format through Friday, December 18. Frank Carmichael:

The show was so lame! So we decided to go in a different direction and try to make it a little more hip.[72]

The ratings weren't very good, and the station wanted to drop the show, but Frank renegotiated. He became the executive producer, and paid for the use of the production facilities. In exchange, the brothers got creative control. Rather than a straight kids' show, the brothers changed the format into a risqué, ad-libbed version, full of sexual double-meanings.

Renamed "Bozo's Breakfast Club," the new version made its debut at 7:00 a.m. on January 18, 1982. While eating breakfast with a group of children in the studio, Carmichael would engage in outlandish behavior – the mildest of which was drinking directly out of a milk carton. He would let loose with "Bozo's butt burner," where he would point his finger at his bottom and let out with a sizzling sound.[73]

Kurt Carmichael as "Bozo" (Courtesy of Kurt Carmichael)

He would also tell the kids that: "You can say anything you want, as long as you say 'just kidding'!" [74] Kurt Carmichael:

> Frank told me to go out there and be funny. Some of that stuff I was doing in my stand-up shows.
> We had some structure, with segments like 'Bozo's Grand Slam Dunk', letter reading, and guests. Sometimes we'd go out to a location and shoot footage.
> The kids were more like props for the comedy. We weren't making fun of the people; it was all about having a good time and laughing. Some of the stuff was intended more for adults, with double-meanings.[75]

Parents began to catch on, and lodged complaints with both the station and sponsor Hostess, who dropped the show. Dolly Madison replaced them. Carmichael fed the sponsor's product to "Sparky" the dog – that happened to be his!

Bill LeMonds had replaced Dick Weis as station manager, and Frank Carmichael found himself at odds with him:

> Bill was having fits with us because he thought it was a little too 'edgy' for mornings with the kids. We had numerous meetings with him because he would tell us: 'You've got to pull back! You've got to cool it!'
> I said, 'Bill, if it's that big of a problem, just pull the show.'
> He said, 'I would, but it's the only show on the station that my kids are watching!'[76]

Because of its content, the show developed a cult following among high school and college students, and the brothers began getting requests to do lingerie parties, and college events.

The parents of smaller children were not as amused, and continued to complain. Sponsors jumped ship, and the time was filled with public service announcements and station promos. As a result, the station cancelled it, with the last show scheduled for May 28. *Milwaukee Journal* media critic Mike Drew wrote a scathing review that appeared on May 4, and encouraged the station to cancel it immediately.[77] They didn't, and the show died as scheduled at the end of the month. Ironically, it was replaced with *The Jim Bakker Hour*, another time-buy.

The Carmichael's later produced a demo for a show geared more toward adults named "Bedtime for Bimbo." Bimbo was also a clown. The show had a catered dinner for a studio audience – and plenty of alcohol. It was never broadcast. Kurt Carmichael:

> It was Frank's idea to produce a show geared to adults. It was a disaster! Bimbo had too much to drink! It was a big party that was shot on videotape![78]

Sinclair Broadcasting had begun running a syndicated children's show called "Take 1." On it, hosts at various Sinclair stations in Baltimore, Pittsburgh, Raleigh, North Carolina and Columbus, Ohio would rotate hosting assignments, with segments on any given show produced by all of the stations.

As a Sinclair station, WCGV-TV picked up the show. It ran Saturday mornings at 11:30, and began in Milwaukee on September 2, 1995. At first the station did not contribute segments, but that changed two months later. The locally hosted version began on September 16, 1990.[79] Amy Hastert, who had hosted "Super 18 Superkids Club" on sister station, WVTV (See chapter 5.), was tapped to host the Milwaukee segments. She remembered:

> 'Take 1' included segments from local attractions (the Milwaukee County Zoo, Discovery World – when it was in the Central Library, a fire house, Noah's Ark in Wisconsin Dells, etc.) and wrap-arounds. So I'd tape wrap-arounds

from the zoo, throw it to a segment from Pittsburgh, have my own segment, finish with a segment from another city and then wrap-up."[80]

In early 1996, Hastert elected to leave her hosting duties and move into a writer/producer role at the station. An open audition for new hosts was held at the Grand Avenue mall on March 23. One hundred seventeen hopefuls showed up.[81] The field was narrowed, and three were selected to host the show: "Andy" (Stephan Roselin), and two gals: "D.J." (Amy Shelander) and "Charly" (Charly Rowe). Charly soon left the show.

Stephan Roselin:

I had heard from some friends of mine that they were casting for a kids' show host. I had never seen the show, and so I didn't know what hey were talking about. I was an actor, and any audition sounded pretty enticing.

It was a little intimidating. I think in that first round they had us say our name, where we were from and why we would make a good kids' show host. Then they had us read a cue card.

They liked me enough to invite me to the second round. There they asked me a surprise question: 'Who is your favorite cartoon character?'

I told them: 'Bugs Bunny because he's from New York – a cross between the Bronx and Brooklyn – and I'm from New York!'

They chuckled about that, and had me read some more cue cards. Then I got a call back for another round. I was supposed to teach kids how to do something in the studio at the station. So, I came up with a nice little program of teaching kids how to take care of their pets.

I think there were ten little kids that I was teaching because they wanted to see you interact with them. It was all recorded. I didn't know that back in the control room were the kids' parents, the promotions manager, the general manager, etc.

I had another interview with the station's top management, and they offered me a job as the kids' host coordinator. I was the writer, director and producer for the station's segments of 'Take 1' as well as for promos, station IDs, contests, public appearances, station appearances, grand openings, parades, etc. It was a pretty big deal![82]

Amy Shelander recalled:

It was pretty easy. I was about nineteen or twenty, and a bit of a goofball. So, I made an appointment for an audition. They asked you a couple of questions and had you read a teleprompter.

One of the guys from the station said that they wanted me to be a host because they thought I had a 'street innocence'. Little did they know! [Laughs]

We didn't really do the show at first. Instead we did promos for the cartoons and entertaining kids at local venues.[83]

The new team produced segments from Six Flags' Great America, on Jolly Good Soda, behind the scenes at a Milwaukee Bucks' game, and taped segments at Walt Disney World – where Roselin interviewed Bill Nye the "Science Guy." He also covered President Clinton's visit to Milwaukee.

Amy Shelander recalled:

Charly did some kind of dance with the kids.

I had done some work at Discovery World and used to teach Girl Scout leaders science. So, on 'Take 1' I did little science experiments. I did things like show the kids why you could stick a straw through a potato because it was hollow.[84]

Roselin recalled that it was a rewarding experience:

It was an extraordinary experience – especially as an actor. It was a wonderful, great time in my life that I wouldn't trade for anything. It was a dream come true to be this local kids' show host/celebrity. I was living in a dream world! It was my first real job coming out of grad school. My parents were happy – I got health insurance! [Chuckles][85]

The last "Take 1" aired on October 5, 1996.

THE HORROR HOSTS

When WCGV-TV dropped SelecTV in 1984, it needed to fill the time. On Saturday nights, it turned to an old formula: hosted horror films. Rather than produce its own, it chose to buy a syndicated show.

Cassandra Peterson had created the "Elvira" character on KHJ-TV in Los Angeles in 1981, after the station tried unsuccessfully to obtain the rights to the "Vampira" character from Maila Nurmi. She later went into nationwide syndication with *Elvira's Movie Macabre*. Originally, twenty-six episodes were released, and later an additional thirteen.

WCGV-TV picked up the show, which ran for the first time on Saturday, July 14, 1984 at 9:00 p.m. It also showed a second horror film at midnight through December 28, 1985. In early 1985, the station held an "Elvira Look-Alike" contest! On January 4, 1986, the show was shifted to midnight or 1:00 a.m. for the rest of its run, which ended on July 8, 1989.

For many years Madison, Wisconsin had enjoyed a horror movie show on WMTV. Sponsored by American TV & Appliances, the show was first called "Ferdie's Inferno" after the store's owner, Ferd Mattioli. The show was extremely popular – especially with students at the University of Wisconsin. Jack Crowley played the original host "Ferdy" beginning in 1964, and he was subsequently replaced by Carl Ames in 1967-68.

Ferd was diagnosed with terminal cancer and his brother Len took over the business. He decided to continue the show, and the name was changed to "Lenny's Inferno." Beginning in 1969, WMTV's art director, Dick Flanigan, hosted the show as "Mr. Mephisto." He was joined by voice talent John Sveum, who played "the voice in the box." Sveum also played various characters on the show. The show's cult following continued, but in 1982, Len Mattioli felt that the store was sufficiently established in the area, and no longer wanted to fund it, so it was cancelled.

Len expanded the business and opened stores in Waukesha and Oak Creek. In 1988, he decided to bring the show back for use as a promotional tool in the Milwaukee area, and contacted WCGV-TV. The original plan was to run the show for

(Courtesy of Hal Erickson)

CHAPTER 9 ~ MCGV: CHANNEL 24   427

"Mr. Mephisto" on the set of his Madison show. At the right is "the box." (WMTV photo, courtesy of Dick Flanigan)

thirteen weeks, and WCGV-TV selected films from its library. "Lenny's Inferno" debuted on July 1, 1988. Flanigan and Sveum would travel to Milwaukee every other week and tape two shows at the WCGV-TV studios. After two months, Mattioli decided to cancel the show, and the last one ran on August 26, 1988.

NOTES

1 "Skiatron Gets FCC Grant," *Broadcasting Telecasting*, November 27, 1950, 94.
2 "Telemeter: Paramount Explains Its System," *Broadcasting Telecasting*, September 3, 1951, 70.
3 "Telemeter TV: Paramount's Test Gets FCC Grant," *Broadcasting Telecasting*, October 15, 1951, 82.
4 "Telemeter: Trade Showing Not Set," *Broadcasting Telecasting*, January 28, 1952, 79.
5 Mervin Block, *Pay Television Background Report*. Telease, Inc., 1974, 3.
6 "Phonevision: Zenith Asks FCC Hearing," *Broadcasting Telecasting*, March 3, 1952, 82.
7 Block, *Television Background Report*, 6.
8 "Skiatron Asks for Pay-TV Approval," *Broadcasting Telecasting*, September 20, 1954, 66.
9 "FCC Squares Off to Face Subscription TV Dilemma," *Broadcasting Telecasting*, November 15, 1954, 31-32.
10 "Senate Staff Urges Toll TV 'Test': Will Commerce Committee Agree to prod FCC for Immediate Approval?" *Broadcasting Telecasting*, February 18, 1957, 27-29.
11 Richard D .Arroyo, *The History and Development of Subscription Television*. MS Thesis, University of Illinois, 1964, 99.
12 "Toll TV Plea OK Favored: Law to Let Concern Negotiate for Use of Wires Urged," *Milwaukee Journal*, September 27, 1957. Also see: "Council Unit Approves Toll Television Resolution," *Milwaukee Sentinel*, September 27, 1957.
13 "Second Plea for Toll TV: Mayor Gets Request," *Milwaukee Journal*, September 29, 1957. Also see: "Caution Urged by Mayor On Pay-See TV Franchise," *Milwaukee Sentinel*, September 29, 1957.
14 "Council Railroads OK for Pay TV," *Milwaukee Sentinel*, October 2, 1957.
15 "Zeidler Vetoes Toll TV Resolution: Mayor Wants Study of All Phases of Medium; Does Not Oppose Principle," *Milwaukee Journal*, October 5, 1957.

16 Frank P. Zeidler, Letter to Mr. Gerald Caffrey, October 7, 1957. Frank Zeidler Papers, Milwaukee Public Library (Box 163, folder 4).
17 "Toll TV Veto Upheld, 18-1: Reverses 12-6 Vote," *Milwaukee Journal*, October 16, 1957. Also see: "Council Backs Zeidler on Toll TV Veto," *Milwaukee Sentinel*, October 16, 1957.
18 "2 Employe Unions, Station Fight Toll TV Proposal," *Milwaukee Sentinel*, October 18, 1957.
19 Gerald P. Caffrey, *Pay TV: A Summary of Current Information*. October 16, 1957. Frank Zeidler Papers, Milwaukee Public Library (Box 163, folder 4).
20 Federal Communications Commission, 24th *Annual Report for Fiscal Year 1958*, 109-110.
21 "FCC Announces Specifications for National Tests of Toll TV," *Broadcasting*, October 21, 1957, 82.
22 Ted Leitzell, Telegram to Mayor Frank Zeidler, October 18, 1957. Frank Zeidler Papers, Milwaukee Public Library (Box 163, folder 4).
23 "Council Gets Ordinance to Control Toll TV," *Milwaukee Sentinel*, November 8, 1957. Also see: Harry G. Slater, memo to the joint committee on utilities and streets-zoning, November 5, 1957, Frank Zeidler Papers, Milwaukee Public Library (Box 163, folder 4).
24 FCC, 24th *Annual Report for Fiscal Year 1958*, Also see: "FCC Bows to Hill, Defers Pay TV," *Broadcasting*, March 3, 1958, 62.
25 FCC, 24th *Annual Report for Fiscal Year 1958*,
26 Laurence C. Ecklund, "What's Happening with Pay TV?" *Milwaukee Journal*, October 4, 1959.
27 Ibid.
28 Block, *Television Background Report*, 54.
29 "First Large Test is Made for Over the Air Pay TV," *Milwaukee Journal*, June 30, 1962.
30 "FCC Group Advises Approval of Pay TV," *Milwaukee Journal*, July 15, 1967. Also see: "FCC Experts Give Pay TV Nod," *Broadcasting Telecasting*, July 17, 1967, 32-34.
31 "Pay TV Hearing Set," *Milwaukee Journal*, August 1, 1967.
32 "Pay TV Rules Adopted," *Broadcasting*, December 16, 1968, 38.
33 "Pay TV's Fate Up to Congress, Top Court," *Broadcasting*, October 6, 1969, 30-31.
34 "End of the Road for Pay-TV Opponents?" *Broadcasting*, March 2, 1970, 23, 26.
35 Robert S. Block, interview with author, March 21, 2007.
36 "Taking a Fling In on Pay TV: Two Midwesterners Gamble on Survey Showing Public Interest in Sports and New Motion Pictures," *Broadcasting*, March 19, 1973, 46, 48.
37 Eileen Alt Powell, "Pay TV Station Gets OK," *Milwaukee Journal*, June 14, 1973.
38 Block, email to author, August 9, 2007.
39 "Pay in the Sky," *Broadcasting*, May 27, 1974, 5.
40 Block, March 21, 2007,
41 Marvin Fishman, interview with author, October 26, 2006.
42 Block, August 9, 2007,
43 Ed Rosenthal, interview with author, July 13, 2007.
44 Mike Drew, "TV-24 Picks Up the 'Tempo,'" *Milwaukee Journal*, April 17, 1980.
45 "Rabb Jury Rejects Sexual Bias Claim; Sets Pay Award," *Milwaukee Sentinel*, November 17, 1983.
46 Block, August 9, 2007,
47 Duane Dudek, "Growing Pains Plague Infant Cable Television," *Milwaukee Sentinel*, March 10, 1983.
48 Rosenthal, July 13, 2007,
49 Helen Pauly, "Storm-Tossed Channel 24 Sees Smoother Sailing," *Milwaukee Journal*, May 24, 1983.
50 Mike Drew, "WCGV, SelecTV Switch Off Pact," *Milwaukee Journal*, July 2, 1984.
51 "Channel 24 Sold in Package Deal," *Milwaukee Journal*, May 14, 1986.
52 Duane Dudek, "Channel 24 to Join Fox Network," *Milwaukee Sentinel*, March 12, 1987.
53 "Bucks, Brewers to TV 24," *Milwaukee Sentinel*, June 21, 1988.
54 Geeta Sharma-Jensen, "Pair Agree to Buy Channel 24 Here," *Milwaukee Journal*, June 5, 1990. Also see: "WCGV Included in Sale Plan," *Milwaukee Sentinel*, June 6, 1990.
55 David I. Bednarek, "Channels 18, 24 to Combine Some Operations," *Milwaukee Journal*, January 14, 1993.

CHAPTER 9 ~ MCGV: CHANNEL 24

56 Joel Dresang, "Channel 24 Sale Brings Shake-Up: With Loss of Fox, Its Status is Unclear," *Milwaukee Journal*, May 25, 1994.
57 "Channel 18 Joins New Network," *Milwaukee Sentinel*, July 27, 1994. Also see: "Paramount Signs WVTV, Other for New Network," *Milwaukee Journal*, July 27, 1994.
58 Duane Dudek, "Protest by Baltimore Station Stops Purchase of WVTV," *Milwaukee Sentinel*, April 20, 1994.
59 Duane Dudek, "WITI Flips to Fox; CBS Left Looking," *Milwaukee Sentinel*, May 24, 1994.
60 Tim Cuprisin, "UPN Network Debuts With 'Star Trek' Classics," *Milwaukee Journal*, January 12, 1995.
61 Paul Drzewiecki, "'Champs' Director Sees Her Efforts Come to Fruition," *Milwaukee Journal Sentinel*, January 16, 1996.
62 Paul Drzewiecki, "Popular TV Bowling Show Returns, But 'Bowling with the Champs' is Reduced to Two Weeks Only," *Milwaukee Journal Sentinel*, December 5, 1995.
63 Tim Cuprisin, "Channel 6 Gains at 10p.m., But Channel 4 Still on Top," *Milwaukee Journal Sentinel*, February 28, 1997.
64 Tim Cuprisin, "Channel 24 to Drop UPN Affiliation," *Milwaukee Journal Sentinel*, December 24, 1997.
65 "SportsDay," *Milwaukee Journal Sentinel*, January 18, 1998.
66 "UPN Lineup Returns to Channel 24," *Milwaukee Journal Sentinel*, August 2, 1998.
67 Joanne Weintraub, "A Fresh New TV Merger: TV's Youngest Networks Will Become One," *Milwaukee Journal Sentinel*, January 25, 2006.
68 Tim Cuprisin, "Wisconsin Native Extends Sitcom Stay," *Milwaukee Journal Sentinel*, March 3, 2006.
69 Frank Carmichael, interview with author, July 25, 2007.
70 Kurt Carmichael, interview with author, July 29, 2007.
71 Carmichael, July 25, 2007,
72 Ibid.
73 Mike Drew, "This Bozo Not Fit for Kids or TV," *Milwaukee Journal*, May 4, 1982.
74 Rich Kirchen, "Bozo's Breakfast Club: No Kidding: Complaints + Poor ratings = Cancellation," Milwaukee *Journal*, May 16, 1982.
75 Carmichael, July 29, 2007,
76 Carmichael, July 25, 2007,
77 "This Bozo Not Fit for Kids or TV."
78 Carmichael, July 29, 2007,
79 Tim Cuprisin, "Kids TV Host Amy Hastert Gets Bigger Market," *Milwaukee Journal Sentinel*, October 26, 1995.
80 Amy Hansmann, email to author, November 7, 2007.
81 Crocker Stephenson, "Kiddin' Around: 117 Vie for Host Job; Contestants Bring Out the Child Inside at Auditions for WCGV's UPN Kids," *Milwaukee Journal Sentinel*, March 24, 1996.
82 Stephan Roselin, interview with author, February 4, 2008.
83 Amy Burkee, interview with author, February 4, 2008.
84 Ibid.
85 Roselin, February 4, 2008.

CHAPTER 10
WVCY-TV
CHANNEL 30

(VCY America photo)

When the FCC issued its Sixth Report and General Order in 1952, channel 31 was assigned to Milwaukee. When the city's UHF assignments were changed in 1958, channel 30 replaced it. Three different entities would hold construction permits, but none would ever broadcast on the channel. Finally, after over thirty years of lying dormant, the channel was used. It would take not only a lot of hard work, but a great deal of faith to make it happen.

On November 13, 1952, Cream City Broadcasting, Inc., which owned WMIL radio, filed an application for channel 31.[1] Cream City was owned by local attorney Gene Posner, and had put WMLO radio on the air on 1290 kHz on April 20, 1947.[2] The call letters "WMIL" had been assigned to an FM station for which Myles H. Johns of Des Moines, Iowa held a construction permit. Johns owned the Kapital City Broadcasting Co., which had applied for VHF channel 6 in Milwaukee in 1948. He later formed a new corporation, the Majestic Broadcasting Co., and assigned his construction permit to it. He dropped his plans to broadcast in Milwaukee after it became apparent that he wouldn't be awarded a television channel, and asked the FCC to dismiss his application. In 1949, Cream City changed WMLO's call letters to WMIL.

At first, Cream City was confident that it would be the only applicant, but in early December of 1952, the North Shore Broadcasting Co. of Shorewood applied for channel 31. Company president Harold R. Murphy owned the North Shore Publishing Co., which published the *Whitefish Bay Herald*, the *Shorewood News*, and the *Glendale News*.

Posner was able to come to an agreement with Murphy, and as a consequence, the FCC dismissed the application of the North Shore Broadcasting Co. on August 18, 1953. The agreement reimbursed Murphy for his $1,000 application fee, and included a clause in which he would be hired as a public relations consultant at $200 per month beginning four months after WMIL-TV began broadcasting, until he was compensated for a total of $12,500.[3] On August 19, the Commission granted

MILWAUKEE COULD HAVE A NEW TELEVISION STATION... SOON!

On November 13, WMIL filed its application with the Federal Communications Commission for TV channel No. 31. This is one of five commercial TV channels assigned to Milwaukee. **It is the only uncontested TV channel in Milwaukee,** so it could be granted soon. WMIL has a firm contract with General Electric for equipment to be delivered quickly after a grant. WMIL has a signed letter of interest from ABC to provide network service immediately. We are ready to go, now!

A word of warning to Milwaukeeans: there has been a lot of misleading information about UHF channels of which channel 31 is one. Here are the facts: To the listener sitting at home, there is no difference between channel 3, which is VHF, and channel 31, which is UHF. Remember the early days of radio? Sets could tune from about 600 to 1400. Then radio stations were granted frequencies from 550 to 1600. Today every radio set can do that.

So it is with TV. Almost any television set made this year can, with minor adjustment, receive any UHF channel. Almost any set with a 16-inch screen or better can, with slight adjustment, receive any UHF channel and even with a real old set, it won't cost a lot of money to adjust it to channel 31.

WMIL believes Milwaukee **wants** and **needs** more than one TV service. WMIL is **bending** every effort to see that Milwaukee gets **additional service SOON!**

If you buy a new TV set, make sure it can receive channel 31; if it's **really** new, it can.

And, you'll be seeing us soon

WMIL

1290 ON YOUR RADIO DIAL NOW...31 ON YOUR TV DIAL SOON!

Cream City a construction permit for the channel, and it was later assigned the call letters WMIL-TV.[4]

Cream City had hoped to begin broadcasting somewhere between November 15 and December 15 of that year. That was optimistic, given the fact that in late September, they had not settled on a location for their studios, transmitter, or tower.[5] Nonetheless, they had a contract with General Electric for a UHF transmitter – with the highest power then available. News was to be a big part of their programming, and they contracted to show Fox Movietone newsreels, and arranged to have a facsimile machine installed so that photographs from United Press International could be shown as soon as they were received.[6]

CHAPTER 10 ~ MVCY: CHANNEL 30   433

Meanwhile, the Hearst Corp., which had lost its fight to have channel 10 reassigned for commercial use, convinced the FCC to assign channel 6 to the village of Whitefish Bay. (See chapters 7 and 8.) Cream City filed the first application for the channel on December 4. At that time, it returned its construction permit for channel 31.

The North Shore Broadcasting Co. asked the FCC to re-instate its application for the channel later that same week.[7] The FCC deleted WMIL's construction permit on December 14. The North Shore Broadcasting Co. withdrew its application for channel 31 on June 1, citing the confused situation regarding the future of UHF.[8]

The Wisconsin Broadcasting System, Inc., had put WFOX radio on the air on 860 kHz in 1946. The company was the brainchild of Charles Lamphier, who had been the general manager of WEMP radio.[9] It was the only applicant for channel 8 in 1948, and was expecting to be granted a construction permit when the FCC froze all television license applications. When the FCC announced its new draft channel assignments in 1951, it filed a joint comment with Hearst, asking that channel 6 be taken from Green Bay and given to Milwaukee. The FCC rejected that request.

After the freeze was lifted, it applied for channel 12.[10] Since there were several other applicants for that channel, it amended its application to specify channel 25 in late December of 1952, after the Northwest Television Corp. amended its application from channel 25 to channel 19.[11] All of the maneuvering was an attempt to be the sole applicant for a channel, as the FCC had adopted a policy of processing unopposed applications first.

After Bartell Broadcasters (WOKY) received a construction permit for channel 33 in Madison, WFOX again amended its application in early March of 1953, this time to channel 19, under the mistaken impression that Bartell would not receive a construction permit for a Milwaukee channel.[12] When it was clear that Bartell might receive a CP, WFOX again amended its application – back to channel 12 – on June 1. In doing so, it stated that it wanted a VHF channel.[13]

The four applicants for channel 12 merged behind the application of the Milwaukee Area Telecasting Co. in exchange for stock. As a consequence, the FCC granted them a construction permit on June 14, 1954, and WTVW went on the air on October 27. It was a marriage of convenience. (See chapter 6.)

The Hearst Corp., purchased the station, and the FCC approved the sale on March 4, 1955. WFOX was out of the television business.

In August of 1954, WFOX had been sold for $100,000 to Joseph A. Clark, the president of Business Management Inc., the owners of the Dutchland Dairy restaurants. That company filed an application for channel 31 on March 11, 1955[14] – a week after the FCC approved the sale of WTVW to Hearst. The Commission granted it a construction permit on May 4, and the call letters WFOX-TV were later assigned to it.

The station was never built. Business Management sold WFOX to Wisconsin Broadcasters, Inc., owned by Chicago disc jockey Howard Miller, on April 24, 1958. It kept the construction permit for channel 31, however.

The FCC shifted UHF channels in Milwaukee on July 31, 1958. Milwaukee received channels 18, 24 and 30 instead of 19, 25 and 31. The order became effective on August 15.

The FCC was not happy with entities which had received construction permits, but had failed to build the stations. On February 20, 1960, it informed Business Management, Inc., and fifty-three others, that they had thirty days in which to inform them that the stations would be built, or their permits would be cancelled.[15]

On November 22, 1960, the construction permit was cancelled along with those for twenty-six other UHF stations.[16]

Faced with demand for both cultural as well as educational programming, the board of the Milwaukee Vocational and Adult Schools asked the FCC to reassign one of the unused UHF channels to educational use. Instead, the Commission assigned channel 36 to Milwaukee, and reserved it for educational use.

Channel 30 remained unused. On April 11, 1968, Standard Broadcasting Co., headed up by Kansas attorney Eugene G. Coombs, applied for it. The FCC granted them a construction permit on December 30, and later assigned the call letters WMKE-TV. Once again, the station was never built.

It would take the efforts and faith of a dedicated religious group to finally utilize the channel.

When Vic Eliason was thirteen years-old, his father gave him an old radio that had belonged to his grandmother. The radio had been struck by lightning, and while sick in bed, young Vic took it apart.

Eliason's father was a minister in his hometown of Cook, Minnesota, and he often accompanied him when he visited radio stations to do religious programs. Vic became fascinated by radio and electronics. When the owner of the local Philco repair shop started a class on electronics for teenagers, young Vic signed up.

The repairman showed the class an oscillator, which he had built, that allowed him to broadcast over his radio. He drew the teenager a circuit diagram, which would allow him to do the same. Eliason played with the circuit for about a year, but couldn't get it to work. He finally took it back to the repairman, who showed him what to change. It worked! Young Vic hooked his oscillator up to an overhead telephone line. He called a friend who lived eight miles away, who turned his radio on, and heard Eliason's first broadcast. He spoke in English, but since all of his records were in Swedish, that's what was played!

His interest in electronics piqued, Vic applied for admission to the Coyne Institute, was accepted, and had put down a tuition deposit for the fall term. That spring, he and his parents paid a visit to relatives who lived in Pasadena, California. While there, he heard a sermon in which the pastor suggested that those listening give their life to the service of God while they were young. The pastor pointed out that they had a school, The California Open Bible Institute, which was enrolling young people. Inspired by the pastor's sermon, Eliason decided to forfeit his tuition deposit at the Quoin Institute, and instead enroll in the bible college.

After graduation, he and his new bride moved to Des Moines, Iowa, where he became an associate pastor at a church. One day, the pastor, knowing that Eliason had some knowledge of electronics, asked if he could help them build a studio, from which they could broadcast their services. The church couldn't afford to hire an outside contractor to build a facility, but if Vic could do the work, they would buy the necessary hardware. He did, and it worked!

In 1959, Eliason was contacted by the head of Milwaukee chapter of Youth for Christ. That organization was started in the 1940s, by a group of businessmen who wanted to provide spiritual activities for sailors from the Great Lakes Naval Training Center, who came up to Milwaukee, as well as others. In 1954, Russ Johnson started a ministry for teenagers, and incorporated the organization in 1954 as Milwaukee Youth for Christ.[17]

Johnson's father Adolph, had been the sheriff in Eliason's hometown, and Russ had taught Daily Vocation Bible School classes. Johnson needed a bible club director, and contacted Eliason, who accepted the position. In September of 1959, the Eliasons moved to Milwaukee. His job was to coordinate twenty bible clubs in high

CHAPTER 10 ~ MVCY: CHANNEL 30

schools around the city. The teens would meet once a week for thirty minutes, outside of the normal school program.

In late 1960, Russ Johnson was asked to head up Youth for Christ nationwide, and announced that he was moving to Des Moines. Twenty-three year-old Vic Eliason was asked to serve as interim director of the Milwaukee chapter. Johnson agreed to provide whatever help he needed, and promised that they would hire another person to manage the high school bible clubs. On that basis, Eliason agreed to serve.

The Milwaukee Youth for Christ storefront office at 2631 West State Street in Milwaukee. (VCY America photo)

In 1961, three teenagers approached Eliason and asked if they could start a Christian radio program. One of the young men had a microphone, another had some records and a turntable, and the third had a borrowed Ampex reel-to-reel tape recorder.

At the time there were few FM stations in town, and those which were on the air had very few listeners. FM tuners were unstable, and tended to drift off of the frequency selected after a few minutes. As such, FM stations were looking for programming that might appeal to some group of listeners.

Eliason saw FM as an opportunity. The first thing he suggested was that they put together a sample program. He and his wife had just rented an apartment, which had no furniture in the front room. The group met there and put together its first fifteen minute demo tape on the carpeted floor!

The goal was to provide a fifteen minute program which would air once a week on an FM station, which would accept the tape as a part of its public service programming. The group had no funds with which to buy air time. The young men took their demo to a number of FM stations in town, but all turned them down.

Discouraged, they turned to Eliason for advice. He wasn't sure what to tell them, so he suggested that they pray, and ask God to provide the air time if it was something he wanted.

Five days later, Eliason was sitting in the Youth for Christ office, when a man walked in the door and changed his life. As he remembered:

> *A man walked in the door and he asked, 'Is there anybody here who could use some free air time?' I was shocked. I came up to the front asked said, 'Who in the world are you?'*[18]

The man was John Harold Clark. He had come from Atlanta and was selling time for WFOX. He mentioned that a new FM station had started in New Berlin, with the call letters WBON, at 107.7 MHz. He was moonlighting there as a DJ, as well as selling time for WFOX. He told Eliason that he was a Christian, but hadn't been living the life of one. He was going to return to Atlanta, and get squared away with the Lord. Clark continued by saying that he had been asked by his boss at WBON to do a religious program named "Sacred Stylings." Eliason remembered:

> *He said, 'The theme of the program was 'unworthy', and I don't feel worthy at all. I have been driving all around town looking for someone to give this air time to.'*
> Coincidence? I don't think so.[19]

Eliason asked how much time he was talking about. Clark told him that it was thirty minutes Monday through Saturday and an hour on Sunday, and that he had to begin the following Monday!

The group got organized, and began accumulating records, and other materials – most from Paul Stewart in Madison. The first show began on May 15, 1961.[20] The show was done live in the WBON studios. That posed some problems, as the group's schedule wasn't conducive to driving out to New Berlin each evening. So, they began to acquire the necessary equipment, and began pre-recording their programming. The show lasted for about eight months. Then the station hired a new program director, Ron Walker, who told Eliason that a half-hour of religion was too much for any single day, and that the program was being terminated as of the end of the week.

One Sunday thereafter, Eliason was home in bed with the flu while his wife was at church services. He began to search the FM dial, and stumbled upon a new station, WTOS on 103.7 MHz. The programming was a hodgepodge of different styles. Thinking that as a new station they would be looking for programming, Eliason came up with the idea of buying a block of time on the station. He called the owner, Bob Purthell, and told him that they had been doing religious programming on WBON, and asked if he would consider selling Youth for Christ eight hours of time per day for five hundred dollars a month. Purthell said that he would sell the group the 4:00 p.m. to midnight block, provided that the group furnished all of the necessary personnel, and asked Eliason to come over and discuss the idea.

The WTOS studios were located in the basement of an old gasoline station in Wauwatosa, to which the tower was attached. Eliason drove there, and the two discussed the idea. During those discussions, he pointed out that he had to discuss the matter with the Youth for Christ board of directors. Purthell countered by offering to give the time block to the group for the next two weeks, free of charge to use as a demonstration. If after that time the YFC board approved the idea, they would sign a contract.

Eliason called Paul Stewart and asked for more programming. Stewart sent him boxes of tapes and records, and the group began programming.

After two weeks they had developed a small listener base, and a number of churches were impressed enough to ask for a half-hour a week, for which they offered to pay $15.00. The Youth for Christ board was impressed. Volunteers helped to run the station during the 4:00 p.m.-midnight time block, and the income was enough to pay for the air-time.

After a few months, they had saved enough to afford a dedicated phone line, with which they could send programming from their office to WTOS. They built their first tiny studio in their offices, which allowed the teenagers to get involved with running the equipment.

As time went on, the air-time became more valuable. Purthell told the group when it came time to renew their contract, that they could keep the block, but that the price would go up to $1,400 a month. Eliason thought about it, and concluded that WBON's power was too low to reach the area they wanted. The price was just too high for what they would receive.

Cream City Broadcasting still owned WMIL on 1290 AM. In 1962, a sister station, WMIL-FM, began broadcasting on 95.7 MHz. At first, it rebroadcast programming from the AM station, but it later started its own programming. The WMIL studios were located at 2625 West Wisconsin Avenue – just a few blocks away from the Youth for Christ office. Eliason went there and spoke to Sol Radoff.

There he explained what he wanted to do. Both owner Gene Posner and Radoff were Jewish, and they said that as long as the programming wasn't anti-Semitic, they would be happy to have Youth for Christ on the air. Eliason told them, "I want you to know that my best friend I have in the whole universe is a Jew – Jesus Christ!"[21] For the same $1,400 a month that WTOS had wanted, the group was now on a 25,000 watt station, which had CBS news at the top of the hour, and other amenities. The contract was for the same 4:00 p.m. to midnight time block that the group had at WTOS, and Youth for Christ's young volunteers continued to program from their small studio.

Therein was a problem. After almost a year, WMIL's union employees began to complain about the fact that volunteers were running the station in that time block. Gene Posner called Eliason and told him that he would be happy to sign another contract, but that the union employees would have to run the control board and perform the other technical functions. Youth for Christ would be limited to dropping the programming off at the station. Eliason knew that one of the benefits for the teenagers was the experience they gained by performing those functions. After thinking about it, he told Posner that he "didn't think that was what God would have us do."[22]

That was in 1964. The group had no where else to go. Eliason told the *Milwaukee Journal Sentinel's* Tim Cuprisin in 2001: "I was praying, 'Lord if you want this thing to continue, you're going to have to open a door somewhere.'"[23] He hadn't told the young people that they were not going to renew their contract. With only three days left before the contract expired he got a telephone call from John Derringer, one of the owners of WBON, who inquired as to how things were going. He didn't know that Milwaukee Youth for Christ's contract with WMIL-FM was about to expire. WBON had a new program director, and the sentiment had changed. WBON was "store casting"[24] on their sideband as a company called "Music Air," and management didn't have much interest in the main over-the-air programming. Derringer had called to see if the group had an interest in returning to WBON. He offered to hire Eliason as their program director for $1.00 a year, and would allow Milwaukee Youth for Christ to broadcast for nineteen hours a day, seven days a week. For that they wanted $3,500 a month.

With only three days left, the group began calling national religious broadcasters for programming, and he got the telephone company to run a line from their small studio to the WBON facilities in New Berlin.

The relationship with WBON continued for four years. Then one day in 1968, John Derringer called Eliason and told him that they were considering selling the

Vic Eliason in the WBON Production Studio (VCY America photo)

station. Because Milwaukee Youth for Christ had been broadcasting for four years, he offered them the first option to buy it. The price was $318,000 – the highest price for an FM station at the time.[25]

The board of directors talked it over, and decided that they had no other option but to pray and ask God to provide the funds. Derringer told them that if they could raise $75,000 for a down payment, the station's owners would self-finance the deal until it was raised.

Vic Eliason, seated at left, in the Milwaukee Youth for Christ studio in the State Street headquarters sometime in the late 1960s. Seated to his left is Gordon Morris who still serves as the radio operations manager for VCY America. Seated at the top right in the white shirt is Alan Knuth, who served as the chief engineer for the first ten years of radio operations. (VCY America photo)

CHAPTER 10 ~ MVCY: CHANNEL 30

In 1968, WVCY purchased an old bank building at 2712 West Vliet Street to use as its headquarters. (VCY America photo)

After making an appeal to the public, donations began coming in. Eventually, $78,000 was raised, and Milwaukee Youth for Christ was able to make the down payment. They obtained bank financing for the balance. The banks insisted that the group keep Music Air, as it provided revenue which would help make the payments. Donations continued to come in, and in 1970, Milwaukee Youth for Christ became the outright owners of WBON.[26] Thereafter, they sold Music Air.

In the meantime, Milwaukee Youth for Christ decided to change its name to reflect the increased emphasis on its broadcast ministry. The name was changed to Wisconsin Voice of Christian Youth, and on June 1, 1973, the radio station's call letters were changed to WVCY. In 1975, the station began broadcasting in stereo.

The radio ministry was going well, but Eliason's thoughts began to turn to expansion. Television was a natural extension, and in 1976, while he was at the National Association of Religious Broadcasters convention in Washington, D.C., Eliason paid a visit to the FCC. There he met Quentin Proctor, and inquired as to whether there were any television channels available in Milwaukee. He was told that channel 30 was available, and was told about Dick Dean in Allentown, Pennsylvania who had just put a UHF station on the air using used equipment. Proctor made a copy of the application that Dean had filed, as an example for Eliason to use.

Eliason took the application back to his chief engineer, John Lafferty, who made the necessary calculations. The application was filed with the FCC in early August of 1977, but the commission didn't act on it. Generally, uncontested applications sailed through the approval process. The FCC

The interior of the bank building was gutted for conversion to offices and broadcasting studios. (VCY America photo)

Wisconsin Voice of Christian Youth moved into its new headquarters on West Vliet Street in 1970. (VCY America photo)

now had rules which prohibited entities from owning both television and radio outlets in the same market. Both the Journal Co. and Hearst had them, but they were "grandfathered" from earlier days. In 1962, the FCC waived its multiple-ownership rule so that the Milwaukee Vocational School could own two educational television stations.

A kickoff dinner for the TV30 fund drive was held in the fall of 1981 at Milwaukee's old M.E.C.C.A. The guest speaker was author Tim La Haye. Eight hundred people attended including John Koss and other interested Christian business men. (VCY America photo)

CHAPTER 10 ~ MVCY: CHANNEL 30   441

The old WMVT UHF transmitter was installed in the former Sealtest ice cream plant where WCGV-TV had its located. (VCY America photo)

One day Eliason got a call from the FCC. The caller asked if Wisconsin Voice of Christian Youth operated the FM station commercially or non-commercially. After he was told that they operated non-commercially, the caller told Eliason that there would be no problem getting the TV application approved. On October 21, 1980 the FCC granted a construction permit for channel 30 to the group, and the call letters WVCY-TV were later assigned to it.

None of the WVCY staff had any experience in television, but the word got out that they were looking for equipment. Bill Witt from WVTV called to offer some old G.E. cameras. Bob Truscott at WITI-TV offered some of their old monochrome image orthicon cameras and other equipment. Since they were moving to new studios in Brown Deer, Truscott also offered to sell Eliason their old microwave tower for $1.00. All of the donations were accepted with thanks – and put to use!

U-Matic ¾" cassette videotape recorders were now available, and the staff purchased some. WVCY-TV would be the first Milwaukee station to use them.[27]

Eliason negotiated an agreement to mount their television antenna on the tower erected for WCGV-TV. The transmitter would be located inside the old Sealtest plant on East Capitol Drive – as was WCGV-TV's.

Milwaukee Public Television was in the process of moving their transmitters and antennas to the new tower they would share with WVTV. They had purchased a new transmitter for WMVT, and had the old one for sale. A broker called Eliason, and offered the old WMVT transmitter to them for $65,000. It was still in the transmitter building at the WITI-TV tower site. It sat there for a number of months. No one at WVCY knew what was involved in moving the unit.

One day, Eliason received a call from an engineer named Nolan Tobias. Tobias asked if WVCY had anyone to move it. Eliason said that he didn't. Tobias then of-

Nolan Tobias (left) and Don Kay install the cooling line for the old WMVT transmitter. Tobias donated all of the time needed to install the unit. (VCY America photo)

The used transmission line that helped put WVCY-TV on the air. (VCY America photo)

fered to disassemble and move the transmitter to its new location in the old Sealtest ice cream plant on one condition – he wouldn't accept payment. He donated his services, and with the help of his father-in-law moved the transmitter.

The transmitter needed a new exciter, and that was installed. At the same time, it was retrofitted with new klystron tubes.

Television engineers from around the area volunteered their services to help put the station on the air. WTMJ-TV had some old consoles, which their chief engineer, Jim Wulliman, offered to Eliason. WISN-TV had just built a new news

CHAPTER 10 ~ MVCY: CHANNEL 30 443

set, and offered their old lights. The WVCY staff picked them up, and refurbished them. Marquette University donated some old camera dollies and tripods.

One day a gentleman from Midland Video Productions called and asked if WVCY had anyone to put together their control room. Upon hearing that they didn't he volunteered his services – for free!

Channel 30 needed transmission line that was in 19'-6" sections. One day the same broker who had sold WVCY the UHF transmitter called to tell Eliason that a station in Knoxville, Tennessee had just disassembled 1,000' of that line. Normally that line sold for $1,000 per section, but the station was willing to sell all of the line for $25,000. Eliason flew to Knoxville and bought it all.[28]

The staff worked diligently to try and get the station up and running. The goal was to make the first TV broadcast on Christmas Eve of 1982, and press releases stated that "a new star would be shining over Milwaukee" that evening.[29] Unfortunately, an ice storm hit the area some days prior to the target date, and the crew installing the antenna refused to climb the tower, as it was covered with ice. Everyone went home for the holidays.

The work continued, and on January 11, 1983, all was ready. No advanced notice was given, save for two announcements on WVCY-FM shortly before 6:00 p.m. that evening. At 6:00 p.m. WVCY-TV began broadcasting. The staff had connected fourteen telephone lines, and viewers were asked to call in if they saw the first broadcast. The station received 665 calls![30]

One of the programs the station began was a call-in talk show called "In Focus." On it issues of interest to the community were discussed. Eighteen phone lines handled calls from viewers.

In 1978, the group purchased a school building on the northwest corner of North 35th Street and West Kilbourn Avenue in Milwaukee. There they ran a school until 1990. That year, Vic's son Andy, who had become the chief engineer for Wisconsin Voice of Christian Youth's broadcasting ministry, wired the building for use as their new headquarters and studios.

WVCY-TV subscribed to CNN until early 1990. It had as a part of its agreement, a clause granting permission to edit out commercials, as well as a segment called "Hollywood Minute," which in Eliason's opinion contained risqué material.[31] During times the network ran commercials, WVCY-TV ran other things, including conservative commentaries, which viewers might misconstrue as being a part of the newscast. One of those commentaries was directed against CNN founder Ted Turner, who was

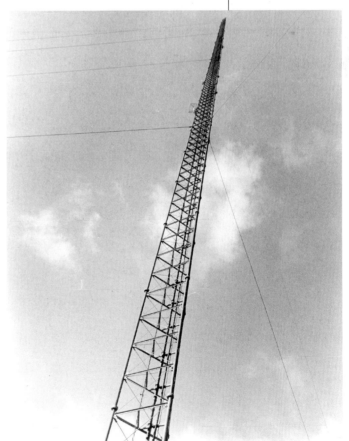

(VCY America photo)

The WVCY-TV antenna was side-mounted on the WCGV-TV tower on the south side of East Capitol Drive – across the street from The Journal Company's Radio City. (VCY America photo)

VCY America's building on North 35th St. (Courtesy of Garrett Wollman)

WVCY-TV's first television studio was located at 12660 W. Beloit Road in New Berlin, and was originally used by the Milwaukee Archdiocese television program. The Archdiocese didn't want anyone to paint over the mural on the building, and the new owners were all too happy to oblige. (Courtesy of Garrett Wollman)

CHAPTER 10 ~ MVCY: CHANNEL 30

The old Milwaukee Archdiocese TV studio became WVCY-TV's first. (VCY America photo)

Dick Anderson and Nancy Petak perform on "Think Life" one of the first shows produced by WVCY-TV. Sponsored by Calvary Memorial Church in Racine, the show was hosted by the church's pastor, Rev. Forrest Williams. Anderson was the church's music director. Petak's husband "Sonny" was the producer and director of the show. He later became State Senator George Petak. (VCY America photo)

Another program produced by WVCY-TV was "Inspiration Time," hosted by Hilton Griswold (left), former pianist for the Blackwood Brothers quartet. Here his son Larry and daughter Barbara joined him in song. (VCY America photo)

called "Humanist of the Year." That contributed to CNN's decision to end their relationship with WVCY-TV.[32]

The station began taking on controversial subjects on its call-in programs. In March of 1990, a bill that would have banned discrimination against homosexuals was defeated in the Wisconsin legislature – with help from Eliason and his audience. He was later asked for a comment by Julie Brenza, a lesbian, who identified herself as a reporter for United Press International. Eliason returned her call, and claimed that she told him that she was working on a story for a Washington, D.C. gay publication. Eliason thought that it was improper for her to be working on an advocacy piece for the publication using UPI's facilities. On Marlow Madox's show *Point of View* he was discussing media bias, and was asked by the host what action listeners could take.[33] Eliason urged the audience to call UPI, and as a result the news service was flooded with calls. Brenza was subsequently fired.[34]

Brenza filed a lawsuit against Eliason and UPI charging that she was fired by UPI because of her sexual orientation, after Eliason began his campaign. In it, she asked for $12.75 million in damages. WVCY's insurance company chose to settle to minimize its litigation costs, and as a result, in 1995 Brenza received $255,000. While reiterating his religious objection to homosexuality, Eliason stated that his concern from the beginning was objectivity in the media and not Brenza's sexuality, and that he accepted "the general principal of equal employment opportunity for gays and lesbians in the media…"[35]

That same year, Milwaukee Archbishop Rembert Weakland held a series of six sessions in which local Catholic women could express their differing opinions on abortion. Following the sessions, Weakland issued a statement on the subject, in which he criticized the literature distributed by some anti-abortion activists, and expressed concern that those groups had formed alliances with Christian Fundamentalist groups that expressed anti-Catholic views. In an interview with the *Milwaukee Sentinel*, he said that "it was possible to be a Roman Catholic in good standing and still take a pro-choice position depending on how one defined being pro-choice."[36]

Weakland's comments were blasted on WVCY-TV's "In Focus" program by host and anti-abortion activist Jan Parshall. Callers took exception to Weakland's comments, as did several other panelists – including three Catholic priests.[37]

In the spring of 1994, the Rev. Matthew Trewhella made a speech at the U.S. Taxpayers Party Convention in Wisconsin Dells. Trewhella was the leader of Missionaries to the Pre-born, a local anti-abortion group. In his speech, Trewhella called for the removal of Wisconsin Attorney General James Doyle[38], because he had brought bills seeking to limit the use of handguns to the state legislature. Planned Parenthood Federation of America released a six-minute tape of the speech in August of 1994.[39] WVCY-TV planned to air the speech in its entirety on August 23, but a technical problem knocked the station off the air.[40] The speech was finally broadcast on September 1, and was followed by a live call-in show.[41]

News Corporation, the parent company of Fox, acquired a 20% interest in New World Communications. As a consequence, all New World stations, including WITI, affiliated with the Fox Network. The switch was announced in May of 1994.[42] WITI had been a CBS affiliate, and the network began looking for a station to purchase – or affiliate with. It made an offer for WVCY-TV, which included some time Sunday mornings for Wisconsin Voice of Christian Youth to program some religious programming.

Wisconsin Voice of Christian Youth was re-evaluating its strategy. Radio was taking off, and it now had stations around the country. Television used resources that might best be redirected toward radio. The group had always prided itself on its programming. It did not want to simply reuse Trinity Network or other programming that was widely available around the country. They had been offered $10,000 a month by Pat Robertson if they would carry his programming, but had turned the offer down.[43]

So, when approached by CBS, Wisconsin Voice of Christian Youth considered selling them station, and falling back strictly on radio. The offer was for $10 million, but they had already been offered that for WVCY-FM.[44] Believing the offer to be too low, the station's board of directors of Wisconsin Voice of Christian Youth unanimously turned it down.[45] In a letter to CBS management, Eliason stated that "We are not for sale!"[46]

Viewers objected to a 1992 decision by the *Milwaukee Journal* to include WVCY-TV under "other Milwaukee stations" in its TV listings.[47] Since 1983, *TV Guide* had refused to list the station, saying that its ratings were too low. In January of

Mary Kay Meeker did a children's show called "The Green Bean Bus" on WVCY-TV. (VCY America photo)

1995, Eliason went on the offensive, and encouraged viewers to call the magazine and object.[48] Later that year, the organization changed its name to VCY America.

As television prepared to move from analog to digital broadcasting, VCY America once again had to decide whether or not to get out of the television ministry. The conversion would be very expensive, and would take resources away from the radio ministry. VCY management put a price on the TV station of $30 million, and prayed. They felt that if that price was offered, it was a sign that they should fall back strictly on the radio ministry. One suitor loosely talked about offering $22.5 million, but none approached the asking price.

So, once again the station turned to its viewers for support. The donations began coming in, and $1 million was raised to purchase digital broadcasting equipment. The station began broadcasting a low-power digital signal in 2003 in order to comply with the FCC's digital mandate. Full-power digital broadcasting began on June 30, 2006.

Channels 31 and 30 sat unused for thirty years until Vic Eliason and his small band of broadcasters finally put a station on the air. With the help of a loyal group of viewers, the station has successfully made the transition to digital broadcasting – without ever airing a commercial. Donations have funded the station since its inception. The station's programming has been provocative – even controversial at times. Nonetheless, VCY America has indicated that their ministry is not for sale, and they have made the commitment to continuing bringing the area programming they think is needed.

NOTES

1 "Station is Sought," *Milwaukee Journal*, November 14, 1952.
2 *Broadcasting Telecasting*, May 5, 1947, 24.
3 "Milwaukee, Owensboro Get TV CPs," *Broadcasting Telecasting*, August 24, 1953, 50.
4 "Go Sign Given for TV Station: FCC Approves Third Ultra High Frequency Application," *Milwaukee Journal*, August 20, 1953.
5 "Third Station Getting Ready," *Milwaukee Journal*, September 27, 1953.
6 "WMIL Begins Telecasting By Dec. 15," *Milwaukee Sentinel*, September 20, 1953.
7 "Murphy Requests Milwaukee Ch. 31," *Broadcasting Telecasting*, December 14, 1953, 11.
8 "Murphy Withdraws Channel 31 Request," *Milwaukee Journal*, June 1, 1954.
9 "Another Radio Station, WFOX is Authorized," *Milwaukee Journal*, April 5, 1946.
10 "Operators of WFOX Apply for TV Channel," *Milwaukee Journal*, June 29, 1952.
11 "WFOX Seeking a UHF Channel," *Milwaukee Journal*, November 19, 1952.
12 "TV Application Channel Changed," *Milwaukee Journal*, January 31, 1953.
13 "WFOX Shifts Channel Plea: Asks VHF 12 For TV," *Milwaukee Journal*, June 2, 1953.
14 "TV Channel 31 Sought by Group," *Milwaukee Journal*, March 16, 1955.
15 "TV Applicants Face Deadline," *Milwaukee Journal*, February 21, 1960.
16 "WFOX-TV Permit is Cancelled by FCC," *Milwaukee Journal*, November 23, 1960. Also see: "FCC Cancels TV Building Permit," *Milwaukee Sentinel*, November 23, 1960. "FCC deletes 26 UHF Construction Permits: Failure to Construct Cited; Dead UHF's Total 234," *Broadcasting*, November 28, 1960, 62.
17 Vic Eliason and Jim Schneider, *God's Continuing Miracle: The VCY Story*. VCY America, Inc., 2001. (Audiocassette)
18 Vic Eliason, interview with the author, August 21, 2006.
19 Ibid.
20 Tim Cuprisin, "WVCY Celebrates 40 Years on the Air," *Milwaukee Journal Sentinel*, May 28, 2001, 6.
21 Eliason, August 21, 2006.
22 *God's Continuing Miracle*.
23 "WVCY Celebrates 40 Years on the Air."
24 Broadcasting background music to stores and restaurants.
25 Eliason, August 21, 2006.

26 Mike Zahn, "Evangelist Expands Broadcast Network," *Milwaukee Journal*, March 28, 1987, Part A, 4.
27 Eliason, August 21, 2006.
28 Ibid.
29 *God's Continuing Miracle*.
30 "New Television Station Now Broadcasting Here," *Milwaukee Journal*, January 12, 1983.
31 Eliason, August 22, 2007.
32 Marie Rohde, "Commander & Servant: As a Leader, Vic Eliason is Certain About the Orders He is Following," *Milwaukee Journal*, July 1, 1990.
33 Eliason, August 22, 2007.
34 "Commander & Servant."
35 Eldon Knoche, "Christian Station Settles Suit," *Milwaukee Journal Sentinel*, April 7, 1995.
36 Mary Beth Murphy, "Weakland Comments Blasted," Milwaukee *Sentinel*, May 22, 1990.
37 Marie Rohde, "3 Priests Critical of Weakland: Madison Cleric Says the Archbishop is Near Heresy," *Milwaukee Journal*, May 22, 1990.
38 Doyle was later elected governor.
39 "Trewhella Targeted Doyle in Gun Speech," *Milwaukee Sentinel*, September 2, 1994.
40 "Channel 30 Problems Delay Airing of Speech," *Milwaukee Sentinel*, August 25, 1994.
41 "WVCY Reschedules Trewhella Speech," *Milwaukee Sentinel*, September 1, 1994.
42 Duane Dudek, "WITI Flips to Fox; CBS Left Looking," *Milwaukee Sentinel*, May 24, 1994.
43 Eliason, August 21, 2006.
44 Ibid.
45 Ernst-Ulrich Franzen, "CBS Rejected by Religious TV Channel: WVCY Nixes Network Offer," *Milwaukee Sentinel*, September 24, 1994.
46 Tim Cuprisin, "WVCY Spurns Purchase Offer From CBS," *Milwaukee Journal*, September 24, 1994.
47 Dominique Paul Noth, "New TV Book: Questions and Answers," *Milwaukee Journal*, October 4, 1992.
48 Tim Cuprisin, "WVCY Fights to be Listed in TV Guide," *Milwaukee Journal*, January 18, 1995.

CHAPTER 11
WKRW-TV/WHKE/WPXE
CHANNEL 55

(Ion Media Networks photo)

In the FCC's Sixth General Order and Report of 1952, Racine was assigned channels 49 and 55. Kenosha was assigned channel 61. UHF channels were not very desirable, and none were applied for. (Kenosha and parts of Racine County already received both Milwaukee and Chicago stations.) In 1964, the FCC dropped Kenosha from its Table of Channel Assignments, as well as channel 55 from Racine. In 1966, channel 55 was assigned to Kenosha.

On July 25, 1969, the Wisconsin Television Corp., headed up by employees of Control Data Corp., applied for the channel. They received a construction permit on October 7, 1970. The company requested the call letters WKSH in January of 1971, but later asked the FCC to change them to WKRL. The FCC granted the request in May of that year, but the station was never built.

On June 23, 1980, Weigel Broadcasting of Chicago applied for a license to operate a low-power, translator station in Milwaukee on channel 55. (See chapter 15.) Weigel owned WCIU-TV in Chicago, and it planned to rebroadcast that station's programming in Milwaukee. On December 11, 1981, Weigel received a construction permit for W55AS.

On July 14, 1982, Family Television 55 applied for channel 55 in Kenosha. On September 8, an application was filed by the Chicago Communications Service. The following day, an application was filed by Midwest Broadcast Associates.

On November 21, 1983, the FCC dismissed the applications of the other two applicants, and granted a construction permit for channel 55 to Midwest Broadcast Associates, who requested the call letters WKRW-TV.

On May 30, 1986, Midwest Broadcast Associates sold the construction permit for WKRW-TV to LeSEA Broadcasting. LeSEA is an acronym for Lester Sumrall Evangelistic Association, in honor of its late founder Dr. Lester Sumrall.

LeSEA Broadcasting requested a change in call letters, which was granted by the FCC on June 1, 1988. The new call letters were WHKE. (The Christian-based LeSEA broadcasts what it calls "World Harvest" programming and all of its stations have "WH" in their call letters. The new calls stood for World Harvest Kenosha Evangelism.) Although licensed to the city of Kenosha, its signal could now be picked up in Milwaukee. Since W55AS could interfere with WHKE, Weigel Broadcasting shifted that station's programming to W65BT on June 17, 1988. WHKE then began programming from a 500' tower located in Pleasant Prairie, with an effective radiated power of 741 kW.

However, the Kenosha station was losing money. Three Kenosha residents, Albert Locante, Dewayne Adamson and Jeff Baas, formed LAB Partnership, and offered $1.35M to LeSEA for WHKE. They filed an application with the FCC on June 18, 1992. The trio planned on showing films as well as reruns of old series. They applied to the Federal Aviation Administration and the Salem Town Board for permission to erect a 1,500' tower, which would allow the station to transmit at 5M kW, and cover all of Milwaukee and Chicago.[1] The FCC granted the license assignment on July 29, but the deal was never consummated.

Because of "must carry" regulations promulgated in 1992, WHKE began to be carried by local cable companies in Milwaukee and its southern suburbs. As such, the programming was expanded beyond religious offerings to include reruns of old network shows.[2]

The station continued to lose money. In early July of 1996, the Christian Network announced that it had purchased it. Its programming ran between 10:00 p.m. and 7:00 a.m. The remainder of the day, Paxson Communications Corp., showed infomercials, for which they bought the time. Paxson was owned by Bud Paxson, the founder of the Home Shopping Network.[3]

Part of the station's plan was to move its transmitter and tower to northern Racine County, and increase its power, so that it could reach all of Milwaukee County. FCC regulations wouldn't allow that while WDJT-TV used the tower atop the Hilton hotel in downtown Milwaukee.[4] That station began broadcasting from its new tower in Lincoln Park on November 29, 1996, allowing WHKE to build its new facility.

Paxson Communications Corp. then purchased the station, and the transaction was approved by the FCC on February 7, 1997. A new tower and transmitter capable of 5MW of power went online that summer from a location near Two Mile Road in Racine County.[5]

Paxson changed the station's call letters to WPXE on January 13, 1998. On May 21 of that year, Paxson sold the station to DP Media of Milwaukee. The reason was that Paxson had purchased WCFC (Ch. 38) in Chicago, and FCC regulations at the time prohibited one entity from owning two stations whose signals overlapped.[6]

At the same time, Paxson was getting ready to launch Pax Net, the country's seventh television network. Featuring family-oriented programming – primarily reruns of old network shows. The new network was launched on Monday, August 31, 1998, WPXE became an affiliate.[7]

In January of 1999, the station moved to new facilities at 700 West Virginia Street in Milwaukee. Later that year, NBC acquired a stake in Paxson Communications, and began time-shifting some of its programming on Pax stations, including WPXE in the Milwaukee area. In a compromise with its affiliates, NBC "encouraged" them to enter into joint sales agreements with Paxson stations in their area. On May 12, 2000, Journal Broadcasting Group revealed that it had entered into such an agreement with WPXE in which WTMJ-TV would take over all operational responsibility, save for programming, on July 3. WTMJ-TV split advertising revenue with WPXE.[8] WTMJ-TV's newscasts were repeated on WPXE, as were some pre-season Green Bay Packer games. During the 2004 Summer Olympics, those games were shown on WPXE.

After the FCC relaxed its multiple-ownership rules, Paxson Communications Corp. acquired DP Media of Milwaukee in a stock purchase on June 5, 2000, which returned ownership of WPXE to them.

WPXE entered the digital age with an antenna on the new digital tower in Milwaukee.

In 2005, Paxson and NBC restructured their investment relationship. As such, WPXE and WTMJ-TV ended their Joint Sales Agreement on June 30.

In early July of that year the Pax Network changed its name to "i" (Independent Television).[9] On August 29, the license for WPXE was transferred from Paxson Holdings, Inc. to the Paxson Management Corporation. The network changed its name to ION Television on January 29, 2007. Throughout the week it ran a locally-originated public affairs program, "ION Milwaukee."

Later that year, Paxson Management Corporation petitioned the FCC for permission to transfer all of its stations, including WPXE, to CGI Media LLC. Some stockholders opposed the transfer, arguing that it was being used as a way to transfer control to NBC. The Commission approved the transfer on December 30, 2007.[10]

After sitting idle for thirty-six years, a station finally began broadcasting on Kenosha's assigned channel. Since its inception it has had religious affiliations, and that continues to this day. After moving to northern Racine County, its signal could be picked up in all of Milwaukee County. Although its ratings are low, it continues to provide family-oriented programming to the area. The digital television transition will result in many changes, and WPXE, like all stations, will have to face them.

NOTES

1 Dave Backmann, "Local TV Station to be Sold," *Kenosha News*, June 20, 1992.
2 Duane Dudek "High Court Ruling Jeopardizes Plans for WHKE Growth," *Milwaukee Sentinel*, July 7, 1994.
3 Rick Romell, "Channel 55 to Show Infomercials: New owner May Ask to Move Kenosha Station's Tower to Racine County," *Milwaukee Journal Sentinel*, July 1, 1996.
4 Tim Cuprisin, "Channel 58 Nears Victory in Tower War," *Milwaukee Journal Sentinel*, July 12, 1996.
5 Rich Kirchen, "'New' TV Station for Milwaukee," *Business Journal of Milwaukee*, May 30, 1997.
6 John Krerowicz, "Paxson Sells Local Channel 55," *Kenosha News*, July 8, 1998.
7 Joanne Weintraub, "7th network Recycles Shows in Shiny New Wrappings," *Milwaukee Journal Sentinel*, August 30, 1998.

8 Rich Kirchen, "Journal Communications Adds a TV Station in Milwaukee – Sort Of," *Business Journal of Milwaukee*, May 19, 2000.
9 Tim Cuprisin, "PAX Puts New 'I' in Identity," *Milwaukee Journal Sentinel*, June 30, 2005.
10 FCC 07-233 (2007)

CHAPTER 12
WDJT-TV
CHANNEL 58

(Weigel Broadcasting Co. photo archive)

On January 11, 1983, WVCY-TV began broadcasting on channel 30. (See chapter 10.) It was the last available television channel assigned to Milwaukee to be used. As such, the FCC assigned channel 58 to the city in September of 1983 and invited interested parties to apply for it. That started the first contest for a Milwaukee channel in thirty years, with more applicants than had ever filed for another.

The first four applicants were all from Knoxville, Tennessee: Ebony Telecasters, KUSA Brewer's Broadcasting Television, High Definition Television and Women in TV Ownership and Management. All applied in October.

On December 19, seven others filed applications: Ronald W. Cochran and William D. Forester of New York, Heriberto B. Colon of Chicago, George Fritzinger of Los Angeles, Glory Ministries of Milwaukee, Enhancement Services, Inc. of Milwaukee (Two of the principals were WISN-TV reporter Brad Carr and John Stone, the son of talent agent/artist Sid Stone.), Milwaukee Broadcasting Limited Partnership of Milwaukee (The principals were State Senator Gary George and the Carley Brothers.), and TV58 Limited Partnership of Milwaukee (Two of the principals were John Torres and Debra Jackson.) On December 22, Greater Milwaukee Broadcasting of Knoxville, Tennessee filed an application. Powell Community Television of Lehigh Acres, Florida later filed one as well. The FCC hearings began in March of 1984.[1]

With thirteen applicants, the hearings promised to be long and contentious. On April 30, the FCC granted a motion by Ebony Broadcasters and dismissed its application with prejudice.[2] The other four applications from Knoxville were dismissed as well.

On June 8, the FCC approved a motion by Glory Ministries to add as an issue in the license hearings for channel 58, whether the applicants' programming proposals demonstrated superior devotion to public service.[3]

Six applicants emerged from the first round of FCC license hearings. On October 24, the FCC granted a joint request for settlement and dismissed with prejudice the applications of George Fritzinger, Enhancement Services, Inc., Milwaukee Broadcasting Limited Partnership, and Glory Ministries. In exchange, TV58 Ltd. and Zodiac Partnership (as Ronald W. Cochran and William D. Forester became known) agreed to reimburse all of the other finalists save Fritzinger, for expenses incurred. Glory Ministries also received a promise of three hours of programming per week.[4]

On March 6, 1985, the FCC announced that it would grant a construction permit to TV 58 Ltd., and that decision would become effective in 50 days if it was not appealed. Zodiac Partnership elected not to appeal, and the FCC issued the construction permit on July 23.

John Torres was no stranger to Milwaukee media. He had been a reporter at the *Milwaukee Journal* and WISN-TV, a reporter and producer at WMVS-TV, and news director at two radio stations: WNOV and WLUM. At the time he received the construction permit, he was the editor of *La Guardia*, a Spanish language newspaper. He also held an FCC First Class license.[5] Jackson was the controller for WNOV radio. Torres remembered:

> *The local applicants thought that they had the best chance. At the time, the FCC was looking for diversity, local ownership and first-time owners. They gave a preference to women and minorities, so most everyone had a woman or a minority in their group.*
>
> *In the end, the administrative law judge decided that we would best serve the public interest, because we were local, and had a broadcasting background.*[6]

One of the next steps was to pick call letters. Torres remembered how he came up with them:

> *I called Debra, who said: 'John, why don't we use your initials, and we can call it WJMT?'*
>
> *That was taken. So I sat down at my desk and started doodling. I put down 'DJ' for Debra Jackson, and added a 'T' for Torres, and had Debra Jackson and John Torres! That's as simple as it was!*[7]

The Commission assigned the new station the call letters WDJT-TV in November, 1985. The pair arranged for interim financing from various banks.[8] Unfortunately, Debra Jackson was diagnosed with a terminal illness, and those banks subsequently backed out of the deal. As a result, Jackson and Torres couldn't make the payments they had promised other applicants as a part of their settlement agreement. Consequently, Milwaukee Broadcasting Limited Partnership forced Torres and Jackson into involuntary bankruptcy in February of 1986.

In May of that year, Torres approached James Carley and Dick Wegner and asked if they would provide financing. Carley was a principal in Milwaukee Broadcasting Limited Partnership – and one of the creditors. On June 12, they came to an agreement with Torres in which they would agree to provide financing to pay off the creditors, pay legal expenses, and construct the station in exchange for a controlling interest. Torres and Jackson would retain the construction permit. State Senator Gary George, who had partnered with the Carley Brothers in their original application, was not approached to be a partner, but remained a creditor.[9]

Carley and Wegner later backed out of the deal. Debra Jackson passed away on January 24, 1987.

Torres was then approached by Weigel Broadcasting of Chicago. Weigel owned WCIU-TV (Ch. 26) there, and rebroadcast that signal on a translator station, W55AS, in Milwaukee. (See chapter 15.) An agreement was reached in 1987 in which Weigel received a controlling interest, and agreed to retain the call letters.[10]

CHAPTER 12 ~ WDJT: CHANNEL 58

They formed a new company, Milwaukee TV58, to own and operate the station, with TV58 Ltd. as a minority partner. That November, Weigel hired Milwaukee broadcasting veteran Lee Dolnick as general manger, and Torres became vice president of operations.

One of their first problems was to find a site for the tower and transmitter. Milwaukee TV58 obtained an option on a part of an abandoned Milwaukee Road right-of-way between North Green Bay Road and I-43 in Glendale, and asked for permission to erect a 1,000' tower. The Glendale Common Council voted against the proposal in a 4-3 vote on June 8, 1987, in which the city's mayor broke a tie.[11]

TV58 then went to Germantown, but the Village Board turned down the plan in a 7-1 vote on March 7, 1988.[12] The City of Glendale asked Milwaukee TV58 to submit a new proposal for a tower there. That idea was rejected on April 12 in a 4-1 vote. WDJT-TV had hoped to begin broadcasting that summer, but without a tower site, that deadline would not be met. The station then approached, and was rejected by the Town of Grafton. John Torres:

> *It was becoming a nightmare trying to find a community that would let us put up a tower. There was a lot of opposition. So I suggested that we go to the Marc Plaza.*[13]

The old WCAN-TV/WXIX/WUHF/WVTV tower atop that hotel was still available. WVTV had moved to a new facility in 1981, and the hotel tower was being used by low-power station, W08BY. WDJT-TV struck a deal for the use of that tower[14], and also rented space in the hotel for studio and office space. Although a newspaper report indicated that a new tower would be erected, the station elected to use the old one, but replaced the transmitting antenna. WVTV had added lights to the tower in 1966 (See chapter 5.), and WDJT-TV installed new ones.[15]

On Thursday, November 10, 1988, WDJT-TV began broadcasting. Its initial broadcast day went from 8:30 a.m. until 12:30 a.m. Old movies were a big part of its programming, with four running daily.[16] Torres wanted to keep the program-

L-R: General Manager Lee Dolnick, Milwaukee Mayor John Norquist and John Torres throw the switch to put WDJT-TV on the air. (Courtesy of John Torres)

L-R: Torres' attorney, Ulice Payne Jr., John Torres and Tony Kalil, the editor of the *Spanish Times* newspaper, on WDJT-TV's first day on the air. (Courtesy of John Torres)

ming family-oriented, and the cartoons and syndicated programs chosen reflected that philosophy. The station billed itself as "Classic TV58." Infomercials had become common, and like many independent stations, WDJT-TV ran them in order to generate needed revenue.[17]

All was not well, however. Soon after the station went on the air, Weigel's principal, Howard Shapiro, forced Torres out by selling the company to another he owned. Torres alleged that Shapiro had undervalued the company, and responded by filing an action in Delaware in which he sought to have the company appraised at a fair-market value. He also filed a breach of contract suit.[18]

After many successful years, WVTV dropped "The Bowling Game" on January 2, 1987. WDJT-TV picked up the show for a thirteen-week run Friday nights at 7:00 p.m., beginning April 28, 1989. The last show was on August 4. Lee Rothman again hosted it. On Monday, January 29, 1990, the show returned Monday-Friday at 7:00 p.m. It ran through Wednesday, July 31, 1991.

Long-time Milwaukee TV veteran Bill LeMonds replaced Lee Dolnick as general manager in 1990.

In August of 1991, Torres and Weigel Broadcasting settled their litigation involving the alleged breach of contract.[19]

In the summer of 1991, Jeffrey Dahmer was arrested for the gruesome murders of a number of young boys and men. His trial began in January of 1992. Rather than interrupt its regular programming, WITI-TV entered into an agreement with WDJT-TV to provide gavel-to-gavel coverage. Since WDJT-TV had no news staff, WITI-TV produced the coverage, which aired on channel 58.[20] Until then, WDJT-TV had struggled in the ratings, but the trial coverage resulted in a viewership increase, and the station actually led several ratings.[21]

CHAPTER 12 ~ WDJT: CHANNEL 58

"SEATOONS WITH CAPT. AL GEE"

Station Manager Bill LeMonds had come from a long tenure at WITI-TV. While there, he had worked on "Cartoon Alley." Some time after joining WDJT-TV, he decided to start a new children's show. The station purchased a package of Warner Bros. cartoons, and developed a show with a nautical theme titled "SeaToons with Capt. Al Gee." LeMonds approached Dick Chudnow at ComedySportz for help casting the role of "Capt. Al Gee," who would be the show's host.

"Capt. Al Gee" (Paul Staszak) hosted "SeaToons" on WDJT-TV. At the right is his nephew Greg. (Courtesy of Paul Staszak)

LeMonds told Chudnow that the person selected should be older, a bit crazy, and look "salty."[22] An audition was held at the station, and Paul Staszak was selected. He remembered:

> They put out a casting call to ComedySportz for the host of a children's show. It sounded intriguing, so I went with a couple of other guys, Rob Schrab and Dan Harmon.
>
> Bill LeMonds told me that they didn't have any money to pay me. He worked out a deal with ComedySportz, where they were giving them commercial time. Dick Chudnow told me that he'd take care of me on the back end. At the end of the show's short run, I think that he cut me a check for about a hundred bucks! It was truly a labor of love. Bill told me that this could develop into something that could lead into action figures and parades, so I had to jump on it!
>
> I had some make-up done, and the first focus group of kids said that it was too ghoulish, so we changed it.
>
> There was no budget, nor anything to speak of. You literally flew by the seat-of-your-pants. On Friday, we would tape all of the shows for the week. There was no preparation. Interns were behind the cameras. Things would fall down. All of the kids on the show were relatives or friends of station employees.

They would bring in a police officer or a fireman. We brought in a person from Discover Wisconsin to do a science demonstration.[23]

The cartoons began running Monday-Friday at 8:00 a.m. on June 28, 1993. The first hosted show was on Monday, July 19. It was short-lived, and ended on Friday, September 10 after a run of only eight weeks.

In 1993, John Torres won his suit with Weigel Broadcasting over the valuation of his stock. The case set a precedent regarding the valuation of assets for Delaware corporations.[24]

News Corporation, the parent company of Fox, acquired a 20% interest in New World Communications. As a consequence, all New World stations, including WITI-TV affiliated with the Fox Network. The switch was announced in May of 1994.[25] WITI-TV had been a CBS affiliate, and the surprise announcement set the network into a search for a new home in Milwaukee.

WCGV-TV had been the Fox affiliate, but the day after the announcement, Sinclair Broadcasting took over that station's operations.[26] The new owners said that they were excited about a potential affiliation with CBS, but industry observers wondered if they would be able to make the investment necessary to start a local news operation – something the network wanted.[27] With new networks scheduled to be launched from Warner Bros. and Paramount, WCGV-TV had other suitors.[28]

CBS approached WTMJ-TV with an offer to discuss an affiliation switch, but the long-time NBC affiliate turned it down[29], and it announced a new seven-year agreement with the network in August of that year.[30]

CBS also approached WISN-TV, but its owner, the Hearst Corporation, signed ten-year contracts with ABC extending the affiliations of five of its television stations – including WISN-TV.[31]

Next, the network approached WDJT-TV, but Howard Shapiro denied reports circulating in New York that Weigel Broadcasting had entered into a deal with them.[32] The station had been clearing CBS' *The Late Show with David Letterman* after WITI-TV elected to run *M.A.S.H.* reruns instead. The station's limited coverage area and its lack of a local news operation were negatives to a possible CBS affiliation.

CBS also approached WJJA with an offer to purchase that station, but was turned down. It did the same with WVCY-TV, and was also turned down.[33] (See chapters 10 & 13.)

After using the old WCAN-TV/WXIX/WUHF/WVTV tower atop the Marc Plaza hotel since 1988, Weigel management sought to boost WDJT-TV's coverage area. While the network maneuvering was taking place, the station began looking for a location to erect a new tower.

Meanwhile, Sinclair affiliated WCGV-TV with the new United Paramount Network (UPN) beginning in January of 1995. It also announced that it had no interest in affiliating WVTV with CBS.[34]

In November, representatives from the station met with Milwaukee County Executive Tom Ament to discuss plans for locating a new tower in a park.[35] Such plans would increase the station's position in negotiations with CBS.

WITI-TV's switch to Fox was scheduled for Sunday, December 11, and a week prior, CBS still hadn't found a home. Finally, on Tuesday December 6, Howard Shapiro and CBS confirmed that they had entered into a ten-year affiliation contract. CBS was looking to buy a station in the city, but Weigel Broadcasting was

CHAPTER 12 ~ WDJT: CHANNEL 58

interested only in an affiliation. The agreement returned the network to UHF in the city.

WDJT-TV continued with plans to boost its signal, and the same day, Weigel Broadcasting announced that it was looking to buy land in the area of East Capitol Drive and North Richards Street for a new tower and transmitter.[36] It also began planning a local news operation.[37]

At 8:00 a.m. on Sunday, December 11, 1994, WDJT-TV began as a network affiliate with "CBS Sunday Morning with Charles Osgood."[38]

After some study, the station narrowed its choice of a tower site to three locations – all of which were in Milwaukee County parks. A site in Lincoln Park next to the WISN-TV tower was deemed the most suitable. Estabrook Parkway near the WITI-TV tower was the next desirable, but required the approval of both the Wisconsin Department of Natural Resources and the Army Corps of Engineers as one of the guy wires would have to be stretched over the Milwaukee River. Kletzsch Park was the third, and least desirable, choice.[39]

In reaction, on February 14, 1995 WISN-TV sued to prevent Weigel from erecting a tower, citing potential interference with its signal to viewers, as well as microwave signals to and from its studios and remote trucks.[40] A Milwaukee County Circuit Court judge issued a temporary injunction on February 27, saying that the new tower would violate a 1984 land-use agreement between WISN-TV and Milwaukee County.[41]

In April of that year, Irwin Starr was named as the station's general manager.[42] The station had signed a contract with Milwaukee County to lease the land for the new tower, but neighborhood residents opposed the project.[43]

While the tower war raged, the station hit a snag as it continued with plans to begin a news operation – space! The studios inside the Hilton (formerly the Marc Plaza) hotel downtown were too small. It began a search for another studio location. It had hoped to begin newscasts by January 1, 1996, but that wasn't possible.[44]

Nonetheless, it began to assemble a news team. Don Shafer was hired as the station's first news director. Mike Strehlow and Lori Stephens were brought on board as co-anchors. Dan Brady and Brad Spakowitz joined to handle sports and weather

WDJT-TV's new facilities on South 60th Street. (Courtesy of Garrett Wollman)

The WDJT-TV staff gathers in its new newsroom. (Weigel Broadcasting Co. photo archive)

respectively.[45] Jana Peterson later joined as entertainment reporter and backup anchor.[46] Others were also hired as the team began to take shape. On February 14, the new team broadcast its first documentary "Dan Jansen: Our Hometown Hero" at 10:05 p.m.[47]

The station began construction of a newsroom in space leased in an old Allis Chalmers plant at 809 South 60th Street that had been used to manufacture casings for atomic bombs for the Manhattan Project during WWII. The newscast would be anchored from the newsroom rather than a dedicated studio.[48]

Finally, at 6:30 p.m. on Monday, March 18, 1996, WDJT-TV broadcast its first, live, local newscast. Its 10:00 p.m. version debuted later that evening; its 5:00 p.m. the following Thursday.[49]

WISN-TV had filed a petition with the FCC seeking to deny the station a new tower location, but in May of 1996, the Commission ruled against it.[50] As a consequence, the City Planning Commission unanimously approved WDJT-TV's plan.[51] WISN-TV then made an offer which would have allowed WDJT-TV to hang its antenna on the Hearst station's tower.[52] That offer was given careful consideration, but rejected. After reportedly spending $500,000 in legal bills to fight the new tower, WISN-TV threw in the towel.[53]

However, it refused to grant WDJT-TV permission to use an access road on its property. In order to get to its new transmitter and tower, WDJT-TV had to construct a bridge over Lincoln Creek.

On Friday, August 2, Weigel Broadcasting dismissed General Manager Irwin Starr as well as the station's creative services director. Starr cited "irreconcilable differences in management style." Chief Engineer Jim Hall was named as interim general manger.[54] Hall was later given the job permanently.

Erection of the new 1,226' tower began that month. At 5:00 p.m. on Wednesday, November 27, the new transmitter and tower were put into operation.[55]

In order to access its new transmitter building and tower, WDJT-TV had to construct a bridge over Lincoln Creek.

From 1971-1997, WITI originated the Milwaukee segments of the annual Jerry Lewis MDA telethon on Labor Day Weekend. WDJT-TV picked it up beginning in 1998.

At 5:00 p.m. on Monday, March 12, 2002, WDJT-TV joined Milwaukee Public Television and WTMJ-TV as digital television broadcasters.[56]

In late November or early December of 2006, a prankster hung a mannequin from the station's transmission tower. Milwaukee Police received a call from a resident indicating that a body was hanging from the tower, but it turned out to be the mannequin.[57]

The news team suffered an embarrassing moment on January 28, 2007, when the driver of a news truck, assigned to do a story on snowmobile safety on the thin ice on area lakes, mistook one of the many ice-covered channels on Big Muskego Lake for a road, and plunged into four-to-five feet of water.[58]

Weigel had produced a Spanish newscast for WCIU-TV in Chicago. Since it owned Telemundo affiliate WYTU-LP in Milwaukee, it decided to use the WDJT-TV news staff to produce a local newscast for use within *Noticiero Telemundo*, beginning on July 2, 2007.

After affiliating with Fox in 1994, WITI started a 9:00 p.m. newscast. WVTV ran one in that timeslot beginning in 2003, but dropped it three years later. WDJT-TV decided to take on WITI when it started a newscast on sister-station WMLW-CA at 9:00 p.m. on Tuesday, January 1, 2008.[59]

WDJT-TV's new 1,226' tower went online in November of 1996.

General Manager Jim Hall enjoys the view from the new tower. (Weigel Broadcasting Co. photo archive)

At 10:30 a.m. on Sunday, June 1, 2008, WDJT-TV started a new interview show, "Eye to Eye," hosted by Paul Piaskoski. It repeated Sunday nights at 9:30 on sister-station WMLW-CA.[60]

Milwaukee Public Television was the city's leader in high-definition programming. No commercial station had attempted to produce its own HDTV – although since 2006, WISN-TV used MPTV's remote truck to produce its coverage of the annual "Big Bang" fireworks. That changed on Friday night, August 29, 2008 when WDJT-TV aired "Harley-Davidson: 105 Years in the Making." It was the first HDTV program produced by a commercial station using its own facilities and equipment.[61]

Born in the first contest since 1952 for one of the city's UHF channels, WDJT-TV grew from its first years as a struggling independent station to become a competitive CBS affiliate. Its state-of-the-art tower, completed in 1996, gave it

The 1999 MDA telethon was hosted locally by WDJT-TV. (Weigel Broadcasting Co. photo archive)

CHAPTER 12 ~ WDJT: CHANNEL 58   465

WDJT-TV broadcast its news from Summerfest for a number of years. (Weigel Broadcasting Co. photo archive)

The CBS 58 Morning News Express team in 2008, L-R: Stephanie Brown (news), Mike Strehlow (news), Emily Engberg (news) and Chris McGinness (weather). (Weigel Broadcasting Co. photo archive)

The CBS 58 Ten at 10:00 News team in 2008, L-R: Paul Piaskowski (news), Michele McCormack (news) and Mark McGinniss (weather). (Weigel Broadcasting Co. photo archive)

coverage area competitive with other stations in the market, and it was the third station here to enter the digital television age. Ratings for its 10:00 p.m. newscast slowly climbed, and it expanded its news coverage to its sister stations. The digital TV transition promises to bring many more changes to all television stations, and WDJT-TV is no exception.

NOTES

1 "FCC Opens Hearings on UHF Channel 58," *Milwaukee Sentinel*, March 14, 1984.
2 If an application is dismissed with prejudice, that party may not apply again for the same channel.
3 "For the Record," *Broadcasting*, June 25, 1984.
4 John Torres, interview with author, March 1, 2004.
5 Jennifer Lieffers, "License in Hand, Torres Seeks Financing for TV 58," *Business Journal of Milwaukee*, November 18, 1985.
6 Ibid.
7 Ibid.
8 Torres, March 1, 2004.
9 John Fauber, "Investors May Rescue Troubled TV 58: James Carley, Dick Wegner Agree on Partnership to Build, Operate Station," *Business Journal of Milwaukee*, June 23, 1986.
10 Torres, March 1, 2004.
11 "Mayor Breaks Tie as Glendale Says No to TV Towers," *Milwaukee Journal*, June 9, 1987.
12 Joe Sandin, "Tower Plans Fall in Germantown," *Milwaukee Journal*, March 8, 1988.
13 Torres, March 1, 2004.
14 "Tower for New TV Station to Top Hotel," *Milwaukee Journal*, September 26, 1988.
15 Michael H, Drew, "Cable Looks Like Key to Future of Struggling Little Channel 58," *Milwaukee Journal*, November 16, 1988.

16 Michael H, Drew, "TV's Sleeze Factor is Zooming," *Milwaukee Journal*, November 10, 1988.
17 Tim Forkes, "Tuning Into Something Different: Milwaukee is Home to Two New, and very Different, Television Stations," *The Shepherd Express*, February 23, 1989.
18 John Torres, interview with author, January 26, 2008.
19 Michael Zahn, "Channel 58 Co-Founder Settles Civil Suit," *Milwaukee Journal*, August 25, 1991.
20 Michael Zahn, "Channels 6, 58 Team Up on Coverage: Local Stations Combine Their Efforts to Show the Full Court Proceedings," *Milwaukee Journal*, January 18, 1992.
21 Michael Zahn, "Ratings Soar as WDJT-TV Covers Trial," *Milwaukee Journal*, January 31, 1992.
22 Duane Dudek, "WDJT is Out to Launch a New Children's Show," *Milwaukee Sentinel*, June 30, 1993.
23 Paul Staszak, interview with author, November 17, 2006.
24 *TV58 Limited Partnership v. Weigel Broadcasting Co.*, Del. Ch. Civil Action No. 10,798 (1993)
25 Duane Dudek, "WITI Flips to Fox; CBS Left Looking," *Milwaukee Sentinel*, May 24, 1994.
26 Joel Dresang, "Channel 24 Sale Brings Shake-Up: With Loss of Fox, Its Status is Unclear," *Milwaukee Journal*, May 25, 1994.
27 Geeta Sharma-Jensen, "Channel 24 Owner Eyes CBS Link: But Sinclair is Uncertain Deal Could be Reached," *Milwaukee Journal*, May 26, 1994.
28 Duane Dudek, "Channel 24 Boss is looking at Other Suitors, Not CBS," *Milwaukee Sentinel*, June 10, 1994.
29 Michael H, Drew, "CBS Still Scrambling for an Affiliate I Iere," *Milwaukee Journal*, June 30, 1994.
30 Duane Dudek, "NBC, WTMJ-TV Reach 7-Year Agreement," *Milwaukee Sentinel*, August 10, 1994.
31 Duane Dudek, "Channel 12, ABC Sign a Long-Term Contract," *Milwaukee Sentinel*, July 26, 1994.
32 "Channel 58 Denies CBS Deal," *Milwaukee Journal*, September 7, 1994.
33 Ernst-Ulrich Franzen, "CBS Rejected by Religious TV Channel: WVCY Nixes Network Offer," *Milwaukee Sentinel*, September 24, 1994.
34 Duane Dudek, "Will Likely Sale of Channel 18 Lead to CBS Affiliation Here?" *Milwaukee Sentinel*, August 31, 1994.
35 Tim Cuprisin, "Meeting May Boost WDJT Signal and Desirability," *Milwaukee Journal*, November 11, 1994.
36 Larry Engel, Channel 58 Eyes Site for Antenna," *Milwaukee Sentinel*, December 7, 1994.
37 Tim Cuprisin, "CBS Gets a Home on Channel 58: Affiliation to Start Sunday When Channel 6 Goes to Fox Network," *Milwaukee Journal*, December 6, 1994.
38 Duane Dudek, "Osgood to Kick Off CBS on WDJT" *Milwaukee Sentinel*, December 7, 1994.
39 Gretchen Schuldt, "3 Parks Eyed as Site for Channel 58 Tower," *Milwaukee Sentinel*, December 28, 1994.
40 "WISN-TV Sues to Block Tower," *Milwaukee Sentinel*, February 15, 1995. Also see: "WISN is Suing to Stop WDJT Antenna Project: Station Claims That Plan of New CBS Affiliate Would Cause Problems," *Milwaukee Journal*, February 15, 1995.
41 Michael Zahn, "Channel 12 Can Block WDJT Tower," *Milwaukee Journal*, March 2, 1995.
42 Tim Cuprisin, "Patrick Brings Sports-Comedy Shtick to WQFM Today," *Milwaukee Journal Sentinel*, April 3, 1995.
43 Lindsey Marcus, "Neighbors Blast Proposed television Tower: More Than 100 Attended Meeting Discussing Plan of WDJT-TV (Channel 58)," *Milwaukee Journal Sentinel*, July 27, 1995.
44 Tim Cuprisin, "Channel 58 News launch Hits a Snag: Jan. 1 Deadline Won't Be Met, Station General Manager Says," *Milwaukee Journal Sentinel*, December 4, 1995.
45 Tim Cuprisin, "At Last, Channel 58 Assembles News Staff: TMJ's Strehlow Will Step Over to Take a Shot at Being the Anchor," *Milwaukee Journal Sentinel*, January 8, 1996.

46 Tim Cuprisin, "Channel 58 News to Have an Entertainment Spin," *Milwaukee Journal Sentinel*, January 25, 1996.

47 Tim Cuprisin, "Documentary is a Taste of 58 News," *Milwaukee Journal Sentinel*, February 14, 1996.

48 Rich Kirchen, "Channel 58 Targets Youth With Noveau Newscast," *Business Journal of Milwaukee*, March 9, 1996.

49 Tim Cuprisin, "The Newest News team in Town," *Milwaukee Journal Sentinel*, March 18, 1996.

50 Tim Cuprisin, "Channel 58 is Helped by FCC Ruling," *Milwaukee Journal Sentinel*, May 20, 1996.

51 "Panel OK's Plan to Erect WDJT-TV Tower in Park," *Milwaukee Journal Sentinel*, May 21, 1996.

52 Tim Cuprisin, "Channel 12 Makes Move in Tower War," *Milwaukee Journal Sentinel*, June 4, 1996.

53 Tim Cuprisin, "TV Tower Battle Finally May Be Over," *Milwaukee Journal Sentinel*, August 22, 1996.

54 Tim Cuprisin, "Owner Fires 2 WDJT-TV Officials: Chief Engineer to be Fill-In as GM at CBS Affiliate," *Milwaukee Journal Sentinel*, August 3, 1996.

55 Tim Cuprisin, "Channel 58 Set to Make Switch Today," *Milwaukee Journal Sentinel*, November 27, 1996.

56 Tim Cuprisin, "Channel 58 Joins Two Others in Digital Era," *Milwaukee Journal Sentinel*, March 12, 2002.

57 Annysa Johnson, "Television Tower Prankster Might Suffer Radiation Poisoning: Someone Strung Up a Mannequin, Leading to Sky-High Recovery Effort," *Milwaukee Journal Sentinel*, December 10, 2006.

58 "TV Truck Gets to Bottom of Ice Danger," *Milwaukee Journal Sentinel*, January 29, 2007.

59 Tim Cuprisin, "Channel 58 Goes Head to Head with Channel 6 in 9 p.m. Newscast Duel," *Milwaukee Journal Sentinel*, December 4, 2007.

60 Tim Cuprisin, "Zakaria's CNN Show Will Give American Viewers a Global Perspective," *Milwaukee Journal Sentinel*, May 30, 2008.

61 Tim Cuprisin, "News Outlets Try To Craft Storyline from Disgruntled Clinton Backers," *Milwaukee Journal Sentinel*, August 29, 2008.

CHAPTER 13
WJJA/WBME
CHANNEL 49

(Weiger Broadcasting Co. photo archive)

In the FCC's Sixth General Order and Report of 1952, Racine was assigned channels 49 and 55. Kenosha was assigned channel 61. UHF channels were not very desirable, and none of those were applied for. (Kenosha and parts of Racine County already received both Milwaukee and Chicago stations.) In 1964, the FCC dropped Kenosha from its Table of Channel Assignments, as well as channel 55 from Racine.

It wasn't until 1966 that channel 49 was finally applied for. United Broadcasting Co., owned jointly by the [Racine] Journal Times Co. and the Kenosha News Publishing Co., filed an application on September 13 of that year. John Weigel Associates later applied for the channel. Weigel owned and operated WCIU-TV in Chicago. The applications were scheduled for a hearing before the FCC on December 16, 1968. Both applicants asked for a continuance for their pre-hearing conference, as well as their hearing. Those petitions were granted on November 15. On November 25, both requested additional time to prepare, but those requests were denied by a hearing examiner two days later. On December 3, the two filed a joint petition for the approval of an agreement that called for Weigel's application to be dismissed with prejudice, while United Broadcasting remained in hearing status. The FCC approved the agreement on January 17, 1969.[1] United Broadcasting later petitioned the Commission to dismiss its application without prejudice. That request was granted on February 19.[2]

The channel remained unused. Finally, on April 30, 1981, the Racine Telecasting Co., owned by Joel J. Kinlow applied for it. Kinlow was the pastor of Greater New Hope Church of God in Christ in Milwaukee. On August 6, Ch. 49 of Racine, Inc., owned by a group of Illinois investors, also filed an application. On February 3, 1983 the Racine Telecasting Co. received a construction permit for channel 49, and the call letters WJJA were later assigned to the station. They stand for the Kinlows' first names: Joel, Joe (son) and Arvis (then wife).

Kinlow formulated plans to affiliate the station with the Home Shopping Network. HSN was available on cable, but penetration was so low that affiliating with an over-the-air station was attractive. He decided to locate his facility at 4311 East

Oakwood Road in Racine on vacant land owned by the Wisconsin Electric Power Co. On February 14, 1989, the Oak Creek Planning Commission approved plans to divide ten acres of the land so that Kinlow could purchase what he needed.³

WJJA's original building in Oak Creek (Courtesy of Garrett Wollman)

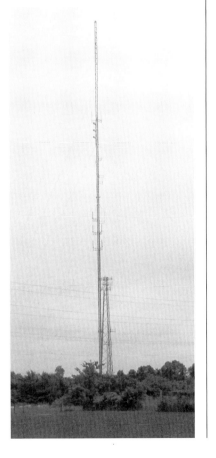

WJJA's original tower. (Courtesy of Garrett Wollman)

He then began looking for financing, and asked Milwaukee County to loan him $101,240 via a community development block grant loan.⁴

Local broadcasting veteran Lee Dolnick was hired as the station's first general manager. Finally, in late January of 1990, WJJA began broadcasting on channel 49. It was 100% minority owned. Although licensed to Racine, its signal could be picked up in Milwaukee. Kinlow planned on offering five minutes of each hour to local advertisers.⁵

The station had trouble attracting them, and Kinlow fired Dolnick in November of 1990. His replacement, Mike Schuster, was similarly unsuccessful, and was fired in November of the following year. Schuster had added old movies to the station's programming, but the results were weak. Those local clients the station did sign reported that had no response from their commercials on the station.⁶ In addition, the station had technical problems that repeatedly knocked it off-the-air.

In July of 1993, the FCC implemented "must carry" regulations. They required local cable companies to carry stations within the "designated market area" (DMA) as defined by Nielsen Media Research.⁷ Kinlow wanted WJJA to be carried on Time-Warner's basic tier, but the cable company balked and asked the FCC for an exemption, citing the fact that they already carried the Home Shopping Network, that the station originated little local programming, and didn't inform the public when that it did provide was scheduled. Kinlow, who is African-American, reacted by charging discrimination.⁸ Time-Warner did begin carrying the channel.

News Corporation, the parent company of Fox, acquired a 20% interest in New World Communications. As a consequence, all New World stations, including WITI-TV affiliated with the Fox Network. The switch was announced in May of 1994.⁹ WITI-TV had been a CBS affiliate, and the surprise announcement set the network into a search for a new home in Milwaukee. After its attempts to affiliate with WCGV-TV, WISN-TV, WTMJ-TV, WVTV and WVCY-TV (which the network offered to purchase) were rejected, the network approached Kinlow in early November of 1994. He told them that he was contractually obligated to the Home Shopping Network.¹⁰

The following year, the station affiliated with the Military Channel, but dropped them in 1996 and affiliated with Shop at Home.

With the development of digital television broadcasting standards, all stations began making plans for the transition. Kinlow wanted to build a new tower near the "tower farm" along the Milwaukee River, and purchased land on North Fratney Street just south of East Capitol Drive. He filed applications with the FCC and the Federal Aviation Administration (FAA) for a 1,053' tower. The FCC approved the plan in September of 1996.[11] The FAA also gave the plan its approval.

In March of 1997, the Milwaukee Common Council adopted a policy designed to reduce the number of tall towers in the city. Kinlow found himself stymied by it. In order to erect his new tower, he needed a zoning variance, but the city's Board of Zoning Appeals denied his request in July of that year, citing safety concerns. Kinlow appealed the ruling to the Milwaukee County Circuit Court, but lost in December of 1998.[12]

He sued the city in Federal Court in May of 1999, alleging that his request was denied because of his race, as two other new towers, for WDJT-TV and Milwaukee Public Television, had been approved earlier. He sought $500,000 in actual damages and $10M for the loss of value to WJJA. The city claimed that the proposal was denied because it did not comply with its new tower policy, and a U.S. District Court judge agreed in an August 8, 2000 ruling that granted the city a summary judgment, saying that Kinlow had failed to prove racial discrimination.[13] Kinlow appealed to the U.S. Circuit Court of Appeals in Chicago, but that appeal was denied on March 16, 2001.[14]

On February 16, 2006, Weigel Broadcasting sued Joel J. Kinlow in Cook County, Illinois Circuit Court. Weigel claimed that it had entered into an agreement to purchase WJJA for $5M, but that Kinlow had then raised the price to $7M.[15]

In June of 2006, Shop at Home owner E.W. Scripps announced that he had sold the network to Jewelry Television. WJJA began carrying Jewelry Television after Shop at Home shut down and then switched to the new Shop at Home channel.[16] Since no other programming was being carried by the station, on January 28, 2007, the *Milwaukee Journal Sentinel* announced that it would no longer carry WJJA in its television listings.[17]

On July 30, 2007, Weigel Broadcasting and Joel Kinlow announced that they had entered into an agreement for the sale of WJJA. The purchase price was $7 million. Weigel, who had sued Kinlow in Federal court as well as in Cook County, Illinois, then agreed to drop all litigation. They promised to convert WJJA to a "full service" station.[18] On September 12, the FCC approved the sale to Channel 49 LLC, a subsidiary of Weigel Broadcasting.

Later that month, Kinlow claimed that the station's tower was in danger of collapsing due to the weight of the TV antenna as well as that of the antennas of wireless carriers and public safety agencies that were also mounted on it. He applied to the FCC for permission to move the station's two antennas to the Weigel Broadcasting tower in Lincoln Park.[19] That request was denied, but upon the advice of the Chief of the Video Division of the FCC's Mass Media Bureau, WJJA filed a request for special temporary authority (STA) to relocate the antennas on October 26. The Commission granted that request on November 8.

In early 2008, Shop at Home announced that it would be discontinuing its network to focus on its internet business. Operations ended at 11:59 m. on March 7. Thereafter, WJJA once again began carrying Jewelry Television. However, Weigel Broadcasting refused to consummate the purchase of WJJA until after the tower was reinforced.[20] Relocating the antenna to their tower would have to wait until spring.

On March 1, 2008, Weigel Broadcasting began carrying Me-TV, which showed classic television programs from the 1950s-1990s, on one of the digital subchannels for WDJT-TV. On Monday, April 21, the deal for the transfer of WJJA was finally consummated. At 12:30 p.m., Jewelry Television disappeared, and was replaced with a set of color bars. Later that afternoon, Me-TV programming began on the station. Technical problems plagued the switchover, but by that evening, it had been completed.[21] On Tuesday, April 29, the call letters were changed to WBME-TV (Be Memorable Entertainment).

Although licensed to Racine, the station hadn't offered any programming targeted to that city and its issues. That changed on Sunday, June 1, 2008 when WBME-TV began running "Racine & Me" at 7:00 a.m.[22]

Racine's only TV channel went unused for thirty-eight years until Joel Kinlow put WJJA on the air. The station's financial status was always tenuous, and Kinlow had to weather a number of set-backs. The sale to Weigel Broadcasting and launch of Me-TV programming brought a new look to the station, and gave its new owners a second full-service station in the area.

NOTES

1 "For the Record," *Broadcasting*, January 27, 1969, 104.
2 "For the Record," *Broadcasting*, March 3, 1969, 80.
3 "Panel Delays Study of TV Station Plan," *Milwaukee Sentinel*, February 15, 1989.
4 "Pastor Seeks $101,240 to help start TV Station," *Milwaukee Sentinel*, June 20, 1989.
5 Michael Zahn, "New TV Station Goes on Air, 2 Others Plan to During 1990," *Milwaukee Journal*, February 4, 1990.
6 Michael Zahn, "Another Morning Team Bites the Dust at 'QFM," *Milwaukee Journal*, November 26, 1991.
7 8 FCC Rcd 2965, 2976-2977 (1993)
8 Gretchen Schuldt, "Black-Owned Shopping Channel Fights to Get on Warner Cable," *Milwaukee Sentinel*, October 25, 1993.
9 Duane Dudek, "WITI Flips to Fox; CBS Left Looking," *Milwaukee Sentinel*, May 24, 1994.
10 Duane Dudek, "TV Movies are Dumb, Dumber," *Milwaukee Sentinel*, November 29, 1994.
11 Rich Kirchen, "Black Broadcaster Tries to Connect to the Towers of Power," *Business Journal of Milwaukee*, August 18, 2000.
12 Ibid.
13 Ibid.
14 Rich Kirchen, "TV Station Owner Lashes Out at City after Losing Tower Appeal," *Business Journal of Milwaukee*, March 30, 2001.
15 Robert Feder, "Tracking: No Sale," *Chicago Sun Times*, February 17, 2006.
16 Tim Cuprisin, "Without Couric, 'Today' Flies High," *Milwaukee Journal Sentinel*, June 23, 2006.
17 "Note to Readers," *Milwaukee Journal Sentinel*, January 28, 2007.
18 Rich Kirchen, "Weigel to Buy Channel 49 for $7 Million," *Business Journal of Milwaukee*, August 10, 2007.
19 "New Tower Sought for Channel 49," *Business Journal of Milwaukee*, September 28, 2007.
20 Rich Kirchen, "Channel 49's Tower Condition Delays Sale," *Business Journal of Milwaukee*, March 7, 2008.
21 Tim Cuprisin, "Shopping Channel gets New Owner, Me-TV Format of Nostalgic Shows," *Milwaukee Journal Sentinel*, April 22, 2008. Also see: Rich Kirchen, "Weigel Completes Channel 49 Deal, Launches 'Me-TV,'" *Business Journal of Milwaukee*, April 25, 2008.
22 Tim Cuprisin, "Zakaria's CNN Show Will Give American Viewers a Global Perspective," *Milwaukee Journal Sentinel*, May 30, 2008.

CHAPTER 14
WWRS-TV
CHANNEL 52

(Courtesy of Trinity Broadcasting Network)

On September 3, 1988, TV-52, Inc., whose principals were Wayne R. Stenz and Lyle R. Evans, applied for a construction permit for channel 52 in Mayville. Evans had owned WLRE (now WGBA) in Green Bay. The pair also applied for a construction permit for an AM daytime station on 990 kHz.[1] On December 5, TV-52, Inc. was granted a construction permit by the FCC. They were later assigned the call letters WWRS-TV (Wayne R. Stenz). Despite having a CP for ten years, the pair made little progress toward actually putting the station on the air.

TV-52 found a buyer in Mayville Communications, Inc., and it filed an application to transfer ownership on October 6, 1998. Approval was given by the FCC on December 17. The second week in January, 1999, an engineer from National Minority Television's station in Portland, Oregon, KNMT-TV, arrived to get the station operating and train a few operators.[2] The sale was consummated on February 16, and broadcasting began on February 28, 1999. Mayville Communications had a relationship with National Minority television, which in turn had one with Trinity Broadcasting, a Christian network headed up by Paul and Jan Crouch, who hosted the "Praise the Lord" variety show. As such, WWRS-TV carried TBN programming.

Many of Trinity's directors also sat on that of National Minority Television. In April of 1999, the FCC revoked a license held by Trinity for a station in Miami. The Commission alleged that Trinity was using National Minority Television as a way to circumvent their multiple-ownership rules. In May of 2000, a United States Court of Appeals ruling overturned the FCC's action and returned the Miami station to Trinity.[3]

WWRS-TV was sold to National Minority Television that year, and an application for approval was filed with the FCC on December 1. The sale was approved by the Commission on December 19, and consummated on February 1, 2001. The sale was made because National Minority TV had the resources to purchase and install a taller antenna, more powerful transmitter, and digital broadcasting equipment.[4]

The WWRS-TV transmitter building and 500' tower. (WWRS-TV photo)

The station had broadcast with enough power (10 kW) to serve Mayville and Dodge County, but after the sale to National Minority Television, a new 500' tower and more powerful (5000 kW) transmitter were installed. That gave it enough power to reach northwestern Milwaukee County. Studios were built in Iron Ridge, Wisconsin. The new facility went online on November 11, 2001.[5]

One result of the power increase was that Time-Warner cable was required to carry the station because of the FCC's "must carry" rule.[6] That rule required all cable companies to carry all full-service, local television stations on its basic cable tier[7], applied to all stations within the same "Designated Market Area" (DMA) as defined by Nielsen Media research. To do so, the cable company had to move WHA-TV to its digital tier. The switch took place on April 1, 2002 in the Milwaukee metro, western and northern areas.

Time-Warner fought the matter in the case of Racine, Kenosha and Walworth, Wisconsin. In a Memorandum Opinion and Order on May 23, 2002, the FCC granted Time-Warner's petition to exempt those communities from must-carry.[8]

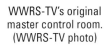

WWRS-TV's original master control room.
(WWRS-TV photo)

Shown in the small studio from which WWRS-TV originates local programming are Public Affairs Director Jackie Kahlhamer and Chief Engineer Gary Wallace.
(WWRS-TV photo)

The WWRS-TV transmitter room: The digital transmitter is on the left; the analog on the right. (WWRS-TV photo)

The new automated master control for WWRS-TV: All five digital subchannels are controlled from here. (WWRS-TV photo)

The station carries the Trinity network exclusively, save for two locally-originated, public affairs programs: "On Wisconsin" and "Public Report," which are seen several times each week.

The station began broadcasting a digital signal on channel 43 in October of 2002. On August 23, 2005, it began full-power digital operations, twenty-four hours-a-day, seven days-a-week. Five networks – Trinity Broadcasting Network (TBN), Enlace (Hispanic), JCTV (Youth), Church Channel (Worship) and Smile of a Child (Children's) – are all broadcast on the station's digital subchannels.[9]

Although only on the air since early 1999, WWRS-TV has had its own impact on the Milwaukee television market. It successfully increased its power, began being carried by local cable companies, and began digital operations. With five digital subchannels – all with Christian networks – it provides alternatives for those seeking religious programming.

NOTES

1 Jeff Schimetz, email to author, August 6, 2007.
2 National Minority TV, Inc., *History of WWRS-TV*, sent to author.
3 Rich Kirchen, "'Praise the Lord,' Trinity Network Targets Milwaukee," *Business Journal of Milwaukee*, March 16, 2001.
4 Ibid.
5 *History of WWRS-TV*.
6 8 FCC Rcd 2965, 2976-2977 (1993)
7 Tim Cuprisin, "Christian TV Station Boots WHA Off Cable," *Milwaukee Journal Sentinel*, January 29, 2002.
8 FCC DA 02-1244 (2002)
9 *History of WWRS-TV*.

CHAPTER 15

LOW-POWER, CLASS A AND TRANSLATOR STATIONS

When the FCC released its final Rules Governing Television Broadcast Stations on November 21, 1945, it provided for three different types of licenses: metropolitan, community and rural. Metropolitan licenses covered a single, major city, and were allowed a maximum effective radiated power (ERP) of 50 kW. Community stations covered smaller cities, were allowed a maximum ERP of 1 kW, and could not interfere with metropolitan stations. Rural stations were allowed to cover larger areas, but were prohibited from covering more than one metropolitan area. Channel 1 was reserved exclusively for community stations, and was assigned to Racine-Kenosha.[1]

When the FCC issued its Sixth Report and General Order, on April 14, 1952, it included new rules for television. The three types of licenses were dropped in favor of a single version.

The Commission's goal had been the development of "a truly nationwide, competitive television system." The Sixth Report failed to achieve that. Local topography meant that some areas of the country wouldn't receive an over-the-air signal from a nearby city.

In late 1952, WSM-TV in Nashville began experimenting with a "booster" system in Lawrenceburg, Tennessee. Boosters rebroadcast television programs from other stations, in communities that were unable to receive the originating station's signal. They did so using the same channel as the originating station. In mid-September of 1953 the Sylvania Electric Products Co. petitioned the FCC to institute rule-making that would allow the use of "satellite" stations. Such stations performed the same function as boosters, but broadcast on a different channel than the originating station.[2] WSM joined Sylvania formally when it too petitioned the FCC for rule-making the first week of November, 1953.[3]

Satellites and boosters were touted as one way to inject life into UHF television. One stumbling block was the "multiple-ownership" rule, which forbade parties from owning two stations serving the same area. Nonetheless, on August 4, 1954, the FCC announced that as of September 1 it would consider applications for stations in the UHF band that did not wish to originate programming, but simply wished to rebroadcast another station's. Because of the limited nature of boosters and satellites, the Commission agreed to consider waivers to the multiple-ownership rule, if the operation of such a facility could be shown to be in the public interest.[4]

Such stations would have to use existing channel assignments (or petition the FCC for rule-making to amend the Table of Channel Assignments), cover the licensed city, and not interfere with other stations.[5]

Commissioner Frieda Hennock dissented to the plan, saying that it would stifle competition by allowing VHF stations to grab more of the spectrum. She also argued that the plan would make UHF "auxiliary" to VHF.[6]

The first construction permit for a "satellite" station under the new rules was granted on November 3, 1954 to KIMA-TV of Yakima, Washington, so that it could broadcast its signal to Pasco-Richland-Kennewick, Washington on channel

19.[7] Exactly two weeks later, the FCC approved the re-establishment of channel 9 at Lufkin, Texas to rebroadcast the signal of KPRC-TV in Houston. It became the first VHF satellite station.[8]

The FCC had reason to be concerned. In September, an appliance store technician in Bridgeport, Washington had built a small booster that picked up the signal of KXLY-TV in Spokane. The communities of Bridgeport, Pateros, Brewster and Manson, had been without TV, as they were separated from Seattle to the west by mountains. They were open to Spokane to the east, but separated by 130 miles. Groups in each community contributed financing and four unlicensed boosters went into operation.

Late in October, the Commission began receiving complaints about interference to aeronautical and other non-broadcast services. They tracked down the illegal boosters and shut them down. The seals they had placed on the devices were broken shortly thereafter, and "persons unknown" put them back into operation. Washington Senators Magnuson and Jackson met with the FCC in late November to discuss the situation, and called for rule-making to permit automated boosters to be used.[9]

On December 15, the FCC issued a notice of proposed rule-making in which it outlined a plan to introduce low-power television stations with 100 watts of power designed to serve communities with less than 50,000 people.[10] The plan drew mixed reactions. Some thought that the proposal would make it easier for radio station owners to enter television, while others argued that such stations would be economically unviable because of their small coverage area.[11]

In early January of 1955, the FCC authorized the use of an experimental, 200 watt booster unit in Manson, Washington.[12] Meanwhile, five more unauthorized units went into operation. The Commission wrote to all Spokane stations to inquire if they had given permission for their signal to be rebroadcast. This was done to build a case against the operators of the boosters.[13]

UHF broadcasters continued to have problems, and the Commission sought ways to help them. In late March of 1955, it called for comments on a new proposal to allow co-channel UHF boosters to fill in the shadows of parent UHF stations. Successful tests of such devices had been conducted by RCA in Vicksburg, Mississippi, in addition to Sylvania and WSM-TV.[14]

The FCC continued to get mixed comments on its low-power TV proposal. Adler Communications had also been conducting tests on such a system, but pointed out that some sort of relay device, owned and operated by the booster station, might be necessary in areas that could not pick up an over-the-air signal, in order to avoid the cost of using a microwave relay system. Seward Community TV, which held franchise agreements for two communities in Alaska filed comments opposing the idea, pointing out that local interests able to serve the needs of individual communities should have priority over satellite stations controlled by distant parents.[15]

The Commission continued to fine-tune its proposal to allow low-power booster and satellite stations. It preferred to use the term "amplifying transmitter" for a booster, but the name hadn't caught on. It then began using the name "translator" for any station that re-broadcast the programming of another, whether UHF or VHF, on the same channel or another. In January of 1956, it asked for comments on the idea. Generating higher frequencies took more electrical power for the same effective-radiated-power (ERP), and as such UHF channels 70-83 were not being used. The FCC proposed that low-power translator stations use them.[16]

Meanwhile, Washington Congressman Don Magnuson introduced legislation in early May that would require the FCC to initiate rule-making to propose regulations for the licensing of VHF translators.[17]

Later that month, the FCC authorized television translator operation as of July 2. Such stations were limited to 10 watts or 100 watts ERP, could not interfere with any other station, could operate via remote control[18], and had to operate in UHF channels 70-83. They used their own call letters, with the form: [W or K, depending on if the station was east or west of the Mississippi River][Channel no.][AA-ZZ, assigned sequentially – the station had no say in what they were assigned]. There was no limit on the number of translators that could be owned by any individual entity. Translator owners had to obtain permission from the parent station to re-broadcast their signal. The Commission rejected suggestions that translators be allowed to operate in the VHF band, that such stations would compete with community TV services, or that such translators be allowed to beam their signal to a central point in the community, from where it could be distributed to viewers via cable.[19] *Broadcasting Telecasting* reported that by April of 1957, twenty to twenty-five of the stations were operating – primarily in the Pacific Northwest.[20] Since full-power stations also originated their own programming, they became known as "full-service" stations.

In September of 1959, the chief of the FCC's Broadcast Bureau made a month-long visit to the Western part of the country. He made a survey of translator stations, and estimated that 1,000 illegal translators were operating! One hundred fifty were identified in Montana alone![21]

Translators began popping up in northern Wisconsin. In the mid-to-late 1960s, Green Bay stations began building them in the Fox River Valley, in order to improve their signal quality in some communities. Two Milwaukee stations followed suit. WTMJ-TV received a construction permit for a translator in Sheboygan on June 28, 1967[22], but the station was never constructed. WISN-TV also applied for one, and W70AO went on-the-air in May of 1968. (See chapter 6.)

In the late 1960s, the FCC was again under pressure from land-mobile users to free up unused television channels for their use. In July of 1968, it proposed rule-making that would make TV channels 70-83 available to them. It made that official in May of 1970. Since that would displace television translators, it allowed them to broadcast on channels 14-69.[23]

No translator station had ever been proposed for Milwaukee. That changed on June 23, 1980, when Weigel Broadcasting of Chicago applied for a license to operate one on channel 55. Weigel owned WCIU-TV in Chicago, and proposed to rebroadcast its programming.

Although many of the UHF channels that had been assigned in 1952 were finally being used, much of the spectrum allocated to television still wasn't. The FCC sought ways to utilize it – especially since they were still under pressure from land-mobile users for more spectrum space. On September 9, 1980, it unanimously approved another rule-making proposal that would allow low-power television stations (LPTV).[24]

The proposal included a minimal number of requirements:

• Studio facilities and locally-originated programming would not be required.

• While no formal ascertainment would be required, applicants would still have to determine community needs and outline how they intended to respond to them.

• The "fairness doctrine" would still apply.

♦ No limit would be placed on the number of stations any single entity could own. However, NBC, CBS and ABC would be precluded from entering the low-power market, and existing one-to-a-market and duopoly rules would still apply.

♦ Unlike full-service stations, the owner of a low-power version would not have to hold it for three years before being allowed to sell it.

♦ Subscription TV operation would not require approval, but rather a simple notification.

♦ Cable systems would not be required to carry low-power stations.

♦ A "paper hearing" procedure would be developed to simplify the application process.

VHF stations would be limited to 10 watts if operated outside the existing Table of Channel Assignments, and 100 watts if they operated within it – provided that they complied with existing full-power co-channel and adjacent-channel mileage separation requirements. UHF stations would be limited to 1 kW if they operated outside the Table.

While studio facilities and locally originated programming were not required, low-power stations could elect to produce their own programming – something translators could not do.

The Commission was flooded with inquiries. Applications were allowed to be filed, even though the proposal had not been adopted, and no rules had been approved. By February 17, 1981, over 3,000 had been received. Because there was no ownership limit, one entity filed over 100 applications![25]

The National Association of Broadcasters (NAB) petitioned the FCC on behalf of full-service stations and the television networks, objecting to the restrictions that prevented them from owning LPTV stations. Because the rules were only in the proposal stage, ABC and NBC had applied for stations, as they feared that the best might be granted before they were finalized. The Commission had dismissed the petition in January, promising to accept and process the applications on a case-by-case basis until the rules were promulgated.[26]

Applications continued to pour in. By March 31, 4,748 had been received. The Corporation for Public Broadcasting filed a motion to stay the entire LPTV interim process on the grounds that conversations between some commissioners and private entities had "tainted" it.[27] The CPB was also concerned that noncommercial stations might lose LPTV stations to commercial interests.

On the recommendation of its staff, the FCC froze all LPTV applications on April 9. The shear number of applications made the freeze necessary. Exceptions were made for: applications for communities served by only one full-service station, and translators wanting to move from channels 70-83 or avoid interference with full-service stations. Using existing mileage separation requirements for full-service stations, the FCC staff first examined each applicant to sort out those that were uncontested or mutually exclusive.[28] Such applications would require less study before grants could be made.

Meanwhile, on December 11, Weigel Broadcasting received a construction permit for low-power translator station W55AS.

Interest was still high, and on March 4, 1982, the FCC finally released new rules for LPTV. Such stations could not interfere with full-service stations, but would have to accept interference. As such, they had secondary status. Existing translators could become low-power stations simply by notifying the FCC of their intention, and could then originate programming if they desired. The freeze on new LPTV applications remained in effect until the backlog of applications was eliminated.[29]

On January 27, 1983, W55AS began tests on channel 55. It officially began broadcasting on February 9, and rebroadcast WCIU-TV in Chicago. The signal was beamed via microwave from the Sears Tower to an antenna mounted atop the First Wisconsin (now the US Bank) Center. The station broadcast from a small studio and switching center in the building.[30] The programming consisted of Polish, Italian, Greek, Serbian, Korean, Chinese, and Indian shows, financial news, religious programming, and sports. Some forty percent of the programming was in Spanish.[31]

On September 10, 1984, the FCC issued a construction permit to Woods Communications for a low-power station, W08BY. In early November of 1985, W08BY began broadcasting on channel 8 from facilities located atop the Marc Plaza hotel. It showed music videos from Canada's "MuchMusic," as well as those selected by its own "VJs,"

On April 6, 1986, W55AS began offering two locally-produced programs for the Hispanic community: a call-in public affairs program named "Yolanda Ayubi Presents" and a ten-minute news program "The Milwaukee Hispanic News," They aired together in a thirty-minute block Sunday nights, and were sponsored by local Hispanic businesses.[32]

By 1987, W08BY had begun originating programming that spotlighted the Milwaukee music scene. That included on-site interviews at local clubs, profiles of new bands, updates on established groups, and features on national and international bands coming to the city.[33]

WHKE in Kenosha was ready to go on the air in 1988 on channel 55. Since W55AS could interfere with it, Weigel Broadcasting shifted that station's programming to W65BT (Ch. 65) on June 17, 1988.

Milwaukee became a center for low-power television activity. The Community Broadcasters Association was incorporated in 1984, and its offices were located in the area for many years. The name came from the fact that many station owners thought that a stigma was associated with the use of "low-power" to describe them, and preferred to use the 1945 designation as a "community" station.

Spanish programming was working so well for Weigel Broadcasting that it decided to add a second translator station to its Milwaukee group. On October 30, 1989, W46AR began operations on channel 46 from facilities in the Marc Plaza hotel. It broadcast programming from Univision, and replaced that network on most local cable systems.[34]

W08BY had dropped its locally-originated programming by September of 1990, and was offering public domain films and infomercials as well as music videos. It had not made a profit since it went on the air, and was put up for sale.[35] The following month, the station began carrying "The Jukebox Network" whereby viewers could dial a 900 number, and for $2.50 select a music video to be played.[36] That network eventually became known as "The Box,"

The Community Broadcasters Association was still seeking to improve the public's perception of LPTV. In January of 1991, it petitioned the FCC to change the name of such stations from "low power" to "community" – bringing back the name used in 1945. The Association also asked the Commission to assign such stations standard, four-letter call signs (six if a suffix was used), rather than the alpha-numeric system used for translators. Doing so, it argued, would make it easier for viewers to fill out the diaries used by some ratings services. It also petitioned the FCC to allow any LPTV station to increase its power to whatever level it needed to cover the communities it served, as long as it did not cause interference. The National Association of Broadcasters (NAB) opposed the requests.[37]

Woods Communications filed for Chapter 11 bankruptcy in on July 27, 1993.[38] As a consequence, on November 19, KM Communications, Inc. of Skokie, Illinois, purchased W08BY.

In May of 1994 the FCC voted to allow LPTV stations to use standard, four-letter call signs. The NAB requested that such stations use the suffix –LP to designate them as "low power,"[39] As such, KM Communications applied for permission to change the call letters of W08BY to WMKE-LP. The FCC approved, and the change was made on December 23, 1994. As the new owners were Korean-American, the station began offering some programming aimed at that community.

After Weigel's new tower went online in November of 1996, the company began moving the antennas for its other stations there. W46AR increased its power three-fold, and added brief local news updates throughout the day hosted by WDJT-TV reporter Saul Garza.[40]

In November of 1998, Univision notified Weigel Broadcasting that it would end its affiliation with W46AR as of April 30, 1999[41], and move strictly to cable – ending its availability on free, over-the-air TV. The decision caused an uproar in the local Hispanic community, whose leaders called for a boycott of Univision.[42]

Weigel challenged the decision in Milwaukee County Circuit Court and received a restraining order against Univision on April 28 that temporarily stopped the move. A U.S. District Judge granted a motion from Univision, and had the case moved to it. He later decided that the move did not violate anti-trust laws, as Weigel had contended.[43]

Weigel claimed that W46AR was a "dealer" for Univision, and that it had not been given adequate notice of the switch. A hearing on the matter was scheduled for July 22. Univision and Weigel then entered into settlement negotiations. The hearing was postponed, and the date for the switch was extended to November 1.[44] The matter was eventually settled. Weigel entered into negotiations with the Telemundo network, and in October, it announced that W46AR would become an affiliate as of November 1.[45]

With the advent of digital television and the establishment of a transition period in which both analog (NTSC) and digital (ATSC) signals would be broadcast by full-service stations, the FCC gave each one a second channel on which to broadcast a digital signal. Those assignments had the potential to displace LPTV stations. In order to preserve the diversity and "localism" that LPTV stations provide, Congress passed the Community Broadcasters Protection Act, which was signed into law on November 29, 1999, and ordered the FCC to establish a "Class A" television service, which would provide primary status (and consequently frequency protection), as well as enhanced commercial viability to LPTV stations. The proposal had been around for some years, and was opposed by the NAB and others. Only those LPTV stations which existed as of November 29, 1999 were eligible for the upgrade. To be eligible, LPTV stations had to meet certain programming requirements within the 90-day period prior to that date. In addition, all Class A stations had to meet some of the same requirements as their full-service counterparts. Class A stations would use the suffix –CA in their call letters. All Class A stations must air at least three hours of locally-produced programming each week.

Since the FCC assigned channel 8 as the digital channel for WMVS, WMKE-LP applied for the use of channel 7. Despite objections from WMVS and WLS-TV in Chicago, the FCC granted its application on February 16, 2000. It began broadcasting on its new channel in August of that year, and relocated some of its facilities from atop the Hilton Hotel to South 27th Street that December.

Meanwhile, Weigel Broadcasting shifted its channels in September of 2000 in order to free channel 46 for WDJT-TV's digital signal. Telemundo programming shifted to W63CU, which began broadcasting on September 13, 2000.[46] Channel 65 then went dark, and W41CI began broadcasting the same day, as a joint venture between Weigel and Bridge Information Systems, Inc. of New York. During the day, W41CI broadcast Web Financial Network (WebFN) programming.[47]

(Weigel Broadcasting Co. photo archive)

WMKE-LP became a Class A television station on January 26, 2001, and changed its call letters to WMKE-CA. MTV merged with The Box in October of 2000, and their management decided to replace its programming with MTV2. As a result, WMKE-CA became an MTV2 affiliate as of January 1, 2001.[48]

On November 13, 2001, W41CI received low-power television status from the FCC and changed its call letters to WMLW-LP.

With the new millennium, WMLW-LP began to expand its programming. As an independent station, it looked to sports as a way to build an audience. University of Wisconsin men's basketball was the first addition, during the 2000-2001 season. In 2001, it added Big Ten football and men's basketball, Marquette and UWM men's and UWM women's basketball. It also signed a three-year deal to cover the WIAA state basketball and wrestling tournaments.[49]

The station struggled for years to get on local cable. With Weigel opting to use WMLW-LP for sports, fans began to call Time Warner protesting that they could not get the WIAA basketball tournament unless they went back to over-the-air TV. Finally the cable company relented – partially. It added the station to its digital cable line-up in March of 2002.[50] Analog cable subscribers were out-of-luck.

On January 14, 2003, the FCC accepted Weigel Broadcasting's application for Class A status for WMLW-LP, and the call letters were changed to WMLW-CA on September 19. It also applied for low-power status for channel 63. That status was granted, and the call letters were changed to WYTU-LP (y tú = Spanish for "and you") on December 16.

On January 2, 2004, Time Warner announced that WMLW-CA would become part of its basic cable package as of the 29th of that month. Telemundo affiliate, WYTU-LP did as well.[51] It was a major victory for Weigel Broadcasting – especially since WMLW-LP would use channel 7.

In 2006, WMKE-CA dropped their MTV2 and Korean programming and became a full-time America One affiliate.

The success of WYTU-LP in reaching the Hispanic community drew competition. On June 13, 2006, the FCC approved the sale of W53CC to Bustos Media LLC, the owner of the area's first Spanish-language radio station, WDDW-FM, and assigned it channel 38. Bustos purchased the station, whose city of license was originally Ludington, Michigan, from MS Communications. They then announced that they would become an affiliate of Azteca America.[52] The call letters originally assigned in 1995 were W55CG, and they were changed to W53CC in 2001. On August 30, 2006, the FCC assigned the station the call letters WBWT-LP.

T63
TELEMUNDO
WISCONSIN
(Weigel Broadcasting Co. photo archive)

The station began over-the-air tests in September of that year by transmitting an ID logo. It began broadcasting formally on December 12.[53]

Milwaukee Brewers' baseball games had not been seen on over-the-air television since the team signed a deal with FSN North in 2003. That changed in 2007 when Weigel entered into a deal to broadcast fifteen games on WMLW-CA. WYTU-LP had been broadcasting the games using Spanish-speaking announcers. They were produced by FSN North.[54]

Weigel had previously produced a local Spanish newscast for WCIU-TV in Chicago. Since it owned Telemundo affiliate WYTU-LP in Milwaukee, it decided to use the WDJT-TV news staff to produce one for use within *Noticiero Telemundo*, beginning on July 2, 2007.[55] It was called "Noticiero Telemundo Wisconsin y tú."

After affiliating with Fox in 1994, WITI started a 9:00 p.m. newscast. WVTV dropped its newscast in that time slot in 2006. The 2007 World Series was carried by Fox, and as such, WITI's 9:00 p.m. newscast was pre-empted. WDJT-TV produced one shown on WMLW-CA beginning on October 24.[56] The experiment worked so well that it was later made permanent. Called "CBS 58 News at 9 on WMLW," the first was broadcast at 9:00 p.m. on Tuesday, January 1, 2008.[57]

Unlike their full-service counterparts, low-power, Class A and translator stations were not automatically granted a second channel on which to broadcast a digital signal. They were assigned digital channels, and were given the choice of making the change whenever they wanted to, or applying for a digital companion channel. In February of 2006, the FCC announced the first filing window for such stations to apply for one.

Milwaukee -LP and -CA
Digital Channel Assignments
WMKE-LD   20
WMLW-LD   13
WYTU-LD   17
WBWT-LD   31

Weigel had broadcast WMLW-CA programming on the digital subchannel for WDJT-DT (46-2) for some time. It was granted construction permits for WMLW-LD and WYTU-LD on March 16, 2007, as was Bustos Media for WBWT-LD. WMKE-CA was granted a construction permit for a digital companion on October 11. WMLW-LD began broadcasting a digital signal in late November of 2007. It broadcast at a lower power so as not to interfere with WZZM-TV in Grand Rapids, Michigan, which broadcasts its analog signal on channel 13. WYTU-LD began broadcasting a digital signal on December 10.

On December 18, 2007, the FCC adopted a Report on Broadcast Localism and Notice of Proposed Rulemaking. In it, the Commission agreed with recommendations that would allow more low-power stations to obtain Class A status.[58]

Low-power and translator stations have been with us since the 1950s. At first they served communities that because of typography might not otherwise have been able to receive an over-the-air television signal. With the advent of LPTV, they began to serve small communities within larger metropolitan areas – as the FCC envisioned when they established "community" licenses in 1945. The Hispanic community in Milwaukee has been the largest beneficiary. The digital transition will challenge full-service stations, and their low-power counterparts will face even greater ones as the internet and streaming devices take over some video distribution.

NOTES

1 "Rules Governing Television Broadcast Stations," *Broadcasting*, December 3, 1945, 76.
2 "Sylvania Seeks 'Satellite' Approval," *Broadcasting Telecasting*, September 21, 1953, 50.
3 "WSM Seeks Booster or Satellite Rule," *Broadcasting Telecasting*, November 9, 1953, 52.
4 "Television for Everybody? Way Opened for Satellites," *Broadcasting Telecasting*, August 9, 1954, 31.
5 "FCC Approves UHF 'Budget' Stations," *Broadcasting Telecasting*, August 9, 1954, 32.
6 Ibid., 22.
7 "FCC Grants Two TVs, One Satellite," *Broadcasting Telecasting*, November 8, 1954, 54.
8 "Texas TV Grant Extends Satellite Policy to VHF," *Broadcasting Telecasting*, November 2, 1954, 80.
9 "A Small Town + TV Repeater Idea: FCC Headache," *Broadcasting Telecasting*, November 22, 1954, 82.
10 "Little TVs Proposed," *Broadcasting Telecasting*, December 20, 1954, 9.
11 "'Coffee Pot' TV Plan Draws Mixed Reaction," *Broadcasting Telecasting*, December 27, 1954, 67-68.
12 "One Way Out," *Broadcasting Telecasting*, January 17, 1954, 84.
13 "Wash. State TV Boosters Cause Concern at Commission," *Broadcasting Telecasting*, March 21, 1955, 104-105.
14 "Comments Sought on FCC's Proposal to permit Co-Channel Boosters," *Broadcasting Telecasting*, April 4, 1955, 66.
15 "FCC Gets Mixed Comments on Low-Power TV Proposal," *Broadcasting Telecasting*, April 4, 1955, 69.
16 "FCC Proposes 'Translators' Pint-Sized TV Satellites," *Broadcasting Telecasting*, January 16, 1956, 67.
17 "Licensing of TV Boosters, Reflectors by FCC Sought," *Broadcasting Telecasting*, May 7, 1956, 72.
18 FCC regulations at the time required that a licensed engineer be present at the transmitter site of television stations.
19 "FCC Opens Gates on TV Translators," *Broadcasting Telecasting*, May 28, 1956, 75.
20 "Translators Give Rural West TV," *Broadcasting Telecasting*, April 15, 1957, 56.
21 "TV's Secret Stations," *Broadcasting*, September 14, 1959, 5.
22 "For the Record," *Broadcasting*, November 6, 1967, 85.
23 "Land Mobile Moves Into the UHF Band," *Broadcasting*, May 25, 1970, 62.
24 "FCC Opens Pandora's Box on Low Power," *Broadcasting*, September 15, 1980, 29-30.
25 "Another Deluge of LPTV Filings Inundates FCC," *Broadcasting*, February 23, 1981, 29.
26 "LPTV" (Special Report). *Broadcasting*, February 23, 1981, 38-66.
27 "LPTV Line Gets Longer at FCC," *Broadcasting*, April 6, 1981, 40.
28 "FCC Whistles Low-Power TV to Standstill," *Broadcasting*, April 13, 1981, 28-29.
29 "LPTV Gets the FCC Go-Ahead," *Broadcasting*, March 8, 1982, pp. 35-36.
30 "Channel 55 to Go On Air Feb. 9," *Milwaukee Journal*, January 20, 1983.
31 John Barron, "WCIU Programs an International Stew," *Milwaukee Sentinel*, March 4, 1983.
32 "Hispanic TV Shows to Be Broadcast Weekly," *Milwaukee Journal*, April 6, 1986.
33 Eugene Kane, "Local Music Channel is Off to a Sound Start," *Milwaukee Journal*, May 5, 1987.
34 Duane Dudek, "New Low-Power TV Station Serving Hispanic Community," *Milwaukee Sentinel*, October 30, 1989.
35 "Technical Woes Take Channel 8 Off the Air," *Milwaukee Journal*, September 17, 1990.
36 "Channel 8 Now Showing Videos," *Milwaukee Journal*, October 5, 1990.
37 HAJ, "CBA Asks FCC for LPTV Name Change" *Broadcasting*, June 17, 1991, 62.
38 JAZ, "Woods's(sic) Five TV Stations to Go to Banks," *Broadcasting and Cable*, August 20, 1993, 56.

39 Christopher Stern, "New Calls for LPTV," *Broadcasting and Cable*, May 23, 1994, 16.

40 Georgia Pabst, "Spanish TV Station Boosts Power, News Staff: More Frequent Reports Will Flow to Wider Area," *Milwaukee Journal Sentinel*, October 25, 1997.

41 Rich Kirchen, "Univision, Weigel Attack Each Other in Battle Over Spanish TV," *Business Journal of Milwaukee*, May 21, 1999.

42 Georgia Pabst, "Boycott of Univision Advertisers Suggested: Network to Switch from Free Channel to Cable," *Milwaukee Journal Sentinel*, April 22, 1999.

43 "Univision Switch to Cable Deemed Legal by Judge," *Milwaukee Journal Sentinel*, June 12, 1999.

44 Georgia Pabst, "Deadline Extended for Univision Switch to Cable: Spanish-Language Network to Stay on Channel 46 Until Nov. 1, Time Warner Says," *Milwaukee Journal Sentinel*, July 31, 1999.

45 Georgia Pabst, "Telemundo to Replace Univision on Channel 46: Station Losing Nation's Top Spanish-Language Network to Time Warner Cable," *Milwaukee Journal Sentinel*, October 18, 1999.

46 "Spanish Language Station on New Channel," *Milwaukee Journal Sentinel*, September 8, 2000.

47 Rich Kirchen, "Channel 41 Brings Milwaukee New Financial Network and 'The Munsters,'" *Business Journal of Milwaukee*, October 20, 2000.

48 Rich Kirchen, "MTV Bops The Box," *Business Journal of Milwaukee*, December 29, 2000.

49 Bob Wolfly, "Channel 41 Jumps Into Local Sports," *Milwaukee Journal Sentinel*, July 29, 2001.

50 Tim Cuprisin "Channel 41 Wins a Spot on Cable, But Only on Digital," *Milwaukee Journal Sentinel*, March 18, 2002.

51 "Channel 41 Joins Basic Cable Service," *Milwaukee Journal Sentinel*, January 3, 2004.

52 Georgia Pabst, "Milwaukee to Get New Spanish TV Station," *Milwaukee Journal Sentinel*, May 12, 2006.

53 Rich Kirchen, "Buestos Premiers Milwaukee Azteca America TV Station," *Business Journal of Milwaukee*, December 12, 2006.

54 "Some Brewers Games to Return to Airwaves," *Business Journal of Milwaukee* (online), February 16, 2007, http://www.bizjournals.com/milwaukee/stories/2007/02/12/daily54.html

55 "Channel 63 to Offer Spanish-Language News," *Business Journal of Milwaukee* (online), June 4, 2007. http://www.bizjournals.com/milwaukee/stories/2007/06/04/daily12.html

56 Tim Cuprisin "Channel 58 to Fill 9 p.m. News Gap; Cuban's Season Over on 'Dancing,'" *Milwaukee Journal Sentinel*, October 24, 2007.

57 Tim Cuprisin "Channel 58 Goes Head to Head with Channel 6 in 9 p.m. Newscast Dual," *Milwaukee Journal Sentinel*, December 4, 2007.

58 Federal Communications Commission, *Report on Broadcast Localism and Notice of Proposed Rulemaking*. Issued: January 24, 2008, 63.

AFTERWORD

So where is Milwaukee over-the-air television headed? The digital TV (DTV) transition promises to change the way we view video information. At first, the local stations will opt for broadcasting a high-definition signal (HDTV), or several programs in standard definition on their digital subchannels. As this book was being prepared, a number of stations are already doing the latter. The following table shows the area's digital channels:

Milwaukee Digital Channel Assignments

Call Letters	Analog Channel	DTV Transition Channel	Permanent DTV Channel
WTMJ	4	28	28
WITI	6	33	33
WMKE	7	(None)	20
WMVS	10	8	8
WISN	12	34	34
WVTV	18	61	18
WCGV	24	25	25
WVCY	30	22	22
WMVT	36	35	35
WBWT	38	(None)	31
WMLW	41	(None)	13
WBME	49	48	48
WWRS	52	43	43
WPXE	55	40	40
WDJT	58	46	46
WYTU	63	(None)	17

The fact that every station except WVTV will switch to a new channel doesn't mean that the stations will necessarily re-brand themselves, however. DTV uses the Program and System Information Protocol (PSIP), in which information about both the old analog and new digital channels is contained. Included are content ratings for shows, electronic program guides, and the ability to use virtual channels. Thus, WTMJ may broadcast digitally over UHF channel 28, but the PSIP will allow it to be displayed as VHF channel 4. (Over-the-air viewers will need to exercise care to purchase antennas appropriate to receive the actual broadcast and not the virtual channels.)

The real revolution however, will involve the merger of video with the world-wide web.

Local TV stations used to be program delivery systems. Once cable and satellite became available, the traditional networks could have gone directly to those companies to distribute their product. Thus far, none of the networks have. (PBS affiliates pay for their programming, and as such are a revenue source for the network.)

The bandwidth available on digital cable allowed for more channels as well as broadband internet and even telephone service. The latter two capabilities upset the phone companies – which had previously enjoyed a monopoly on voice and data transmission, and in 2007 they won the right to provide television service in Wisconsin.

Digital cable allowed a degree of interactivity that analog cable hadn't. Previously, one had to call the cable company to order a film or special program. Now one can order it directly using one's remote control. On-demand servers now allow one to watch a film when one wants to, rather than at some scheduled time.

One can extrapolate that capability to envision a situation where one can order any program that has been made available from an on-demand server. Films, reruns of old programs, sporting events, etc. will be able to be ordered whenever one wants to see them. Digital recording technology will allow one to save it for later use. The program source could be anywhere in the world, and distributed via the internet.

There will be problems to be sure, but the historical precedent is there. Hollywood films were released slowly to television, and not all were made available. Still, problems involving rights, residual payments, etc. were eventually worked out. The Writers' Guild of America strike in 2007-2008 involved a dispute over residuals for programming distributed via the internet. Subsequent agreements with the Directors' Guild of America and the American Federation of Television and Radio Artists (AFTRA) included additional residual payments for product distributed there.

The pornography industry has already begun to distribute its product via the Web. It provides previously released, as well as made-for-streaming material on the Web. It's a billion dollar, world-wide industry.

Mainstream video lags behind the porn industry, but they will eventually catch up. Younger viewers are used to a degree of interactivity that their parents never had. Wireless, broadband internet promises to bring a degree of mobility to video that has not been possible previously. One might not use their HDTV monitor to surf the internet, but one could. U-Tube®, MySpace® and other online sites are already used to share videos produced by their users from around the world.

The interesting question is where these changes might leave local television stations. Certainly local news/weather/sports will continue to be an important offering. Will that be enough to sustain the many stations already on-the-air? Further, since wireless broadband will use the public airwaves, will it be subject to tighter regulations than cable and satellite, the way over-the-air broadcast stations currently are?

In December of 2007, the FCC issued a Report on Broadcast Localism and Notice of Proposed Rulemaking. Although some considered it to be a weak attempt to revitalize local programming, it was a start. One of the ways local stations can continue to be relevant in their respective markets will be to originate much more of their own programming. Whether viewers (who will have even more choices than they do now) will watch is a question yet to be answered.

Will free, over-the-air television survive? (Actually, it's not free. It's paid for by those who purchase goods and services from advertisers. In the case of noncommercial broadcasting, tax monies, and those who make direct contributions, or purchase goods and services from program underwriters pay for it.) That depends on whether there are enough viewers who want it. Until wireless broadband is available in every part of the country, over-the-air TV will be the only way many can receive a signal if they don't have cable or satellite.

It's unlikely that we'll see the quantity and variety of locally-produced programming so common in the early days of Milwaukee television. Nonetheless, we are living through a period of transition that promises to be as, or more significant than the introduction of UHF, educational television, cable or satellite.

Hopefully, this book has done more than simply provide a trip down memory lane. I hope that is has framed the historical context of some of the coming changes.

Dick Golembiewski
September, 2008

INDEX

A

ABC, 53, 56, 58, 77, 79, 82, 118, 125, 128, 142, 152, 153, 155, 164, 166-167, 178-179, 192, 206, 217, 219, 225, 232, 241-242, 246, 250, 260, 265, 268, 284-285, 287, 289, 302, 315, 322, 334, 379, 460, 467, 482
ABC Evening News with Ron Cochran, 179
ABC Nightlife, 179
ABRY Communications, 197, 420-421
Adams, Dave, 64
Adams, Nick, 232
Adamson, Dewayne, 452
Addams Family, The, 261, 324
¡Adelente!, 384
Adler Communications Labs, 145, 480
Advisor's Mystery Theater, 9, 172, 205-206
Affiliated Taxpayers' Committee, 335, 343, 350, 352
Affiliates Advisory Board (CBS), 33
African Patrol, 202
After School with Hugo, 202
Afternoon Edition, 276-277
Albert and Friends, 322
Albert the Alley Cat, 67, 292-293, 295-296, 303, 317
Aldridge, Lionel, 96, 240
Alice the Alligator (DuBlon puppet), 317, 320
All-Channel Receiver Act, 135, 177, 364
All-Star Wrestling, 192
Allen, Ward, 15, 285, 289, 292-294, 296, 328-329
Allen-Bradley, 374
Alm, Adrienne, 181
Amaro, Filemon, Jr. (murder trial), 374
Ament, Tom, 461
America One, 485
American Bandstand, 179, 282
American Federation of Musicians, 50
American Federation of Television and Radio Artists (AFTRA), 411, 490
American Meteorological Society (AMS), 294-295
American Society of Newspaper Editors, 92
American Subscription Television (AST), 413, 415-416, 418-419
American Tower Corp., 381
American TV & Appliances, 426
Ames, Carl, 15, 426

Ampex, 230, 284, 361, 435
amplifying transmitter, 480
AnDave, 160
Anderson, Bill, 188
Anderson, Dick, 445
Anspach, Elden, 251, 279, 314
Anthony, John, 276, 282, 289, 291
Antlers Hotel, 38-39, 115
Apex Radio, 23-24, 34-35, 42, 332, 398
Appalachia: Rich Land, Poor People, 365
Aquaramma, 82
Archdiocese, Milwaukee, 297, 359, 360, 362, 444-445
Argyle Television Films, 154
Arlington Broadcasting Group, 420
Armstrong, Edwin Howard, 29, 33, 125, 128, 138
Armstrong, Stu, 15, 277, 281, 328
Army Corps of Engineers, 461
Army-McCarthy hearings, 167
Arnold, Chuck, 235
Ask Gus, 309
Associated Press Managing Editors Association, 92
Association of Land Grant Colleges and Universities, 333
Association of Maximum Service Telecasters, 136
At Twelve with Howard and Rosemary, 239-240
AT&T, 19, 46-47, 53, 58, 125, 183, 378, 413-414
Autry, Gene, 72, 109, 315
Award Theater, 177, 195
Axtell, Tom, 15, 376, 378, 405
Ayers, Liz, 246
Azteca America, 485, 488

B

B & F Broadcasting, Inc., 372, 413
Baas, Jeff, 452
Bach, Bob, 15, 195-196, 209-210
Baden, Mark, 250
Badger Television Co., 163
Badger Television Network, 230
Baird, Audrey, 302
Baird, John, 19
Balaban & Katz, 30
Balaban, Elmer, 145, 163
Balaban, Harry, 145, 163

Balanced Budget Act of 1997, 137
Balloons, The, 264
Balopticon, 357, 403
Bandstand Review, 314
Banks, Andrew, 420
Banzhaf, Peter, 373
Barbara Becker Sings, 317
Barber, Red, 148
Barbie, Lloyd, 372
Barg, Hy, 353
Barkey the Barker, 368, 390
Barnes, Patt, 235
Barry, Bob, 7, 15, 289, 356-357, 403
Barrymore, Lionel, 38
Bartel, Henry, 390
Bartell Broadcasters, Inc., 145, 154, 161-164, 199, 214
Bartell, David, 159-160
Bartell, Gerald (Jerry), 160, 162, 199, 207, 326, 342
Bartell, Lee, 159-160, 162
Bartell, Mel, 200
Baum, Werner, 295
BBC, 361
Bear E. Tone (puppet), 389-390
Beasley, Bob, 80
Beauregard Boo Boo (puppet), 389-391, 393, 395-396
Beaver Dam, Wisconsin 162, 170
Beavers, Roger, 380
Becker, Barbara, 15, 289, 292, 300, 317-318, 320, 322, 330
Becquerel, Alexandre Edmond, 17
Bedtime for Bimbo, 424
Beginning Slide Rule, 360-361
Behan, Ken, 264
Behee, Bob, 227, 276
Behling, Jim, 322
Beilfuss, Trudy, 147, 166, 169, 202, 230
Bell, Ken, 241, 243
Bennett, Bruce, 242
Berg, Darlyne (Also See: Haertlein, Darlyne), 320-322, 394
Beringer, Bob, 7, 206-207
Berkley Fudge, 192
Berle, Milton, 58, 119
Berndt, Mary, 389
Bernie Bear (puppet), 393, 395-396
Betty (Tolouse NoNeck's girlfriend), 263
Bewitched, 261, 324
Bi-Tran, 412

Because of their frequent occurrence, the current call letters of full-power full-service stations are omitted.

Bierman, John, 264
Big Lee, 393
Big Movie, The, 260
Big Muskego Lake, 463
Big Picture, The, 214
Big Time Wrestling, 284
Billy Bounce and Witi, 314
Binford, Al, 359, 390-391, 393, 395
Birge, Edward A., 37-38, 114
Birkholz, John, 382
Bishop, Billy, 314
Black and White in Milwaukee: the First Hundred Years, 375
Black Like Me, 365
Black Nouveau, 378
blanking period, 29, 280, 376
Blatz, 79-80, 148
Bloch, Robert, 231
Block, Robert, 15, 412-415, 418-419, 428
Blonder-Tongue Laboratories, 412
Blumenthal, Cy, 144-145
Bob Newhart Show, The, 420
Bodovinac, Marcus, 390
booster station, 479-480, 487
Borchert Field, 53, 55
Borchert, R. C., 142
Boston Store 47, 50
Bowling for Dollars, 185-186, 242, 268
Bowling Game, The, 186-188, 242, 458
Bowling Proprietors Association of Milwaukee, 185
Bowling with the Champs, 10, 80-82, 185, 421, 429
Box, The, 483, 485, 488
Boyd, Jayne, 183, 190
Bozo, 259, 422-424, 429
Bozo and Stubby, 259-260
Bozo's Big Top Circus, 422-423
Bozo's Breakfast Club, 423-424, 429
bracket standards (for color TV receivers), 129
Bradley–Uihlein, Jane, 368-369
Brady, Dan, 461
Bramhall, Bill, 218, 265
Brauer, Nick, 74, 82
Brechlin, Dennis, 15, 151, 184, 209
Brenza, Julie, 446
Bridge Information Systems, Inc., 485
Bromberg, Ellis, 15, 383, 402
Brown, Les, 317
Brownie Bear (puppet), 390
Bruce, Chuck ('Curley'), 254-255
Buckett, Pat, 15, 165, 199-200, 202, 211
Bundy, Jack, 57
Bush, George W., 137

Business Management, Inc., 361, 362, 433
Business of Wisconsin, 373
Bustos Media, LLC, 485-486
Butler, Jim, 237, 241
Byrd, Phillip, 388

C

C&C Development Co., 25
C&C Super Corporation, 72
C&C Television, 72
Cable TV, 73, 409, 411
Cadaverino, Dr., 9, 264, 298, 324, 325, 330
Caldwell, Orestes, 20
California Open Bible Institute, 434
call letters
 for translator stations, 481, 483
 suffix, 47, 142
 suffix for Class-A stations, 484
 suffix for low-power stations, 483-484
Calligan, Van, 166
Camera Three, 178
cameras in courtrooms, 373
Camplin, Bill, 371
Canada – Land of Color, 367
Canadian Broadcasting Corporation, 394
Cappy Presents Miss Chris, 110, 123
Capt. Al Gee, 459
Captain Jet's Space Funnies, 202
Captain Kangaroo, 179, 209, 315, 322, 405
Captain Witi, 315
Carley Brothers, 455, 456
Carley, James, 456, 466
Carlsen, Bill, 10, 40, 61, 62, 64-7, 88, 96, 119, 170, 291, 292
Carlson, Jill, 103
Carmichael, Frank, 15, 422-4, 429
Carmichael, Kurt, 15, 423, 424, 429
Carnegie Commission on Educational Television, 366, 368
Carnegie Corporation, 366, 368
Carousel, 75-76, 83
Carr, Brad, 455
Carrie, Josie, 388
Carroll College, 205
Cartoon Alley, 10, 292, 316-319, 322, 459
Cartwright, Angela, 192
Cash on the Line, 73
cathode-ray tube (CRT), 278
Catholic Knights Insurance, 214

CBS, 24, 30-4, 36, 46, 47, 53, 56, 58, 72, 77-80, 105, 117, 120-3, 125, 128-31, 138, 139, 146-50, 152-4, 157, 168-71, 177-9, 183, 193, 197, 198, 202, 205, 208, 211, 215, 217, 225, 231, 232, 235, 236, 241, 242, 246, 253, 255, 256, 260, 267, 268, 274, 282, 284, 285, 292, 302, 315, 322, 324, 328-30, 362, 406, 420, 422, 429, 437, 447, 449, 460, 461, 464-8, 470, 472, 482, 486
CBS 58 News at 9 on WMLW, 486
CBS Evening News with Walter Cronkite, 179, 236, 260
CBS field-sequential color system, 30-31, 128-131
CBS Late Movie, 179
CBS Sunday Morning with Charles Osgood, 461
CBS Sunday News with Harry Reasoner, 179
Celebrity Game, 179
CGI Media, LLC, 453
Ch. 49 of Racine, Inc., 469
Channel 1 (Deletion of), 126
Channel 10 Auction, 370
Channel 10/36 Friends', 375, 376, 382, 406
Channel 37, 136, 170
Channel 49 LLC, 471
Channel, Table of Assignments, 33, 45, 125, 126, 152, 155, 163, 176, 214, 272-4, 340, 341, 346, 451, 469, 479, 482
Chan, Charlie, 207
Chase, Ward (Wardwell Chase Rosenberg), 13-14, 16, 202, 315
Cheney, Dick, 137
Chet Huntley Reporting, 179
Chicago Communications Service, 452
Chicago Cubs, 184, 240
Chicago Tribune, 37
Chicago White Sox, 185, 190
Chief White Buck, 165, 199-200
 Chief White Buck's Council Fires, 200
Children's Corner, 107, 353, 356, 388
Children's Fair, 10, 110, 368, 390, 393, 395
Children's Hour, 251
Children's Television Workshop, 394
Chilton, Wisconsin 179
Chopper 12, 249
Christ King Church, 74
Christensen, Richard, 276
Christian Network, 452, 473
Christian, Spencer, 379
Christina's Cottage (unsold pilot), 322

Christopher, Nancy, 241, 243
Christopherson-Schmidt, Joan, 15, 110, 123, 390-391, 393, 407
Chroma-Key, 68, 280
Chuck Wagon, 254
Chudnow, Dick, 459
Church Channel, 477
Ci-Ci (Cynthia Shove), 255-256
Cinema 6, 277
Circuit Court of Appeals for the District of Columbia, 77, 149, 273, 348
Citizens' Committee to Preserve Some Non-Commercial Television Channels, 350
City of Festivals Parade, 377
Clarion Corp., 414
Clark and McCullough, 255
Clark, John Harold, 436
Clark, Joseph A., 433
Clark, Larry, 55, 80, 106, 107, 230
Clark, Ted, 147
Clary, Robert, 192
class A stations, 484
Classic Car Shop, 380
clear channel radio stations, 40-41, 161, 331
Clifford's Book Drive, 397
Clinton, Bill, 307
Cloak of Mystery, 179
closed-captioned programming, 374
closed-circuit broadcast, 224, 276, 338, 342-342, 359, 409-410
Clow, Keith, 236
Club 60, 317
Clubhouse Gang, 314
Clyde (DuBlon puppet), 317
CNN, 443, 446, 468, 472
Cochran, Ronald W., 455-456
Coleman, John, 237
College of the Air, 371
Colnik, Gretchen, 230
Colon, Heriberto B., 455
Colonel Caboose, 315
Color Technology, Inc. (CTI), 129
Color Television
    First Report on, 129
    Second Report on, 129
Combs, Bryce, 15, 378, 379, 382, 405, 406
ComedySportz, 459
Commander Kimban, 149
commercial television, , 27, 29, 31, 32, 34-6, 42, 47, 105, 116, 302, 339, 345, 368
Communications Act of 1934, 20, 134, 241, 369, 397, 411

Community Broadcast Council, 368, 370
Community Broadcasters Association, 483
Community Broadcasters Protection Act, 484
community station (1945), 22, 126, 130, 479, 483, 487
Comte, George, 62, 94, 99
Concannon, Mark, 309-310
Concentration, 179
Concentration of media, 92, 226
Concertina Millie, 192
Conciencia, 377
Condella, Vince, 312
Consultants, 92, 179, 226
Contact 6, 301
Control Data Corp., 451
Cooky (Steve Hildebrandt), 202
Corporation for Public Broadcasting (CPB), 369, 371, 375, 482
Cotey, Roger, 276, 324
Cotter, Carol, 86
Cottone, Benedict, 336
Cousins, Norman, 394
Cowboy Bill, 393
Cowboy G-Men, 202
Cowboy Mike, 250
Cowley, Fred, 289
Cox, Marvin, 15, 221, 229
Cox, Steve, 15, 256, 270
Coy, Wayne, 58, 128
Coyne Institute, 434
Cramer-Kasselt advertising agency, 285
Crane, Bob, 192
Cravy, Katrina, 311
Cream City Broadcasting, Inc., 149, 225, 273-5, 282, 431
Crouch, Jan, 473
Crouch, Paul, 473
Crowley, Jack, 15, 167, 200-2, 208, 426
Crown Room Tonight, 100
Crusher, the (See: Lisowski, Reggie)
CW (network), 422

D

Dagen, Marvin, 142
Dahmer, Jeffrey, 458
Damm, Walter J., 36, 38, 43, 50, 117-9
Dan Jansen: Our Hometown Hero, 462
Dance Party, 282, 291
Danny Peil and the Tigers, 236
Dark Shadows, 179
Darwin (Trent puppet), 257-258
David Letterman Daytime Show, 179

Davis, Carol Milman, 318
Davis, Henry, 294, 304, 322
Davis, Sharon, 378
Davis, Willie, 240, 268
de Castro, Alison, 103, 105
de-intermixture of UHF and VHF In the same market, 134
Dean, Dick, 439
Dearholt, Stephan, 288
Death of a Princess, 374
Defenders, The, 178
Defense Communication Board, 31
Deficit Reduction Act of 2005, 137
DeGraves, Rick, 423
Demos, Karen, 418
Department of Health, Education and Welfare (HEW), 366, 372
Derringer, John, 437
Descriptive Video Service (DVS), 377
Designated Market Area (DMA), 470, 474
Designed for You, 359, 360
Detroit News, 47
Deusing, Murl, 87, 107, 121, 179, 355, 373, 393
Dialing for Dollars, 73, 237, 238, 240, 263
Dick Cavett Show, The, 178-179
Dick Tracy Show, The, 258
digital companion channel, 486
Digital TV (DTV), 137, 489
Ding Dong School, 202
Directors' Guild of America, 490
Discovery, 352
Discovery (Space Shuttle), 381
Disneyland, 87, 217, 220
Dittloff, Edward, 276
Dobiesz, Wally, 321-322
Doerfer, John, 347-348, 402
Doerfler, Robert (See: Barry, Bob)
DOLLAR SIGNS, 379
Dolnick, Lee, 276, 457, 458, 470
Donohue, Beulah, 60
Doodles (monkey), 324
Doodles (*Wee Weekly* character), 389
Double Shock, 324-325
Doyle, James, 447
Doyne, John, 244
DP Media, 452, 453
Dr. Bop (Hoyt Locke), 180
Dr. Cadaverino, 9, 264, 298, 324, 325, 330
Dr. Cadaverino's Halloween Special, 325
Dr. Eon's Lab, 220, 251
Drake, Debbie, 85
Drew, Mike, 16, 209, 424, 428, 429
Drexel, Burnham, Lambert, 307

Dreyfus, Lee, 303
Drilling, John, 290, 300, 304
Du Mont, 11, 29-32, 58, 60, 61, 80, 120, 127-130, 134, 139, 140, 155, 166, 219, 222, 223, 260, 267, 277, 279-282, 284, 285, 315, 329, 335, 368, 369
    Vitascan color system, 9, 29, 275, 278-283, 314, 327-328, 367
Du Mont, Dr. Allan, 125-126
DuBlon, Jack, 289, 292-5, 297, 298, 316-20, 322, 329
Dudley the Dragon, 205
Dunn, Kathleen, 383
Dunphy, Jerry, 170
Dutchland Dairy restaurants, 433

E

Ebert, Larry, 289
Ebony Telecasters, 455
Ed Sullivan Show, 314
Educational Television and Radio Center, 354, 356, 361
Educational Television Facilities Act, 364
Educational Television, Joint Committee on, (JCET), 342
Educational Television, Special Committee on, 337-338
Edwards, Charlie, 187
Edwards, Eddie, Sr., 197, 421
Eisenhower, Dwight David, 82, 134, 317
11th Hour News, 170
Eliason, Vic, 15, 434, 435, 438, 448, 449
Ellis, Julie (Miss Julie), 113-114
Elvira (Cassandra Peterson), 264, 426
    Elvira's Movie Macabre, 426
Emphasis Wisconsin, 377
Empire Building, 218
Empire State Building, 24, 27, 135
Enlace, 477
Erickson, Hal, 16, 170-2, 175, 177, 178, 181, 184, 188, 204, 261, 269, 270, 281, 292, 316, 328, 419
Errol, Leon, 255
Estabrook Parkway, 68, 285, 364, 461
Estes, Billie Sol, 373
Evans, Lyle R., 473
Evans, Ralph, Sr., 162, 163, 166, 167, 207
Evans, Rosa, 159-160
Eye to Eye, 464
Eyewitness, 179

F

Faber, Chuck, 110
Facsimile, 19, 67, 402, 432
Fairness Doctrine, 93-94, 241, 481
Family Television, 55, 452
Famous Adventures of Mr. Magoo, 179
Farmer Vic, 114, 192
Farnsworth, Philo, 25-26, 28-29, 35
Fay, Molly, 103, 105
FCC Television Committee, 29
Federal Communications Commission (FCC), 10, 15, 20-21, 23-24, 27-36, 42-43, 45-47, 56-58, 60-61, 71, 74, 77-78, 80, 91-94, 125-137, 141-143, 145-146, 148-155, 159-164, 168, 170-172, 176-177, 182, 184-185, 191, 196-198, 213-217, 223-226, 228, 240, 247-248, 271-276, 282, 284-285, 310, 332-349, 352-353, 361-366, 371, 380-381, 409-414, 420-421, 431, 433-434, 439-441, 448, 451-453, 455-456, 462, 469-471, 473-474, 479-486, 490
Federal Radio Commission (FRC), 19, 20, 39, 223, 331
Feeley, Jim, 17, 15, 264
Feeleystein, Dr., 262-263
Felski, Rick, 9, 15, 262-4, 270, 325
Ferdie's Inferno, 426
Fernsehturm Stuttgart, 174
Fessler, Earl M., 163
Fetchin' Food, 147
Fiedler, Arthur, 231
Field Communications Corp., 154, 409
Fielding Mouse (Trent puppet), 256
Fielding, Lisa, 198
Fields, W. C., 255
Filbert (DuBlon puppet), 317
Fillmore, Henry, 255
Finius T. Badnick (Trent puppet), 256
First Amendment Congress, 373
First Wisconsin Center, 483
Fischer, Kevin, 383
Fishman, Marvin, 413, 428
Flanagan, Ralph, 317
Flanigan, Dick (See: Mr. Mephisto)
Fleischman Rug and Carpet Co., 273
Fleischman, Lawrence, 273
Fleissner, John A., 142
Fletcher, C. Scott, 342
flicker, 17, 22
Florentine Opera, 387
Floyd (DuBlon puppet), 317
Fly, James, 43
flying-spot scanner, 18-19, 24, 72, 221, 278, 280-281, 366

FM, 23-24, 29-33, 35-36, 42, 47, 55, 76, 88, 116-117, 125-126, 128, 138, 141-142, 146, 161, 163, 249, 332, 431, 435, 436, 438, 441
Fontanne, Lynn, 388
Ford Foundation, 176, 333, 342, 345, 347, 351-3544, 357, 361-362, 365-366, 369-370, 392, 403
Foreman Tom, 108-110, 199, 250
Forester, William D., 455-456
4th Street Forum, 385
frame rate, 22, 30, 31
Frank McGee Report, 179
Freedom of Information Committee, 92
Fried Osterman Co., 273
Fried, Richard G., 273
Frieda the Elephant (puppet), 389-391
Friendly Giant, 356, 388, 394
Fritzinger, George, 455-456
FSN North, 486
Fudge, Berkley, 192
Fun House, 255, 257
Fund for Adult Education, 342
Fund for the Advancement of Education (FAE), 342
Funny Farm, 318, 320, 322, 330
Funny Manns, 257, 259
Funny Manns and Stubby, 257, 259
Fuzy, Luise, 382

G

Gagne, Verne, 192
Gambrinus Society, 370
Gangler, Diane, 203
Garcia, Jesse, 103
Gardner, John, 94, 301
Garland, Patrick, 376
Garza, Saul, 484
Gay, Duane, 195-196
Gaylord Broadcasting, 186, 194, 196-197, 210, 374, 421
Gaylord Entertainment Co., 196
Geisler, Jill, 15, 242, 268, 301, 304, 307, 308, 329
Gellerup, Dan, 38
General Electric (GE), 21, 31, 151, 432
General Instruments, 378
General Order 40, 40, 331
General TeleRadio, 72
General Tire, 72
George Devine's Wisconsin Roof Orchestra, 40, 62
George, Gary, 455, 456
George, Ken, 264
Germantown, Wisconsin, 457

Gernette, Howard, 237, 238, 244
Gernette, Rosemary, 7, 240
Gernetzke, Howard (See: Gernette, Howard)
Gernetzke, Rosemary (See: Gernette, Rosemary)
Gernsback, Hugo, 21
Geyer, Hans, 326
Gherkin, Homer, 318
ghosting (See: multi-path distortion)
Gibbons, Jane, 203
Gilbert, Billy, 255
Gilda (Berg puppet), 322
Gill, John, 221, 229
Gillespie, Earl, 289, 290, 296
Gillespie, John, 244
Gillette, George, 306
Gilmore, Ralph ('Gump'), 326
Gimbels, 38, 50, 115
Glencairn Broadcasting, 197, 421
Glendale, Wisconsin, 214, 431, 457, 466
Glenn, John, 381
Glory Ministries, 455-456
Gnorski, Gus, 309
Goebel, Msgr. E. J., 337
Goeden, Henry, 49, 74, 82
Gogeweosh (Frank Smart), 200
Golden G Ranch, 202
Goldsmith, Thomas, 333
Goldwater, Barry, 233
Goll, Frederick, 366
Good Housekeeping, 230
Good Morning America, 322, 379
Gould, Chester, 259
Gousha, Mike, 99-101, 105, 250
Grafton, Wisconsin, 457
Gran, L. F., 214, 216, 221, 225
Grand Ole Opry, The, 195
Grandma Boo Boo (puppet), 393
Grant, Bob, 169
Grant, Harry, 37
Gratton, Wayne, 389-391, 393
Gray, Dennis, 236
Great Circus Parade, 365-366, 377, 383
Great Lakes Gardener, 384
Great Lakes Naval Training Center, 434
Greater Milwaukee Broadcasting, 455
Green Acres, 179
Green Bay, Wisconsin, 13, 58, 64, 88, 105, 131-133, 213-214, 224, 230, 240, 271-272, 303, 306, 314-315, 336, 340, 433, 453, 457, 473, 481
Green Bay Packers, 58, 64
Green Bean Bus, The, 447
Grenadiers, the, 57, 75

Gresser, Barbara ('Miss Barbara'), 253, 315
Griem, Breta, 59-60, 62
Grimsby, Roger, 170
Griswold, Hilton, 446
Grobschmidt, Eugene, 98
groundwave propagation, 23, 126
Grunert, Fred, 390
Grzegorek, Larry, 15, 321, 322, 325
Gurda, John, 16, 383, 385

H

H&E Balaban Corp., 145, 163
Haberlan, John, 182-4
Haertlein, Darlyne (Also see: Berg, Darlyne), 15, 320, 321, 396, 407
Hal Roach Studios, 420
Haley, Bill, 144
Half-Pint Party, 252
Hall, Jim, 15, 462, 464
Harlow Figley, 393
Hammond, Laurence, 372
Handy Workshop, 68-69
Hanson, Charlie, 230, 234
Happenings, 422
Harmon, Dan, 459
Harmon, Larry, 259, 422-423
Harrison, Gene, 164, 166-167, 200-202, 208
Harry the Horse (DuBlon puppet), 317
Harvey, Nels, 15, 367, 404
Hastert, Amy, 205, 424, 429
Haswell, Rob, 312
Hat-O the Clown, 110, 393
Hatha Yoga, 370
Hattori, John, 205
Haunted, 323
Haushalter, Alan, 390-391
HBO, 417
HDTV, 249, 377-378, 381, 383, 405-406, 464, 489-490
Hearst Corp., 33, 38, 46-47, 126, 131, 133-134, 148-149, 153, 156-157, 161, 213, 221, 223-227, 229, 232, 246-248, 250, 266-267, 269, 271-275, 282, 314, 326-327, 331, 334, 336, 339, 341, 343-346, 348-349, 399, 401-402, 433, 440, 460, 462
Hearst-Argyle Stations, Inc., 248
Hearst-Argyle, Inc., 249
Hegan, Mike, 196
Heinie (Jack Bundy), 57
Heiss, Bob, 80, 83-84
Hemdu Co., 142

Hennock, Frieda, 130, 134, 153, 168, 226, 332, 333, 479
Herbert, Carol, 185
Herbert, Ed, 185, 192, 193, 195
Heredity in Everyday Life, 359
Hersh, Robert, 323-324
Herzog, Lewis, 46
Herzog, Robert (Bob), 235
Hi Kids, 107
Hicks, Brad, 311
High Definition Television (company), 455
High-Definition Television (HDTV), 249, 377-378, 381, 383
High School Bowl, 297
Hildebrandt, Noel, 393
Hildebrandt, Steve (See: Cooky)
Hildegarde, 166
Hill, Dr. Ruane, 16, 191
Hinkley, Gordon, 7, 15, 71, 75-76, 120
Hinshaw, Ed, 15, 89-91, 94, 96, 121-122, 373, 405
Hirst, Bill, 110-111, 393
Hitchcock, Kathleen, 370
Hitchhikers, The, 236
Ho Ho the Clown (puppet), 393, 396
Hoffa, Jimmy, 233
Hogan, John V. L., 41
Holeproof Hosiery Co., 273
Hollywood Matinee, 314
Holmes, Barbara, 378
Holmes, John, 276
Holt, Thad, 154, 168-169
Home, 79-80
Home Shopping Network (HSN), 469
Homemakers' Holiday, 230
Homework Hotline, 377
Homme, Bob, 394
Honeck, Lynn, 233
Hooper, Tom, 289, 296, 301, 303
Hooten, Mickey, 245, 268
Hootenanny, 236
Hoover v. Intercity Radio (1923), 20
Hoover, Herbert, 19-20
Hope, Bob, 239
Horowitz, Rick, 383
Horton, Edward Everett, 394
Horton, Win, 394
Hot Line, 97
Hot Shots, the, 75-76, 111
Houle, Dr. Cyril O., 363
Hour Magazine, 246
How to Marry a Millionaire, 281
HR Broadcasting Corp., 420
Hubert the Hog (DuBlon puppet), 317
Huffman, Tim, 303
Hughes, Howard, 72

Hughes, Tammy, 198
Hullabaloo, 179
Humphrey, Hubert, 233
Hunt, Nile, 349
Hyde (DuBlon puppet), 317
Hyde, Rosel H., 348, 402
Hygo Television Films, Inc., 154

I

i (Independent Television), 453
I Remember, 381
I Remember Milwaukee (See: *I Remember*)
iconoscope, 25
Igor, 298, 324-326
image dissector, 26
In Focus, 443, 447
In the Shadow of the Cross, 229
Independent Television, Inc., 149, 171, 225, 273-275, 281
Ingerson, Mark, 276
Inghram, George E., 141-143
Inquiring Mind, The, 363
Inside North Vietnam, 365
Inspiration Time, 446
InterCHANGE, 383
International Brotherhood of Electrical Workers (IBEW), 411
Ion Television, 453
ionosphere, 22-24, 34
Iowa State University, 34, 333
Irwin, Jim, 96, 98

J

Jack Benny Program, 179
Jackson, Debra, 455-456
Jackson, Jesse, 198, 211
Jacobs, Mike, 101, 104
Jaye, Aye, 15, 113, 114, 124, 192, 193
JCTV, 477
Jenkins, Charles Francis, 19
Jeopardy, 179
Jeremy the Jogger, 321-322
Jetsons, The, 289
Jewelry Television, 471-472
Jim Bakker Hour, The, 424
Jim Dandy, 389
Jirikowic, Otto A., 335
Joey Bishop Show, The, 179, 206
Jogues, Sister M., 360
Johnny Jupiter, 315
Johns, Myles H., 431
Johnson, Arte, 193, 192

Johnson, Dick, 80, 185-186, 234-235, 240
Johnson, Larry (the legend), 303
Johnson, Lyndon, 366
Johnson, Paul, 15, 264, 298, 300, 319, 325, 329, 330
Johnson, Robert, 356
Johnson, Russ, 434-435
Johnston, Patsy, 236
Johnston's Cookies, 257
Joho, Thomas R. (See: Richards, Tommy)
Joint Committee Against Toll TV, 412
Joint Committee on Educational Television (JCET), 333, 342
Joint Sales Agreement, 453
Jones, Art, 255
Jones, Dan, 383
Jones, Thomas, 190
Jordan, Donna, 241, 243
Joseph, Paul, 15, 65-7, 98, 99, 101, 105, 119, 294, 329
Journal Co., 10, 22-4, 27, 30, 33-43, 45-7, 49, 55, 60, 76, 83, 87, 89-94, 106, 115-9, 122, 130, 141, 145, 186, 223, 232, 284, 331, 397, 401, 415, 440
Journal Times Co., 469
Judge Roy Bean, 202
Judge, Barry, 244
Jukebox Network (See: Box, The)
Jung, Mary Jane, 147, 152, 165
Jungle Jim, 202, 315
Junior Science, 202

K

Kahlhamer, Jackie, 475
Kahn, Jack, 273, 276, 281
Kahn, Sol, 273, 281
Kalil, Tony, 458
Kal's Korner, 149
Kanitz, Bruce, 172, 288
Kapital City Broadcasting Co., 126, 161, 431
Karr, Tony, 15, 298, 329
Kasdorf, George, 55
Kay, Don, 442
Kay, Elizabeth, 379
Kay, Sharon, 188
Kay, Sophie, 239
KCZXAK, 128-129
Keer, Frank, 334
Kennedy, Robert, 183
Kenosha News Publishing Co., 469
Kenosha, Wisconsin, 33, 126, 422
Kesselman, Lou, 38-39

Kesselman-O'Driscol Music Co., 38
KFRE-TV, 176
KHTV, 182
Kids in the Kitchen, 396
Kids Karnival, 149
Kids' Klub, 10, 83, 110-114, 123
KIMA-TV, 479
kinescope, 11, 14, 354, 355, 357, 358, 389, 392
King Louis, 393
Kings and Queens Bowling, 185
Kinlow, Joel, 471-472
Kleiman, Lil, 300
Klein, Michael W., Jr., 250
Kletzsch Park, 461
Klotsche, Dr. J. Martin, 337, 354, 355
KM Communications, Inc., 484
KNMT-TV, 473
Knowles, Warren, 92, 374
Knuth, Alan, 440
Knutzen, Bob, 72, 110-111, 113
Kocjan, Irene, 228
Koehler, Glenn, 342
Koester, Tom, 15, 303
Kohl, Herb, 99
Kohl, Tom, 186
Kohlberg, Kravis, Robert & Co. (KKR), 307
Kohler, Walter J., Jr., 77, 347
Kolero Telecasting Corp., 214-216
Koo-Jee-Boo (Trent puppet), 257
Koss, John, 440
KPRC-TV, 480
KPTV, 132
Krueger, Grant, 83, 111
Krueger, Jack, 115, 117, 122
Krug, Richard, 337
Krupp, Roger, 232
KS2XBS, 77, 410
KSD, 47
KSD-TV, 56
KTLA, 410
KTVT, 182
KUHT, 348
Kupcinet, Irv (See: *Kup's Show*)
Kup's Show, 181, 188
KUSA Brewer's Broadcasting Television, 455
KXLY-TV, 480

L

La Haye, Tim, 440
LAB Partnership, 452
Laeser, Phil, 43, 46, 65, 76
Lafferty, John, 439

LaForce, Charlie, 231, 232, 235, 261
Lake Park Lutheran Church, 38
Lamphier, Charles, 433
land-mobile, 32, 136, 140, 481
Landass, Bob, 379
Langsdorf Baseball League, 206
Larsen, Bob ('Coffeehead'), 252
Larson, Duke, 219
Lasky, Byron, 419
Late Show with David Letterman, The, 460
Late Show with Joan Rivers, The, 420
Late Show, The (WITI-TV), 178, 206, 298
Laugh-In, Rowan and Martin's, 179
Lawler, Jim (See: Shamus O'Hara), 167
Lawrence, Carolyn, 231
Lawrence, David, 334
Le Grand, Roger, 92, 285-7, 292, 293, 301, 311
Leader Newspapers, Inc., 273
League of Women Voters, 350
Lease management agreement (LMA), 197, 421
Lee, Cheri, 15, 110-113, 123
Lee, Jack, 15, 94, 123, 192, 210, 370, 405
Lehrer, Jim, 371
Lemberg, Sister Gilmary, 15, 359, 403
Lemke, Cliff, 68, 70
Lemke, John, 358, 367, 393, 396
LeMonds, Bill, 298, 424, 458, 459
Lenny's Inferno, 426-427
Leonard, Dick, 92
LeSEA Broadcasting, 452
Letters to Santa, 407
Let's Experiment, 352
Let's Go Bowling!, 219-220, 223
Let's Remember, 70, 109
Leuders, Tom, 416
Levy, Stanford, 356
Lewis, Jerry, 308
Liberatore, George, 15, 180, 182-183, 205, 209
Lifetime, 351
Lincoln Park, 214, 217, 221, 246-247, 251, 452, 461, 471
Lipman, Bill, 159
Lippy Lucy (Trent puppet), 256-257
Lisko, Diane, 376
Lisowski, Reggie (The Crusher), 192, 303
Little Amateurs, 107
Little Lulu, 314-315
Little Moonbeam, 393
Little Moose, 223

Local TV Personality Most Worthy of Network Recognition, 200
Local TV, LLC, 310-311
Locante, Albert, 452
Looney Tunes, 253
Loose, Don, 66, 96, 97, 99
Lorenz, Larry, 242
Lorimar Pictures, 305
Los Angeles County Sheriff's Department, 136
Lost City, 201
lottery, Wisconsin state, 245-246
Loughlin, Joe, 15, 182-184, 186, 187, 191-194, 209
Louis Rukeyser's Wall Street, 383
Love of Life, 179
low-power television (LPTV), 481-484, 486
Loyalty Building, 224
Lucius the Lion (DuBlon puppet), 317
Luczak, Tom, 188
Ludington, Michigan, 170, 485
Lunts: A Life in the Theatre, The, 388
Lynde and Harry Bradley Foundation, 377
Lyons, Walt, 67

M

M. Carpenter Tower (See: Tower Hotel), 164
Mac the Mailman, 13, 202, 203, 315
MacNeil, Robert, 371
Madison, Wisconsin, 23, 33, 37, 40, 81, 115, 121, 133-135, 140, 145, 160, 163-164, 168, 202, 207-208, 214, 230, 246, 294, 342, 345, 348-349, 378, 388, 394, 416, 426-427, 433, 436, 449
Madox, Marlow, 446
Magic House, 254
Magid, Frank, 291, 329
Maier, Henry W., 89-94, 240-241, 287
Majestic Broadcasting Co. (See Kapital City Broadcasting Co.),
Major, Jim, 17, 15, 289, 292, 298, 318, 322, 329-330
Make Room for Daddy, 179
Making of Milwaukee, The, 385
Making of ..., The, 100
Malan, John, 68, 104
Malone Sisters, 70, 80, 109
Malone, Janice, 109
Malone, Marilyn, 70, 109
Man Without a Gun, 281
Manhattan Project, 462

Mann, Don, 200
Mannequin (hanging from tower), 463
Marasco, Maury, 290
Marc Plaza Hotel, 194, 374, 460, 461, 483
March, Robert, 202
Marino, Budde, 15, 148, 153, 156, 169, 208
Marino, Hank, 81
Marks, Judy, 15, 64, 66, 72-73, 83, 85, 96, 119-120, 157, 165, 168-170, 193, 208, 283, 292, 317
Marquette University, 4, 7, 15-16, 23, 38, 39, 49-50, 82, 100, 114-116, 121, 153, 164, 167-168, 199-200, 202, 214, 223, 236, 242, 251, 299, 331, 337, 354, 359, 373, 397, 443
Marquette, Michigan, 133, 224, 272
Mathews, Jim, 263
Mattioli, Len, 426
Mattioli, Ferd, 426
Matz, Ken, 301
Mayville Communications, Inc., 473
McCall's, 394
McCarthy, Dean, 276, 281
McCarthy, Joseph, 150, 272, 274, 344
McCarty, Harold, 351
McCormick, Maureen, 192
McCullough, John, 95, 96, 98, 101, 377, 423
McCurdy, Pat, 264
McDonald, Ronald, 113, 114, 192
McGhee, Marlon, 195
McGovern, George, 97
McNally, Joel, 92, 383
McNeil, Barbara, 282
Meeker, Mary Kay, 47
Meekins, Carole, 102, 104
Melody Top Theater, 240
Melody, Miss (Melody Wiken), 255-256
Mequon, Wisconsin, 154-155, 157, 160, 275-279, 281, 283, 353, 355, 409, 411
Meredith Publishing Co., 281
Merrie Melodies, 205
Merrill, Eugene H., 346
Metric Man, 322
Metropolitan Broadcasting, 162
metropolitan station (1945), 33, 60, 141-142, 479
Meyer, Roy, 299
Mickey Mouse Club, The, 259, 270
Mid-Day, 76, 83, 84
Midland Video Productions, 443
Midwest Broadcast Associates, 452

Midwest Program on Airborne Television Instruction (MPATI), 176
Mika, Jim, 241, 243
Mila Scopa, 199-200
Miller, Fred, 201
Miller, Howard, 433
Miller, Irv, 15, 146, 150, 156
Miller, Sam, 159-162
Miller-Armstrong Costume Company, 262
Milwaukee Archdiocese, 359, 362, 444, 445
Milwaukee Area Broadcast News Association, 91
Milwaukee Area Technical College (MATC), 13, 370
Milwaukee Area Telecasting Corp., 152, 214-217, 225
Milwaukee Art Institute, 352, 355
Milwaukee Art Museum, 110, 395
Milwaukee Athletes Against Childhood Cancer (MACC), 102
Milwaukee Auditorium, 39, 53, 89, 117
Milwaukee Ballet Company, 387
Milwaukee Board of Vocational and Adult Education, 338, 342, 344, 363, 371
Milwaukee Board of Zoning Appeals, 248, 381
Milwaukee Braves, 148, 219, 290, 354
Milwaukee Brewers (major league team), 82, 114, 194, 197, 303, 420-422, 486
Milwaukee Brewers (minor league team), 53, 55
Milwaukee Broadcasting Co. (See: WEMP)
Milwaukee Broadcasting Limited Partnership, 455-456
Milwaukee Bucks, 82, 194, 195, 303, 413, 420, 425
Milwaukee City Planning Commission, 247, 462
Milwaukee Civic Broadcasting Association, 38
Milwaukee Common Council, 50, 130, 232, 248, 269, 272, 326, 334-335, 339, 341, 346, 381, 398-400, 411, 471
Milwaukee County Council CIO, 226, 337
Milwaukee County Park Commission, 175
Milwaukee County Radio Council (See: Milwaukee Radio and Television Council)

Milwaukee Educators' Committee on Television, 339-340, 355, 399
Milwaukee Electric Railway & Light Co., 223
Milwaukee Federated Trades Council, 226
Milwaukee Hawks, 166
Milwaukee Hispanic News, 483
Milwaukee Home Show, 47
Milwaukee Institute of Technology (MIT), 370
Milwaukee Journal, 11, 15, 24, 34-41, 43, 47, 49, 53, 58, 65, 74, 79-80, 82, 83, 90, 93, 102, 113, 115-124, 138-140, 155-158, 192, 207-211, 240, 265-270, 293, 295, 326-230, 378, 397-407, 424, 427-429, 437, 447-449, 453-454, 456, 466-468, 471-472, 477, 487-488
Milwaukee Lutheran Schools, 229, 337
Milwaukee on Camera, 351
Milwaukee Press Club, 240, 373
Milwaukee Public Museum, 87, 224, 337, 352, 355, 373, 375, 392-393, 395
Milwaukee Public Schools, 224, 229, 336-337, 354, 357, 359, 362, 372, 390
Milwaukee Public Television (MPTV), 383
Milwaukee Radio and Television Council, 177, 255, 368, 390
Milwaukee Radio Show, 38
Milwaukee Repertory Theater, 387
Milwaukee Reports, 233
Milwaukee School Board, 337, 346
Milwaukee School of Engineering, 9, 38, 222, 224
Milwaukee Sentinel, 37, 90-91, 101, 115, 122-124, 155-157, 208-211, 223, 232, 265-270, 274, 276, 326-230, 341, 344, 350, 378, 400-405, 407, 427-429, 446, 448-449, 453, 466-467, 472, 487
Milwaukee Symphony Orchestra, 302, 387
Milwaukee Technical College (MTC), 370
Milwaukee Tonight, 380
Milwaukee Turners, 385
Milwaukee TV58, 457
Milwaukee Urban League, 374
Milwaukee Vocational School, 153, 169, 339, 345-349, 351, 353, 358, 360-361, 363, 365, 370, 440
Milwaukee Youth for Christ, 434-435, 437-439

Milwaukee: Behind the Headlines, 242
Milwaukee's Talking, 247
Minnesota Twins, 184-185
Minow, Newton, 135, 363, 366
Minute Memos, 191
Miss Chris, 110, 123, 390-391, 394
Mister Rogers' Neighborhood, 365, 394
Mitchell, Ray, 38-39
Mobil Oil Corporation, 374
Modrzyk, Mary, 326
Mokeski, Paul, 303
Moment of Fear, 179
Money Game, The, 256
Monkees, The, 179
Monona Broadcasting, 163
Moody, Blair, Sr., 273
Moore, Ted, 64, 193
Moore, Tom, 287
Moquin, Andrew D., 303
Moran, Marvin, 70, 80
Morning Blend, The, 103
Morris, Gordon, 438
Mosley, Dwayne, 196
Movie Quick Quiz, 150
Movies from the Combat Zone, 261
Movies from Tomorrow, 261, 324
MPTV on Demand, 384
Mr. Letterbags, 320, 322
Mr. Mephisto, 426-427
Mr. Magoo, Famous Adventures of, 179
Mrs. Karl's bread, 230
MSNBC, 383
Mt. Sinai Hospital, 192
MuchMusic, 483
Mueller, Bob, 371
multi-path distortion, 135
Multi-Scanner, 278, 280, 327
multiple-ownership rule, 440, 479
Munn, Bob, 315
Munsters, The, 261, 324
Murl Deusing Safari, 87, 179, 373
Murphy, Harold, 431
Murphy, Keith, 378
Murphy, Kim, 310
Murray, Lee, 255, 257, 258, 260, 369
Murrow, Edward R., 150
Murtaugh, James, 236
Muscular Dystrophy Association (MDA), 257, 308, 463
Museum Expeditions, 373
Museum Explorers' Club, 87, 107, 352
must carry, 452, 470, 474
Mutz, John, J., 335
Myers, Melinda, 384
Mykleby, Kathy, 247, 250
MyNetwork TV, 199, 422
MySpace, 490

N

NAACP, 90, 374
Nasal (Trent puppet), 256
Nason, Bruce, 15, 290, 299, 329
National Association of Broadcasters (NAB), 363, 482, 483
National Association of Educational Broadcasters, 135, 332, 333, 341, 351
National Association of Program Executives, 293
National Association of Public Television Stations, 136
National Association of Radio and Television Broadcasters (NARTB), 278
National Association of Theater Owners, 412
National Citizens' Committee for Educational Television (NCCET), 342
National Committee for Education by Radio, 332
National Educational Television (NET), 361
National Educational Television and Radio Center, 361
National Minority Television, 473-474
National Press Photographers, 373
National Public Affairs Center, 371
National Radio Conferences, 20
National Telefilm Associates, 154
National Telemeter Corp., 410
Natoli, Joe, 421
NBC, 25, 27, 31, 39-40, 43, 46, 50, 53, 56, 58, 60, 72, 76, 78-80, 82-83, 87, 105, 118-119, 121, 123, 125, 128-130, 138, 139, 153, 157, 164, 178-179, 206, 266, 277, 297, 327, 453, 460, 467, 482
NBC Saturday Night at the Movies, 179
NET Journal, 365
NET Playhouse, 365
Network Recognition, Local TV Personality Most Worthy of, 200
network, state educational television, 346-347
New World Communications, 103, 246, 307-308, 421, 447, 460, 470
New World Entertainment, 307
Newburgh, NY, 29
News Corporation (Fox), 103, 246, 307-309, 421, 447, 460, 470
Newsweek 4, 99
Niedermeyer, Fred, 233
Nielsen Media Research, 474
Nieman, Lucius, 37
Night of the Living Dead, 264
Nine O'Clock Nightly News, 195, 197
Nipkow Disc, 19, 21, 22
Nipkow, Paul, 17, 34
Nightlife, ABC, 179
Nixon, Richard, 371
No Doubt About It, 392, 407
NoNeck, Tolouse (See: Tolouse NoNeck)
Norquist, John, 457
North Shore Broadcasting Co., 431, 433
North Shore Publishing Co., 431
Northwest Television Corp., 145, 163, 433
Norton, Cliff, 257
Norton, Kenneth (FCC engineer), 32
Noticiero Telemundo, 463, 486
Noticiero Telemundo Wisconsin y tú, 486
Noveltoons, 314
Novik, M. S., 332
NTSC (National Television System Committee), 21, 29-31, 42, 72, 78, 128-130, 278-280, 484

O

O.P.E.C. oil embargo, 388
Oak Hill Capital Partners LP, 310
Office of Defense Mobilization, 129
Oklahoma Publishing Co., 182, 194
Olen, Walter, 357
Oliver, Bob, 292, 318
Oliver, Pat ('Miss Pat'), 253, 314
Olson, Chuck, 181, 418
Olszyk, Arthur, 15, 43, 50, 58, 60, 66, 91, 97, 99, 221, 225, 285, 292-293. 295
Omni America, 381
Omnibook, Inc., 273
On the Record, 169
On Wisconsin, 477
on-demand servers, 490
Open House 12, 233
Operation Alphabet, **364, 404**
Operation Three-R, 229
Orteig, Barbara, 233, 235
Osnos, Max, 273
Other 98, The, 232
Ott, Jim, 101, 105
Outdoor Wisconsin, 375
O'Brien, Pat, 233
O'Donnell, Rev. Edward, 337
O'Hara, Shamus, 167
O'Leary, Susan, 387

P

P.M. Magazine, 241, 268
Pabst Theater, 39
Pack, Leo, 82
Packers, Green Bay, 58, 64
Packer Preview, 240
Pal, George, 281, 314-315
Parade, Great Circus, 365-366, 377, 383
Paramount, 30, 77, 197, 211, 284, 410, 421, 427, 429, 460
Paramount Communications, Inc., 197, 421
Parcher, Don, 96, 98
Parker, William, 332
Parkinson, Dr. George, 337, 354, 355
Passerby, The, 281
Patterns in Arithmetic, 363
Pay Television
  First Report on, 413
  Second Report on, 413
  Third Report on Pay Television, 412
  Fourth Report and General Order on, 414
Pax Net, 453
Paxson Communications Corp., 452, 453
Paxson Management Corporation, 453
Paxson, Bud, 452
Payne, Ulice, Jr., 458
Payola, 282
Peak of Sports, 148
Peck, Jim, 7, 8, 16, 99, 191, 381, 406
Performing Arts Center, 303, 370
Perrin, Bill, 393
Perry, Ted, 311
Petak, George, 445
Petak, Nancy, 445
Peterson, Cassandra (See: Elvira)
Peterson, Jana, 462
Petrie, Bob, 112-113
Pfaff, Ken, 371
Pfister Hotel, 47, 50, 100, 240
Philco, 28-30, 50, 434
Phonevision, 77, 171, 172, 410, 412, 427
photocell, 17-18
Photogram, 352
Piasecki, Charlene, 114
Piaskoski, Paul, 464
Pick a Pet, 203
Pig 'N' Whistle, 284
Pilot Radio Corporation, 129-130
Pins Over, 188
Pinsker, Donald, 356
Pipens, Tom, 312

Planned Parenthood Federation of America, 447
Plante, Bill, 233, 235
Playtime for Children, 199
Pluta, Jim, 290
Point of View, 446
Poller, Lou, 9, 144, 148-149, 151-153, 155, 157, 168, 208, 216, 225, 272-274, 326, 346, 361-362, 402, 409
Poor Pay More, The, 365
Pops, 10, 231, 239, 254-7, 270, 303
Pops' Theater, 257
pornography industry, 490
Porter Wagoner, 188
Posner, 171, 174-177, 189, 197, 209, 275, 282, 431, 437
Post Office Box 6, 315
Powell Community Television, 455
Praise the Lord, 473, 477
Pretzel Party, 230-231
Pride of the Braves, 232
Proctor, Quentin, 439
Program and System Information Protocol (PSIP), 489
programming, building block theory of, 183
Proxmire, William, 94
Pryor, Jeff, 293
PTL Club, 416-417
Public Broadcasting Act of 1967, 369
Public Broadcasting Laboratory, 369
Public Broadcasting Service (PBS), 366, 369-370, 374-375, 383-384, 388, 394-395, 489
Public Relations Society of America, 367
Public Report, 477
Puelicher, Gertrude, 232
Pugal, Peter, 185
Punky and His Pals, 255, 269
Puppetoons, 202, 281, 314, 315
Purthell, Bob, 436

Q

Quintex Entertainment, Inc., 420

R

Raasch, Bunny, 15, 83, 84, 86, 96, 242, 244
Rabb, B.J., 416-417
Racine & Me, 472
Racine Telecasting Co., 469

Racine, Wisconsin, 22, 126, 159, 202, 306, 422, 445, 451-453, 469-470, 472, 474, 479
Radio Act of 1912, 20
Radio Act of 1927, 19-20, 39
Radio and Television News Directors Association, 92
radio astronomy, , 136
Radio City, 42-44, 47-49, 51-52, 60-61, 68, 71, 75, 78, 80-81, 85, 87, 115-117, 119-120, 398, 443
Radio Manufacturers Association (RMA), 21, 78, 129
Radio Patrol, 201
Radio Wisconsin, Inc. (See: WISC)
Radolph, Sol, 437
Rainbow/PUSH Coalition, 198
Ramar of the Jungle, 202, 315
Randall, Clifford A., 142-143
Randall, Gerard, 383
Ranger Don, 393
Rapunzel (Berg puppet), 322
Rasche, Dr. William, 336-339, 342, 344, 345, 347, 353-355
Raskin, Max (judge), 374
RCA, 2424, 26-30, 35, 36, 42, 51, 53, 78-80, 116, 128-30, 138, 139, 167, 177, 232, 275, 278, 281, 282, 357, 358, 367, 480
Reading Rainbow Young Writers and Illustrators Awards, 395
Ready to Learn, 394
Reagan, Nancy, 375
Reagan, Ronald, 190
Real McCoys, 179
Rebel, The, 234
Red O'Rourke, 167, 201, 202
Red O'Rourke, Space Adventures, 201-202
Reddin, John, 75, 89
Reddy, John, 160, 166
Referendum on state educational television network (1954), 349-351
Rennebohm, Oscar, 520
Report on Broadcast Localism and Notice of Proposed Rulemaking, , 488, 492
Republic Pictures, 72, 206
Reth, Budd, 15, 63, 68, 70, 111, 119, 120
Reuss, Henry, 374
Rexall, 150, 151
Reynolds, John, 372
Ribicoff, Abraham, 363
Rice, Crawford, 186
Richards, Tommy, 231, 235, 255, 270
Richgels, Jeff, 81

Riddiough, Bruce, 371
Rivers, Bobby, 241, 246
RKO, 72, 284, 323, 324, 412
Robedeaux, Cliff, 108
Roberta (Berg puppet), 322
Roberts, Julie, 302
Robertson, Jim, 15, 49, 51, 53, 60, 118, 120, 365, 398
Robertson, Pat, 416, 447
Robinson, Bob, 264
Robinson, Jerry, 15, 227, 232, 240, 252, 268
Rock River Broadcasting, 162
Rocky (DuBlon puppet), 317, 320
Rodent Sisters (Trent puppets), 256
Rogers, Fred, 353, 356, 388, 394
Rogers, Will, 39
Rogers, Roy, 72, 254
Romney, George, 233
Romper Room, 189, 203, 205, 227, 252-254, 314
Ronald McDonald, 113-114, 192
Roosevelt, Eleanor, 47, 366
Roosevelt, Franklin Delano, 28, 31, 332
Roselin, Stephan, 15, 425, 429
Rosenman, Alex, 145
Rosenthal, Ed, 15, 305, 415-416, 418-419, 428
Rosing, Boris, 25
Ross, Rosemary (See: Gernette, Rosemary)
Rothman, Lee, 15, 185-7, 192, 458
Roundup Time, 165, 220, 250, 251
Route 66, 179
Rowan and Martin's Laugh-In, 179, 184
Rowe, Charly, 425
Rowlands, Hugh (See: Uncle Hugo)
Roxanne (Berg puppet), 322
Roy the Cabin Boy, 315
Rueppel, Carol, 308
Rufus (Berg puppet), 322
Rukeyser, Louis, 383
Rule 103.8, 27, 42
Rulemaking, Report on Broadcast Localism and Notice of Proposed, 486, 490
Runnion, Guy, 169-170
Rural station (1945), 22, 60, 479
Rukeyser's, Louis, Wall Street, 383

S

Sacred Stylings, 436
Saints Five, The, 236
Sales, Soupy, 100
Sam's, Inc., 273

INDEX

Sampson, Bernard, 171
Sampson, Harold, 177
Sanabria, Ulises, 21-22, 41
Safety, Sandy, 389
Santa, Letters to, 407
Santa Claus Party, 319
Sarnoff, David, 26, 42, 79-80, 121
Satellite Forum on the Nation's Economy, 374
satellite station, 479-480
Saturday Afternoon Movie, The, 261
Saturday Night Movie, 206
Savage, Joseph, 356
Scales, Harvey, 15, 180, 209
scanning, 17-19, 22, 24-26, 28-29, 41, 278-280, 332
Schaefer, George, 388
Scheidecker, Ruth ('Miss Ruth'), 252
Scherbarth, Bill, 15, 262
Schermerhorn, Kenneth, 303
Schlaak, Otto, 349, 357, 362-364, 369, 376, 388, 390, 392-393, 407
Schlitz Brewing Co., 141, 177
Schlitz Circus Parade, 182
Schmidt, Mary, 254
School of Engineering of Milwaukee (See: Milwaukee School of Engineering)
Schorr, Daniel, 242
Schrab, Rob, 459
Schroeder Hotel, 23, 42, 47, 145, 168, 171, 173, 174, 282
Schuster, Mike, 470
Schuster's (department stores), 50
SCI Television, 307
Screen Actors Guild (SAG), 71-72
Scripps Howard Broadcasting, 197
Sears Foundation, 394
Season's Greetings from Barbara Ann Becker, 300
Season's Greetings from TV6, 300
SeaToons with Capt. Al Gee, 459
Second Audio Program (SAP), 377
Seebach, David, 326
SelecTV, 413-414, 416-417, 419-420, 422, 426, 428
Selig, Bud, 303
Senate Foreign and Interstate Commerce Committee, 346, 410
September 11th Commission, 137
Sergeant Lee, 258, 260
Sesame Street, 394
Severson, John, 191
Seward Community TV, 480
Sgt. Preston, 202
Shafer, Don, 461
Shake Shop, 319

Shamus O'Hara, 167
Shanahan, Tom, 15, 214, 215, 219, 265
Shapiro, Howard, 458, 460
Sheena Queen of the Jungle, 277
Shelander, Amy, 425
Sheldon (DuBlon puppet), 317
Sherwood, Bob, 7, 16, 97, 99
Shirley (tarantula), 206-207
Shock, 324-327
Shock! (movie package), 206, 284, 323
Shock Rock, 264
Shock Theater (WISN-TV), 263-264
Shock Theater (WUHF), 206
Shock Theater (WVTV), 206
Shorewood Players, 323
Shorewood Village Board, 285, 287
Shove, Cynthia (See: Ci-Ci)
Showcase, 371
Shubert Theater, 38
Shuster, Scott, 16, 189-191, 210
Siegrist, Mark, 247, 383
Sigma Delta Chi, 92
Sinclair Broadcast Group, 197-198, 421
Singer, Lan, 147, 149
Singin' Here Tonight, 236
Sir Lancelot, 315
Sixth Report and General Order, 74, 77, 131-132, 139, 152, 213, 265, 274, 326, 340, 399-400, 451, 469, 479
Sixty, Billy, 80-81
Skiatron Electronic Corp., 409, 412
Skilling, Tom, 294, 301
Skinner, Paul, 75
Skip (Trent ventriloquist's dummy), 259-260
Skycamera 6, 305
Slayton, William, L., 335
Small, Dan, 375
Smile of a Child, 477
Smith and Company, 377, 380
Smith, Carolyn, 198
Smith, David, 198
Smith, Joe, 377
Smothers Brothers, The, 236
Snyder, Tom, 9, 15, 100, 206, 208
Society of Professional Journalists, 373
Sodality Union Milwaukee Archdiocese (SUMA), 297-298
Son of Shock (movie package), 206, 284, 323
Sony Corporation, 377
Sophie Brandt Opera Company, 38
Soupy Sales, 100
South Side Armory, 10, 49-51, 53, 219, 228, 284
Space Needle, 174
Spakowitz, Brad, 461

Spanish Times, The, 458
Sparks, Ned, 255
Special Committee on Educational Television, 337-338
Special Radio Committee, 336-337
Spheeris, Andrew, 219, 221, 225
Sports-A-Rama, 367
Sportsmanlike Driving, 352
St. Louis Post Dispatch, 47
Stand by for Crime, 58
Standard Broadcasting Co., 434
standards, television, 21, 27, 30, 31, 129
Star Award Theater, 72
Star Trek Voyager, 422
Starr, Irwin, 461-462
Stassen, Harold, 47
Staszak, Paul, 16, 459, 467
State Assembly Committee on Education, 345
State Coordinating Committee for Educational Television, 365
State Educational Communications Board, 376
state educational television network, 346, 347
State Radio and Television Council, 346, 376
State University of Iowa, 332, 397
Steetle, Ralph, 355
Steinmetz, Chuck, 16, 308
Stenz, Wayne R., 473
Stephens, Lori, 461
Steve Swedish Orchestra, 192
Stewart, Paul, 436
Stoddard, Hank, 7, 16, 81, 82, 96, 98, 100, 121, 421
Stone, John, 16, 269, 455
Stone, Shanah, 230
Stone, Sid, 230-231, 252, 455
Stoneman Family, The, 188
store casting, 437
Storer Broadcasting Co., 154, 170-171, 241, 282, 284-288, 302, 304-305, 311, 328
Storer, George, 287
Storer, George, Jr., 286-287
Story Princess, The, 392-393
Strachota, Bernie, 201
Strange, Glenn, 206-207
Stratovision, 176
Straus, Max, 273
Strehlow, Mike, 461, 465
Strictly for Women, 367
Stubby the Clown, 257-258
Student Operations, 376
Studentvision, 376
Subscriber-Vision, 409

Subscription Television (STV), 409
Sumrall, Lester, 452
Sumthin' Else, 236
Sunday Night, 99-100
Sundt, Jerry, 16, 235, 251, 269
Super 18 Superkids Club, 205, 424
Super Band, 302, 329
Super Mario Brothers, 205
Suppan, Dr. Adolph, 147
Sutton, Jim, 387
Sveum, John, 16, 426
Sykes, Jay, 190-191
Sylvania Electric Products Co., 479
Sync-Lite, 280
Synnes, Rod, 83
Szot, Joe, 75

T

Table of Channel Assignments, 33, 45, 125, 126, 152, 155, 163, 176, 214, 272-274, 340-341, 346, 451, 469, 479, 482
Taff, Jerry, 247
Taff, Paul K., 275, 349, 353-354, 359, 361-362, 376, 389, 393-394, 402-404, 407
Take 1, 205, 424-6
Take Back the Night, 245
Talbot, Liz, 195-196
tarantula (Shirley), 206-207
Taylor, Beverly, 311
Taylor, Bill, 95-96
Taylor, Telford, 336, 398
Technicolor, 71
Telcon (color effect), 289
Tele-Movie Development Co., 411
Telease, 413, 427
Telecine, 72
Telecommunications Act of 1996, 137, 197
Teleglobe 410, 410,, 412, 413
Teleglobe Pay-TV, 412
Telemovies, 410
Telemundo, 463, 484-486, 488
Television of Wisconsin, Inc., 163
TeleVisionaries, 51, 118, 119, 398, 400, 403
Tempo 24, 416-418
Terry, Earle M., 37, 114
Texaco Star Theater, 58
That Was the Week That Was, 179
Theater at Four, 72
Think Life, 445
This is Alice, 281
Thole, Rod, 389

Thomas, Gordon, 61
Thompson, Joe, 416, 418
Thompson, Pat, 147
Thompson, Tommy, 382
Three Musketeers, 202
Three Stooges, The, 257
Three-Thirty Theater, 73
Thurwachter, Loren F., 219
Time for Terror, 261
Time Out for Thomas, 61-62
Time-Warner, 198, 384, 422, 470, 474
Timmerman Field, 154
Tiny Toon Adventures, 205
Tobey, Charles, 346
Tobias, Nolan, 441-442
Tobin, Pat, 110
Tobo the Clown, 110
Today, 80
Today for Women, 85
Togie, Dave, 181
Tokyo Tower, 286, 287
Toleman, Justin, 25-26
Tolkan, Phil, 412
Tolouse NoNeck, 9, 260, 263, 264, 325
Tolouse NoNeck and the Zombie Zone Radio Hour, 264
Tomczak, Tom, 418
Tonight, Show, 170, 179
TooLoose & Company, 264, 265
TooLoose & Company Halloween Special, The, 264
TooLoose NoNeck, 264
Torres, John, 16, 455-458, 460, 466-467
Tournament of Roses, 79
Tower Hotel, 164
Tower of Light, 285-288
Towercom Ltd., 381
Towne Hotel, 142, 146, 148, 152-154, 157
Tracks Ahead, 379
Trammel, Niles, 50
transmitter, amplifying, 480
translator station, 451, 456, 481-483
Travelogue, 367
Trent, Bob, 7, 237-238, 256-260, 270
Trewhella, Rev. Matthew, 447
Tribune Co., 310
Trinity Broadcasting Network (TBN), 477
tropospheric ducting, 126-127
Truman, Harry, 332
Truscott, Bob, 16, 217, 218, 227, 284, 441
Tubb, Ernest, 188
Tubby the Clown, 255
Turet, Larry, 172, 205, 323, 412
Turner, Ted, 443

Turtles, The, 246
TV Exhibitors of America, 154
TV Guide, 11, 15, 156-157, 200, 208, 211, 219, 266-267, 269, 297, 327, 330, 447, 449
TV Weatherman, 62
TV-52, Inc, 473
TV58 Limited Partnership, 455, 467
TVQ, 417
Twistin' Harvey and the Seven Sounds, 180

U

U-Tube, 490
U.S. Conference of Mayors, 334
U.S. Supreme Court, 90, 131, 154-155, 343, 373, 412-413
Uahnke, Ernest Lee, 219
UHF, 5, 8-10, 31-34, 36, 46-47, 57, 61, 74, 80, 117, 121, 125-140, 145-146, 148, 151-157, 1621163, 168-71, 176, 188, 194, 199, 207-209, 213-214, 223-224, 265, 271, 273-274, 282, 310, 333-334, 336, 339-340, 342, 344, 347-349, 361-364, 378-379, 386, 404, 409-413, 431-434, 439, 441, 443, 448, 451, 461, 464, 466, 469, 479-482, 487, 489, 490
UHF converter, 132
Uihlein, Herbert E., 141-142
Uihlein, Myrtle, 142
Ultra High Frequency Television Association (UHFTA), 133, 139, 148, 156, 273, 327
UN in Action, 178
Uncle Al, 390
Uncle Geek, 263
Uncle Hugo, 202, 253-254
Uncle Natco, 149
Uncle Otto, 113
United Broadcasting Co., 469
United Paramount Network (UPN), 197-198, 211, 421-422, 429, 460
United Press International (UPI), 191, 432, 446
United States v. Zenith Radio Corporation (1926), 20
University of Wisconsin, 23, 37, 39, 114-115, 159, 294, 304, 342, 347-348, 426, 485
University of Wisconsin-Milwaukee (UWM), 13, 15, 189-191, 255, 337, 354, 389-390
Univision, 483, 484, 488
Up Front with Mike Gousha, 250

INDEX

Urich, Howell, 422
US Bank Center (See First Wisconsin Center)
UWM News Focus, 189-191

V

V-Me, 384
Vacation Station, 395
Van Vooren, Tim, 312
Variety Club of Wisconsin, 191
Variety Club Telethon, 191-193
VCY America, 415, 431, 435, 438-446, 448
VHF, 10, 22-4, 27, 29-34, 42, 45, 46, 61, 74, 80, 121, 125, 127, 128, 130-40, 145, 146, 148, 149, 151-3, 155-7, 162-4, 168, 171, 176, 194, 208, 209, 213-6, 223, 224, 250, 265, 266, 271-4, 282, 284, 327, 328, 334, 336, 339-41, 343, 344, 348, 386, 399, 402, 431, 433, 448, 479-82, 487, 489
Viewpoint, 297, 332
Vincent, Harold S., 337, 354, 355
Virginian, The, **87, 179**
vision, persistence of, 17, 22
Vivian, Oliver J., 142
Vogt, Ken, 113
Von, Eric, 383
Vonier, Sprague, 16, 49, 58, 59, 62, 67, 70, 74, 76, 82, 107, 110, 118-20, 123, 255, 269

W

W08BY, 457, 483, 484
W2XB, 21
W2XBS, 28-31
W2XWV, 30-31
W3XE, 30-31
W3XK, 21
W41CI, 485
W46AR, 483-484
W53CC, 485
W55AS, 451, 452, 456, 482, 483
W55CG, 485
W55M, 43, 117
W63CU, 485
W65BT, 452, 483
W70AO, 240, 481
W9XAO (Chicago), 24-25
W9XAO (experimental FM), 24, 42
W9XAP, 24
W9XAZ (Apex radio station), 23-24

W9XAZ (State University of Iowa TV station), 332
W9XBK, 30-31
W9XD, 27, 41, 42, 116
W9XK, 332
W9XKY, 33, 47
W9XMJ, 30, 42
W9XMK, 47
WAAK, 38
WABD, 31
Wade, Clement, 332
Wagner, Harold, 366
Wagner-Hatfield Act, 332
Waldo the Bear (DuBlon puppet), 293, 317
Waldon, Lori, 249
Walker, Hal, 147, 169, 283
Walker, Paul, 336, 341, 344, 345
Walker, Rodd, 378
Walker, Ron, 436
Wallace, Gary, 475
Walsh, Blaine, 80, 88
War Production Board, 31, 43, 141
Waring, Fred, 317
WARL, 144
WARL-FM, 145
Warner Bros. Network (WB), 197-198, 211, 421-422
Washington, Toya, 250
Watergate hearings, 371
WAWA, 180
WB 18 News at Nine, 198
WBAA, 162
WBAL-TV, 224
WBAY, 13, 315
WBBM-TV, 41, 120, 170
WBCS, 416
WBKB, 31, 51
WBME-TV, 472
WBON, 436-439
WBWT-LP, 485
WCAN, 127, 145, 146-147, 153
WCAN-TV, 5, 9, 134, 143, 145-157, 165-166, 168-170, 174, 215-216, 224-225, 231, 265, 272-274, 283, 301, 327, 346, 361-362, 374, 409, 416, 457, 460
WCAU, 145
WCAY, 38, 39, 115
WCBD, 39, 115, 222, 224, 266
WCBW, 31
WCFL, 21, 24
WCIU-TV, 451, 456, 463, 469, 481, 483, 486
Weakland, Rembert, 446
Weather in the Weather, 232, 235
Weather Vane with Mary Jane, 147

Web Financial Network (WebFN), 485
Webster, Anita V., 355
Wee Weekly, 388, 389, 407
Wegner, Dick, 456, 466
Weigel Broadcasting, 246, 451-452, 455-456, 458, 460-462, 464-467, 471-472, 481-485
Weis, Dick, 422-424
Weissgerber, Leon, 392, 393, 395
WEMP, 57, 92, 116, 126, 131, 139, 141, 143, 153, 157, 161, 164, 167-169, 208, 213-215, 217-219, 221, 252, 265, 283, 335-336, 338, 340, 342-344, 353, 399-400, 433
WENR, 25, 43, 163, 164
WENR-TV, 56
Wenzel, Dick, 368, 390, 404
Western Marshall, 202
Western Television Corp., 24, 41, 332
Westinghouse, 25, 26, 37, 176, 241
Westmore, Ern, 85
Wetzel, Theodore A., 129
WEXT, 126, 127, 160, 161
WFAN-TV, 413
WFLD-TV, 154
WFOX, 57, 126, 131, 145, 156, 161, 163, 208, 213, 214, 219, 265, 271, 335, 336, 338, 341, 345, 361, 399, 433, 436, 448
WFOX-TV, 134, 135, 170, 433, 448
WFRV-TV, 230
WGN-TV, 295, 354
WGY (see W2XB)
WHA, 37, 40, 114, 115, 159, 199, 342, 351, 477
WHA-TV, 349-51, 356, 388, 394, 474
WHAD (Marquette University), 15, 38-40, 223, 331
WHAD (Wisconsin Public Radio), 387
Whalen, Jayne, 83-5
What's This Song?, 179
What's New in the Kitchen, 59
What's New?, 87, 365, 392-393
WHCT, 171, 412
White, Jack, 353, 393-394
Whitefish Bay, Wisconsin, 57, 133, 148-149, 152, 155, 224, 272-274, 284, 317, 349, 431, 433
Whiteman, Paul, 165-166, 317
WHKE, 5, 451-3, 483
Who Knows?, 297-298
WIAO, 15, 38, 39, 115, 222, 266, 331
WIBA, 163
Widoe, Russ, 315
Wiken, Melody (See: Melody, Miss)
Wilde, Walter, 390

Wilk, Herbert, 171, 177
Williams, Rev. Forrest, 445
Willoughby, John A., 127
Wilson, Melodie, 101, 102, 307
Wilson, Pete, 100
Winfrey, Oprah, 97
Winkler, Henry, 192
Winnie, Russ, 23, 76, 77
Winstrom, Allan, 323-324
WISC, 163
Wisconsin Association for Vocational and Adult Education, 346
Wisconsin Broadcasters, Inc., 433
Wisconsin Citizen's Committee for Educational Television, 343-345, 347, 350, 400
Wisconsin Committee on State-Owned, Tax Supported Television, 350
Wisconsin Department of Natural Resources, 461
Wisconsin Electric Power Co., 298
Wisconsin Gas Co., 303
Wisconsin News, 38-40, 115, 221, 223, 235, 266, 397
Wisconsin Roof Orchestra, George Devine's, 40, 62
Wisconsin State Astronautics Commission, 154
Wisconsin State Fair Park, 58, 108, 110, 363, 370
Wisconsin State Teachers' College, 147, 341
Wisconsin Supreme Court, 373-374
Wisconsin Television Corp., 451
Wisconsin Tower, 42, 55
Wisconsin Voice of Christian Youth, 439, 440, 443, 447
Wisconsin's Lawn and Garden, 384
WISN, 14, 33, 40, 57, 92, 93, 116, 117, 131, 149, 213, 223-5, 230, 232, 249, 255, 266-9, 271, 273, 274, 283, 285, 326, 327, 331, 335, 336, 338, 344, 397, 399, 401, 402, 467
Witi, Captain, 315
Witliff, Phil, 303
Witt, Bill, 441
Wittenberg, Lionel ('Witty'), 217
Witzke, Paul, 360
WJIM-TV, 132, 272, 340
WJJA, 5, 460, 469-472
WKAF, 39, 40, 223
WKOW-TV, 230, 294
WKRL, 451
WKSH, 451
WKTI, 93, 330
WKY, 182, 183

WKY-TV, 182
WKZO-TV, 74
WLEX, 21
WLIP, 159
WLPX, 264
WLS, 161-162
WLS-TV, 484
WLTQ, 249
WLUM, 456
WMAQ, 24-25
WMAW, 57, 127, 141-146, 155-156, 174
WMFM (Madison), 163
WMIL, 113, 126, 161, 171, 175, 176, 189, 225, 431, 433, 437, 448
WMIL-FM, 176, 437
WMIL-TV, 146, 431, 432
WMJT, 33, 43, 47
WMKE-CA, 485-486
WMKE-LP, 484-485
WMKE-TV, 434
WMLO, 335, 431
WMLW-CA, 463, 464, 485, 486
WMLW-LP, 485
WMTC, 371, 405
WMTV, 163, 202, 426, 427
WNBT, 31, 129
WNDT, 370
WNET-TV, 370, 384
WNOV, 456
WNTA-TV, 281
WNUV-TV, 197
WNYC, 332
WOC-TV, 132, 133, 224, 271, 272, 340
WOI-TV, 333
Wok Through China, A, 376
WOKY, 13, 92, 97, 126, 145, 162-164, 166-167, 169, 201, 207-208, 214, 217, 289, 342, 356, 433
WOKY-TV, 5, 9, 64, 80, 146, 152-4, 157, 161, 163-5, 167-9, 171, 173, 175, 177, 179, 181, 183, 185, 187, 189, 191, 193, 195, 197, 199-203, 205, 207-209, 211, 214-215, 217, 230, 253, 272, 274, 353, 362, 364
Woman's World, 60, 69, 85
Women in TV Ownership and Management, 455
Wometco Broadcasting, 307
Wood, Hi, 39
Woodbine, 371
Woods Communications, 483-484
Woods, Jane ('Miss Jane'), 253
Woodward Broadcasting Co., 273
WOPT, 154, 157
WOR-TV, 409

Word for Word, 179
World, 374
World's Fair (New York), 28
WPAW, 141
WPGH, 197
WPTT, 197
WPTZ, 31
WPWA, 144, 152
WQED, 353, 356, 388, 394
Wright, Dennis, 81
WRIT, 92, 153, 157, 168, 185, 189, 191, 353, 400
Writers' Guild of America, 490
WRNY, 21
WSM-TV, 96, 479, 480
WSOE, 15, 39, 40, 115, 222, 223, 266, 331
WSUI, 162, 332
WTMJ, 7, 23, 35, 40-41, 45, 50, 51, 56-57, 59, 61-62, 64, 71, 75-76, 85, 92-96, 111, 115-117, 119-123, 223, 242, 245, 266, 309, 335, 489
WTOS, 436-437
WTTO-TV, 420-421
WTVO, 145
WTVT, 181-3, 185
WTVW, 5, 80, 152-153, 157, 202, 208, 215-221, 223, 225-231, 233-235, 237, 239, 241, 243, 245, 247, 249-255, 257, 259, 261, 263, 265-267, 269, 275, 283, 314, 327, 433
WUHF (Milwaukee), 5, 16, 121, 151, 159, 161, 163, 165, 167, 169, 171, 173, 175, 177, 179-183, 185, 187, 189, 191-193, 195, 197, 199, 201, 203, 205-207, 209, 211, 324, 413, 457, 460
WUHF (NYC experimental station), 135
Wulliman, 16, 349, 361, 367, 404, 442
WVCY, 439, 441, 443, 446, 448, 449, 467, 489
WVCY-TV, 5, 441-7, 455, 460, 470
WVUE, 282, 328
WWJ, 47
WWMT-TV, 74
WXIX, 5, 9, 13, 16, 64, 151, 159, 168-74, 176-9, 182, 197, 202, 205, 206, 208, 209, 229, 233, 282, 283, 288, 301, 315, 317, 328, 359, 374, 413, 415, 416, 457, 460
WXIX, Inc., 171, 176, 177, 182, 197, 282
WYTU-LP, 463, 485, 486
WZZM-TV, 486

X

X-Cleavers, The, 264

Y

Yaeger, Jack, 380
Year of Decision: The Milwaukee School Desegregation Case from 1965-1974, 372
year of grace (for educational television reservations), 342
Yokes, Ron, 16, 278, 284, 327
Yolanda Ayubi Presents, 483
You and I, 321, 322, 394
Young Set, The, 179
Youth for Christ, 434-439
Yudkoff, Royce, 420

Z

Zeidler, Carl, 43
Zeidler, Frank, 56, 76, 80, 92, 120, 122, 219, 272, 326, 336, 355, 381, 382, 398, 401-402, 411, 428
Zeman, Otto, 145, 163
Zenith Corp., 77, 378
Ziarnik, Robert, 303
Zielsdorf, Lydia, 175
Zimmermann, Carl, 16, 214, 215, 218, 265, 283, 285, 289, 291, 294, 296-297, 299, 304, 328, 423
Zimmers, Wilke M., 142
Zodiac Partnership, 456
Zoning, Neighborhoods and Development Committee, 248
Zworykin, Vladimir, 25